THE ROUTLEDGE HISTORY OF DISABILITY

The Routledge History of Disability explores the shifting attitudes towards and representations of disabled people from the age of antiquity to the twenty-first century. Taking an international view of the subject, this wide-ranging collection shows that the history of disability cuts across racial, ethnic, religious, cultural, gender and class divides, highlighting the commonalities and differences among the experiences of disabled persons in a global historical context.

The book is arranged in four parts, covering histories of disabilities across various time periods and cultures, histories of national disability policies, programs and services, histories of education and training and the ways in which disabled people have been seen and treated in the last few decades. Within this, the 28 chapters discuss topics such as developments in disability issues during the late Ottoman period, the history of disability in the Belgian-Congo in the early twentieth century, blind asylums in nineteenth-century Scotland and the systematic killing of disabled children in Nazi Germany.

Illustrated with images and tables and providing an overview of how various countries, cultures and societies have addressed disability over time, this comprehensive volume offers a global perspective on this rapidly growing field and is a valuable resource for scholars of disability studies and histories of disabilities.

Roy Hanes is Associate Professor at Carleton University, Canada. He was a founding member of the Canadian Disability Studies Association and is well known for his disability rights activism.

Ivan Brown was Head of the Centre of Excellence for Child Welfare at the University of Toronto, Canada, and a founding editor of the *Journal on Developmental Disabilities*.

Nancy E. Hansen is Director of the Interdisciplinary Master's Program in Disability Studies at the University of Manitoba, Canada, and past president of the Canadian Disability Studies Association.

THE ROUTLEDGE HISTORIES

The Routledge Histories is a series of landmark books surveying some of the most important topics and themes in history today. Edited and written by an international team of world-renowned experts, they are the works against which all future books on their subjects will be judged.

THE ROUTLEDGE HISTORY OF DISEASE
Edited by Mark Jackson

THE ROUTLEDGE HISTORY OF AMERICAN SPORT
Edited by Linda J. Borish, David K. Wiggins and Gerald R. Gems

THE ROUTLEDGE HISTORY OF EAST CENTRAL EUROPE SINCE 1700
Edited by Irina Livezeanu and Árpád von Klimó

THE ROUTLEDGE HISTORY OF THE RENAISSANCE
Edited by William Caferro

THE ROUTLEDGE HISTORY OF MADNESS AND MENTAL HEALTH
Edited by Greg Eghigian

THE ROUTLEDGE HISTORY OF DISABILITY
Edited by Roy Hanes, Ivan Brown and Nancy E. Hansen

THE ROUTLEDGE HISTORY OF NINETEENTH-CENTURY AMERICA
Edited by Jonathan Daniel Wells

THE ROUTLEDGE HISTORY OF ITALIAN AMERICANS
Edited by William J. Connell and Stanislao G. Pugliese

THE ROUTLEDGE HISTORY OF DISABILITY

Edited by Roy Hanes, Ivan Brown and Nancy E. Hansen

Routledge
Taylor & Francis Group

LONDON AND NEW YORK

First published 2018
by Routledge
2 Park Square, Milton Park, Abingdon, Oxon OX14 4RN

and by Routledge
52 Vanderbilt Avenue, New York, NY 10017

First issued in paperback 2020

Routledge is an imprint of the Taylor & Francis Group, an informa business

British Library Cataloguing in Publication Data
A catalogue record for this book is available from the British Library.

Library of Congress Cataloging in Publication Data
Names: Hanes, Roy (Associate professor) editor. | Brown, Ivan, 1947- editor. | Hansen, Nancy E., editor.
Title: The Routledge history of disability / Edited by Roy Hanes, Ivan Brown and Nancy E. Hansen.
Description: Milton Park, Abingdon, Oxon ; New York, NY : Routledge, 2017. | Series: The Routledge
histories | Includes bibliographical references and index.
Identifiers: LCCN 2017023119| ISBN 9781138193574 (hbk : alk. paper) | ISBN 9781315198781 (ebk)
Subjects: LCSH: People with disabilities—History—21st century.
Classification: LCC HV1552 .R68 2017 | DDC 362.409—dc23LC record available at https://lccn.loc.
gov/2017023119

ISBN 13: 978-0-367-65999-8 (pbk)
ISBN 13: 978-1-138-19357-4 (hbk)

Typeset in ITC New Baskerville Std
by diacriTech, Chennai

CONTENTS

CONTENTS

CONTENTS

CONTENTS

LIST OF FIGURES

LIST OF TABLES

xiii

LIST OF TABLES

LIST OF CONTRIBUTORS

Paul M. Ajuwon, PhD, is Professor of Special Education at Missouri State University, U.S.A. Previously, Professor Ajuwon served as the Director of Idaho School for the Blind, U.S.A., and Special Education Consultant in Cleveland Municipal School District of Ohio, U.S.A. In addition, he was Lecturer in Special Education for several years at two Nigerian universities. He has researched and published extensively on international education and leadership effectiveness in schools, inclusive education policies and practices, enhancing the quality of life of families and their children with disabilities, and Braille literacy and assistive technology applications.

Martin Atherton is Course Leader for British Sign language and Deaf Studies at the University of Central Lancashire, UK. He holds a BA (Hons) in Deaf Studies and History and a PhD in Sports History for research into the leisure and sporting history of Deaf Club members in north-west England, 1945–1995. He has published extensively on the social and cultural history of deaf people in Britain and has been lead researcher on various research projects and publications. He is currently reconstructing the deaf population of 1901 Lancashire for a forthcoming book on living, learning and working as a deaf person.

Anna Balcells, PhD, is Professor at the Faculty of Psychology, Education and Sport Sciences Blanquerna, Ramon Llull University, Barcelona, Spain, and Researcher of the research group "Disability and Quality of Life: Educational Issues". She is also a member of the coordinating team of the Master on Early Intervention and Family at Ramon Llull University. Her main areas of research focus on working with families, particularly in the first years, to improve the quality of life of the whole family.

Luc Brants is an independent researcher and writer. He defended his PhD thesis on the history of Dutch extramural care for people with mental disabilities in 2004. He has since then worked on (the history of) marginalised groups and published, among other things, on sexual abuse of people with disabilities. Recently (2016) he published a study on the history of the emancipation of gay and lesbian people in the city of Eindhoven, the Netherlands.

Gildas Bregain holds a doctorate in Contemporary History. His PhD thesis focuses on the construction of disability-related public policies over the twentieth century on the international and national scale, with a focus on Spain, Argentina and Brazil. He is now conducting post-doctoral research about the policy for the blind in the French Empire (1900–1960) at the School for Advanced Studies in the Social Sciences (EHESS,

Paris). He has published various articles, including "An Entangled Perspective on Disability History: The Disability Protests in Argentina, Brazil and Spain, 1968–1982", in S. Barsch, A. Klein and P. Verstraete (dir.), *The Imperfect Historian: Disability Histories in Europe* (2013).

Ivan Brown, PhD (Special Education), is an internationally recognized expert in intellectual and developmental disability, with a long-standing interest in the history of disability. He has published widely in the academic literature and has written or edited 14 scholarly books and numerous journal articles and book chapters. He has initiated and supervised several major research studies, and has demonstrated active leadership in international organizations in the field of intellectual disabilities. Dr Brown was the founding editor of the *Journal on Developmental Disabilities* in 1992, and continued to serve for many years as its editor. He has been active in local disability organizations, and his work there has been recognized by several awards. He has been an active presenter at scientific conferences, with more than 200 presentations, keynotes and workshops to his credit in the past 25 years. Dr Brown is currently the Director of IASSIDD's Academy on Education, Teaching and Research and, although retired, continues to teach graduate students as an adjunct Professor of Applied Disability Studies at Brock University in Canada.

Steven E. Brown, Historian, is a retired Professor of Disability Studies from the University of Hawaii Center on Disability Studies, and Co-Founder of the Institute on Disability Culture (IDC), currently located in California, USA. Brown received the first U.S. funding to research disability culture, and wrote *Investigating A Culture of Disability*. Books include *Movie Stars and Sensuous Scars: Essays on the Journey from Disability Shame to Disability Pride* (2003); *Surprised to be Standing: A Spiritual Journey* (2011); *and Ed Roberts: Wheelchair Genius* (2015), a Middle Grade biography. Brown writes, advocates, teaches, and is an international speaker.

Eli Carmeli, BPT, PhD, Professor, Department of Physical Therapy, Faculty of Social Welfare and Health Sciences, Haifa University, Mt Carmel, Haifa, Israel. Postdoctoral research was conducted at the University of Florida in Gainesville. His publications and research interests are investigating the aging process both on the cellular and clinical level, physical activity and people with intellectual and developmental disabilities and public health issues. E-mail: ecarmeli@univ.haifa.ac.il

Joanna L.P. Chung, M. Soc Sci (Counseling), BSW, is a professional social worker with more than 20 years working experiences in the disability field. At present, she is working as lecturer and fieldwork supervisor in a tertiary institution.

Luigi Croce, Medicine Doctor, specialized in Psychiatry and Cognitive Psychotherapy. Professor of Child Neuropsychiatry at Catholic University, Milan, he is now president of the Scientific Board of ANFFAS, Rome, an organization serving more than 30,000 people with Intellectual and Developmental Disabilities, and Scientific Director at SIR, Milan, providing support to children and adults with IDD. Affiliated to AAIDD and IASSIDD, he has long been a clinician and a researcher in the field of challenging behavior, psychopathology, health and education integration, and quality of life of people with Intellectual/Developmental Disabilities. He is an author of many papers and partner of an international network of experts in this specific area.

Marc Depaepe is professor of history of education and psychology at the KU Leuven, where he was deputy chancellor (2013–2017). Co-editor-in-chief of Paedagogica Historica. Former president of the International Standing Conference for the History of Education and member of the Board of directors of the International Academy of Education. In 2015 he was awarded an honorary doctorate at the University of Latvia in Riga.

Federica Di Cosimo is a doctor in Political Science with specialization in International Law. She also has Masters in Education and Social Psychology and Philosophy. She works for the Italian Ministry of Education, University, and Research, and is now senior officer at Region Lombardy School Authority, and professor of Economy and Law at High School and Catholic University, Brescia, Italy. She is past president and advisor of Italian Association of Families and People with Intellectual and Developmental Disabilities, a local Association, and Brescia Foundation for People with Intellectual and Developmental Disabilities in Brescia. She has published papers in social, education, and psychological fields.

Gisela Dimigen is a social psychologist with many different interests. She ran a blindness research unit at the University of Glasgow with Archie W.N. Roy from 1992 until 2003 and was the principal research lead in numerous funded projects on processing information graphics by auditory and haptic means, accessing statistical analysis software and challenging the barriers to employment experienced by blind graduates. She has also advocated for a multidisciplinary approach to tackling the mental health issues of children brought into local authority care. Her articles have appeared in *Nature, Journal of Visual Impairment and Blindness, Behaviour Research and Therapy*, and other journals.

Diane Driedger has been involved in the disability rights movement in Canada and internationally since 1980. She is author or editor of nine books, including *The Last Civil Rights Movement: Disabled Peoples' International* (Hurst, 1999). Her latest publication is *Red with Living: Poems and Art* (Innana, 2016). She holds an MA in History and a PhD in Education and lives in Winnipeg.

Dave Earl is a PhD candidate in the Department of History at the University of Sydney. His dissertation is titled "Help Us/Help Them: How Australian Parents Understood the Problem of Mental Retardation, and What They Did about It, 1945–1970." Dave is currently based in the Race and Ethnicity in the Global South Research Collaboration, and lectures in the Department of Education and Social Work's Indigenous Education Program. His research interests include histories of youth, gender, welfare, education and disability. Dave sits on the New South Wales History Council and has a broad interest in public history.

Martin A. Elks is an independent human services consultant. He began his career working in residential institutions for the department of Mental Retardation Services, Victoria, Australia. He completed graduate work in disability studies at Syracuse University, NY, and has worked in various, including psychologist, behaviour support specialist, school inclusion advocate, case manager, citizen advocacy coordinator, adjunct professor and assistant court monitor. Martin and his wife Darcy are parents of an adult daughter with Down syndrome.

Mualla Erkilic (BArch, MArch, PhD), Received B. Arch. and M. Arch. Degrees at METU, Department of Architecture, and PhD Degree at the University of Edinburgh in 1994. Her field of interest includes Theory and Criticism in Architecture. She has been dealing with the issue of disability and the strategies of Universal Design since 2002. Prof. Erkilic currently is teaching at METU, Department of Architecture, and conducts undergraduate- and graduate-level design studios and seminar courses.

Lea Ferrari, PhD, is Associate Professor at the University of Padova. She actively collaborates with the Larios Laboratory. Her research activities focus on variables that characterize quality of life of individuals with disabilities and their self-determination, on the development of assessment instruments and intervention programs related to these variables. These research activities are also related to the study of career construction across lifespan according to a life design approach and socio-cognitive model. More recently her interests have focused on disability and diversity management, on factors involved in job placement processes and in the job search of adults with disability and psychosocial distress.

Susan Ferguson is a researcher, writer and educator with an interest in interpretive social inquiry, autobiography and writing pedagogies. Her work is informed by transnational feminist theory, disability studies and decolonizing methodologies. Susan has a Master's degree in Sociology and Equity Studies in Education from OISE/University of Toronto, and she has published work on disability, gender and equity in higher education. Susan is the Director, Writing & Learning Centre at OCAD University in Toronto, Canada, where she advances excellence and innovation in student learning and writing pedagogy in art and design education and leads a university-wide Writing Across the Curriculum initiative.

Climent Giné, PhD, is Professor Emeritus and former Dean at the Faculty of Psychology, Education and Sport Sciences Blanquerna, Ramon Llull University, Barcelona, Spain, and a Fellow of the American Association on Intellectual and Developmental Disabilities (AAIDD). Previously he was principal and psychologist of the special education school "Sants Innocents" in Barcelona, and he has held positions in Educational Administration at local and national levels. Since 1998 he is the principal researcher of the research group "Disability and Quality of Life: Educational Issues". His main areas of research focus on the contribution of services to the quality of life of people with intellectual disabilities and their families.

Roy Hanes, PhD, is an Associate Professor of Social Work at Carleton University, Ottawa, Canada. He is recognized for his work in the area of disability history, disability policy, direct social work practices with individuals and families with disabilities, and for his work in the area of community organizing. Dr Hanes is a founding member of the Persons with Disabilities Caucus of the Council on Social Work Education; he is also a founding member of the Canadian Disability Studies Association. He is an active promoter of Disability Studies, and he is involved with advocacy organizations such as the Council of Canadians with Disabilities.

Nancy E. Hansen, PhD, is an Associate Professor and Director of the Interdisciplinary Master's Program in Disability Studies at the University of Manitoba. She is a human geographer, and her research interests in disability studies range across a variety of areas, including disability in spaces of culture education, literacy social policy, employment and healthcare access. Nancy is a former President of the Canadian Disability Studies Association. She is co-editing two disability history books and has written numerous book chapters and contributed to various international academic journals.

Aamir Khan

Margaretha Kristoffersson is a senior lecturer, Department of Education, Umeå University. Her research area is parental involvement in School practice connected to parents and teachers relationship and building bridges between home and school. Involved in the Nordic network Families, Institutions, and Communications in Educational Context (FICEC/NORNAPE) and in the European Research Network About Parents in Education (ERNAPE). Both networks include the relationship of parents to school systems and the contributions parents and families make to their children's learning outside school.

Rafael Lindqvist is Senior Professor in the department of Sociology, Uppsala University, Sweden. His main research interests are the emergence of the Nordic Welfare States, with an emphasis on reforms and organisation in sickness insurance, vocational rehabilitation and disability policy.

Dr Myrtle Hill is a visiting Research Fellow in the School of History and Anthropology in Queen's University, Belfast, where she was formerly a Senior Lecturer and Director of the Centre for Women's Studies. She has published widely on Protestant evangelicalism and Irish Women's History, with many book chapters and articles on the Irish Suffrage movement, nineteenth-century female missionaries, Ireland and Empire and Disability and Conflict. She is currently researching links between "feminism" and "the left" in Irish history and is active in the wider women's and community relations sectors in the north of Ireland.

Marco Lombardi is a psychologist working as a researcher and lecturer at HoGent University College in Belgium, for the Department of Special Education in the Expertise Centre on Quality of Life (E-QUAL). His field of interest is promotion of quality of life outcomes for people with disabilities. He serves as a consultant to associations and service providers in Italy and internationally, and is an author of many papers in the field.

Carles Llombart is a psychologist and speech therapist. He began working as an educator and psychologist in a special school for people with intellectual disabilities, learning difficulties or deafness. Later, at the beginning of mainstreaming in Catalonia, he was involved prominently in the education of deaf children in public and private schools in Barcelona. Finally he moved to CREDAC Pere Barnils (Educational Resource Centre for Students with Deafness or Severe Language Difficulties), Barcelona, where he works as a psychologist with the students, teachers and families.

Joana Mas, PhD, is Professor at the Faculty of Psychology, Education and Sport Sciences Blanquerna, Ramon Llull University, Barcelona, Spain; Researcher of the research group "Disability and Quality of Life: Educational Issues", and member of the coordinating team of the Master on Early Intervention and Family at Ramon Llull

University. Her main areas of research focus on working with families, particularly in the first years, to improve the quality of life of the whole family.

Hazel McFarlane is a disability researcher and activist. Her PhD dissertation, "Disabled Women and Socio-Spatial Barriers to Motherhood" (2005), explored disabled women's experiences of having (or not) children. The experiences of women who participated spanned six decades. Hazel's dissertation included a historical review; as a lifelong blind person, she felt she needed to explore blind women's history to make sense of encounters in the present day. Her chapter in this book is drawn from this review. Hazel works in the voluntary sector, promoting participation, inclusion and rights of sensory impaired people.

Joav Merrick, MD, MMedSci, DMSc, was born and educated in Denmark, and is Professor of Pediatrics, Child Health and Human Development, affiliated with the Division of Pediatrics, Hadassah Hebrew University Medical Center, Mt Scopus Campus, Jerusalem, Israel; Kentucky Children's Hospital, University of Kentucky, Lexington, United States; Professor of Public Health at the Center for Healthy Development, School of Public Health, Georgia State University, Atlanta, United States; the Medical Director of Health Services, Division for Intellectual and Developmental Disabilities, Ministry of Social Affairs and Social Services, Jerusalem; and the Founder and Director of the National Institute of Child Health and Human Development in Israel.

Mohammed Morad, MD, FRCP (Edin), MRCPS (Glasg), a specialist in family medicine, is the Medical Director of Yaski Community Medical Center, Ben Gurion University of the Negev, Clalit Health Services, Beer-Sheva, Israel; Senior Lecturer in family medicine, Department of Family Medicine, Division of Community Health, Faculty of Health Sciences, Ben Gurion University of the Negev, Beer-Sheva, Israel; Associate Director of the National Institute of Child Health and Human Development in Jerusalem, Israel; and Professor of Pediatrics at the Department of Pediatrics, University of Kentucky, Lexington, Kentucky, United States. His publications are on family medicine, Bedouin health, health aspects, spiritual health and aging in persons with intellectual disability.

Karen K.H. Ngai, PhD, MPA, MSW, is a professional social worker who has had frontline work experiences in services for families and people with disabilities before she joined a tertiary institution in early 90s. Now her work focus is in training of personnel working in different settings for people with disabilities.

Laura Nota, PhD, is associate professor, Rector Delegate for Inclusion and Disability Issues and Director of the Larios Laboratory at the University of Padova. Her research efforts are focused on social abilities and inclusion processes, devising procedures and instruments for career counselling and work inclusion. More specifically, research efforts are focused on variables and processes in Life Design models, setting up instruments and intervention programs characterized by an inclusive approach. She is associate editor of the *Journal of Policies and Practice in Intellectual Disabilities* and member of the editorial boards of *Journal of Vocational Behavior* and *Journal of Career Development.*

Kenneth Poon is Associate Professor of Early Childhood and Special Education at the National Institute of Education, where he also serves concurrently as Associate Dean, Research Quality. He has over twenty years of experience working with individuals with developmental disabilities and their families in various capacities as a researcher, early interventionist, clinical psychologist, and special education consultant.

Bodil Ravneberg is a Professor at Bergen University College, Norway. She holds a doctorate in political science. Her work has been oriented towards the development of welfare state professions within the areas of special education, health and social policy. She has conducted several studies on professional work and professionaliza-tion in a historical perspective, and has in particular analysed the conditions for the development of the special teacher profession in Norway between the 1880s and 1990s. She has also studied the field of assistive technology with a special focus on design issues and the user-expert relationship.

M. Lynn Rose is Professor of History in the Social Sciences at the American University of Iraq, Sulaimani; she has also held faculty positions in the U.S. and, as a Fulbright Scholar, in Germany. Dr Rose teaches the history and humanities of the premod-ern world; her scholarship focuses on disability studies in the ancient Graeco-Roman world, sometimes considers the modern world and non-western societies, and almost always overlaps with gender studies. Her book *The Staff of Oedipus: Transforming Disability in Ancient Greece* was published with the University of Michigan Press in 2003, coming out in paperback in 2013.

Archie W.N. Roy gained a BA (Hons) in psychology in 1982 and a PhD in social-cognitive developmental psychology in 1987 from the University of Strathclyde. He worked for the Royal National Institute of Blind People (RNIB) as a student adviser and educational consultant, advising visually impaired students and running training sessions for college staff keen to improve accessibility. From 2004, he has worked as a Careers Manager at the University of Glasgow. His work on albinism with Robin Spinks and the New York–based photographer Rick Guidotti, Real Lives, appeared in 2005. His articles on education and disability have appeared in *Nature*, the *British Journal of Visual Impairment*, and other journals.

Soresi Salvatore, PhD, is Senior Professor and founder the Larios Laboratory and the University Centre for Disability and Inclusion. His research efforts are directed toward the development of social abilities; issues raised by school, work and social inclusion of individuals with disability; and family and social health workers' involve-ment. A deep attention is also devoted to the study of Life Design models and preven-tive intervention programs. Recently he studied career counselors competencies and training. He received an award from the Society of Counseling Psychology (2008) and the award 'For Distinguished Contributions to International Counseling Psychology' from the International Association of Applied Psychology (2014).

Alice Schippers, MSc, PhD (interdisciplinary social sciences), has been General Director of Disability Studies in the Netherlands since 2009, and has worked for 20 years in policy, management, research and higher education in the disabilities field. She also holds a coordinating senior research position at the Disability Studies unit of the Medical Humanities department of the VU University medical centre in Amsterdam. Her publications are on community support and (family) quality of life. She is chairing the International Special Interest Research Group on Quality of Life of the Disabilities (IASSIDD) and is the incoming Vice President for Europe of IASSIDD. Disability Studies in the Netherlands is a partner organization of the IASSIDD Academy, striving to further the knowledge of disability professionals around the world.

Teresa Maria Sgaramella, PhD, is adjunct professor and research associate University of Padova. She is member of the Larios Laboratory. As regards disability and vulnerable individuals, research activities focus on assessment and development of life skills, such as problem solving and future time perspective; on the role of executive skills on Life Design dimensions (namely career adaptability and preparedness); qualitative career assessment in positive rehabilitation counselling; preventive and counselling activities for social and work inclusion of vulnerable adolescents and adults; and setting up career education programs and verifying their efficacy in fostering change and impact on at risk and vulnerable individuals.

Fady Shanouda is a fourth-year PhD Candidate at the University of Toronto at the Dalla Lana School of Public Health, in the Social and Behavioural Health Sciences division. His award-winning research explores the consequences and benefits of disclosure in higher education for disabled students, including students with multiple non-visible identities. Fady is also a Course Instructor at Ryerson University and the University of Toronto, teaching Disability Studies and Mad Studies, respectively.

Tim Stainton is Professor at the School of Social Work and Director of the Centre for Inclusion and Citizenship, University of British Columbia. He holds a PhD from the London School of Economics on disability rights and social policy. His focus is primarily on intellectual disability, and he has published widely on individualized funding, disability rights, history, ethics and theory.

Ariel Tenenbaum, MD, born in Argentina, graduated from the Hadassah Hebrew University Medical School in Jerusalem, Israel, and is a specialist in pediatrics and the Director of the Down Syndrome Center at the Department of Pediatrics, Hadassah Hebrew University Medical Centers, Mt Scopus Campus, Jerusalem. He has publications in the field of pediatric medicine and especially around medical conditions in persons with Down syndrome.

Paul van Trigt is postdoctoral researcher in the ERC-project Rethinking Disability: The Impact of the International Year of Disabled Persons (1981) in Global Perspective at the Institute of History, Leiden University. After the defence of his PhD thesis (2013), he was lecturer in political history and has worked from different angles on disability in collaboration with societal partners and researchers from the Netherlands and abroad. He has published about the modern history of the welfare state, human rights, disability and religion.

Evelyne Verhaegen

Pieter Verstraete works as an assistant professor at the Research Unit Education, Culture and Society of the KULeuven (Belgium). In his research he focusses on the history of education for persons with disabilities as well as the role played by conta-gious diseases and emotions in the history of education. He is author of different academic books and co-editor of several scientific volumes. For some of his publica-tions he has received international awards, like the DHA Best Book Award and the Mauritz De Vroede Award. He is also co-founder of the annual Disability Film festival in Leuven, the KULeuven Disability History lecture Series and the *Public Disability History* blog journal.

Kim Wickman, PhD, is Associate Professor and senior lecturer, Department of Education, Umeå University. Her research focuses on the question of identities, gender, disability and sport. Her current research reflects an interest in interactive processes in the special educational practice and is about students and teachers in physical education.

Meng Ee Wong is Associate Professor at the Early Childhood and Special Needs Education Academic Group at the National Institute of Education, Nanyang Technological University. He teaches special education, and has published in topics including special education, assistive technology, disability sociology, visual impair-ment and inclusion. He is also an active advocate for disability issues in the community.

Simon W.K. Wu, MA Disability Studies, MA Gender Studies, is a professional social worker and has been director of a self-help organization of people with disabilities for years. The mission of the organization is to advocate equal opportunities and full participation of people with disabilities in society. Now he works as a free-lance trainer in the disability field.

Karen K. Yoshida, BSc PT, MSc PhD, Associate Professor, Department of Physical Therapy, Rehabilitation Science Institute, Dalla Lana School of Public Health, University of Toronto. Dr. Yoshida has published extensively, using a critical dis-ability studies lens on disability history, lived experience, and disabled women and their health. She was a contributing artist to the *Breathing Installation to the Out From Under: Disability, History and Things to Remember* exhibit, which is now a translated and permanent exhibit in the Canadian Museum of Human Rights. Dr. Yoshida was a Fellow, Columbia University, Oral History Institute and was President of the Canadian Disability Studies Association.

Andrea Zittlau is Assistant Professor at the department of North American Studies at the University of Rostock, Germany. She received her PhD in 2011, writing about ethnographic museums, the performance of objects and notions of haunting. Her current work concerns the body, identity politics and performance art as a strategy to overcome the limits of normativity. She has worked with and about performance artists such as the group La Pocha Nostra, Verbo*bala and Natalie Brewster Ngyuen. Andrea's current work deals with nineteenth-century trial reports, psychiatry and theories of disorder and absence. Her publications include the edited volume (with Anna Kerchy) *Exploring the Cultural History of Continental European Freakshows and Enfreakment* (2012).

ACKNOWLEDGEMENTS

To those disabled people throughout history who have always been present but rarely visible. (Roy Hanes, Ivan Brown and Nancy E. Hansen)

For Mindy, my life partner, and to our children Ilana, Jesse and Rachel, my greatest supports – always. (Roy Hanes)

INTRODUCTION

Roy Hanes

Authors' note: Throughout this text the readers will come across terms such as "crippled", "lame", "mental defect", "physical defective", "imbecile", "idiot", and "dumb", and while these terms are no longer considered acceptable when referring to disabled people, the terms do represent a professional and lay culture of a particular era, so please keep the context and the culture of the era in mind when reading this text. Similarly, the editors are well aware that some categories of people that were once identified as disabled or part of the defective classes are no longer identified as such. We refer here to deafness, wherein Deaf people of contemporary society do not recognize or accept references to being deaf as an impairment or as a disability. Deaf advocates and their allies suggest that Deaf people have a distinct language (sign language) as well as distinct culture, and they maintain that Deaf people are disabled not because of the inability to hear and to speak aurally but they are instead disabled because of the societies in which they live. The authors accept and support the legitimacy of Deaf culture and Deaf language, but the few chapters dealing with deaf education address time periods during which being deaf was considered a disabling condition, hence the inclusion of deaf histories as part of this histories of disabilities text.

Additionally, the editors use the term "disabled person" rather than the term "person with disabilities" or "people with disabilities". The choice is a deliberate one, as we write from a position of disability rights and inclusion wherein we borrow from the social model of disability (Oliver, 1990) and the United Nations definition of disability. Briefly stated, the social model asserts that people with impairments are disabled throughout their daily lives because of structural and attitudinal barriers. The United Nations definition reasserts the social model framework and suggests that disabled people are "those who have long-term physical, mental, intellectual or sensory impairments which in interaction with various barriers may hinder their full and effective participation in society on an equal basis with others" (United Nations Convention on the Rights of People with Disabilities, www.un.org/disabilities/ convention/conventionfull. shtml. *Retrieved May 19, 2016*)

Disabled people have always been part of humankind, but in terms of historical investigation the history of disabled peoples is relatively new. In suggesting that the historical accounting of disability and disabled people is relatively recent, this is not to suggest that there aren't historical accounts of disabled individuals in religious texts, including the texts found in Hinduism, Judaism, Islam and Christianity. Similarly, there are numerous accounts of disabled individuals found in oral histories and folklore, and literature is full of disabled characters such as Charles Dickens' Tiny Tim or Herman Melville's Captain Ahab, but as an academic discipline disability history is paid little or no attention worldwide, and this handbook is an attempt to address this underdeveloped realm of history.

Disabled people compose approximately 1.6 billion of the earth's population, making this group one of the largest minority populations on the planet. Interestingly, while there have been copious numbers of historical texts regarding other populations, including people of colour, Indigenous peoples, women, LGBTQ persons, the rich, the poor, immigrants, warriors, politicians, religious leaders, kings and queens and so on, there is little mention about disabled persons in these histories. Indeed, most disability-related texts deal with personal accounts about living with a disability; there are various texts pertaining to family and disability, enumerable texts pertaining to disability policies and scores of texts regarding disability theories, yet there remains minimal literature relating to histories of disabled persons. It is as though disabled people as individuals and as a collective have no social membership, have no social identity, have no history. In short, until recently (excluding traditional fields of medicine, nursing, physiotherapy, occupational therapy and other health sciences) the study of disability and disabled people has not been part of the broader academic investigation in fields such as anthropology, sociology, history, classics, religious studies or other social sciences and humanities. Moreover, it is most likely that scholars and likewise students connect disability and disabled people to what is considered formal "academic inquiry" rooted in medicine and rehabilitation. And, as such, the examination of disability is overwhelming guided by social constructs which view disability in terms of individual difference and inferiority, and as something that can be cured or fixed or rehabilitated. Hence, it is most likely that disability will be investigated through the lens of an undesired social status which must be avoided, and the desire of avoidance has led most scholars, including those in the discipline of history, to avoid exploring disability as a legitimate element for historical enquiry.

As a form of human variation (Higgins, 1992), disability and impairment – whether physical, intellectual, sensory or a combination of the three, or whether one is born with impairments or one acquires impairments during one's life – are universal. Disability cuts across all elements of the human species and applies to all forms of human diversity, including racial diversity, diversities in culture or religious beliefs or social norms, differences in sexual orientation, distinctions in economic class and diversity in age, including the very young to the very old. In brief, there is no element of any society or culture where disability does not exist. In fact, if one lives long enough, one will most likely become disabled at some point in one's life. Simply put, it is difficult to live life without either being disabled or having a family member or close friend who is disabled in some way. These observations about the universality of disability as being part of human existence are not meant to shock the reader, but to show that disability is as natural a human trait as is non-disability. Despite the universality of disability, this does not mean that disability is viewed the same way from one cultural context to the next or from one historical epoch to the next. In fact, there is great diversity in disability designations worldwide, and that which may be considered disability in one society may not be considered as such in another (Shuttleworth and Kasnitz, 2005). Similarly that which may be considered a disability or impairment in one particular historical period may not be defined as a disability in another era. In other words, disability is considered to be a socially constructed human category (Wendell, 1996), and disability definitions change over time: that which is considered disability in the present era of human history may not have been considered as such in the past and may not be defined as disability in the future (Conrad and Schneider, 1992).

Hanes, Brown and Hansen, each of whom has been involved in various elements of disability studies and disability advocacy for close to 40 years, are acutely aware of the underdevelopment of disability history, especially at the international level, and it is through their collective interest that this handbook was pursued and developed. The intent of the handbook is to provide the reader with an overview as to how various countries, cultures and societies have addressed disability over time. Hanes, Brown and Hansen realize that not all histories are told in this text, and to be more expansive and inclusive would be beyond the scope of this one text, but they do note that the handbook is a beginning opportunity for much further historical research.

The writing of histories of disabilities is a recent academic development, and there are few histories which take a broad international focus such as the material provided for this handbook. This text includes material from 49 authors representing 19 countries who have come together to compose a text of 27 chapters. In the following pages the reader will be informed about histories of disability from the age of antiquity to the twenty-first century. In terms of geographic location the histories include material from around the world. And while the scope of the text is very comprehensive, the authors note the limitations of the text, as it has no material from South and Central America. Notwithstanding these limitations, the authors believe that a comprehensive history of disabilities is nonetheless offered in this text. This international historical text aims to address and redress many of the misunderstandings about disability. While often stigmatized, persecuted and silenced, disabled people do have histories which need to be examined and shared, especially during this era wherein more and more governments are beginning to address past harms as this population becomes a greater part of the mainstream of the global community.

The volume is unique in that it represents the first large-scale history of disability research ever carried out at the international level. The volume shows that disability and disability histories cut across all racial, ethnic, religious, cultural, gender and class divides, and it provides an opportunity to explore disability history on a truly international scope. The volume shows that disabled people have always been and always will be part of humankind, and it is now time to tell that story and to provide a voice to a population that has been "historically" silenced. This handbook aims to provide the reader with an understanding of the depth and breadth of disability history worldwide, as the text offers a collage of different social, political and cultural disability histories from around the world by covering many different time periods, locales, issues and populations by the various authors who contributed to this handbook. It should be noted that the contributors represent diverse countries such as Canada, Turkey, Italy, Israel, Spain, Nigeria, the Netherlands, Hong Kong, Singapore, Belgium Congo, England, Scotland, Ireland, Australia, Sweden, Nigeria, Norway, Germany, Zambia and the United States.

Hanes, Brown and Hansen recognize that texts pertaining to disability have been published in recent years, but it is their contention that no history of disability text represents such an expansive international exploration of disability histories as the *Routledge Handbook of International Histories of Disabilities*. As the title suggests, this comprehensive text offers a distinct approach from other histories of disabilities texts, which remain for the most part nationally based histories, or histories about specific populations, or histories about specific institutions. This handbook covers a number of time periods, representing significant diversity in disabled populations, diversity in countries, and diversity in topics.

Readers will note that the handbook is not a march-of-progress representation of disability history. Hanes, Brown and Hansen recognize that over generations, the quality of life for many disabled people worldwide has improved but so too have the lives of people in general. It should be therefore pointed out that despite improvements, disabled people, for the most part, continue to have fewer opportunities for life advancement when compared to their nondisabled peers. Moreover, readers will also note some interesting contradictions in the histories provided in the handbook, as some of the chapters denote an element of care and concern toward disabled people, while others show a high degree of distain, distrust and hatred toward the same population. For example, some chapters deal with the rise of education and training programs for disabled youth; others call attention to the rise of supports for people with intellectual impairments and psychiatric disabilities, and many of these developments occur at the same time as there is a demand for segregation, removal from the community, sterilization and/or eradication.

As an entity, the "impaired body and or mind" is a neutral status; there is nothing about disability which should conjure up notions of difference, especially in terms of social role, but this is not the reality, nor was it ever the reality for disabled people. But, as indicated earlier, disability is a socially constructed social category which is very much influenced by cultural, societal, religious and economic variables which extend far beyond individual impairment, and it is these variables which influence the rejection or acceptance of disabled people. The various chapters of the handbook attest to the various social constructs of disability rooted in history. For example, many of the histories pertaining to the rise of programs and services for disabled people are very much linked to a countries' political economy, wherein programs and services are connected to the need for a better trained and or educated workforce. Similarly, history also shows the reverse, wherein shifts in economies from agrarian to industrialized economies led to programs which called for the elimination of some disabled populations through eugenics policies and practices. Scheer and Groce (1988) also note that in societies where life is harsh and poverty and hunger are rampant, infanticide of disabled babies is often a common practice, but they also point out that some forms of impairment are viewed as sacred gifts which empower the disabled individual. The point being raised here is that the examination of disability histories is more than the investigation of the individual and of individual impairment: the investigation should make a connection to the social, cultural and historical context.

Although some of the chapters in the text explore histories dating back to ancient Greece, the majority of the histories centre on the development of programs and services for disabled people beginning in the mid 19th century and continuing on to the end of the 20th century. While this "lumping" of history was not intentional, it does attest to many of the realities of disability histories, in that until the rise of organized programs and services, relatively few records were maintained about disabled people. Along with the rise of public institutions, including asylums, hospitals, charities, sheltered workshops, schools, and trades training facilities, came record keeping and "scientific research"; and many institutional records and period texts are used to inform the material of the various chapters.

The handbook not only presents histories of local and national programs, but also some of the chapters indicate the international connectedness of disability programs beginning in the mid 19th century and continuing well into the 20th century. In many ways the period between the mid 1800s and the mid 1900s can be considered a period of isolation and segregation, as we see that most of the services and programs, whether they were developed in Canada, the United States, Norway, Italy, Sweden or Australia, etc., all were based on large institutions. Moreover, this institutional approach became the preferred method internationally and as the Bregain chapter depicts, international research, collaborations and conferences were the common practice by the early post–World War 1 era. Besides the sharing of ideas through conferences and collaborations, disability-related services and programs were also influenced by emigration and migration. For example, many of the disability-related institutions established in Canada, Australia, Zambia, Hong Kong and the United States were influenced by the development of policies and programs for disabled people established in Britain. Similarly, countries which were colonized by other countries, such as the Belgian Congo, adapted programs of their colonizers (Verstraete et al.). Briefly stated, much of the catalogued disability history covering the past 200 years in this handbook shows a shift from a history of segregation and exclusion toward greater inclusion and the provision of civil rights for disabled people, as noted in the chapter by Brown.

In closing, it is important to note that this histories of disabilities handbook comes at a time when academia is finally beginning to address disability through programs and courses relating to disability culture (Brown, 2002), disability theory (Spiers, 2008), crip theory (McRuer, 2006) and disability and gender (Garland, 2002), as well as numerous texts found in the fields of disability policy, disability rights, disability and gender, disability and sexuality and many others. Disability history is a "thematic" thread that could and should traverse all these areas of study, but it is the area which is least addressed among academic literature. Indeed, most of the academic literature found in these topic areas highlights personal accounts of living with a disability, or "triumphing" over one's disability. There are numerous texts regarding family and disability, various texts pertaining to gender and disability, many public policy and disability texts as well as a large number of texts addressing disability theories, but there are relatively few texts on disabled peoples' history. This observation is not intended to suggest that disability history is being neglected, but rather it is meant to suggest that this is a new area of academic enquiry; many of the histories that do exist are often locally or nationally focused and there are no broad-based international texts relating to disabled people's histories – this handbook is intended to address this missing element. As noted earlier, the handbook shows that disability histories cut across all racial, ethnic, religious, cultural, gender and class divides, and the text will show what many disability scholars have known for many years: disabled people have always been and always will be part of humankind, and it is now time to reveal that story and to provide a voice to a population that has been "historically" silenced.

References

Brown, S.E. (2002) What is disability culture? *Disability Studies Quarterly.* Spring 2002, Volume 22, No. 2, pages 34–50

Conrad, P. and Schneider, J.W. (1992) *Deviance and Medicalization: From Badness to Sickness Deviance and Medicalization.* Philadelphia: temple University Press.

Higgins, P. (1992) *Making Disability: Exploring the Social Transformation of Human Variation.* Springfield, ILL.: CC Thomas.

McRuer, R. (2006). *Crip Theory: Cultural Signs of Queerness and Disability.* New York: New York University Press.

Oliver, M. (1990) *The politics of disablement: A sociological approach.* London: St. Martin's Press.

Scheer, J. and Groce, N. (1988) Impairment as a human constant: Cross cultural perspectives on variation. *Journal of Social Issues* 44(1), 23–37.

Shuttleworth, R. and Kasnitz, D. (2005) The cultural context of disability in *Encyclopedia of Disability*, G. Albrecht. Thousands Oaks: Sage Publication.

Spiers, T. (2008) *Disability Theory.* Ann Arbour, Michigan: University of Michigan Press.

Garland, T. R. (2002) Integrating Disability, Transforming Feminist Theory. *National Women's Studies Association Journal* 14(2), 1–32.

Wendell, S. (1996) *The Rejected Body.* New York: Routledge.

PART I

HISTORIES OF DISABILITIES
ACROSS TIME
AND CULTURES

A brief overview of the *Routledge History of Disability*

The handbook has four sections and it includes 26 chapters spread across these four thematic categories, including Histories of Disabilities Across Time and Cultures, Histories of National Disability Policies, Programs and Services; Histories of Education and Training; Histories of Spectacle, Science, Services and Civil Rights.

Introduction to Part I: Histories of disabilities across time and cultures

Roy Hanes

The first section of the handbook begins with a generic presentation of disability beginning with the ancient Greek era and it ends with a presentation of national disability programs and policies. The section helps to establish an important theme of this histories of disability handbook in that disability has always been part of humankind and this section's first two chapters present disability during the age of antiquity as an example of disability issues dating back thousands of years. This section also attempts to establish that disability is moulded by social, cultural and religious roots as represented in the history of disability in Italy as well as the portrayal of disability during the Ottoman era. Additionally, this section includes a chapter which addresses services and programs for disabled people in Israel, and while the chapter provides specific discussions about specific programs, it also discusses the portrayal of disability according to Romantic era. He uses the conceptualization of reason to explore different societal responses to those defined as having an inability to reason and to think, those we would define today as having intellectual impairments. Stainton's chapter incorporates the works of notable theorists including Aristotle, Saint Augustine, Thomas Aquinas, Martin Luther and John Locke to deconstruct stereotypes of people with intellectual impairment such as "children of God, the holy innocent or the menacing feeble minded" (Stainton).

Similar to Stainton's examination of disability beginning with ancient Greece and the work of Aristotle, M. Lynne Rose's chapter "The courage of subordination: Women and intellectual disability in the ancient Greek world" explores the intersection between gender and disability. Rose presents an interesting stand on the social construction of disability in history by examining the role of women in ancient Greece. In particular, she points out that because of gendered stereotypes women were identified as being less intellectually capable than their male counterparts. In this regard, by definition and because of the societal image of women as intellectually backward, they were disabled by what Aristotle referred to as "possessed a bouleutikon" (Rose, abstract) which affected women's leadership abilities. In short, Rose's chapter provides an interesting case study of the construction of disability, gender and social control.

In the chapter entitled "Jane Austen and me: Tales from the couch" Dianne Driedger explores the social construction of disability through a historical lens by examining some of the works of Jane Austen. Driedger notes her own location in the re-reading of Jane Austen's novels and what they meant to her as a young teenager and then what these novels meant to her as an adult with disabilities wherein she found many characters similar to herself in books such as *Mansfield Park, Mansfield Hall, Pride and Prejudice, Emma,* and *Persuasion.* Driedger's examination of Jane Austen challenges many of the portrayals of some characters as malingerers and the like, and she contends that these characters may have had serious and debilitating impairments ranging from lupus to mental health difficulties such as depression. In today's parlance, many of the conditions portrayed in the Jane Austen novels would be coined as being "invisible impairments", and Diane Driedger makes important linkages between the impairments of Austen's characters and contemporary societal attitudes toward invisible impairments such as chronic pain, and she shows that significant stigma is still assigned to many invisible impairments.

Diane Driedger's chapter is followed by M. Erkilic's investigation of disability during the Ottoman Empire. Her chapter, entitled "Developments in disability issues during the late Ottoman period of Turkish history from 1876 to 1909", primarily focuses on disability during the late 19th and early 20th centuries but the chapter does provide some insight into the plight of disabled people during earlier periods of the empire's existence. M. Erkilic's chapter incorporates both primary and secondary sources from the era, and she includes material not only from Turkish authors of the time but also primary source accounts of people who visited Turkey during the latter 19th and early 20th centuries. An interesting element of this chapter is the manner in which Erkilic examines the influence of Islamic values and beliefs over the development of programs and services for disabled people. Included in this chapter is not only a depiction of attitudes toward disabled people but also a detailed discussion as to the manner in which support services programs were built around Islamic principles of charity. In addition to the examination of the influences of Islam, Erkilic provides a detailed discussion of "secular" influences over the development of programs for disabled youth, especially educational and training programs. Erkilic points out that Turkey's programs and services for blind youth were influenced by similar programs being developed throughout Europe at the time.

Groce, Di Cosimo and Lombardi's chapter entitled "A short history of disability in Italy" provides a broad overview of disability in Italy from the Roman era to the late 19th century. This broad retrospective of history highlights the manner in which disability and disabled people were defined and treated over time. The chapter falls in line with the book's focus pertaining to the social construction of disability by exploring social influences toward disability during the Roman period, the influences of superstition (disability as punishment) during the Middle Ages and the shifts toward more humane attitudes with the rising influence of the Catholic church. The chapter ends with an examination of disability toward the end of the 19th century when there was a greater influence of secularism, particularly in the areas of education, trades training and health support.

Merrick, Tenenbaum, Morad and Carmeli's "A short history of disability aspects from Israel" rounds out the section on broader histories of disabilities. Since the chapter pertains to the history of the state of Israel, the history of disability is relatively new and dates back to the creation of Israel in 1948, but these authors provide an interesting review of Judaic, Islamic and Christian influences over the the development and delivery of supports and services for disabled peoples and in particular people with intellectual and developmental disabilities. Having stated this, however, it should be noted that the primary focus of this chapter is on the development of health care facilities for people with intellectual and developmental disabilities since 1948. The authors end their chapter by drawing attention to the need for multi-services health care centres wherein people with intellectual and developmental disabilities receive services that could be provided to the broader population.

1

REASON, VALUE AND PERSONS: THE CONSTRUCTION OF INTELLECTUAL DISABILITY IN WESTERN THOUGHT FROM ANTIQUITY TO THE ROMANTIC AGE

Tim Stainton

Introduction

The discourse of reason has been central to western thought since the time of antiquity. The role of reason in defining what constitutes a person, or a citizen, and the relationship between reason and the value of a person has, not surprisingly, been a key determinant of the social response to people with intellectual disabilities.[1] The "children of God", the "holy innocent", the "mass of flesh", the "menacing feeble-minded", or the deconstructionist dialogue of the present all reflect to a greater or lesser degree this discourse of reason, value and persons and consequently, the pre-vailing social attitude towards intellectual disability.

The concept of social response is used here in a broad sense, encompassing daily life, public, academic and political attitudes and explicit policy responses. There is of course no absolute unanimity of social response. At any given time a variety of atti-tudes and responses can be identified. While it is tempting to argue for a dominant ideology, this strikes me as a rather stronger claim than is warranted in most cases. In the foregoing I want to focus less on the actual conditions, although this will enter into the work, and more on the relationship between ideas about reason, persons and value, and how these affected general social attitudes and ideas about intellectual disability both in the contemporary history and in subsequent periods. I will focus pri-marily on the work of Aristotle, Saint Augustine, Thomas Aquinas, Martin Luther and John Locke. The approaches each of these thinkers take to the relationship between reason, persons and value are to a large degree paradigmatic of dominant western ideas, which have, and continue to have, a critical impact on the construction of and response to intellectual disability. I will deal with both the general impact of their thought as well as specific textual references. In order to contextualize these main concerns of this chapter, I will also consider specific social responses, which are either contemporary with, or ontologically related to, the central ideas of these thinkers.

Reason, persons and value in classical thought

The classical age provides a useful starting point for considering the role of rea-son in defining the nature and value of persons. Socrates' belief in the importance of knowledge and the development of the mind set the stage for ideas about the domination of those with superior intellect over those with lesser endowments. Plato's doctrine of "the three parts of the soul" set out in *The Republic* (206–17) clearly indicates the primacy of reason over the passions.[2] Plato's Philosopher King's where the naturally superior by virtue of their superior reason. In the Republic, Plato sets out his eugenics scheme for mating:

> "… the best of our men with the best of our women as often as possible, and the inferior men with the inferior women as seldom as possible, and bring up only the offspring of the best …. officers will take the children of the better Guardians to a nursery and put them in the charge of nurses living in a separate part of the city: the children of the inferior Guardians, and any defective offspring of the others, will be quietly and secretly disposed of …. They must be if we are to keep our Guardian stock pure", he argued. (240–1)

'Guardians' is the term used by Plato for his ruling elite (see 122–25), those considered to possess the highest degree of reason. The idea of infanticide would not have been particularly shocking to the Greeks or Plato, as it was widely practiced. Plato's eugenics programme included the limiting of ages of men and women between whom mating could take place; if infants were conceived at other ages they were to be disposed of either by abortion or infanticide (236–43). Two thousand two hundred years later, similar positive and negative eugenics schemes would be proposed. One interesting facet of Plato's scheme is that it was to be done in secret, suggesting that there would have been a negative reaction to the idea of selective breeding. No such circumspection was shared by 19th- and 20th-century eugenicists.

Aristotle continued in much the same vein as Plato in striving to develop virtuous citizens. He describes procedures for restricting marriage to those who would produce the best offspring, care of the mother's health during pregnancy and, most interesting here, the comment "let there be a law that no cripple child shall be reared" (*The Politics*, 439–44).

Also in Aristotle we see the strong association between reason, goodness and humanness. In *De Anima* he sets out his tripartite definition of the soul. The nutritive soul, common to all living organisms, is that which is concerned with basic self-nurturing, i.e. plants, animals, man; the sensitive, characterized by the capacity to perceive through sight and sound and to experience pleasure and pain, and this soul is common to man and animals; and the rational soul, which is characterized by the capacity for cognition (W.T. Jones, 238–43).

This natural hierarchy of the soul allows for a differentiation between animals: "It is, however, clear that perceiving and understanding are not the same. For while all animals have a share of the former, only a few have a share of the latter" and "thinking admits of being false and is enjoyed by no animal that does not have rationality" (*De Anima*, 197–8). In other words, it defines "Man".

The idea of a natural hierarchy is also evident in divisions between people. Thus Aristotle in the *Nichomachean Ethics* can argue for the superiority of freemen over slaves and men over women as reflecting the natural order. "It is clear, then, that some men are by nature free, and others slaves, and that for these latter slavery is both expedient and right" (in Jones, 301). The related themes of rationality as definitive humanness and the natural superiority of those with greater intelligence or rationality would recur throughout the history of social attitudes toward people with intellectual disabilities.

While it is not clear exactly how intellectual disability was viewed in classical antiquity, the dominant themes of classical thought would suggest that it was not viewed in a particularly favourable light. Some forms of mental illness, however, were treated with great respect and as evidence of prophetic powers (Dodd, 1964). The actual response of the Greeks is, however, of less interest here than the association among rationality, goodness and humanness inherent in the thought.

Grace and innocence

In the classical period we see the roots of many of the attitudes which characterized the later history of the social response to intellectual disability. There was, however, with the advent of Christianity, a significant change in attitude, which would to some degree mitigate the harsher attitudes of the classical age. While many abhorrent practices would continue throughout this period, the doctrine of Grace would serve as the lifeline, which ensured, in theory at least, an acceptance of the essential humanness of people with an intellectual disability.

Several Biblical passages have either direct or related significance, but offer somewhat contradictory messages. In Leviticus particularly we find what would appear to be a rather negative attitude towards disability in general:

> For no one who has a blemish may approach to offer the bread of his God. For no one who has a blemish shall draw near, a man blind or lame, or one who has a mutilated face or a limb too long … or a hunchback, or a dwarf … He may eat the bread of his God … but he shall not come near the veil or approach the alter, because he has a blemish, that he may not profane my sanctuary. (Lev. 21:17–23).

This passage, concerned with the laws of cleanliness and uncleanness, is interesting in that, while those described cannot approach the alter, they can still receive the bread. So this would seem to suggest that while people with disabilities were viewed as "blemished", they remained human and worthy to worship their God. In the New Testament we see a somewhat more compassionate view. In Paul's letter to the Thessalonians, he writes: "Now we exhort you brethren … comfort the feebleminded, be patient with all men" (1 Thessalonians 5:14). While the doctrines of compassion, universal love and charity all had and continue to have an impact on both attitudes and the social response towards intellectual disability, it was the doctrine of Grace that was paramount in restraining the classical equation of goodness and reason.

With the emergence of Christian theology, a struggle to define orthodoxy and its obverse, heresy, ensued. Saint Augustine (354–430 AD), more than any other, was to define this orthodoxy. He more than any other established the orthodoxy that it was not by man's acts or reason that he would be saved, but by the Grace of God. So great was the weight of original sin that any inequality of status or endowment between persons was insignificant in the eyes of God. Under the doctrine of Grace the person with an intellectual disability achieves an equality of status unknown in classical thought.

Augustine's Anti-Pelagian writings were directed at confirming the doctrine of grace against the challenge of the English Monk Pelagius and his followers. The crux of the Pelagian heresy was the emphasis on free will and the denial of the Fall and the necessity of grace (Warfield, xiii).[3] In essence, the Pelagianians argued that Man, through the powers that God had endowed him with, could live without sin, and thereby achieve salvation. In the Anti-Pelagian writings Augustine makes several references to Moriones.[4] In arguing against the idea that we receive our earthly body and power based on our conduct in a previous life, Augustine tells the story of a man:

> ... of this class [Moriones], who was so Christian, that although he was patient to the degree of strange folly with any amount of injury to himself, he was yet so impatient of any insult to the name of Christ, or, in his own person, to the religion with which he was imbued ... Well, now, such persons are predestined and brought into being, as I suppose, in order that those who are able should understand that God's grace and the Spirit, ... does not pass over any kind of capacity in the sons of mercy, nor in like manner does it pass over any kind of capacity in the children of Gehenna, so that "he that glorieth, let him glory in the Lord". They, however, who affirm that souls severally receive different earthly bodies, more or less gross according to the merits of their former life, and that their abilities as men vary according to the self-same merits, ... -what will they have to say about this man? How will they be able to attribute to him a previous life of so disgraceful a character that he deserved to be born an idiot, and at the same time of so highly meritorious a character as to entitle him to a preference in the award of the grace of Christ over many men of the acutest intellect? (27–8)

We can see in this passage the clear recognition of the humanness, (of having a soul), and the relative unimportance of capacities (Moriones versus "men of acutest intellect"). This runs directly counter to the Aristotelian notions of virtue or Platonic perfectionism. We can also see however that people with an intellectual disability were not exactly seen in a positive light. The downside of grace was and remained pity.

In another section of the same work, Augustine gives us an even clearer picture of the life of "idiots", and more important, of how they came to be associated with the idea of "innocence". Augustine is discussing the nature of original sin and children. He argues that children are baptized not because they have sinned as children, but to cleanse them of original sin. He goes on to point out that because they cannot yet reason, their "folly" can not be considered sins for which they can be held responsible, thus they are considered "innocents". Later in the section he compares children to the folly of "Moriones"; he writes:

> ... by their own will-without which there can be no sin in their own life-infants could never commit an offense, whom all, for this very reason, are in the habit of calling innocent? Does not their great weakness of mind and body, their great ignorance of things ... the absence in them of all

perception and impression of law, either natural or written, the complete want of reason to impel them in either direction,-proclaim and demonstrate the point before us ... (41)

This view of innocence and the inability to sin is important to note in that it is the key point which separates Augustine's view of intellectual disability from that of Luther who was in many other key respects an Augustinian. We will return to Luther shortly.

A final citation from Augustine gives us a remarkably clear description of contemporary social attitudes and practice towards people with an intellectual disability in the late Roman period.

> We see, also, how those simpletons whom the common people call Moriones are used for the amusement of the sane; and they fetch higher prices than the sane when appraised for the slave market. So great, then, is the influence of mere natural feeling, even over those who are by no means simpletons, in producing amusement at another's misfortune. Now although a man may be amused by another man's silliness, he would still dislike to be a simpleton himself; and if a father, who gladly enough looks out for, and even provokes, such things from his own prattling boy, were to foreknow that he would, ... turn out a fool he would without doubt think him more to be grieved for than if he were dead. (41)

So in these passages we see not only how the notion of "holy innocent" (the inability to knowingly sin) came to be associated with people with an intellectual disability, but we also have a remarkably lucid description of both the life of many people with an intellectual disability and the prevailing social attitude ("more to be grieved"). The comment regarding the value of "fools" as slaves also indicates how widespread and accepted the practice of keeping fools was. A practice that was to continue for many years and which represents one of the most prevalent features in the history of intellectual disability into our current century (see: Welsford; Blillington; Bogdan). We can also see the association between people with an intellectual disability and children. Again, an idea that would continue into the present day.

Medieval interlude

Our knowledge of intellectual disability is limited for medieval times. This period saw the growth of Christian charity provided mainly by Monastic orders. One of the most famous examples was the Belgian Town of Gheel, where it was believed St. Dympna, upon her beheading for spurning the King's advances, caused several mentally afflicted people to become sane. This led to Gheel becoming a place of pilgrimage in the seventh century and it became a haven for people with a variety of mental disabilities. A hospital was established and subsequently the main focus was a programme of family care, remarkable in its relevance to more modern ideas of community care (Scheerenberger, 34).

During the Middle Ages the ideas of Folly and the Fool were common. The Medieval Feast of the Fools was a time of license, when "as fools" one was freed from the responsibility of reason. Porter suggest that in England, though not so much as Russia and other European countries, the church was sympathetic towards "simpletons", and the "holy fool" was often revered (20). The vast majority of people with an intellectual disability most likely continued to live with their families, and particularly in the case of mild handicaps, were not likely to be differentiated from the mass of people.

An interesting indication of how people with an intellectual disability were viewed in England can be gleaned from the record of a 13th-century legal case (PRO) involving a dispute over the estate of a man whose heir was "found to be an idiot". The case sets out the story of how, upon the father's death, the son was convinced to sign over the ownership of the family mill. The record states that "Saffrid's [the son] state is to be inquired by the sheriff of Kent and by all the Knights of the county. They all say that Saffrid was an idiot from birth". Based on this the transfer of the Mill ownership was cancelled and "Saffrid along with his land is to be committed to John of Sandwich's custody [thereafter] to find reasonable sustenance for him [Saffrid] from his land and to answer for the remainder when necessary." The man who caused Saffrid to sign away the mill is committed to goal for trespass and fined forty shillings.

While the question of responsibility had been around since the Classical age, we can note several interesting things from this case. The fact that Saffrid seems to have lived with his family and that the estate was transferred to him does not seem remarkable. The committal of Saffrid to another's custody suggests that no formal state provision existed or was thought necessary. Finally the seriousness which with the fraud was viewed is evident in the treatment of the accused.

The way the determination of "idiocy" was established is also of interest in that it did not involve either a medical or ecclesiastical opinion. This would seem to support the idea that it was not viewed as a question of why or how he became an idiot, but merely a fact pertaining to this individual. The reason the whole matter became an issue for the state is the question of property, which is also reflected in the laws on competence passed in the reign of Edward II at the beginning of the 14th century (Abbott and Sapsford, 5). What is also interesting is that the estate is to be used for the support of Saffrid and that the guardian will have to account for the use of the funds. Guardianship was however a very lucrative role for the guardian during this period. This not withstanding, this reflects in many ways a very modern attitude towards guardianship and a view of the individual as entitled to protection from the state. Guardianship here, it should be noted, is established to protect the individual and his property, not to protect the state as would in part be the case in the late 19th and early 20th centuries.

In an interesting article Haffter (1968) traces the idea of the Changeling in European folklore. The Changeling was usually described as having a large head, staring eyes and other features typical of hydrocephalus and cretinism. The general view of the changeling during the Middle Ages, as a replacement for a human child taken by fairies, reflected the secular view of the abnormal as having otherworldly origins. The response to these changelings, Haffter suggests, was mixed. In Ireland, they were well treated as it was felt this would ensure good treatment of the human child. In other parts of Europe they were treated badly to force the denizens of the underworld to change the child back. Later as these ideas were incorporated into the church orthodoxy, they would support the notion of the disabled as the result of sin and the work of the devil.

Before we leave the Middle Ages it is important to take note of the work of Saint Thomas Aquinas, the 13th-century Scholastic. During this time there was a major philosophical struggle between Augustinian and classical thought which had reached Western Europe through the Arab world. The Augustinian view of the world and man as corrupted by original sin but who would achieve salvation through the grace of God was being challenged. Saint Thomas's great contribution was essentially the resolution of Augustinian and Aristotelian thought. Through him reason and virtue return centre stage with, however, the retention of grace. God as the "first unmoved mover" remains prior to free will and reason and retains the unknowable power to award grace. In simple terms, Aquinas was concerned with the earthly exercise of reason, order and virtue in this world which are not equated directly with the ultimate award of grace. In his *Summa Contra Gentiles* (1959) Aquinas addressees the question of ordering between men and other creatures and between themselves:

> ... there is an order to be found among men themselves; for men of outstanding intelligence naturally take command, while those of who are less intelligent but of more robust physique, seem intended by nature to act as servants; as Aristotle points out in the Politics ... So, just as in the case of a man there is a lack of balance if his reason follows the dictates of his senses, or his sensible powers are affected by some bodily infirmity, as happens for instance in lameness, so also in human government. (BK III, Chp. 81)

Here we see Aquinas's Aristotelianism as it equates with earthly affairs. The retention of grace and the dictates of virtue combine to present an orderly vision of society where justice and charity combine. In his discussion of property we see the dictates of charity:

> What pertains to human law can in no way detract from what pertains to natural law or to divine law ... material goods are provided for the satisfaction of human needs. Therefore the division and appropriation of property, which proceeds from human law, must not hinder the satisfaction of man's necessity from such goods. Equally, whatever a man has in superabundance is owed, of natural right, to the poor for their sustenance. (*Summa Theologica*, Q. 60, Art. 7)

In this passage we see the distinction between human and divine law, which would mitigate the force of ordering along lines of intelligence, as well as the positive duty of charity.

While this brief review of Aquinas is far from adequate we can see the wedding of classical ideas of reason and goodness, but restrained by the role of grace and divine law. What we can draw directly from this as to the particular social response to people with intellectual handicaps is in no way clear; however, it would seem to support the continuance of Christian charity but affirm an inferior social position.

Of devils, witches and the *massa carnis*

One of the most frequently cited passages in the history of intellectual disability is that of Martin Luther and the story of the changeling of Dessau. I cite this rather lengthy passage here as it captures well a particular change in attitude, but also as it has often been misinterpreted as to its meaning and what it represents.

> Eight years ago, there was one at Dessau whom I, Martinus Luther, saw and grappled with. He was twelve years old, had the use of his eyes and all his senses, so that one might think that he was a normal child. But he did nothing but gorge himself as much as four peasants or threshers. He ate defecated and drooled and, if anyone tackled him, he screamed. If things didn't go well, he wept. So I said to the Prince of Anhalt: "If I were Prince, I should take this child to the Moldau River which flows near Dessau and drown him." But the Prince of Anhalt and the Prince of Saxony, who happened to be present, refused to follow my advice. Thereupon I said: "Well, then the Christians shall order the Lord's Prayer to be said in church and pray that the dear Lord take the Devil away." This was done daily in Dessau and the changeling died in the following year. When Luther was asked why he had made such a recommendation, he replied that he was firmly of the opinion that such changelings were merely a mass of flesh, a massa carnis, with no soul. For it is in the Devil's power that he corrupts people who have reason and souls when he possesses them. The Devil sits in such changelings where their soul should have been! (Cited in Scheerenberger, 32)[5]

The vehemence of this statement and its seeming clarity led Kanner to label this as the period when "mental defectives were at their worst"(6). This view has in the main been accepted by most subsequent histories but with little analysis of what Luther actually meant by terms such as "massa carnis", a mass of flesh.

To understand Luther's comment fully we need first to consider Luther's use of the term "flesh". Luther used this term as a general designation for all things worldly or sinful as opposed to a specific designation of body. For example he speaks of "fleshy reason" (Althaus, 66), the reason of fallen man, sinful and unable to see God. So to speak of a "mass of flesh", is not, as Ryan suggests, a reference to the child as an animal, but in fact affirming his humanness, a human being possessed by sin and worldliness.

The devil to Luther is in constant struggle for man's soul. He is in fact the "Lord of this world". He is the instrument of God's wrath on earth. He is for Luther "at work in everything that particularly contradicts God's own ultimate will for his creation and for men"(Althaus, 163). He is indeed a devil more terrible and majestic than the devil of the Middle Ages. So in this context Luther's comments are less a specific condemnation of handicap as a comment on how the devil creates obsession which blinds men to the Word, which for Luther was the only true path to salvation. The use of this metaphor however does suggest a rather less than positive view of intellectual disability. The use of this metaphor in secular discourse, which we will discuss shortly, would confirm this opinion.

We can also gain some insight into Luther's ideas, and how they may have affected views of intellectual disability by considering Luther's view of reason and free will which through Aquinas and the Scholastics had once again become central to the thought of the late Middle Ages and early Renaissance. Luther's views on reason are at first glance seemingly contradictory. Reason is both the greatest of God's gifts to men and a "whore", the "wisdom of the flesh" (Althaus, 64:69). Gerrish explains this paradox by distinguishing three forms of reason in Luther's thought:

> (1) natural reason, ruling within its proper domain (earthly Kingdom); (2) arrogant reason trespassing upon the domain of faith (the Heavenly Kingdom); (3) regenerate reason, serving humbly in the household of faith, but always subject to the word of God. Within the first context, reason is the excellent gift of God; within the second, it is ... the Devil's Whore; within the third, it is the handmaiden of faith. (Gerrish, 27)

Luther was essentially an Augustinian, grace once again becoming central, the "mass of flesh" echoing the Augustinian notion of a "mass of sin", all of fallen humanity. So what does this tell us about attitude towards the intellectually disabled? Although he rejects the strong association of reason and goodness, he retains the view of reason as essential in understanding the word of God, and ordering the affairs of man in the world: "All laws have been produced by the wisdom and reason of men ... Human wisdom or reason produces laws and determines what is right, just as all the other arts which we have, have been born of human talent and reason" ("The Disputation Concerning Man", in Althaus, 64fn). By interfering with our reason, the devil blocks the path to God's word, and our capacity to contribute to good in the world. So he has in essence removed the safeguard of Grace which had shielded intellectual disability from the classical view of goodness and reason and through corruption associated the devil directly with people with an intellectual disability.

On a practical level, Luther's attack on monasticism, and the "doing of good works" as a means of gaining merit in the eyes of God, would have very direct consequences on the social response to intellectual disability. The two main tenets of Luther's thought were "by faith alone" and "by scripture alone" (Garraty and Gay, 522), so the doing of good work could not lead to salvation and monasticism merely protected the privileged ecclesiastical role as intermediary between persons and God. For Luther God was a personal God which the individual must seek through the Word. On a practical level, this encouraged the dissolution of the monasteries as did the reformation in England, the primary means of formal support for people with intellectual disabilities. Luther's view also led to the association of handicap or misfortune as punishment for sin: "God indeed uses the devil to afflict and kill us. But the devil cannot do this if God does not want sin to be punished in this way" (Luther quoted in Althaus, 165fn). Thus the Holy innocent became the soulless brute, corrupted by sin, possessed by the devil and unable to free himself.

The change in attitude can be glimpsed in the Bourse Francaise, founded in the mid 16th century by John Calvin and others in part to replace the welfare function of the monastic orders and the Roman Catholic church (Olson, 12). Olson relates how a women is refused support because "the deacons did not want to support fools." (142). This would again support a general negative attitude towards the intellectually disabled and the lack of any positive association on the part of reformation Christianity with "holy innocence".

While these changes were no doubt real, how original were they, and how far did their influence extend with regard to the social response to intellectual disability? As we noted earlier, the idea of the changeling was current well before Luther. In fact the "Christianization" of the changeling began sometime before Luther, as Haffter and Scheerenberger both note. The *Malleus Maleficarum* published in 1487 cites numerous religious sources for the association of intellectual disability and demonic possession dating well back into the Middle Ages (Haffter, 58–9; Scheerenberger, 32–3). The Inquisition and the burning of witches predates both Luther and the reformation. As such it is properly understood as a doctrine of the late Middle Ages which carried on and likely gained strength in the Renaissance. The other important point to note is that it was by no means limited to intellectual disability, but represented a broad spectrum of those whose "humanness" was somehow suspect or flawed, a recurrent theme into the present day. Women were at least equally suspect and at times doubly damned as both giving birth to changelings, a sure sign of having slept with the devil, and as themselves directly being led into temptation (Ryan, 88).

Paracelsus, the Swiss physician, writing in 1530, produced a remarkable document, which exemplifies the coming together of the doctrine of Grace and the interest in explanation and knowledge. In *De Genartione Stultorum* he is quite clear on the equality of "fools" in the eyes of God. He sets out a dichotomy of the animal body and the true soul or spirit, trapped within the defective animal body. He writes:

> And Know ye also withal that the fools reveal greater judgment, more shrewdness, more wisdom than the wise. Because wisdom comes from the true man, who does not die, and it does not come from the animal body, yet through the animal body it show itself and is revealed. (Cranefield and Federn, 70)

He goes on to state:

> … thus the animal reason that is with us, which we regard as great and intelligent, and of which we think highly, and through which we want to accomplish much, stands in relation to the reason which the true man has [the inner reason of the soul] as such fools are regarded in relation to us. That is we scorn them because they do not control their reason. (Cranefield and Federn, 72)

No sign of the devil here. But we do see the idea of the Fool as object lesson to the wise. A subtle chastising of Man who may be tempted to grow arrogant in his animal reason. An idea similar to Luther's fleshy reason, but without the devil to blame and retaining the protection of Grace for the "fool".

While the impact and extent of "witch-hunting" or possession by the devil is perhaps overstated (Abbott and Sapsford, 8), it is clear that the association of intellectual disability and individual sin, as opposed to original sin, gains an important foot hold at this point (Ryan, 88). But the devil himself was not the cause of the change in the social response to intellectual disability. Rather it was the re-emergence of the individual and his reason, which is the fundamental shift which influences attitudes and responses to intellectual disability.

Of reason and folly

What a piece of work is man! how noble in reason! how infinite in faculty! ... the paragon of animals! [*Hamlet*, II.ii]

The discourse on free will and the rise of Humanism, exemplified by Pico della Mirandola's "Oration on the Dignity of Man" (1486), was central to the whole of the Renaissance (Kristeller, I.1). While it was not a period of secularism, it sets up the secular humanism of the Enlightenment: it frees the discourse from its reliance on a remote and merciful God and places man and his reason back in the centre of social and political thought. As this discourse of reason and Man develops, a parallel discourse of unreason forms.

The idea of the fool was, as has been noted, at least as old as classical Rome. Although the designation "fool" represented a broad range of meanings from psychiatric disabilities to the "professional" fool with no identifiable disability, in all cases, it represented a real or presumed deficit in reason, substantive or instrumental and clearly included people with intellectual disabilities. During the Renaissance the "Fool" and the discourse of folly became central. Charles the V of France issued an exclusive contract to the Province of Champagne for the supply of Fools to court. Many Fools become famous throughout Europe and Fools are common in both households and courts (Kanner, 1964).

In Shakespeare the Fool's wisdom is set against the earthly reason of Man. Man, grown weak and distracted by licenses and reliance on divine mercy, has disassociated from his reason. As the discourse of Man and reason is beginning, so too is the satiric voice of folly, the traditional truth-sayer, left to speak of the folly of man:

> Fool' had ne're less grace in a year;
> For wise men are grown foppish,
> And know not how their wits to wear,
> Their manners are so apish.
> (*King Lear*, I.v.)

And on a larger scale in *King Lear*, the heath where Lear's madness rages, that harrowing realm of unreason, stands as a vast metaphor for the perils inherent in unreason. The vast land beyond the city walls would have been a place of very real fear to the people of Shakespeare's time. Not an abstract or other world, but a place inhabited by the dangerous beings whose very humanity might now be suspect, where man is reduced to "a poor, bare, forked animal ... "(*Lear*, III.iv.).[6]

In Brant's 1494 book *The Ship of Fools* (1944) the Fool or the Idiot, those lacking in reason, are used metaphorically to show the folly of Man. "For fools a mirror shall it be, Where each his counterfeit may see" (Prologue). This was the most popular book of its day and was widely read and influential throughout Europe (Zeydel, vii). It was not the first book to use the fool as a metaphorical subject (Zeydel, 8–10) but given its popularity it was the most influential.

Erasmus's *Folly* (Praise of Folly, 1515), suckled on Ignorance, set out the satiric castigation of indolence and indulgence. Erasmus, unlike Brant the Scholastic, challenged directly the orthodoxy of the church. Erasmus attempted to reconcile the doctrine of Grace with Man's free will. This led ultimately back to Pelagianism. The orthodox scholars could never fully free themselves from this dilemma (Levi, 30–1).

In paintings such as Bosch's *Ship of Fools* and Bruegel's *The Beggars* we again find the Fool as a satiric challenge to the debased church and state. So as the dialogue of reason emerges so too does the Fool, laid bare in art, literature and society, an object of scorn and ridicule and associated with all that is dissolute and reprehensible. This is in essence the secular parallel of Luther's "mass of flesh", the embodiment of corruption. It is this attitude, spurred by reason not the devil, which is the central feature of the Renaissance concept of intellectual disability. And with this we begin to see the beginnings of control.

Laws for the control of idiots were introduced in several European countries. In England Bethlem opened as an insane asylum in 1377 and laws were passed for the guardianship of idiots and lunatics (Scheerenberger, 33–36; Abbott and Sapsford, 8–9). The Idiot, once a subject on the borders of society, was now revealed, a subject to be controlled.

This increasing subjectification and control continued throughout the 16th and 17th centuries. Now that the "subject" was recognized in law, there began the work of identifying and classifying the subject. The first attempts to devise intelligence tests emerged. In 1534 Sir Anthony Fitzherbert published the *New Natura Brevium*. In it he writes "And he who shall be said to be a sot and idiot from his birth, is such a person who cannot account or number twenty pence, nor can tell who was his father or mother … " (quoted in Scheerenberger, 36). In 1700 the laws in England which had evolved in this period were sufficiently numerous to be collected in *Law Relating to Natural Fools and Mad Folks* by John Brydall. The potential for abuse and the malleability of definition is clearly seen in a case described in a mid-18th-century document, "The case of Henry Roberts, Esq; a gentlemen, who, by unparalleled cruelty was deprived of his estate, under the pretense of idiocy". The title is, I think, sufficiently self-explanatory. The document relates how both the proceedings of the Lunacy Commission, and the definition of idiocy were manipulated to deny the unfortunate Mr Roberts his estate (Hunter and MacAlpine, 373–5). While the "Idiot" had become an object of scorn, degeneracy and pity, he was not alone. He was also caught up in, to use Foucault's term, "the great confinement".

In England the enclosure movement, the dissolution of the monasteries, rising population and economic crisis, in part precipitated by the cost of war with France and the debasement of the currency, created great masses of poor and vagrants (Foucault, 48–9; Olson, 21; Abbott and Sapsford, 8–12). In 1575 an act for "the punishment of vagabonds and the relief of the poor" called for the building of houses of correction. Later the opening of private houses or hospitals was encouraged by the abolishing of the need for permits. Porter notes the proliferation of these private institutions was fuelled less by any grand strategy of state control or by the scientific establishment as by pure entrepreneurial zeal (Porter, 164–5). In 1598 the poor laws were codified and by 1630 Poor Law Institutes were being established. By the late 17th century workhouses were being established throughout the country (Foucault, 43–4). These would become the main institutional provision for people with an intellectual disability until the beginning of the 20th century.

While for most of these institutions the basic criterion for support was poverty or vagrancy, Foucault notes that "confinement had become the abusive amalgam of heterogeneous elements". But as was recognized at the time, poverty was both a cause and an effect, a great unifier among the superfluous, despised population. Burton wrote in 1621, "for to be poor is to be a knave, a fool, a wretch, a wicked odious fellow, a common eye sore, say poor and say all." (350).

Porter however convincingly argues that Foucault's "great confinement" was at best vastly overstated in the case of England. He shows that while there was development of asylums and other institutions of confinement, there were by the 1810s somewhat more than 5000 lunatics incarcerated in them. He further notes that there was no systematic attempt to control any but those considered dangerous to themselves or others (Porter, 110–19). It is likely that most people with an intellectual disability remained in the community during this period. A "great confinement" would come, but not until the 20th century, when paternalism was mixed with a strong measure of fear. Those with families who would care for them, some of whom received a small sum to assist in this; and those who were not perceived as a social menace in any way, remained in their homes and communities. Similarly, those without significant means would not have fallen within the purview of the laws on guardianship and property (Abbott and Sapsford, 10–11). But what we see is the beginning of a new idea:

> For the first time, purely negative measures of exclusion were replaced by measures of confinement; the unemployed person was no longer driven away or punished; he was taken in charge, at the expense of the nation but at the cost of his individual liberty. (Foucault, 48)

It would not be until the beginning of the 20th century that the right to support from the state on the basis of disability, as opposed to poverty, was established, but we can see in this period the roots of what was to come: the beginning of the problematization and subjectification of people with an intellectual disability coupled with the general movement towards confinement and regulation. While confinement served a range of purposes – regulation of the labour force; control of "deviants"; centres of moral correction – the legacy of isolation and confinement would outlive its original purposes. The objects and rationales would change, but confinement would continue to the present day.

Reason, rights and sensualism

Kanner suggests that the Enlightenment was a bleak time for people with an intellectual disability, as indeed it may well have been. We can discern much of the structure that, as the Enlightenment dawned, was to characterize the coming social response to intellectual disability. But amidst this growing control and regulation the seeds of a much more positive vision were being sown.

Many of the late 17th-century humanists reacted against the enclosure movement in England and its effects. Daniel Defoe called for a wealth of social reforms and charitable works in his "An Essay Upon Projects" published in 1697. In it he calls for Academies for women and, of most interest here, that a "Fool-House be erected, either by Publick Authority, or by the City, or by an Act of Parliament; into which, all that are Naturals, or born Fools, without Respect or Distinction, should be admitted and maintain'd" (Defoe, 179–91). Defoe's essay is interesting for a number of reasons. On the one hand he explicitly rejects the notion that "fools" have no soul or are being punished for past fault or sin. He also speaks quite positively of "Bedlam … a Noble Foundation" but wonders why no similar provision was made for "fools". While he clearly sees such provision as a positive step, both with respect to the "fools" and society, his view reflects the general view that to be without reason, is "the greatest unhappiness that can befal Human Kind". It is also a reasonable reflection of the general attitude towards confinement at the time, and the benevolent paternalism that would be the lighter side of the increasing social control.

Finally Defoe's method of raising and funding the house is interesting. He proposes in the first instance to tax books, as these reflect the ultimate use of reason, and as such is the gift of God's providence, it is fitting that they should fund those who have been less fortunate. In the second case he proposes that a lottery be set up so that "fools can be supported by their own folly". In both cases we see an inclination towards a "natural justice". Whether Defoe was completely serious about these proposals is debatable, however they do reflect the emerging expansion of what was considered appropriate State action. Defoe in this sense was reflective of the early enlightenment in England: a humanist, pragmatic, paternalistic, concerned with law and the responsibilities of the state, and with natural justice.

While Defoe provides an interesting "period piece", John Locke is central in several ways to the future social response to intellectual disability. As a means of reflecting the impact of the ideas, I want to consider two aspects of Locke's thought: His ideas on law, rights and Man; and, his ideas on the source of knowledge. The former would have resonance to the present day, the latter, more immediate impact.

Locke's impact is somewhat paradoxical. While his ideas about rights and the social contract are at the root of the claims made in our present age, Locke (1924) was clear that those rights were contingent upon reason, as the basis of participation in the liberal state. In his second Treatise he states:

> But if through defects that may happen out of the ordinary course of Nature, any one comes not to such a degree of reason wherein he might be supposed capable of knowing the law, … he is never capable of being a free man, … So lunatics and idiots are never set free from the government of their parents. (142)

In this Locke was following in the natural law tradition. Samuel Pufendorf (1717) notes, "To make a Man capable of (I) giving a ferious and firm Consent, tis above all things necessary that he be master of his Reason … ". He goes on to state that if one is incurably lacking in reason that he "is in all Legal and Moral Consideration to be accounted Dead". The latter reference is to the notion of civil death, an exclusion from society and civil life (56; fn5). This view has remained the dominant liberal view into the present day with some notable and increasing exceptions. The idea of civil death is an evocative description of the situation of many people with intellectual disabilities into the present day.

Locke's ideas on how a person's humanness is defined are also of interest. One might expect Locke to adopt the idea of people with an intellectual disability as less than human given their deficiency in reason, but Locke was too much the empiricist to engage in idle metaphysical speculation. In the Essay Concerning Human Understanding (1975), he notes that:

> ... if several Men were to be asked, concerning some oddly-shaped Foetus, as soon as born, whether it were a Man, or no, tis past doubt, one should meet with different Answers. ... so far are we from certainty knowing what a Man is ... (454–5)

Given this scepticism, Locke would likely have agreed with Hobbes that "upon the occasion of some strange and deformed birth, it shall not be decided by Aristotle and the philosophers, whether the same be a man or no, but by the laws." (Hobbes, 189).

In the Essay, as the title implies, Locke sets out to explain how we come to acquire knowledge. Locke rejects the idea of innate ideas that we are born with any "Characters, as it were stamped upon the Minds of Man, which the soul receives in its very first Being; and brings into the world"(48). One of his arguments to support this is interestingly that "all Children and Ideots, have not the least apprehension or Thought of them" (49). Rather Locke sees the mind as a blank slate upon which ideas are imprinted through our senses or reflection, that is the ideas developed from the mind reflecting on its operation within itself. (105). It is essentially deficits in these two faculties that characterize "naturals" (160–1).

So while views of intellectual disability were less dependent on interpretation of scripture, they now faced the problem of reason and membership in the liberal state. This is a problem as yet not fully resolved. This loss of theological rationales, as Porter notes, humanized madness [and "idiocy"]. In so doing it removed the remnants of protection of Grace and left it open to amelioration by man (192: 279). While Locke's general scepticism about amelioration of idiocy likely prevented any real interest in them in terms of early psychiatry, his ideas on education deriving from his association-ism would be an important stimulus to early attempts at the education of people with an intellectual disability.

Many of Locke's ideas on "ideots" were likely influenced by Thomas Willis, a phy-sician whose lectures he attended at Oxford and who both directly and indirectly influenced Locke's early medical and scientific thinking (Cranston, 74; Dewhurst, 4–7). In 1672 Willis published *De Anima Brutorum*, later translated into English as *Two Discourses Concerning the Soul Of Brutes*. The title refers to the mortal soul that is common to all animals, a vague complex of "anatomical and physiological pro-cesses which underlie psychological processes" (Cranefield, 106). Willis devotes a chapter to the discussion of the causes and treatment of intellectual disability. In discussing how the brain and nervous system operates he describes how animal spirits, moving through various nerve passages and passages in the brain, cause, if outward from the brain, movement, and if inward how they carry sensations to the brain. He states" ... from this manifold way of sensation, proceeds the Knowledge of all things, according to the philosopher, All Knowledge is made by the sense" (57).

Willis attributes mental deficiency to either a defect in the animal spirits or in the brain itself. In general problems are related to the free flow and motion of the animal spirits which slows the operation of the brain and nervous system (207–8). All of this seems consistent with Locke, who does not deal with the physiology but draws similar conclusions. There is much of interest in Willis's book, his discussion of causes and of differing levels of handicap are as accurate as anything to come out in the next two centuries. What is of most interest here is his recommendations for treatment. For those with more mild "affliction" he suggests the "mechanical arts" or "agricultural pursuits". For those more seriously affected, he writes "though it may not be cured, yet it is often wont to be amended. Wherefore it must be the work both of a Physician and a Teacher" (301–2). The teacher he suggests by repetition of simple lessons, can cause an improvement in the brain by improving the passage of spirits.

This is a remarkable suggestion for the 17th century, but one that flowed logically from the new spirit of empirical and sceptical acquisition of knowledge. Locke, who as noted would have been familiar with Willis's work, became the inspiration for many of the French philosophers of the 18th century, among them Condillac, whose sensualism would in turn would influence the first serious attempts to "improve the idiots" as Willis had recommended. These ideas would return to Britain and to North America in the mid-19th century, when the first schools for "idiots and imbeciles" were opened.

Of remarkable men and the education of the idiot

There is a certain irony in the fact that the "Age of Reason", is in many ways one of the most positive in the history of intellectual disability – not necessarily in the actual conditions, but in developing the ideas that in many ways remain the most positive perspective on intellectual disability. The optimism of the age regarding human potential and the power of unfettered humanity is nowhere more evident than in the interest and faith in the power of education. The paradigm work is of course Rousseau's *Emile*.

In *Emile* Rousseau seeks to demonstrate his belief that Man is naturally good and free, but is corrupted and enslaved by the society. The positive side of this is that given the proper training and education, or put another way, the right environmental and sensory experiences, Man can retain or regain his natural goodness. While Rousseau borrowed much from Locke's writings on education, he was the first to attempt a coherent presentation of a course of education emphasizing a natural progression beginning with physical education through more complex learning (Jimack, xiii–xv). While Rousseau himself had little time for "the care of a feeble, sickly child" (Rousseau, 21),[7] his ideas and writings capture the spirit of the age which led to the beginnings of a more positive approach to intellectual disability.

It was in this spirit that Johann Pestalozzi began his pioneering work in education and Jacob Pereire began teaching deaf-mutes, as noted by Rousseau (Kanner, 9–12; Scheerenberger, 48–50). This was also the age of Pinel and Tuke and the "liberation" of the mentally ill from their chains. In reply to the revolutionary Couthon's query "are you mad yourself to unchain such beasts" Pinel replied "Citizen, I am convinced that these madmen are so intractable only because they have been deprived of air and liberty" (in Foucault, 242). It was in this spirit that Jean Marc Gaspard Itard (1774–1838) began what is often cited as the beginning of educational efforts for people with an intellectual disability, the education of Victor, the "wild boy of Aveyron".

The story of Victor, the "wild boy", and Itard's efforts towards his education is in many ways a study in the conflict of ideas which raged at this time; particularly the struggle to prove the sensualist claims of the primacy of sensual experience in the development of man. The subject for much of this debate was of course, the "noble savage". While much of this interest centred on native people such as the American Indian, there was also keen interest in "feral man". Linnaeus, Condillac and Rousseau all used examples of "wild men" to support their arguments.[8]

The sensualist philosophy of Locke and Condillac was the driving force for Itard. With Victor, Itard hope to deliver the coup de grace in this debate by showing that, with the proper sensory stimulation, Victor could be raised from his savage state. In the preface to his first report on Victor, Itard states:

> On this account we have reason to hope, that, if ever a similar individual (a "wild child" untainted by society), presented, (we could) employ, in order to produce his physical and moral development, all resources to be derived from (our) actual knowledge: or, … if this application proved impossible, there would be found in this age of observation some one individual, who, carefully collecting the history of a being so astonishing, would ascertain what he is, and would infer, from what is wanting to him, the sum, as yet not calculated, of that knowledge and of those ideas for which man is indebted to his education.
> May I dare confess that it is my intention to accomplish both of these important objects? (1799, 93)

Itard of course did not believe that Victor was in fact an "idiot" to begin with despite an intensive study and diagnosis to the contrary by Pinel. Pinel based his diagnosis on rigorous comparison with "idiots" in Bicetre and La Salpetriere, the French asylums for incurable men and women respectively. In his report on the subject to the Society of Observers of Man, he concluded that "the boy was not an idiot because he was abandoned in the woods; he was abandoned in the woods because he was an idiot" (in Lane, 56).[9] Itard was not convinced and undertook a 5-year course of sensory education. Although neither of Itard's original goals were achieved, his work was seminal in changing the prevailing view that "among children suffering from idiocy … there is no hope whatever of obtaining some measure of success through systematic and continued instruction" (Pinel in Lane, 69).[10]

In reading Itard's work one is struck not only by the compassion which he showed, but also the astuteness of his observation and methodology, much of which has become standard practice in education. In his Report to the Academy of Sciences we see again the compassion of Itard, and the astuteness of his mind. Despite not having achieved his original goals, he recognizes what his legacy would show to be his true achievement:

> … from whatever point of view one looks at this long experiment, whether one sees it as the methodical education of a wild man, or whether one restricts oneself to considering it as the physical and moral treatment of one of those creatures born ill-favored, rejected by society and abandoned by medicine, the care that has been lavished on him, the care that is still his due, the changes that have taken place, those one hopes are still to come, the voice of humanity, the interest aroused by so cruel a desertion and so strange a fate, all these things combine to commend this extraordinary young man to the attention of scholars, the solicitude of our administrators and the protection of the government. (179)

27

While it is certainly true that during this period many who were exposed languished in the unspeakable horror of Bicetre, La Salpetriere, and similar places of confinement, the optimism and humanism of the age brought hope. There is too, the paternalism of the idea that one need be "raised up", a feature which would continue into present day policy. These early efforts however were the link between the ideas and vision of the Enlightenment and intellectual disability. A link which would in the next century bring a line of reformers whose vision we can only marvel at today, whose vision born of hope and faith in humanity, was to come to an abrupt end with the century. With this period also comes the rise of explicit policy. The idiot, exposed and for some, actively supported to join in the human community and to take his place as a citizen, would come to regret that exposure as our current century dawned.

In reading of the pioneers in the field of education of people with an intellectual disability one is struck by their commitment to social change and the commitment they showed to the causes with which they were connected. These are not disinterested professionals pursuing careers for professional and personal gain. They were people who could (and often did) have excelled in a variety of areas, but chose to concern themselves with people who until that time were thought worth little more than pity at best. They were products of the Romantic age, passionate in the belief that society could be re-organized to end exploitation and suffering.

Edouard Seguin (1812–1880), often called the father of special education, was active in the Christian socialist movement of Claude-Henri Saint-Simon who wrote in his *Nouveau Christianisme* (1825) "The whole of society ought to strive towards the amelioration of the moral and physical existence of the poorest class; society ought to organize itself in the way best adapted for attaining this end" (in Scheerenberger, 69). In the "poor idiot", Seguin found his "poorest class". Samuel Gridley Howe (1801–1876), perhaps the greatest of the early American reformers, served as a volunteer in the Greek war of liberation, and was imprisoned for attempting to carry funds to Polish revolutionaries on behalf of Lafayette (Kanner, 40). Caught up in the revolutionary zeal of America and France, these men saw their work on behalf of people with an intellectual disability not as some detached clinical exercise, but as part of the struggle for the liberation of humankind. A key element in Seguin's theory was his belief that education must yield liberty and freedom (Kraft, 405).

Seguin was perhaps the most influential of these early reformers both because of his seminal educational work and his influence in both Europe and North America. Seguin was a student of Itard and Esquirol and at the age of 25 was asked to take on the education of a "young Idiot" to which he agreed despite Esquirol's belief that idiots could not be improved. Within 14 months, using methods adapted from Itard "M. Seguin has taught his pupil to make use of his senses, to remember, to compare, to speak, to write, to count, etc." (in Lane, 264).[11]

Seguin went on to open his own school and after Bonaparte turned on his comrades of the revolution, fled to the United States to escape persecution. There he directed the Pennsylvania Training School for Idiots for a brief period and was influential in the development of training schools throughout the U.S. Eventually he helped found and became the first President of the Association of Medical Officers of American Institutions for Idiotic and Feeble-Minded Persons.[12] While in Paris he was visited by the Superintendent of the English Northern Counties Insane Asylum, who was much impressed with Seguin's methods and success (Lane, 270–8).

Seguin's physiological method emphasized several key elements. One of the most basic dealt with the relationship between the teacher and the student. Seguin states that the beginning and end of his system is "to make the child feel he is loved, and to make him eager to love in his turn" (Seguin, 244). He also emphasized physical exercise and social interaction. He stressed that schools should be in or near the centres of activities so that students could visit museums, attend church etc. (Scheerenberger, 70). He was also against corporeal punishment as "oppression everywhere creates opposition" (Seguin, 227). Throughout the process the child's freedom was to be respected, thus coercion was to be kept at a minimum (Kraft, 406).

As noted above, liberation was the goal of Seguin's method, to make the child will his freedom. The school was seen as an educational facility, as such children were to return to their homes when suitable gains were made. Seguin did however propose that those who failed to make sufficient gains might remain in long-term asylums. A proposal which was to have chilling consequences (Scheerenberger, 70).

Johann Jakob Guggenbuhl (1816–1863), a Swiss contemporary of Seguin, is the other great figure of the age. As the story goes, Guggenbuhl, the young physician, was passing through the village of Seedorf when he was taken by the sight of a young "dwarf crippled cretin of stupid appearance"[13] reciting the Lord's prayer at a shrine by the roadside. Guggenbuhl was so struck by the sight that he determined to dedicate his life to the "cure and prophylaxis" of cretinism. After researching the scientific literature he determined that what was needed was the kind of personal commitment "of the kind which John Howard and Elizabeth Fry had in prison inmates, Thomas Clarkson, William Wilberforce … had in slaves … ". Fired by the belief that God had chosen him for this mission, he established the first recognized institution for the intellectually disabled at Abendberg, 4000 feet high in the Swiss Alps.[14]

Guggenbuhl's method included exposure to mountain air and natural beauty, a good diet, care of the body and physical exercise, some rudimentary medications and sensory training. The latter included progressive introduction of stimuli from simple to more complex. Speech and memory training and a regular routine were also integral parts of his regime. At one point he even introduced two non-disabled children into the school, an idea which would be considered progressive today (Kanner, 23–4).

Guggenbuhl's and Abendberg's fame soon spread throughout Europe and North America. Howe, who visited Abendberg, declared "The holy mount it should be called" (Kanner, 25). He was especially influential in England. In 1842 he was visited by William Twinning who wrote glowingly of Guggenbuhl's achievements on his return to England. The first residential school in England, Rock Hall House, was inspired by Guggenbuhl and begun in Bath by a Miss White in 1846. In 1847, urged on by Andrew Reed who had visited Abendberg, Park House at Highgate, the first major institution for people with intellectual disabilities in England was established. In 1848, a sister from Abendberg came to Highgate House to assist in the establishment of the nascent institution. Guggenbuhl himself wrote to Lord Ashley, M.P., urging that intellectual disability become a matter of public concern (Kanner, 55–6).[15]

Unfortunately Guggenbuhl's fame led to travel and lectures throughout Europe which kept him away from Abendberg much of the time. Without his guidance the school quickly deteriorated. As early as 1850 there were questions about Abendberg and Guggenbuhl. Down wrote that Guggenbuhl, "was seduced by the English drawingroom" and "on reaching the summit of Abendberg, which I mounted as a pilgrim to a shrine, I found the pupils in a state of physical and mental neglect while the patron saint was enervated by the Capua-like influence of the West End of London" (in Scheerenberger, 72). The final blow came when the British Minister in Berne visited and his report regarding the "disgusting disorder" of the place led to an official investigation which cited a variety findings. These included: that "not a single cretin had ever been cured; initial educational supervision by well trained instructors had deteriorated and that no educator had been employed for several years; heating and other physical plant was inadequate; no records concerning residents progress were kept (Kanner, 28–9). Guggenbuhl died in 1863 a broken man and Abendberg closed in 1867.

How did Abendberg, the model for many subsequent institutions, plummet so quickly from "Holy Mount" to "disgusting disorder"? Beyond the rapidity, what is remarkable is the pattern, a pattern that would be repeated throughout the western world in the next century. The descriptions of Abendberg's degraded state are hauntingly reminiscent of descriptions of its scandal plague progeny of the 1950s and '60s. Hindsight suggests that Abendberg was in fact a model institution in the paradigmatic sense, a model whose history would be replicated for decades in all its glory and degradation.

While Abendberg's demise was rapid, the vision of these pioneers was more often repeated in its positive form during the late 19th and early 20th centuries. One is struck by the photographs of early institutions and their residents. They resemble much more an English public school than the crowded warehouses of humanity which burst into prominence in the middle of the 20th century.[16] Indeed they were intended as pedagogical institutions, not hospitals or asylums. In fact one of the things that separates these early pioneers from the superintendents of latter institutions, is that, though they were medical men, their concentration and purpose were educational. From Willis, through Itard, Seguin, Howe, and Guggenbuhl, this was the case. However, as we moved towards the turn of the century these men were replaced by medical men, and men of the emerging discipline of psychology, whose search for scientific legitimacy would find a rich yet passive vein in those labelled intellectually disabled.

Another striking feature of this early period was the lack of emphasis on classification and grading. While this was certainly something the early pioneers were aware of they did not assert that only a few could benefit from education. "Not one in a 1000 has been entirely refractory to treatment, not one in 100 who has not been made more healthy and happy" (in Wolfensberger, 49). "THE IDIOT MAY BE EDUCATED" declared a pamphlet for Park House triumphantly (K. Jones, 183). While the belief that all "idiots" could derive benefit from education would continue, the increasing interest in classification would lead to increasingly differentiated support and greater circumspection regarding the potential of people with intellectual disabilities. Again a legacy that would continue into the present age.

The age of the institution had now begun, and with the coming of the eugenics movement, these early pedagogical facilities would transform in places of exclusion and regulation. Evil would once again be associated with a perceived deficit in reason and the eugenic vision of Plato and Aristotle would return through segregation, sterilization and elimination, most recently in vitro through the brave new world of new reproductive technology.

Conclusion

In this chapter I have explored the interplay between ideas of reason, value and personhood. As the last paragraph makes clear, it is discourse still very much in evidence. As such there can be no final conclusion at this point. As this chapter has demonstrated, there is little that is new about reproductive technologies from a moral perspective. Perhaps by understanding and study of what our intellectual predecessor had to say on these issues, and the consequences of their ideas, we can bring some measure of perspective to our current ethical and moral debates.

Notes

1 The term "intellectual disability" is used to denote a real or perceived, permanent deficit in intellectual capacity. While the "name debate" is an important and complex area I do not pursue it here. The above term is used to represent the construct which encompasses "mental handicap", "mental retardation", developmental disabilities and in the U.K., learning difficulties. Contemporary terminology is used where appropriate as the semiotics of labels is crucial to understanding the contemporary construction.

2 The third element is translated as spirit, which acts similar to desire but usually in support of reason, i.e. indignation. (see, 208).

3 It is important to note that Augustine did not deny free will but its scope and role in the affairs of men and God.

4 This usage, derived from the Greek, is interesting in that Augustine prefaces his usage with "and whom the vulgar call" suggesting this was a derisive colloquial usage which seems to die out, not to reappear until Goddard's usage in the early 20th century (OED, 1976 Supp., Vol. 2). It is also interesting to note the semiotic pattern this suggests. Beginning with a standard Greek usage, this is then translated into a derisive colloquial term. A process that is repeated with the same word some 1500 years later!

5 Roy Porter notes this generally attitude of the state would continue to the end of the 18th century where a "feudal paternalism" governed judicial regulation first through the Court of Wards and after the restoration through the Chancery (111–117). This passage is also cited in Kanner; Sapsford & Abbott; Blatt and Ryan.

6 See Michael Ignatieff, *The Needs of Strangers* (Chp. 1), for a similar but more extensive interpretation of Lear.

7 The full passage is somewhat contradictory. While he "approves" of the charity of others who undertake this task, he states he has no gift for such a task himself. The main thrust of his comment seems to be that those of weak bodies, who "need all their strength to stay alive", could never learn "the art of living". This is of course directly related to the idea derived from Locke on the importance of physical education, "The body must be strong enough to obey the mind". He makes no direct comment about the mind being strong enough to direct the body, but this would seem to be a reasonable assumption as to Rousseau's belief. This is all the more strange given that Rousseau had a physical disability himself.

8 For a discussion of the history of "wild children" and their significance in the contemporary philosophical discourse see: Lucien Malson, *Wolf Children*. This volume also includes translations of Itard's *Of The First Developments of the Young Savage of Aveyron* (1799), and *Report on the Progress of Victor of Aveyron* (1806). Linnaeus cites ten cases in *Systema Naturae*, Rousseau's five cases in *Discourse on the Origins of Inequality*, and Condillac's two cases in five cases in "An Essay on the Origins of Human Knowledge". In total Malson lists sixteen reports on "wolf children" in the 18th century alone. For a review of both the context and legacy of Itard's work with Victor see Harlan Lane, *The Wild Boy of Aveyron*.

9 Lane reproduces extensive excerpts of Pinel's report (57–69). The report gives an interesting view of the contemporary perspectives and understanding of mental handicap as well as conditions at the two institutions. This whole debate seems oddly topical in light of the current debate on "the social construction of mental retardation". Within this paradigm, it would seem that Itard was in fact correct in his approach and his discoveries are somewhat less "accidental" within this view.

10 Esquirol, a fellow student of Itard under Pinel, who was to become the inheritor of Pinel's mantle as the leader in "mental medicine" echoed this view; "Idiots are what they must remain for the rest of their life" (*Dictionnnaire des Sciences Medicales*, cited in Lane, 261).

11 Esquirol did not however change his view as he attributed this remarkable success to the fact that the pupil had not been an idiot in the first place, a comment heard frequently today in regards to successful returns to the community and educational success.

12 Later the "American Association on Mental Deficiency".

13 Cretinism was perhaps the most studied and recognized form of mental handicap and was endemic in the Swiss Alps. For a history see: Paul Cranefield, "The Discovery of Cretinism".

14 The story of Guggenbuhl and Abendberg is told in virtually every history of mental handicap. The most comprehensive include: Leo Kanner "Johann Jakob Guggenbuhl and the Abendberg", 17–34; Scheerenberger, 70–73.

15 Daniel H. Tuke in his *History of the Insane* also credits Guggenbuhl for early English interest in the area.

16 For descriptions of these early schools and methods see: Kraft; Radford & Tipper; Wolfensberger.

Bibliography

Abbott, P. and Sapsford R. (1987) Community Care for Mentally Handicapped Children. Milton Keynes, UK: Open University Press.

Althaus, P. (1966) *The Theology of Martin Luther.* Translated by Robert Schultz. Philadelphia, PA: Fortress Press.

Anon, T. (1847) Visit To Bicetre. *Chamber's Edinburgh Journal.* (series 2), Vol. 7: 20–22.

Anon, T. (1848) Hospital for infant cretins. *Chambers' Edinburgh Journal.* Vol. 9: 296–299.

Aquinas (1959) *Selected Political Writings.* Introduction and edited by A.P. D'Entreves. Translation by J.G. Dawson. Oxford, UK: Blackwell.

Aristotle (1981) *The Politics.* Translated by T.A. Sinclair. Revised by T.J. Saunders. Harmondsworth, UK: Penguin.

Aristotle. (1986) *De Anima.* Translated by H. Lawson-Tancred. London, UK: Penguin.

Augustine. (1956) Anti-Pelagian writings, In *A Select Library of the Nicene and Post-Nicene Fathers of the Christian Church*, Vol. 5, Edited by P. Schaff. Grand Rapids, MI: W.R. Eerdmans Publishing Company.

Billington, S. (1984) A Social History of the Fool. Sussex, UK: The Harvester Press.

Blatt, B. (1987) The Conquest of Mental Retardation. Austin, TX: Pro-Ed.

Bogdan, R. (1988) Freak Show. Chicago, IL: University of Chicago Press.

Brant, S. (1944) *The Ship of Fools.* Translated, Introduction and Commentary by E. Zeydel. New York, NY: Columbia University Press.

Burton, R. (1932) *The Anatomy of Melancholy*, Vol. 1, Edited by H. Jackson. London, UK: J.M. Dent.

Cranefield, P. (1961) A seventeenth century view of mental deficiency and schizophrenia: Thomas Willis on 'stupidity or foolishness'. *Bulletin of the History of Medicine,* Vol. 35: 291–316.

Cranefield, P.F. and Federn W. (1967) The Begetting of Fools: An annotated translation of Paracelsus, *De Genartione Stultorum. Bulletin of the History of Medicine,* Vol. 41: 56–74.

Cranefield, P. (1962) The discovery of cretinism. *Bulletin of the History of Medicine,* Vol. 36, No. 6, 489–511

Cranston, M. (1985) John Locke. Oxford, UK: Oxford University Press.

Defoe, D. (1969) An Essay Upon Projects. Menston, UK: Scholar Press.

Dewhurst, K. (1963) John Locke, Physician and Philosopher: Medical Biography. London, UK: Wellcome Historical Medical Library.

Dodd, E.R. (1964) The Greeks and the Irrational. Berkeley, CA: University of California Press.

Erasmus. (1971) *Praise of Folly*. Introduction by A.H.T. Levi. London, UK: Penguin.

Flew, A. Ed. (1979) A Dictionary of Philosophy. London, UK: Pan.

Foucault, M. (1967) Madness and Civilization: A History of Insanity in the Age of Reason. London, UK: Tavistock.

Garraty, J.A. and Gay P., Eds. (1972) The Columbia History of the World. New York, NY: Harper & Row.

Gerrish, B.A. (1962) Grace and Reason. Oxford, UK: Clarendon Press.

Haffter, C. (1968) The changeling: History and psychodynamics of attitudes to handicapped children in European folklore. *Journal of the History of the Behavioral Sciences*, Vol. 4: 1.

Hobbes, T. (1889) The Elements of Law. London, UK: Simpkin, Marshall and Co.

Hunter, R. and MacAlpine I. (1963) *Three Hundred Years Of Psychiatry*, 1535–1860. London, UK: Oxford University Press.

Ignatieff, M. (1986) The Needs of Strangers. Harmondsworth, UK: Penguin.

Jimack, P.D. (1974) Introduction, in Jean-Jacques Rousseau, In *Emile*, Translated by B. Foxley. London, UK: J.M. Dent.

Jones, K. (1972) A History of the Mental Health Service. London, UK: Routledge & Kegan Paul.

Jones, W.T. (1970) *The Classical Mind: A History of Western Philosophy*, Vol. 1, 2nd ed. New York, NY: Harcourt Brace Jovanovich.

Kanner, L. (1959) Johann Jakob Guggenbuhl and the Abendberg. *Bulletin of the History of Medicine,* Vol. 33: 6, 489–502.

Kanner, L. (1964) The History of the Care and Study of the Mentally Retarded. Springfield, IL: Charles C. Thomas.

Kraft, I. (1961) Edouard Seguin and the 19th century moral treatment of idiots. *Bulletin of the History of Medicine*, Vol. 35: 5.

Kristeller, P.O. (1972) Renaissance Concepts of Man. New York, NY: Harper Torchbook.

Lane, H. (1977) The Wild Boy of Aveyron. London, UK: George Allen & Unwin.

Locke, J. (1924). Two Treatises of Government. London, UK: J.M. Dent.

Locke, J. (1975) An Essay Concerning Human Understanding. Oxford, UK: Clarendon.

Malson, L. (1972) *Wolf Children*. London: NLB. [This volume also includes translations of Itard's *Of the First Developments of the Young Savage of Aveyron* (1799) and *Report on the Progress of Victor of Aveyron* (1806).]

Olson, J.E. (1989) Calvin and Social Welfare. London, UK: Associated University Presses.

Plato. *The Republic.* (1974) Translated by D. Lee, 2nd ed. Harmondsworth, UK: Penguin.

Porter, R. (1987) *Mind Forg'd Manacles*. London; UK: Athlone Press.

Public Record Office Document Just 1/873, membrane 14 dorse. Translated from the Latin by A. Heresy, unpublished.

Pufendorf, S. (1717) *Of the Laws of Nature and Nations*, 3rd ed, B. Kennet translator with the notes of Jean Barbeyrac.

Radford, J.P. and Tipper A. (1988) Starcross: Out of the Mainstream. Toronto: G. Allan Roeher Institute.

Rousseau, J.-J. (1974) *Emile*. Translated by Barbara Foxley. London, UK: J.M. Dent.

Ryan, J. (1987) The Politics Of Mental Handicap. London, UK: Free Association Books.

Scheerenberger, R.C. (1983) A History of Mental Retardation. Baltimore, MD: Paul H. Brookes.

Seguin, E. (1866) Idiocy: Its Treatment by the Physiological Method. New York, NY: William Wood & Co.

Tuke, D.H. (1882) History of the Insane. London, UK: Kegan Paul Trench.

Twinning, W. (1843) Some Account of Cretinism and the Institution for its Cure on the Abendberg, Near Interlachen, in Switzerland. London, UK: Parker.

Warfield, B.B. (1956) Introductory essay on Augustine and the Pelagian Controversy, In *A Select Library of the Nicene and Post-Nicene Fathers of the Christian Church*, Vol. 5, Edited by P. Schaff: Saint Augustine: Anti-Pelagian Writings. Grand Rapids, MI: Wm. B. Eerdmans Publishing Company.

Welsford, E. (1935) The Fool: His Social and Literary History. London, UK: Faber and Faber.

Willis, T. (1971) *Two Discourses Concerning the Soul of Brutes.* Translated by S. Portage. Gainsville, FL: Scholars Facsimiles & Reprints.

Wolfensberger, W. (1976) The origin and nature of our institutional models, In *Changing Patterns in Residential Services for the Mentally Retarded*, revised edition, Edited by R. Kugel and A. Shearer. Washington, DC: U.S. Government Printing Office.

2

THE COURAGE OF SUBORDINATION: WOMEN AND INTELLECTUAL DISABILITY IN THE ANCIENT GREEK WORLD

M. Lynn Rose

Introduction and overview

Ancient Greece incubated the Greek Miracle of city planning, comedy, competitive sports, history, individual excellence, philosophy, rational medicine, and tragedy, and we in the west like to claim ancient Greece as our cultural ancestor, especially when it comes to Classical Athens and the roots of democracy. We have been less enthusiastic to claim, or even acknowledge, the oppressive fundamentals upon which the Greek Miracle rested, i.e. systematic imperialism, slavery, and the subordination of women.

In one of my earliest essays, I argued that female physical disability had little to do with somatic configuration. A woman's most important function was to produce sons, and the female who failed the task of serving as incubator was the one who lacked ability. Barrenness, in other words, was the most significant female physical disability. Now, a couple of decades later, I turn to the criteria for female intellectual disability in the ancient Greek world, though I have come to see over the interceding years that separating body from mind is anachronistic (Edwards/Rose 1998; Goodey and Rose forthcoming).

In this essay, I argue that the conditions in which the ideal ancient Greek female lived went hand in hand with intellectual impairment, but I argue that the criteria for intellectual impairment had specific ancient meaning and status that has little to do with modern definitions. The similarity, though, is the timeless tendency to classify people in such a way that we are "us" and they are "them".

The essay begins with gender relations in ancient Greece, followed by discussion of its title, "The Courage of Subordination". From there follow four interrelated points. First, ancient Greek women's unmanaged cleverness was dangerous; second, men were responsible for managing their wives' intellect; third, the conditions in ancient Greece were in fact ripe for creating disabled intellect in women; but, fourth, intellectual disability was integral to the maintenance of ancient Greek socio-economic systems.

35

Gendered hierarchy

The intellectual subordination of women in the ancient world was deeply ingrained in the socio-economic system. A summary of gender relations in Greece provides a context for this discussion of women and intellectual disability. Pandora, in Greek cosmology the world's first female, and the source of the world's troubles, is an appropriate place to begin (Panofsky and Panofsky 1956/1991). In his narration of the origin of the gods, Hesiod, writing in the seventh century BC, recites legends that had been handed down to his generation, and that remained part of the ancient mythological fabric for centuries. In his narration of the origin of the gods, Hesiod describes scatterbrained (*hamartinoon*) Epimetheus, a scourge to men (*Theogony* 29). Scatterbrained Epimetheus is the brother and antithesis of the more familiar fire-giving Prometheus, whose cleverness and pragmatism enabled humankind to survive. Among other mistakes, Epimetheus first accepted Zeus's malicious gift of a woman, Pandora, thus bringing misery to men (*Theogony* 511). In modern popular culture, Pandora and her proverbial box are shorthand for the cause of all evils, but the meaning of this tale in particular is prone to getting lost in cultural translation: as an example, Pandora never even had a box (Panofsky and Panofsky p. 3). The ancient focus of the story is Epimetheus's mistake of allowing a woman to harm the whole human race eternally; Pandora was the mere vehicle, crafted by clever gods, whose terrible female potential was unleashed. The tale of Pandora illustrates several principles of ancient gender relations: women are potentially dangerous; the man who emulates Prometheus will use his wits to domesticate everything in his household; he who falters in the footsteps of Epimetheus will not be in control of his own Pandora.

The courage of subordination

The title of this essay, "The Courage of Subordination", comes from Aristotle's *Politics*, his analysis of the best possible state. Aristotle, who wrote in the politically turbulent fourth century BC, explains the hierarchy of human beings, putting forth his careful observations of ordinary social phenomena. It is only human to conflate observation of the way things are with the conclusion that this is the way things must be, or in other words, that the way things are is the natural order. Aristotle explains that "between the sexes, the male is by nature superior and the female inferior, the male ruler and the female subject" (Aristotle *Politics* 1.2.12–13 [1254b14–21]).

Aristotle established what he perceived to be obvious: one type of human being rules over other types. He provides a simple example, which anyone could have seen just by looking around any ancient community: "For the free rules the slave, the male the female, and the man the child". Who is a slave? Aristotle answers: "he is by nature a slave who is capable of belonging to another and that is why he does so belong". A slave is a slave because he is a slave. He then goes on to explain why each of these three categories of people is capable of being ruled, each in a different manner. All three categories – slaves, females, children – "possess the various parts of the soul, but possess them in different ways; for the slave has not got the deliberative part [bouleutikon] at all, and the female has it, but without full authority, while the child has it, but in undeveloped form". This deliberative part that Aristotle names, the bouleutikon, is the ability to consider and advise. The term has a tangible, archaeological connection: the Bouleutikon referred to the special seats in the Athenian theater, those closest to the orchestra and belonging to the members of the Boule, an archeological reflection of high social status and the accompanying, assumed privilege of participating prominently and meaningfully in public life (Goodey 1999).

Men and women, Aristotle observes, have very different natures. It is obvious to him that "the temperance of a woman and that of a man are not the same, nor their courage and justice, as Socrates thought but the one is the courage of command, and the other that of subordination, and the case is similar with the other virtues" (*Politics* 1.5.8 (1260a20-24). The female virtue that corresponded to the courage of subordination was silence. Aristotle quotes a line from a tragedy of Sophocles to make his point: "Silence gives grace to a woman". Just in case there might be any doubt, Aristotle is quick to clarify that this virtue "is not the case likewise with a man". Women's bouleutikons, or deliberative parts, he explains, were without full authority. They were without validity (*akuros*); the same term was used legally to refer to laws that were no longer in force, no longer valid. The ideal woman acknowledged the invalidity of her deliberative part (bouleutikon) and submitted courageously – preferably silently – to being ruled. Clever women are able to lie, and lying, when it is done well, can ruin a man. We learn in the Hippolytus, in the wake of the chaos wrought by female lies, that "a woman's silence is her greatest asset". A woman's deliberative function, activated, threatens social order.

This concept of silent and courageous subordination provides a starting point from which to examine the contextualized meaning of female intellectual ability and disability. Greek legends tell tales of both extremes: some women embodied the courage of subordination; other women were very insubordinate indeed.

The idea of courageous subordination is not unique to ancient Greece. With few exceptions, women have been praised for their willing, even defiant, insistence on submission to the men to whom they are accountable throughout human history, and various ideologies have justified, promulgated, and glorified the subordination. The physical mark resulting from foot binding provides a dramatic example of institutionalized female acquiescence to pain and loss. Female subordination is not necessarily marked on the body; psychological oppression is just as effective. It is important not to read any system of female subordination as a conscious patriarchal plot in which men forcibly oppressed women who yearned to run free and make legal decisions. The subordination of women is a system in which women participated, not one to which they merely acquiesced. A graphic example is an image of women with bound feet sewing their own tiny slippers.

It is also very important not to sensationalize ancient society. One culture's beauty is another culture's barbarianism. Lest we think that courageous subordination is some kind of ancient (or Oriental) exoticism, I offer Marabel Morgan's *The Total Woman,* as well as the more recent *Rules* or the best-selling *Surrendered Wife.*

> Like millions of women, I wanted my marriage to be better. But when I tried to get my husband to be more romantic, helpful and ambitious, he withdrew – and I was lonely and exhausted from controlling everything. Desperate to be in love with my man again, I decided to stop telling him what to do and how to do it.

> When I surrendered control, something magical happened. The union I
> had always dreamed of appeared. The man who had wooed me was back.
> (Doyle 2001)

More recently, *A Wife After God's Own Heart* was a best-seller in the U.S. God, apparently, does not want wives to make the big decisions (George 2004).

Dangerous female intellects

Courageous subordination has many faces. In Greece, one of the manifestations of the ideal was the danger of women's intellect. In the earliest Greek literature, the Homeric *Iliad* and *Odyssey*, the stick-figure female characters had two characteristics – or more precisely, formulaic epithets – that determined their value: beauty and cleverness (MacCary 1982). These Homeric women survived through the ancient world and into the modern world. Penelope of the *Odyssey* demonstrates the cleverness of handiwork in her endless weaving by day and unraveling by night, stalling her suitors during her husband's 20-year absence by saying she will marry one of them once she has finished her work. Weaving was the quintessential female skill, and Penelope was the archetypal good wife, literally weaving together her own interests and those of her absent husband's household.

But female ingenuity, just like female beauty, is a double-edged sword. Helen, whose face launched the thousand ships, is the best example of a Greek woman whose physical appearance created catastrophe, an "'Iliad of woes' for Greeks and barbarians", as the biographer Plutarch put it, a thousand years later (Plutarch "Advice to Bride and Groom" 21F Moralia 141). Helen's twin sister, Clytemnestra, had an clever nature that created an Odyssey of woes. Like Penelope, she was also spinning while her husband, Agamemnon, was off in Troy – but unlike Penelope, she was spinning a web of deceit culminating in the murder of Agamemnon in his own bathtub. In some versions of the story, she even wove a royal welcoming carpet on which he strutted to his doom.

The good ancient Greek woman does not misuse her cleverness to usurp her husband's domain. She surrenders her intellect to male authority, and this principle is as alive in Plutarch's time – the second century AD – as it was in the Homeric epics a thousand years earlier. Plutarch illustrates the courage necessary for women to surrender to appropriate male authority in his "Bravery of Women." He opens with what is, at first glance, a startlingly feminist statement that qualities of men and women ought to be compared on the same grounds (*Moralia* 242E); the intelligence of Tanaquil, for example, the wife of an Etruscan king of early Roman mytho-history, he proclaims, should be judged on the same scale as that of King Servius (*Moralia* 243C). But any misinterpretation of feminism dissolves quickly in Plutarch's cultural milieu, in which, after all, equal grounds of comparison were simply inconceivable. The impossibility of equal comparison is exposed in his account of Aretaphilia, whose name literally means virtue (*arête*)–loving. Aretaphilia personifies the courage of subordination, for she was beautiful and as clever as Penelope, and, quoting Plutarch, "reputed to be unusually sensible and not deficient in political wisdom" ("Bravery of Women" 19, *Moralia* 255 E). Notably, though, after using both of these qualities to topple the despots of Cyrene through her own sacrifice and cleverness, and when she could have had anything she wanted, including political clout, "when she saw the city free, withdrew at once to her own quarters, among the women, and rejecting any sort of meddling in affairs, spent the rest of her life quietly at the loom in the company of her friends and family" (*Moralia* 257E). Aretaphilia transcends even Penelope in subordinating her clever instincts for the greater good, and ultimately fulfilling the Thucydidean role that nature intended.

Women's cleverness was damned far more often than it was praised – good behavior does not make a juicy story – and female wiliness is the subject of many a cautionary tale. The man with a clever wife such as Penelope was blessed, but the flip side was always lurking. She could be clever enough to deceive, clever enough to undermine the household. The legend of Medea, best known to us through Euripides' fifth-century tragedy of the same name, takes ingenious villainy of the feral woman to its fullest extent. Medea, with her bitter skills unmonitored, illustrates further the danger of unharnessed clever women. The courageously subordinate Greek woman is silent. Not only does she not talk (or appear in public, lest her beauty invite rape or launch a thousand ships); no one even talks about her. Medea is not Greek, though: she is a barbarian, and Euripides has her howl that she will be talked about, and for years.

Language of cleverness and foolery abounds in *Medea*. At the beginning of this play, the household slave speaks of Medea as a fool, or, more literally, a moron (*môros*) ("if I may speak this of my masters"). The slave calls Medea moronic because she is still ignorant of her latest trouble. On top of having been abandoned by her husband, Jason, in favor of the Corinthian king's young daughter, she is now going to be exiled from Corinth (*Medea* 61). But the audience knows that Medea is no fool. As she pleads tenderly for a little more time before she is driven from the land, King Creon wonders out loud if she could be plotting some harm while speaking soothing words. "A hot-tempered woman", he says, "and a hot-tempered man likewise – is easier to guard against than a clever woman who keeps her own counsel" (Medea 316–320).[1] But he succumbs, and, granted that bit of time by King Creon, Medea tricks Jason into taking poisoned gifts for his new bride back to the palace. To lull him into submission, she dismisses her previous anger as womanly folly (*aboulian*; that is, lacking the particularly male sense that it would take to serve in the Boule, the sense that Aristotle claims is latent in females) and says that she realizes that she was the fool (*aphrôn*, un-minded) (*Medea* 882).

The audience still knows better. Medea was very strong-minded, not un-minded at all. She delights in learning that she was successful in murdering both Jason's bride and King Creon, and, taking ultimate revenge on Jason, she kills his prize possessions, the two sons she bore to him. As opposed to Agave, the son-slaying mother in Euripides' Bacchae, who is horrified by her gruesome act when she recovers from her Dionysiac trance, Medea was never in a trance. Agave was restored to sanity after hearing rational words and gazing at the sun, the rational light of Apollo; Medea's partner is the moon. Jason, seeing the corpses of his sons, cries out, "O children most dear!" to which Medea replies, "Yes, to their mother, not to you". "So you killed them?", Jason asks; "Yes", Medea replies calmly, "to cause you grief" (*Medea* 1396–1398).

Medea is infamous today, just as Euripides had her predict, because the tale of betrayal and revenge is gruesomely enduring. The *Medea* is many things; it is, among them, a cautionary tale of a woman's untended cleverness run amok. Sometimes *Medea* is misunderstood as a cautionary tale about the dangers of leaving the wife and kids even if family life is getting a little stale, sort of a prototype of *Fatal Attraction*, though in the latter, Glenn Close ends up dead in the bathtub instead of victorious in a divine, snake-driven chariot. *Medea* is a cautionary tale, but the fifth-century warning is economic, not moral in the modern sense: it illustrates the danger of mismanaging one's household. It is not Medea's anger or even her jealous rage that is scary, it is her uncontrolled deliberative intelligence. She is not so much a woman scorned as a woman mismanaged. The marriage was unpropitious in the first place: she was already trained in magical arts, and worse, she came from a non-Greek family. She entered into marital partnership with Jason, using her cleverness first on his behalf and then against him. In the end she destroyed her natal family and her husband's. Jason's should have been the dominant, rational authority. Instead, his weak foresight led to his inability to control his own household. Jason ends up the fool.

Taming the female

The role of the ideal wife and the perceived dangers of diverting from this role remain fairly consistent throughout the long expanse of ancient Greek history. Throughout, men were responsible for harnessing and shaping their wives' latent intellects into mirrors of their own, active intellects. From the earliest Greek literature – that is, Homeric writing – and on, the idea that women were bothersome but necessary, and that they had to be supervised, is readily apparent. The management of wives, the Greek tales tell us over and over, cannot be left to chance. One might be blessed with an unsupervised Penelope waiting at home, but a twist of fate could arrange Clytemnestra, axe in hand. In the Homeric tales in 800 BC and in Graeco-Roman literature a thousand years later, the ideal wife was the well-supervised wife; that is to say, the ideal wife reflected her husband's household.

That a woman should serve as a mirror for her husband is not hyperbole: in his marriage manual, "Advice to the Bride and Groom", Plutarch suggests that "the wife ought to have no feeling of her own" so as to reflect more accurately her husband's feelings ("Advice to the Bride and Groom" 14, *Moralia* 140A). The woman should reflect her husband not only emotionally but also intellectually, and Plutarch warns of the consequences of a wife who is left to her own thoughts, rather than shaped by her husband's doctrine. He compares the resulting thoughts to a gynecological symptom, calling them "misshapen, fleshlike, uterine growths originating in some infection, which develop of themselves and acquire firmness and solidity" ("Advice to Bride and Groom", *Moralia* 145D 48). Plutarch turns to the established adage that the best cure for female illness is pregnancy. Literally, girls should be be well-impregnated with the sperm of good doctrine. Otherwise, again quoting Plutarch, "they, left to themselves, conceive many untoward ideas and low designs and emotions" ("Advice to Bride and Groom, *Moralia* 145 E, 48/139A). The courage that it took for a woman to subordinate herself to her husband, emotionally and intellectually, was facilitated by the proper ancient Greek marriage, ideally between a man in his thirties and a barely pubescent girl.

The mechanics of such a marriage are outlined by the fifth and fourth century BC historian Xenophon in his household manual *Oeconomicus* (Pomeroy 1994).

In Xenophon's view, it was the husband's duty to manage his household and everything in it, as a shepherd manages his sheep. One should blame the husband if the wife manages badly, just as one blames the shepherd for a sick sheep, not the sheep itself (*Oeconomicus* 3.11). Xenophon illustrates this concept of sheep management by manufacturing a dialogue between Socrates and Isomachus, the ideal householder. This ideal householder has an ideal wife, an anonymous child bride. Socrates asks Isomachus if his wife came to him already trained, and Isomachus scoffs his well-known reply that of course she did not; she was not yet 15 years old, and he goes on to brag that she "had spent her previous years under careful supervision so that she might see and hear and speak as little as possible" (*Oeconomicus* 7.4–6). The day came when the wife – this girl – was flustered because she could not find some items that her husband wanted, but Isomachus did not become angry with her; instead, he gallantly blamed himself for his failure to teach her how to arrange things (*Oeconomicus* 8.1–2). Isomachus goes on to narrate how he himself (shepherd) trained the wife (sheep) gently and thoroughly. "How beautiful it looks", he claims to have told her, "when shoes are arranged in rows, each kind in its own proper place, how beautiful to see all kinds of clothing properly sorted out, each kind in its own proper place, how beautiful bed-linens, bronze pots, table-ware!" (*Oeconomicus* 8.18–19). He goes on, verging on the compulsive, to point out that not only do the objects themselves look so nice when they are arranged well, but, like dancers, even "the interval between them looks beautiful when each item is kept clear of it" (*Oeconomicus* 8.20).

The ideal situation, outlined explicitly by Xenophon, suggests that girls were deliberately kept from knowing anything at all, beyond weaving, so that they could go to their husbands as blank slates. This lack of education was not cruelty, deprivation, or neglect; indeed, plenty of evidence suggests that Greek female children were cherished by their parents. Lack of exposure to intellectual stimulation was thought to keep females pure. The priestess of the god Apollo at Delphi was, according to Plutarch, who served as a priest at the Temple, "utterly unlettered as she goes down into the shrine". Plutarch goes on to make a noteworthy parallel. He writes: "Just as Xenophon believes that a bride should have seen as little and heard as little as possible before she proceeds into her husband's house, so this girl, inexperienced and uninformed about practically everything, a pure, virgin soul, becomes the associate of the god" ("The Oracles at Delphi" 22 [*Moralia* 405C-D]). Here, utter ignorance marks female purity.

At first glance, the ideal of women's ignorance is contradicted by Aristophanes' comedy *Lysistrata*. In Lysistrata's soliloquy, as she arranges the Reconciliation between the warring Greek states, she says: "I am a woman, but I have got a mind (nous): I am not badly off for intelligence (gnomes) on my own account, and I am not badly educated either, having heard a great deal of the talk of my father and of other older men" (1125–1126). But Spartan Lysistrata, for the Athenian audience, was a joke. Everything in comedy is topsy-turvy, playing on underlying social order. Women couldn't really influence international military policy any more than Aristophanic birds could rule kingdoms.

The collective literary lesson is this: there were no bad women, only men's bad management of women. Isomachus' bride was an anonymous teenage lump of moldable substance just like Pandora, but the enterprising Isomachus, modeling Prometheus' careful planning and not Epimetheus' scattered thoughtlessness, was able to use her potential to its fullest. If only Jason had been a good shepherd, all would have been well in Corinth. But Jason misused his authority, and allowed invalid female authority to reign instead.

Isomachus' anonymous wife was a real prize: not only did she arrive with an empty mind and the basic skill of spinning wool, but she had already acquired another sign of subordination: she had been trained to control her appetites (*Oeconomicus* 7.6). The relationship between women and food was highly charged by the time Xenophon described the ideal wife. Here, we can return to Pandora again, the first woman, who "astounds men by her god-given beauty and ruins them by her thievish gluttony" (Zeitlin 1995, p. 59). The female appetite was almost as dangerous as her potential cleverness. Sarah Pomeroy notes that the appetites (*ta gastera*) included not only appetite for food but all physical appetites. Pomeroy also explains that the female was thought to have a "vast and empty" belly and thus had the tendency to be insatiable (Pomeroy p. 71). Semonides' infamous poem describing the varieties of women a man might be unfortunate enough to acquire includes this type:

> Another the Olympians fashioned out of earth and gave to man with wits impaired; for such a woman understand nothing, bad or good. The only thing she knows how to do is eat: not even when the god brings on a bad winter does she feel the cold and draw her stool nearer to the fire. [Semonides 7.21–26]

To this point, I have discussed the ideals of cultivating and maintaining female ignorance through literature. Ken Dowden, addresses the dangers of relying on myth: myth explores and expresses cultural data, but cannot be the source of cultural data. Myth, he goes on to explain, illustrates what we already know, but does not add to that knowledge (Dowden 1992). Heeding this caution, I now turn to the implications of ideals of feminine intellect in their relation to everyday life.

The environment of disabled intellects

It is worth repeating my bedrock assumption here that intellectual disability is a fluid concept, and perhaps nothing more than a concept, that varies widely over time and between cultures. I have argued that the ideal Athenian woman repressed her intellect, and that the cultural ideal was that women's intellects should be curtailed for the good of the household. This ideal woman should be kept from knowing too much or learning too much, and, with some exceptions, an educated woman was laughable, foreign, or worse.

I would like to pad this ideal with the caveat that no matter how clearly the surviving literature instructs women to be blank slates for their husbands, the reality of daily life would have intruded on the ideal. Life for a female peasant would have conformed to the secluded, silent ideal to a much smaller degree than that of the aristocratic wife. By necessity, the peasant woman was outside, working, and participating in the marketplace to some extent. Lacking or repressing one's inherent deliberative intellectual function did not result in mass stupidity. Still, it is worth considering the basic principle behind the modern measurements, even if the modern measurements do not have the same ramifications for ancient societies. Ill-educated mothers, especially mothers who begin giving birth at an age at which their physical bodies are not developed, are likely to provide an environment for their offspring in which intellectual disability in the modern sense can manifest. By the same token, disabled intellect, in the ancient sense, can be fostered.

In modern terms, the education of women, combined with the age of women at the beginning of childbearing, has implications not only for the lives of women themselves but also for their subsequent generations. Epidemiologically, maternal age and education are important factors in predicting intellectual disability (in all its rapidly varying terms, from "low-grade moron to "delayed learning") in children. Today, low maternal education corresponds with delayed or permanent intellectual development of the offspring; younger mothers with fewer than 12 years of education give birth to babies with the greatest proportion of intellectual disability.

In ancient Greece, girls became mothers, or more to the point became pregnant, at a very young age relative to modern western standards. As for education, with a very few notable exceptions, women (and, for that matter, the vast bulk of men) had no sort of formal education. Our modern measurements reflect our own society, in which 10 or 12 years of education is, remarkably, the standard; the same number of years would never apply to any ancient society as a standard for the whole population. This is the point: standards and expectations varied among the ancient population between station and gender. Logically enough, individuals and populations tend to fulfil deeply ingrained expectations. Even if not, what is expected tends to be perceived anyway, and any notable exception usually proves the rule.

Material culture mirrors and perpetuates social expectations in tangible ways. Nutritional factors, for example, play a role in intellectual development. Nutritional deprivation, especially of proteins and of vitamins A and E, contribute to the presence of what we today term "intellectual disability". The ancient literary theme of greedy and insatiable women, on one hand, and women with controlled appetites, on the other, reflects the gendered issue of food. Peter Garnsey, in his 1999 study of food and society in antiquity, offers a balanced narration of the relationship between women and food. He points out that while it would not have been sensible to deprive women of nutrition to the point of incapacitating them, even if anyone had wanted to, when push came to shove, food was rationed to those in power, and those in power were male. Garnsey writes: "The dilemma facing the male head of household is clear. If women were confined to the home, as they more or less were in upper-class society, then they were handed the power to indulge their alleged weaknesses in the matter of food and drink" (Garnsey 1999).

Some ancient beliefs about nutritional needs for females were born of a misogynistic culture and reflect that culture, but nevertheless hold true, as far as we know, in any culture. Aristotle observed that women need less food than men (History of Animals 608b14–15), which is generally true, in terms of basic caloric intake. Then again, pregnant women were thought to need even less food than usual, which is false, unless one subscribes to the nutritional philosophy of supermodel Giselle Bundchen.[2]

Women in agricultural households would probably have been allotted more calories than those in urban households. The ancient Mediterranean diet was fairly healthful; even when one eliminates the image of today's tomato-laden choriatiki, cereals had good nutritional qualities, though they were short of Vitamins A, C, and D. Cereals comprised the general population's subsistence, and Garnsey points out the basic fact that our extant sources make so easy to erase: the vast bulk of the ancient population was composed not of aristocrats, but of farmers. He hypothesizes that women took part in agricultural work and that the distribution of food was commensurate with their labour, but adds the sensible reminder that the nutritional situation was not the same for all women throughout the ancient Mediterranean world (Garnsey).

Here again Pandora displays female appetite. Women, urban or rural, were portrayed as literally insatiable; again, their physiology consisted largely of a vast and empty belly that could never get full. A man had to take a wife to have children, but as Sarah Pomeroy explains, "after a woman had borne the requisite number of children she could be considered as little more than a parasite, a consumer, like the first human bride, Pandora" (Pomeroy).

In these terms, the best wife of all was perhaps not Homer's Penelope but Euripides' Alcestis. Queen Alcestis bore sons, and then got out of the way by offering her death in exchange for her condemned husband's life. Once the divine deal was carried out, King Admetus immediately embarked on decadent funereal dining as quickly as possible after a brief and formulaic statement of woe for the wife he had lost. Euripides leaves us to ponder if the scheme worked, though, and if Admetus is rewarded or punished when the shell of his woman, mute and veiled, is delivered to his door.

The environment of disabled intellect seems at first look not to match that of the women of Sparta. Spartan women, i.e. the women who belonged to the Spartan elite, need to be considered as a possible exception to the rule, as there is some indication that Spartan women were educated, fed decently, encouraged to take exercise, and that they started giving birth later in life than the wives of other Greek men. But most of our information about Spartan daily life comes from reports one millennium after the fact. In short, I am suspicious of Plutarchian propaganda about Spartan society.

Plutarch's ideal woman comes not even from his own second century Graeco-Roman tumult, but from his imagination of how Spartan women acted in the bygone days of Spartan glory. He tells the story of a Spartan woman who was being sold as a slave. When asked what she knew how to do, she replied laconically: "to be faithful". He says that another Spartan woman, in similar style, answered: "to manage a house well" ("Sayings of Spartan Women 27 and 28, *Moralia* 242C.) Even in the imagination of the Spartaphile Plutarch, women were the models of subordination, albeit formidable ones.

Intellectual impairment and desire

The conditions in the ancient Greek world were favourable for women to be inferior intellectually to men, inferior even to the *agroikos* men who were already considered by the upper classes to be stupidity embodied (Ronell 2001). The ideal wife was a clear pool in which to reflect her husband's intellect and emotion, a vehicle for bearing her husband's children, and an automaton for arranging her husband's household. Ancient intellectual fitness was determined by how one measured up according to one's station; gender was lockstep with station. The concept of a universal test of social skills, speaking ability, and economic dexterity did not exist and could not have existed. Females, at least those living their prescribed role, were reflections of the men who owned them. When Aristotle concluded that women did not have a fully valid bouleutikon, he was making an observation, not a judgment.

We all know about cultural relativity. What might appear horrifying in one time and space might be delightful in another. What looks like female mutilation in one time and place is attractive femininity in another. What disables people in one society enables them in another. The core of Disability Studies is recognizing that the meaning of disability is not inherent in the individual, but shifts over time and across cultures.

To borrow the saying about a tree falling in a forest with no witness, if a woman is, by modern standards, intellectually disabled, but the concept of intellectual disability had not yet been invented, was that woman really intellectually disabled? To take it another step, if a female is by her own culture's standards basically ignorant, but this lack of knowledge is the desired quality – fostered from a young age – can we say that she is disabled in any way?

At one extreme we have Penelope, waiting and weaving; possibly better yet, Alcestis bears sons and then willingly prepares for Charon's journey.[3] At the other extreme, at the same time (that is, long long ago, in the collective memory of the Trojan War), Clytemnestra devises plots to usurp her own house, an act more brazen even than her sister Helen's treachery of being beautiful and abducted. The ideal, obviously, is that barely pubescent female blank slates be trained into submission so as to bar women's unharnessed thinking, which could damage the household.

Comparing ancient and modern attitudes about taking a person with an intellectual disability as a spouse provides a small but interesting window through which to view change over time. We get a glowing portrayal of compatibility between people who differ in labels of intelligence in the novel and subsequent film Tim, a romance between an attractive intellectually disabled young man and a clever, older, wealthy woman, in which there was no problem that could not be solved by a lot of open mindedness and money (McCullough 1974). The more common arrangement in real life, unsurprisingly, is between a man without identified intellectual disabilities and a woman who has been labelled intellectually disabled, rather than an older benefactress and a young hunk.

The surface characteristics are striking in their parallels between the Greek arrangement of the dominant kind man and the submissive trainable woman in Robert Edgerton's now-dated anthropological reports of "normal" men who married what he termed, 50 years ago, mentally retarded women. Edgerton traced the lives of over 100 deinstitutionalized people over 30 years and summarized his findings in *The Cloak of Competence*. He was surprised by the large number of women labelled mentally retarded who married men without intellectual disabilities (Edgerton 1967/1993). Four examples follow. While the terminologies and measurement of modern diagnosis of intellectual disability have changed quite a bit, the scenario is the same. Women who had been trained to be dependent on relying on someone else for the process of reasoning are intellectually dependent on men who tell them what to do.

Billie Mae says: "My husband just does everything for me. He shops; he buys everything; ... I like it that way.... I think a man's place is to tell a woman what to do. I don't have to worry about anything now". Edgerton records the point of view of Billie Mae's spouse: "Sure, she's sort of stupid. When I met her she didn't know nothing about nothing. But I got her trained. She's OK now. I take care of her and she's OK. She cooks real good" (Edgerton p. 167).

Of another woman, June, Edgerton reports her husband's assessment. "My first wife was a real bitch, if you'll pardon me. Nothing was good enough for her. June is what I've always wanted. She appreciates everything. Everything is new and enjoyable for her. She stays home and takes care of the house, and that's what I want" (Edgerton p. 168).

Myrtle's husband perceives that he rescued his wife from a life of being exploited. "Now she's well taken care of. All I ask is that when I come home from work she has dinner ready and the house cleaned up" (Edgerton p. 170).

Finally, a man says about his wife, Corliss: "I'll admit she's a problem sometimes. She needs so much supervision, but I don't mind – it works out all right" (Edgerton p. 170).

Conclusions: Context and community

Edgerton carried out his research in an age when "mental retardation" was a standard, even respectful word, and the validity of the IQ test had only just come into question. In the United States, the American Association on Mental Retardation, a government agency, set the diagnostic formula to establish who was mildly, moderately, or profoundly mentally retarded. Borderline Mental Retardation was a grey and contested zone. Even then, in the middle to late twentieth century, when we were so confident in our ability to apply scientific measures to human intelligence, one of the AAMR's assumptions essential to the application of their definition of mental retardation is that "limitations in present functioning must be considered within the context of community environments typical of the individual's age peers and culture" (AAMR 2002).

Intellectual ability and disability takes meaning from its community's context. Ancient Greek women, courageously subordinating their intellect and appetite, were merely part of the ancient Greek system of expectations and resources, just as Chinese women who lovingly broke their little girls' feet were part of theirs, and just as American teenagers suffering and dying in the name of fashion are part of theirs.

The meaning behind intellectual ability and disability is dependent on expectations and resources, and on the dizzying circular relationship between expectations, and only a generation or two ago, babies born with Down Syndrome were not expected to live very long, and so they were routinely placed in institutions, where, denied the basic comforts of childhood, they didn't live very long. Since the early 1980s, the life expectancy for people with Down Syndrome has doubled, not because of some breakthrough medical advance, but because of higher expectations coupled with appropriate resources. When we look at disability, we are looking at hierarchies of resource allocation and configurations of authority. Female idiots in ancient Greece were women who allowed their intellects to develop.

Notes

1 Jason enumerates all the benefits that he has garnered for Medea by taking her away from the barbarians and bringing her into the rational light of Greece. "All of the Greeks have

learned that you are clever (sophên), and you have won renown. But if you lived at the world's edge, there would be no talk of you". (539–540) This is a poisoned compliment, for two reasons: women are not supposed to be renowned; also, what she will ultimately be renowned for is the worst evil possible. Later, Aegus tells Medea the obscure oracular advice he received about his childlessness. Medea asks if it is acceptable for her to hear the oracular pronouncement, and Aegus replies that it's acceptable: "It calls for a wise mind". (epei toi kai sophês deitai phrenos) (677).

2 Some beliefs were born of a misogynistic culture and reflect that culture, but are nevertheless true scientifically, e.g., Aristotle states that women need less food than men (History of Animals 608b14-15) and Garnsey points out that this is true that women require fewer calories than men.

3 Alcestis, in dying so that her husband might live, at first glance might appear to represent the ultimate model of subordinated courage, but Euripides prevents this by referring to the mindedness of Alcestis and Admetus. Pheres, Admetus' father, says (line 615) "For you have lost, as no one will deny, a noble and virtuous wife". (sôphronos – to be of sound mind, discreet, prudent, self-controlling). But later, toward the end of the squabble, Pheres says that she lacked sense in this self-sacrificing act (aphrôna) (line 728).

References

Aristotle, *History of Animals* vol 3, ed. and trans. D.M. Balme, Loeb Classical Library 439 (Cambridge, MA, 1991).

K. Dowden, *The Uses of Greek Mythology* (New York, NY: Routledge, 1992).

L. Doyle, *The Surrendered Wife: A Practical Guide for Finding Intimacy, Passion and Peace with a Man* (New York, NY: Simon and Schuster, 2001).

R.B. Edgerton, *The Cloak of Competence, 1967*, Revised edition (Berkeley, CA: University of California Press, 1993).

M. Edwards [L. Rose], Women and physical disability in ancient Greece. *Ancient World* 29, no. 1 (1998): 3–9.

P. Garnsey, *Food and Society in Classical Antiquity* (Cambridge, UK: Cambridge University Press, 1999).

E. George, *A Wife After God's Own Heart: 12 Things That Really Matter in Your Marriage* (Eugene, OR: Harvest House, 2004).

C.F. Goodey, Politics, nature, and necessity: We're Aristotle's slaves feeble- minded? *Political Theory* 27, no. 2 (1999): 3–23.

C.F. Goodey and M. Lynn Rose, The construct of disability in ancient Greece and Rome, in *Oxford Companion to Disability History*, ed. M. Rembis, C. Kudlick, and S. Burch now (forthcoming).

R. Luckasson et al., *Mental Retardation: Definition, Classification, and Systems of Support*, 10th ed. (Washington, DC: AAMR, 2002).

W.T. MacCary, *Childlike Achilles: Ontogeny and Phylogeny in the* Iliad (New York, NY: Columbia University, 1982).

C. McCullough, *Tim* (New York, NY: Fawcett, 1974).

A.M. Miller, *Greek Lyric: An Anthology in Translation* (Indianapolis/Cambridge: Hackett Publishing, 1996), 23

D. Panofsky and E. Panofsky, *Pandora's Box: The Changing Aspects of a Mythical Symbol, Bolingen Series 52*, 1956 (Princeton, NJ: Princeton University Press, 1991).

S. Pomeroy, Trans. and Commentary, Xenophon, *Oeconomicus* (Oxford, UK: Clarendon Press, 1994).

A. Ronell, Stupidity (Urbana, IL: University of Illinois Press, 2001).

F.I. Zeitlin, Signifying difference: The myth of Pandora, in *Women in Antiquity: New Assessments*, ed. R. Hawley and B. Levick (London, UK: Routledge, 1995), 59.

3

JANE AUSTEN AND ME:
TALES FROM THE COUCH

Diane Driedger

I read Jane Austen's (1775–1817) novels as a teenager, and I loved *Pride and Prejudice* for its thrust and parry between men and women. But, rereading her novels as an adult, I noticed that there were many characters like myself in her books. There were characters that had ongoing health issues, who needed to lie on the couch a lot (*Mansfield Park*, *Persuasion*), who took to their beds and worried when their nerves were frayed (*Pride and Prejudice*, *Emma*), who could sometimes go out for long walks and at other times not (*Mansfield Hall*). I have had fibromyalgia for over 20 years and the experiences of these characters resonated with me. I'm being written about, at last, I thought.

Jane Austen critics, who have discussed Austen and the body, have the interpretation that the characters with lingering health issues were malingerers, hypochondriacs, and hysterics (Miller, 1990; Wiltshire, 1992). In my literature review, I have not encountered critics who understand that perhaps these characters had chronic illnesses that we now know as lupus, chronic fatigue, fibromyalgia, arthritis, depression etc.

This chapter will discuss the Austen characters that relate to my own life with chronic illness and disability. I will discuss the current state of social attitudes towards my disability and how this relates to Austen's characters and attitudes towards invalidism in her day. I will examine the novels, the work of literary critics about the novels, and current-day film versions of the books for their view on invisible disability and chronic illness.

Austen also experienced chronic illness 1816–1817, perhaps Addison's disease, (Miller, 1990; Austen-Leigh & Austen-Leigh, 1965), and wrote letters about taking to her couch and about the damp weather affecting her back. She wrote the unfinished novel, *Sanditon*, during this time, which focuses on many people with chronic illnesses going to the sea for relief. I will discuss her illness' possible impact on her writing.

In–valids in the late 18th and early 19th centuries

A key concept to consider in all of the books is the notion of "the invalid". In Jane Austen's day, England in the early 1800s, an invalid was seen as a person with delicate health who stays at home a lot and lies around or sits around being quiet, so as not to aggravate his/her "condition." An invalid was a person whose physical condition was not fixable, was not going to get better. Therefore, the person was mostly house bound and bedridden for a long period of time. I have thought about this word— in-valid—if you break it down. So, if I act like an invalid, am I in—valid? Not valid?

Have no place? There was a role for in-valids in the 1800s. Maria Frawley, in her book *Invalidism and Identity in Nineteenth-Century Britain* (2004), claims that even though invalids were seen as delicate, they still did a lot of work and they also travelled. In addition, invalids were seen as morally superior in many ways to those others who were part of the rat race of working in a rapidly industrializing society.

Invalids as workers and socializers

Florence Nightingale was a well-known invalid in the mid to late 19th century, who actually did a lot of her important work building the nursing profession from her sequestered bed: "Responding to an admirer who had written to ask after her health, Florence Nightingale once wrote: 'I am an incurable invalid, entirely a prisoner of my bed (except during a periodical migration) and overwhelmed with business'" (Frawley, p. 1). Nightingale, even though she spent most of her time in bed, still did work. Being in one's bed afforded a place of contemplation, quiet, a place to write letters, articles and books, and a retreat from a busy work world outside the home. England was fast industrializing and people were becoming much busier. There were even male workers who became invalids themselves through working too hard, too many hours, with too much stress (Frawley, 2004).

Invalids were also not expected to participate in going out to events or socializing outside their bed. Even so, invalids held court at their bedside to social gatherings and friends. In fact, Elizabeth Gaskell, a well-known novelist and short story writer at the time, in her book, *Round the Sofa* (1913), featured a "crippled" woman who hosted a weekly Monday night soiree of friends, which was well-attended.

Invalids had a lot of time on their hands. Some wrote books and shared their experiences with other invalids. One such author was Harriet Martineau, a pioneer in the field of sociology and a woman who wrote about her own life experiences as an invalid. She experienced gynaecological problems that were deemed incurable by doctors and the symptoms were very painful and disabling. During this time, she wrote about her experience of the sickroom, saying that she dedicates the book to fellow invalids, as a way of telling her story to others who know what she is experiencing. She ends her dedication with a wish that her words may help other invalids:

> If they [words] should have the virtue to summon thoughts, which may, for a single hour, soften your couch, shame and banish your foes of depression and pain, and set your chamber in holy order and something of cheerful adornment, I may have the honour of being your nurse, though I am myself laid low. (Martineau, 1844, p. xii)

Thus, on one hand invalids were in-valid as they did not participate in everyday life with its work tensions and social obligations, and on the other, they were still contributing their productivity to society.

Invalids as morally and religiously enlightened

Frawley posits that invalids in the 1800s saw that they had an opportunity to become closer to God through their suffering and "Illness, many nineteenth-century invalids argued, conferred on the sufferer a far more valuable form of status, the status that came with the priceless opportunity to experience and exhibit grace" (p. 158). Invalids believed that God provided them the stoicism and strength to bear the pain and suffering of their illnesses which they have shared about in diaries, letters and books of devotions meant for other invalids.

Invalids, such as Harriet Martineau, thought that being couch-ridden afforded her the time and space to think about the larger issues of humanity such as good and evil, pain and suffering. She was not rushing about doing things like the rest of the industrializing society around her. She discovered that, there were lessons she learned: "while the troubles of that night-season [pain and suffering] are thus sure to pass away, its products of thoughts and experiences must endure" (Martineau, p. 24).

Invalids as travellers

There were invalids who travelled to better their health. There was a movement led by Henry Matthews through his diaries written while travelling as an invalid in 1817–1819. He believed that moving around from place to place could help invalids feel better, having "ventured from England to Lisbon and on to Pisa, Florence and Rome as an invalid traveller, Matthew came to believe that motion helped to restore 'equilibrium' between mind and body and bestow tranquility on the anxiety-ridden sick person" (Frawley, 2004, p. 113). It was also believed by some invalids that there were climates that made them feel better, climates other than the city, or the winter weather of England. Indeed, in Jane Austen's time and for the rest of the 19th century, going to Bath, a seaside town, to take the waters was seen as an act of healing or at least feeling better for invalids.

Are all of these invalids' experiences apparent in the writings of Jane Austen? I will now look at three of Austen's novels and their images of "invalids".

Mansfield Park

Mansfield Park is a novel about Fannie, an orphan, who is taken in by her Aunt and Uncle Bertram. As the book unfolds it is apparent that Fannie became the Lady Bertram's companion. Lady Bertram lies on the couch in the parlour everyday and most evenings with her dog, Pug. She appears to be an invalid, laid up with chronic fatigue and languor. Austen describes her as indolent and not having interest in going out with her daughters—and one of the duties of a mother is to show interest in her daughters: "Lady Bertram did not go into public with her daughters. She was too indolent even to accept a mother's gratification in witnessing their success and enjoyment at the expense of any personal trouble" (Austen, 2008a, *Mansfield Park*, p. 34). Instead, Lady Bertram's sister took on these duties in her place. The use of the word "indolent" gives a negative connotation to the motives of Lady Bertram, that she does not care at all, perhaps. This brings to mind the "moral" issues of having a chronic illness.

When I first experienced my onset of fibromyalgia, I was unable to fulfil a lot of social functions, as I was so exhausted I had to cancel or postpone plans. I did not want to, but my body was not willing to leave the couch. Some friends impugned that I did not want to be with them and was not a good friend. They are no longer in my life. Over the years, the issue of "what is a good friend" has loomed with its moral imperative to "be there" physically at all times, otherwise, you are not a good friend.

Morally, Lady Bertram and I are accused of not caring and in fact, being bad because we are "indolent". The notion of being indolent is a big slap in the face in Western capitalist cultures. With the industrial revolution in England, hard work was deified and those who worked hard and were busy kept the devil away (Frawley, 2004). After all, the industrial complex needed hard workers to keep the system going. People who lie around and do not contribute to society outside their couches and beds are not productive and are therefore suspect.

Paradoxically, this notion of being productive does become part of the invalid's narrative in the 19th century, as people who are chronically ill find ways to be productive. Indeed, Lady Bertram does do productive work. It is apparent that she is the middle of things in the family, lying on her couch in the middle of the parlour. This is shown well in the film *Mansfield Park* (BBC, 1996). Lady Bertram directs the activities of the family and the home, as the lady of the house should in Austen's times. She finds people to accompany her daughters when she cannot. She is part of the decisions made in the family. They come to her and family life happens around the couch. She requests accommodations in the process.

Firstly, she is resting. Secondly, she has a companion, an attendant (?) to assist her with her food and fetching items and keeping her company. Finally, she has her therapy dog, Pug, with her at all times. The small pug dog stays with her on the couch, or when she moves to the table the dog accompanies her. She talks to the dog as to a beloved child. Pug obviously provides emotional support to Lady Bertram and improves her quality of life.

I, too, work and direct from a lying position at various times of the day. I work for a few hours at the computer and then continue reading, talking on the phone, and directing activities for most of the days when I don't teach classes. When I was Provincial Coordinator at the Manitoba League of Persons with Disabilities, I requested that a couch be put in my office, so that I could lie down when I needed to, to rest my body from the sitting position that is the hardest for me to maintain for hours. I hung a photo of Frida Kahlo, the disabled Mexican artist, above the couch. She is lying in bed with an easel on her body and she is painting while propped up on pillows. I was hoping that some visitors to my office to comment on the juxtaposition of the photo and my couch and my situation, but that did not happen.

Instead, people when entering my office commented, "Oh, every office should have a couch!" "How inviting to have a couch!" Then the visitor would sit down on the couch to meet with me. I thought that people would have problems with the couch, a symbol of leisure, in a work environment—I didn't get the reactions I thought I'd get. Instead, my office was welcoming in their eyes.

Persuasion

In the novel *Persuasion*, Anne, a single woman, goes to stay with her married sister, whose health is not good. When Anne arrives at Mary's home, she is lying on the sofa in the drawing room. Mary complains that Anne has not come quickly enough to be by her side. Why did she not come to visit sooner, she has been so ill? Anne replies to Mary, who is on the couch: "My dear Mary, recollect what a comfortable account you sent of yourself! You wrote in the cheerfullest manner, and said you were perfectly well, and in no hurry for me" (Austen, 1997, *Persuasion*, p. 27).

Anne is perplexed that her sister now lies on the sofa and says she is ill. Why, just a little while ago, Mary said she was fine. This is puzzling for anyone who has not experienced an illness that goes up and down, gets worse and better, never stays still. Our society has a poor understanding of things that do not have the kind of narrative we are used to. How can one's health change so drastically over a few days, or indeed, a few hours? This has been my experience with fibromyalgia. One day, I am very well, out and about, meeting with many people, writing a lot and working a lot. The next day, I may be feeling fatigued and stiff and experiencing pain. Maybe the weather changed since the day before, maybe I overdid it the day before, or maybe none of these are the reason I feel badly—it just happens.

Indeed, Frawley points out in *Invalidism and Identity in Nineteenth-Century Britain* (2004) that various invalid authors in 19th-century Britain realized that the story of their lives was not the usual story. She cites Elizabeth Gaskell an invalid writer, whose character, Mrs. Dawson, says her life story is "an old-world story, which after all, would be no story at all, neither beginning, nor middle nor end" (Frawley, 2004, p. 247). Frawley points to the importance of this view of narrative: "Elizabeth Gaskell could not have found a more apt way to capture invalidism's inherent challenge to the ideals of resolution and closure embedded within traditional linear narrative" (p. 247). In other words, those of us whose health goes up and down do not adhere to the usual story convention. There is supposed to be a beginning, middle and end. In the case of illness the story is: you get sick, you go the doctor to treat it, you rest and voila, you are well again.

Indeed, Anne, assuming then that her sister Mary has been sick does not ask about whether she attended a dinner the night before. Mary is perplexed that Anne does not ask how her dinner went. Anne says she didn't ask because she assumed that Mary was too sick to go (as Mary is sick this next day). Mary responds, "Oh yes, I went, I was well yesterday; nothing at all the matter with me this morning" (p. 27)—a confusing narrative for Anne, who was expecting that the middle part of the story, treatment and resting, would have happened the night before. This after all, is part of the illness narrative.

I have experienced the confusion of others without chronic episodic illnesses about the narrative of my life. I'm often asked by people I have not seen for a while, particularly those who live at a distance, "Do you still have that fibromyalgia problem?" The narrative of my illness must be over—aren't I well yet? Our Western fixation with fixing has led us to the medical model being a dominant paradigm. Those of us who are "incurables" do not fit into the medical narrative—we are rogue patients, who must be making up symptoms, because medicine cannot cure them. Therefore, we must be totally in-valid, not able to do anything, because we do not have static good health, we are assumed to have static bad health. We, as a society, tend to deal in binaries: if you are not always well, then the least confusing narrative to understand is that you are always *not* well. Austen depicts a good example of this dilemma later in *Persuasion* when several members of the family want to go on a walk and no one invites Mary. She then says that, oh, she can go on walks and can do this. This was not the answer the others were expecting, as she was lying on the couch a little while ago. Mary sets out with the group and when they reach the hill that leads to her aunt's home, she tells her husband she is too fatigued to climb down the hill and then up again. She will wait at the top of the hill for him to return.

It appears in the book and in the film version of *Persuasion* (Faber & Eaton, 1995) that she is conveniently fatigued at the right time—she does not like this aunt and she is feigning fatigue to not go. This kind of situation happens to me often—I set out to be a part of an activity and then sometimes run out of energy and other times I can go the whole way. It appears that we, Mary and I, are just making an excuse to get out of something unpleasant. We are indeed tired, however, and the notion of climbing up and down that hill doesn't wash with our bodies. We know we cannot drag ourselves up the hill and pay the pain consequences, maybe for the day or for the next week. I am a great walker when I'm a great walker, just like Mary.

Sanditon

In Austen's short fiction, *Sanditon*, she introduces the Parker sisters, who come to the sea for relief of health issues. At the time, going to the town of Bath, by the sea, was something that people did to feel better, to get better air. As Frawley (2004) explains, "Most influential for invalids who embarked on a search for health was the emergence of climatotherapy, a form of nature therapy based on the assumption that fresh air, exercise, and removal from sources of stress and fatigue were essential to recovery … The emerging field constructed and classified types of invalids, each with distinctive medical needs that could be best served by particular climates" (p. 126). The field originated in medical science, but then it became quickly popularized, with invalids believing that they could take their own health regimes into their own hands by relocating to these locations.

I, too, after exhausting medical routes that declared that nothing could be done to help me manage my pain and fatigue effectively, decided to move to a warmer climate for the winters. Winnipeg's winters span 5 months and the temperature is steadily under −25° Celsius. I spent three winters in Trinidad and Tobago in the Caribbean in the late '90s. Afterwards, I did indeed feel more rested, relaxed and had less pain. Perhaps, in the back of my mind, I related to the 19th-century ideas about certain climates being good for certain maladies. I had observed that my symptoms of pain, fatigue and stiffness were worse in cold weather.

Austen describes the Parker sisters as women who have "Disorders and Recoveries so very much out of the common way" (Austen, 2008b, *Sanditon*, p. 334). Austen, as narrator, appears to doubt that the sisters are actually ill, as sometimes they don't feel well and sometimes they do. When they do feel well, they "must be very busy for the Good of others or else extremely ill themselves" (p. 334). Austen explains that the women seemed to want to help others as a part of their vanity. "They had Charitable hearts and many amiable feelings—but a spirit of restless activity, and the flurry of doing more than anybody else, had their share in every exertion of Benevolence—there was Vanity in all they did, as well as in all they endured" (p. 334). Again, Austen says that they have been fancying their illnesses a lot and have had contact with quacks trying to heal them early on in their lives.

The narrator believes that the illnesses are in their heads, especially because they can do good works, want to do a lot and be seen as doing good. Here, again, I can relate, as when I am ill, I cannot go out and "do good works", but when I am well

I can go out and help others. Especially as part of my Mennonite upbringing, doing service for others is the essence of life. In my case, when I am not well and cannot "do service", I feel that I am not doing my part, that I am letting people down, and a lot of people indeed do not understand why today you cannot volunteer, whereas yesterday you looked just fine. Austen depicts the sisters' urge to help others as restless and them trying to do better than others at helping.

Could it be, as it is for me, that when they felt well, they needed to maximize their energy and get a lot done, as tomorrow they may not be able to do it? This is true in my case—I want to continue to contribute to my society through work and volunteer work and writing, just like others, to be seen as a "good person" in my own mind and to be seen as having a role. Perhaps the sisters were not actually trying to "outdo" anyone, but were merely participating when they felt well.

Frawley (2004), in her study of invalidism in the 19th century, points out that many invalids who were bedridden or could not leave their houses due to illness, were very productive. Frawley's book is about the narratives that invalids told through writing and publishing for a wider public, beyond their sickbed. This was being productive, helping others in similar situations, to provide them with solace and encouragement from a person who also experienced being an invalid. There was an element of peer counselling and support here and also the belief that this illness has to be good for something. This is definitely the main reason why I continue to write my own experiences in poetry and in nonfiction. I want to share the experiences to help all of us understand what is happening in the case of episodic illnesses. I also want to tell society that I am still here, even if you don't see me at every art show or reading, like I used to be. I have to be very selective and pace many aspirations and priorities in a day, just to complete the must-do tasks.

The invalid's narrative is a Christian voice in the wilderness in the 19th-century world, according to Frawley (2004), and Austen was part of that world. There was a sense that invalids had the corner on developing themselves morally and spiritually because of their unique position. They had time to contemplate away from the rest of the hurrying world. They could retreat from "the competitive world of status seeking" (Frawley, 2004, p. 157). It could be that the Parker sisters also prescribed to this view—they were being upright, even if they were sick sometimes.

Jane Austen's invalidism

Jane Austen herself experienced illness in 1816–1817 (Austen-Leigh & Austen-Leigh, 1989). Austen's letters to her niece, Charlotte, refer to a mysterious decline in her strength and that she needed to lie down more. But, her niece, Charlotte, visiting Chawton Cottage, where Jane resided, relates that Jane would not take the sofa in the living room even if it was unoccupied. Her grandma usually laid down there. Jane would arrange three chairs to lie on, which looked very uncomfortable to her niece. Even when Grandma was not there, June did not lie on the sofa. Her niece, Charlotte, asks her why and learns, "I often asked her how she *could* like the chairs best—I supposed I worried her into telling me the reason of her choice—which was, that if she ever used the sofa, Grandmama would be leaving it for her, and would not lie down, as she did now, whenever she felt inclined" (Austen-Leigh & Austen-Leigh, 1989, p. 215). Jane's mother was not ill, she was elderly and needed to rest at different intervals from time to time. It is interesting that Jane foregoes the sofa altogether, thinking her mother needs it more. Is this a denial of her own illness state? A refusal to play the role of the invalid?

During this year, Austen's illness symptoms were up and down, and she was writing *Sanditon* January to March 1817. She was writing about the fluctuating symptoms of the Parker sisters and their brother while she experienced her own symptoms. Jane wrote in a letter to Fanny Knight, another niece, "I am got tolerably well again quite equal to walking about and & enjoying the Air" (Austen-Leigh & Austen-Leigh, 2004, p. 221). Ten days later Jane Austen reported to Fanny that she was not well, and that "Sickness is a dangerous Indulgence at my time of life" (p. 221, Austen-Leigh). It seems again that she sees sickness as an indulgence, perhaps like her previous characters. Was she thinking that it was a matter of choosing to be well? Because she had appeared to satirize the symptoms and lifestyles of invalids in her novels, could it be that she didn't want to be one?

Jane died in July 1817 at the age of 41.

References

Austen, J. (1997). *Persuasion.* New York, NY: Dover Publications.

Austen, J. (2008a). *Mansfield Park.* New York, NY: Bantam Dell.

Austen, J. (2008b). Sanditon. in J. Austen, *Northanger Abbey, Lady Susan, The Watsons and Sanditon.* Oxford, UK: Oxford University Press.

Austen-Leigh, W. & Austen-Leigh, R.A. (1965). *Jane Austen: Her Life and Letters, A Family Record,* 2nd ed. New York, NY: Russell & Russell.

Austen-Leigh, W. & Austen-Leigh, R.A. (1989). *Jane Austen, A family record.* New York, NY: Konecky & Konecky.

British Broadcasting Corporation (1986). *Mansfield Park* [Motion Picture]. London, UK: BBC.

Faber, G. (Executive Producer) & Eaton, R. (Executive Producer). (1995). *Persuasion.* [Motion Picture] London, UK: BBC Films, Millesime Productions.

Frawley, M.H. (2004). *Invalidism and Identity in Nineteenth-Century Britain.* Chicago, IL: The University of Chicago Press.

Gaskell, E.C. (1913). *Round the Sofa.* London, UK: Oxford University Press.

Martineau, H. (1844). Life in the Sickroom: Essays. Boston, MA: William Crosby.

Miller, D.A. (1990). The late Jane Austen. *Raritan,* vol. 10 (Summer), p. 55.

Wiltshire, J. (1992). *Jane Austen and the Body: "The Picture of Health."* Cambridge, UK: Cambridge University Press.

4

DEVELOPMENTS IN DISABILITY ISSUES DURING THE LATE OTTOMAN PERIOD OF TURKISH HISTORY FROM 1876 TO 1909

Mualla Erkilic

Introduction

During the era of the Ottoman Empire, which lasted approximately six centuries, from 1299 to 1923, the historical record notes some shifts pertaining to the care and treatment of disabled individuals over the years, but the historical record also notes deep-rooted religious, social, and cultural beliefs pertaining to disability that remained through the centuries. Scholars of history will note that the Ottoman Empire controlled vast areas of land throughout the Middle East, parts of Africa, Southeastern Europe and beyond. Over the centuries the Ottoman Empire ruled over thousands of people representing different cultures and ethnic groups and different religions including Muslims, Jews and Christians. Considering the vastness of the rich history of the Ottoman Empire, examining disability from all parts of the realm is beyond the scope of this chapter; hence, it will deal with disability as portrayed in Anatolia, which encompasses much of modern-day Turkey.

For the most part, the care and treatment of disabled people is and was very much connected to social, cultural and economic variables, which in turn were influenced by Islam and Islamic understandings of disability. Briefly stated, societal attitudes towards disabled individuals were typically reflected in the belief that it is "God's will". The influence of the Islamic faith is noted in ideas of compassion toward disabled individuals and to provide charitable relief to those who were unable to care for themselves. For example, the historical records notes many instances of relief for the *meczup* (crazy), *divane* (lunatics) or *mecnun* (madly in love with God) and being cared for in a *darussifa* (hospital). In compliance with the traditional Islamic perspective, disabled people's needs were to be met through individual assistance, such as *sadaka* (charitable giving), *zekat* (stipulated in the Quran as required giving of alms) and *fitre* (charitable giving connected to religious days such as Ramadan) or through institutional support, such as *vakif* (foundations), *sifahane* (hospitals) and *imarhane* (charitable kitchens).

Disabled individuals who were able to provide for themselves were expected to do so. For example, blind people who were able to work played music and served as hafiz (read the Quran by memory). Research also reveals that deaf individuals and dwarfs often served the needs of the royalty, and by the 15th century deaf courtiers had developed sign language that eventually dispersed throughout much of society.

Similar to other societies, there is a shift over time from viewing disabled persons as being totally in need of charitable relief and aid to viewing disabled individuals as being trainable and capable of being educated. Although there is some evidence of the education and training of disabled people beginning in the 14th century, it is not until the 19th century that educational and training programs take root on a large scale. It appears that the 19th century developments were heavily influenced by educational and trades training reforms that were taking root in Europe at the time. Sultan Abdulhamid II (1876–1909), who ascended to the throne as the first constitutional monarch, implemented a series of European-inspired changes in the military, technology, social life and particularly education. The purpose of these reforms was to assist with the modernization of the Turkish state, and they are discussed in the *Tanzimat* (1839) and *Islahat* (1856), which were additional social and legal reforms aimed at giving more rights in areas of education, government appointments and legal rights to religious minorities such as Christians and Jews. By the late 19th century, the care and treatment of disabled Turkish people incorporates European models such as institutional, segregated living and training such as the Istanbul School for the Deaf and the Mute (1889), which also began to accept blind students by 1891, or in the form of alms houses (*darulaceze*), which emerge by 1896. Much of the material pertaining to this chapter is based on primary and secondary sources of the Turkish state archives.

Tracing the historical roots of care of disabled people during the Ottoman reign

Anatolia (Asian portion of Turkey) is a mixture of civilizations, including Hittite, Lydian, Phrygian and Genoese, Greek, Roman, Byzantine, Seljukian and Ottoman. Moreover, many of today's modern methods of treatment have deep historical roots which reflect these diverse cultural beliefs regarding disabled people. For example, contemporary psychotherapeutic treatments such as music therapy and hydrotherapy can be traced back to the ancient Anatolian civilizations and are evidenced throughout the Ottoman period. The Asclepion at Pergamon was the first healing centre in the ancient Greek and Roman period for people deemed to be mentally ill, in which methods of inculcation, music, sound and water sound therapies were used (Greek 4th-century BC and Roman 1st-century BC (Taskin 1995). In many ways the historical record contests the common belief that disabled persons were always treated as outcasts, and in fact there is evidence which suggests that disabled people were often treated with compassion and care.

There may not have been an in-depth understanding of impairments such as mental illness, but the historical record suggests that attempts were made to treat this population in local "hospitals", even though there may have been no "medical diagnosis" of the impairment. During the Ottoman period, for example, mentally disabled people were regarded as *meczub*, meaning that they were "tempted" by God or ecstatically in love with God and thus had lost themselves and their minds. In the case of an insane person, the mind is described as having left that person; however, in the case of *meczup*, the person is regarded as having lost his/her mind due to having lost him/herself (Sari and Akgun 2008). Moreover, instead of "insane", the words *mecnun, seyda* and *divane* (meaning to lose one's mind as a result of unrequited love) were used colloquially to refer to mentally disabled people. There are records indicating that mentally disabled people were neither excluded from society nor despised; on the contrary, they were protected and tolerated, and they held no criminal liability according to the Islamic law (Sari and Akgun 2008). Additionally, during the Ottoman period, *darussifas* (healing centres) were founded and dedicated to serve all types of patients, including people with mental health impairments. The words *bimarhane, bimaristan* and *timarhane*, which were originally used to refer to mental hospitals, came to mean "a house or place for patients" and "a house for treatment" (Sari and Akgun 2008, 8). Healing centres/ *darussifas* were not merely custodial institutions such as the European insane asylums, and staff were required to treat mentally disabled people compassionately and kindly, and this included entertainment by musicians who played various styles of music to the "patients" (Sari and Akgun 2008, 7 and 8). This is an interesting juxtaposition to Europe of the time, wherein disabled individuals such as mental defectives, physical defectives, blind persons and deaf persons were often characterized as being sinful. Disability was commonly viewed as a punishment from God, and such individuals were put away in very demeaning and punitive institutions (Winzer 1993, 23–28; Yildirim 1997, 305).

Attitudes towards disabled individuals such as the *sagir* (deaf), *dilsiz* (mute), *kulaksiz* (earless, deaf), *bizeban* (blind and dumb in Persian) and *ama* (blind) were shaped by beliefs and values rooted in Islamic religion and culture, which emphasizes care for those who are unable to care for themselves. For example, following Islamic tradition, institutionalized forms of charity, such as *vakif*, and individual acts of charity through *sadaka, fitre* and *zekat* were practiced for the benefit of disabled people who were unable to provide for themselves. In Islam, the term *vakif* literally means "detention" and refers to the dedication and donation of property owned by God for righteous purposes (Ghaly 2010 p. 151). The emphasis here is that withholding an object owned by God is only appropriate if it is used to benefit other people. Accordingly, goods and properties collected for *vakif* could be used only for religious purposes, charity and aid. While *sadaka* refers to an individual charitable act, *fitre* and *zekat* refer to a defined amount of alms that each Muslim is expected to offer at certain times of the year to people in need. As outlined in Islamic guidelines, alms are given at a rate proportional to a person's income. For example, *fitre* refers to the amount of alms individuals are expected to give during the month of Ramadan. In addition to individual acts of charity, charitable relief of poor disabled individuals were also provided through taxation measures collected and dispersed through institutional relief systems rooted in the values of social care and responsibility toward fellow humankind (Ozbayrak 2011, 27; İnalcık 1994, 35). When possible, individuals with some forms of impairments such as "deaf" individuals were expected to work, and there is evidence which suggests that deaf individuals were employed as palace servants during the Ottoman period.

In an article published in 1910, *The Silent Worker Journal* includes the observations of a political essayist who served in the Ottoman Palace.

Sigmund Muenz, the political essayist, who has just returned from Constantinople, will soon publish a striking account of his odd experiences in the Turkish capital. …During his investigations of conditions in Turkey under the new regime, he discovered that at cabinet councils a number of deaf and dumb secretaries are present during deliberations of the Sultan's ministers. Behind the chair of each Cabinet Minister stands also a deaf and dumb domestic. On the inner side of the table sit the mute secretaries.... This practice is maintained to prevent important secrets from reaching the outside world. (*The Silent Worker* 1910, 11–2, 38)

This experience that Muenz regarded as somewhat odd (that deaf-mutes were assigned to secret meetings of officials) had actually become a part of a tradition inherited from past periods of the Ottoman Empire and was in fact quite common place by the beginning of the 20th century. There is ample evidence which details the inclusion of deaf individuals and dwarfs in everyday palace life. Deaf individuals and dwarfs, for example, accompanied Ottoman sultans during meetings and travels; they lived on the palace grounds, including the harem; and it appears that the numbers of deaf persons and dwarfs involved in palace life increased over time. In his article entitled "Signing in the Seraglio: Mutes, Dwarfs and Gestures at the Ottoman Court 1500–1700", Miles (2000) writes that since the era of Sultan Mehmed (1470s), deaf-mutes who privately served the members of the palace court had developed a type of lip and body language among themselves and even among the members of Sultan's family and extended family, including small children. Over time the signing system became popular, and was regularly used by hearing people, including successive Sultans:

> There is evidence for the adaptation of the Ottoman Sign Language by hearing users because of its practical usefulness, and perpetuation of the Ottoman Sign Language over several centuries. At present, no historical parallel is known, anywhere in the world, for a sign language continuing through five hundred years or more. ... Yet the continuation of Ottoman Sign Language might actually reflect some of the ill-defined and incremental home – and street – processes that are much more widespread, in the 'handing-on' of signed communication to the next generation. (Miles 2009, 1.0)

Miles (2000, 115) notes that deaf mutes worked in the Turkish Ottoman court from the 15th to the 20th century in various "confidant" roles and likewise so too did dwarfs, whose primary role was one of entertainer.

The sign language that developed in the Ottoman court was transferred to the broader society from generation to generation, and over the course of time had spread throughout the Ottoman Empire. Sign language was practiced in various provinces, including Albania, Armenia, Bulgaria, Croatia, Greece, Iraq and Syria, which had been, according to Miles,

> the Ottoman Court mutes' early achievements, at a time when deaf education and employment was barely considered feasible in Western Europe, have been obscured through literary critics' reactions against later travelers' stereotyping of Middle Eastern countries. Detailed, contemporary sixteenth and seventeenth century accounts of the mutes' activities and signing system are collated and appraised by modern linguistic and historio-graphical criteria. (Miles 2000, 115)

Deaf-mutes, who were selected to the Ottoman court regardless of their race or ethnicity, were assigned to several locations within the various palaces, including the esteemed Topkapi Palace. Interestingly, there appears to have been hierarchical organization of the deaf-mute servants, and, depending on the level of seniority, various titles and designations were given, which of course meant different responsibilities and rewards. Duties for the deaf-mutes ranged from servant work, entertainment for the sultan, family and other courtiers. Yildirim (1997) reports on the various roles of the deaf servants who were part of the royal households over the centuries; the employment of deaf persons as receivers to the court became very engrained throughout the Ottoman era, and the tradition of employing deaf people for the various Ottoman Palaces continues today in the National Assembly of the Turkish Republic as a parliamentary tradition. These officials, known as *kavas* (attendants), are assigned to the auditorium of the National Assembly and serve at private functions.

Care and treatment of disabled individuals in the Late Ottoman period

According to Yildirim (1997), the development of educational and training programs for disabled individuals, including blind, deaf and crippled populations in Ottoman Turkey, reflected similar programs which emerged in Europe at the time. For example, poor laws which permitted cripples as well as blind and deaf individuals to beg for alms had existed in Europe since the 17th century. An example is the rise of Elizabethan Poor Laws of 1601. In addition to these state laws, mental and physical defectives who were unable to provide for themselves were given alms through churches, monasteries and other religious organizations. Similarly, throughout the Ottoman Empire at the same time, the disabled population was offered charitable relief through religious organizations based on Islamic tradition and laws, and like many European states, disabled individuals who were unable to provide for themselves were offered relief through legislated measures such as poor laws.

In addition to measures of relief through state- and religious-sponsored mechanisms, there were similarities in the delivery of educational and training programs for various disabled populations. For example, rudimentary educational training programs for deaf persons emerged in France and Spain during the 16th century, and they were followed by the development of deaf education programs throughout other parts of Europe, including Germany and the United Kingdom, as well as the United States by the mid 1800s. And during this same time period, we find the introduction and development of educational and training programs for blind individuals, especially with the development of Braille during the early 1800s (Yildirim 1997; Stokoe 1960).

Although it is likely that the Turkish elites and educators of the Ottoman era learned a great deal from their European counterparts, it should be noted that institutional care for some disabled populations such as blind people emerged during the 14th century. In fact, the first *korhane*, or home for the blind, was established by Surahan Bey in the Manisa region of Antolia in the 1400s, and it remained active until the 17th century (Unver 1944). By the 1800s educational institutions for the blind had spread throughout the empire, with schools for the blind opening in such cities such as Cairo (Sayi 2008; Yildirim 1997).

Like so many leaders of empires before them, the Sultans of the Ottoman Empire began to have their authority challenged. By the late 1800s cracks begin to emerge with the rise of political, religious and cultural nationalism throughout the empire, from southern and eastern Europe to the Balkans to the Middle East to North Africa, and by 1876 Sultan Abdulhamid II introduced the first constitutional monarchy. While it is argued that Sultan Abdulhamit II was known as being very authoritative, indeed despotic in his attempts at control, he is also noted as being a reformist (İnalcık 2004). It appears that one of the sultan's many concerns was preventing total encroachment and dominance from Christian Europe in the internal affairs of the Ottoman Empire, yet in his attempts to bring about reforms for the empire he sought advice from a number of Europeans living in Istanbul at the time. Among the many reforms introduced by Sultan Abdulhamid II were those which were directed at providing support for individuals who were not capable of providing for themselves, and this included poor and disabled individuals of the empire. It is quite likely that Sultan Abdulhamid II was acting in an altruistic manner in his attempts to bring about social reforms, but it is also very likely that he brought about many of these reforms as a means to gain trust and support from the citizenry and to show the Europeans that the Ottoman Empire was moving toward greater modernization, and that Europeans should remain out of the affairs of the Ottoman Empire.

Many of the reforms introduced by Sultan Abdulhamit II included the establishment of a representative government, the complete equality of Muslims and non-Muslims under the law, women's rights, developments in the legal and economic systems, innovations in education, the establishment of new schools, modern farms, hospitals, quarantines and universities in compliance with Western standards, the proliferation of communication and printing industries, the use of new technologies in agriculture and the acknowledgement of Western arts, including theatre and music along with intensified efforts to construct roads, telegraph lines and railways (Shaw 1992, 1–15; Shaw 1977; İnalcık 2004, 890–891). Apart from these modernizing movements and reforms, Sultan Abdulhamit II stood against the Westernization of religion and culture by emphasizing Islamic values (İnalcık 2004, 891). As part of overseeing the many reforms Sultan Abdulhamit II attempted, as much as possible, to centralize and directly control the management and internal organization of the newly established institutions, as he was always concerned that Europeans would attempt to disrupt and possibly dismantle the Ottoman Empire if given the opportunity to do so (Shaw 1992, 3, 9–10).

Sultan Abdulhamid II and educational reforms for blind, deaf and physically disabled individuals

As noted above, Sultan Abdulhamid II was influenced by the social and political reforms movements taking root in Europe during the mid to late 19th century, and many of the reforms pertaining to the education, training and social care of blind, deaf and physically disabled individuals reflected European programs of the era. To begin, the sultan established programs for sick and injured soldiers (a common practice to care for disabled soldiers and sailors began during the Napolenic era). The *Mecruhin-i Askeriye Iane*, "Community for Helping the Sick Soldiers", was established in 1868, and the institution survives as the *Turkiye Kizilay Dernegi* (Turkish Red Crescent) today (Ozbayrak 2011, 28).

During his reign, Sultan Abdulhamid II brought about a number of educational reforms for the broader society, and as part of these reforms people who were blind, deaf and physically disabled were provided with a number of educational and training programs which were based on European educational and trades training programs.

The first institutional school for deaf children and youth opened in 1889 (Ergin 1941; Yildirim 1997) under the direction of Ferdinand Gratin of Austria, who earlier had founded the *Hamidiye Ticaret Mektebi* (Hamidiye Trade School). In his book titled *Türk Maarif Tarihi* (*History of Turkish Education*), written in 1939, the renowned historian Osman Ergin notes that the school was open to students between the ages of 6 and 20, regardless of language, religion or race. Unlike many of the schools for deaf students and schools for blind students that opened in North America and Europe from the mid 19th century to the early 20th century, this school was not a boarding school. Courses taught in the school were *ilm-i hal* (behavior), *husn-i hat* (calligraphy), *ilm-i hesap* (math), *coğrafya-yı umumi ve hususi* (geography), *resm-i hat* and imitation (painting/drawing), *ilm-i ahlak* (religion), composition, cosmography, *mimariye* (architecture), *tezyinat* (decoration), coloring and gymnastics (Yildirim 1997, 315; Ozbayrak 2011, 32) (Figures 4.1 and 4.2).

The *Amalar Mektebi* (School for the Blind) was opened in Istanbul in 1891 (as part of the School for the Deaf, later known as the School for the Deaf, Dumb and Blind), and similar to the School for the Deaf, it appears that there were no restrictions based on religion, ethnicity, race of economic status. Reports indicate that poor children and youth did not have to pay to attend the school, but that economically advantaged students took private lessons from the schoolteachers. For the most part the students who attended the school were viewed as part of the community, and they (the boys) were easily identified by their school uniforms, which consisted of a red blazer and trousers with red stripes. The students often attended places of public entertainment

Figure 4.1 School for the Deaf-Mute and Blind in the era of Sultan Abdulhamid II (1889): Students saying 'Long Live Sultan'. (Published originally in Servet-i Fünun no 648. The original photo is kept in the Rare Books Library, Istanbul University (90834/36), Ottoman Yıldız Palace Collection no:20161031-135435: Photographer: Abdullah Biraderler 1891.)

Figure 4.2 The photograph of the building of the School for the Deaf-Mute and Blind. (Ottoman Yıldız Palace Library collection: 20161031-135439. Published also in the special collection book Imperial Self Portrait: The Ottoman Empire as Revealed in The Sultan Abdulhamid II's Photographic Albumes, presented as gifts to the Library of Congress (1893), and British Museum (1894). Edited by Sinasi Tekin and Gonul Tekin. Harvard University Publisher, 1988. LC Album no: 9544.8 -9544.9 (LC neg: 81984-81985), pp:174–175.)

and music, and they participated in religious activities such as the *Hirka-i Serif* (a religious rite-of-passage ceremony in the Festival of Ramadan) (Ergin 1941, 966). The inclusion of the students into the broader community is evidenced in warnings for automobile drivers to be aware of the students as they could not hear the oncoming vehicles (BOA.1893, MF.MKT.D.154 G.25). In addition, public records of the era recommend that deaf and blind students should be taught to use public transportation such as the trolley cars and ferry boats (Turkish State Archive 1890, MF.MKT.D.113,G.110). European methods of teaching were adapted to the Ottoman context; for example, the sign language that was developed for deaf students was slightly different than the European model. It is interesting to note how the blind students and the deaf students were expected to work in tandem when away from the school. Kadir Bey in Ergin, 1941, describes how the students of the school walked to school together:

> The blind and mute students were always in rows of two, arm-in-arm when they were going to school and coming back home. On the condition that one among the two was blind and the other was deaf, the deaf would first [find] the blind [person], and together they would act like a one person with the blind [person's] ears and the deaf [person's] eyes. On the way, the blind [person], upon hearing voices in his ears, would warn the deaf [person] by poking, and the deaf [person] would then inform the blind [person] similarly about what he saw. (Ergin 1941, 967) (Figures 4.3 and 4.4).

Interestingly, the school's Department for the Blind closed in 1897, and it appears that the closure was associated to a decline in enrolment, which in turn was affected by a shift in the delivery of curriculum wherein music education was shifted from a

Figure 4.3 Photographs of students with visual and hearing disabilities. (Ottoman Yıldız Palace Collection no: 20161031-135452 and 20161031-135459. Published also in the special collection book Imperial Self Portrait: The Ottoman Empire as Revealed in The Sultan Abdulhamid II's Photographic Albumes, presented as gifts to the Library of Congress (1893), and British Museum (1894). Edited by Sinasi Tekin and Gonul Tekin. Harvard University Publisher, 1988. LC Album no: 9531.4-9531.6 (LC neg: 81481-81483), pp:176–177.).

Figure 4.4 Photographs of students with visual and hearing disabilities. (Ottoman Yıldız
Palace Collection no: 20161031-135452 and 20161031-135459. Published also in the
special collection book Imperial Self Portrait: The Ottoman Empire as Revealed
in The Sultan Abdulhamid II's Photographic Albumes, presented as gifts to the
Library of Congress (1893), and British Museum (1894). Edited by Sinasi Tekin
and Gonul Tekin. Harvard University Publisher, 1988. LC Album no: 9531.4 -9531.6
(LC neg: 81481-81483), pp:176–177.)

secular focus to a religious focus (Yildirim 1997, 318; BOA. İ. Talt. 164 (28 Ra. 1314/6
Eylül 1896).

Not unlike many of the European and North American schools for deaf and blind
students of the late 19th and early 20th centuries, the Hamidiye School for the Deaf,
Mute and Blind had a strong focus on vocation training and skills development, and
graduates of the school received assistance in securing employment (BOA, MF.MKT.
1897, D.323.G.76).

It is interesting to note that at the same time as the non-boarding School for the Deaf, Mute and Blind in Istanbul was developing during the early 1890s, "institutional" facilities were being constructed as well. By 1895 the Darulaceze (Istanbul) was completed after three years of construction. In many ways this institution became a testament to the "reforms" brought about by Sultan Abdulhamid II, and it has been in continuous operation from its founding until the present day. *Dar* means home and *aceze* refers to incapable, weak and powerless people. Yildirim (1996) notes that the origins of the concept of *darulaceze* date back to the Seljukian era, and that such institutions had been considered a part of *kulliyes* (Islamic-Ottoman social complexes) called *imaret* (alms houses) in the 16th century. Yildirim (1996) describes *darulaceze* as a typical example of Ottoman tolerance that emerged with the purpose of helping poor, desolate, sick and disabled people without differentiating on the basis of language, religion, race or sect. The institution consisted of 18 buildings modelled upon their counterparts in Europe, and it included a kindergarten, orphanage, hospital, school of arts, workshops, laundry room, *hamams* (Turkish baths), kitchens, pharmacy, carpenters' shop and a tailors' shop (Yildirim 1996). In addition to the collection of financial aid from every province for the construction of the institution, Sultan Abdulhamid II also provided personal financial support as well (Yildirim 1996, v–vi). Early in the institution's establishment, the *darulaceze* symbolized the intersections between the secular and the religious. On the one hand, Sultan Abdulhamid II decreed that all blind students should memorize the *Quran* and hymns, to gather and pray in mosques, to visit *tekkes and zaviyes* (Islamic monasteries and hermitages), and on the other hand, to be educated in line with how blind, deaf and mute students were educated and trained in Europe.

International relations and the education of disabled people during the era of Sultan Abdulhamid II

As noted above, Sultan Abdulhamid II brought about a number of reforms which promoted the education and training of disabled individuals in Turkey, and as part of his endeavours to develop these programs, the sultan borrowed and adapted European methods. By the early 20th century, Sultan Abdulhamid II was funding Turkish professionals in the fields of medicine and education to travel abroad to learn about methods of medical treatment as well as methods directed at education and vocational training. But as we will discuss later, most attempts at developing programs for disabled individuals in Turkey were disbanded in 1909.

Dr. Esad Bey (a renowned Turkish ophthalmologist) was sent to the International Congress for the Amelioration of the Living Standards of the Blind, which was held in Brussels, Belgium, in 1902. Dr. Bey was very concerned about the quality of life facing many blind Turkish people, and he believed that the best way of reducing dependency was through education and trades training. He adapted many of the European programs he learned about through his European, North and South American contacts made at the Brussels Congress.

The following notes from Dr. Esad Bey provide an example of the influences of European programs:

In Belgium, the visually disabled made their living through [assistance], and music and piano teaching were important. Other than these, there were disabled [people] working in the production of brush and wire and wattle, making chairs; and visually disabled women made their living through learning knitting jobs such as undershirts and socks. In Italy, the visually disabled made their living from basketry but according to the thought of delegate member Monsieur Martochelli, it would be more proper to employ the visually disabled in telephone and telegraph enterprises rather than arts. In Portugal, the visually disabled could find jobs in handcrafts and in assistant roles, in parallel with the development of the industry as described by Monsieur Sepapen. In addition, in Portugal, the visually disabled took on illustrator/artist jobs, carpentry, bookbinding, [manufacturing] cork stoppers, brushing, teaching music and serving as musicians in the churches. In the report Monsieur Moldonhaverek presented on Denmark, the visually disabled took on music, piano-tuning, basketry, rope, brush, wickerwork, straw, armchair-production and sewing jobs by hand and machine. In Denmark, the visually disabled could acquire more than one job. Moreover, massage and exercise began to be taught to the visually disabled. According to the report of Father Narsis, in France, visually disabled [peoples'] most important means of subsistence were teaching music, tuning pianos, serving as church musicians, and making armchairs. According to Monsieur Shanuval Nekhel, among the visually disabled in the Netherlands, basketry, chair making and wickerwork production were common. In coastal areas of the country, visually disabled [young women] were successful at making their living by sewing fish-nets and laces. (Esad Bey, 1903, 648 in Keskinbora 2008, 356–359)

It appears that Dr. Esad Bey had numerous questions and concerns about European and other foreign methods of education and training, as well as the provision of care and treatment of blind individuals, including methods of education, the creation of trades training opportunities, questions regarding employment, concerns about recreation, questions about germ-related causes and prevention of some forms of blindness, and he raised concerns about living and working conditions which also contributed to blindness.

It appears that Dr. Esad Bey was quite progressive in his thinking about the development of programs and supportive services for blind people as well as creating changes in living and working conditions which could reduce levels of blindness. He noted, for example, that

the causes of blindness must be eliminated even in the most remote villages. The following precautions should be taken: health compliance in workplaces, factories and schools must be controlled; the places where the workers live must be rehabilitated; the working conditions must be improved; work accidents must be prevented; hospitals must be established exclusively for eye diseases; and contagious eye diseases must be quarantined. (Esad Bey, 1903 in Keskinbora 2008, 356–359)

Bey suggested that the methods of education and vocational training of blind individuals had to be adapted to the context/country in which people lived, and he maintained that government departments and charitable organizations had to work together to develop education, training and employment programs for blind individuals such as with telephone and telegraph companies. And while Dr. Bey advocated for specific jobs for blind persons, he did not necessarily support totally segregated employment and suggested that it was appropriate to employ non-blind people in these workplaces to assist the visually impaired (Esad Bey 1903 in Keskinbora 2008, 356–359).

Upon his return from Brussels, Dr. Esad Bey's attempted to solicit funding from the sultan to establish a comprehensive school for the blind. However, despite the support of Sultan Abdulhamid II, who approved Dr. Esad Bey's proposals, it appears that, following many years of debate and discussion, that the training school for blind students was abandoned when the sultan was overthrown in 1909. This initiative remained unrealized as well, as Sultan Abdulhamid II was dethroned the following year (Yildirim 1997, 327; Sayi 2008, 75).

There may have been various reasons for the failure of the initiatives to establish a school for the disabled Turkish people during Sultan Abdulhamid II's reign, but there are some very important elements which should not be overlooked, as the debates reveal some very detailed reforms for the era:

> it was decided that a school would be established to teach visually and hearing disabled people to read, write, religious rules and necessary manual work; that this school would include a *masjid* for Muslim students, a special place of worship for non-Muslims, dormitories that are in compliance with sanitary regulations, a proper pharmacy; that the revenue of one of the state farms would be allocated for its administration; …. that a teacher specialized in educating people with speaking and hearing disabilities and other teachers would be employed; that its budget would be included under the Ministry of Education; that a commission would be formed to supervise the construction; that a *nizamname* (constitution) would be prepared by the Ministry of Education concerning its administration. (Sayi 2008, 69–70).

It is likely that the postponement for developing training and educational programs for disabled children and youth in the pre–World War I era were related to the political environment of the period, wherein many parts of the Ottoman Empire were under revolt and the political turmoil led to the downfall of Sultan Abdulhamid II. In addition, Turkey and Istanbul endured a devastating earthquake in 1894, and it was still recovering from its devastation into the early 20th century. Much of the funding which could have been applied to the development of the school was shifted to the development and the construction of the Hospital of the Faculty of Medicine. Although the initiatives for the Deaf, Mute and Blind School to be established within the context of the modernization and reformist activities of Sultan Abdulhamid II proved to be insufficient, these initiatives did lay the foundation for future reforms undertaken in later periods.

References

Ergin, O. 1941. *Türkiye Maarif Tarih Cilt 3i*. İstanbul: Osmanbey Matbaası.

Esad, M. 1903. Amaların Talim ve Terbiyeleri, Servet-i Fünun no 648:362–373.

Ghaly, M. 2010. *Islam and Disability*. London, UK and New York, NY: Routledge.

İnalcık, H. and Ş. Pamuk. 2001. *Osmanlı Devlet'inde Bilgi ve İstatistik*. İstanbul: Başbakanlık Devlet İstatittik Enstitüsü Yayınları.

İnalcık, H. and D. Quataert. 2004. *Osmanlı mparatorluğu'nun Ekonomik ve Sosyal Tarihi C2: 1600–1914*. Eren Yayıncılık, Turkey.

İstanbul Sağır ve Dilsizler Cemiyeti Nizamnamesi. 1939. İstanbul: Ahmet Said Basımevi, Publisher.

Keskinbora, K. 2008. 1902 Brüksel Körlerin Durumlarının Düzeltilmesi Kongresi ve İsanbul'dan Katılan Göz Hekiminin Değerlendirmesi. T.Oft. Gaz. 38:353–360.

Miles, M. 2000. Signing in the seraglio: Mutes, dwarfs and gestures at the Ottoman Court 1500–1700. *Disability and Society*, vol. 15, no. 1:115–134.

Miles. M. 2009. Deaf People, Sign Language and Communication, in Ottoman and Modern Turkey. Accessed February, 2012. http://www.independentliving.org/miles200907.html

Ozbayrak, K.İ. 2011. *II Abdülhamid Döneminde Uygulanan Sosyal Yardım Politikaları (1876–1909)*. İstanbul: Libra.

Sari, N. and B. Akgün. 2008. Türk Tarihinde Psikiyatriye Bakış. *TSKPH Dizisi* 62:1–24.

Sayi, H.B. 2008. Osmanlı Belgeleri ışığında Dr. Esat Bey'in Biyografisi ve Görme Engellilere Yönelik Eğitim Çalışmaları. Yüksek Lisans Tezi, Selçuk Üniversitesi, Konya.

Shaw, S.J. 1977. History of the Ottoman Empire and Turkey v2: *Reform, Revolution, and Republic, The Rise of Modern Turkey*. New York, NY: Cambridge University Press.

Shaw, S.J. 1992. Sultan Abdülhamid II: Last Man of Tanzimat. UCLA Program for the study of Ottoman and Turkish History Publication Series no.1:1–15.

Stokoe, Jr. W.C. 2005. Sign Language Structure. *Journal of Deaf Studies and Deaf Education*, vol. 10, no. 1: Oxford University Press (originally published as Studies in Linguistics, Occational Paers 8 (1960), By the Department of Anthropology and Linguistics, University of Buffalo, New York) Accessed on 8 February, 2012. http://www.bris.ac.uk/Depts/DeafStudiesTeaching/dhcwww/chapter2.htm

Taskın, S. 1995. Bergama Hümanizması. İzmir: Anadolu Matbaası.

The Silent Worker. 1910. *News*. Vol. 23. no. 2: 38. Accessed February 8, 2012. http://www.independentliving.org/miles200907.html?page=)

The Silent Worker. 1912. *News*. vol. 11, no. 2:19. Accessed February 8, 2012. http://www.independentliving.org/miles200907.html?page=)

Unver, S. 1944. Amalar ve Körhaneler: Manisa'da Saruhan Körhanesi. *Göz Kliniği* vol. 1, no. 6:231–235.

Yildirim, N. 1997. Sağır-Dilsiz ve Amaların Eğitimi. In *İstanbul Armağanı 3: Gündelik Hayatın Renkleri*, editid by M. Armağan, 305–330. İstanbul: Büyükşehir Belediyesi Kültür İşleri Daire Başkanlığı Yayınları.

Yildirim, N. 1996. *İstanbul Darülaceze Müessesesi Tarihi*. İstanbul: Darülaceze Vakfı Yayınları.

Winzer, M.A. 1993. The History of Special Education. Washington, DC: Gallaudet University Press; Michigan University.

5

A SHORT HISTORY OF DISABILITY IN ITALY

Luigi Croce, Federica Di Cosimo
and Marco Lombardi

Introduction

This chapter is structured around two different components: a historical overview of disability in Italy from Roman times up to the 19th century, and the evolution of the considerable number of changes over the past 100 or more years that have led up to the disability framework in use today. That framework increasingly views disability as a common and legitimate experience of human functioning but, as the historical overview shows, this was not always the case. Scientific, psychosocial, advocacy, protection and right-promotion approaches have all contributed to these progressive changes.

When presenting the history of mental and intellectual disabilities in Italy, we need to consider our historical heritage and the variegated influences produced by different cultures and social factors due to the specific geographical and geopolitical position of this country. Even during the Roman age, anthropological and social conventions and values in the field, reflect the combination of autochthonal and Mediterranean, Greek and eastern roots.

Continuing with our time travel, the authors describe the main topics around humanity and disability, pointing out the paradigmatic changes that have emerged at theoretical and practical levels. If the evolutionary key is important to encompass all the longitudinal development of disability as image and icon of poor and deteriorated humanity, a real emancipation of Human Nature from the attribution of disability as a problem of functioning in life environments (World Health Organization ICF, 2001) might be traced in the second part, with the synchronic view of the current-day period.

The Roman age

"Portentosos fetus extinguimus, liberos quoque, si debiles monstrosique editi sunt, mergimus; nec ira sed ratio est a sanis inutilia secernere"(Lucio Anneo Seneca, De ira, libro I, 15.2) ["We destroy extraordinary babies, even our children, if they are born with weakness or abnormalities, we drown them: it is not done in anger, but in reason, to separate the useless."]

Roman culture identified a citizen with his own body, and the condition of usefulness of that body to the community was interpreted as a unique condition for the maintenance and integrity of the society. A person who was "un-able" was considered to be useless to work, to procreate, or to engage in military defence. He was thus a weight, and not acceptable to the community.

In ancient Rome, the solution to the "un-able" body was not an option, but an obligation that was prescribed in the Twelve Tables, the ancient legislation that stood at the foundation of Roman law (Section IV: *Cito necatus insignis to deformitatem puer esto*): "kill the baby visibly deformed; the monstrosity is impossible because it is not tolerated". Killing the baby was not considered to be murder. In fact, the birth, with the legal status of a citizen and member of the Gens, the paternalistic family, took place not with the emergence of the baby into the world or even the cutting of the umbilical cord, but only with the act completed by the *pater familias*, the male head of the family, raising the child in the air and presenting him or her to the world. If a deformity or impairment was discovered later, the child or the youth was "exposed" – literally removed from the family home, condemned to death by starvation, freezing, drowning, or being eaten by wild animals. This practice was commonly followed, especially by the poor, although there is some evidence that children with disabilities were kept hidden in the homes of wealthy families. Even Seneca was said to have a severe form of asthma, and Julius Caesar had epilepsy.

Disability as a physical anomaly was not perceived as a matter of health, but rather as an expression of monstrosity. It was explained by magical thinking as a sign of divine wrath, the result of a fault known or unknown, for an action performed or yet to be performed, or as a harbinger of misfortune. The etymological ambiguity of the Latin term *monstrum* (meaning monster or monstrous, but also evil omen), coupled with *admonitio* (meaning warning, or stern reminder), reveals the underlying cultural approach to disability. These conceptualizations of guilt, admonition and punishments of the gods came to Rome from Greek culture, with philosophers Aristotle and others decrying the value of any deformity to society, and exerted an influence that would last for many centuries.

Different types of disability may have been perceived differently. We do not have historical information about intellectual disability from Roman times but, if it is similar to other cultures, it might have been seen as the work of the gods or predicting the work of a demon. When the person was presented as physically able-bodied and useful to society, he or she would inspire awe and respect, be socially recognized, and be explained as the result of magic. Other conditions such as dwarfism, blindness, and muteness might be perceived and treated differently, such as the surgical cutting of the frenulum of the tongue.

In Roman civilization, belligerent and legally very structured, there is the figure of *deminutus* (diminished, limited), the soldier returning from battle with permanent disabilities. This figure was recognized as an hero, but was excluded from the right to vote and was confined on the edges of civilian life and regarded as useless. The explanation for this lies in the fact that, in Roman culture, the stigma – literally, marks applied to the body – had a broader moral meaning. Maiming and deformation produced a rift between the idea of the person and the real person. Physical appearance upheld one's social status, and the disabled, stigmatized person who survived was downgraded and lost social status. This represents well the sociological concept of symbolic violence: the stigma is literally a prejudice that emerges before any rational reflection, and thus the violent death or exposure (abandonment) of a person with disabilities was not considered immoral.

Roman culture is imbued with Greek culture, right from the first colonization of southern Italy and Sicily. The Hellenic heritage emphasized the dyad body-citizen, and one form of this was the construct of the scapegoat (*pharmakos*): those "useless" or "degraded" people maintained at the expense of the State and housed in a separate enclosure outside the polis who were sacrificed to the gods of Olympus, to propitiate them. By Roman times, this practice had been modified considerably to marking a person with fire or blade to let them be recognizable to the community as slaves or criminals. The function of the goat, *pharmakos*, is also *pharmakon*, the therapeutic practice of medicine (although, paradoxically, it could refer to either helpful drugs or poisons).

In the Greek-Roman world, then, the main "solution" to disability was to purge society of disfigured offspring at birth. It marginalized and inactivated those who later became disabled, through military activity or natural causes, as unable and useless. It established procedural and substantive differences between different types of disabilities, using the integrity of the body as criteria to determine the degree of stigma. It excluded people with disabilities from civil and religious life using the logic of class structure, that is, following the rules of a society structured in a pyramidal way. It was a world imbued with a protective magical thinking, which exerted social violence to protect the healthy people, because they were active and useful.

The Christian age

According to Christian tradition, the Church in Rome was founded by Peter, the disciple of Christ, who came to pagan Rome as bishop of Antioch in Syria. The principles of equality, the actions for a good life and eternal salvation were inconceivable and even dangerous to the Empire. For this reason, principally, Peter was killed by crucifixion under the dynasty Giulio-Claudia by Nero in 64 AD.

The evangelic ethic and morality of Peter's Christianity introduced the disruptive and revolutionary principle of equality between all humans and God the creator. This direct relationship between every person and God implies the choice of liberation from original sin for every person, originated from disobedience to the divine will for human presumption, through the gift of faith and practice of the theological virtues of faith, hope and charity. Furthermore, the coming to the Earth of Christ, the Son of God, gives to every person the possibility of being recognized as a sinner. This condition results in eternal salvation, after death, with the exercise of the Ten commandments, prescribed by Moses on Sinai, and the virtues, described by the theology of the Catholic Roman Church as cardinals, with an obvious derivation from the Platonic virtues: prudence, justice, fortitude, temperance.

Throughout the High Empire (27–23 BC to c. 284 AD), Christians were both feared and persecuted, but their influence continued to spread slowly. During the reign of Roman Emperor Constantine (306–337), the persecution of the Christians that had taken place sporadically over the previous three centuries ended, Christian worship was allowed, and Christians became Roman-accredited citizens. The Edict of Milan in 313, which decreed tolerance for Christianity within the empire, was a turning point in these events. Although this was a period when people of all religions were allowed to worship freely, Christianity steadily gained ground as the preferred religion and, increasingly over the period of his reign, the preferred religion of Constantine and thus subsequent emperors. Historical data confirm a slow cultural transition from paganism, whose signs we can find in some festivities and events in the Christian calendar.

By this time, the Roman Empire was fragile, with uprisings in Gaul by the Barbarians and Germans who plundered the territories to the north, and on the Iberian Peninsula. This disruptive condition lasted until the autonomy of Britain and the death of Theodosius I in AD 395, who, since 380, had decreed the Christian religion to be the faith of the Roman Empire. In 395, the Empire was formally divided under the influence and the power of his two sons Arcadius and Honorius, marking the end of the single Empire and also the division between the Latin Church and the Orthodox Church.

Through this political and cultural turmoil, Christianity emerged as the dominant religion and its values strongly affected the way disability was perceived. But here there seems to be a dual message. Christ overcomes evil – any evil – discrimination, stigma, and failure to respect the sanctity of life. To attain eternal life, children born with physical disabilities should not be killed, nor later abandoned, but welcomed and helped to compose, "each according to his talents", a place in the Christian community. Similarly, the Gospels, in their description of Christ life, describe the world of the poor in spirit and the poor in material wealth, and give a unique centrality to each human body as the guardian of the immortal soul. But, descending from this principle, a crippled body shows the stigma of sin, thus resurrecting the Platonic model of the dichotomy between body and spirit. The evil of the body, in the miracles of Christ, hides the power of the devil. Lucifer, an angel who became the Devil for his disobedience to God, one and triune, seduces human minds through the body and represents Evil. In other words, if the body is impaired, it reveals the deterioration of the soul; that is the sin. The model shows an evident and deep contradiction between the ethical and theological model expressed in early Christian evangelical practices and the prescriptions of the Church that have a dramatic development in the Middle Ages with the burning of witches and the possessed, mostly people with disabilities and psychopathology. Such contradictions are still alive at the present time.

Today, the Latin Church is the Vatican State, which is governed by the Code of Canon Law. On one hand, the Code ratifies the universal equality of persons to access the sacraments of initiation and the baptism; on the other hand, it excludes people with disabilities from access to other sacraments, such as marriage – if there is physical or mental impairment to procreation or to the possibility to receive the sacrament of the Eucharist, which corresponds to the communion with God. At the time of writing of this chapter, the Vatican State had not ratified the *UN Convention on the Rights of Persons with Disabilities* (United Nations, 2006), although it had opened a great debate in theological circles.

The medieval era

476 AD, the year of the fall of Occidental Roman Empire, is considered the beginning of the mediaeval era, which lasted approximately 1,000 years. The perspective on people with disabilities in the medieval times has to be considered separately for various disabilities – intellectual disability, physical disabilities, sensory deficits, and pauperism – although what was common to all these was a condition of marginality (Geremek, 1992).

The Lex from the 12 tables from the Roman era that prescribed suffocation for babies born with abnormalities was no longer in use, but as for the practices themselves, little changed. Even the practice of "exposing" children who were not desired or had some "deficits" was still in use.

In the *Codex Iustinianus,* one part of the the *Corpus Iuris Civilis* (body of civil law) which is a classification of Roman laws ordered by the Emperor Justinian (482–565 AD), there are some indications about the restrictions imposed on the deaf and dumb subjects. If a subject was deaf and dumb from birth, this person had no civil rights, but if the condition was acquired and if the person was able to read and write, the subject had civil rights. However, the subjects with these kinds of disabilities were excluded from marriage, unless they had specific permission from the Pope.

In the Codex there was a distinction for people who were not able to work and people who were. Those in the first category were allowed to live off alms and to beg for charity, but the second group were subject to punishment if they were caught in the act (usually they were forced to work or they were taken back to their "owner").

The pope Saint Gregorius Magnus (590–604 AD) maintained that a healthy anima should never have its house in an ill home. Applied to common practice, this meant that if a person acquires a disability in his life, he is no longer a full citizen. The personal and social conditions of a person with disability were similar to those of a person with a terrible sin.

During this period, many authors wrote about the relationship between disability and sin. People with disability were perceived as "monstrous" because of the terrible sins committed by their parents, usually mothers, and for this reason their condition was a sign of divine anger. The origin of the word "monster", associated with persons with disabilities, comes from the Latin word *monstrum,* which derives from *monere,* meaning to warn and from the word *monstrare,* meaning to show, and was considered to be proof from the divinity for misdeeds and sins committed (Schianchi, 2013). In what is now Italy, this conceptualization became popular, with various books written on the topic. For example, Mauro Rabano developed a classification of illnesses based on sins committed. From this time forward, persons with disabilities and illness were perceived by others as demonstrating the evil they committed (Schianchi, 2013). The mother who had a child with physical deformity, during this time, was accused of having slept with the devil, or worse. Many women were condemned to burn in public with their babies (Castellani, 1963). In one such case, reported by Girolamo Magi in the XVI century, a woman gave birth to a child with a normal head but with a body and arms that resembled those of a dog. Under interrogation, the woman admitted that she had sexual relations with a dog. For this reason, the woman and beast were both burned.

An interesting "excuse" for having a child with a visible disability emerges in the idea of the *changeling*. The notion here was that the mother had given birth to a healthy and well-formed baby but, during the night, a demon or nefarious fairy came by and snatched the baby, leaving a deformed baby (the changeling) in its place (Brown, 2007). The art of medieval Europe provides us with a great many examples of what both the babies and those spirits who perpetrated the change looked like. What is not so clear is whether the myth of the changeling was actually believed or whether it was adhered to for cultural and practical purposes. The "monster" baby was not the mother's fault, nor the fault of sin, but rather the mischievous work of an other-worldly being.

Nevertheless, to the people considered *bruti* (with monster appearance) or fools or demented, baptism was refused, as described by Saint Thomas of Aquino in his opera *Summa Theologica* (Tommaso, 1996). But the condition (at least the physical condition) of the person with disabilities began changing, as described in two famous books: *De Monstruorum Natura, Caussis, Natura, et Differentiis Libri Duo* (Liceti, 1616) and *Monstrorum Historia* (Aldrovandi, 1642), where the authors classified the different manifestation of "monsters". The important aspect of Liceti's book is that the condition of being a monster was given because the person created surprise or admiration in others, not because of sin or blame. Thus, at the end of the medieval era, the perspective of disability shifted toward something that is more socially valued and might be considered from a slightly more scientific point of view (Figures 5.1 and 5.2).

Still, it would take almost three more centuries before the idea that the human bodies of the monsters were possible dimensions of human beings took hold (Freud, 1955 Jentsch, 1906).

People with disabilities and mental problems are difficult to locate in the medieval town. They are probably blended into the great mass of indigents living off charity and begging. If the behaviour of the person went beyond what was acceptable and too difficult to tolerate, the person was condemned to a life of wandering from town to town or banished to a solitary life in the county. If the person manifested inappropriate behaviours in the town, he or she was often consigned to the caravans of pilgrims and usually left in the fields outside the city walls (Fioranelli, 2011).

The Catholic Church in the 9th and 10th centuries was actively supporting "the afflicted" – the people representing the poor part of the society. In this age, the conceptualization of a person with disability was changing, moving from the concept of a person unusual to society to a person who has an illness or is in a condition of need. This change of perception brought about, at this time, the first places to segregate and control the poorest parts of the population. The connections and flourishing of commercial contacts among European cities were creating the necessity to control the people who were simply, in the previous times, left outside of the walls of the cities. The first place dedicated to people with leprosy opened in 1217, as the "San Lazzaro" in Reggio Emilia, then was converted for people with Black Death in the 1348. In the same period in various other cities, similar structures opened: Aversa (1269), Turin (about 1390, not certified data), Bergamo (1352), and Feltre (1369–93). The main stated purposes of these establishments was to regulate and control the beggars, and to limit the spreading of diseases to the society.

R Monſtrum marinum Dæmoniforme. 357

Figure 5.1 Illustration from the *Monstrorum Historia* by Ulisse Aldrovandi. (Courtesy of the Wellcome Library, London.)

In the 15th and 16th centuries, the Inquisition, featuring the persecution of witches and heretics, was one strong way of controlling the social order and the marginality that existed in society. At this time, the city-countries that formed the political units of the Italian territory began to partially assist the vagabonds, the beggars

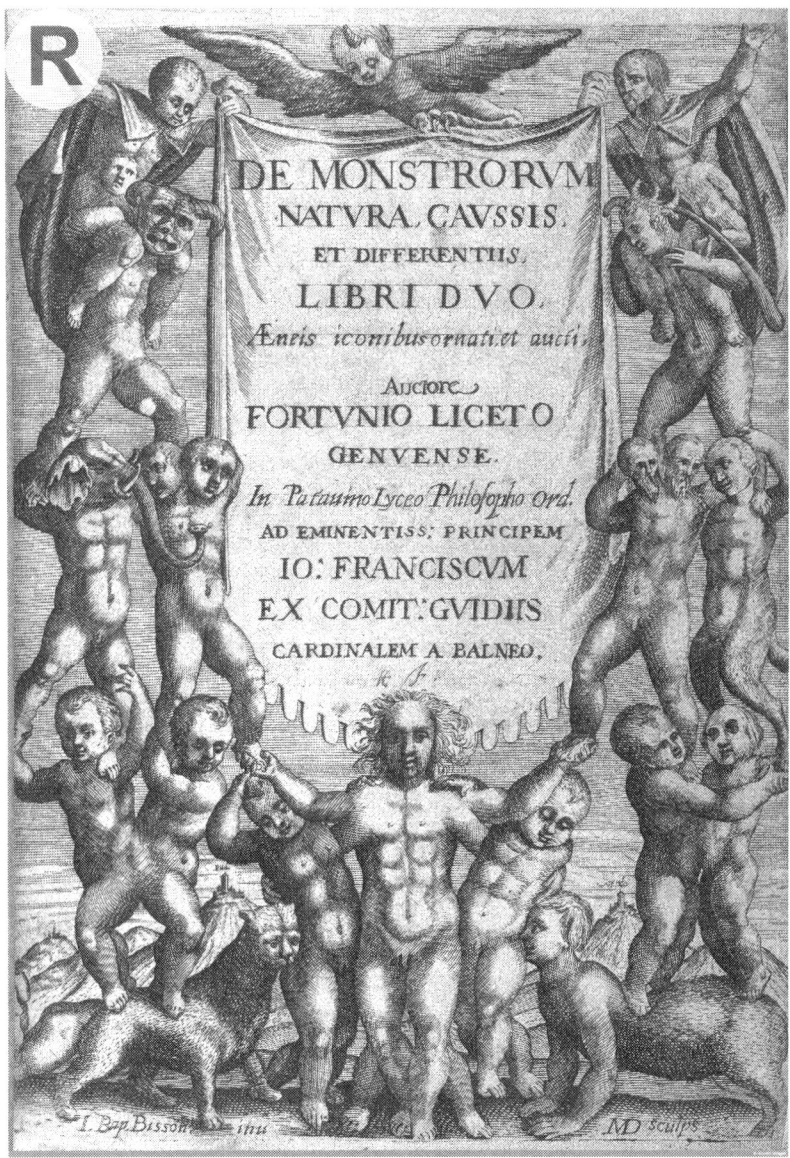

Figure 5.2 The frontispiece to *De Monstrorum Natura Caussis* by Fortunio Liceti. (Courtesy of the Wellcome Library, London.)

who were in need and not in a condition to work. In the 14th century, a Guild of Blind Beggars was established in Padua, Italy, which regulated begging and organized pensions for older blind beggars. In the mean time, The Venetian Republic founded the first publicly funded health service in Europe, and required licensed doctors to attend an annual course in anatomy, attend monthly meetings, and exchange notes on new cases and treatments (NHS, 2013).

77

During this period, also, the missions of the hospitals began to result in a segregation of people in need. This occurred first in 1427 in Brescia, then in 1456 in Milan and Bergamo. For the first time, hospitals had the function of segregating and controlling people who were marginalized by society.

With the end of the medieval age, which might be thought of as concluding in 1492 – the year Spain was overtaken by the Arabs and America was discovered by Columbus – little had fundamentally changed in the daily lives of people with disabilities. It would be some years later before a religious order of monks, the *Fatebenefratelli* – inspired by the scientific and human perspective of their Founder, St. John of God (1495–1550) from Granada, Spain – diffused throughout Italian territory, beginning in Rome, a new approach to people with mental and intellectual disabilities.

1500–1800: From humanism to renaissance and to the beginning of the age of enlightenment

In this era approximately 40,000–50,000 people, mainly women, were put to death across Europe, accused of being witches (Gaskill, 2010). Many were disabled women, whose impairment was seen as the badge of their evil. Others were mothers of disabled children. Various symptoms of mental illness were described as witchcraft. This activity took place mainly in northern Italy and Tuscany in the first part of the 16th century. Valley Camonica (1518–1521) had the biggest witch hunting (62) and 80 fires, Como (1510), had approximately 60 fires, Val di Fiemme (1501–1505) had 11 fires, Mirandola (1522–1523) had 10 fires, and Peveragno (Cuneo) (1513) had 9 fires (Col, 2008; Di Gesaro, 1988; Muraro, 1976).

In the second half of the 1500s, deviance began to be considered as a normal condition and manifestation of society. People who were not able to work and to be productive and had visible limitations started to receive assistance. In support of this, was the 1561 edict from Pope Pio IV, *Ad Insaniam Curandam ...*, establishing S. Maria della Pietà, an institution in the central Colonna square of Rome. The institution was founded in 1549 for the purpose of assisting the poor, pilgrims, and vagabonds, by the Spanish priest Ferrante Ruiz and private citizens Angelo Bruno and his son Diego. Ten years later, its activity was re-directed to help the "poveri pazzerelli" (poor crazy little people). By 1572, this hospital housed more than 80 people, and its name changed to Ospedale di Santa Maria della Pietà dei poveri pazzerelli.

The first documents known to exist concerning the practices in the hospitals are the *Ordini Statuti e Costituzioni della Compagnia della Madonna della Pietà della casa ove hospitale delli poveri forestieri e pazzi dell'alma città di Roma*, published in 1563 by Antonio Blado. Four chapters described the tasks undertaken and the assistance given to the "poor fouls" by the hospital during the time. Those who were assisted had a totally free stay for at least 3 days. The Statuti also described the personnel involved: a medical doctor, an expert on herbs *speziale*, and a *barbero*, a figure who had the duty of coordinating the assistance to the "poor ills". Normal practices included the use of contempions, laxatives, salaxis and, in some cases, exorcisms. A preliminary form of occupational therapy for the female residents was practiced, in the form of daily "ergotherapy" activities (a treatment approach based on work, where the therapeutic factor consists of rationally programmed work activities). Once a week there was a special meeting and once a month a collective one, with many people involved, for

Figure 5.3 Tiberina Island. (Courtesy of the Wellcome Library, London.)

the purpose of discussing outcomes and monitoring the actual supports and treatments provided. A similar form of assistance was developed in Reggio Emilia (1536), Bologna (1560), and Verona (1565).

In the meantime, the order of "Fatebenefratelli" was officially constituted in 1572, and shortly after was founded the first hospital devoted to the poor and fouls in Granada, Spain. In Italy, the order started to operate hospitals in Naples and Rome in 1584, where the order bought the monastery and the church of San Giovanni Calibita on Tiberina Island. The structure was then converted to a hospital, and it is still in use as a hospital today (Figure 5.3).

By 1653, there were eight distinct Italian provinces – Rome, Naples, Milan, Sicily, Bari, Calabria, Basilicata, and Sardinia – that had, among them, more than 150 active hospitals (Francini, 1985). These structures were different from the structure of the normal hospitals in four ways: the people who were hospitalized were usually people with mental problems; there was a small number of people hospitalized in the institutions; there was an explicit intention to heal those housed; and the main practice was to house people almost in isolation for limited periods of time (Fioranelli, 2011).

In the 17th century, the French model dominated the approach to how to cure foulness. The hospitals became places where people who were living off begging and were on the margins of society became concentrated. The idea that led to the recover and treatment of many people with disability in the previous century is destroyed by the return of the contention as the form of therapy. The hospitals, during these times, were opening their doors not only to people with disabilities but also – on the request of the families (with a donation for the subsidy of the person) and institutions – to keep and evaluate people who were refusing to comply with the family's directions or whose heredity was in question.

In this period, the house of "Santa Dorotea dei Pazzarelli" in Florence was founded, and in the year 1643 Carmelita Alberto Leoni opened this establishment to host mentally ill people who were in poor condition. The humanitarian purpose was to release the poor fouls from the place where they were previously locked: the jails of the "Stinche" (Magherini & Biotti, 1997).

In Italy, Pavia, Bologna and Rome, one century before, Girolamo Cardano (1501–1576) was the first physician to recognize the ability of deaf people to reason. A study about deafness and sign language, implemented by G. Bonifacio, was published in 1616: "Of the Art of Signs". During the 17th century in Germany, France, Italy and England, the first schools for deaf people were set up. Tommaso Silvestri, who had studied in France, established the first Italian school for deaf people in Rome in 1748. His practice was based on a combination of sign language and labial recognition. This experience permitted the expansion and settlement of other schools for deaf people in Italy, from Naples to Genova, for a total of more than 40 schools in the whole Italian territory.

The 17th century was a time when people with disabilities were still primarily living in cities and villages. Their daily lives were with their families, often wandering from one town to another, begging. The most capable worked in informal jobs. But during the 17th century, an increasing number of institutions and asylums were built for the purpose of housing, educating, and rehabilitating people with disabilities, and of escaping the unhealthy conditions of cities and towns (Brown, 2007). Many people were housed within these structures, although they were only a portion of the total number of people with disabilities. This was especially the case for children, who mostly continued to live with their families (Schianchi, 2013).

New hospitals were spreading all over Italy during the age of Enlightenment. In Turin, a new hospital was built in 1727–29. In Milan, Lombardy Senavra House was opened in 1780; an institution for females opened its doors in 1750 in Parabiago, and Voghera opened in 1786. Significant growth in institutions occurred in the area of Tuscany and Emila: Bologna 1710, Reggio Emilia 1754, Lucca 1773, Siena 1775, Firenze 1788, and Parma 1793. In the Papal States, innovations were introduced, moving S. Maria della Pietà from the centre of Rome to Lungara in 1726, and introducing two new institutions in Ancona and Pesaro in 1749.

An innovative approach to such hospitals was S. Bonifacio Hospital in Florence. The building was modelled after S. Dorotea the pazzerelli in Rome, and operated under the direction and mentorship of the physician Chiarugi, who standardized the interventions provided in 1789. Chiarugi explicitly identified the structure with a psychiatric and medical model of treatment and curing. In this sense, S. Bonifacio in Florence can be considered as the first psychiatric hospital in history. But Chiarugi was a reformer and, with Pinel in France, he promoted a scientific approach while maintaining a cultural dignity to the disabled person – providing both cure and hospitality.

Chiarugi promoted the idea of a scientific approach to the cure of the mental illness, as opposed to earlier-used methods of exorcism, the benediction, and torture. He was "breaking the chains" by redefining the social rules of treating the patients, and by classifying the pathologies and their specific scientific treatments. He reclassified people admitted at the Hospital, using five categories: mania, melancholia, delirium, dementia, and imbecility (Chiarugi, 1793). Attitudes toward the people changed as well, especially when chains were abolished. Other forms of physical restrains were used instead with the most difficult cases. This change resulted in a considerable reduction in the number of wounds produced by the constriction of chains. Under Chiarugi's influence, the hospital lost its main characterization as a segregating place. However, some limits to the success of the hospital emerged, mainly because of overcrowding. The limited internal spaces, especially in summer, had particularly painful effects on the lives of those who lived in the hospital.

The 1800s: Education, re-education and large institutions

During the 19th century in Europe, there was a major paradigm shift in the approach to disabilities toward rehabilitation. In Italy, there began a process of implementing treatment for all the different types of disabilities. One example of this was the invention of the Braille alphabet as an aid to the education of people who were blind. The first institution for blind pupils was founded in Naples in 1818, and another opened in Padua in 1840. Another example was the invention of the first typing machines for blind people by Giuseppe Ravizza in 1846. The experience of Augusto Romagnoli, the first person to be born blind but to graduate and become a teacher in a public school, set a precedent for the benefits of educating people who were blind.

Also at this time in Italy, the first institution for the education of people with intellectual disabilities opened in Aosta in 1848 for the cure of cretinism, followed in the 1884 by a structure in Rome specifically for "idiots and imbecils". The positive reasons for these institutions rapidly diminished, and it was not long before they turned into places of segregation. By the end of the century, there was a recognizable change in society's view of disability, and in the way people with disabilities were served.

Nevertheless, many positive developments continued. In 1889, Antonio Gonnelli Cioni founded two institutions for the treatment of people with intellectual disability. This pedagogist was also the author of many publications about the necessity of education for children with intellectual disabilities. Sancte de Sanctis, one of the fathers of neuropsychiatry in Italy, was the founder of the first kindergarten and school for children with intellectual disabilities. In his career, he introduced the first ambulatories for neurodevelopmental psychiatry (1899) and introduced the clinical practice of maintaining a file containing biographical information for each person (Cimino, 2004). During this period, Andrea Verga was a supporter, with his writings, of the necessity of educational intervention for the people with disabilities in special institutions. In the meantime, Montessori, Montesano, and Bonfiglio founded the National League for the Protection of Deficient Children.

Maria Montessori, a scholar of pedagogical science, brought together her interest in scientific knowledge of people with intellectual disabilities and the practice of the psychiatric clinic of the Rome University to develop what was then called "The Montessori Method" in education. Maria Montessori was also the first woman with a medical degree in the Italian State. Using her unique position, she promoted laws for children "frenastesici" in the Italian parliament, she persuaded institutions to perform medical-pedagogical treatments, and she established special classes for disabled children in the regular schools.

Montessori became the director of the school Ortofrenica in Rome in 1900. This institution was formerly a municipal asylum for the "deficient and insane" children of the city – probably autistic or mentally disabled children – that principally provided a caretaker role in very barren surroundings. Supported by her colleagues, she initiated numerous reforms. She began by dismissing the staff who had provided a caretaking role and who did not share her vision of rehabilitation. She recognized the children's need for stimulation, purposeful activity, and self-esteem and, although acquiring competent staff was a major challenge, Montessori began to teach the more able children, through her innovative methods, how to care for themselves and how to care for the less able children (StateUniversity.com., 1870–1952).

Montessori's school even had a second purpose: the training of teachers who would assist children with disabilities. This degree required two years of training in a multidisciplinary field: medicine, neurology, hygiene, education, and language. At the core of her practice was the notion that children with disabilities could learn and improve their skills through their relationships with adults and with specific training (Schianchi, 2013). Montessori took the idea from her mentors that a scientific approach to education, based on observation and experimentation, was possible. She constantly implemented her work with the careful training and objectivity of the scientist. She studied her mentally disabled patients, listening and carefully noting their responses to her attempts to implement De Sanctis and Séguin's educational methods, as well as their progress in becoming increasingly independent and verbal (Montessori, 1992).

Slowly the children of the school learned to perform most of the everyday tasks involved in preparing the meals and maintaining the environment of the residential school. Her success in training the children with disabilities received international attention when, after 2 years, many of Montessori's adolescents were able to pass the standard exams given by the Italian public schools.

Acclaimed for this miracle, Montessori responded by suggesting that newborn human beings normally enter the world with an intellectual potential that was barely being developed by schools in the early years of the 20th century. Her challenge to the education system was that if she could attain such results with children who were disabled, schools should be able to get dramatically better results with normal children.

The 1900s: The contemporary age: Human rights, science, laws, and advocacy

As was the case throughout Europe, the Industrial Revolution in Italy (especially in the North) had resulted in a sizeable increase in the numbers of people with physical disabilities caused by accidents at work. One result of this was a first rudimentary model of a public pension system. However, people with intellectual disabilities and those with psychopathology were excluded, as they were considered to have limited work capacity in any case.

This was also a time when medicine took on a prominent role in the care of people, particularly to readjust and re-educate. People with disabilities were accepted by institutions and other establishments, run almost exclusively by Christian Catholics according to the spirit of Pietas, a welcoming and acceptance for the "lasts," a tradition that endured from previous centuries. These "lasts" were a mixture of people who were poor, had physical and mental disabilities, or were marginalized in other ways.

The first Italian law that recognizes and establishes clear rules for the management of the institutions and asylums was the Giolitti law No. 36 of 1904. This law established the power of the State through psychiatric social issues and marginalization and defined the criteria to consign people to institutions: "social dangerousness" and "public scandal". These persons were interned in a mental hospital, then, not because they are ill but because they were considered to be harmful, dangerous, unproductive, and involved in public scandal. In this way, the "crazy people" were identified in the court records as common criminals and legally excluded from civil society.

The impact of World War I

The disability scenario changed significantly due to the Great War between 1914 and 1918 that involved more than 50 countries. This war left 15 million dead, 8 million disabled (crippled, blind, deaf) and an unknown number of "dumb war" alienated and suffering of post-traumatic disorders. In Italy, it is estimated that half a million soldiers were disabled. Veterans with disabilities were honoured as war heroes, but were neglected as citizens with rights, even with the introduction in 1917 for the first time in Italy of Law 481 that changed social security rules to require the compulsory employment of disabled war veterans. Similarly but even more dramatically, the Second World War of 1939–45 resulted in 55 million people dead, and 24 million soldiers and 32 million civilians wounded.

The Fascist period

Between the two wars, the Fascist period in Italy (1922–1943), which featured the totalitarian power of Benito Mussolini's national socialism, aligned with German Nazism in Hitler's desire for purification of the race. This had profound effects on the perception and treatment of disability. The link with eugenics, the ideology that Hitler eventually took to horrifying extremes, was that syphilis and tuberculosis were considered hereditary in the same way disability was, and thus subject to measures of racial hygiene. Based on this thinking, Mussolini, in the Sermon on the Ascension in 1927, declared the principle that the state has the right and duty to prohibit weddings to ensure the "overflow of life force of Latin origin".

This principle was badly misused by the Fascists. History has recorded the many misuses, but one example was that the internment of people disliked for personal or business reasons became common. Mussolini himself set a precedent with his first wife, Ida, and his natural son, Benito Albino: both died in reclusion.

Another practice, regulated first in Germany in 1935 and then with the racial laws in Italy, was the prohibition of mixed marriages between Jews and non-Jews, purportedly to protect against disease and deficiency. Eugenic sterilization and even therapeutic abortions became mandatory for people with disabilities, vagabonds, and other socially excluded persons, such as those with "frenastenia congenital disorder, schizophrenia, folie circulaire, hereditary epilepsy, St. Vitus' dance hereditary, hereditary blindness, severe hereditary physical deformity, and severe alcoholism"

(Sterilization Law, ReichsgesBblatt, July, 25th, 86, 1933, art. 1.). The Latin Catholic Church, in its 1931 encyclical *Casti Connubii*, condemned eugenic sterilization measures, but supported eugenics in general and the more moderate acts of Mussolini by being in favour of a "moral selection of breeding" based on education, abstinence, and accountability.

The impact of World War II

In Germany, the T4 project was begun in 1939 shortly after the war began. It was the systematic, but secretive, planning and killing more than 70,000 German adults with disabilities, mostly people who were living in psychiatric institutions. Over-medication and starvation were the principal methods of causing death, although deaths were often conveniently attributed to another cause such as pneumonia. The project also included the systematic killing, using similar methods, of about 5000 children with disabilities in Germany in about 20 killing hospitals. The full extent of these killings was not commonly known because family members and others were not told the truth about the causes of death, and the war served as a major distraction but, even so, pressure from public opinion and of the Church brought about an end to the project as overt public policy in 1941.

In Italy, action against people with disabilities was much more secretive. It remained the secret task of the midwife, at the time of birth when the impairment was evident, to take action. The degree to which there was compliance from midwives is not entirely known.

The Jewish people with disabilities, on the other hand, began to experience even more blatant discrimination at this time. The decade-long persecution of the Jewish people accelerated and those with disabilities were included in the euthanasia program for their ethnicity, not just because of their disabilities. As much of continental Europe fell under the control of the German Nazis, the extermination of Jews and especially disabled Jews was carried out in occupied countries. There were dramatic episodes of this in Italy. Jews were interned in psychiatric hospitals in Venice, and deported to Auschwitz-Birkenau. A close reading of the documented evidence shows that very few of the Jews admitted to St. Servolo and San Clemente in Venice had real mental illness. There is also evidence that, in 1943, Dr. Dietrich Allers, the former director of the administrative office of T4 in its second phase, had been the architect and manager of the transit camp in the Italian Rice Mill of San Sabba.

Even asylums were described as camps by Ugo Cerletti and Lucio Bini who, in 1938, invented electroconvulsive therapy, so-called electroshock, for the partial or total remission of mental illness. This therapy was indicated where there existed a state of material and moral degradation in the patients. The conditions of the interned patients were very poor: normally they were kept dirty, naked, and tied up. (It has been only since the 1950s that psychotropic drugs came into use in psychiatric hospitals, and thus when sedation replaced physical restraints.) Ironically, the events of World War II – and especially the gruesome discovery of the concentration camps at the end of the war – worked to promote rights and inclusion for people with disabilities throughout the world (Brown, 2007). The world's leading cultures, perhaps still reeling from their experience of war, turned their attention to human rights, beginning with the United

Nations' 1948 Declaration of Human Rights, and eventually including people with disabilities very specifically (Rioux, Lindqvist, and Cuthbert, 2007).

Human rights and support for the beginnings of inclusion

In the second half of the 1900s, after the carnage of two world wars had ended, the impact of disability in Italy changed due to advances in science and medicine. But new causes of disability opened up in the form of accidents at work (today there is still a rate of 20,000 permanent disabilities per year) and in the streets (currently about 20,000 per year). There were new causes of disability, such as thalidomide, used in the 1950s to combat morning sickness in pregnant women and withdrawn from the market in Italy only in 1959. These additional causes brought about the realization that disability is a broad social phenomenon, something that can affect any social group. Disability is not just something that affects others, but something that could also relate to me and to my offspring: it is a real threat.

The Italian Constitution, promulgated in 1948, made a clear and elegant statement in support of formal and substantive equality and freedom (Articles 2 and 3), attained through political, economic, and social means. Article 38 more specifically established the right to ongoing support and social assistance by two separate categories of citizens: those who are incapacitated, and those without a means of support. The citizen is referred to as worker, in keeping with concepts from the Greco-Roman, Catho-social, and production-capitalist cultures. Equality is sustained with a guarantee of formal rights and economic support upon official recognition of disability, whatever its origin.

The welfare state that emerged at this time can be thought of as the juxtaposition of two separate life realms: work and care. Its roots can be recognized in earlier forms of social protection, sketched out at the end of the 19th century. The principal idea of the welfare state was to use the proceeds of economic prosperity to promote the equality of all citizens, particularly those who were socially and economically marginalized. Although many advances were made in Italy and other countries over the next 50 years, these goals would not be fully reached, as the high cost of care and economic support, combined with a series of downturns in the world economy, sank the welfare state in favour of a less certain Community State, where the goal became inclusion rather than equality.

Republican Italy, in keeping with the standards of the time, enacted Law 66/1962 on the management of blind civilians by the Blind National Opera in 1954, which was replaced in 1970 by the Italian Union of Blind. In 1962, Law 1539, under pressure from the newly constituted associations, and Law 743/1969 progressively extended the economic benefits to persons with more severe disabilities. Law 482/1968 regulated the compulsory employment, in both the public and private sectors, of military and civil people with disabilities, and for those who were blind, deaf and mute. However, its application was not universal, but rather just to those who were financially needy.

Receiving the disability pension was, therefore, the prerequisite status to access other disability benefits. The first general legislation on disability was Law 118/1971, which widened the definition of disability to citizens suffering from congenital or acquired disabilities, including a progressive nature, including irregular psychic caused by oligofreny, organic or dysmetabolic, mental deficiencies resulting from defects in sensory and functional features who have suffered a permanent reduction in working capacity of not less than one-third, or, if under the age of 18, who have persistent difficulties to perform the duties and functions of their age.

This law introduced health care benefits, fully paid by the National Health Service, as well as drug prescriptions, specialized visits, hospital assistance, and prosthetics to the categories of people listed, which in 1978 came under the jurisdiction of the regional Sanitary System. The Ministries of Health and Education also ensured inclusive education with Law 118/71, but still excluded students with certification of gravity (severe disabilities). A diagnosis of the "condition of disability" carried out through a medical examination by the health system's Provincial Commissions, was the requirement to obtain such rights. In addition, Law 118/71, for the first time, introduced the principle of removal of architectural barriers.

Beginning in 1973, eligibility for economic benefits followed a complex system: a disabled adult with total work incapacity was eligible for a disability pension; a person with a reduction to work greater than or equal to 74%, in the age range 18–64, received a monthly allowance (as well as a social pension); a person younger than 18 and non-ambulatory was provided a payment for an attendant caregiver, but only if he or she was attending school; the civilian disabled or invalids were assigned a per diem pay on the condition that they attend training courses organized by the Ministry of Labour. There are also special provisions for interruptions from work to care for people in extraordinary circumstances.

Law 517/1977 introduced the complete integration of pupils with disabilities into regular classes, with an obligation to support the educational programming of all students with educational certification. Together with the subsequent Law 104/1992, Italy reached its goal of total inclusive education for all children and young people with disabilities in all levels of school, with classroom support of a specialized teacher and a series of administrative bodies and organizational tools to promote inclusion. These Italian laws regarding school inclusion have been exemplary in their specification of pedagogic and rational approach, methods of instruction, and strength of legislation (e.g. not following ad hoc rules for students with disabilities, but rather designating the school as an inclusive system for everyone). One ongoing challenge, though, is to invest in training of specialized professionals among the teaching staff.

Returning to institutionalization, the Italian Law 180/1978, known by the name of Basaglia – a psychiatrist from Trieste and a fierce promoter of citizenship rights for people with disabilities – addressed the closure of the institutions and mental hospitals in Italy. This law defers to each of 20 regions across Italy, now empowered to implement the closure of psychiatric hospitals and the deinstitutionalization of persons with disabilities. This was to be completed with the support of local community services, with the goal of full social integration. Law 180/1978 also re-established psychiatry within the broader field of medical practice, after its exclusion by the legislation in 1904 that had relegated its practice to matters of public order. Decentralization (further to the power given to the 20 regions in Law 180/1978) was extended through federal legislation by Constitutional Law 3/2001, and this resulted in the development of very different set of accredited and contracted services, from one region to another, that support people with disabilities and their families. As a result, today there are different costs for disability services and, across regions, a very different quantity and quality of supports for the same citizens of the Italian Republic.

Throughout the 1980s, the population of those entitled to the disability allowance expanded to disabled adults and minors who were unable to perform the acts of everyday life. This took place primarily because the fragmentation of responsibilities for disabilities across Italy from State to Regions produced differences in attributing the status of "person with disability" and the consequent eligibility to receive financial compensation (Canevaro, 2006).

In fact, a complete reorganization of the conceptualization of disabilities occurred as a result of Law 104/1992, the "Law for the assistance, integration, and social rights of disabled people", and expanded later by Law 162/1998, Law 53/2000, Decree 151/2001, Law 183/2010, and Law 114/2014. This new view reflected and incorporated the evolution of the contextual conceptual model introduced by the World Health Organization (ICF, 2001). According to such a model, functioning and disability derive from the interactions between the Person and his/her environments. The same laws reaffirmed Italian constitutional requirements with respect to the principles of equality, equal opportunities, solidarity, as expressed through personal autonomy and social integration. The legal and cultural implications of Law 104/1992 were that the public would take charge of the person with disabilities – regardless of cause and severity of the disability – from birth and throughout the whole of life, including family and school (Canevaro, D'Alonzo, & Ianes, 2009), work, and leisure time. The Law decentralized, from Central authority to local authority, ensuring that the rights of people with disabilities were being respected. It also opened space for the participation of voluntary associations, co-operation with other bodies, and the use of private capital. This specific rule illustrates the transition from assistant state to welfare state: the care of the person with disability and his or her family by the community.

More than 20 years have passed since Law 104/1992 was enacted, and its impact continues to be strong. But, at the same time, there continues to be a lack of identified ways to implement and support in an ongoing way the rights and protections stated. Perhaps this is because the way in which the welfare state is expressed has already veered towards a community one.

The 1999 Law 68, "Standards for the right to work of persons with disabilities", regulated the mandatory recruitment of people with disability for employment, repealed previously in Law 482/1968. It stated an obligation for private and public companies to recruit workers with disabilities, following an evaluation of work capacity, environmental modifications, and inclusive support needed to carry out the work. The law is complex and leaves considerable room to avoid putting it into practice to its full extent. At the date of writing, it is estimated, in absence of official data, that employment positions for people with disabilities in the open market pursuant to Law 68/1999 constitute about 21% of all positions.

Following World War II, one of the constitutionally guaranteed rights was participation in free associations. Advocacy from family members of persons with disabilities resulted in numerous service associations being funded, beginning in 1954: AIAS, Italian Association for the Assistance of Spastics; ANMIC, National Association of

Table 5.1 Chronology of normative references

Law 6144/1889	Public safety: ban on begging; internment of beggars filed by local authorities.
Law 6972 /1890	Establishment of charitable institutions for the poor, the disabled, the sick, and those unable to work.
Year 1898	Establishment of a National Fund for pension for disability, and a non-compulsory old age insurance
Law 36/1904	Social control of deviance through psychiatry: the reason of internment in a mental hospital is danger to society and public scandal, not disease.
Law 481/1914	Social Security. The inclusion of measures of compulsory employment for war invalids.
Law 70/1895 and regulation of its application R.D. 835/1920	Establishment of civil and military pensions to survivors in case of death. Grinding with R.D. 2480/1923: Due to the limitation of service as a determinant of illness / death.
Law 1132/1924	Social Security. Introduction of mandatory quotas for recruitment of disabled war veterans.
Legge 416 /1926	Compensation for "anatomical damage" to a civil servant of the kingdom with a compensation or pension at the rate score assigned by gravity.
Royal Decree 1765/1935	Extension of accidents at work, Consolidated Safety. Identify categories of dangerous people who must be interned in charitable institutions on the basis of inability to work, including the beggars.
1923–1943	National Socialist Fascist period in Italy – Fascism.
1925 and 1926 1938	Fascismo Totalitarian regime. Read "fascist": A: Q: 1848/1925, Law 2029/1925, Law 237/1926, RD 1848/1926, Law 2008/26, Law 2693/1928 The Fascist racial: set of administrative and legislative measures.
Law 66/1962	Management of the National Opera for Blind civilian replaced in 1970 by the Italian blind Association.
Law 1539/1962	Progressive extension of the economic benefits to the disability more than two-thirds (until the law 743/1969).
Law 482/1968	Discipline compulsory employment in the public and private sectors for war invalids military and civil, labour, blind, deaf and dumb.
Law 118/1971	First disability civil organic framework. First introduction of the principle of removal of architectural barriers. First mandatory school integration in mainstream classes, except the certificates of gravity (severely disabled).
Law 517/1977	Inclusive education in mainstream classes with compulsory educational programming for educational support.
Law 833/1978	Establishment of the National Health Service and transfer of some powers to the Regions.

(continued)

Table 5.1 Chronology of Normative References (*continued*)

Law 180/1978	Framework Act which empowers the regions to implement the closure of psychiatric hospitals, and provide community-based services for people with disabilities with the goal of full social integration.
Sentence 215 – 5 -year 1987 Constitutional Court	Full and unconditional recognition of the right for pupils with certification of gravity (severe disability) to be educated in mainstream secondary schools.
Law 13/1989	Provisions to support the adaptation and removal of architectural barriers in public buildings.
Law 104/1992	"Law for the assistance, integration, and social rights of disabled people" further added to later by L. 16271998, by Law 53/2000, the Decree. 151/2001, by Law 183/2010, by Law 114/2014.
Law 68/ 1999	Recruitment protection made obligatory: Regulations for the right to work of persons with disabilities.
Law 328 /2000	Law for the implementation of integrated system of interventions and social services.
Law 67/2006	Non-discrimination: "Measures for the legal protection of persons with disabilities who are victims of discrimination".
Law 6/2004	Integration to the Civil Code art. 404–413. Legal protection: establishment of a Support Administrator for people with limited ability to act.
Law 18/2009	Ratification of the UN Convention on the Rights of Persons with Disabilities and the Protocols annexed to the Convention.
Interministerial decree 166/2010	Regulation governing the National Observatory on the status of Persons with Disability, under article 3 of Law 18/2009
Law 112/2011	Supervisor Institution of Childhood and Adolescence.
Decree of the President of the Republic 12/28/2013	Adoption of the biennial program of action for the promotion of the rights and the integration of people with Disability.

Civilian Disabled or Invalids; ANFFAS, National Association of Families of Mentally Handicapped Children; and UILDM, Italian Union Fight Against Muscular Dystrophy. In 1962, ANMIC obtained recognition in law, and had a representative in both parliament and ANFFAS (Comitato Tecnico-Scientifico Anffas Onlus, 2007). AIAS, as public interlocutors, focused on establishing local public services. These associations were followed by a plethora of associations related to specific disability conditions and categories, bringing about the risk of further fragmentation of services and, consequently, of political irrelevance. In Milan, LEDHA was founded in 1979 as the league for the rights of disabled persons, an initiative that brought together various associations in Lombardy to defend the rights of people with disabilities and their families. Law 104/1992, which assigned an explicit role to the associations, established two large federations of associations: in 1993, FISH, the Italian Federation to Overcome

Handicaps (characterized by a progressive approach) and, in 1997, FAND, a federation that combined the existing associations, ANMIC, UIC, ENS, AMNIL, UNMS (characterized by a more moderate approach). The road was now open to the federated associations to be a political force when dealing with the legislature and public administrators.

In 2000, the Charter of Fundamental Rights of the European Union was published. It contained a guideline for all Member States whose intent was to reaffirm those rights already present in the Italian Constitution of dignity, freedom, equality, solidarity, justice, and citizenship. This was expressed, in particular, in the Article 26:

> The Union shall respect and ensure the rights of persons with disabilities to benefit from measures designed to ensure their independence, social and occupational integration, and participation in the life of the community.

In Italy, in keeping with the trend in other Western countries, there was a steady increase in the number of certifications, and today it is estimated that there are approximately 3 million people with disabilities, although only 700,000 are under the age of 60. In 2014, Italy was in seventh position among the 28 EU countries for all social spending, which included health, social security, and assistance. This has important implications for future policy development.

The United Nations' 2006 *Convention on the Rights of Persons with Disabilities* was ratified in Italy by Law 18/2009. This law is the most recent summary, in chronological order, of scientific, cultural, and legal aspects of disability, and of what is in Italy a key input in the dialectic between the gaps of the welfare state and activism associations and the third sector. The Convention became binding law in Italy, including the obligation to adjust legal and policy options to support the Convention. Law 18/2009 also transformed the rights of people with disabilities from soft law to active and positive law. It was binding on the ratifying States, and created a universal change. This change was based on the long history of regulatory and scientific knowledge of the United Nations, which has estimated that there are about 650 million disabled people in the world. The law has a double legal implication: as a statement of values through the enunciation of legal principles also clearly stated in specific rights, and as coherence of legislation and administration for the ratifying states. The aim is to change Italian culture regarding disability, and to adapt current national practices.

The assumption is that our conceptualization of disability is immediate and changeable, rather than definitive. The Convention sees disability as a dynamic construct, one that cannot be defined by default (thus surpassing the previous definitions of the WHO ICF in 2001 and 2007). Further, the assumption is that disability is expressed through two variables: one objective, relating to the living environments and interests of people; and the other subjective, relating to the perspectives of human diversity.

The legal text of Law 18/2009 does not focus on positive aspects of disability, as perceived by the person functioning and experiencing life in here and now. Nor does it focus on the person's life to this point, and to the personal history that may affect the present. Instead, it focuses on the variety of rights of persons with disabilities, and on ensuring that applicable policies and practices are developed and activated to guarantee the rights agreed to by ratifying governments. The entire document revolves around a matrix of two components – human rights and citizenship – expressed through the two areas of self-determination: self-determination as an expression of freedom and non-discrimination, and self-determination as an expression of the need to protect and safeguard.

The two categories for putting Law 18/2009 into practice are reasonable accommodation, and universal design. Reasonable accommodation requires application of the legal principles of fairness, proportionality, and appropriate investment of community resources, to ensure that people with disabilities can exercise their rights as declared. Universal design is a conceptual and physical tool to ensure non-discrimination and the possibility of access to programs and services for everyone, defined by individuals' needs for specific supports.

Italy, like other Western countries, is therefore in a time of change between the crisis of the welfare state and the application of the ratification of the Convention through Law 18/2009.

The chronology of normative references is reported in Table 5.1.

All the information about the current laws in favour of People with disability can be found on specified websites (handylex.org, osservatoriodisabilita.it, 3istat.it, istruzione.it)

Other information about the development of politics, rights and support systems can be retrieved from the following websites

www.anffas.net
www.cnd.it
www.europarl.europa.eu
www.fishonlus.it
www.handylex.org
www.istruzione.it
www.osservatoriodisabilità.it
www.superando.it

Conclusion

At the end of this two-part chapter, we suggest that the reader capitalize on two different sets of key information that might be useful as interpretation criteria of what has been synthetically presented. First, regarding the historical overview, we stressed the progressive efforts over the centuries, and especially in Italy, to enrich the identity of the Person with disability as a valid part of human diversity. Person and disability are not the same: value, meaning, sense, and quality of life do not discriminate but belong to every human being, despite their physical condition or perceived social disadvantage. Disability is a set of problems, a complex attribute of human functioning, and refers to natural and psychological phenomena interacting with social and contextual factors. Second, regarding the more recent developments, we wish to emphasize the attempt today to integrate scientific knowledge with the legal and rights approach, with providing efficient services and supports, with advocacy, and with family participation. Such initiatives serve the purpose of creating an innovative system of supports for fully participating people with disabilities.

The historical perspective helps to understand the gradual separation between the person and the disability – or, to borrow from anthropology, the progression from an emic perspective (view of the person from within the social group) to an etic perspective (view from outside a social group). Over time, disability became something different from the person with disabilities. In ancient times, stigma was imposed because the identity of the person was inseparable from his/her low social or economic functioning, and thus low value. Over the centuries, as the idea grew that each person had rights and value just for being a human, the person him/herself was slowly revealed and extracted from the person/disability mixture (Harris & Enfield, 2003) After this necessary separation, a debate emerged in Italy about how best to reintegrate the person and his/her disability/functioning by means of rights, personal supports, and contextual supports.

Such a new integrative perspective might be embedded into standard practice by the complete implementation of the United Nations' *Convention or the Rights of Persons with Disabilities* and, addressing technical and scientific concerns, by further development of the quality of life and support models. These should be promoted by all the stakeholders, including support users, families, and society (Brown, Schalock, & Brown, 2009).

The shared "agorà" of this new perspective might be represented by what in Italy is called "Progetto di Vita" – Life Project. This is the normative, law-based agreement between the community and its citizens who have a condition of disability, supported by best practice assessment and plan development (such as an Individualized Support Plan). When these are based on evidence and human paradigms, we can build pathways towards lives of quality and meaning (Butkus,Rotholz, Lacy, Abery, & Elkin, 2002).

References

Aldrovandi, U. (1642). *Monstrorum Historia. Cum Paralipomenis Historiae Omnium Animalium.* Bologna:Typis Nicolò Tebaldini.

Brown, I. (2007). Historical overview of intellectual and developmental disabilities. in I. Brown & M. Percy (Eds.), *A Comprehensive Guide to Intellectual & Developmental Disabilities* (pp. 17–33). Baltimore, MD: Paul H. Brookes Publishing.

Brown, R. I., Schalock, R. L., & Brown, I. (2009). Quality of life: Its application to persons with intellectual disabilities and their families: Introduction and overview. *Journal of Policy and Practice in Intellectual Disabilities, 6*(1), 2–6.

Butkus, S., Rotholz, D. A., Lacy, K. K., Abery, B., & Elkin, S. (2002). Implementing person-centered planning on a statewide basis: Leadership, training and satisfaction issues. in S. Holburn & P. M. Vietze (Eds.), *Person-Centered Planning: Research, Practice and Future Directions* (pp. 335–359). Baltimore, MD: Paul H. Brookes Publishing.

Canevaro, A. (2006). *Pedagogia speciale. La riduzione dell'handicap.* Milan: Mondadori.

Canevaro, A. L., D'Alonzo, L., & Ianes, D. (2009). *L'integrazione scolastica di alunni con disabilità dal 1977 al 2007: Risultati di una ricerca attraverso lo sguardo delle persone con disabilità e delle loro famiglie.* Bolzano: Bozen–Bolzano University Press.

Castellani, C. (1963). *Le donne e il Diavolo.* Milano: Longanesi.

Cimino, G. P. L. (2004). *Sante de Sanctis tra psicologia generale e psicologia applicata.* Milano: Franco Angeli.

Chiarugi, V. (1973). *Della Pazzia.* Firenze: Luggi Carleri.

Col, A.D. (2008). La persecuzione della stregoneria in Italia dal medioevo all'età moderna. Retrieved from http://www.incontritramontani.it/Files/Atti/ITM2008%20-%20Del%20 Col.pdf

Comitato Tecnico-Scientifico Anffas Onlus. (2007). A cura di I sostegni per incrementare la qualità di vita della persona con disabilità intellettiva e relazionale. Una sperimentazione, in *American Journal on MentalRetardation: Edizione Italiana, Brescia, Vannini, 5*(3), 397–398.

Di Gesaro, P. (1988). *Streghe: L'ossessione del diavolo, il repertorio dei malefizi, la repressione.* Bolzano: Praxis 3.

Fioranelli, M. (2011). *Il decimo cerchio: Appunti per una sotriadella disabilità.* Bari: Laterza.

Francini, M. (1985). *San Giovanni di Dio e i suoi seguaci in Italia.* Milano: Frassinelli.

Freud, S. (1955). The 'Uncanny'. In trans: J. Strachey, A. Freud & S. Freud (Eds.), *The Standard Edition of the Complete Psychological Works of Sigmund Freud* (Vol. 17, pp. 217–256). London: Hogarth; Also in Dickson, A. (1985). *The Pelican Freud Library.* trans: J. Strachey (Vol. 14, pp. 335–376). Harmondsworth: Penguin. For Freud's German text, see the Freud, A. et al. (Eds.). (1947). Gesammelte Werke (Vol. 12, pp. 227–268). London: Imago; or the Mitscherlich, A. et al. (Eds.). (1970). Studienausgabe (Vol. 4, pp. 241–274). Frankfurt: Fischer.

Gaskill, M. (2010). *Witchcraft, A Very Short Introduction.* Oxford: Oxford University Press.

Geremek, B. (1992). *Uomini senza padrone: Poveri e marginali tra Medioevo ed età moderna.* Torino: Einaudi.

Jentsch, E. (1906). Zur psychologie des Unheimlichen. *Psychiatrisch-Neurologische Wochenschrift, 8.22* (25 Auguest 1906), 195–198 and *8.23* (1 September 1906), 203–205.

Harris A., & Enfield, S. (2003). *Disability, Equality and Human rights: A Training Manual for Developmental and Humanitarian Organisations.* Oxford: Oxfam Publishing.

Liceti, F. (1616). *De monstruorum natura, caussis, natura, et differentiis libri duo.* Padova.

Magherini, G., & Biotti, V. (1997). *Luogo della città per custodia de' pazzi: Santa Dorotea dei Pazzerelli di Firenze nelle delibere della sua Congregazione, 1642–1754.* Firenze: Le lettere.

Montessori, O.N. (1992). *Maria Montessori: Il pensiero il metodo* (Vol. 1). Teramo: Lisciani & Giunti Editori.

Muraro, L. (1976). *La Signora del gioco, episodi di caccia alle streghe.* Milano: Feltrinelli.

NHS. (2013). *A Disability History Timeline.* NHS North West, Manchester.

Pope Pio XI. (1930) *Casti Connubi.* Vatican. https://w2.vatican.va/content/vatican/it.html

Rioux M.H., Lindqvist B., Carbert A. (2007). *International Human Rights and Developmental Disabilities,* in Brown I., Percy M., *A Comprehensive Guide to Intellectual and Developmental Disabilities.* New York: Brooks.

Schianchi, M. (2013). *Storia della disabilità.* Roma: Carocci.

StateUniversity.com. (2015). Maria Montessori. (1870–1952). Biography, work with disabled children. Retrieved from http://education.stateuniversity.com/pages/2244/Montessori-Maria-1870-1952.html

Tommaso, D.A. (1996). *La somma teologica.* Bologna: PDUL. Retrieved from www.fulvionapoli. it/sommateologica.somma.htm

World Health Organization (WHO). (2001). *International Classification of Functioning, Disability and Health* (ICF). Geneva: Author.

World Health Organization (WHO), Division for Social Policy and Development Disability (2006), *United Nation of the Rights of People with Disability.* Geneva

6

A SHORT HISTORY OF DISABILITY ASPECTS FROM ISRAEL

Joav Merrick, Ariel Tenenbaum,
Mohammed Morad and Eli Carmeli

Introduction

Disability studies have since the 1980s evolved into an interdisciplinary field, where scholars think about disability not as an isolated or individual medical pathology or issue, but instead as a key defining social category on par with race, class and gender (Kudlick, 2003). In this chapter we will try and give a snapshot of some of the disability history from the Middle East region, but with a major focus on Israel.

Disability and Islam

In the Middle East the topic of religion is a very important factor of people's lives, and religious organisations have since early days been associated with providing health and welfare services to persons with a disability (Selway & Ashman, 1998).

In 706, the Caliph Al-Walid Ben Abed Al-Malik permitted the establishment of the first Islamic hospital and declared the medical profession official (Nader, 1995). He also ordered the assignment of a caregiver for each disabled and needy person and permitted allowance from the imperial treasure to these workers (Nader, 1995). Khalid Ibn Yazid (end of the seventh century), gave up his wealth for the study of medicine and chemistry. One anecdote from the first years of Islam shows the interest and understanding of the Moslem society for the needs of the disabled. One person complained to the Caliph Omar Ibn Al-Khatab that his son was physically disabled and unable to reach the mosque. The Caliph ordered his subordinates to arrange a closer shelter to the mosque for this disabled person (Anwar, 1973).

By the ninth century Islamic medical practice had advanced greatly. From talisman and theology to hospitals and wards of those afflicted with fever, the insane were treated with gentleness, and pain was relieved by walking in gardens, parks and listening to music and storytelling. The prince and the poor man got equal medical attention. Hospitals were crowded with patients and staff of both genders. Permanent and mobile clinics were caring for the disabled and other sufferers (Anwar, 1973).

Medical licensing became a central issue and patient education and legal measures were taken to protect the patients and the rights of the disabled. The famous

Islamic physician, Ibn Sinna, known to the West of the medieval period as Avicennum, allocated a great deal of his knowledge to this topic of health of the disabled and practiced psychotherapy and made great effort to develop a healthy lifestyle for the sick and disabled (Anwar, 1973) In the year 1500, the Islamic physician Al-Hafez published his book on disablities in an encyclopedic fashion, including details on different disabilities in a special scientific classification (Anwar, 1973).

Egypt was the first Arab state to pay attention officially to the disabled and their needs by allocating three classes at elementary schools for the disabled in 1955 (Nader, 1995). In 1965 this number reached a total of 20, and four institutions were providing care to this population. In Kuwait two centres were built in 1960 to provide care to the population of persons with intellectual disabilities. One provided care for males and the other to females. In 1965 a centre for severely intellectually disabled persons was established (Nader, 1995). In Syria and Lebanon, the initiative to establish two facilities for persons with intellectual disabilities was taken in each country in 1960 (Nader, 1995). Jordan joined in 1967, when Christian and civil Islamic organisations initiated the movement to establish institutions for the disabled. The Ministry of Social Welfare also participated in opening a number of centres for the intellectually disabled, including the Al-Manar centre in Amman, during 1977 (Nader, 1995). In Israel the first residential centres for Arabs with intellectual disability were established in 1973. Today there are 13 centres with a total population of 921 persons (13.5% of the total residential care population). Of the 921 persons in 2006, 58 were children aged 0–9 years and 260 were aged 10–19 years, with the majority having severe or profound intellectual disability (Merrick et al., 2008). The centres for Arabs are either privately or publicly administrated, but supported by the Ministry of Social Affairs and Social Services, who provides the budget and supervision.

The Jewish view on deafness

According to ancient Jewish laws, deaf people were in the same category as minors and the insane or imbecile, meaning that they could not be held responsible for their actions. The Rabbis considered deaf people to be more like children than like the insane. On the other hand, the Rabbis realized that the deaf person was mentally superior to the imbecile.

In the Talmud (Babylonian Talmud, Seder Moed, Sabbath) there is a discussion on whom to leave your purse with, if Sabbath falls while you are traveling on the road. In this passage the Rabbis grade in descending order the minor, the deaf-mute and the imbecile. The deaf person was excluded from public life and could not serve as a witness, lead public prayer or be involved in property transactions, but on the other hand it was accepted that the deaf person could be married and divorced using sign language, if both parties understood. Marriage could be to either a hearing person or another deaf-mute person. The details of the manner in which a marriage or a divorce should take place were described in great detail and has been the subject of a special responsa (*Encyclopaedia Judaica*, 1972).

In the past century the stigma of intellectual disability has been removed from deaf persons. In Vienna there was a school for teaching deaf children to speak and read Hebrew, and in 1864 the principals tried to get the acceptance of the deaf persons in the Jewish community (Strassfeld & Strassfeld, 1976), but they talked to "deaf ears".

In 1963 the Rabbinal Court of London, Beth Din, ruled that deaf persons can be called to the Torah reading and recite the blessings, just like a person without hearing impairment (Strassfeld & Strassfeld, 1976).

The Jewish view of blindness

The blind person in the Jewish law is regarded as fully normal, and most of the legal and religious restrictions placed upon him are due to the physical disability. The Bible twice warns us not to mistreat the blind, once with the statement "You shall not insult the deaf or place a stumbling block before the blind" (Leviticus 19:14) and next with "Cursed be he who misdirects a blind person on his way" (Deuteronomy 27:18).

On the other hand, there is also some ambivalence in the Bible, because Itzak (Isaac), our forefather, being visually impaired in old age, was easily deceived by his wife and son. A blind Cohen or priest is disqualified from Temple service: "No man of your offspring throughout the ages who has a defect shall be qualified to offer the food of his God … no man who is blind, or lame, or has a limb too short or too long … he shall not profane these places sacred to Me" (Leviticus 21:17–23).

The blind person can be called to the Torah and recite the blessings, he can testify as a witness and, even though it was not recommended, it was also not forbidden for a totally blind person to act as a Judge.

The Jewish view of intellectual disability

The Talmud puts the person with an intellectual disability into a category together with the deaf and the minor who is bound to appear at the Temple:

> "Mishnah. All are bound to appear (at the Temple), except a deaf man, an imbecile and a minor, a person of unknown sex, a hermaphrodite, women, unfreed slaves, the lame, the blind, the sick, the aged and one who is unable to go up on foot. Who is a minor? Whoever is unable to ride on his father's shoulders and go up from Jerusalem to the Temple Mount. This is the view of Beit Shammai. But Beit Hillel said: Whoever is unable to hold his father's hand and go up from Jerusalem to the Temple Mount, for it is said: Three regalim" (The Babylonian Talmod. Seder Moed, Hagigah 2a)

The Rambam, Rabbi Moses Maimonides (1135–1204), one of the great leaders of Judaism and a physician, wrote many books commenting on the Torah, on philosophy, Jewish Law, science and especially medical books. His books are still studied in many universities today and by many Jews every day. He was one of the first scholars who specially referred to and described the person with intellectual disability (he referred to them as *petti* or, plural, *pettaim*, meaning feebleminded). He looked upon persons with intellectual disability as people, and even if they are not complete in their body or mind, their position should not suffer. He ruled in his work (Rambam) that the testimony of a petti or *shoteh* could not be accepted in the Court:

> one must testify about what has already happened and there is concern that what the witness might, at that moment, imagine is really true, actually is not

and was exchanged for something else and he will not testify about what he saw at first.

So the Bible, in spite of the differences, truly emphasizes that the person with intellectual disability is in fact like any other person, despite his deficiencies. The Rabbis have also determined that even though a person with intellectual disability is exempt from *mitzvot* or commandments, it is absolutely forbidden to use him for the violation of any commandment.

It seems that Judaism and Jewish Law have had a practical approach to intellectual disability and a flexible view on the complex issues involved during a long history. Education and respect for the person with intellectual disability also seem to have been important points of interest.

To illustrate the respect Rabbis gave to the person with intellectual disability (ID) the story of Hazon Ish (Avraham Yeshayahu Karelitz, 1878–1953) comes to mind: As the teacher, scholar and author of many books, he received many visitors for advice and support. One day a father came to visit him together with his son with ID. The father entered the study of Hazon Ish and when his son entered, the Hazon Ish stood up and gave respect to the other visitor. The father did not understand why the great Rabbi had stood up and wondered if another visitor had entered the room without his notice. When the father asked the Hazon Ish why he had stood up, Hazon Ish simply answered that he had risen out of respect for his son.

Services for people with intellectual disabilities in Israel 1929–1995

The first school for children with intellectual and developmental disability (IDD) was opened in Tel Aviv in 1929 (Hovav & Ramot, 1998). The first residential care centre or boarding school for children with IDD was established in 1931 in Jerusalem, and the first centre for assessment of children with IDD was established in Tel Aviv in 1936. The second residential care centre, also established on a private initiative, was opened in Herzliya in 1945 (Hovav & Ramot, 1998). At the time that the modern State of Israel was established in 1948, there was a total of four residential care centres for 150 children with IDD and 25 special education classes with 350 students (Hovav & Ramot, 1998).

The history of the development of services was reviewed in 1998, and the changes divided into different time periods: 1948–1961, 1962–1976, 1977–1985 and 1986–1994 (Hovav & Ramot, 1998). The 1948–1961 period started with the Ministry of Education establishing a separate department for special education in 1950, with about 400 children registered. Official records from 1957 showed there were 22 classes with 252 children with moderate IDD, and 276 classes with 5,284 children with mild IDD (Hovav & Ramot, 1998). In 1951 the Israeli Parent Association for Children with IDD (called AKIM) was established in Tel Aviv as a response to the level and quality of service provided. Today they have several branches with a variety of services: nurseries and kindergartens, support for families, respite care centres, hostels and apartments, community centres, employment programs, summer camps, Special Olympics and other sport programs, arts activities and guardianship. These activities are mainly funded by the government, but AKIM also is supported by donations and fund-raising activities.

At this period in time welfare services for children with IDD at the Ministry of Welfare were provided through the Child, Adolescent and Youth Protection Services, while practically no adult services were in place. Residential care was provided by government (695 persons registered in 1962) or private institutions (469 persons registered in 1962). The first sheltered workshop was opened in Jerusalem in 1955 by AKIM (Hovav & Ramot, 1998).

The 1962–1977 period saw the establishment of a separate Service for Persons with Mental Retardation in 1962 (Hovav & Ramot, 1998). Now all the services for both children and adults were gathered under one roof. This process was not easy for political reasons, but both internal and external pressure helped this reorganization that coincided with the efforts of the John F. Kennedy (1917–1963) administration in the United States to focus on mental retardation with the establishment of the National Institute of Child Health and Human Development in 1962 and University Affiliated Centers of Excellence in 1963. The policy trend in the United States also influenced parents, professionals, administrators and politicians in Israel to establish better standards for residential care. The Ministry formulated standards and criteria for placement, and three assessment centres (for both children and adults) were also opened in Jerusalem, Haifa and Tel Aviv, and in 1970 the first medical director of the Ministry was appointed. Kindergartens, day care centres and sheltered workshops for adults were established throughout the country. In 1965 the "Residential Care Center Law" was passed in the Israeli Parliament to regulate supervision. In 1969 the "Welfare Law for Persons with ID" came into effect. Training of care staff in residential care centres and community settings (hostels) was established in 1968 when the first certificate course was opened (Hovav & Ramot, 1998).

The 1977–1985 period (Hovav & Ramot, 1998) began when the Ministry of Welfare merged with the Ministry of Labour in 1977 to be named the Ministry of Labour and Social Affairs (MoLSA). Reflecting the increasingly important role of governmental support of individuals with IDD, the Service for Persons with Mental Retardation was given its own administration, personnel, and budget in 1978, becoming the Division for Mental Retardation (DMR).

In 1977, the "father" of normalization and de-institutionalization, Niels Erik Bank-Mikkelsen (1919–1990) from Denmark, came to Israel to explain his ideas, and to visit facilities for persons with ID. His report on the situation in Israel for persons with IDD with his recommendations, together with reports from the parent advocacy organization AKIM, resulted in a period of reorganization and improvement of services. Rather than focus solely on residential care, the DMR worked on a clear definition of the target population to serve. Services in the community were adopted, and supervision of residential care was improved. Because treatment and care were not up to the standard of the Ministry, several facilities were closed. Concern for the legal and social responsibilities of individuals with IDD led to the need to formulate a clear policy concerning criminal acts carried out by persons with IDD. Mandatory education was introduced for children with IDD due to pressure from parents that children with IDD also needed education. Laws were passed concerning guardianship, disability allowance, marriage and payment for productive employment. A campaign to educate the Israeli public on mental retardation and intellectual disability was also put in effect (Hovav & Ramot, 1998).

During this period several universities became interested in the field of intellectual disability, although nursing and medicine demonstrated little interest in the study of IDD. Scholars and clinicians from the fields of psychology and social work accomplished early work in the field of IDD, and several masters and doctoral dissertations were published (Hovav & Ramot, 1998). Beit Issie Shapira in Raanana took the initiative to organize the first international conference on developmental disabilities in 1994, which brought international and national researchers together in Israel.

The 1986–1994 period (Hovav & Ramot, 1998) could be characterized as a period of development and expansion. The second medical director was appointed in 1991, and over this period till today expanded the scope of medical and health care with the introduction of new standards of care and supervision. In 1992 he took initiative to vaccinate against Hepatitis B all persons with intellectual disability in Israel in residential care centres and community residence together with personnel in order to prevent the spread of hepatitis B (Merrick, 1998) and also introduced routine annual influenza vaccination to all persons in residential care.

The DMR now felt responsible for all persons with IDD, from infancy to old age. The DMR also started to work with parents and families in a partnership. In 1993, toward the end of this period, a new Minister secured more resources to the DMR from the Minister of Finance, which resulted in several changes. The waiting list for residential care was abolished due to the opening of more centres, community services were expanded, and parents were encouraged, through financial incentives, to keep their children at home as long as possible.

Services for people with intellectual disabilities in Israel 1995–2012

From 1995 until today we have also seen many new directions, especially with many health research projects that had never before been conducted in this population, but we will mention only some here. In 1998 the second medical director (the first author of this paper) established the National Institute of Child Health and Human Development (NICHD) as the research arm for the activities of his position. In the first years of activities the focus was in the south of Israel due to collaboration with various professionals at the Faculty of Health Sciences at the Ben Gurion University of the Negev, and since 2000 an affiliation with the Zusman Child Development Center at the Pediatric Division of Soroka University Medical Center resulted in collaboration around the establishment of the Down Syndrome Clinic at that centre. In 2002 a full course on "Disability" was established at the Recanati School for Allied Professions in the Community at Ben Gurion University, and in the academic year 2005–2006 a one-semester course on "aging with disability" was started as part of the master of science program in gerontology. In 1998 the Office of the Medical Director also started an annual national survey of all medical clinics in the residential care centres (Merrick, 2005), which has provided important data for planning and development of services and information on trends over the years.

Together with the social worker Shlomo Kessel and the chief nurse Hilmi Arda in 1999, the medical director took the initiative to focus on a new generation of people with intellectual disability who had reached the "golden age" – in fact, the first generation of older people with intellectual disability (earlier these people did not survive to an old age in great numbers). This resulted in a multidisciplinary work group, who proposed guidelines for this population, several research projects and later a book (Arda et al., 1999; Kandel, Schofield & Merrick, 2007). This work led to a collaboration with researchers from the University of Rochester, Albany, and the University of Chicago to study the health status of persons aged 40 years and older with intellectual disability, which resulted in the largest database in the world with 2,282 persons from Israel (Merrick et al., 2004), 1,373 persons in Rochester and 1,128 from Taiwan (Robinson et al., 2010). Results showed that age is a significant factor in health status. The frequency of different disease categories (e.g., cardiovascular disease, cancer, and sensory impairments) increased significantly with age for both genders. Cardiovascular disease in this population was less prevalent when compared to the general population, suggesting that under-diagnosis of some diseases or conditions may be prevalent in this population. The patterns of organ-system morbidity with increasing age were similar to those in other studies conducted in several countries, suggesting that health status and outcomes could be independent of cultural factors (Merrick et al., 2004).

In 1999, together with the chief psychologist Chaia Aminadav (the former director of the Division for Intellectual and Developmental Disabilities), a project was conducted with a focus on people with severe and profound intellectual disability, nursing aspects and multidisciplinary intervention and activity, which also produced several studies on visual impairment in this population (Koslowe et al., 1999).

From the year 2000 the NICHD and the Office of the Medical Director have focused on many aspects of people with Down syndrome. Together with professor Shlomo Wientroub, the chairman of Pediatric Orthopedics at Dana Children's Medical Center in Tel Aviv and the European Paediatric Orthopaedic Society, an initiative was taken to survey musculoskeletal problems in persons with Down syndrome in Europe, vision problems were investigated, cancer incidence studied, and in the year 2000 a clinic for children with Down syndrome was established at the Soroka University Medical Center, where today over 200 families are followed. In 2004 the National Down Syndrome Center at Hadassah Hebrew University Medical Center, Mt Scopus Campus, was established, that today follows over 700 families (Merrick et al., 2000; Boker & Merrick, 2002; Carmeli et al., 2004; Vardi et al., 2006; Luxenburg et al., 2006; Tenenbaum et al., 2008).

In 1991 the Office of the Medical Director established a database on all cases of death in persons with intellectual disability from residential care centres. This way it can be seen and proven that since 1991, the average lifespan of IDD care centre residents has improved by 15 years (Merrick, 2002). It is our hope that this project will result in the establishment of a mortality register that can be used to evaluate risk factors and improve the service.

Several surveys around HIV/AIDS, *Helicobactor pylori* infection and PKU (phenylketonuria) have have been conducted in this population (Merrick & Morag, 2000; Morad, Merrick & Nasri, 2002; Merrick, Aspler & Schwarz, 2001) and the research into PKU resulted in a change of the national policy concerning lifelong diet treatment.

In the field of allied health professions we have collaborated with both the Department of Physical Therapy at Tel Aviv University and Ariel University Center of Samaria around physical activity, exercise, assistive technology and other interventions to facilitate better health and well-being in this population, which also led to other research projects and interventions. A recent study focused on the lack of physical exercise in the age group of adults with IDD (Carmeli et al., 2012) as recommended by health authorities, which may be related to lack of appreciation of the benefits of physical activity, lack of support from their caregivers and difficulty finding experienced personnel to train them. Of special interest is also the Snoezelen or controlled multisensory stimulation, a Dutch intervention, which we have managed to introduce to practically every residential care centre in Israel, resulting in many research projects where Israel seems to have been a leader in this field over the past many years (search PubMed for Snoezelen and intellectual disability to find papers published from Israel). This method has also been used in the dental clinic and treatment of people with IDD.

Since 1991, when the second medical director was appointed, dental treatment of this population has been improved dramatically and today this service is conducted via close to 20 clinics spread all over Israel with state-of-the-art treatment and service that include dental implants. In the past persons with IDD were often neglected by the dental profession because of different barriers like insufficient knowledge and experience to treat this population; problems in the regular dental consultation of mixed populations for dental visits; lack of collaboration with the patient; patient fear of treatment; lack of awareness by caregivers; and inadequate facilities and low compensation for treatment of patients who take much longer to approach, assess and treat. In general, people with IDD have poorer oral health and oral hygiene than those without this condition. Data indicate that people who have IDD have more untreated caries, higher prevalence of gingivitis and other periodontal diseases than the general population, affecting their ability to chew, speak and look attractive. With increasing age and life expectancy, this population will be in need of good dental care on a regular basis to prevent disease and increase their quality of life (Feldberg & Merrick, 2011).

The overall prevalence of disability in childhood has also been studied, the issue of poverty has been studied, the issue of physical fitness and also the development of osteoporosis in children and adults with severe and profound intellectual disability have been looked upon in collaboration with several universities (Merrick, 2010).

The time period since 1995 has also been characterized by increased seminars, teaching and local, national and international conferences. The DMR in 1999 started a biannual national conference, which over the years has seen an increased number of participants (over 3,000 participants in 2011) and the Office of the Medical Director in 2006 took the initiative to start an annual World Down Syndrome Day (every year on March 21) together with the Singapore Down Syndrome Association, which now is taking place in many countries every year. We first started this annual event in collaboration with Ben Gurion University in Beer-Sheva and since 2010 it has been conducted with Hadassah Hebrew University Medical Center in Jerusalem. In 2006 the Office of the Medical Director also decided to initiate a biannual national conference on "health and intellectual disability", where we started the first conferences at one of our larger residential care centres, but in the past few years at a conference centre in the central part of Israel with close to 500 participants.

As mentioned above, Beit Issie Shapira in 1994 started with international conferences on developmental disabilities (the fifth in 2011) and in 2012 the NICHD in collaboration with Hadassah Hebrew University Medical Center and Cincinnati

Children's Hospital Medical Center conducted the Third International Conference on Pediatric Chronic Diseases, Disability and Human Development in Jerusalem.

Teaching medical, nursing and allied health professionals about IDD has also increased over the past decade at several universities in Israel; at some it has become a part of the curriculum, and at several other universities there are also site visits at residential care centres and other facilities servicing this population.

Division for intellectual and developmental disabilities in recent years

In the year 2009 a reconstruction of the Division for Mental Retardation (DMR) took place with the establishment of four services–Assessment and Planning, Family and Community Service, Residential or Supported Living Service and Health Services in order to provide comprehensive services for about 35,000 people with intellectual disability.

In recognition of an increasing number of intensive nursing care patients within this population and several years of discussions between the Ministry of Social Affairs and Ministry of Health, it was decided in 2010 to establish six intensive nursing or long-term nursing care departments at six of our residential care centres certified as hospital departments by the Ministry of Health in collaboration with our Health Services. These places are slowly starting operation and in the future it is also expected that a joint psychiatric facility or facilities will be established to deal with the complex problems of dual diagnosis.

In 2011 at the biannual national conference the Ministry invited several international professionals and researchers to come to Israel, and in a public hearing over several days investigate the level of service and care provided to this population compared to the international standard and recent discussion about human rights. This international group recommended for Israel to continue the focus on community services and downsizing of residential care facilities and finally in 2012 the division changed name to the Division for Intellectual and Developmental Disabilities.

Medical care

Israel has never had large institutions, like. for example in the United States, but rather continues to have smaller residential care centres or supported living with an average of about 112 persons. As a result, only a third of the total registered population of persons with IDD resides in these centres, with the majority remaining at home or in community settings, but they all receive some services from the Division for Intellectual and Developmental Disabilities.

In order to ensure that all medical clinics in residential care centres for people with IDD in Israel use the same standard of annual report, institute self-control of their performance, increase competence and generate a national team spirit, the Office of the Medical Director of the Division for Intellectual and Developmental Disabilities in 1997 developed an instrument to monitor the health service provided for people with intellectual disability (Merrick, 2005).

The annual survey of residential care centres is conducted in order to obtain a picture of this population and to analyse trends in service provision. The last survey in 2009 (Tenenbaum et al., 2012) showed that 78% of the population with IDD in residential care in Israel was between the ages of 20 and 60 years old, 45% with severe or profound IDD, 41% with moderate and 13% with mild IDD (see Tables 6.1 and 6.2). This distribution, weighted towards severe and profound IDD, is due to the large number of persons with mild and moderate IDD who are served in the community and not in the residential centres. Twenty-five percent were nursing patients, and 19% were confined to a wheelchair, thus making a high workload for the care staff. The 33% with epilepsy, which is much higher than the usual 0.5% to 1% in the general population, also demands monitoring and work by the nursing staff.

It is clear that this population of persons with IDD in residential care has many associated medical problems and therefore a higher prevalence of daily medication than the general population. In the 2009 survey (Tenenbaum et al., 2012), 87% were found to be receiving medication daily for chronic illness, and 54% received psychotropic medication for psychiatric illness. Ambulatory (out-patient clinics) or specialist service in this survey showed that the sub-specialties of ophthalmology, orthopaedics and gynaecology were the most requested specialist visits, but dialysis for 14 patients resulted in 1,288 visits to the hemo-dialysis clinic for treatment, usually several times per week.

In the 2009 survey (Tenenbaum et al., 2012). questionnaires were received from all 63 residential care centres (100% response rate). There were 9 government, 41 private, and 13 public (not-for-profit) centres serving a total of 7,067 persons (see Table 6.1). The average number of persons percentre was 112.17 (range 21 to 324). The level of IDD in the population of residential care centres is shown in Table 6.2.

Children between the ages of 0 and 19 years constitute 12% (845) of the population, which has declined since 1999, when children comprised 18% of the population in residential care. In the aging group we have seen an increase since 1999 from 261 persons aged 60 years and older in 1999 to 717 in 2009. The profile of the population is shown in Table 6.3. There were 1,476 nursing patients and 261 intensive nursing care patients. This again is an increase since 1998, when there were only 1,439 nursing patients (Merrick, 2005). The "educational category" is used for persons with a moderate level of self care, functioning social skills and ability to work.

Table 6.1. The population of persons with intellectual disability by age and gender in 63 residential care centres in Israel, 2009

Age in years	Males	Females	Total	Percent
0–9	70	45	115	1.63
10–19	448	282	730	10.33
20–39	1,619	1,147	2,766	39.14
40–49	803	606	1,409	19.94
50–59	707	623	1,330	18.82
>60	330	387	717	10.14
Total	3,977	3,090	7,067	100.00
%	56.28	43.72	100.00	

103

Table 6.2. The level of intellectual disability by age in persons in 63 residential care centres in Israel, 2009

Age in years	Mild	Moderate	Severe	Profound	Other	Total	Percent
0–9	6	15	39	43	12	15	1.63
10–19	108	267	233	121	1	730	10.33
20–39	372	994	997	387	16	2,766	39.14
40–49	212	567	437	189	4	1,409	19.94
50–59	161	659	368	141	1	1,330	18.82
>60	84	400	160	63	10	717	10.14
Total	943	2,902	2,234	944	44	7,067	100,00
Percent	13.34	41.07	31.61	13.36	0.62	100.00	

MILD IDD: IQ 55–70; MODERATE: IQ 35–54; SEVERE IQ 20–34; AND PROFOUND: IQ < 20. "OTHER" REFERS TO 10 PERSONS WHO WERE PLACED FOR OTHER REASONS, OR LEVEL OF IDD NOT YET DETERMINED.

Table 6.3. Profile of the population in residential care in 2009 according to educational, treatment, rehabilitation, nursing, and challenging behaviour

Profile	Numbers	Percent
Educational	521	7.37
Treatment	1,415	20.02
Rehabilitation	372	5.27
Nursing	1,476	20.89
Intensive nursing	261	3.69
Challenging behaviour	3,022	42.76
TOTAL	7,067	100.00

The "treatment category" refers to persons with normal-to-moderate self-care functions and social skills, able to accomplish simple tasks and skills in a limited number of activities. The "rehabilitation category" describes persons with poor adaptive skills, in need of support, instruction and assistance. The "challenging behaviour" categories includes persons that are hyperactive and in need of constant supervision.

The population of persons in residential centres is in need of a level of support that families are not able to provide at home. The profiles shown in Tables 6.3 and 6.4 demonstrate that this population has mental and medical needs that surpass the capabilities of community care and thus requires placement in residential centres.

Table 6.4. Nursing profile of the population in residential care, 2009 (*N* = 7,067)

Profile	Numbers	Percent
Gastric tube feeding	15	0.21
Urinary catheter	41	0.58
Gastrostomy	196	2.77
Pressure sore (decubitus)	49	0.69
Dialysis	14	0.20
Oncology treatment	84	1.19
Down syndrome	574	8.12
Fragile X	73	1.03
Rett syndrome	16	0.23
Epilepsy	2,313	32.73
Diabetes mellitus	419	5.93
Hypertension	605	8.56
Asthma	157	2.22
Phenylketonuria (PKU)	12	0.17
Self-injurious behaviour (SIB)	351	4.97
Blindness	317	4.49
Wheelchair users, manual	1,303	18.44
Wheelchair users, electric	43	0.61
Walkers	217	3.07

Working with this population is a multidisciplinary task and involves many professionals, as charted in Table 6.5. In each residential care centre, a daily medical clinic is held for the purpose of acute problems and routine health surveillance. Table 6.6 shows the number of examinations for the year 2009. Treatment is monitored by regular blood tests performed in the residential care centre as well as samples sent to laboratories run by the local area health maintenance organizations (HMOs). Primary preventive medicine is an important aspect of the practical work in residential care centres, as illustrated in Table 6.7. Every year nearly all (97%) residents are vaccinated with the seasonal influenza vaccine, but in 2009 due to the swine flu (influenza A H1N1) pandemic the "other vaccination" category was 92%. This high coverage was due to a national effort to vaccinate all persons in Israel, and via our health service we were successful in reaching this high number.

Table 6.5. Medical and allied professional staff in 63 residential care centres, 2009

Profession	Number of equivalent full-time positions
Physicians	50.27
Chief nurse	59.93
Other nurses	318.22
Psychiatrist	23.96
Other medical specialist	5.60
Pharmacist	2.72
Physiotherapist	46.49
Communication and speech therapist	15.34
Nutritionist	16.55
Medical secretary	10.63
Occupational therapist	20.35

Table 6.6. Number of examinations at the 63 residential care centres in 2009

Examination/treatment by	Total 2009	Exams/person with ID/y
Physician	100,566	14.23
Psychiatrist	26,825	3.80
Other physician	4,512	0.64
Physiotherapist	98,596	13.95
Blood test, urine, stool, other	69,405	9.82

Table 6.7. Preventive medical aspects in 63 residential care centres, 2009

Measure	Number	Percent of population
Influenza vaccination	6,846	96.87
Hepatitis B vaccination	189	2.67
Hepatitis A vaccination	17	0.24
Other vaccination	6,488	91.81
Breast examination (females)	413	13.37
Gynaecological examination (females)	982	31.78

N = 7,067, 3,090 females.

In this population more than 87% were in need of daily medication (see Table 6.8), 33% received anti-epileptic drugs and 54% received psychotropic medication. Daily medication is typically given three times per day and for acute situations (usually challenging behaviour) extra medication is given (SOS).

Infectious disease rates in this population can be high, as the close-quarter living conditions are conducive to disease transmission. Rates of common infectious diseases can be seen in Table 6.9 for the year 2009.

The medical clinics in the residential care centres are usually staffed by nurses, 24 hours of the day, every day of the year. A staff physician sees patients daily, but there is not full-time call coverage. When a physician is not available, the medical clinic at the residential care centre may send the resident to the emergency room or for hospitalization. A few residential care centres have a small number of beds for observation (called internal institutional hospitalization, see Table 6.10). Emergency and hospital utilization in 2009 is shown in Table 6.10.

The physician in each adult residential care centre is usually a family physician or an internist, while paediatricians are utilized for the centres with a paediatric population. The number of specialist referrals outside the residential care centre in 2009

Table 6.8. Medication for persons with intellectual disability in residential care, 2009 (*N* = 7,067)

Type of medication	Number	Percent
Chronic medication	6,173	87.35
AED (for epilepsy)	2,298	32.52
Psychotropic	3,813	53.96
Oral contraception (females)	93	3.01
Depo-Provera (females)	360	11.65
SOS	6,144	

Table 6.9. Infectious diseases in 63 residential care centres, 2009

Disease	Number of cases
Sepsis	12
Meningitis	1
Hepatitis	20
Campylobacter	1
Salmonella	6
Varicella	6
Scabies	870
Lice	150

Table 6.10. Emergency room visits and hospitalizations in 63 residential care centres, 2009

Activity	Number	Days	Rate per 1,000
Emergency room	1,933	0	273.52
Internal medicine	878	4,697	124.24
Paediatrics	143	1,229	20.23
Surgery	182	1,061	25.75
Other	225	1.073	31.84
Total somatic hospitalization	1,428	8,060	202.07
Psychiatric hospitalization	55	1,191	7.78
Total hospitalization	1,483	9,251	209.85
Internal institutional Hospitalization	277	5,709	39.20
Total external and internal hospitalization	1,760	14,960?	249.04

Table 6.11. Use of outside ambulatory services for 63 residential care centres in 2009 (7,067 persons). Total number and rate per 1,000 are shown below.

Type of service	Visits	Rate/1,000
Surgery	669	94.67
Internal medicine	120	16.98
Eye	1,503	212.68
Optometrist	251	35.52
Dermatology	957	135.42
Orthopedics	1,095	154.95
Gynaecology (females)	1,012	327.51
Neurology	903	127.78
Oncology	155	21.93
ENT	938	132.73
Diabetes	242	34.24
Cardiology	255	36.08
Endocrinology	304	43.02
Pulmonology	101	14.29
Child development	19	2.69

Type of service	Visits	Rate/1,000
Urology	335	47.40
Gastroenterology	501	70.89
Auditory	156	22.07
Proctology	88	12.45
Rehabilitation	100	14.15
Vascular	109	15.42
Haematology	217	30.71
Physiotherapy	146	20.66
Plastic surgery	148	20.94
Oral surgery	128	18.11
Haemodialysis	1288	182.26
Psychiatrist	125	17.69
Other	320	45.28
TOTAL	12,185	1,724.21

is shown in Table 6.11, and the number of special examinations in laboratories or clinics outside the residential care centre is shown in Table 6.12. It should be noted here that ECG is also done in the centres (3,042 in 2009), at the sites where they have ECG equipment, especially to monitor psychotropic medications and their cardiac effects.

Dental services have been developed over the years for this population, and today even dental transplantations are provided to this population. Information on the dental visits for 2009 can be seen in Table 6.13.

People with intellectual disability and especially those with associated challenging behaviour are prone to injuries. Each injury (intentional, unintentional or death) must be reported to the medical director (see Table 6.14) (4).

Dreams for the future

We have several dreams and wishes for the future. We would like to see more registered nurses coming to work with this special population. We have finally in 2003 received moral and financial support on this from the Ministry, so that hopefully all future nurses employed will be registered nurses. There are challenges to be overcome, such as a shortage of nurses in Israel, and that residential care centres must compete for nurses with hospitals and HMOs, because working in a residential care centre with this population is less prestigious. A first goal is that all chief nurses in each residential centre will be registered nurses, which we have practically achieved today.

Table 6.12. Use of outside laboratory services for the 63 residential care centres, 2009 (7,067 persons)

Type of laboratory	No. exams	Rate/1,000
Chest X-ray	469	66.36
Other X-ray	763	107.97
Ultrasound	893	126.36
ECG	1,473	208.43
EEG	138	19.53
Mammography (females)	357	115.53
ECHO	160	22.64
CT	351	49.67
MRI	48	6.79
Other	354	50.09
TOTAL	5,006	708.36

Table 6.13. Dental treatments provided to the residents of the 63 residential care centres, 2009

Examination	Numbers	Rate/1,000
Dental examination	7,309	1,034.24
Dental hygienist	12,797	1,810.81
Treatment under GA	21	2.97

Table 6.14. Reported cases of injuries from 63 residential care centres, 2009

Injury	Numbers	Percent of population
Death (unintentional injury)	0	0
Burns	23	0.33
Fractures	160	2.26
Wounds	1,075	15.21
Runaway	151	2.14
Care staff injured resident	8	0.11
Resident injured other resident	622	8.80
Abuse of resident	15	0.21

Injury	Numbers	Percent of population
Drowning	0	0
Other	946	13.39
TOTAL	3,080	42.45

We would like to see a sub-specialty in intellectual and developmental disability for health professionals (physicians, psychiatrists, nurses and others) and have had discussions with the Ministry of Health, but so far without any operational solutions. We would like to see some kind of university affiliation to facilitate education of student health professionals in our field of work and, as in the Netherlands, establish a university chair(s) in this field. Such an educational partnership could bring students on site in our residential care centres, and nurture more research projects and interventions for this population.

As we have shown in several research and intervention studies. promoting physical exercise in aged people with IDD is particularly important, since these individuals are prone to high risk of chronic morbidity and sedentary lifestyle resulted from being overweight, difficulties in active daily living (ADL), frequent hospitalization, frailty, falls and mortality. However, for persons with IDD, participation in regular physical activity is not that simple and is considered somewhat incomprehensible, challenging and complex due to environmental barriers, inappropriate facilities, lack of motivation, and consistency. Therefore, educating the staff and organizing the environment are indispensable in facilitating physical activity engagement, better quality of life and well-being.

Many countries around the world have adapted the Scandinavian model of normalization and deinstitutionalization, which developed in the 1970s, where persons were transferred from large state institutions into services in the community. Several states in the United States of America (Braddock et al., 1998) have completely closed down their institutions and today serve this population in the community. The transfer has not been without complications, such as earlier death, more health problems or lack of health services (Strauss, Kastner & Shavelle, 1998) and therefore we believe that it is not a question of either/or, but instead a combination of both residential care in small residential care centres and community settings.

We would like to see the future development of IDD services in Israel move toward both community care and institutional care for the population of persons with IDD. We would like to have future residential care centres for persons with IDD established within selected areas around the country to provide services for persons unable to stay in the community or at home. Regional university-affiliated centres of excellence would provide a medical home for people with IDD (one-stop centre) in that specific region along the lines of the centres established by president John F. Kennedy (1917–1963) in 1963 in the United States. These services should include prevention programs, primary care, rehabilitation and treatment in the health field, mental health, dental health, nutrition, preventive medicine (vaccination, women's health etc.), physical therapy, speech and language therapy and occupational therapy with home visitation and outreach provided.

Finally we would like to see the National Institute of Child Health and Human Development in Israel established as an independent national research, policy and practice institute with resources and manpower to fullfil its vision and mission.

In 2017 the Division for Intellectual and Developmental Disabilities merged with the Division for Rehabilitation and the Service for Autism into a new entity called the Disability Administration, which will serve all three populations.

References

Anwar, A. (1973) *The History of Science in Islam* (Arabic). Beirut, Lebanon: Dar Al fikr.

Arda, H., Merrick, J., Habusa, H., Cahana, C., Murover, M., Shalem, G., & Kessel, S. (1999) Aging in Persons with Mental Retardation in Institutions in Israel. Jerusalem: Division for Mental Retardation (Hebrew).

Babylonian Talmud. *Seder Moed*, Sabbath 153a.

Boker, L.K., & Merrick, J. (2002) Cancer incidence in persons with Down syndrome in Israel. *Down Syndrome Research and Practice*, 8(1), 31–36.

Braddock, D., Hemp, R., Parish, S., & Westrich, J. (1998) *The State of the States in Developmental Disabilities*. Washington, DC: American Association on Mental Retardation.

Carmeli, E., Kessel, S., Bar-Chad, S., & Merrick, J. (2004) A comparison between older persons with Down syndrome and a control group: Clinical characteristics, functional status and sensori-motor function. *Down Syndrome Research and Practice*, 9(1), 17–24.

Carmeli, E., Merrick, J., Imam, B., & Levy R. (2012) Exercises and sports participation in healthy older adults with intellectual disability. A pilot study. *Health*, 4(1), 769–774.

Encyclopaedia Judaica (1972) Jerusalem: Keter, 5:1419–20.

Feldberg, I., & Merrick, J. (2011) Dental aspects. In: Patel, D.R., Greydanus, D.E., Omar, H.A., & Merrick, J., eds. *Neurodevelopmental Disabilities. Clinical Care for Children and Young Adults*. Dordrecht: Springer, 341–352.

Hovav, M., & Ramot, A. (1998) The development of welfare services for the mentally handicapped in Israel. *Social Security*, 5, 142–162.

Kandel, I., Schofield, P., & Merrick, J. (2007) *Aging and Disability. Research and Clinical Perspectives*. Victoria, BC., Canada: International Academic Press.

Koslowe, K., Yinon, U., Arda, H., Aminadav, C., & Merrick, J. (1999) A multi-disciplinary diagnostic and treatment approach with institutionalized mentally retarded adults: Initial report of ocular and visual findings. *Journal of Behavioral Optometry*, 10(3), 59–61.

Kudlick, C.J. (2003) Disability history: Why we need another "other". *The American Historical Review*, 108(3), 763–793.

Luxenburg, O., Arda, H., Shemer, J., & Merrick, J. (2006) Down syndrome in Israel: Health care utilization from a national survey. *International Journal on Disability and Human Development*, 5(4), 381–383.

Merrick, J. (1998) Hepatitis C prevalence in persons with mental retardation. *Public Health Review*, 26, 31–36.

Merrick, J. (2002) Mortality of persons with intellectual disability in residential care in Israel 1991–1997. *Journal of Intellectual and Developmental Disabilities*, 27(4), 265–272.

Merrick, J. (2005) National survey 1998 on medical services for persons with intellectual disability in residential care in Israel. *International Journal on Disability and Human Development*, 4(2), 139–146.

Merrick, J. (2010) *Publicationlist on Intellectual Disability* 1999–2010. Jerusalem: Office of the Medical Director, Ministry of Social Affairs.

Merrick, J., Aspler, S., & Schwarz, G. (2001) Should adults with phenylketonuria have diet treatment? *Mental Retardation*, 39(3), 215–217.

Merrick, J., Davidson, P.W., Morad, M., Janicki, M.P., Wexler, O., & Henderson, C.M. (2004) Older adults with intellectual disability in residential care centers in Israel: Health status and service utilization. *American Journal on Mental Retardation*, 109(5), 413–420.

Merrick, J., Ezra, E., Josef, B., Hendel, D., Steinberg, D.M., & Wientroub, S. (2000) Musculoskeletal problems in Down syndrome. European Paediatric Orthopaedic Society Survey: The Israeli sample. *Journal of Pediatric Orthopaedics Part B*, 9, 185–192.

Merrick, J., Merrick-Kenig, E., Kandel, I. & Morad, M. (2008) Trends in the number of Arabs with intellectual disability in residential care in Israel 1998–2006. *International Journal of Adolescent Medicine and Health*, 20(1), 93–96.

Merrick, J., & Morag, A. (2000) Human Immunodeficiency Virus (HIV) in institutions for the mentally retarded in Israel. *International Journal of Rehabilitation Research*, 23(3), 173–175.

Morad, M., Merrick, J., & Nasri, Y. (2002) Prevalence of helicobacter pylori in people with intellectual disability in a residential care centre in Israel. *Journal of Intellectual and Disability Research*, 46(2), 141–143.

Nader, A. (1995) *Teaching the Disabled Children* (Arabic). Jordan: Dar Al fekr.

Rambam. *Mishneh Torah*, Laws of Evidence, 69:9–10.

Robinson, L.M., Davidson, P.W., Henderson, C.M., Janicki, M.P., Merrick, J., Morad, M., Wang, K.Y., Hsieh, K., Heller, T., Bishop, K.M., & Wexler, O. (2010) Health trends from an international sample of older adults with intellectual and developmental disabilities. *International Journal on Disability and Human Development*, 9(4), 329–338.

Selway, & D., Ashman, A.F. (1998) Disability, religion and health: A literature review in search of the spiritual dimensions of disability. *Disability & Society*, 13(3), 429–439.

Strassfeld S., Strassfeld M., eds. (1976) *The Second Jewish Catalog*. Philadelphia, PA: The Jewish Publication Society of America, 151–166.

Strauss, D., Kastner, T., & Shavelle, R. (1998) Mortality of adults with developmental disabilities in California institutions and community care 1985–1994. *Mental Retardation*, 36, 360–371.

Tenenbaum, A., Fuchs, B.S., Raskas, M., Carmeli, E., Aspler, S., & Merrick, J. (2012) National survey 2009 on medical services for persons with intellectual disability in residential care in Israel. *International Journal on Disability and Human Development*, 11(1), 75–79.

Tenenbaum, A., Kastiel, Y., Meiner, Z., Kerem, E., El-Salam Abu Libde, A., & Wexler, I.D. (2008) Multidisciplinary care of persons with Down syndrome in Jerusalem. *International Journal on Disability and Human Development*, 7(3), 355–357.

Vardi, G., Merrick, J., Lubetzky, H., Eshed, R., Virgin, A., Yishai, H., Morad, M., & Galil, A. (2006) Multidisciplinary clinic for persons with Down syndrome in the south of Israel. *International Journal on Disability and Human Development*, 5(4), 377–380.

PART II

HISTORIES OF NATIONAL DISABILITY POLICIES, PROGRAMS AND SERVICES

7

THE ROLE OF INTERNATIONAL INSTITUTIONS IN THE PROCESS OF CATEGORIZATION OF 'DISABLED PEOPLE' (1930s–1975)

Gildas Bregain

At the end of the 19th century, soldiers mutilated during military conflicts are referred to as invalids (*invalides* in French, *invalidos* in Spanish), likewise the individuals injured during their professional activity. That occurs in Spain, where one can find a *Cuerpo de Invalidos de Guerra* and a *Instituto Nacional de Reeducación Profesional de Inválidos del Trabajo*. However, very often, there is a wide variety of names people give to the 'civil' physically disabled persons. These identifications have generally pejorative connotations. In Spain, terms like *inutiles, cojos, tullidos*, and *impedidos* are very frequently used. The persistence of these various names is partly explained by the fact that these individuals had never been subject to categorization of administrations or of powerful private institutions.

During the 19th century, invalidity is defined only on the basis of medical criteria that justify the destructive incapacity (as a soldier) or the productive incapacity (as a worker) of the person. After the First World War, the practice of professional rehabilitation for war-disabled and for industrial work-disabled was strongly developed among several European countries. Politics about vocational rehabilitation are in fact correction and accommodation procedures intended to allow the people to return to a social normality (Stiker, 1996, p. 30). By developing this practice intended to use the residual capacities of the individual with lesions or with disabilities in order to integrate him into the world of production, this is impossible to view the disabled person as non-productive. This new reality makes the medical specialists review the name 'invalids' (*invalides* in French, *inválidos* in Spanish), now inappropriate, and to question the definition criteria for unemployability. Much more than a simple linguistic modification, semantic changes often reflect the willingness to impose a new meaning for the disability. Some other actors (the people with disabilities themselves, the social workers, the policy makers, et al.) episodically participate in this debate that aims to impose a new definition on a medical profession and on the entire society.

Representatives of disabled people reappropriate very often foreign categorizations or categorizations used by international institutions included in international resolutions or in reports of international experts (ILO, WHO, UN). They try sometimes to make a suitable translation of this foreign definition to the local context. The reports of these commissions of international experts, as well as the international documents approved during this period, play a key role within the categorization changes of the disabled group at the international and national levels. However, the influence of these international categorizations varies in intensity and in temporality across countries. These variations depend on the manner in which the local actors learn about the categorizations and also on the manner in which they appropriate them.

These international documents endorse and institutionalize the dynamics of existing conceptual and semantic changes concerning disability at an international level. Two spheres of rehabilitation gradually appear, the vocational rehabilitation and the medical rehabilitation. They are respectively promoted by the International Labour Organization (ILO) and by the World Health Organization (WHO). These two spheres of rehabilitation lead to different conceptual and semantic transformations.

We focus our analysis on the manner in which the representatives of the disabled people, and first of all the international experts, identify the disabled in a collective way in front of the international public opinion. This research perspective leads us to pay less attention to the other ways of naming the disabled that are used by the same representatives in front of different interlocutors or that are used by different actors. Indeed, as Frederick Cooper reminds us, the manner in which somebody identifies himself appreciably varies according to the context and to the interlocutor whom he addresses. All of this can change over time (Cooper, 2005, p. 71). Identifications used by some disabled leaders in order to name their comrades in front of the society are very different from those they employ when they speak only to their peers, in a small group.

It is not easy to date these semantic and conceptual changes about disability, as they are not linear processes. The dynamics of construction and consolidation of new identifications often combine themselves, and they overlap and sometimes contradict one another at national and international levels. Our knowledge of these dynamics of conceptual and semantic transformation is limited by our sources. The last sources are mainly reports of committees of international experts, so we can get to only a minor part of the public debates. Furthermore, while it is quite easy to identify the semantic changes, it is more difficult to see the conceptual transformations as the authors rarely mention the definition they give to the word 'disabled'.

New definitions of disability intrinsically related to the exercise of a professional activity within the area of vocational rehabilitation (1918–1955)

The first transformation, which mainly starts after the First World War, aims to show the potential productive capacity (and eventually destructive capacity) of the people with important impairments and lesions. In order to do this, the representatives of the disabled people discard the previous conception of incapacity, which linked systematically serious impairment with entirely productive or destructive incapacity. As main actors of this transformation, doctors – together with the war-disabled and work-disabled – underline the necessary difference between the physical impairment and the incapacity (permanent or temporary, total or partial) to have a professional activity.

This dynamic is related to the birth of legislation concerning invalidity insurances and the industrial accident insurances within many countries starting from the end of the 19th century. In response to the introduction of these laws, some doctors and lawyers, sometimes together with entrepreneurs and employee representatives, are asked to evaluate the degree of incapacity of the injured or ill people. This evaluation has two main purposes: to figure out the different ways towards their vocational rehabilitation and to fix the amount of the compensatory pension for earning incapacity they should receive.

At the international level, the assessment procedures of this incapacity are very heterogeneous. Laws from some countries (France, Italy, Belgium) establish the degree of incapacity on the basis of only the physical integrity prejudice, by following a compulsory or indicative scale. In this case, the pension allotted to the individual is permanent and cannot be modified. But already by the middle of the 1920s, the biggest majority of international experts believe that this assessment procedure is not judicious, as it does not measure the real economic prejudice.

As a matter of fact, a very big number of national laws concerning the invalidity-insurance and the compensation for work injuries are based on the notion of *professional incapacity* (*incapacité professionnelle*). They assess the unemployability by taking into account the diminution of working capacities. Examinations are no more based on the physical impairment, but on the reduced function (related to this impairment), which restricts the working capacity. In that case, specialists often define the group of disabled people based on their diminution of wage-earning capacity (*capacité de gain*) related to their lower productivity (A-Type of definition). In some cases, this professional incapacity is based on only the physical condition and on the previous regular occupation of the person. In other cases, some other criteria are considered, like the individual's age, gender and social group. Some national laws say that this assessment has to be based on the unemployability inside a specific occupation (seaman, miner, etc.) or a group of occupations (administrative staff), while others say that this assessment has to be based on the unemployability within a company, a group of companies, or even an industry.

Although various, these assessment procedures imply that the possibilities for vocational rehabilitation are seen inside only a very small job circle (inside the same company, the same industry or the same group of occupations). They are therefore criticized by some experts who think they do not take into account the possibilities for vocational rehabilitation of the disabled people within another industry, or another company that is not affiliated to the insurance scheme. These possibilities of professional reclassification are even more important when the process of vocational rehabilitation is set up. These experts are convinced by the need to maximize the boundary of professional reclassification in order not to lose the many efforts made within the vocational rehabilitation. But experts agree with the need to keep this restrictive way of conceiving the professional incapacity (*incapacité professionnelle*) in a small labour circle with respect to some specific dangerous and extremely tough occupations (miner, seaman).

The willingness to widen the boundaries of the professional reclassification makes the experts value a new way of conceiving the unemployability. That is the *general earning incapacity* (*incapacité générale de gain*). In November 1936, ILO set up a meeting for the international experts on the social insurances. It strongly recommends applying the conception of *incapacité générale de gain* (Bureau International du Travail, 1937, p. 367). This one considers the possibilities of reclassification and of earning inside the general labour market, by taking into account the nature and the severity of disabilities, the age and the previous occupation of the disabled person. In this case, the residual working capacities of the individual are completely taken into account and the perimeter of vocational rehabilitation is very large, which makes it possible to find a job adapted to him more easily, and to stop assigning him a pension. Adopting this conception allows the legislator to conceive the unification of its insurance system to all employees and all workers, to take into account the possible outcomes of the vocational rehabilitation, and to diminish the number of invalidity paid pensions.

The economic crisis of 1929 and its disastrous social effects at the unemployment level make the international experts understand that the evaluation of the earning incapacity is closely related to the situation on the labour market. In this context of crisis, the least productive and the sick people are the first ones to be laid off, and the disabled people do not manage to find any employment because the employers raise their requirements to select the workers. This depreciation of the work of the disabled on the labour market is very perceptible in England. In this country, the House of Lords issued a judgment that set precedent in England at the beginning of the 1930s. It considers that there is a total earning incapacity in the case of disabilities that make the work of the victim as 'unsaleable' on every market reasonably accessible to him and that there is a partial earning incapacity when disabilities decrease the value of this work on the mentioned market (Bureau International du Travail, 1937, p. 65). In England, the depreciation of the work of a disabled person on the labour market is thus taken into account to evaluate the degree of wage-earning incapacity. That generates a very important rise of the declarations of disability submitted to the administrative institutions during the 1930s (Whiteside, 2002).

This makes the experts recommend in 1936 to take into account the real conditions on the labour market in the evaluation of the wage-earning incapacity. They recommend that the invalidity insurance should give pensions in the event of partial permanent disability for the applicant who could not manage to have an adequate payment for his work, and also for the applicant "who, in view of the conditions of competitions within the labour market, has no reasonable chance to find a proper job" (Bureau International du Travail, 1937, p. 382).

The focus on the highly discriminatory labour market brings some doctors to define the group of disabled people on the basis of the professional disadvantage they experience because of their disability (B-type of definition). For them, this professional disadvantage must be analysed in view of the real conditions on the job market, by taking into account the disability, the age of the person, his professional experience, his social and cultural conditions. This approach is the one adopted within the *Disabled Persons (Employment) Act* in England in 1944 (United Kingdom, 1944). In this text, the disabled person means

> a person who, on account of injury, disease, or congenital deformity, is substantially handicapped in obtaining or keeping employment, or in undertaking work on his own account, of a kind which apart from that injury, disease or deformity would be suited to his age, experience and qualifications.

The expression "disease" includes "physical or mental condition arising from imperfect development of any organ".

Whatever their methods of classification were, by doing their examination, doctors and lawmen have to differentiate at this time the individuals having a permanent partial incapacity ('recoverable' disabled), potentially capable to successfully follow the process of vocational rehabilitation, and the individuals who have a permanent total incapacity and are unable to work, the 'unrecoverable'. The norms set by the German disability insurance are an international reference for many European countries. The German disability insurance sets the unemployability around a threshold equal to one-third of a normal worker's average salary. Only the individual who cannot earn the third of this salary is allowed to have this pension.

This separation of individuals having an impairment into two different groups makes some specialists ask themselves if they have to limit the category of the *invalides* to those considered unable to work, or, more broadly, to those having a permanent total or partial disability. Defending the definitions A and B means to keep the unity of the group of disabled people, including from a semantic point of view. Some other actors choose to define the disabled people on the basis of their productive capacities, which are inferior to the norm, but real (C-type of definition). All of this induces the exclusion of the 'unrecoverable'. The choice of this interpretation leads their zealots to the semantic split of the group of disabled people into two opposite categories. In the French and Spanish linguistic areas, some of the actors wish to promote a new word in order to name the recoverable individuals, while maintaining the word *invalide* (in French), *invalido* (in Spanish) in order to name the unrecoverable disabled people. This threat of split between the two categories is real during the 1940s. In Spain, a disabled intellectual, Fernando Cebreros Poch, affirms in a conference from 1953 the need to differentiate between the word *inútiles* – or *invalidos* – and the word *impedidos*, which shows those who are more likely to be 'adapted to the society" (Diario *ABC*, 1953), briefly, those who have enough energy to work and to participate in the social life.

In the middle of the 1940s, the international experts are in a great uncertainty regarding the manner of defining the 'disabled'. The combination of a very broad scale of impairment (physical, sensory, mental, etc.) and of the relativisation of vocational disablement places the experts of the ILO in a great perplexity. On the one hand, they admit that "only a very small percentage of the population in any country is free from any kind of physical or mental disability", and that, on the other hand, "there is no clear or permanent relationship between physical or mental disablement and vocational disablement" (International Labour Organization, 1945, p. 1). But in the same time, they consider that those who can be categorized as 'disabled' for the purpose of special measures on the training and employment form only a small percentage of those who have a physical or mental deficiency. For the experts, "the problem of terminology is almost insoluble" (ibid., p. ii). The experts criticize the existence of restrictive definitions of the word "disabled" in certain countries, "on the ground that it implies a separate classification which it is both impossible and undesirable to delineate in practice" (ibid., p. ii).

However, this threat of split into two differents semantic categories disappears in the middle of the 1950s at an international level when ILO choose to keep the term 'disabled' (*invalides* in the French translation) in its Vocational Rehabilitation of the Disabled Recommendation no. 99. At the moment of the preparation of the project of recommendation, in 1953, the editors from ILO inform the different governments of their wish to elaborate a definition of the disabled depending on the right of admission to the services of vocational rehabilitation (Organisación Internacional del Trabajo, 1953, p. 9). This procedure would mean adopting a limited definition that includes only the disabled people who can be rehabilitated. Finally, negotiations reach a compromise: the recommendation no. 99 adopted in June 1955 maintains the word "disabled", largely defined as "an individual whose prospects of securing and retaining suitable employment are substantially reduced as a result of physical or mental impairment" (General Conference of the International Labour Organization, 1955). This definition is quite similar to the definition B that sees the disability as a professional disadvantage. But the text implicitly confirms the existence of a dichotomy between the unrecoverable disabled people and the recoverable ones, as one paragraph of the text stipulates that

> vocational rehabilitation services should be made available to all disabled persons, whatever the origin and nature of their disability and whatever their age, provided they can be prepared for, and have reasonable prospects of securing and retaining, suitable employment.

The dynamic of conservation of the unity of the disabled group is facilitated by the difficulty of the doctors to assess the real productive potential of an individual. Indeed, this classification is sometimes weakened by the fact that some disabled people considered as suitable for rehabilitation, and therefore rehabilitated, cannot manage to become productive. On the other side, doctors have to take care of disabled children for whom it is difficult to assess a productive potential. Finally, several actors disagree with this dissociation, as its use is likely to exclude and to marginalize even more the disabled people unable to be rehabilitated.

The ratification of the ILO recommendation no. 99 confirms another dynamic that is the widening of the category of the disabled to some other groups of individuals different from the war and work injured: the blind, the deaf, the people born with a disability, as well as the mentally disabled. In the United Kingdom, the widening of the category of *disabled persons* to the mentally disabled is recorded since 1944. The equalization of these categories is allowed by the fact that all these individuals are seen as receivers of the vocational rehabilitation policy. As a consequence, these different categories, which were in part seen before as opposite, can now be unified under one single identification linked to the process of vocational rehabilitation.

The emergence of new definitions of disability that are not related to the exercise of a professional activity within the area of medical rehabilitation (1952–1975)

A new way of considering disability emerges in conjunction with the development of medical rehabilitation intended for children with different illnesses (poliomyelitis, arthritis, etc.). The aim of this rehabilitation is to prepare the individual to do daily actions in the most independent way possible. The medical rehabilitation claim to coordinate all the actions intended for the disabled people of all ages, including the educational or vocational training questions. For this reason, this rehabilitation is also named 'integral' or 'total' rehabilitation a few years later. The defenders of the medical rehabilitation define the disabled person on the basis of the difficulty to carry out the daily activities. However, several versions of this definition can be identified during the 1960s and the 1970s.

The 'original' version is given by the definition ratified by the specialists from the international institutions (World Health Organization, United Nations), based on the difficulty to fully participate in the educative, social and professional activities because of the physical impairment (D-type of definition). In 1950, a joint committee of experts on physically handicapped children is created under the auspices of WHO. It brings together international experts belonging to the four organizing bodies (WHO, ILO, UNESCO, UN) under the chairmanship of Harry Platt. This committee does not link the definition of the disability to a professional activity:

> a child is considered handicapped if, over an appreciable period, he is prevented by a physical condition from full participation in childhood activities of a social, recreational, educational, or vocational nature. (Joint Expert Committee on the Physically Handicapped Child, 1952, p. 5)

This choice of definition allows legitimating the children's right to access a range of different services (education, vocational rehabilitation, assistance, etc.).

During the 1950s and the 1960s, a version of this definition gradually emerges, inspired by the definition B (the disabled persons as a group of individuals suffering from a professional disadvantage). Some Western medical rehabilitation specialists begin to define the disabled person on the basis of the social disadvantage caused by his impairment within the practice of social activities (E-Type of definition). Although it does not assign explicit responsibility to the society with the exclusion from social activities, this interpretation implies the idea of rights to compensate.

Starting from the late 1960s, inside several countries, associations of people with disabilities consider that society plays an important role within the construction of the professional and social disadvantage affecting the disabled persons (importance of employers' negative prejudices; lack of accessibility of the public buildings and of the public transport). These radically social interpretations of the *disability* vary, however, over the degree of responsibility assigned to the society within the construction of this social and professional disadvantage.

Some groups of people with disabilities built a Marxist interpretation of the *disability*, by assigning the whole responsibility of their marginalization to the way in which the capitalist society is organized. In London, the Union of the Physically Impaired Against Segregation (UPIAS) defends 'a social definition of disability' by considering that it is not something personal and by totally dissociating it from the *physical impairment*. According to them,

> it is society which disables physically impaired people. Disability is something imposed on top of our impairments, by the way we are unnecessarily isolated and excluded from full participation in society. (Union of the Physically Impaired Against Segregation, 1976, p. 13)

More precisely, the *disability* is

> the disadvantage or restriction of activity caused by a contemporary social organization which takes no or little account of people who have physical impairments and thus excludes them from participation in the mainstream of social activities. Physical disability is therefore a particular form of social oppression.

In other cases, some actors understand the *disability* as a social disadvantage based, at the same time, on the functional diminution and on other problems in which society could be involved (as the mobility and the job access). This interpretation implies a questioning of the responsibility of the society within the construction and the maintenance of the services which are not accessible to the disabled persons.

In Spain, at the end of the 1970s, some physically disabled leaders from the association *Minusvalidos Unidos* from Madrid disagree with the medical definitions of the *disability*. But they criticize this in a more subtle way than the English association UPIAS, who radically dissociates the *disability* from the *impairment*. According to one of the members of *Minusvalidos Unidos*, we have to understand the disabled people 'as a social group which is marginalized by society because of (?) its physical and psychical impairments (Gabinete de Estudios y Asesoramiento, 1979, p. 5). The question mark is used here in order to register doubt about the 'fatal cause-effect relationship' between the physical impairment and the marginal situation. The author wishes therefore to show that a certain physical defect "does not lead by itself to the social marginalization" (ibid., p. 57), as the contemporary capitalist society contributes to the marginalization of disabled people.

At the end of the 1960s, the medical rehabilitation experts confirm their definition of the disabled person on the basis of the difficulties to assume his social and professional needs and obligations. Gathered in Geneva in November 1968, the WHO committee of experts on medical rehabilitation brings together experts specialists on rehabilitation from the entire world, as well as representatives from the other intergovernmental institutions as the UN or Unesco and representatives of some NGOs. The committee decides after several debates to define the *Handicapped person* as

> a person whose physical and/or mental well-being is temporarily or permanently impaired, whether congenitally or through age, illness, or accident, with the result that his self-dependence, schooling, or employment is impeded. (Expert Committee on Medical Rehabilitation, 1969, p. 7)

This definition change endorses the widening of the receivers of medical rehabilitation to include the mentally disabled persons. This version is definitively confirmed inside the UN Declaration on the Rights of Disabled Persons approved in December 1975, in which the term disabled person

> means any person unable to ensure by himself or herself, wholly or partly, the necessities of a normal individual and/or social life, as a result of deficiency, either congenital or not, in his or her physical or mental capabilities. (General Assembly of the United Nations, 1975, p. 1)

Resolving the conflicts of interpretations related to the term *disability*

After 1955, the approaches of disability through the medical rehabilitation and through the vocational rehabilitation strongly diverge, but they are also confused because of the shared use of the term "disability" with different meanings. The ILO recommendation implicitly confirms the need to differentiate between the organic deficiency (*impairment*) and its consequences on the chance to find or maintain a proper job (*disability*). Aware of the institutionalization of this definition of the term *disability* at the international level, the specialists on medical rehabilitation show their willingness to choose another term in order to characterize the degree of difficulty to execute the daily actions. To this end, they choose at the beginning to give a new meaning to the term *impairment*.

In February 1958, WHO set up a committee of experts on medical rehabilitation in Geneva. Chaired by the doctor G. Harlem, the Health Minister of Norvegium, the committee decides that their task is to evaluate the *Impairment* (in French *infirmité*), defined as "the presence of a medically diagnosed physical defect in the individual which reduces his fitness to cope with the requirements of everyday life" (Expert Committee on Medical Rehabilitation, 1958, p. 8). This committee differentiates between this *impairment* and the *disability* (translated in French as *incapacité de travail* or *invalidité*), which is "a complex evaluation of the reduction in the patient's ability as regards gainful employment" (ibid, p. 8). But the specialists aren't quite satisfied with this classification, and they call for a rapid homogenization of definitions and for the adoption of a concise definition for each one of the terms *impairment* and *disability*.

During the 1960s, the definition prevailing into the area of medical rehabilitation also becomes predominant inside the area of rehabilitation (which includes medical and vocational rehabilitation, educative services). Because of this, the primacy of the definition of *disability* from the area of vocational rehabilitation is questioned. In 1968, the committee of experts on medical rehabilitation (who also brings together specialists from ILO, Unesco, UN) maintains the distinction between *impairment* and *disability*, but they also modify their definition. They adopt a definition of *disability* totally dissociated from professional capacity, as it underlines 'the reduction of functional ability to lead a fruitful daily life' (Expert Committee on Medical Rehabilitation, 1969, p. 7). We must stress that the definition adopted about the disability states that the individual himself can worsen his degree of disability if he badly reacts to his impairment: 'It is the result not only of mental and/or physical impairment but also of the individual's adjustment to this' (ibid., p. 7). On the other side, the specialists on rehabilitation define from now on the *impairment* as a 'permanent or transitory pathological condition resulting in a diminution of functions' (ibid., p. 7).

Furthermore, specialists add a new term, *invalidity* (in French *invalidité*), defined as "a measure of the diminution of the individual's capacities" (ibid., p. 7). The absence within the classification built by the specialists of a definition intrinsically linked to the professional capacity could be explained by their wish to build a measurement instrument that is not specifically dedicated to the assessment of the vocational incapacity. The specialists search for ranking procedures and operating definitions inside all the areas of the rehabilitation. It means that these definitions have to be useful as measuring tools for the services responsible for assessing, for providing support services, and allowances in the educational, professional and medical areas.

Nevertheless, the choice of a definition available for all areas turns out to be very difficult, as the receivers of the rehabilitation are not necessarily the same category of persons as the receivers of the specialised education services, etc. During the 1970s, some governments (as in France) avoid including a precise definition of the disabled person within their legislation of integral protection of disabled people, in order to elude this difficult question or in order to avoid the exclusion of an individual from these services because of a too restrictive definition.

Starting from the 1960s, definitions of the group of disabled on the basis of the social disadvantages they experience in order to ensure the necessities of their social life become increasingly important inside the area of rehabilitation. In order to qualify this condition of social disadvantage, the local actors sometimes modify the meaning of the word *disability* (as the English association UPIAS do), or they promote the term *handicap*. American professionals have used the word *handicap* since the 1940s in order to speak about the professional disablement. If the classification made by the specialists of WHO in 1968 does not include the term *handicap* within its definitions, it still confirms the victory of the interpretation of the group of disabled people on the basis of their social disadvantages by adopting the terms *handicapés* and *handicapped persons*.

The efforts of the specialists on rehabilitation to reconcile the approaches of medical and vocational rehabilitation remain imperfect and confusing for a long period of time, including for the insiders themselves who admit that they are not satisfied with the adopted classifications. It is within this background that Dr Philip Wood is named responsible by WHO at the beginning of the 1970 for the creation of a new consistent classification. This new classification is published in 1980 under the name *International Classification of Impairments, Disabilities and Handicaps: A Manual of Classification Relating to the Consequences of Disease*. This classification distinguishes between the *impairment* that is a personal characteristic of a person, the *disability* that represents the functional limitation due to this impairment, and the *handicap* that represents the social disadvantages resulting from this disability. This classification is intended to give the possibility of ranking and measuring to the different institutions in charge of providing support and services (Stiker, 2005, p. 191). The official French translation is made in France by Inserm and by the *Centre technique National d'Etudes et de Recherches sur les Handicaps et les inadaptations*, with the name *Classification internationale des Handicaps: Déficiences, incapacités, et désavantages* (1988). The official Spanish translation is made in 1983 by the *Instituto Nacional de Servicios Sociales* from Madrid, into *Clasificación Internacional de las Deficiencias, Discapacidades y Minusvalías* (Instituto Nacional de Servicios Sociales, 1983).

The institutionalisation of the expression *disabled persons* at the international level

Starting from the 1930s, inside the English-speaking countries and European ones, where vocational rehabilitation is very developed, the dynamic is clearly in favour of the creation of an alternative identification against *invalides* and *infirmes* (within the French-speaking world) and against *cripples* (within the English-speaking world). Although the *International Society for the Welfare of Cripples* keeps its name until the 1960s, the English-speaking specialists are already very critical towards the word *cripples*, which seems pejorative to them. Moreover, the United States and Great Britain's governments have already endorsed the need for a semantic and conceptual change. In 1944, the British parliamentary monarchy approves the *Disabled Persons Employment Act*. In the United States, it is the name *handicapped*, appeared during the first decades of the 20th century (Stiker, 1996, p. 20), that is preferred by the most specialised doctors and by some disabled persons. This name is then institutionalised at the federal level by the introduction by President Truman of a *President's Committee for the Employment of the Physically Handicapped* starting from 1945 (Groce, 1992, p. 32). Intended to steer the policy of vocational rehabilitation at the federal level, this committee acquires very quickly a considerable status at the international level. Finally, we have to underline that other terms are also used, but less often, for instance the expression *impaired workers*.

Inside the French-speaking countries, two identifications appear during this period. The first one is *déficients (physiques et mentaux)*, which replaces the term *anormal* within the area of specialised education. It has spread across the area of rehabilitation. The second one that tries to impose itself on the French international arena is *diminués physiques*. In France, Suzanne Fouché creates the *Ligue pour l'adaptation du diminué physique au Travail* in 1929 (Stiker, 2005, p. 193).

Inside the Spanish-speaking countries, debates about semantics appear starting from the beginning of the 1940s. During the 1940s and the 1950s, the specialists from the Latin American countries and the Spanish specialists suggest multiple alternative identifications, both by inspiring themselves from the French names (*deficientes, disminuidos*) and by trying to adapt English names (*lisiado* as synonym for *cripples, dishabil* and *incapacitado* as synonyms for *disabled*, and *impedido, handicapeado* as synonyms for *handicapped*). During a conference on disability organised in Buenos Aires in 1946, E. Mira y Lopez advises to adapt the word *disabled* to the Spanish background:

> maybe we can use in Spanish some words like *hipoérgico* (if we wish to have a scientific term) or *dishabil, dishabilitado* (by copying the English word) or hence the term *readaptado*. (Asociación de Ayuda y Orientación al Inválido, 1947, p. 266)

Some other people suggest new original identifications, like *menor-valido*. During a conference on disability organised in Buenos Aires in 1943, a Chilean doctor, Dr Osvaldo Quijada, suggests the term *menor-valido*, in order to define the individual who has a limited productive capacity because of his illness (Asociación de Ayuda y Orientación al Inválido, 1944, p. 191).

At the beginning of the 1950s, the dynamics of the semantic transformations within the English and French areas are confirmed by the United Nations and WHO. In 1952, the specialists from the WHO committee are using the term of *enfants physiquement diminués* in their report. In the English version, the authors are using the term *physically handicapped child* (Joint Expert Committee on the Physically Handicapped Child, 1952, p. 5). The victory of the terminology from the United States explains itself by the presence of the American specialists at the head of this committee. As shown by Groce (1992), the United States vision on rehabilitation quickly dominates within the different bodies of the United Nations.

During the 1950s, the United Nations contributes in a decisive way to the progressive unification of the disability public policy (education, rehabilitation, assistance, etc.) for all the categories of disabled people. This unification of the public policy of disability leads to the unification of the identifications concerning disabled persons existing in all the sectors of disability public policy within a unique identification: *Handicapped (mentally handicapped, visual handicapped, physically handicapped, etc.)*. In 1951, United Nations sets up a *Working Group on Rehabilitation of the Physically Handicapped* in order to coordinate the programmes of action among all the intergovernmental agencies (ILO, UNESCO, WHO, UNICEF). This group works on medical, psychological and social rehabilitation, and on special education for mutilated, crippled, blind and deaf-mutes (Brunel, 1951). The constitution of this intergovernmental administrative organization encourages the various NGOs interested by this subject (*Fédération Internationale des Mutilés, des Invalides du travail et des Invalides civils, International Society for the Welfare of Cripples, World Council for the Welfare of the Blind, World Veterans Federation*, etc.) to join themselves into a *Conference of International Non-Governmental Organisations Interested in Rehabilitation of the Physically Handicapped*. The first meeting of these organizations takes place in New York on the 9th and 10th of February 1953, a few days before the meeting of the United Nations *Working Group on Rehabilitation of the Physically Handicapped*. In November 1953, the conference officializes its existence, by modifying its title into *Conference of World Organizations Interested in the Handicapped* (Conference of World Organizations Interested in the Handicapped, 1954). This modification is due to the incorporation of organizations related to the cause of the mentally deficient in the conference. This new title thus confirms the unification of all the sectors of disability public policy (with the suppression of the term rehabilitation), and the unification of all the categories (physically handicapped, mentally deficient, blinds, deaf, etc.) in a unique identification, *Handicapped*. The CWOIH very quickly encourages the members of the United Nations Working Group to widen their concern to the mentally deficient. Thus, in January 1954, Kurt Jannsson suggests extending the programs studied by the working group to measurements useful for the "mentally deficient" (Jansson, 1954). A few years later, the United Nations Working Group widens its focus to include the mentally deficient, and modifies its heading to *Technical Working Group on Rehabilitation of Handicapped* (early 1960s). Within the intergovernmental institutions, the unification of the public policy of disability takes place without the disappearance of the term *rehabilitation*, because this term covers from now on the totality of the public policies intended for the social integration of the handicapped people.

The promotion of the term *handicapped* quickly extends to the French-speaking sphere. In 1955, the Department of Social Affairs of the United Nations publishes a booklet named *L'assistance aux Handicapés* (Département des Questions sociales de l'Organisation des Nations Unies, 1955, p. 1). Two years later, the members of the French Parliament use for the first time the term *handicapés* within the law 57-1223 from the 23rd of November 1957 on the professional reclassification of the disabled workers.

In 1955, the English version of the ILO recommendation no. 99 institutionalises the name *disabled person* at the international level (Vocational Rehabilitation of the Disabled Recommendation, 1955). The translations in French and Spanish of the recommendation seem to be far behind the ongoing semantic evolutions, as they maintain the terms *invalides* and *invalidos*. Furthermore, the substantival adjective disappears in favour of a name in these translations, while the English version stresses the fact that we talk about people above all. This recommendation reinforces the legitimacy of terms that have already lost most of their credibility in the French- and Spanish-speaking spheres.

Because of its presence inside the recommendation of ILO, the expression *disabled persons* becomes compulsory and gradually invades the area of rehabilitation. In 1960, the members of the *International Society for the Welfare of Cripples* decide during a general assembly organised in New York to replace the title of their association with the *International Society for the Rehabilitation of the Disabled*. However, the international specialists on medical rehabilitation have been reluctant to use this word for a very long period of time. In 1958, the WHO committee of experts on medical rehabilitation is mostly using in its first report the word *handicapped*, but also the term *disabled* (Expert Committee on Medical Rehabilitation, 1958, p. 9). The French version is using the terms *diminués physiques* and *invalids* (Comité d'experts de la réadaptation médicale, 1958, p. 9). Ten years later, the WHO committee of experts on the medical rehabilitation meeting in Geneva in November 1968 decides after many debates to promote the use of the expression *Handicapped persons* (Expert Committee on Medical Rehabilitation, 1969, p. 7), and *Handicapé* in its French version (Comité d'experts de la réadaptation médicale, 1969, p. 7). By the end of the 1960s, the word *handicapé* becomes stronger inside the French-speaking area, to the detriment of the expression *diminué physique*. It is this word *handicapé* that is then used in the French translation of the *Declaration on the Rights of Disabled Persons* in 1975.

This period ends in 1975 when the word *disabled* is definitively established inside the Anglo-Saxon world. In December 1975, the English version of the *Declaration on the Rights of Disabled Persons* adopted by the UN Assembly reuses the expression *disabled persons*.

The Spanish translations of the international documents use once again the term *impedido* starting from the 1950s, probably as a synonym for *handicapped*. (See Table 7. 1) The Spanish translation of the WHO report in 1958 uses the word *impedido* in order to name every person having a diagnosed medical impairment that limits his ability to cope with the requirements of daily life (Comité de expertos en rehabilitación médica, 1958). The translation of the UN *Declaration on the Rights of Disabled Persons* from 1975 also maintains the term *impedidos*. In the Spanish-speaking area, several specialists on rehabilitation support the term *incapacitados* as a synonym for *disabled*, considering that the best synonym for *disability* is the term *incapacidad*, stemming from the French word *incapacité*. This tendency is strengthened by the fact that the *International Society for the Rehabilitation of the Disabled* used the term *incapacitado* in their Spanish documents. However, soon enough, none of the expressions used by the different international governmental or non-governmental organisations (*invalido, impedido, incapacitado*) seem to be totally appropriate for the representatives of disabled people who create other alternative identifications (*minusvalido, discapacitado, minusfisico,* etc.) starting from the 1960s. The word *minusvalido* is promoted in Spain inside the area of sportive medicine starting from the middle of the 1960s. The *Asociación Nacional de Invalidos Civiles* organizes some annual sports competitions, the *campeonatos nacionales de minusvalidos*. At the end of the 1960s, the manager of the rehabilitation department of the Madrid Clinic Hospital, Ricardo Hernandez Gomez, promotes the term *discapacitado* with great passion. This term is created by analogy with the word *disabled* (Gomez, 1965).

Table 7.1 Summary table of the international semantic changes concerning the group of disabled

	English original version	French version	Spanish version
OMS, *Joint expert commitee on the Physically Handicapped, First report, 1952.*	Physically Handicapped child	*Enfants physiquement diminués*	
OIT, Vocational Rehabilitation of the Disabled Recommendation, 1955	Disabled person	*Invalides*	*Invalidos*
OMS, technical report no. 158, 1958	Disabled	*Diminués physiques*	*Impedido*
OMS, second technical report no. 419, 1969	Handicapped persons	*Handicapés*	*Impedido*
ONU, Declaration of rights, 1975	Disabled persons	*Personnes handicapées*	*Impedidos*
ONU, International Year, 1981	Disabled persons	*Personnes handicapées*	*Impedido*

Conclusion

The international institutions (ILO, UN, WHO) play a fundamental role within the transformations of the categorization of the group of disabled people at an international level. During the 20th century, the meanings of incapacity promoted inside the area of vocational rehabilitation (intrinsically linked to the exercise of a professional activity) are gradually marginalised in favour of some other ways of understanding disability built inside the area of medical rehabilitation and having no connection with the exercise of a professional activity. It is one of these alternative meanings, defended especially by the WHO committee of experts, which is institutionalised at the international level by the adoption of the Declaration on the Rights of Disabled Persons in 1975. This definition of the group of disabled people on the basis of the difficulties they experience participating in the social, professional, educational life because of their impairments does not assign any direct responsibility to the society in the construction of the social disadvantage affecting the disabled people.

The semantic changes inside the international documents are operating according to different temporalities depending on the linguistic areas (English, French, Spanish). The expression *disabled persons* is twice institutionalised inside the English-speaking sphere, through the ILO recommendation in 1955, and through the Declaration on the Rights of Disabled Persons in 1975, despite the promotion of the expression *Handicapped persons* by the medical rehabilitation specialists and by the *Council of World Organizations Interested in the Handicapped* (CWOIH). The name *diminué physique* is depreciated inside the French-speaking sphere during the 1950s and the 1960s in favour of the word *handicapé*. This can be seen in the semantic changes from the international documents. On the other hand, the semantic debates taking place in the Spanish-speaking sphere in the 1940s which lead to multiple proposals of identification (*menor-valido, dishabil, minusválido, incapacitado, discapacitado, handicapeado*, etc.) have less influence on the semantics used by the international institutions (ILO, UN, WHO) until the beginning of the 1980s. Starting from the 1960s, these organisations are always using the old term *impedido* (however, as a synonym for *Handicapped*) in their translations.

References

Asociación de Ayuda y Orientación al Invalido (1944). *Primera Conferencia Argentina, Relatos oficiales, contribuciones y discusiones, Buenos Aires, octubre de 1943*, Buenos Aires, Argentina: Orestes A. Capello, 312 pages.

Asociación de Ayuda y Orientación al Invalido (1947). *Segunda Conferencia para el bienestar del Lisiado, relatos oficiales, contribuciones y discusiones, Buenos Aires, octubre de 1946*, Buenos Aires, Argentina: Orestes A. Capello, 572 pages.

Brunel, F. (1951). Letter to the General Director of UNESCO., Dated January 5, 1951. UNESCO Archives, 371.91 A 022 UNSA.

Bureau International du Travail (1937). *L'évaluation de l'incapacité permanente de gain dans les assurances sociales*, Etudes et Documents, Série M no.14, Genève, Switzerland: BIT., 404 pages.

Comité de expertos en rehabilitación médica de la Organización Mundial de la Salud (1958). *Primer informe*, serie de informes técnicos no. 158, Ginebra: OMS., 58 pages.

Comité d'experts de la réadaptation médicale de l'Organisation Mondiale de la Santé (1958). *Premier rapport*, service des rapports techniques. no. 158, Genève, Switzerland: OMS., 56 pages.

Comité d'experts de la réadaptation médicale de l'Organisation Mondiale de la Santé (1969). *Deuxième rapport*, série de rapports techniques, no. 419, Genève, Switzerland: OMS., 25 pages.

Conference of World Organizations Interested in the Handicapped (1954). Document joined to Jansson K. (1954). Letter to Dr W. D. Wall, Dated January 13, 1954. UNESCO Archives, 371.91 A 022 UNSA.

Cooper, F. (2005). Identity. In Cooper F., *Colonialism in Question. Theory, Knowledge, History*, Berkeley, CA: University of California Press, 59–90.

Département des Questions sociales de l'Organisation des Nations Unies (1955). *L'assistance aux handicapés*, no. 1954.IV.10., Suisse: ONU., 32 pages.

Diario *ABC* (1953). Sevilla, Dated July 4, 1953.

Expert Committee on Medical Rehabilitation of the World Health Organization (1958). *First report*, technical report series no. 158, Geneva, Switzerland: WHO., 52 pages.

Expert Committee on Medical Rehabilitation of the World Health Organization (1969). *Second report*, technical report series no. 419, Geneva, Switzerland: WHO., 24 pages.

Gabinete de Estudios y Asesoramiento (1979). *Minusvalidos Fisicos. Marginación y Opresión*, Madrid, Spain: Grafiprint.

General Assembly of the United Nations (1975). *Declaration on the Rights of Disabled Persons. Resolution 3447 [XXX]*, Dated December 9, 1975.

General Conference of the International Labour Organization (1955). *Vocational Rehabilitation (Disabled) Recommendation* no. 99, Dated June 22, 1955.

Gomez, R. H. (1965). Evolución Historica del concepto de discapacitado ante la sociedad. *ASCLEPIO*, XVII., 261–271.

Groce, N. (1992). *The U.S. Role in International Disability Activities: A History and a Look Towards the Future*, New York, NY: World Institute on Disability.

Instituto Nacional de Servicios Sociales (1983). *Clasificación Internacional de Deficiencias, Discapacidades y Minusvalías*, Madrid, Spain: Instituto Nacional de Servicios Sociales.

International Labour Organization (1945). *The Training and Employment of Disabled Persons. A preliminary Report*, Studies and Reports, Series E (The Disabled), no. 7, Montreal, Québec, Canada: ILO., 305 pages.

Jansson, K. (1954). Letter to Dr W. D. Wall, Dated January 13, 1954. UNESCO Archives. 371.91 A 022 UNSA.

Joint Expert Committee on the Physically Handicapped Child of the World Health Organization (1952). *First report*, technical report series no. 58, Geneva, Switzerland: WHO., 28 pages.

Organisación internacional del Trabajo (1953). *La Rehabilitación Profesional de los Invalidos. Informe IV. Conferencia Internacional del Trabajo. Trigésima Séptima reunion, 1954, cuarto punto del orden del dia*, Ginebra, 66 pages.

Stiker, H. J. (1996). Handicap, handicapé. In Stiker H.-J., Vial M., Barral C. (dir.), *Handicap et Inadaptation. Fragments pour une histoire: Notions et acteurs*, Paris, France: Alter, 15–34.

Stiker, H. J. (2005). *Corps infirmes et sociétés. Essais d'anthropologie historique*, Paris, France: Dunod.

Union of the Physically Impaired against Segregation and the Disability Alliance Discuss Fundamental Principles of Disability, London, UK., November 1976. The Union of the Physically Impaired against Segregation and the Disability Alliance discuss Fundamental Principles of Disability. Being a summary of the discussion held on 22nd November 1975 and containing commentaries from each organization, London, November 1976.

United Kingdom, Act of Parliament (1944). *Disabled Persons (Employment) Act*, 1st March 1944.

Whiteside, N. (2002). Chômage et inaptitude en Grande Bretagne de la fin du XIXe siècle aux années trente. In Omnès C. et Bruno A.S. (coord.), *La construction sociale de l'inaptitude au travail en Europe, volume II. Actes du colloque international 8–9 novembre 2001*, Université Versailles-Saint-Quentin-en-Yvelines.

8

DISABILITIES AND DISABILITY SERVICES IN NIGERIA: PAST, PRESENT AND FUTURE

Paul M. Ajuwon

Social and economic conditions in Nigeria

Nigeria, which is more than three times the geographical size of Britain, has been described as "the giant of Africa" (Fagbadebo, 2007). The country has a population of approximately 165 million people, representing about a quarter of the total African population (Nations of the World, 2014). It is bordered to the west by Benin, to the north by Niger, to the northeast by Chad, to the east by Cameroon, and to the south by the Atlantic Ocean. The main rivers, the Niger and Benue, merge in the centre of the country, dividing it into three major regions of north, south, and east. The north consists of dry savannah, the south of jungle with mangrove swamps nearer the coast, and the east of a plateau leading into the country's only major mountain range along the Cameroon border.

Nigeria as a nation emerged in 1914 under an amalgamation led by Sir Frederick Lugard, the colonial Governor-General (Nduka, 1964; Taiwo, 1980). The country is characterized by diverse and complex social and religious values, which are visible along ethnic and geographical lines. In the northern part of the country, approximately half of the population accepts a feudalistic, hierarchical social system, traceable to earlier kingdoms whose driving unifying force was, and remains, Islam. In the south, both the Yoruba and Igbo ethnic groups, combined with their subgroups, mainly practice Christianity, while they adhere again primarily on traditional lines to a more spirited, entrepreneurial and socially active society than what exists in the north.

About 10% of the Nigerian population is said to practice traditional religion. This statistic is, in all likelihood, much higher, given the fact that both Islamic and Christian believers secretly practise traditional religion in their daily lives (Abimbola, personal communication, 2014). From the foregoing religious and social patterns derive both the strengths and weaknesses of Nigerian society, which significantly impact persons with disabilities and their families.

In recent years, Nigeria has enjoyed a robust economy. However, in spite of its abundant natural resources (including its position as the eighth largest petroleum exporter in the world), the country continues to face rising unemployment, a high incidence of poverty, a fragile health care system, and a high degree of social deprivation

(Federal Ministry of Health, 2006; Osain, 2011; Sulaiman, 2008). The unemployment rate rose from 19.7% in 2009 to 21.1% in 2010, and to 23.9% in 2011 (Nations of the World, 2014). Income distribution continues to be skewed, with a Gini coefficient of 0.44 in 2011; 63% of Nigerians live below the poverty line of U.S. $1 per day; 42% lack access to potable water; and 69% do not have access to basic sanitation (Nations of the World, 2014). According to *Africa Report* (2014), most Nigerians are poorer today than they were at independence from Britain in 1960 – victims of the resource course and rampant, entrenched corruption that has characterized the country's leadership for decades. It is against this background that the group called Boko Haram (usually translated as "Western or secular education is forbidden") emerged. Boko Haram is an Islamic sect that believes that corrupt, false Muslims control northern Nigeria, and the sect intends to remedy this by establishing an Islamic state in the north with strict adherence to Sharia (Islamic) law.

Despite Nigeria's abundant natural resources, the National Assembly (2013) has observed that the overall economic improvements in the country in recent years have not translated into gains in the welfare and quality of life of the average Nigerian. This has resulted in a deteriorating condition for the 22.5 million people with disabilities (Ajuwon, 2012).

Languages, traditions, and religious beliefs on disabilities

Nigeria has an extremely diverse population, with over 250 languages spoken. Of these, three major languages – Hausa, Yoruba, and Igbo – are spoken by approximately half the population. Other minor languages include Efik, Edo, Kanuri, Tiv, Fula, and Ijo. However, English remains the *lingua franca*. Most Nigerian languages have not developed appropriate terms to describe disabilities in ways that are inclusive and less degrading.

A review of available literature shows that there are varied beliefs, attitudes, and practices related to the causes of disabilities and to how the society perceives persons with disabilities. The varied beliefs of many Nigerian cultures regarding the causes of disabilities can be summed up as a curse on the family or the wider community for offenses against God or the gods, anger of the ancestral spirits for neglect or breached promises, a punishment on the child for offences committed in a previous incarnation, punishment on the parents' misdemeanour, a potential evil person curtailed by the gods, offenses against the laws of the land or breaches of customs, and wicked acts of witches and wizards (Abang, 1988; Mba, 1978; Onwuegbu, 1988).

In precolonial times, most communities in Nigeria were structured around the system of kinship – made up of families and other types of kin groups. The kin groups of a society tended to contribute in practical terms to the upkeep of its members and solving societal problems. According to Johnson (1960), under the kinship system, those members with physical disabilities, the elderly, and those with diseases were assisted to a large extent by other members of the group. Unfortunately, today the forces of urbanization and the dependency pattern of industrial development have created incursions into the kinship system, thereby weakening its structure and functions. These forces of social change set in motion those processes, particularly in urban areas, that have led to problems associated with begging among persons with disabilities, the needy, and the aged.

There is a widely held belief among the Yoruba ethnic group of southwestern Nigeria that there are gods who are malevolent by nature and who cause children with disabilities to be born for sheer pleasure. Such "bad gods" are believed to roam villages at midday and midnight, so it is believed that any pregnant woman who moves around outside her home at these times will bear a child with a disability. The mother is thus seen as the culprit and will bear the brunt of the family and community anger while the child will probably be accepted (at least on the surface) and well treated in order not to further offend the malevolent gods (Onwuegbu, 1988, cited in Hill, 1985).

Some ethnic groups poison or starve a baby with a disability. Alternatively, he may be taken to a shrine or thrown into a river so that he may be transformed into a snake, thus preventing reincarnation as a disabled human baby. All these customs result from the belief that there is no place for people with disabilities in the kingdom of the gods, so they are doomed to perpetual reincarnation as disabled children unless drastic measures are taken to prevent their return (Ogbue, 1981, as cited in Hill, 1985).

In many cultures the soothsayer is consulted to determine who is responsible for the birth of the disabled child, and that person is then punished by exile, serfdom for a specified period, or by ostracism. Such punishment may be for a limited period, for life, or even extend to subsequent generations.

In traditional Igbo society, titles and status are earned by accumulating wealth and by merit. Thus, an Igbo is what he is on his own merit, so if a person with a disability achieves success in business or other spheres of life he is "absolved" from his impairment. If he fails, then his family must provide for him, as it would disgrace the whole family if any member of it were reduced to begging (Levine, 1966, cited in Hill, 1985).

In the current Delta and Edo states of Nigeria, the extended family has a traditional responsibility for members of the community who experience disabilities (Ojo Eweka, 1975, as cited in Hill, 1985). In rural areas, the whole community assists a farmer with a disability to clear, plant, weed, and harvest his farm. Apart from mental disability, a disability does not preclude a man from family headship nor from acting as a priest at the ancestral shrines. The chief danger is that the person with a disability will be pampered and overprotected (Hill, 1985). However, such kindly treatment toward people with disabilities may result from false sympathy. Ogbue (1981, as cited in Hill, 1985) argued that it is more accurate to regard the Nigerian culture as being hostile toward disabilities, in that where sympathetic treatment is given its intention is most often to avert further calamities.

Islamic beliefs of disabilities

In the predominantly Islamic region of the north, the people readily succumb to the fatalism of "In Shah Allah" – "It's God's Will." This implies that the Muslim perspective is that of a fatalist, accepting good fortune and misfortune alike as the will of God. A belief in this part of the country is that Muslims are born into their social positions and cannot earn a higher status. For this reason, persons with disabilities accept their lowly status as beggars (Levine, 1966, cited in Obani, 1982), and positive actions to better the lot of people with disabilities are not usually contemplated.

On the other hand, one of the pillars of Islam is almsgiving, and beggars may be considered to be bringing a blessing to others by providing them with the opportunity of almsgiving and thus of earning merit (Okediji, 1972). Thus, in Muslim areas of Nigeria, people with disabilities normally receive alms in fulfilment of religious obligation, as they are regarded as those whom "Allah the supreme God has created that the laws may be fulfilled."

An example of this custom and the beliefs that accompany it is an article in the *Light Bearer* of 1953 (Hill, 1985). This article described a Guild of Blind Beggars, which included men, women, and children, in the large city of Kano. Their chief, the "Sarkin Makafi," claimed that "the guild serves a vital function in the city," and "if all the blind became craftsmen, to whom would the faithful give alms?" adding "Allah has made them blind; it is not for men to interfere."

Under Muslim (Sharia) law, the punishment for many crimes is mutilation, for example, amputating the hand of a thief. Ironically today, the Boko Haram Sect in northern Nigeria has engaged in propaganda that seeks to introduce Sharia law to the country, beginning with northeastern Nigeria. This set of beliefs and practices, in itself, increases the negative attitudes of Muslims toward those with disabilities, as it associates disability with wrongdoing.

Christian beliefs of disabilities

Generally, among Christian followers in Nigeria, the concept of disease and disability is usually interpreted as a punishment for sin or wrongdoing. This belief is now widespread in the Nigerian Christian community of all denominations. Examples abound in the Christian Bible that reference common diseases and conditions such as blindness, deafness, dumbness, paralysis, leprosy, and others. For instance, in the Old Testament, the general perception is that God creates disability as punishment for sin or as an expression of God's wrath for people's disobedience. Similarly, in the New Testament, the link between sin and disability is well documented, in spite of instances where the gospels portray Jesus as positively disposed toward people with disabilities.

These interpretations of the Bible continue to shape the attitudes of Nigerian Christians toward disabilities and people with disabilities. As a result, the Pentecostal churches organize miracles and prayer sessions for these special populations, with the promise of "healing" them and elevating them to new levels of spiritual and physical status. This is a growing ideology across the country, and one that potentially interferes with modern rehabilitation practices.

Development of formal education and rehabilitation services

Hill (1985) provided a concise historical development of Christian missionary work related to education and care of people who are blind and, to a limited extent, those who are deaf and/or have speech limitations. Much of the information presented in the paragraphs that follow is derived from her research. Hill (1985) reported that early education of people who are blind began in 1916 in the predominantly Islamic region of northern Nigeria. Northern Nigeria was then characterized by a high prevalence of blindness, illiteracy, and poverty (Audu, 1973). At that time, the region was a vast area dominated by the emirs or rulers (Ogunsola, 1974). The emirs had, for many years, resisted Christian missionary incursions into their emirates (Fafunwa, 1974). Western forms of education had been well established in the mainly Christian region of southern Nigeria for over five decades prior to 1916 (Ikejiani, 1965; Taiwo, 1980), but southern Nigeria had no formal system of special education during that period.

Research conducted by this author in the Sudan United Mission (SUM) Archives in the United States reveals that as early as 1916, Rev. David Forbes of the Sudan United Mission taught Braille to Milkatu Batu, a girl who was blind in the Freed Slaves Home, Umaisha, in the current Nasarawa State (Hill, 1985). The Freed Slaves Home had been established earlier in 1909 in response to the colonial government directive to abolish slavery (Hill, 1985). Subsequently, as an experiment, the Home admitted children who were blind, beginning in 1916 (Hill, 1985), signalling formal specialized instruction of the pupils.

When Rev. G. P. Bargery inspected the Freed Slaves Home for government assistance from June 1919 through October 1920, he found three infant classes, three primary classes, and one blind class (*sic*) (Bargery, as cited in Hill, 1985). Interestingly enough, and as noted in his report, "This is probably the only school in Nigeria where any attempt is made to train the blind." The report also alluded to the presence in the ordinary classes of "four somewhat mentally deficient (*sic*) children."

Forbes also reported on the presence of a girl with physical disabilities who was taught spinning and weaving, and of two boys with deafness and speech limitations (cited in Hill, 1985). The whole school was taught sign language to communicate with them (Hill, 1985). Furthermore, Hill commented that the SUM school at Du had a boy with deafness and speech impairment who was proficient at reading and writing.

As Christian missionary activities flourished in the region, "blind people came from long distances seeking instruction" (LB July/August 1937, as cited in Hill, 1985). These students received instruction at various times from missionaries in Ibi, Kano, and Gindiri, among other places in northern Nigeria. It was reported that the competent teachers among the blind who had converted to Christianity were hired to provide instruction, while the missionaries also helped to develop reading and writing skills in the Hausa language, primarily to read and write the scriptures (Audu, 1973).

The establishment of the Sudan Interior Mission (SIM) Eye Hospital in 1943 in Kano was a landmark feat in ophthalmological care. The hospital attracted patients from both inside and outside the country for several decades. Audu (1973) reported that in 1944, the Sudan Interior Mission School was set up adjacent to the Eye Hospital. However, the school could provide only limited education (notably the teaching of the scriptures) to mainly young pupils in the first three elementary grades. As expected, the hospital creditably served as a referral source, steering children who had sight problems to the school. The school operated until the mid-1970s, when it discontinued all services.

In 1953, the Sudan Interior Mission (SIM) officially commissioned the School for Blind Children, Gindiri, in Plateau State. Hill (1985) commented that older elementary pupils from the School for the Blind in Kano attended the Gindiri School, under a successful collaborative training scheme that lasted until the mid-1970s, when the Kano state government set up its own school for the blind under the Universal Primary Education arrangement.

137

From the preceding information, it can be seen that the formal education of children who were blind was uppermost in the minds of Christian Missionaries like David Forbes of the SUM, as early as 1916. The early introduction of special education to benefit blind children in northern Nigeria is similar to the trend in the United States that emerged in the late 1820s and early 1830s, when the first three residential schools for the blind were first established. Thus, in a significant way, Forbes' success in this aspect of education in northern Nigeria was revolutionary. His efforts paved the way for other Christian missionaries and educators who operated in conjunction with competent local blind persons to provide training to their pupils.

Development of specialized care and education in southern Nigeria

European and North American missionaries were the first to introduce to southern Nigeria the system of formal care and training of vulnerable groups and people with disabilities (Blindness Report, 1948; Hardage, 2008; Schram, 1971). Hardage (2008) reported that the missionaries arrived in Calabar with preconceived ideas about the status of the society. The missionaries decried cultural practices that were unacceptable to them, notably human sacrifice, killing of orphans and twins, and the banishment of twin mothers. Prominent among these missionaries was Mary Slessor from Scotland, who worked assiduously until her death in Nigeria in 1915 to evangelize the people, to cater to the vulnerable children, and to empower the women (Hardage, 2008). It is interesting to note that missionary enterprise in disability care and special education services in Nigeria continues to some extent to the present day.

Compared to northern Nigeria, formal special education services for children with disabilities began later in southern Nigeria. It was not until 1956 that a school for children with physical disabilities (other than leprosy patients who had been receiving help since the 1920s) was established at the National Orthopedic Hospital, Igbobi, Lagos (National Orthopaedic Hospital in Lagos, n.d.). The Orthopedic Hospital itself was established in 1945 to cater to disabled ex-servicemen who had sustained injuries while serving with British forces during the Second World War. In later years, the hospital became renowned, and its services were extended to other African countries (International Labour Office, 1960).

Provision for children who were deaf was established relatively late compared to provision for the blind and those with physical disabilities as a result of leprosy. For instance, the Wesley School for the Hearing Impaired initially started with special classes at Yaba Primary Methodist School in 1957, and at Olowogbowo Methodist Primary School in 1958 (Schram, 1971).

Lally (2011) reported that the Lagos Roman Catholic Diocese, in conjunction with the government of Nigeria, officially opened the Pacelli School for the Blind in June, 1962. Today, Pacelli School remains a leading residential primary school in the country under the management of the Catholic Archdiocese of Lagos. The Oluyole Cheshire Home School in Ibadan, inspired by Group Capt. Leonard Cheshire, began in 1959, primarily to educate children and youth with deafness and physical disabilities.

Almost at the same time, G. Salisbury of the Royal Commonwealth for the Blind, pioneered the Open Education (integration) scheme for the blind in Katsina, northern Nigeria (Salisbury, 1964). The training scheme was subsequently introduced to other parts of the country in the 1960s, in collaboration with various state governments

(Sykes & Ozoji, 1992). However, the Open Education scheme has floundered, due, in part, to underfunding, inadequate specialized manpower, and parents' preference for residential schooling.

Today, in most of the residential schools, the curricula focus on compensatory courses as well as general public school subjects. These subjects are aligned to standards set by the Ministry of Education in each state. In the final year of elementary school, pupils are encouraged to sit for the National Primary School Certificate Examination. Over the years, successful children have been admitted into regular secondary and vocational schools, while others have graduated from universities within and outside Nigeria. Currently, several of these university graduates have been employed in various walks of life, including, but not limited to, teaching, broadcasting, law, civil service, mosque and church leadership, banking, and self-employment.

The training of adults with disabilities in southern Nigeria also gained prominence in the 1950s. According to Schram (1971), Dr. George Ademola of the Lagos Ministry of Health spearheaded the establishment of Farmcraft Centres, beginning in Ikeja, Lagos. This was carried out under the auspices of the federal government and the Royal Commonwealth Society for the Blind. Somewhat later, the idea of the Centres spread to other towns in the country, namely, Bida, Barna, and Maiduguri. A vocational training centre was also opened at Kaduna, with an annual grant from the Ministry of Social Welfare and Cooperatives, providing a 2-year course for 40 trainees.

Later, sheltered workshops were set up in Adamawa, Bauchi, Jos, Kano, Katsina, Sokoto, and Zaria. In all the Farmcraft Centres, occupational facilities were available for making baskets, rugs, mats, and mattresses, in addition to training in agriculture. These Centres were all staffed by sighted instructors, most of whom were trained locally (Schram, 1971).

Earlier in 1956, the Federal Nigerian Society for the Blind founded a vocational training centre in Oshodi, Lagos (About Us, n.d.). Besides the training in crafts, the Centre's curriculum focused on telephone switchboard operation and, until recently, several of their graduates were successfully placed as telephonists in government offices and industries across the country. Today, this aspect of vocational training has become obsolete, due to the proliferation of mobile phone technology.

In June 1960, the American Baptist Mission, under the leadership of Mrs. Frances West, launched the Training Center for the Blind in Ogbomoso, western Nigeria (Nigeria Faithful Works Report, 2009). In the same year, the CMS established the multipurpose Special Education Center for both leprosy patients and the blind at Oji River in Enugu State. This later developed into a school with units for young pupils with blindness, deafness, and those with physical and health challenges.

In 1969, The Modupe Cole Memorial Child Care and Treatment Home School was set up in Akoka, Lagos. Following the inauguration of the Universal Primary Education program, the home-school was taken over by the Lagos state government. Today, with about 110 staff, the home-school caters to about 200 residents with various cognitive and physical disabilities. The home has a school, a vocational training centre, a library, a physiotherapy room, and dormitories. The residents, who are between 6 and 60 years of age, are grouped into different units, depending on their level of independence. Some of the residents complete their education up to university level, all funded by the state government.

As can be seen from the preceding discourse, the pattern of special educational provision beginning in the 1950s was mainly missionary-inspired and/or voluntary agency residential centres, with minimal grants from the government. Today, most of these schools and centres have been taken over by their respective state governments. However, these institutions are known to be chronically underfunded, poorly equipped, and unable to recruit specially trained teachers, counsellors, and therapists.

Care and rehabilitation of individuals with leprosy in Nigeria

In the 1920s, Christian missionaries first became involved in setting up leprosy colonies throughout the country. At that time, leprosy had ravaged several communities, notably in eastern Nigeria. In that region of the country, the Igbo people coined the word "Opo" to describe leprosy (Onwuegbu, personal communication, June 20, 2014). So serious is the apprehension of being afflicted with the disease that the local word "Opo" is seldom used for fear that the utterance could cause the speaker to contract the disease (http://www.ilep.org.uk/ilep-co-ordination/leprosy-around-the-world/africa/nigeria/).

Beginning in the 1930s, leprosy control programs sprang up in various parts of the country, with missionaries and the colonial government working collaboratively to tackle the clinical and social problems associated with the disease. It was reported then that the areas surveyed showed an incidence rate as high as 50–60 per thousand of the population, with only a small percentage receiving treatment in asylums or leper colonies. This was clearly an unsatisfactory situation from the standpoint of effective and quality health care and social programs.

The mounting social problems associated with leprosy culminated in the 1936 report by Dr. Ernest Muir, Medical Secretary of the British Empire Leprosy Relief Association. This report resulted in increased measures aimed at leprosy control in the provinces, particularly in eastern Nigeria, where distinguished European leprologists were actively engaged not only in treatment, but also in cutting-edge research that significantly advanced the production of drugs for this population (Ten-Year Development Plan, 1946).

The leprosy control program of the government faced setbacks in the 1960s and 1970s due to the impact of the Nigerian civil war. Eventually, the government launched the National Tuberculosis and Leprosy Control Program to control the increasing prevalence of leprosy and tuberculosis. Unfortunately, many of the leper settlements that were adequately equipped several decades earlier have now been abandoned, and affected persons struggle to eke out a living in the colonies and/or are reduced to begging on the streets (tribune.com.ng/quicklinkss/features/item/11786-iberekodo-lepers-colony-tales-of-a-blighted-hope).

At the beginning of 1992, the World Health Organization estimated that there were 360,000 people with leprosy in Nigeria. Around 1996, approximately 30% of past or present people affected by leprosy in Nigeria, were affected by a disability or impairment (www.ilep.org.uk/ilep-co-ordination/leprosy-around-the-world/africa/nigeria/). Studies conducted in Nigeria revealed health workers' knowledge and attitudes toward leprosy to be inadequate and identified the need for appropriate curricula on leprosy (Awofeso, 1992; Ayanniyi, Duncan, & Adeniyi, 2013; Iyor, 2005).

For several decades, Nigeria has been struggling to overcome discrimination against people with obvious signs of the disease and to address the disability it causes. Many find it hard to seek help because they fear being stigmatized.

In 2006, Nigeria was one of seven countries in Africa reporting more than 1,000 new cases of leprosy a year (the other six being Angola, the Democratic Republic of Congo, Ethiopia, Madagascar, Mozambique, and Tanzania) (www.ilep.org.uk/ ilep-co-ordination/leprosy-around-the-world/africa/nigeria/). Today there are plans to integrate HIV/AIDS control measures into the tuberculosis and leprosy program so as to facilitate early case detection of tuberculosis among persons living with HIV/AIDS.

Special programs in
Nigeria after independence in 1960

In the late 1960s, Nigeria began to indigenize its education policies and programs (Fafunwa, 1974). But the efforts met with setbacks because of the Nigerian civil war. The civil war (1967–1970) brought to the forefront the need for resettlement and rehabilitation of children, youth, and adults, particularly in the war-ravaged south-eastern region of the country. But the thrust of the policies was on setting up special institutions for long-term care of persons with disabilities, tackling the perennial problems associated with street begging in cities and towns, and correcting the lopsid-edness in the geographical distribution of opportunities across the country.

In the mid-1970s, the government affirmed:

> Considerations of justice and equity demand that every Nigerian child should have comparable opportunities for self-development and fulfilment irrespec-tive of where he lives and the economic and social circumstances into which he has been born. (Third National Development Plan, 1975–1980)

This was undoubtedly a lofty aim, and one that successive governments have struggled to implement effectively due to underfunding and a limited number of trained pro-fessionals. Nonetheless, in the plan, the government was committed to the policy that aimed to tackle the problems of "blindness, deafness and dumbness (*sic*)," which the government said "has become more complex with the substantial increase in recent years, in the number of such cases in the country." Subsequent national develop-ment plans and numerous policy memoranda continued to stress the importance of allocating sufficient funds to support institutions to provide services. In the face of mounting disability problems in the country, these efforts have yielded few dividends, leading to declining quality of life for millions of people who have disabilities.

Another reason for the setback in program implementation has been the inability of the government to create a national database, or conduct a credible census on the number of persons with disabilities, including the beggars and the destitute. Needless to say, the lack of adequate statistics continues to be the bane of effective rehabilita-tion and social planning in the country today.

The national education policy

Following the Universal Primary Education (UPE) scheme of the federal government in 1976, Nigeria released the landmark publication entitled *National Policy on Education* (Federal Republic of Nigeria, 2004). According to Section 10 of the policy, the government classified persons with exceptionalities into three broad categories:

I *People with disabilities* – the visually impaired, the hearing impaired, the physically/ health impaired, the emotionally disturbed, the speech impaired, the learning disabled, and the multi-handicapped.

II *The disadvantaged* – the children of nomads, migrant fishermen, migrant farmers, hunters, etc. who, due to their lifestyles and means of livelihood, lack access to the conventional educational provision, necessitating special education services to meet their unique circumstances.

III *The gifted and talented* – those who possess very high IQ and are naturally endowed with special traits (in arts, creativity, music, leadership, intellectual precocity, etc.), but find themselves insufficiently challenged by regular school programs.

The aims and objectives of special education in the National Policy on Education incorporated several of the objectives previously built into the nation's development plans. Overall, government recognized the need to give concrete meaning to equalizing educational opportunities for all children with disabilities, to provide opportunities for exceptionally gifted and talented children to develop at their own pace in the interest of the nation's economic and technological development, and to design diversified and appropriate curricula for all the beneficiaries.

Several other aspects of the policy are worth mentioning. First, the government declared that "[t]he education of children with special needs shall be free at all levels." Second, government shall conduct regular census and monitoring of people with special needs to ensure adequate educational planning. Third, schools shall be required to arrange regular sensory, medical, and psychological screening assessments to identify any incidence of disability. Fourth, all necessary facilities that would ensure easy access to education shall be provided, for example, "inclusive education or integration of special classes and units into ordinary public schools under the Universal Basic Education (UBE) scheme." (The inclusive education movement with specific reference to Nigeria will be discussed briefly later in this chapter, in *Inclusive Education in Nigeria – Trends and Challenges*).

Nigerians with Disability Decree

In what appeared to be a major step toward codifying special education and rehabilitation laws in the country, the erstwhile Federal Military Government promulgated the *Nigerians with Disability Decree* of 1993 (http://dredf.org/international/nig1 .html, the Disability Rights Education & Defense Fund). Its main purpose was to provide comprehensive legal protection and security for Nigerians with disabilities, and to establish standards for enforcement of the rights and privileges guaranteed under the decree and other laws applicable to persons with disabilities.

The decree, which could be likened to the *Americans with Disabilities Act* of 1990 (Maes, 2000), spelled out in clear terms government's commitment to the provision of

opportunities for persons with disabilities in the areas of education, vocational rehabilitation and employment, housing, accessibility, transportation, supportive social
services, sports and recreation, telecommunications, voting access, and legal services.

Within the decree, and for the first time, it was proposed that a National Commission
for People with Disability should be established. The objectives, among others, were
to: promote the welfare of persons with disabilities in general; promote the full utilization of people with disabilities in the development of human resources and to bring
about their acceptance as full participants in every phase of national economy and
development with equal rights and corresponding obligations; stimulate and encourage actions to improve the civic, political, cultural, social, and economic education
of persons with disabilities; and play a coordinating role between government and
citizens with disabilities.

Other objectives as stipulated in the decree were to work toward total elimination
of all social and cultural practices that tend to discriminate against or dehumanize
persons with disabilities, coordinate in the various states of the country government
efforts to enhance the integration of people with disabilities into the community, and
to enhance the rights of persons with disabilities in any existing legislation in all ways
deemed proper and appropriate. These were far-reaching objectives which, at that
time, were well received by the disability community and the stakeholders. However,
as with previous policies, the decree has remained largely unfunded, and the objectives unattainable.

The political will to contemplate effective introduction of specialized services,
similar to those that exist in high-income countries, has been lacking in Nigeria. The
profound social and economic changes of the past 25 years have resulted in disequi-
librium in the family, and innocent children have been made enemies of parents who
vent the frustrations of their failures on vulnerable children. This has given rise to the
growing incidence of stigmatization of children locally referred to as *ifot* or witches,
particularly in the Akwa Ibom state (Oladipo, 2010). The situation has been fueled
by the proliferation of a fundamentalist sect that "has re-injected the fear of the devil
into religion" (Chineyemba, 2010). Thus, the need to employ education as a weapon
for eradicating the belief in *ifot* should be vigorously pursued.

Private initiatives in specialized services in Nigeria since independence

In the stagnation of services that ensued, particularly in the years after the 30-month
civil war, concerned parents emerged to set up schools and centres to meet the myriad needs of children with special needs. These advocates have been motivated by
the need to challenge assumptions about children's capacities, and to encourage the
development of environments in which children can build and demonstrate capacities. In the section that follows, the author describes four specialized institutions that
responded to his survey for this project.

Torrey Home for People with Intellectual Disabilities
Elizabeth Torrey, who might be described as the forgotten *"Nigerian"* mother
of special education in Nigeria, founded the first Beth Torrey Home in 1965
in Lagos, Nigeria. Ms. Torrey, an American missionary, previously worked in
Angola and Ghana. While in Nigeria, she worked tirelessly for children who were

orphaned and those with intellectual disabilities. The Lagos home she founded currently has 25 children and adults in its long-term care. In later years, Beth Torrey established similar homes in Kano and Zaria, to cater to the needs of orphans with disabilities.

The home relies primarily on charitable funding and support. Over the years, religious organizations, service clubs, and philanthropists have contributed generously toward the day-to-day running of the home, including staff salaries.

The children and adults in the home are taught how to read and write, and are trained to develop domestic, social, theatrical, and singing skills. Some of the students have severe intellectual disabilities, and require more sustained training before they can successfully carry out certain tasks like housekeeping, feeding, and self-care. The fact that Ms. Torrey very much touched lives in a very personal way is illustrated by the many children who boastfully say, "I am Beth Torrey's child." In November 1977, Beth Torrey passed away after being struck by a motorcyclist while crossing a Lagos street.

Therapeutic Day Care Centre

The Therapeutic Day Care Centre, Enugu, was founded in January 1979 by Mrs. Hildegard Maria Ebigbo, from Fremdingen in Bavaria, Germany, with the help of her Nigerian husband (http://www.foerderkreis-tdcc.de). The initial aim was the early education of children with intellectual disabilities, learning disabilities, multiple handicaps, and severe emotional disturbance. It has now developed into an inclusive education centre with a nursery school, a primary school, a secondary school (comprised of junior and senior secondary school classes), and a sheltered workshop. Currently, there are about 700 children and adolescents with intellectual, emotional, sensory, and physical disabilities who study alongside typically developing students. The school runs a small boarding facility of about 110 children with various disabilities who find commuting from home arduous (Mrs. Ebigbo, personal communication, July 2014).

Since 1997, the Centre has been fending for itself with the help of public-spirited individuals and organizations. It therefore needs the generous support of philanthropists and the government to continue its good work, since the fee charged by the Centre is minimal.

Open Doors for Special Learners, Jos

The Open Doors for Special Learners, Jos, in the Plateau state, was established by Professor Joanne Umolu in 1998, as a registered non-government and not-for-profit organization (www.opendoorsnigeria.org). The primary goals of the school are to provide quality educational opportunities for children and youth with learning disabilities who have not been successful in regular schools; provide such pupils with specialized literacy skills; expand the quality of education for children with special needs; enhance the opportunities for the young learners to participate in music, arts, indigenous crafts, and sports; and counsel and advise families and caregivers on how to cope with the disabilities in their children. The school has been approved as a collaborating, non-governmental organization with UNICEF/Nigeria.

The overarching philosophy of the school is to assist the pupils who require compensatory training because they have a learning disability such as autism, Down syndrome, cerebral palsy, epilepsy, specific learning disabilities, or other developmental problems. The focused curriculum of Open Doors is therefore unique, given the lack of expertise of teachers in public schools and the over-whelming prejudice and discrimination against children with intellectual disabili-ties in society.

Some of the children at the school have conditions that need to be treated by a physical therapist; hence, the setting up of a Physical Therapy Clinic within the facility. The full-time physical therapist not only treats each child who requires therapy, but also assists parents or caregivers in implementing follow-up therapeu-tic activities to sustain the physical development gains of each child. Currently, 15 of the children use this specialized service. Furthermore, some therapeutic devices that have been fabricated with the ingenuity of local craftsmen are being successfully utilized within the clinic.

The curriculum of Open Doors places a high priority on vocational training. Indeed, the belief is to inculcate in the pupils useful skills that would prepare them for independent and self-reliant adulthood. The pupils learn how to cook, garden, and make petroleum jelly cream and candles. The plan is to expand the scope of the centre's vocational training to include the manufacture of other popular products for distribution within the region.

In terms of promoting public awareness of disabilities, teachers at Open Doors frequently conduct workshops in public schools, agencies, the Ministry of Education, as well as the Ministry of Social Development. These professional development activities have contributed immensely to the participants' level of awareness of cognitive disabilities, and increased their understanding of instruc-tional methodologies.

Down Syndrome Foundation of Nigeria

The Down Syndrome Foundation of Nigeria (DSFN, 2014) was formed in December of 2001 by Rose Mordi, a parent of a child with Down syndrome (see http://downsyndrome-ng.org/). Mrs. Mordi was motivated by the desire to improve nega-tive attitudes of Nigerian society toward parents of children with Down syndrome, and to enhance the quality of life of their children through appropriate education and training. She observes that Nigerian society defines people with Down syndrome by what they do not have rather than what they do have, and by what they cannot do rather than what they can do. The commitment set forth by the Foundation is embedded in the belief that if given adequate encouragement and support to grow like their peers, people with Down syndrome can and will actualize their potentials to live a fulfilled life.

In the entire West African region with a combined population of over 230 mil-lion people, the DSFN, a mainly residential school located in Surulere, on the Lagos mainland, is the leading non-governmental, not-for-profit association pro-viding leadership and support in all areas related to people with Down syndrome. The Foundation's mission is to improve opportunities to people with Down syn-drome by identifying how to support their development through guidance and training.

The Foundation's curriculum emphasizes educational programs, such as liter-acy development, numeracy skills, communication and language competencies, social development, vocational skills, and perceptive skills. The DSFN also pro-vides services in social welfare, that include relocation programs for street boys and girls with Down syndrome, sports competitions, enlightenment and interactive services in local languages through the media, a help line telephone service, and house-to-house emergency respite. The Foundation provides services in the realm of rehabilitation and counselling of pupils, and counselling services for parents and siblings of children with Down syndrome. Officers and members of the Board of Trustees meet quarterly to review the centre's activities and assess the success and challenges of the various programs.

Inclusive education in Nigeria – Trends and challenges

Looking at the preceding examples of specialized programs in Nigeria to date, it is evident that the major efforts have been undertaken, largely within institutional settings. The pioneering schools and settlements for the blind and lepers, and the numerous state residential schools for children and rehabilitation facilities for adults that were built after independence, clearly illustrate this. Often, these institutions were located in remote parts of the town or city, with limited connection to their immediate community.

In the past 3 decades, Nigeria has been a signatory to a number of international agreements and protocols, notably the *Salamanca Statement and Framework for Action on Special Needs Education* (UNESCO, 1994), and the *Convention on the Rights of Persons with Disabilities* (United Nations, 2006). Both protocols, among other things, seek to promote the inclusive development and education of persons with disabilities in each country.

On the basis of these international agreements, Nigerian politicians and civil servants now engage in empty rhetorical discussions about inclusion, with little or no practical strategies for operationalizing the scheme (Ajuwon, 2012). This is in contrast to what occurs in western countries, where it is common to hear about practical issues of inclusion that bear on such factors as teacher-pupil ratio; the educational approach that should be implemented; the presence of typically developing peers; the number of hours of intervention; how associated services such as audiology and speech pathology, guidance and counselling, orientation and mobility, transportation, etc. are utilized; Universal Design Learning (UDL) principles; and proximity to the home of the child with a disability (McLeskey, Rosenberg, & Westling, 2013).

The way forward

As has been shown in this chapter, efforts at creating effective special education and rehabilitation services in Nigeria have been carried out at a gradual pace, and are largely devoid of practical commitment. Yet, there is evidence of an increase in the number of persons with disabilities and other vulnerable individuals, due to cultural, environmental, economic, and social factors (2011). In light of the concerns that have been identified, and the documented pitfalls in planning effective services, it is pertinent to conclude this chapter with the recommendations that follow:

1 *Establish a national database on disabilities.* Although this idea was first presented to the Nigerian government in 1960 (ILO, 1960), it has not been possible to create

such a database. It is imperative that more comprehensive data about the extent of disability throughout the country be obtained. The national census could be used as a platform to collect specific information concerning any obvious disability: congenital deformity, speech impairment, leprosy, deafness, blindness, albinism, and so on. Policymakers and implementers of special education and rehabilitation services could then utilize such data to define health, education, social and employment needs, plan interventions, and evaluate progress.

2 *Empower consumers with disabilities and their families.* If services are to be meaningful, it is critical to recognize the needs, wants, and choices of consumers and their families or caregivers. In recent years in the more affluent countries, this paradigm of care has been adopted to improve the "quality of life" and "family quality of life" of consumers, and their nuclear or extended families (Ajuwon & Brown, 2012). From what has been highlighted in this chapter, it is clear that the lack of involvement of persons with disabilities in the development and running of services in Nigeria has largely accounted for their continued marginalization and vulnerability in all aspects of life. The situation has also been exacerbated by the absence of an effective national parent advocacy body. It is recommended that the Nigerian Association of Parents of Exceptional Children (NAPEC) be duly constituted, with local and state branches. This Association would recommend, initiate, monitor, and assist with implementing programs and services in the 774 local government areas of the country.

3 *Develop an operational policy framework for inclusive education.* Inclusion has become an important movement in special education worldwide, and it is likely that the philosophy and practice of inclusive education will dominate the special education discourse for many years to come. Odeme (2016) argued that although Nigeria's National Policy on Education (2004) is clear on the inclusive education approach as the current trend in the special education system, it lacks an operational policy framework for the implementation of this approach to the education of special needs children. In his words, "This is needed to establish the source of funding, who provides resources, personnel training, stakeholders' involvement, and modalities of monitoring and implementation" (p. 6). It should be stressed, however, that unless such policy becomes law, there is little strength in it. If inclusive educational settings are a goal, then any efforts toward getting that policy legislated will support that idea and give it more power.

4 *Strengthen standards and curricula in all tertiary institutions that prepare special education and rehabilitation of professionals.* Currently, some post-secondary institutions in Nigeria are known to train professionals in this field: the University of Ibadan, the Federal College of Education (Special), Oyo; Kaduna Polytechnic; University of Jos; Bayero University, Kano; University of Calabar; University of Uyo; and Nsukka University. The governing councils of these institutions of higher education must ensure that their students are given quality education, while also guaranteeing that their degrees, diplomas, or certificates are recognized worldwide. It is imperative that the accrediting agencies pay attention to the professional competence and dispositions of lecturers; the provision and maintenance of specialized teaching devices, libraries, and laboratories; adapted recreational centres; and the general physical development and layout of their campuses. The campuses must be barrier-free and accessible to trainees, staff, and faculty with disabilities. Other

PAUL M. AJUWON

priority areas should include examining the content of all course syllabi, including each institution's formative and summative systems of evaluation, and understanding how instructions and teaching practice experiences are being adapted to local or community circumstances that impact learners with disabilities. Lecturers will need to explore innovative ideas to produce instructional materials that positively portray Nigerian children, youth, and adults with disabilities in education, home, and community settings. Such resources should be used to supplement teaching of large classes, for example, in an introductory course to exceptionalities, where field-based observations are almost impossible due to large class sizes. The current requirement for all colleges of education and universities to include in their curricula a general introductory course on special education is a positive measure that can improve the knowledge base of prospective general educators.

5 *Promote research into disabilities, inclusion, and other special education practices.* Researchers must determine empirically the educational, cultural, social, and emotional effects of disabilities on inclusive education and other practices on children with and without disabilities, their teachers, parents, counsellors, and others. The Special Needs Section of the National Policy on Education (2004) already identifies learners with all types of disabilities. There are also students in nomadic and other special programs, including those identified as gifted. The Nigerian Educational Research and Development Council (NERDC) must set aside substantial competitive grants each year to conduct comprehensive, methodologically sound research on the specific needs and interests of each group. Such rigorous research efforts should (a) examine the various disabilities and their causal factors, including standardizing names in all Nigerian languages for describing each disability category to facilitate communication among medical service providers and parents and teachers; (b) establish culturally sensitive, ecologically valid assessments and instructional strategies for all children with disabilities; and (c) ensure that teachers, social workers, counsellors, medical specialists, and parents form mutually beneficial partnerships that will contribute to the social, psychological, and educational growth of all children.

References

Abang, T. B. (1988). Disablement, disability, and the Nigerian society. *Disability, Handicap & Society, 33*(1), 71–77.

About Us. (n.d.). Retrieved from http://www.nigsocblind.org/about-us/

Abimbola, W. (Prof.)(2014). Traditional religion in Nigeria. Personal interview, February 24.

Africa Report. (2014). *Curbing violence in Nigeria (II): The Boko Haram insurgency.* Belgium: International Crisis Group. Accessed 2014 March 23. https://www.crisisgroup.org/africa/west-africa/nigeria/curbing-violence-nigeria-ii-boko-haram-insurgency

Ajuwon, P.M. (2012). A study of Nigerian families who have a family member with Down syndrome. *Journal on Developmental Disabilities, 18*(2), 36–49.

Ajuwon, P.M. (2012). Making inclusive education work in Nigeria: Evaluation of special educators' attitudes. *Disability Studies Quarterly, 32*(2).

Ajuwon, P.M., & Brown, I. (2012). Family quality of life in Nigeria. *Journal of Intellectual Disability Research, 56*(1), 61–70.

Ajuwon, P. M., Lesi, F.E.A., Odukoya, O., & Melia C. (2015). Attitudes of medical students toward disabilities in Nigeria. *International Journal of Disabilities and Human Development, 14*(2), 131–140.

Audu, J. (1973). *The establishment and growth of SIM School for the Blind, Kano from 1930s–1972.* Unpublished B.A. Thesis, Zaria, Nigeria.

Awofeso, O. (1992). Appraisal of the knowledge and attitude of Nigerian nurses toward leprosy. *Leprosy Review, 63*(2), 169–172.

Ayanniyi, O., Duncan, F. O., & Adeniyi, A. F. (2013). Leprosy: Knowledge and attitudes of physiotherapists in Nigeria. *Disability, CBR and Inclusive Development, 24*(1), 41–55.

Blindness Report. (1948). *Blindness in British Africa and Middle East Territories.* London, UK: HMSO.

Chineyemba, L. I. (2010). Chapter 1 The emergence of and worries over child-witches. in A. J. Ademowo, G. Foxcroft, & T. D. Oladipo (Eds.), *Suffereth Not a witch to Live: Discourse on Child-witch Hunting in Nigeria* (pp. 1–8). Mokola, Ibadan, Nigeria: Ayomide Publications.

Down Syndrome Foundation of Nigeria. (2014). Retrieved from http://downsyndrome-ng. org.

Ebigbo, H. M. The Therapeutic Day Care Center, Enugu, Nigeria. Personal communication. July 2, 2014.

Fafunwa, A. B. (1974). *History of Education in Nigeria.* London, UK: George Allen Unwin.

Fagbadebo, O. (2007). Corruption, governance and political instability in Nigeria. *African Journal of Political Science and International Relations, 1*(2), 28–37.

Federal Ministry of Health. (2006). *National child health policy.* Abuja, Nigeria.

Forbes, D. (1916). Work for the blind. *Lightbearer, 12*(3), 37.

Galadima, M. *Overcoming the skeptical attitudes of regular teachers towards inclusive education approaches in Sokoto State, Nigeria.* Ministry of Education, Sokoto State, Nigeria. Retrieved from www.afri.can.org/Ghana/Mamuda.doc

Hardage, J. (2008). *Mary Slessor – Everybody's Mother: The Era and Impact of a Victorian Missionary.* Eugene, OR: Wipf & Stock Publishers.

Hill, K. E. (1985). *Provision for the visually handicapped in Plateau State, Nigeria.* Unpublished B.Phil. thesis, University of Birmingham, England.

Iyor, F. T. (2005). Knowledge and attitude of Nigerian physiotherapy students about leprosy. *Asia Pacific Disability Rehabilitation Journal, 87*(16), 85–92.

Ikejiani, O. (1965). *Education in Nigeria.* New York, NY: Frederick A. Praeger.

International Labor Office (ILO). (1960). *Report to Government of the Federal Republic of Nigeria on vocational rehabilitation and employment of the disabled.* Geneva, Switzerland: Author.

Johnson, H. M. (1960). Sociology: *A Systematic Introduction* New York, NY: Harcourt, Brace & World.

Lally, A. (2011). *History of the Religious Sisters of Charity in Nigeria, 1961–2011.* Dublin, Ireland: Specialty Printing.

Maes, A. (2000). The Americans with Disabilities Act – time to measure the efficacy of this legislation. *Michigan Bar Journal, 79*(12), 2–4.

Mba, P. O. (1978). *Priority needs of special education in developing countries: Nigeria. International Perspectives on Future Special Education.* Stirling, Scotland: CEC World Congress.

McLeskey, J. M., Rosenberg, M. S., & Westling, D. L. (2013). Inclusion: *Effective Practices for All Students.* New York, NY: Pearson.

Nations of the World. (2014). *A Political, Economic and Business Handbook.* New York, NY: Grey House Publishing.

National Assembly. (2013). *The Senate: National Assembly Federal Republic of Nigeria, 2*(5). Retrieved from http://www.nassnig.org/nass/news.php?id=420

National Orthopaedic Hospital in Lagos. (n.d.). Retrieved from http://www.nohlagos .org.ng/

Nduka, O. (1964). *Western Education and the Nigerian Cultural Background.* Oxford, UK: Oxford University Press.

Nigeria Faithful Works Report. (2009). Retrieved from http://www.nigeriafaithful.org/wp-content/uploads/2010/10/December-2009-Newsletter.pdf

149

Obani T.C. (1982) 'A Study of some Factors Affecting Attitudes to Teaching the Handicapped Among Nigerian Teachers', Doctoral Dissertation, University of Birmingham, U.K.

Ogunsola, A. F. (1974). *Legislation and Education in Northern Nigeria.* Oxford, UK: Oxford University Press.

Okediji, F. O. (1972). Sociological aspects of the rehabilitation of beggars. in F. O. Okediji (Ed.), *The Rehabilitation of Beggars in Nigeria* (pp. 24–37). Ibadan, Nigeria: Ibadan University Press.

Oladipo, T. D. (2010). Education for eradication of the belief in Ifot. in A. J. Ademowo, G. Foxcroft, & T. D. Oladipo (Eds.), *Suffereth Not a Witch to Live: Discourse on Child-witch Hunting in Nigeria* (pp. 85–88). Mokola, Ibadan, Nigeria: Ayomide Publications. 85–88.

Omede, A.A. (2016). Policy framework for inclusive education in Nigeria: Issues and challenges. Public Policy and Administration Research, 6(5), 33–38.

Onwuegbu, O. I. (1988). The Nigerian culture: Its perception and treatment of the handicapped. in O. C. Abosi (Ed.), *Development of Special Education in Nigeria* (pp. 4–8). Ibadan, Nigeria: Fountain Books.

Open Doors for Special Learners, Jos. Retrieved from opendoorsnigeria.org/

Osain, M. W. (2011). The Nigerian health care system: Need for integrating adequate medical intelligence and surveillance systems. *Journal of Pharmacy and Bioallied Science, 3*(4), 470–480.

Salisbury, G. (1964). Open education. in A. Taylor, & F. H. & Butcher (Eds.), *Education of the Blind in Africa* (pp. 4–8). Ibadan, Nigeria: Caxton Press.

Schram, R. (1971). A History of Nigerian Health Services. Ibadan, Nigeria: Ibadan University Press.

Sulaiman, S. (2008). *Rich nation, poor citizens: The missing links for increasing output and alleviating poverty in Nigeria.* Retrieved from http://www.africaeconomicanalysis.org/authors/30/Sa%E2%80%99idu-Sulaiman

Sykes, K. C., & Ozoji, E. D. (1992). *Teaching Blind and Low Vision children.* Zaria, Nigeria. Ahmadu Bello University Press.

Taiwo, C. O. (1980). *The Nigerian Education System: Past, Present and Future.* Lagos, Nigeria: Thomas Nelson Nigeria.

Ten-Year Development Plan (1946). *Ten-year plan of development and welfare for Nigeria.* (1946). Lagos, Nigeria: Government Press.

Third National Development Plan, 1975–1980. Lagos, Nigeria: Government Press.

UNESCO. (1994, June 7–10). *The Salamanca Statement and Framework for Action on Special Needs Education.* Salamanca, Spain. June 7–10.

United Nations. (2006) *Convention on the Rights of Persons with Disabilities.* http://www.un.org/disabilities/documents/convention/convoptprot-e.pdf

9

A SHORT HISTORY OF APPROACHES TO DISABILITY IN THE NETHERLANDS

Luc Brants, Paul van Trigt and Alice Schippers

Introduction

On the 19th of September 2011, one day before Budget Day, many people with disabilities demonstrated in The Hague against the budget cuts in social and health services that were planned by the Dutch government. Among the protesters was a group of disability activists operating under the name *Terug naar de bossen* (Back to the woods). The name of this group refers to the situation before the 1990s, when many people with disabilities were housed in institutions in the countryside. Since then, many people with disabilities have left these institutions and have taken their place in society. This recent activism has emerged because "this state of equality is threatened by measures of the government" (www.terugnaardebossen.nl, 2012). *Terug naar de bossen* places itself explicitly in the tradition of disability activism as it was developed during the 1970s (www.terugnaardebossen, 2012). But, as was the case 40 years ago, Dutch disability activism is not very strong and does not receive much attention in the media. Why this is the case is one of the issues that we want to explore in this chapter.

Although disability (history) has not received much attention in Dutch historiography, with the exception of mental illness and intellectual disability, it is possible to give a historical sketch. We start with presenting the so-called new disability history as the perspective from which we, as far as possible based on the existing literature, write a modern Dutch disability history. The starting point is the notion that disability is at least partially a sociocultural construction. Thereafter, we outline the most important political developments of Dutch history (1800–2012) to set the general context. Then we describe the main developments in the way people with disabilities have been approached in society, following the themes of education, work, housing, and care. We trace the continuing and changing perspectives on various disabilities throughout this time period. We end the chapter with some concluding remarks.

New disability history

The history of people with disabilities in the Netherlands that is available to date is dominated by three different perspectives: the history of education, institutional history, and medical history (Van Trigt, 2013).[1] In recent years, such perspectives in other countries have been enriched by other perspectives, especially the American tradition of new disability history, a viewpoint of disability history that has not been used frequently up to now in the Netherlands. Fundamental to this view is that, as in disability studies in general, in disability history social constructivism has replaced the medical view on disability. A landmark book that described this shift was *The New Disability History: American Perspectives* by Longmore and Umansky (2001). These and other authors espousing new disability history have postulated that disability should become a standard analytical category in the toolbox of the historian, alongside such concepts as gender, race, and class. We need another "other," argued Catherine J. Kudlick (Kudlick, 2003, p. 763) in a well-known review article. The emphasis historians like Longmore and Kudlick place on disability as a concept marked a shift in the field: in the 1970s and 1980s disability history in the US was a history of a discriminated minority, but from the 1990s onwards historians became increasingly concerned with the question of how disability functions as a socio-historical construction. People with disabilities were no longer reduced to their impairment (as in the medical model), but according to the so-called social model of disability – and other concepts – they were considered within the complex and interwoven set of relationships between the biological and social worlds (Kudlick, 2003).

The perspective of new disability is fruitful for two reasons. First, this perspective challenges us to look beyond the dichotomy health/illness to the way in which society constructs normality and deviation. The second reason lies in the plea of new disability historians for a "history from below," where people with disabilities and their sources are made central. Because of the current state of historic research, it is not possible to write this article radically from a new disability perspective, but, inspired by this perspective, we take as our guide as much as possible the inclusion and exclusion of people with disabilities in Dutch society.

The Dutch nation, pillarization and the welfare state

Disability is mainly perceived as a modern phenomenon, which began to be described as a category onto itself at the end of the eighteenth century. In the decades around 1800, much of the modern Western European states were formed. The Dutch kingdom was established in 1813 after a period of revolution and French occupation. Under the absolute monarch William I, the provinces of the premodern Dutch republic were forged into a Dutch unitary nation-state. Relations between the different levels of government (national, provincial, and municipal) were reorganised, and measures were taken to give the state, rather than the dominant churches, a role in poor relief. Meanwhile, the (liberal) bourgeois elites took various initiatives to help and to educate certain groups of those who were both poor and disabled (De Haan, 2003).

In 1848, a relatively liberal constitution was introduced in which the power of the king was restricted in favour of the parliament. In this new political order, citizens were given the right of free association. The Protestant and Catholic elites used this right as an opportunity to organize themselves politically and to mobilize "their" people. In later decades, socialism emerged in the Netherlands and grew into a new, non-religious community. All these developments led towards a process of ideological pluralism often described as pillarization (Stuurman, 1983). The Dutch historian Peter van Rooden has argued that the social imagery of the pillarized society was dominant between 1880 and 1960. In the pillarized society, religion and ideology were used as a method of distinguishing between people and of creating social groups. Van Rooden described the emergence of what he called social worlds, especially built up by Catholics and Orthodox Protestants, as "starting with separate educational systems, but spilling over, eventually, into almost all aspects of social life" (Van Rooden, 2007, p. 147). Regarding the care for people with disabilities, pillarization meant that the state gave a general policy framework, but the actual execution of these policies was left to private organizations of the different "pillars."

The Dutch welfare state was built up during what is called the "long sixties" (1958–1973). Compared with other western countries, this occurred later, but it was very extensive and developed in a short period of time. Within 15 years, a fully state-financed social security system was realized, which no longer was seen as a favour but rather as a right. In the execution of these rights, the "pillarized" organizations remained important players, at least until the 1970s. The new social security system was introduced, without undue political turmoil, in a period of unprecedented economic growth and subsequent wealth (Harinck, 2009; Van Kersbergen, 2009). But soon after its realization, it began to be contested. The economic recession of the late 1970s and the 1980s was diagnosed in terms of economic politics: maintaining the welfare state would be too large a burden for the working population and the business community. This debate is still going on, as illustrated by the demonstration described in the first sentence of this chapter.

"Uplift" of the blind and deaf

We situate the beginning of Dutch disability education history in the last decade of the eighteenth century, when Daniël Guyot founded his school for the deaf-mute in Groningen (Josephus Jitta et al., 1938, p. 141). Together with the first school for the blind, which began operations in 1808 in Amsterdam (Joshephus Jitta et al., 1938, p. 171), this initiative can be seen as the first specialized form of education for people with a well-defined disability. Both schools were initiated by so-called enlightened Protestant elites, who were fascinated by the lack of sensory abilities and wanted to "uplift the people" by developing specific education for specific groups (Rietveld-van Wingerden & Tijsseling, 2010; Vos, 2008). When religion became a dividing factor in Dutch society, new initiatives for people with sensory disabilities were taken by the different religious groups. Catholics started their own institute for the deaf in 1840 and for the blind in 1859, followed by orthodox Protestant institutes for the deaf in 1891 and for the blind in 1919 (Josephus Jitta et al., 1938, pp. 141, 171).

These institutes all started as schools that taught their students how to deal with their disabilities. The goal was to make their students "useful" citizens. For reasons of distance between homes and school, the students were also housed in a boarding school or in foster families. In this way, education and housing became indiscernibly connected. But this connection, and thus the whole policy of "uplifting" people with disabilities in this way, also had segregating effects because it set these students apart in society. When students had finished school and had to return to their own social environments, it was difficult in many cases for them to find work. To resolve this, these early institutes established separate homes for adults, in some cases with workshops for sheltered employment attached to them. Although some people with

153

sensory disabilities remained outside the institutes, segregation was the dominant way Dutch society approached people with sensory disabilities.

The deaf and the blind were virtually the only groups with a bodily impairment who were subject to public interest in the nineteenth century. Other groups with bodily impairments were neglected. It was only at the very end of the nineteenth century when, under pressure from industrialization that made productivity of citizens especially important, a facility for the care of physically disabled children was erected. It opened a home and school in 1900 (Dietz & Ketelaars, 1990).

This lack of interest can be explained as follows. First, people with bodily disabilities did not form a well-defined group with clear-cut measures that could be taken. They were primarily seen as "ill" and treated within the regular healthcare system. Second, medicine was preoccupied with other problems that were seen as more urgent. During the whole nineteenth century, the combat of infectious diseases took much energy (Houwaart, 1991). Furthermore, towards the end of the century, worries around the (supposed) increase in numbers of "idiots" and the "feebleminded," as they were increasingly called, grew. This concern became the subject of the Mental Hygienic movement, that was concerned with improving overall societal mental health (Brants, 2004, p. 21).

Mental disorders as a problem

People with a mental disorder, whether categorized as psychiatric or intellectual, were the subject of many discussions. These grew in number and intensity towards the 1910s. As in many other European countries, the Dutch approach to care for people with mental disorders had its roots in the late Middle Ages, when towns and cities began offering special houses for these groups. These so-called *dolhuizen* (madhouses) were mostly intended for the "raging mad" – those who caused problems or danger for themselves or other people (Mans, 1998). In the nineteenth century, some statutory regulations for the care of the "insane" were made by the national state. The risk for society was one of the driving forces behind this: the "insane laws" of 1841 and 1884 were first and foremost instruments of public order. But safety for the public was combined with the idea that the insane were ill, could be treated, and, at least in theory, could be cured in the medical institutions that emerged beginning in the middle of the nineteenth century (Van der Grinten, 1987, p. 38). The key to these institutions was given to physicians: they could write a "declaration of insanity," which led to admittance in a medical institution. This meant that they could mark the difference between what was considered to be mentally normal and abnormal.

Recent research shows that it was primarily people who caused too much nuisance or danger for their surroundings who were sent to these institutions (Vijselaar, 2010). But the boundaries between society and institutions were not as rigid as was often assumed in the Foucaultian narrative of the "great confinement." Like those in other countries (Brown & Radford, 2015), residents of institutions often returned to society and to the care of their families when their behaviour showed amelioration (Vijselaar, 2010).

The inhabitants of these institutions formed a very diverse group. Besides patients with psychiatric diseases like schizophrenia, depression, and manic-depression (now called bipolar disorder), people who were known as idiots, and people with dementia and seizure disorders were also admitted (Vijselaar, 2010). From the middle of the nineteenth century onwards, people referred to as idiots were increasingly treated separately, often living in separate quarters. This was the beginning of the differentiation of *mental disorder* and *mental disability* in the Netherlands, which had already become standard practice in the surrounding countries.

In education, there was already a specific treatment for idiots, thanks to vicar Cornelis Elisa van Koetsveld, who opened his School for Idiots in The Hague in 1855. It was a boarding school with special education for children we now think of as having intellectual disabilities, and was based on the framework provided by the schools for the deaf and blind. The idea that mentally disabled children could be taught originates from this institute. It led to a growing conviction that this education should be available to all mentally disabled children. In 1896, the first classes for children were introduced into general education, when Daniël Köhler began an experiment at his own public school in Rotterdam. This "special" education was soon moved to separate schools, which in the first decades of the twentieth century grew considerably. This growth occurred for two important reasons. First, "normal" education embraced it as a way to get rid of children who slowed down or disturbed regular education. Second, the teachers in special education showed that mentally disabled children could be successfully taught, an idea that was embraced by the government (Graas, 1996).

Aspects of class

The approach towards people with disabilities in the nineteenth and early twentieth centuries was possible because disability was highly entangled with class – people with disabilities were mainly considered as poor people. Legal measures and charitable institutes that affected disabled people's lives were often part of the way in which elites dealt with the poor, be it in the oppressive sense (via legal measures such as the Insanity Acts) or the "uplifting" sense (via charitable societies). Disabled members of the elites were helped within their own families or in private institutions and were kept out of the scope of public interest. Even some public medical institutions had class systems (e.g., the Catholic Voorburg in Vught) in which the quality of care depended on the amount of money that was paid by the patient's family (Vijselaar, 2010).

The way disability was associated with class is also illustrated by the striking absence of the disabled people's voice. Measures were taken *for* them, discussions were held *about* them, but almost never were their voices heard. The idea that people with disabilities, or even their parents, could have their own opinions did not appear to have popped up in the minds of the elites who organized care.

Social Darwinism and eugenics

The view that people with mental disabilities were a danger to society grew in the Netherlands into "common sense" only after World War I. The teachers in Dutch special education saw the risk as manageable, which could only grow into a danger when the mentally disabled were neglected (Brants, 2004, pp. 75–76). It was enough to take social measures to help them. Against this conviction stood the belief, shared mostly by professionals with a medical background, who pleaded for more restrictive measures to limit or forbid procreation.

155

Eugenic measures were, in contrast to some surrounding countries (Germany, Scandinavia), never taken in the Netherlands. The most important reason for this was the pillarization system: Catholic and Protestant morality was opposed to eugenics, and their politicians effectively blocked any eugenic measure (Brants, 2004, pp. 116–117). Nevertheless, there is a dark chapter. During the Second World War the inhabitants of a Jewish psychiatric hospital were deported and murdered (Van Wijnen, 2014). Also, there are indications that the Nazis who occupied the Netherlands planned steps against people with minor mental disabilities in 1944 (Graas, 1996, pp. 77–78).

Disability as functional deficit

As in many of the surrounding countries, in the early decades of the twentieth century, labour was increasingly seen as essential for developing human potential. It was intrinsically good and, despite its internal religious and ideological differences, Dutch society in general shared this view. Part of this common view was that education should prepare people for work, and this view applied also to people with disabilities. To attain the goal of students in special education acquiring meaningful work in their communities, organizations began to operate in the 1920s for the purpose of matching special education students with work opportunities. The main activity of this so-called "After Care" was to find students a job and to support them in their first period at work. This grew into a system of *social pedagogical care*. Work was important to the extent that the "social usability" of children was measured by their (in)ability to work (Brants, 2004, p. 89).

Sheltered employment was set up for people with mental disabilities who under no circumstances could find a regular job. This meant that they could work and did not have to be sent to institutions, an argument that was used to convince municipalities to subsidize these workshops. Sometimes, it was even possible to place people from institutions back into their former communities. An important aspect of this movement was that it formed a counterweight against the Social Darwinism movement, that saw people with disabilities primarily as the most "unfit" in society, the least likely to make a positive contribution, and the most likely to thus be subjected to measures that would reduce their numbers in society. It showed that people with disabilities could positively contribute to society and were not simply a burden.

Sheltered employment diversified throughout the 1920s and 1930s, and was developed for more and more different disabilities (Josephus Jitta et al., 1938), although attention to people with physical disabilities alone was still not strong. In this period, the word *handicap* emerged in the Dutch language and was used as a general term for all people with a functional deficit in their ability to work (www.etymologie.nl, 2011).[2] Establishing and maintaining workshops remained, in this period, the responsibility of municipalities and charities, which lead to a patchwork system without a central policy from the Dutch national government.

In spite of these changes, the discourse and practice of rehabilitation was considerably less dominant in the Netherlands than in other countries, where wounded war veterans sparked the development of many new services, because of the relative small military involvement of the Dutch in the two world wars (Van Trigt, 2013).

From charity to right

Soon after World War II, things began to change in the Netherlands. In 1950, the central government obliged municipalities to maintain workshops for people with disabilities. It was the first intervention of the National government in these matters, but it was only the beginning (Moes, 1997).

With the unprecedented economic growth of the late 1950s and the 1960s, the general idea grew that care for people with disabilities was not a matter of charity, but a right guaranteed by the state. This thinking led to reforms of the welfare system in the 1960s, in which the association of poverty with disabilities was broken by separating poor relief from the financing of the care for people with disabilities. Under the *Social Employment Law* of 1969, the financing of workshops for people with disabilities was lifted to the national level. The *Act on Extraordinary Medical Expenses* from 1968 meant that the costs of care for people with disabilities became part of a general insurance for all inhabitants of the Netherlands. The state distributed the finances mainly among already existing social and care systems. This strengthened the segregation of people with disabilities, who now often became financially dependent on an anonymous government.

Normalization?

Was the changing role of the state in the 1960s accompanied by a changing attitude towards people with disabilities? Until the 1960s, the defect perspective, reflected in the medical model, was uncontested. People with disabilities were seen as patients and had to be treated. A new paradigm emerged, the *normalization principle*, which meant making available to people with mentally disabilities, as much as possible, the norms, patterns, and conditions of everyday life in mainstream society (Nirje, 1969; Van Gennep, 2007; Vos, 2008). This principle was rooted in the social policies of the social-democratic government of Sweden and aimed to mainstream public services like housing facilities, education, and work.

In the Netherlands, the normalization principle was never fully embraced, mainly because disability services continued to be segregated in character. Segregated special education kept expanding, in numbers as well as in types of education. What began as education for the blind, the deaf, and the mentally disabled grew into 15 forms of special education and, in 1994, almost 5% of all children in the primary age group attended special education (Graas, 1996, p. 235). The increase in numbers can also be seen within the realm of the sheltered employment. Based on the idea that people with disabilities had the right to work, in 2006 approximately 90,000 people were involved in sheltered employment (www.canonsociaalwerk.eu, 2015).

"Dutch" normalization showed most clearly in the way facilities for people who needed extensive care and support were organized. From the 1970s onwards, there was a building boom of small-scale facilities constructed in neighbourhoods and villages (Mens & Wagenaar, 2010, pp. 90, 132, 192; Weijers, Tonkens, & Mans, 1998, p. 319). This was normalization "in bricks," because little attention was paid to the development of social interaction with the surrounding "normal" society. Policy planners and care professionals still had the lead, not people with disabilities or their advocates. This style of normalization mostly reflected the concerns of professionals and their services, rather than the social context that is essential for integration (Chappel, 1997).

As a result of this paternalistic normalization, self-advocacy emerged slowly. Only the sensory disabled communities had organized themselves in the pre-war period, partly in pillarized groups. In the 1950s, parents of people with intellectual disabilities organized themselves according to the Dutch pillarized model. These associations became very powerful and even established care facilities themselves. But because it was the parents who were the organizers, the voice of people with disabilities them-selves was still not heard. In the 1970s and 1980s, self-advocate associations were founded by people with mental disorders and by people with intellectual disabilities. These were no longer based on different ideologies, and the number of self-advocate associations has increased since that time.

Pressure for change

Since the 1980s, special education, sheltered employment, and decentralized living accommodations became more and more questioned. The government has tried to reduce costs of special education and sheltered employment by reducing the num-bers coming into these systems. Special education was reformed by the slogan *together to school again* and was renamed in 2011 into *fitting education*, in which support of chil-dren with disabilities in regular education is now a core government policy.

Regarding sheltered employment, since the 1980s workshops have had to operate in an economically competitive manner. The demands on employees increased, and more vulnerable groups were excluded from this type of work. This led to a new type of workshop for these groups, operated mostly by care providers. However, in later reforms, initiated in 2011, the government made a full swing in policy: sheltered employment is, according to these plans, meant only for those people who under no circumstance can work in the broader economy.

The trend in government policy for living accommodation since the 1990s has been towards providing respite and short-term care (in order to postpone admission to residential care), and integrated places of living (Oosterhuis & Gijswijt-Hofstra, 2008, p. 1232). The initial idea of community support seems to have failed here, but not because of a lack of "bricks." To the contrary, most people with disabilities who require housing now live in small-scale living accommodations in "normal" society. The problem is that the development of social interactions within the living environ-ment has been neglected. In many cases the only interaction with people outside the homes is with family and professionals (Van Berlo et al., 2011, p. 36).

Disability activism and disability studies

One striking aspect of Dutch disability activism is the lack of strong, independent cross-disability groups, as were organized in the United Kingdom, the United States, and elsewhere. In the 1970s there were some disability-related protests, but this did not grow into a strong Dutch grass-roots disability movement.

An explanation for this phenomenon might be found in the way the self-advocate associations have been structured since the 1970s. They are fragmented along the lines of distinct diseases and syndromes and do not have a national platform from which to operate. Thus, there are separations between people with mental disorders, people with intellectual disabilities, people with physical and sensory disabilities, users of care institutions, and others. Existing self-advocate associations serve much more as a discussion partner of the government and care providers than as a pressure or advocacy group. Moreover, Dutch self-advocate groups do not focus to any great extent on civil rights, but rather direct their attention to the improvement of social and care services, which are difficult to address because of the dominance of large care providers. These providers place an emphasis, as already mentioned, on physical-structural changes and have a strong orientation towards the medical point of view. This reflects in the way people with disabilities are organised – as patients and consumers of care.

Parallel to, and at least partly because of, this lack of disability self-advocacy, several attempts to establish disability studies as a field in the Netherlands failed during the 1980s and 1990s. In addition, Dutch scholars did not contribute substantially to the emerging international field of disability studies. Only seven of 1300 articles published in the journal *Disability Studies* between the years 1986 and 2010 are of Dutch origin (Blume & Hiddinga, 2010). In the Netherlands, expertise and knowledge has been developed in some areas of disability, but there seems to be little awareness of scholarly and professional work among these areas.

In research, a recent initiative to establish disability studies as a coherent scientific field with its own body of knowledge seems to be fruitful. This program aims to contribute to the quality of life for people with disabilities and to promote an inclusive society by means of developing research and education that includes people with disabilities in all stages of development. Disability studies is an interdisciplinary science field, covering social, behavioural, human, and medical sciences. Technical and applied sciences, history, law, arts, and economics are also highly relevant. Synergy between these scientific fields and involvement of people with disabilities, professionals, and the public sector may bridge the gaps that currently exist between people, policy, practice, and science (Parmenter, 2011).

An integrated future?

The dominant conceptual models used in the past in the field of disabilities – medical model, social model, ecological model, and critical disability model (Bach, 2007; Hosking, 2008) – still guide Dutch disability-related research and practice to varying degrees today. However, they have increasingly been combined with cultural and historic concepts, and referred to as a contextual model. The contextual model, with its focus on integration, has slowly been adopted in recent years, as old structures fade away and people with disabilities are seen as one of the last groups to be included into society. Principles of inclusion and integration (the "next step" after inclusion) are now being implemented in educational, employment, and care systems.

Inclusion and inclusive policy and practice began in the lifestyle and care domains of disability, but were subsequently adopted in broader life domains such as work and education. Thus, inclusion and its "next-step" concept, integration, focus on all aspects of the lives of people with disabilities, but are also the focus of how systems and organizations operate. This shift is driven by an emphasis on human rights and the so-called citizenship paradigm. The emergence of this rights-based and inclusion-oriented paradigm can be seen in recent Dutch policy and practice and research. In policy and practice, a cross-disability NGO the Coalition for Inclusion was established in 2007 and is a serious partner for policymakers in striving for ratification of the United Nations' *Convention on the Rights of Persons with Disabilities* (www.coalitievoorinclusie.nl, 2015). At the time of publication, legal and financial implications of ratification are being studied closely by the government, which has promised ratification by 2016. Recent partnerships among self-advocates, scientists, and policymakers indicate that lessons from the past and from abroad are being taken into account.

Summary and conclusion

Looking at the trends in the conceptual and practical approaches to disability in the Netherlands, it is apparent that Dutch developments have typically mirrored developments in surrounding countries but followed them by a delay of some years or decades. For example, at the end of the eighteenth century and the beginning of the nineteenth century, Dutch liberal bourgeois began to pay attention to their own people with (sensory) disabilities, following French examples. The emphasis at this time was on support in dealing with the disability for positive reasons, namely to "uplift" people. Later on, in the nineteenth century, society leaders began to intervene for reasons that were not positive for people with disabilities: in order to ensure public order, people who might endanger this were (temporarily) segregated. This was largely the product of the Social Darwinist and eugenic discourse that dominated the most affluent countries of the world in the late nineteenth century and first half of the twentieth century, although its influence in the Netherlands was not as strong as in some neighbouring countries. The Christian view on the care for people with disabilities, as a duty and a service, prevailed until the end of the 1960s, and charity remained the predominant approach in dealing with this group. Following this, the care for people with disabilities became a right, and finances were provided for disability services by the national government.

The unintended consequence of this development was the loss of ties with local communities who had previously taken care of their "own" people with disabilities. Instead, people with disabilities became financially dependent on an anonymous government. From the 1980s onwards, when on the national political level neo-liberal influence grew, economic developments started to govern much of the financing of the care for this group.

In the meantime, at the care provision level, the attitude towards people with disabilities shifted from the medical model towards a social-contextual model, in which members of the target group got a voice and were involved in the organization of their own care, although this was on a much lower level than in the surrounding countries. Care providers often merged over the past 20 years into large organizations, which still have much power. This has led to the paradoxical situation where, physically, many people with disabilities live within "normal" society, but in a social sense they are functioning in a separate world. This is a situation that is changing now very slowly.

Acknowledgements

The authors are very grateful to Prof. Dr. A.Th. G. van Gennep and Prof. Dr. J. Vijselaar, who commented on an earlier version of this chapter.

Paul van Trigt acknowledges the support of the ERC Consolidator Grant Rethinking Disability under grant agreement number 648115.

Notes

1   In two recent dissertations a more explicit link is made with the tradition of (new) disability history: Paul van Trigt, *Blind in een gidsland. Over de bejegening van mensen met een visuele beperking in de Nederlandse verzorgingsmaatschappij* (Hilversum: Verloren, 2013) and Corrie Tijsseling, *'School, waar?' Een onderzoek naar de betekenis van het Nederlandse dovenonderwijs voor de Nederlandse dovengemeenschap, 1790–1990* (Proefschrift Universiteit Utrecht, 2014).

2   www.etymologie.nl (retrieved December 2, 2011) shows the word was first used with the meaning of deficit in the interwar period. In the US the development of handicap was also closely linked to work; see Devlieger, P. J. (2001). "Handicap" and Education in the United States of the 1930s: Discursive formations in the *New York Times, Paedagogica Historica, 37*(2), 279–289.

References

Bach, M. (2007). Changing perspectives in developmental disabilities. in I. Brown & M. Percy (Eds.), *A Comprehensive Guide to Intellectual & Developmental Disabilities* (pp. 35–43). Baltimore, MD: Paul H. Brookes Publishing.

Blume, S., & Hiddinga, A. (2010). Disability studies as an academic field: Reflections on its development. *Medische Antropologie, 22*, 225–236.

Brants, L. (2004). *Leiding moeten zij hebben. Geschiedenis van de sociaal pedagogische zorg voor mensen met een verstandelijke handicap in Nederland tussen 1900 en 1945.* Antwerpen/Apeldoorn, the Netherlands: Garant.

Brown, I., & Radford, J. P. (2015). The growth and decline of institutions for people with developmental disabilities in Ontario: 1876–2009. *Journal on Developmental Disabilities, 21*(2), 7–27.

Chappel, A. (1997). From normalisation to where? In L. Barton & M. Oliver (Eds.), *Disability Studies: Past Present and Future* (pp. 45–62). Leeds, UK: The Disability Press.

Devlieger, P. J. (2001). '"Handicap" and Education in the United States of the 1930s: Discursive Formations in the New York Times', in: *Paedagogica Historica 37*, 2 (2001) 279–289.

Dietz, H., & Ketelaars, T. (1990). *Johanna Stichting 1900–1990: Negentig jaar zorg voor kinderen met een lichamelijke handicap.* Arnhem, the Netherlands: Stichting Fonds Johanna Stichting.

Graas, D. (1996). *Zorgenkinderen op school. Geschiedenis van het speciaal onderwijs in Nederland, 1900–1950.* Leuven/Apeldoorn, the Netherlands: Garant.

Haan, I. de. (2003). *Het beginsel van leven en wasdom. De constitutie van de Nederlandse politiek in de negentiende eeuw.* Amsterdam, the Netherlands: Wereldbibliotheek.

Harinck, G. (2009). *Religion and the Dutch Welfare State.* Paper presented to the conference 'Religion, values, and the welfare state,' Münster, Germany.

Hosking, D. L. (2008). *Critical disability theory.* Paper presented at the 4th Biennial Disability Studies Conference at Lancaster University, Lancashire, UK., September 2–4, 2008.

Houwaart, E. (1991). *De Hygiënisten. Artsen, staat en volksgezondheid in Nederland 1840–1890.* Groningen, the Netherlands: Historische Uitgeverij.

Josephus Jitta, N.M. (1938). Verslag van de Staatscommissie inzake onvolwaardige arbeidskrachten, ingesteld bij Koninklijk Besluit van 12 April 1929. Gravenhage, Netherlands: Algemeene Landsdrukkerij.

Kudlick, C. (2003). Disability history: Why we need another 'Other'. *American Historical Review 108*, 763–793.

Longmore, P., & Umansky, L. (Eds.). (2001). The New Disability History: American Perspectives. New York, NY: New York University Press.

Mans, I. (1998). *Zin der Zotheid, vijf eeuwen cultuurgeschiedenis van zotten, onnozelen en zwakzinnigen.* Amsterdam, the Netherlands: Bert Bakker.

Mens, N., & Wagenaar, C. (2010). *Architectuur voor de gezondheidszorg in Nederland.* Rotterdam, the Netherlands: NAi Uitgevers.

Moes, J. (1997). *Van bedelstaf tot marktwapen. Sociale werkvoorziening in Leiden na 1795.* Leiden, the Netherlands: Dirk van Eek–stichting.

Nirje, B. (1969). The normalization principle. In *Changing Patterns in Residential Services for the Mentally Retarded* (pp. 179–196). Washington, DC: President's Committee on Mental Retardation.

Oosterhuis, H., & Gijswijt-Hofstra, M. (2008). *Verward van geest en ander ongerief: Psychiatrie en geestelijke gezondheidszorg in Nederland 1870–2005.* Houten, the Netherlands: Bohn Stafleu van Loghum.

Parmenter, T. (2011). The study of intellectual disability. in H. Reinders (Ed.), *Authenticity and Community* (pp. 11–31). Antwerpen/Apeldoorn, the Netherlands: Garant.

Rietveld-van Wingerden, M., & Tijsseling, C. (2010). *Ontplooiing door communicatie: Geschiedenis van het onderwijs aan doven en slechthorenden in Nederland.* Antwerpen/Apeldoorn, the Netherlands: Garant.

Stuurman, S. (1983) *Verzuiling, kapitalisme en patriarchaat.* Nijmegen, the Netherlands: SUN.

Terug naar de Bossen (2012, September 14). Retrieved from: www.terugnaardebossen.nl

Van Berlo, W., De Haas, S., Van Oosten, N., Van Dijk, L., Brants, L., Tonnon, S., & Storms, O. (2011). *Beperkt weerbaar. Een onderzoek naar seksueel geweld bij mensen met een lichamelijke, zintuiglijke of verstandelijke beperking.* Utrecht, the Netherlands: Rutgers WPF/Movisie.

Van der Grinten, T. (1987). *De vorming van de ambulante geestelijke gezondheidszorg, een historisch beleidsonderzoek.* Baarn, the Netherlands: Ambo.

Van Gennep, A. (2007). *Waardig leven met beperkingen.* Antwerpen-Apeldoorn, the Netherlands: Garant.

Van Kersbergen, K. (2009). Religion and the welfare state in the Netherlands. In K. van Kersbergen & P. Manow (Eds.), *Religion, Class Coalitions and welfare States* (pp. 119–145). New York, NY: Cambridge University Press.

Van Rooden, P. (2007). Dutch concepts to express religious difference, 1572–2002. In L. Hölscher (Ed.), *Baupläne der sichtbaren Kirche. Sprachliche Konzepte religiöser Vergemeinschaftung in Europa* (pp. 136–150). Göttingen, Germany: Wallstein Verlag.

Van Trigt, P. (2013). *Blind in een gidsland. Over de bejegening van mensen met een visuele beperking in de Nederlandse verzorgingsmaatschappij.* Hilversum, the Netherlands: Verloren.

Van Wijnen, A. (2014). Het Apeldoornse Bos. De moord op joodse verstandelijk gehandicapten. in A. Van Gennep, J. Van der Lans, M. Van der Linde, T. Post, & P. Van Trigt (Eds.), *Canon sociaal werk* (pp. 38–40). Amsterdam, the Netherlands: Vereniging Canon Sociaal Werk.

Vos, J. (2008). *Tastend door de tijd: Twee eeuwen onderwijs en zorg voor slechtziende en blinde mensen.* Amsterdam, the Netherlands: Boom.

Vijselaar, J. (2010). *Het gesticht: Enkele reis of retour?* Amsterdam, the Netherlands: Boom.

VNG. Vereniging van Nederlandse Gemeenten (2015, December 28). De WSW in beweging. Retrieved from: www.canonsociaalwerk.eu/1920_werkvoorziening/wsw%20in%20beweging%20www.pdf.

Weijers, I., Tonkens, E., & Mans, I. (1998). Verstandelijk handicap en burgerschap. Een historiografische schets. *Comenius, 18*, 310–324.

10

A JOURNEY OF CHANGE – HISTORY OF DISABILITY IN HONG KONG 1841–2014

Karen K.H. Ngai, Simon W.K. Wu and Joanna L.P. Chung

Setting the scene

Hong Kong is a unique place in the world. It has encountered enormous economic, social, and cultural changes in the past one-and-a-half centuries. From a relatively unpopulated territory at the beginning of the nineteenth century, Hong Kong has grown into one of the most important international financial centres in the world. Hong Kong was only a small fishing village when it came under British colonial rule in 1841, but it underwent a rapid and successful period of industrialization from the 1960s that captured much attention from economists and sociologists in the 1980s and 1990s. Effective on July 1, 1997, the sovereignty of Hong Kong was returned to the People's Republic of China (PRC), in accordance with the "one country, two systems" principle entrenched in the 1984 Sino-British Joint Declaration signed between the United Kingdom and the PRC. Regarding its population, it grew from 7,450 in 1841 (Ng, 1984) to 7.23 million in 2014 (Census and Statistics Department, 2014). With a total area of 1,092 square kilometres, Hong Kong has become one of the world's most densely populated places.

Disability issues also evolved during this period of time in Hong Kong. Like other social issues, this evolution is closely related to the local context, although it is sometimes influenced by the international scene. This chapter seeks to identify and discuss some of the significant events/incidents related to disability in Hong Kong from 1841 to 2014.

Traditional views of disability

Hong Kong is basically a Chinese society. According to the latest Census Report, 93.6% of the population is of Chinese ethnicity (Census and Statistics Department, 2012, p. 25). Thus, before providing an account of the history of disabilities in Hong Kong, it is important to identify the significant Chinese traditional values that may have influenced thinking about disability in Hong Kong. As it is unrealistic to aim at an exhaustive description, a few highlights and their implications are described.

It is generally considered that three major systems of thought – Confucianism, Buddhism, and Taoism – contributed to traditional Chinese values and the traditional way of life of Chinese people.

Confucianism was founded by Confucius (551–479 B.C.). Confucian philosophy emphasizes harmony in society, which can be materialized only through a series of structured hierarchical relationships where senior members are always in positions of power with respect to their juniors. Family is an essential unit in society. In *Yijing*, one of the "Five Classics" that are the basic texts of Confucianism, it is written, "The families that accumulate goodness will have good fortune; the families that accumulate bad things will have misfortune" (Tang, 1999, p. 164). This implies that Chinese people believe in some kind of retribution.

Chinese people are taught that they should behave themselves for the present life; otherwise, they will be punished in their coming life. In the same vein, Chinese people believe that those who are disabled are consequences of evil acts they performed in a previous life. Alternatively, parents of children with disability think that they must have done something very wrong in their previous life such that they are being punished by having a child with a disability. This means that Chinese people regard it as personal fate to have an impairment. Even worse, it relates to the fate of other family members.

Confucianism also stresses perfection. Chinese people do not feel comfortable having a child with disability because it brings disgrace to the family. They feel very shameful about disclosing the existence of a disabled member in their family. The issue of "face," which is also highly valued by Chinese people, contributes to feelings of shame (Bond, 1986). Besides, the value of family cohesiveness is significant, such that problems within the family need to be solved internally. There is a popular saying in Chinese culture: "Family's dirt should not be spread." So if there is a member with disability in a family, he or she should be kept at home rather than be taken out to the public world. Some families, with the intention to cover up the truth forever, simply abandon the child at a very early age. Some even do so when the child has grown up. In fact, most abandoned children in Chinese society are either disabled or girls, or both, since ancient China was absolutely a patriarchal society where females were always treated unequally.

Buddhism began in India 2,500 years ago. Buddhism is based on the teachings of an Indian prince named Siddharta Gautama, who lived around 500 B.C. Buddhists believe in the doctrine of karma. That is, each person is responsible for his/her behaviour. When one performs good deeds, he or she will earn positive consequences. Conversely, bad deeds will lead to negative results. Relating this to disability, having an impairment is perceived as the destiny or a punishment for one's wrongdoings in the past. Such a line of thinking is similar to the views in Confucianism. However, it seems to be more rational, in the sense that one has to be responsible for one's misdeeds, but not those of others.

Taoism, also known as Daoism, arose about the same time as Confucianism. Taoism is a philosophical, ethical, or religious tradition that has had a profound influence on Chinese culture. The belief systems of Confucianism and Taoism are viewed as complementary. While Confucianism focuses on the social and moral side of life, Taoism is more concerned with the individual spiritual life.

Taoists believe in harmony between humans and nature. Yin and yang is the best-known concept of Taoism. It describes how opposite or contrary forces are actually complementary, interconnected, and interdependent in the natural world. In Taoism, disability results from "a disharmonious fusion of nature and man" (Lam et al., 2006, p. 274). The presence of a person with disability implies an imbalance of yin and yang, a problem that needs to be fixed. For Taoists, harmony is the goal, and the practical way to achieve it is to maintain the balance of yin and yang. In ancient China, people encountering health problems visited temples or Taoist priest houses to worship or perform rituals for treatment.

To sum up, the traditional Chinese concept of disability is rather negative, as it is associated with shame and guilt. Such stigma attached to disability may cause the person with disability and/or the family to fear exposure to criticism and disgrace. Unless such thinking is altered and changed, it may create barriers for people with disabilities to lead healthy and independent lives. Luckily, as time goes by, real change has become evident.

Paradigm shift: The journey of change

In Thomas Kuhn's (1962) influential book, *The Structure of Scientific Revolutions*, the term "paradigm shift" was first used. Initially, the term referred to revolutionary science and denoted a change in the basic assumptions, or paradigms, within the ruling theory of science. Since the 1960s, the term has been used in non-scientific contexts to describe a profound change in a fundamental model or perception of constructs, issues, or events. This term is also considered relevant in describing the disability-related changes that unfolded in Hong Kong in the past one-and-a-half centuries. Shifts have been evident in various areas of disability, and are described in the major subsequent sections of this chapter: *mindset of government, terminology, roles of stakeholders, legislation, service and practice*, and *the Welfare Sector Subvention Reform*. All these changes have, in fact, occurred as a result of the combined impacts of international trends and forces from the local civil society.

Change of mindset of Government: From non-development to development of disability policy

Significant disability-related events: 1841 to 1976

Following its defeat in the First Opium War, China was forced to cede Hong Kong to Great Britain in 1841. Sir Henry Pottinger became the first Governor of Hong Kong in August 1841. As noted in various sources (e.g., Hodge, 1981; Yee, 1989), from the early years of British rule to the end of the Second World War, the British Government had to devote much effort in maintaining law and order in the territory. By that time, crime was prevalent and there were threats of piracy from the sea. Services for people with disabilities were delivered mainly by local missionaries. For example, the first home for people with visual impairments was built in 1863 (Chow, 1980) and a temporary lunatic asylum was established in 1875 (Fan, 1994). During this time, the Government seemed to focus more on mental (psychiatric) problems; for example, in 1885 a small wing of the Government Central Hospital was designated to accommodate mental patients (Lo, 1981). Another psychiatric hospital, the Victoria Hospital, was built in 1891 (Foo, 1981). During that period of time, only acute treatment and temporary custodial care were offered to mentally disturbed patients. Once their condition became stable, these patients were then sent to the Fong Chuen Mental Hospital in Canton, China, and the Hong Kong Government paid for all the expenses incurred by these patients annually (Liu, 1990).

In 1935, the first school for people with hearing impairment was established by local missionaries (Hong Kong Government, 1977). A camp to provide temporary shelter and relief for people with disabilities was set up in 1938 (Hong Kong Government, 1977). Medical social service was introduced in 1939 (Hong Kong Government, 1977). From December 1941 to August 1945, when Hong Kong was under Japanese occupation, it was said to have entered into a dark era of "3 years and 8 months," during which no significant developments regarding disability or services occurred.

In the 20 years from 1946 to 1966, the development of Hong Kong was greatly influenced by disastrous events in the PRC. Following a series of civil wars between the Communist Party and the Nationalist Party that led to the establishment of the PRC on 1 October, 1949, there were the Korean War (1950–53), the Great Leap Forward (1958–1961), and a severe drought and a serious famine (1958–1962). Since its establishment, the PRC entered a period of isolation from the international arena. In those years, not surprisingly, Hong Kong became a shelter for PRC refugees, most notably from 1966 when the Cultural Revolution began. Unexpectedly, Hong Kong took advantage of this influx of refugees, entrepreneurs, and capital from the PRC, which helped accelerate its industrialization from this time onward.

In the post–Second World War period, there were modest developments in services in relation to people with disabilities, yet most were shouldered by voluntary agencies (termed as non-governmental organizations (NGO) in the early 1990s, following the international trend). The Hong Kong Council of Social Service (HKCSS), a federation of non-governmental social service agencies of Hong Kong, was established in 1947 with the aim to plan and coordinate large-scale post-war relief work and social welfare, while the colonial Government set up the Social Welfare Office (SWO) in the same year to tackle welfare issues in the territory. Counselling services for people with disabilities only commenced 7 years after the establishment of the SWO in 1954 (Hong Kong Government, 1977). The SWO was renamed the Social Welfare Department (SWD) in 1958. The Mental Health Association of Hong Kong, with the primary objective of promoting and educating the general public on mental health, came into existence in 1952 in the form of a Mental Health Study Group. In 1954, the Study Group was formally registered as an NGO called the Mental Health Association of Hong Kong.

In 1955, simple handwork training was provided for people with intellectual disabilities (Hong Kong Government, 1977). The Hong Kong Society for the Blind, which mainly supported people with visual impairments, was established as an NGO in 1956. In 1958, the Government initiated voluntary registration of people with intellectual disabilities (Hong Kong Government, 1977). The Hong Kong Society for Rehabilitation (HKSR) was founded in 1959 under the strong leadership of the late Professor Sir Harry Fang. The HKSR set as its mission to provide services to enhance the quality of life of people with disabilities, and to advocate for their equal opportunities in the social, civil, and economic arenas in building a caring and equal society.

In 1960, the Hong Kong Government released the Hilliard's Report (Hilliard, 1960), according to which there was to be a division of labour with regard to service provision for people with intellectual disabilities: people with an IQ of below 25 were to be taken care of by the Medical and Health Department (later split into two entities: the Hospital Authority and the Department of Health Services); people with an IQ from 25 to 50 were to be looked after by the SWD; and those with an IQ of 51 to 70 were to be served by the Education Department. Besides this, a new section was established in the Education Department to deal with the education of people with intellectual disabilities in 1960, and in-service training for teachers of handicapped children began in 1961 (Hong Kong Government, 1977).

In 1960, the Mental Hospital Ordinance was also enacted. It was the first ordinance for the certification, detention, and treatment of people with mental problems in Hong Kong (Hong Kong Government, 1972). The Castle Peak Hospital was opened in 1961 with a capacity of 1,000 beds. This hospital was built to replace the Victoria Mental Hospital (Lo, 1981).

The Medical Rehabilitation Centre, the first in-patient medical rehabilitation centre in Hong Kong, was opened on 18 September 1962, and was subsequently renamed the Margaret Trench Medical Rehabilitation Centre (MTMRC) in 1971. The Hong Kong Society for the Blind began operating a factory and a centre for people with visual impairment. The factory was the first of its kind in Asia and was officially opened in March 1963. Two other prominent organizations were also formed in the same year. The Heep Hong Society was founded by a group of women focusing on the lack of postoperative care for children recovering from poliomyelitis. The Hong Kong Association for the Spastic Children was established by Professor Field and other pioneers. Its aim was to provide tailor-made training and caring services for children with neurological impairment. It was renamed as the Spastics Association of Hong Kong in 1967.

Most significantly, the first self-help organization for people with visual impairment, the Hong Kong Association of the Blind, which is now the Hong Kong Blind Union, was established in 1964. In the same year, organizations for people with disabilities and interested individuals formed the Joint Council for the Physically and Mentally Disabled – Hong Kong (the Joint Council, later renamed the Hong Kong Joint Council for People with Disabilities). In 1965, the Joint Council was incorporated into the Hong Kong Council of Social Service (HKCSS) and was also called the Rehabilitation Division of the HKCSS. The Joint Council was a strong advocate for a comprehensive development of a caring, rather than charitable, approach to handling disability issues.

The first male halfway house, a kind of transitional accommodation for discharged mental patients, Irene House, was started by the Mental Health Association of Hong Kong in a public housing estate in 1967. The Hong Kong Society for the Deaf was founded in 1968, positioned as a non-profit organization with the aim of promoting the well-being and equalization of opportunities for people with hearing impairments. In the same year, the New Life Farm was initiated by the New Life Psychiatric Rehabilitation Association as the first industrial rehabilitation farm in Hong Kong (New Life Psychiatric Rehabilitation Association, 1990). The Hong Kong Federation of Handicapped Youth, a self-help organization founded in 1970 by a group of young people with physical disabilities, operated under the mission of promoting equal rights of people with disabilities.

The Kowloon Hospital Psychiatric Unit was opened in 1971 as the first psychiatric unit providing comprehensive psychiatric services, with a day hospital, and outpatient and inpatient sections within a general hospital setting (Lo, 1981). Later, the Siu Lam Psychiatric Centre, a treatment and retention centre for 200 offenders with mental problems, was established in 1972 (Lo, 1981). The first sheltered workshop, the Kowloon Sheltered Workshop, and the first halfway house for female survivors of mental problems were opened by the New Life Psychiatric Rehabilitation Association in 1972 (New Life Psychiatric Rehabilitation Association, 1990).

167

The idea of PHAB ("Physically Handicapped and Able-Bodied") originated in the United Kingdom in the 1950s. The PHAB concept, "Opportunity Not Pity," was first introduced to Hong Kong in the early 1970s by its founder, Mary Robinson. A Working Group was subsequently formed by the HKCSS, which eventually led to the inception of the Hong Kong PHAB Association in October 1972, targeting as its main aim the overall coordination and promotion of PHAB work in the community.

The Hong Kong Sports Association for the Physically Disabled (now the Hong Kong Paralympic Committee & Sports Association for the Physically Disabled) was established in 1972 under the leadership of the late Professor Sir Harry Fang and a group of rehabilitation enthusiasts. The Association planned, organized, developed, and promoted sports for people with physical disabilities. This is the only organization in Hong Kong that has gained recognition from the International Paralympic Committee (IPC) and authorization to select Hong Kong Team members to participate in the Paralympic Games, World and Regional Games, and Championships sanctioned by the IPC.

Two other important developments also occurred in the 1970s. In 1973, the Disability Allowance scheme, similar to the basic single individual entitlement in Public Assistance payment, was implemented (Hong Kong Government, 1977). The Hong Kong Association of the Deaf, the first self-help organization of people with hearing impairment, was set up in 1976.

The above brief overview of disability-related developments from 1841 to 1976 is provided to illustrate that, during this long period, a large share of disability services were operated by NGOs, and the Government played only a small part, confined mostly to some governance issues. Some people with disabilities were aware of the significance of self-help to the extent that they started to form their own organizations. However, disability work that developed in this period seemed to be spontaneous and free-flowing, without any comprehensive planning. In response to this, the Government started to take the lead for policy formulation and service planning for people with disabilities in 1976.

The first White Paper on rehabilitation

Following persistent advocacy for more than a decade by the Joint Council for a comprehensive rehabilitation service plan, the Government eventually issued the first Green Paper on Rehabilitation in 1976. It was a practice of the British Government at that time that a Green Paper was issued with some policy proposals, aimed at calling for the public's comments and suggestions, followed by the publication of a White Paper that incorporated the public's ideas.

In July 1976, a Program Plan for Rehabilitation Services was prepared by an inter-departmental Working Group of the Hong Kong Government. The Plan covered the 10-year period from 1975 and was prepared in consultation with Government departments providing rehabilitation services and with the Joint Council. A summary of the main findings and recommendations contained in the Plan were tabled in the Legislative Council on 13 October 1976, as a Green Paper entitled "The Further Development of Rehabilitation Services in Hong Kong." (Hong Kong Government, 1976)

Incorporating the comments and suggestions made by the concerned parties and the public, the Government issued the first White Paper on Rehabilitation, "Integrating the Disabled into the Community: A United Effort," in October 1977.

This White Paper gave a cursory account of the development of rehabilitation services from 1863 to the 1970s. Moreover, it expressly admitted that

> much of the burden of rehabilitation during this remarkable period of development has been carried by voluntary agencies ... The role played by the voluntary organizations in this field needs to be stressed, for it is their devotion and commitment which were largely responsible for the development and expansion of many of the services available to the disabled. (Hong Kong Government, 1977, p. 4)

It further stated that the overall policy objective was

> [t]o provide such comprehensive rehabilitation services as are necessary to enable disabled persons to develop their physical, mental and social capabilities to the fullest extent which their disabilities permit. (p. 6)

To achieve this objective, it proposed to establish a Rehabilitation Development Co-ordinating Committee (later renamed the Rehabilitation Advisory Committee) with the following terms of reference:

- To advise on the development and phased implementation of rehabilitation services in Hong Kong;
- To advise on the principles of subvention applicable to such services;
- To co-ordinate rehabilitation services in Government departments and voluntary organizations and to ensure that available resources are put to the best use;
- To advise on the respective roles of Government, voluntary organizations and other bodies providing rehabilitation services; and
- To make recommendations on the training of rehabilitation workers. (Hong Kong Government, 1977, p. 6)

The White Paper also called for the setting up of a Central Registry for the Disabled (presently named the Central Registry for Rehabilitation) in 1978–1979. The statistical information kept by the Registry was to be used for long-term projections of demand and supply of services.

The White Paper clearly listed the specific objectives for the various rehabilitation services and targets for future development in the coming decade, including prevention and early diagnosis, education and training, medical treatment and rehabilitation services, as well as social rehabilitation services.

The White Paper seemed to have signalled the Government's serious commitment to addressing disability issues, that is, moving from inaction to action in relation to formulating disability policy and services. But, why did the Government take action at that point in time? A considerable amount of important disability work had been carried out by the voluntary organizations, but this was a patchwork system of services that left obvious gaps. This is recognized in the White Paper:

> [T]he severely disabled ..., who are regarded as being the least able to support themselves .... However, there are gaps in them *(services for people*

with disabilities). Demand has increased and is increasing, both because of the growth in the size of the population and because many disabled persons, who would in the past have been cared for by their families, are prepared to seek the professional help, advice and services provided by Government and voluntary agencies. (Hong Kong Government, 1977, p. 5)

Obviously, the Government realized that a great deal of work had been done by the NGOs, but that it was time for a more co-ordinated effort. For this reason, the Government emphasized setting up a body to co-ordinate all disability services. In addition, the White Paper mentioned that people with disabilities were the group who were least able to support themselves, and that the growing demand for professional help was becoming apparent as help from families was not as effective as had previously been the case. Numerous studies (Jones, 1990; Miners, 1975; Schenk, 2008) pointed out that in the 1970s, Hong Kong's economy was flourishing with its influx of refugees, with their capital and skills, from the PRC during and after the Cultural Revolution. The market needed a large number of workers for development of labour-intensive industries such as textiles, electronics, toys manufacturing, and others. As more and more women who had previously taken up the caring roles at home to look after the elderly and people with disabilities joined the labour market, the Government assumed more responsibility with a view to releasing caregivers for economic growth.

It is also worth mentioning that during the administration of Governor MacLehose from 1971 to 1982, welfare services were greatly expanded, particularly those related to people with disabilities, elderly people, and troubled families (Hong Kong Government, 1974). Castells et al. (1990) regarded the 1966–1967 riots in Hong Kong, which "symbolized the emergence of a new local generation" (Matthews, Ma, & Lui, 2008, p. 32), as central to MacLehose's thinking behind such expansion. It was their hypothesis that MacLehose identified social reform as one of the critical elements to fulfilling his fundamental political assignment to pacify and stabilize the colony after the 1966–1967 riots.

Notwithstanding the intention behind it, the issuance of the first White Paper on Rehabilitation in 1977 at that time was considered a major step forward. In fact, it laid the foundation for future development of policy and services for people with disabilities in Hong Kong. Subsequently, development of services for people with disabilities in Hong Kong continued to gain momentum. The Government and the disability sector began conducting regular reviews of the Rehabilitation Program Plan with a view to addressing the needs of people with disabilities in a timely manner.

The second White Paper on rehabilitation

It was not until 1995 that the Hong Kong Government issued the second White Paper on Rehabilitation. But, since the publication of the first White Paper, various disability issues had called for the public's attention.

In 1978, the Hong Kong Society for Rehabilitation started to run Rehabus to provide a fully accessible transportation service for people with disabilities, with the objective of improving their mobility and thus promoting their equal opportunities in employment, education, training, and social participation. The Hong Kong Sports Association for the Mentally Handicapped, with an overall objective to develop the potentials of people with intellectual disabilities through promotion of sports activities, was also founded the same year.

In the mid-1980s, various major services for people with disabilities experienced rapid development, both in terms of quality and quantity: preschool training, day activity centres, hostels for people with intellectual disabilities, halfway houses for survivors of mental problems, and vocational services. The Selective Placement Division of the Labour Department, with the aim of helping people with disabilities enter open employment, came into operation in 1980. In the following year, the Office of the Commissioner for Rehabilitation was set up under the Health and Welfare Branch (now the Labour and Welfare Bureau) to coordinate policy formulation and services provision for people with disabilities. A Report of the Working Party on Pre-school Care, Education and Training of Disabled Children was released in 1984. In 1985, mandatory requirements for barrier-free access for persons with disabilities were first imposed on various kinds of buildings under the Buildings Ordinance (Cap. 123). Supported employment was introduced in 1988.

The 1990s marked a milestone decade in the promotion of equal opportunities and full participation for people with disabilities in Hong Kong. In 1995, the Disability Discrimination Ordinance (Cap. 487) was enacted to ensure equal opportunities for people with disabilities in areas such as employment, access to education, housing, and daily living in the community. In the same year, the Government developed, from the Green Paper issued in 1992, the second White Paper on Rehabilitation titled "Equal Opportunities and Full Participation: A Better Tomorrow for All." In this second White Paper, the Government reiterated its commitment to sustainable development of rehabilitation services.

The overall policy objective of the 1995 White Paper, which has been followed up to the present time, is to ensure that persons with disabilities can fully participate and enjoy equal opportunities in their personal and social development through a range of measures in the following areas:

a) Preventing disabilities
b) Helping persons with disabilities develop their physical, mental and social capabilities
c) Creating a barrier-free physical and social environment (Hong Kong Government, 1995)

Compared to the first White Paper, which had been published nearly 20 years earlier, the second White Paper carried significant changes to various aspects of disability. Some of the most important of these are discussed in the following sections.

Change in terminology

Politics of language

Terminology is of crucial importance, since language is central to our understanding of the world. We use words to ascribe meanings to situations and objects. As Patton (1990) contended, "Language is a way of organizing the world" (p. 227). Spradley (1979) maintained that language functions "not only a means of communication, it also functions to create and express cultural reality" (p. 20). More importantly, when human beings are actively involved in the creation of meanings, they also produce outcomes that they neither intended nor anticipated (Giddens, 1986). Terminology in disability is a true reflection of this.

The traditional Chinese term for disability is *canfei*, which means both *handicap* and *useless*. Later, it is modified as *canji*, that refers to *handicap* and *illness*. Similarly, in the earlier years of Hong Kong, people with disabilities were addressed in a humiliating way. For example, people with intellectual disabilities were called "the idiots," "the mentally retarded," and people with mental problems were called "the crazy people," "the insane" or "the mentally ill." In fact, some of these terms like "the mentally retarded" and "the mentally ill" were also used in some old documents, including the Green Papers and White Papers.

However, there has been a growing realization that people's understanding of social issues such as disability can be transformed through the use of language. The fact that definition and terminology are regarded as important – and as a tool that can be used for specific purposes – arises from what is termed the politics of language. Here, a change in terminology is viewed as an attempt to alter social attitudes. Terminology used for groups of people about whom there are negative connotations and who are devalued in society results in the terms themselves carrying negative connotations. For this reason, definitions and terminology relating to disadvantaged groups are constantly challenged and changing.

Similarly, the disabled people's movement has shown that definition and terminology play a significant role in their oppressed status. Terms such as "cripple" and "spastic" are offensive when used to refer to an individual. Other terms that depersonalize and objectify the disability community are also regarded as unacceptable. Examples include "the deaf," "the blind," or "the mentally retarded."

Thus, the changes to terminology relating to disability in Hong Kong are of considerable significance. Ever since the second Green Paper on Rehabilitation was issued in 1992, all official documents have adopted the "people first" principle. Hence, terms like "people with a disability," "persons with disabilities," or "people with disabilities" are always used. With regard to the Chinese translation, frequent changes have also been adopted. The result is that all terms with negative meanings or humiliating connotations have been banned, as they have been deemed to contravene the Disability Discrimination Ordinance.

Along the same vein, some NGOs have also changed their agency names. The Hong Kong Association for the Mentally Handicapped was renamed the Hong Chi Association, which means "an organization helping the people with intellectual disabilities." The Society of Homes for the Handicapped, established in August 1977, was renamed the Fu Hong Society in January, 2001. In Chinese, "Fu" refers to support or assistance, whereas "Hong" implies health.

Even the term "rehabilitation," commonly used to refer to disability issues, is disputed, as it denotes the concept of "help to recover." Some impairments experienced by people with disabilities are permanent and cannot be "recovered" from.

The ICIDH and ICF

The International Classification of Impairment, Disability and Handicap (ICIDH) was published in 1980. It used a threefold typology: *impairment, disability*, and *handicap*.

According to its classification system, *impairment* means "any loss or abnormality of psychological, physiological, or anatomical structure or function," whereas *disability* means "any restriction or lack (resulting from an impairment) of ability to perform an activity in the manner or within the range considered normal for a human being." Handicap denotes "a disadvantage for a given individual, resulting from an impairment or disability, that limits or prevents the fulfilment of a role that is normal (depending on age, sex and social and cultural factors) for an individual" (Wood, 1980, p. 29). The first White Paper on Rehabilitation issued in 1977 also adopted this ICIDH classification.

By the end of the twentieth century, the World Health Organization (WHO) embarked on a revision of the entire scheme of ICIDH (WHO, 1998). Eventually a classification of health and health-related domains, termed the International Classification of Functioning, Disability and Health (ICF), the WHO framework for measuring health and disability at both individual and population levels, was proposed. The ICF encompasses a list of environmental factors in recognition of the fact that the functioning and disability of an individual necessarily arise in a context. Officially endorsed in May 2001 as the international standard of describing and measuring health and disability, the ICF looked beyond a purely medical or biological conceptualization of dysfunction, and instead took into account the other critical aspects of disability, such as environment and other contextual factors. It further considered the impact of these factors on the functioning of an individual or a population. What it did not do was take into account, to any substantial degree, views on societal responsibility as reflected in the emerging literatures on the Social Model and the Critical Disability Model (Bach, 2007; Oliver, 1990).

In the latest Hong Kong Rehabilitation Program Plan Review (Hong Kong Government, 2007), the Working Group for the Review also explored the concepts of the ICF. The Group agreed that the ICF would likely be an international trend for the interpretation of disabilities. Nonetheless, considering that its application might have major impacts on the existing mechanism, the Group recommended that the Government make reference to other countries and explore the feasibility of its application to Hong Kong (Hong Kong Government, 2007). Recently, there have been heated discussions over implementing the ICF framework in the formulation of policy and planning of services for people with disabilities in Hong Kong. Local academics and self-help organizations for people with disabilities are keen on advocating the use of the ICF in Hong Kong.

Categories of disabilities

Categories or classification of disabilities evolve over the passage of time. This is significant, as what we deem to be legitimate categories and classifications of disability will determine who is eligible to receive the services provided by Government or NGOs. The first White Paper on Rehabilitation issued in October 1977 did not include a section specifying any group of people to be considered as "people with disabilities." However, in the first paragraph of the Foreword, it states that

> the services recommended in the Plan [the Programme Plan which is the blueprint of the White Paper] were intended to cater for the needs of the deaf (and partially hearing), the blind (and the partially sighted), the mentally ill,

the mentally retarded, slow learning and maladjusted children, the physically disabled and those with multiple disabilities.

Hence, it implied that the service users were people identified with the above six categories of disabilities and those with multiple disabilities.

The second White Paper on Rehabilitation, published in 1995, mentioned the review of the categories of disability and the adoption of nine categories (Hong Kong Government, 1995, pp. 9–10):

- Hearing impairment
- Autism
- Mental handicap
- Maladjustment
- Physical handicap
- Visual impairment
- Mental illness
- Visceral disability
- Speech impairment

The inclusion of the category visceral disability on this list is worth mentioning. The Government was cognizant of its duty to meet the changing needs and aspirations of this group of people. According to the White Paper, visceral disability is "a disability resulting from a disease or its treatment, its nature not being limited to locomotor functions, and which constitutes a disadvantage or restriction in one or more aspects of daily living activities, including work" (Hong Kong Government, 1995, p. 10). The term "visceral disability" is interchangeably used with "chronic illness," a term that is more popular in the disability sector in Hong Kong.

Thereafter, slight changes were made to the categories in other official documents. In the recent Rehabilitation Programme Plan Review (Hong Kong Government, 2007), which is the most updated Government document describing the policy and services for people with disabilities, further revisions were made with regard to categories of disability. Compared with the above list, the category of maladjustment no longer existed, whereas two new categories, namely Attention Deficit/Hyperactivity Disorder and Specific Learning Difficulties, were now included. Such a change reflects the demands from the community and the Government's willingness to respond to their needs.

Shift in roles of stakeholders

From service recipients to customers and persons-in-charge

Traditionally, services for people with disabilities in Hong Kong were mostly run by non-governmental organizations and managed by professionals. Such was the case, for example, with the Hong Kong Society for the Blind, Hong Kong Association for the Deaf, Hong Kong PHAB Association, the Mental Health Association of Hong Kong, and others. Hence these organizations and the professionals who worked in them were the service providers, and people with disabilities were the service recipients. As service recipients, they were put into passive, powerless, and dependent positions. Take the existing home help service as an example for the purpose of illustration. Since the home help service was subvented by the Government, people with disabilities wanting to use the service would have to apply for it. Then helping professionals who had been vested with the authority would assess and determine whether or not a particular applicant, that is, the person with a disability, satisfied the eligibility criteria. When they succeeded in getting the service, a home helper would be assigned to them without their involvement whatsoever in the service management. That is, all matters concerning the recruitment, appraisal, and supervision of the home helper were beyond their control. Furthermore, service recipients had no say in the entire process. All that they could do is to lodge a complaint if they found anything wrong. Then the professionals would conduct an investigation to see if the complaint was genuine. Those who were the end users of the service, people with disabilities, under such circumstances, were placed in a totally passive position. To them, the service seemed more like a charity than a kind of entitlement or right, which further reinforced the dependent and inferior position of people with disabilities in society.

The wave of self-help organizations

As time went by, more and more people with disabilities felt uncomfortable and questioned such assigned roles. As a result, they joined hands and formed their own organizations. In Hong Kong, the first organization run and managed by people with disabilities, the Hong Kong Society of the Blind, then renamed as the Hong Kong Blind Union, was founded in 1964. People with disabilities in the early days were not as active as they are at the present time. It was not until the 1970s that self-help organizations for people with disabilities started to bloom in Hong Kong. During the 1980s and 1990s, more and more organizations of people with chronic illnesses were formed. According to Mok's study (2001), there are currently more than 200 self-help organizations in Hong Kong, and the majority of them are organizations of people with disabilities.

What is a self-help group or organization? A self-help organization refers to

a group of individuals with the common goal of furthering their own welfare and interests. Among the members, a sense of group solidarity will be developed through experience sharing and exchanges of information to address their common problems. (Hong Kong Government, 2007, p. 60)

Rappaport (1993) noted that self-help groups can promote shared experience, enhance emotional support and social learning, and help constitute a social identity. Along the same vein, Yalom (1995) maintained that self-help groups provide a unique opportunity for growth, social experimentation, and change.

The Hong Kong Stoma Association, registered as a non-profit organization in 1979, was the first patients' self-help organization found in Hong Kong. It was set up by and for ostomates to advocate mutual support and information sharing. Afterwards many other patients' self-help organizations were formed. Some examples include the Hong Kong Rheumatoid Arthritis Association, founded in 1989 by people with rheumatoid arthritis; the Regeneration Society, set up in 1991 by people with systemic lupus erythematosus; the New Horizon Club of Hong Kong, founded in 1993 as a self-help organization of cancer patients; the Retina Hong Kong (formerly known as Hong Kong Retinitis Pigmentosa Society), set up in 1995 by people with retinitis pigmentosa; and the Care for Your Heart, formed in the same year by people with heart diseases.

The rapid growth of self-help organizations of people with chronic illness injected much strength into the disability field in Hong Kong. Before the HKSR launched the two Community Rehabilitation Networks (CRNs) for people with chronic illness on Hong Kong Island and Kowloon in January 1994, there had already existed a number of self-help groups of people with chronic illness (some of which are mentioned above). With the investment of resources, the existing groups were helped to grow much stronger and faster, while more and more new groups emerged.

Seventeen self-help organizations of people with chronic illness joined together to form the Alliance of Patients' Mutual Help Organizations (APMHO) in February 1993. At present, the number of self-help organizations under the APMHO has reached 43, with total membership exceeding 40,000 persons. These groups had been very active in mobilizing public support for the inclusion of people with chronic illness into the second White Paper on Rehabilitation. Their goal was finally achieved, with the recognition of the category termed visceral disability. Besides, the Alliance worked closely with the media to promote both public awareness of the needs of people with chronic illness and health consciousness for all. To gain the attention of the public, they had been very keen on conducting or initiating research on the needs and experiences of people with chronic illness (APMHO, 1996; Community Rehabilitation Network, 1994; Wong, 1993).

In the area of intellectual disability, self-help organizations have likewise been formed. The Society for the Welfare of Autistic Persons, founded in 1982, focuses on the welfare of people with autism; the Parents' Association of Pre-school Handicapped Children was established in 1986 to advocate for the rights of preschool children with disabilities; and the Hong Kong Down Syndrome Association started in 1987 as a self-assistance organization for parents, with the objective of offering emotional and information support to families with members with Down syndrome.

In addition, parents' associations have also been set up under the organizations for people of the intellectual disabilities. In the late 1980s, the Parents' Association of People with of the Mentally Handicapped declared independence from its mother organization, the Hong Kong Association for the Mentally Handicapped (later known as the Hong Chi Association), to form the Hong Kong Joint Council of Parents of the Mentally Handicapped in 1987. Since then, it has played a prominent role in advocating for the rights of people with intellectual disabilities. The founding Chairman, the late William Cheung, devoted his entire life to striving for equal rights for people with intellectual disabilities in the territory, gaining much respect and support from other parents from similar backgrounds. His influence is not limited to Hong Kong, but has extended to other Chinese communities, such as Taiwan and the PRC. The Macau Association of Parents of the Mentally Handicapped was said to have been formed with his encouragement and guidance. As suggested by Schopler and Galinsky (1981) and by Mok (2001), leadership is an important factor in contributing to the success of self-help groups.

The Rehabilitation Alliance Hong Kong (RAHK), which was founded in 1992 after the release of the Green Paper on Rehabilitation, is another important self-help organization in Hong Kong. Its membership, different from other self-help organizations, comprises people with different types of disabilities, including physical impairment, intellectual disability, hearing impairment, visual impairment, mental health survivors and people with chronic illness, as well as allies of people with disabilities; that is, people without disabilities are also welcome to enrol as members. Yet an emphasis is placed on the control and management of the organization by people with disabilities, with the overall goal of promoting equal opportunity and full participation of people with disabilities in society.

The RAHK positions itself as an advocate for the equal rights of people with disabilities. Despite its relatively short history, under the strong leadership of the late Peter Chan, a professional accountant who had become paralyzed while pursuing his university studies abroad, it undertook numerous tasks that garnered attention from the public and resulted in actual change. Examples include the campaign for separate legislation for people with intellectual disabilities (RAHK, 1993), voting rights of people with disabilities (RAHK, 1995), physical access to public buildings (RAHK, 1995), accessibility to Mass Transit Railway and public buses (RAHK, 1993; 1995), employment rights of people with disabilities (RAHK, 1993; 1995), and integrated education (RAHK, 1995; 1997). In 1997, following the death of Peter Chan, the RAHK lost its momentum and had been stagnant for a short period of time. At the time of writing, the Chairman of the RAHK, Cheung Kin-Fai, very often acts as the representative and spokesman of self-help organizations or people with disabilities in Hong Kong. Mr. Cheung is also the elected Chairperson of the Joint Council/the Rehabilitation Division of the HKCSS.

People with intellectual disabilities, with their parents, also formed their own organizations. The Chosen Power with 'People First' in brackets was first established in November 1995. They said that they were inspired by their participation in the People First Conference held in Toronto in 1992. Their vision is to strive for a stronger voice in society, and their goal is to achieve independence, promote mutual acceptance, gain respect in the community, and promote equality for all people. The Chosen Power worked in collaboration with the Hong Kong Joint Council of Parents of the Mentally Handicapped to organize three conferences focusing on people with intellectual disabilities in Hong Kong in 2003, 2005, and 2009 respectively. A large number of people with intellectual disabilities were empowered by these conferences. Similarly in 1995, a group of people with severe physical disabilities, most with tetraplegia, came together to form the Direction Volunteer Service for the Handicapped to strive for their own welfare, resources, and opportunities. It then changed its name to Direction Association for the Handicapped in 1995. This is the first self-help organization of people with severe physical impairment.

After the establishment in 1996 of the first self-help organization of survivors of mental illness, the Amity Mutual Support Society, a few more self-help organizations were formed for this population, such as the Concord Mutual Aid Club Alliance in 1998 and the Alliance of Ex-mentally Ill of Hong Kong in 1999. This represented a breakthrough in Hong Kong as a predominantly Chinese society where, traditionally, very serious stigmatization is held towards people with mental illness. Anyone who has once been diagnosed with mental illness would usually seek to cover it up and try to conceal it from others, even close relatives. So it is with very exceptional courage that members of these alliances stand up and disclose such a status to others.

Furthermore, a unique self-help organization, the Association of Women with Disabilities Hong Kong, focusing on combating double discrimination of the dual role of "women" and "disability" in Chinese culture, was established in 2000. Apart from striving for equal rights of women with disabilities locally, the Association is also keen on networking with other similar organizations in the region as well as in the international arena. The Association has initiated the Asian Pacific Network of Women with Disabilities, and also participated in the International Network of Women with Disabilities. Seeing the need for mainstreaming in society, this organization also plays an active role in the local Women's League, which represents a variety of women's groups, such as female labourers, lesbians, sex workers, and others in the territory.

As seen from the above, the self-help movement has clearly developed very rapidly in Hong Kong in the late twentieth century. Why and how did this happen? It appears that the driving factors included the stability and prosperity of the territory at that time, the public's attitude change towards the Government, inspiration gained from overseas exposure, and the rise of the Social Work profession. These are explored in more detail in the following section.

Rapid development of self-help: 1980s and 1990s

Stability and prosperity of the territory

Since the explosion of industrialization in the 1960s, Hong Kong experienced several unstable periods economically and politically. First, the onset of the Cultural Revolution in the PRC in 1966 resulted in the 1966–1967 riots in Hong Kong. Second, the global oil crisis from 1973 to 1975 had a strong impact. Third, the negotiation talks over the future of Hong Kong in the early 1980s produced uncertainty. Fourth, the Asian Financial Crisis in 1998 interfered with progress. Finally, the attack of Severe Acute Respiratory Syndrome (SARS) in 2002–2003 was centred, among other cities of the world, in Hong Kong, creating an immediate crisis that had to be met and a barrier that lasted for some time. However, Hong Kong's economy has always survived, and recovered very quickly on each of those occasions. During the period from 1962 to the onset of the oil crisis in 1973, the average growth rate in GDP was 6.5% per year. From 1976 to 1996, GDP grew at an average of 5.6% per year (Schenk, 2008). During the 1980s and 1990s, people in general enjoyed a dramatic rise in living standard. As one of the most disadvantaged groups in society, people with disabilities began to think that they should have a share in the growing prosperity of Hong Kong. They therefore stood up to strive for their interests and rights, by means of their own efforts.

The public's attitudinal change towards the Government

During the 1980s, the public's thinking towards the Government had changed. The refugees' ideology of "borrowed place, borrowed time" (Hughes, 1976) was no longer valid. There were a large number of "baby boom" young people who planned to settle down in their place of birth. They had expectations of positive action from the Government. The adoption in 1971, from western education, of the system of 9-year compulsory free education, in particular, brought to people's attention the concepts of equality, welfare, and citizenship. People with disabilities, being an oppressed group, also started to be aware of their rights. Forming self-help groups was a means to claim their rights in society.

Inspiration gained from overseas exposure

The blooming of self-help organizations is also a result of the overseas exposure of people with disabilities. Hong Kong, as a British colony, gradually obtained its status as an international city in the 1980s. Hong Kong people were able to gain more opportunities to visit other countries. Coincidentally, the 1980s and 1990s were the most active phase of the disability movement in the Asia-Pacific region.

The United Nations International Year of Disabled Persons (IYDP) in 1981 marked the beginning of the global community's serious attention to disability issues. Hong Kong was no exception. After the IYDP, there was the World Program of Action Concerning Disabled Persons, declared in 1982, followed by the United Nations Decade of Disabled Persons 1983–1992. In December 1992, the Asian and Pacific initiative was launched at a meeting held in Beijing where Full Participation and Equality of People with Disabilities in the Asian and Pacific Region were proclaimed. At that meeting, the Asian and Pacific Decade of Disabled Persons, 1993–2002, was adopted.

The most influential measure of this Asian and Pacific Decade of Disabled Persons was the campaigns held every year during the Decade (Price & Takamine, 2003). As the Decade progressed, campaigns were held in Japan (1993), the Philippines (1994), Indonesia (1995), New Zealand (1996), Republic of Korea (1997), Hong Kong, China (1998), Malaysia (1999), Thailand (2000), Viet Nam (2001) and, the final one, in Osaka, Japan (2002). Needless to say, these campaigns had a strong impact on the host country of each campaign, which resulted in many steps taken by Governments to promote equal opportunities for people with disabilities in the respective countries, and thus in the region as a whole. Hong Kong hosted the campaign in 1998, and as a consequence positive influences were brought not only to the Government and civil society, but also to people with disabilities.

In fact, during this Asian and Pacific Decade, Hong Kong organized a large team of delegates to attend each annual campaign. On a few occasions, the number even exceeded 100 persons, the majority of whom were people with disabilities and their caregivers. As Price and Takamine (2003) stated, some of the side effects of these campaigns were the strong networks formed. They particularly pointed out that self-help organizations in the region were strengthened. It is true that the self-help organizations in Hong Kong that developed rapidly in the 1990s were to a certain extent inspired by the international trend.

Some individuals were highly influential as well. One such person who merits specific mention was the late Professor Sir Harry Fang, the "Father of Rehabilitation" in Hong Kong, who helped make the dream of people with disabilities come true. In his autobiography (Fang, 2002), Professor Fang mentioned that he had "probably raised over HK$1.5 billion" (p. 83) in his career. Much of the money came from the Hong Kong Jockey Club, and all those funds were used for people with disabilities. That explained, to a considerable extent, why during the 1980s and 1990s Hong Kong could support such a large number of people with disabilities to attend the different kinds of training and conferences overseas. Sir Harry Fang regarded those activities as most rewarding and effective in helping people with disabilities engage in independent living.

Following the second Asian and Pacific Decade of Persons with Disabilities, 2003–2012, the third Decade, 2013–2022, was launched in Icheon, South Korea. It aimed at consolidating and taking forward the achievements of the previous two decades and the realization of the rights of the estimated 650 million persons with disabilities in the region. With the passing away of Sir Harry Fang, Hong Kong now lacks a similarly prominent and influential figure to take a leadership role. It is therefore probable that this Decade will not involve as many people with disabilities as previously. However, the regional and international exchange in the past 2 decades has already enlightened a large number of people with disabilities in Hong Kong. They are well equipped with self-help spirit and skills, and appear highly competent to advocate for the rights of people with disabilities in Hong Kong.

The rise of the social work profession

In the late 1960s, social work education was formally introduced in Hong Kong. Owing to its appealing philosophy and ideology, a great many young people sought to study Social Work at universities. In the 1970s and 1980s, more and more young people graduated and joined the profession. "Self-help," being the central theme in social work, was naturally applied by these young professionals. Hence, the majority of the self-help organizations of people with chronic illness were started by social workers, most in medical settings. Even in some cases that were not initiated by social workers, people with disabilities would employ social workers to help them manage their organizations, whenever funding would allow. The reasons were simple. Social workers were trained to understand and apply self-help concepts. They were knowledgeable in social and disability policies, and skilful in interpersonal relationships. All these are essential elements for effective management of self-help organizations. However, it is perhaps somewhat ironic that, although part of the thrust of "self-help" is to get rid of professionalism, people with disabilities in Hong Kong favoured the involvement of professional social workers in their self-help organizations to help them achieve their goals.

Work in coalition or alliance

People with disabilities understand very well the meaning of "united we stand, divided we fall," so they form coalitions or alliances in some battles of common ground. For example, those concerned with the deficit in residential services initiated the Alliance for Subvented Residential Care Service. Those who wanted to strive for more job opportunities joined together to establish the Coalition for Securing Job Opportunities and Quota System for People with Disabilities. Other groups planning to work on accessibility issues formed the Alliance for Public Transport Fare Concession Scheme for People with Disabilities. As Mok (2001) maintained, "When these (self-help) groups are pulled together to form an organized power base, they will be more likely to assert greater influence on social policies" (pp. 14–15). Chesler (1991) also contended that self-help groups were not purely about individual gains and self-empowerment, but also about policy change and collective empowerment. Thus, such kinds of coalitions or alliances are more effective in the negotiation process, be it with the Government or any other entities. For example, regarding the case of public transport fare concession referred to above, following concerted efforts by the Alliance, both the Government and some public transport operators agreed to subsidize the expenses. As a result, since 2012, eligible people with disabilities can travel on the Mass Transit Railway, franchised buses, and ferries at any time at a concessionary fare of $2 per trip.

Last but not least, there is the Hong Kong Coalition for the Rights of Persons with Disabilities. This coalition was formed by a number of self-help organizations of people with disabilities, NGOs, and human rights organizations. Its aim is to oversee the implementation of the United Nations Convention on the Rights of Persons with Disabilities (UNCRPD) in Hong Kong. The UNCRPD was entered into force for the PRC and extended to Hong Kong on 31 August 2008. The purpose of the Convention is to promote, protect, and ensure the full and equal enjoyment of all human rights and fundamental freedoms by all people with disabilities, and to promote respect for their inherent dignity. In September 2012, people with disabilities representing different groups, legislative councillors, and members from human rights organizations and civil society formed a joint delegation to travel to Geneva to present to the UN review of the Hong Kong Government's implementation of the UNCRPD. There, they interacted with international experts in the open hearings, aiming at the realization of the full range of rights of people with disabilities in Hong Kong.

The above illustrates that the influence of self-help organizations is not limited to the local context, but also extends well into the global scene. Various approaches are taken to achieve self-help goals, although in most cases milder approaches such as lobbying, arranging meetings, issuing press releases or press conferences are most typically followed. Only when these do not achieve results are more radical approaches, such as mobilizing mass protests or demonstrations, adopted (Ling et al., 1999). By employing less radical ways, self-help organizations have been able to gain acceptance from politicians and government officials, and to make many gains by staying on good terms with the Government.

Self-help organizations for people with disabilities were first recognized by the Government in the 1992 Green Paper on Rehabilitation. At present, there are people with disabilities or their caregivers sitting in the Rehabilitation Advisory Committee and its subcommittees in their personal capacity. They are also involved in the working group tasked with the responsibility of drafting the Hong Kong Rehabilitation Program Plan. Moreover, some are invited to participate in advisory committees on matters relating to transport, building access, and employment and vocational training, either in their personal capacity or as a representative of a self-help organization (Hong Kong Government, 2007). It appears that people with disabilities are now given more opportunities to voice their opinions in matters that relate to them.

Beginning in 2001, the Social Welfare Department started a Financial Support Scheme for Self-help Organizations of People with Disabilities/Chronic Illness. As of July 2014, there are 68 organizations receiving funding from the Scheme. However, the funding forms a double-edged sword for the organizations: they are truly in need of funding for their survival, yet their autonomy may be undermined by their receipt of financial support from the Government. This will be an area worthy of further investigation.

Change in roles of other stakeholders

Interpersonal relationships are interactive. If roles of people with disabilities change from service recipients in the past to customers (the term "customer" is now commonly used to replace the term "service recipients/clients" in NGOs), then roles of the staff of NGOs have to be changed accordingly. Since their work is to meet the customers' needs, they have to consult them, and involve them in decision-making as far as possible. Hence, NGO staff have now moved more toward playing the role of facilitator. At present, it is not unusual to invite people with disabilities or their caregivers to participate in the management level of NGOs. Such practice is significant, as the Social Welfare Department approves projects or tenders of NGOs that stress user participation.

Similarly, changes also occur in the academic field. Nowadays, the emancipatory approach has become popular in disability studies. The view here is that emancipatory research in the disability context should be enabling, not disabling. It should be carried out by people with disabilities and aimed at challenging routine oppression in their daily lives (Oliver, 1992). Research that aspires to be emancipatory has to be characterized by rigorous evaluation of questions of control. Who decides what the research will be about, how it will be conducted, and to what extent are people with disabilities engaged in the central decision-making processes of a project and its outcomes are all critical determinants of emancipatory research.

The entire question of emancipatory research is vested with one core value: let the researched be the director of the research, not the researcher or the funding institution. "Nothing about us without us" is the essence of emancipatory research. Hence, the traditional role of researcher has been changed completely. All the research conducted by self-help organizations of people with disabilities is of an emancipatory nature, with the ultimate aim to combat oppression of people with disabilities in society.

Change from discrimination to equal opportunities in legislation

In the early 1990s, when the Hong Kong government attempted to take a community approach with respect to service provision for people with intellectual disabilities and people with mental health problems, they faced tremendous opposition from the community. The most well-known incidences of protest were from residents of Tung Tau Estate and of Laguna City. In fact, such response stemmed from an incident that occurred in 1982 that illustrated the public's misunderstanding towards people with intellectual disabilities and mental illness. The incidents that followed throughout the 1980s and 1990s eventually resulted in some significant changes in legislation in relation to disability in Hong Kong.

Significant events

In 1982, a massacre took place in which a non-compliant psychotic outpatient killed his mother and sister at home, another three victims on the staircase of the building where he resided, and a number of children in a kindergarten. This shocking incident aroused the concern of society towards the potential threat of similar patients. Soon after, the Working Group on Ex-mental Patients with a History of Criminal Violence or Assessed Disposition to Violence was appointed by the Government to suggest and implement preventive measures. A report with two important recommendations was subsequently published (Hong Kong Government, 1983). First, a community nursing service was proposed in Kwai Chung (Psychiatric) Hospital, and later introduced to other medical settings (Lee, 1986). Second, a 24-hour hotline service was set up in Castle Peak (Psychiatric) Hospital, which was later turned into a regular service for psychiatric patients, their families, and the general public (Hong Kong Government, 1987). Following this, improvements to the standards of halfway houses were proposed, and other measures, such as "priority follow-up" and the "sub-target" label, were introduced to patients with a disposition to violence.

Such measures met with some resistance, however, and were implemented with some difficulty. In 1983, the first halfway house with new standards for discharged mental patients was planned in Sun Tsui Estate, a public housing estate in Shatin. However, there was strong protest from the residents, and the opening of the facility was held up until 1986 after a series of community education projects had been carried out. In December 1992, there were protests again from residents of a public housing estate, the Tung Tau Estate, where it was planned to establish a residential home for people with intellectual disabilities. The construction work was disrupted until March 1993, when the Legislative Council unanimously adopted the continuation of the construction. The dispute was then settled. In May 1993, a group of residents of Laguna City, a middle-class community, organized a strong opposition to the Governor for having a social centre for the discharged mental patients in the community (Chan, 1993, Leung, 1995).

At that time, resistance from the general public was frequently encountered when facilities for people with disabilities were proposed in the community. This reflected the generally held discriminatory attitude of many Chinese people towards people with disabilities. In support of this observation, a survey on the protesting residents revealed "their ignorance about disability and their extremely heavy sense of prejudice against people with disability" (Hong Kong Council of Social Service, 1993, p. 1). On the surface, there might have been inadequate neighbourhood consultation and education before the setting up of those facilities. In reality, though, these incidents showed that the implementation of the cherished "community-based" or "community care" approach in social services was in jeopardy. In dealing with the resistance, the Government could only claim that public education was essential. However, it was argued,

> The present public education efforts suffer from a lack of long term planning and an absence of feedback on the effect of various campaigns. Most activities are carried out on an ad hoc basis, with a minimum of co-ordination and continuity. (Hong Kong Council of Social Service, 1993, p. 2)

Chan (1993) contended that this kind of discrimination was a major barrier to full participation and equal opportunity. Seeing such unjust happenings, Anna Wu, former Legislative Councillor, put forward the equal opportunity legislation in the form

183

of a private bill in early 1994, which then forced the Government to introduce its own anti-discrimination legislation in late 1994.

The anti-discrimination legislation

The anti-discrimination pieces of legislation that are of particular relevance here are the *Sex Discrimination Ordinance* (SDO) and the *Disability Discrimination Ordinance* (DDO). The latter, enacted on 3 August 1995, had its non-employment-related provisions put into effect on 20 September 1996 and became fully operational on 20 December 1996, following the commencement of a Code of Practice on Employment issued by the Equal Opportunities Commission (EOC) under the DDO.

The DDO was the first piece of anti-discrimination legislation to protect the rights of people with disabilities in Hong Kong. Largely modelled on the Australian Disability Discrimination Act, the DDO prohibits discrimination, harassment, and vilification on grounds of disability. Its aim is to ensure the equality of opportunity between people with and without disability in all major spheres of public life, such as employment; education; access to and use of premises; provision of goods, services, and facilities; and participation in clubs and sporting activities. The Ordinance, which has provisions for its enforcement through the court by allowing aggrieved persons to take civil proceedings, is mainly implemented by the EOC. To combat discrimination, the intent is that the law provides protection for people with disabilities against less favourable treatment in various areas of public life. In addition, it is hoped that the promulgation of the legislation coupled with vigorous enforcement will lead to the improvement of the public's attitude towards people with disabilities.

Most recently, a public consultation on disability law review was carried out by the EOC. Proposed changes to the current DDO for the public input included, among other things, the introduction of the prohibition of inter-disability discrimination, and a review of the Productivity Assessment Scheme. It remains to be seen whether this will lead to any positive legislative changes for persons with disabilities.

The role and function of the EOC

With regard to the role and function of the EOC in relation to the DDO, Tong (1997) provided the following explanation:

> The role of the EOC is to implement the Ordinance. The chief function of the EOC is to work towards the elimination of discrimination, harassment and vilification and promote equality of opportunity between people with disabilities and people without disabilities. For such purposes the EOC may issue codes of practice to provide practical guidance in respect of certain areas of activities.
> The EOC is specifically required to deal with complaints lodged with it under the DDO and to encourage parties concerned to settle the matter by concili-ation. The EOC is also empowered to conduct formal investigations for any purpose connected with its functions.
> Broadly speaking, the EOC has three major areas of work: investigation and conciliation, education and promotion, and legislation and guidelines. (p. 4)

However, self-help organisations of people with disabilities were critical for the success of the DDO and the EOC, as ambiguity and exemption existed in the DDO, and there was a lack of real power and independence in the EOC. It was a matter of some speculation whether equal opportunities could be realized by such provisions (Rehabilitation Alliance Hong Kong, 1995). In fact, according to the findings of a follow-up survey in 2002 commissioned by the Sub-committee on Public Education on Rehabilitation of the Rehabilitation Advisory Committee, and conducted by the Chinese University of Hong Kong, public discrimination against people with disabilities had undergone positive changes compared to the results of the benchmark survey conducted in 1994. These changes included the general acceptance of integration of persons with disabilities into society and the willingness to have social interaction with them. That said, no significant changes were found in other aspects; for example, acceptance among the respondents of people with mental health problems was still at a level lower than that of people with intellectual disabilities. However, the survey also found that 60% of the respondents were aware of the Disability Discrimination Ordinance.

There is still public misunderstanding and resistance towards people with disabilities, as evidenced by the opposition from local residents against the setting up of facilities for people with disabilities, difficulties in introducing barrier-free physical environments, and the low employment rates in open market for persons with disabilities.

Separate legislation for people with intellectual disabilities and people with mental problems

The Government's and the professionals' gross neglect of people with intellectual disabilities can be illustrated by governmental and professional historical consent to the same application of the Mental Health Ordinance (MHO) to people with intellectual disabilities and people with mental problems. As early as the late 1980s, parents' groups and people from a number of NGOs did see the severity of the problem. A working group was then formed to look into the situation. In the report submitted to the authorities, several significant points were highlighted to justify the separation of legislation (Hong Kong Council of Social Service, 1992).

First, the MHO was said to focus only on control and supervision, while protection and care would be the genuine needs of people with intellectual disabilities. Illustrated by real-life case examples, the report stressed the need of guardianship and the monitoring of proper guardianship for people with intellectual disabilities. This applied equally to those over the age of 18. For example, there were adults with intellectual disabilities deprived of immediate medical treatment owing to their inability to understand and sign the consent forms. Also, some people abused and even deserted their family members or relatives with intellectual disabilities (Hong Kong Council of Social Service, 1992).

Second, regarding the judicial procedure that involved investigation, court hearing, retention, and sentencing, the working group pointed out that it was unfair to apply this general practice to people with intellectual disabilities. Special assistance during an investigation and court hearing, and alternatives for the places of retention and sentencing, should be provided to address the special needs of this group of people, with an emphasis on caring and training. Police training in interviewing people with intellectual disabilities (Yu, 1989) and videotaping for the court hearing were also proposed.

However, it was not until a case in 1993, which resulted in strong protest from the community, that the government began to treat the issue in a more serious manner.

The case of 1993

On 15 September 1993, an accused was acquitted of a charge of attempted rape and indecent assault against a 25-year-old woman who was born with hearing impairment, speech difficulties, and low intelligence. The Justice dismissed the case in the trial process on the grounds of communication difficulties and emotional distress experienced by the victim. The public and parents' groups were greatly alarmed, and saw this as a case of gross injustice. Acting on this opportunity, the parents' groups and advocates exerted a great deal of pressure on the Government to reactivate the once-heated issue of separate legislation for people with intellectual disabilities.

In response to the public outcry, the Chief Justice set up a Working Party in October 1993 to look into the procedures of giving evidence in Court by persons with intellectual disabilities. The Working Party came up with a series of recommendations in their Interim Report in January 1994. The key recommendations included that the Court should consider the clinical psychological report on the conditions of a defendant or witness with intellectual disabilities, the trial be fixed for an early date, and the case was heard in a courtroom furnished like a juvenile court. Other points were that persons other than those authorised should be excluded; the trial be conducted in Cantonese (the dialect of Hong Kong Chinese); the judge and counsel should wear ordinary attire; a social worker or teacher be allowed to accompany the defendant/witness while the latter gives evidence; and counselling by a clinical psychologist should be rendered before, during, and after giving evidence (The Working Party, 1994a). In the second report submitted in March 1994, apart from the items already proposed, the Working Party further recommended firmly that legislation be introduced to make available a video link and that videotaped statements be admissible in court (The Working Party, 1994b).

Separate legislation for the protection of rights, which was the ultimate goal of parents' groups of people with intellectual disabilities, was finally realised in 1997 with the enactment of the Mental Health (Amendment) Ordinance 1997. This legislation incorporated the proposals made by the Working Group (Hong Kong Council of Social Service, 1992). Since then, all parties concerned have made strong efforts to facilitate the enactment of the recommendations, such as installation of video linking systems in courts and provision of a disability sensitivity training program to the police and court staff. As a result, the incorporated procedures were applied with satisfactory results. Clearly, the separate legislation was a human rights issue for people with intellectual disabilities, yet it took nearly a decade to become functional. This reflected the fact that the rights of people with intellectual disabilities were very much neglected in Hong Kong at that time.

Setting up of the Guardianship Board

As mentioned, the need for guardianship and the monitoring of proper guardianship for people with intellectual disabilities over the age of 18 had been a genuine concern of the parents' groups for long time. Usually, these parents faced difficulties when their adult children were in need of medical treatment for which consent forms were required (Hong Kong Council of Social Service, 1992). With the staunch efforts made by these parents and numerous self-help organisations, the Government finally agreed to set up the Guardianship Board to safeguard the rights of people with disabilities in 1999.

Recent thoughts and critique

Recently, parents of people with intellectual disabilities proposed revisions to the Guardianship Order, based on some of its drawbacks. For example, it has been stated that due to the complicated application procedure, the medical treatment of persons with intellectual disabilities has been delayed on some occasions. This shows that every rule, no matter how well supported it was at the time when it was established, has to go through and pass the test of time. Perhaps it is time to revise the whole Guardianship Board scheme. Furthermore, no one, other than the parent/carer of a person with disability, and the person with disability himself or herself, is in a better position to understand the essence of the scheme. Hence involvement of the end users in the revision exercise is of utmost importance.

Shift in service ideology and mode of practice

Following the global trend of community care and an integrative approach for services for people with disabilities in the 1970s, the Government also attempted to apply that service ideology and mode of practice with regard to services for people with disabilities in Hong Kong. Significant changes in the three areas of education, social care, and vocational services are discussed in the following sections.

Education service – from segregated to integrated approach

The drawbacks of segregated education have been analysed by a great many western researchers (e.g., Christophos & Renz, 1969; Guranlnick, 1976; Galloway & Goodwin, 1979; Potts, 1982). Warnock (1978) stressed in his report that children with special education needs (SEN) should be offered learning opportunities in ordinary schools. The principles and philosophy of inclusive education was affirmed and gained full support as stated in the UNESCO Salamanca Statement (1994).

Integrated education in Hong Kong can be traced to 1969. Before 1969, all children with disabilities could either stay at home or study in special schools. Children with hearing impairments were first allowed to attend classes in ordinary schools in 1969 (Yung, 1977). Although the policy of integrated education was suggested in 1977 (Hong Kong Government, 1977), there was no concrete plan to implement the concerned policy before 1982 (Hui, 2003). In 1982, the Education Department started to provide intensive remedial teaching services for children with learning difficulties, and behavioural or emotional problems. Integrated education was mentioned again in the Education Commission Report No. 2, which suggested that children with SEN should enrol in ordinary schools so that they could receive comprehensive education and benefit from the normal environment (Hong Kong Government, 1986).

187

In response to the urging of a number of self-help organizations of people with disabilities, in September 1997, the Hong Kong Government initiated a two-year Pilot Project on Integrated Education. With the positive results gathered from the Pilot Project, the Government started to promote the whole-school approach to Integrated Education, as advocated by the United Nations Educational, Scientific and Cultural Organization, to enhance the quality of local integrated education. In September 2000, 40 schools adopted the whole-school approach in providing integrated education (Hong Kong Government, 2000). Subject to the assessment and recommendation of the specialists/physicians, and with parents' consent, children with more severe or multiple disabilities are placed in special schools for intensive support. Other children with SEN could attend ordinary schools.

In the 2013/2014 school year, 60 aided schools, including a hospital school (operating classes at 18 hospitals), provided places for children with visual impairment, hearing impairment, physical disability, emotional and behavioural difficulties, and intellectual disability (Information Services Department, 2014). All these special schools are subvented by the Government and operated by NGOs. Some NGOs served as resource centres to support ordinary schools in catering to students with SEN.

The learning support grant for each school was $1,500,000 in 2013/2014 (Information Services Department, 2013). The grant was further increased by 30% in 2014/2015. With more resources, schools are expected to employ additional teachers and teaching assistants or hire professional services to render appropriate support to the students with SEN (Hong Kong Government, 2014).

Other concerns regarding educational issues

Before 2002, students with SEN had to end their schooling at the age of 16. In June, 2002, the Education Bureau announced a 2-year Pilot Project on Extended Education in Special Schools to allow students with SEN to continue schooling until the age of 18, provided that the schools concerned had their own resources and no extra subvention from the Government was required. In order to make the extended education a regular practice, several parents' groups joined together and formed the Parents' Alliance on Special Education System. They launched a series of campaigns and did a great deal of lobbying. With their persistence and support from a few Legislative Councillors, in 2009 they eventually succeeded in securing 6+3+3 (i.e., six years of primary + three years of junior + three years of senior secondary education) – free 12-year education for their children that all students with SEN were entitled to take part in up to the age of 18.

There was another concern – not yet addressed – about students with mental problems who are not yet included in the integrated education policy. It was suggested that additional resources should be granted and training be provided to the staff of the schools, so that students with mental problems can also be enrolled in ordinary schools (Hong Kong Professional Teachers' Union, 2013).

Recent developments

Recently, a parents' group called the Parents' Alliance on Concern of Rights to Special Education is advocating the extension of school age from 18 to 20 for students with intellectual disabilities. They expressed the concern that students with intellectual disabilities need to take more time to complete the secondary schooling and that the maximum age set at 18 constituted discrimination. Judicial review proceedings have also been initiated to challenge the exclusion of special schools for students with intellectual disabilities from the Native English Teacher Scheme, which covers mainstream schools as well as special schools for students with physical disabilities. Parents of students with intellectual disabilities regard it as a case of discrimination, as their children are excluded from the support solely on ground of their category of disability.

Significant changes in education policy and services for people with disabilities in the recent decades have been met with optimism. However, unfairness is still found in some areas, as described in the preceding sections. Parents of children with disabilities are more empowered compared with their counterparts in the past. They understand that should they want to strive for equal educational opportunities for their children, they have to fight for changes in the existing policy and culture. They have to join together in a united front and seek assistance from other parties where appropriate.

Social care services – from institutional care to community care

Although the first White Paper on Rehabilitation in 1977 was titled *Integrating the Disabled into the Community: A United Effort*, in fact not much was accomplished in terms of integrating people with disabilities into the community. Most of the services (various kinds of residential services, day activity centres, etc.) were specialized and segregated in nature. It is little wonder that, nearly 20 years later, the second White Paper published in 1995 included the words "More needs to be done to enhance integration of people with a disability into the community" (Hong Kong Government, 1995, p. 17). It was only after 1995, and particularly after 2000, that the Social Welfare Department encouraged NGOs to propose innovative community support projects. To support these, the Government made efforts to provide extra funding to develop community support services. This marked the first real progress in integrated and community-based services for people with disabilities.

As there were more than 30 integrated or community support services or projects launched after 2000, several significant ones are mentioned in the following discussion. For easy reference, all can be grouped under the following categories:

a) Centre-based training or care, for example, the District Support Centre for Persons with Disabilities (DSC), the Gateway Club;
b) Home-based training or care, such as the Home Care Services for Persons with Severe Disabilities, Specialized Home-based Training and Support Service;
c) Transitional or respite services, such as the Transitional Care and Support Centre for Tetraplegic Patients, Place of Refuge; Residential Respite Service;
d) Parents/caregiver support, such as the Parents' Resource Centre; and
e) Paramedical support, such as the Central Psychological Support Service Unit and the Central Paramedical Support Service Unit.

However, there is overlap, and nearly all services belong to two or even more categories. The District Support Centre for Persons with Disabilities (DSC) can be used as an example for illustration. There are 16 DSCs covering all districts of the territory. The website of the Social Welfare Department states that a DSC, by adopting a district-based approach, provides one-stop community support services for persons with disabilities and their family members/caregivers. It aims at enhancing domestic living and community living skills for persons with disabilities so as to facilitate their integration into the community through the provision of a range of community support services. It also provides training and support services to the family members/ caregivers of persons with disabilities so as to strengthen their caring capacity and to relieve their stress.

As such, it is clear that despite its centre-based nature, it also delivers services, including paramedical support services in the homes of the service users, and even day respite service if there is a genuine need.

It is also worth mentioning that recently, in order to facilitate people with severe disabilities who were much neglected in the past to live independently in the community, more support services are delivered. These services include, just to name three, the Home Care Service for Persons with Severe Disabilities, the Integrated Support Service for Persons with Severe Physical Disabilities, and the Day Care Service for Persons with Severe Disabilities.

The Home Care Service for Persons with Severe Disabilities, which was set up as a Pilot Project in two districts in 2011, evolved into a regular service and extended to all districts in Hong Kong, beginning in March 2014. It aims at providing a package of home-based support services to meet the service users' daily needs. Besides, it also helps relieve the stresses of their family members/caregivers and improve their quality of life. The home-based support services include personal care, escort service, occupational therapist/physiotherapist rehabilitation training service, nursing care service, and caregiver support service.

The Integrated Support Service for Persons with Severe Physical Disabilities (ISS) aims at strengthening support services for persons with severe physical disabilities, to prepare for their discharge from hospital and follow up with integrated home-based services, with a view to facilitate their full integration into the community. Support is provided to those who need constant attention and care by relieving them of the burden of medical equipment and medical consumables, and to enable them to continue living in their familiar community. The ISS includes a cash subsidy for renting Respiratory Support Medical Equipment (RSME) and purchasing medical consumables. It also provides integrated home-based support services, such as case management service, pre-discharge support service, and post-discharge home-based professional support services such as nursing care, rehabilitation training, meal services, social work service, and more.

The Day Care Service for Persons with Severe Disabilities provides centre-based day care for persons with severe disabilities. Its objective is to promote care in the community by strengthening the caring capability of families or caregivers through provision of regular day care, including nursing, rehabilitation, and social and personal care services, so as to enhance opportunities of persons with severe disabilities to continue living in the community.

Besides these, there are other community-based services catering to people with specific categories of disabilities. For instance, the Integrated Community Centre for Mental Wellness (ICCMW) provides one-stop, district-based and accessible community supports to meet the needs of survivors of mental problems, people with suspected mental problems, and their families/caregivers through a single-entry point. Similarly, the Multi-service Centre for Hearing Impaired Persons aims at providing a full range of services solely for persons with hearing impairments, including casework and counselling service, sign language interpretation and training, and speech therapy service.

Standardized assessment mechanism for residential services

Although integration and community care constitute the main approach of social care for people with disabilities, there are people with disabilities who opt for residential services. In the past, there was no specific screening procedure to assess applications for residential services for people with disabilities. The usual practice was that anyone who wanted to enter a residential home would be offered a place once it became available.

To further align with the integration and community care policy, and to maximize the utilization of the various residential services for people with disabilities, the Social Welfare Department set up a multidisciplinary Steering Group on Admission Procedures for Residential Care Homes for People with Disabilities in 2001, to review the admission criteria and process of residential homes for people with disabilities. In 2002, the Steering Group formed a Task Group, comprising rehabilitation professionals and parents, to devise a Standardized Assessment Tool to identify those people with disabilities with genuine need for residential services and to match them with appropriate types of residential homes. Starting from January 2005, all people with intellectual disabilities or physical disabilities who intend to apply for residential services have to undergo a standardized assessment arranged by social workers. Only those with confirmed need for residential care may be on the waitlist for, or be admitted to, residential service.

Applicants assessed to have residential service need are registered on the waiting list in accordance with the types of residential service matched. For those assessed not to have such need, the social workers will refer them for other services, such as day training programs or community support services.

Licensing scheme for residential care homes for persons with disabilities and the Bought Place Scheme (BPS) for private residential care homes for persons with disabilities (RCHDs)

To ensure that residents of residential care homes for persons with disabilities (RCHDs) receive services of acceptable standards physically, emotionally, and socially, the Residential Care Homes (Persons with Disabilities) Ordinance commenced operation on 18 November 2011, and was fully implemented on 10 June 2013. The Ordinance provides for the control of residential care homes for persons with disabilities through a licensing system administered by the Director of Social Welfare. All RCHDs that began operation on or after 18 November 2011 are also subject to regulatory control by way of the issue of a license, in an effort to ensure that the services meet the statutory standards and to protect the interests of people with disabilities more effectively. Under the Ordinance, it would be an offence for any person to operate, keep, manage, or in any other way control a residential care home for people with disabilities without a valid license or certificate of exemption.

The Social Welfare Department launched the pilot Bought Place Scheme (BPS) in October 2010 to encourage private RCHDs to upgrade their service standards. With this licensing scheme, the quality of the private RCHDs is further monitored. As of December 2013, the Government had purchased 245 places in six private RCHDs under the Scheme. By doing so, the supply of subsidized residential care services was increased and more service options were developed for people with disabilities. The pilot BPS has become an ongoing regular service since October 2014.

Care for older persons with intellectual disabilities

Due to medical advancements and improved health care, more and more people with intellectual disabilities, who typically died at a young age in the past, now can live longer and longer. Caregivers, both formal and informal, have become increasingly aware of the issue of ageing in the population of persons with intellectual disabilities. For this reason, new programs have emerged to address the needs of this group of people.

Both the Extended Care Program (ECP) and the Work Extension Program (WEP) were launched in 2005 by the Social Welfare Department. The ECP is targeted at people with intellectual disabilities who are trainees of day activity centres, but could no longer benefit from prolonged or intensive training due to old age or deterioration of health conditions. Instead, simple training or social and leisure activities are provided.

The WEP aimed to meet the service needs of the trainees of sheltered workshops/ integrated vocational rehabilitation services centres. As the trainees get older, they can no longer perform normal work tasks due to deterioration in work abilities. Services, including work activities for sustaining residual work abilities, social and recreational programs, and caring activities for meeting their health and physical needs began to be delivered.

In addition, to prepare people with intellectual disabilities and their parents or caregivers to enter to the "older" and the "double ageing" stage (when both the people with intellectual disabilities and their parents or caregivers are getting old), many NGOs started to offer life-and-death education, palliative care, and bereavement counselling to the service users (Tung Wah Group of Hospitals, 2010; Caritas-Hong Kong, 2010). These services are all new in the field of intellectual disability, yet are the genuine needs of the service users. Practitioners whose work covers these issues need to be well equipped to respond to such change.

Vocational services

Vocational services can cover various areas, such as vocational assessment and training, vocational counselling, job search and matching, on-the-job training, job coaching, and others. However, the discussion below focuses on employment services that can help people with disabilities obtain and maintain remunerated jobs.

Scenario before 2000

The Government first officially mentioned employment of people with disabilities in 1977. It contended:

> Most disabled persons have more abilities than disabilities. With suitable training and education, many of them will be able to secure and maintain remunerative employment in the open commercial and industrial sector and in the Civil Service. The Government will provide services to enable as many disabled persons as possible to find employment in the Civil Service and in commercial and industrial undertakings. (Hong Kong Government, 1977, pp. 16–17)

However, apart from the commencement of the Selective Placement Division of the Labour Department in 1980, not much progress was noted in this area. The Selective Placement Division of the Labour Department was set up to help people with disabilities with aspects of employment. It operated on the principles of placing the right person in the right job, and emphasizing the working abilities of the disabled job seekers.

In a survey conducted in 1987, it was found that, in a sample of 3,415 people with disabilities randomly drawn from the Central Registry of the Disabled, 35.7% were in open employment (32.8% employees, 2% employers or self-employed, and 0.9% home workers), 9.9% were unemployed job seekers, 22.1% were unemployed non-job seekers, 7.5% were sheltered workers, and 24.8% were economically inactive (Hong Kong Council of Social Service and the Rehabilitation Development Co-ordaining Committee, 1987). The results of the survey also indicated that people with hearing or visual impairments, or with orthopaedic disability, were the groups with relatively more employment in the open labour market compared to the groups with mental problems and people with intellectual disabilities (at that time, people with chronic illness were not classified as people with disabilities). Regarding the nature of the jobs that people with disabilities held, 58% were production and related workers; 20.5% were service workers; 10.9% were clerical workers; 4.9% were sales workers; and 4.3% were professionals, technicians, or administrators. Surprisingly, 47.8% of the employed people with disabilities did not rely on any formal assistance in job seeking, but rather they sought their jobs through personal relationships. Only 13.9% were placed by the Selective Placement Division of the Labour Department.

In another study on the employment situation of people with chronic illness, among the 308 persons in the study, only 45.7% of those who held a job before the onset of the illness could continue the employment afterwards. Of the 45.7%, 69.6% were able to maintain their full-time jobs. In general, participants in the study said they had experienced discrimination in employment (Alliance for Patients' Mutual Help Organisations, 1996). Even the Hong Kong Government has admitted that the unemployment rate of people with disabilities was as high as 49% (Hong Kong Government, 1992).

The last governor of colonial Hong Kong, Christopher Patten, took a very keen interest in the issue of disability. In response to the concern raised by groups of people with disabilities, he called and chaired two summit meetings on the employment of people with disabilities in 1994 and 1995, respectively. Despite his high profile with regard to the employment issue, it is disappointing to the groups of people with disabilities that the Government, being the largest employer, only paid lip service to enhancing the job opportunities of people with disabilities. With the total number of more than 180,000 civil servants by that time, less than 4,000 were people with disabilities (RACSCE, 1999). The lack of real commitment on the part of the Government in promoting the employment of people with disabilities was further reflected by its inaction in assisting people with disabilities to be self-employed. It said:

> Self-employment is a very important source of employment opportunities for people with a disability. Either individually or in small groups, they may set up their own small business at home or outside (e.g. desk-top publishing, snack bars in public parks, mobile cleaning crew), provided that they have adequate funds to meet the setting up costs of such a business. (Hong Kong Government, 1995, p. 73)

Thus, people with disabilities who intended to run a business needed to make sure that they had adequate funds for the setup costs. Self-help groups of people with disabilities urged the government to allocate funds to help people with disabilities to start their businesses, but their efforts were in vain (Chan, 1994; Mak, 1994). In view of the difficulties in gaining access to open employment, the Government attempted to develop supported employment. Supported employment, which serves as a midway measure between sheltered employment and open employment, was first introduced in Hong Kong in 1988. Real jobs and real pay are the essence of this approach to employment. With practical assistance and advice, it aims to enable people with disabilities to work in integrated, open settings. However, it was only from March 1995, when the programme was widely implemented, that funding was allocated to increase the number of people supported from 30 to 360. By 1997, the number was more than 1,000.

Major changes after 2000

i) Promoting self-reliance of people with disabilities through support to social enterprise

As revealed by the "Special Topics Report No. 48: Persons with Disabilities and Chronic Diseases" (Hong Kong Government, 2008), about 86.8% of the 347,900 persons with disabilities aged 15 and over were economically inactive. That meant that only 13.2% were economically active. This figure was rather alarming, given that the Government had made an effort to promote more job opportunities for people with disabilities in recent years.

The Government began to implement the Enhancing Employment of People with Disabilities through Small Enterprise Project in 2001. Its aim was to promote an enterprise-driven approach to create employment opportunities for people with disabilities and train those with lower work abilities for open employment. NGOs or organizations of people with disabilities could apply for a maximum grant of $2 million as seed money to support the initial capital expenditure and the first-year operation of a small business or social enterprise.

According to the Hong Kong Government, social enterprise is a business to achieve specific social objectives such as providing the services or products needed by the community, creating employment and training opportunities for people who are socially disadvantaged, protecting the environment, funding its other social services through the profits earned, and initiatives along those lines. Its profits would be principally reinvested in the business for the social objectives that it pursues, rather than distributed to its stakeholders.

The business of a social enterprise should be self-sustaining in the long run and employ people with disabilities to fill no less than 50% of its total number of employees. By the end of 2013, a total of more than $65 million had been granted, sponsoring 84 different small businesses and creating more than 630 job opportunities for people with disabilities. Hence, social enterprise became a trendy service mode in the disability field as it brought more people with disabilities into the real job market.

This was a breakthrough to the field of social services, since those involved needed to alter their mindsets from supporting people to supporting successful business activities. Running a social enterprise involves a dual emphasis of "social" and "business," which is very different from the traditional view of managing a social service unit. Thus, this is truly a paradigm shift in service ideology and practice.

ii) From service fragmentation to service integration

Responding to an inflexible deployment of resources that caused considerable difficulties to the service users in fragmented vocational services, the Social Welfare Department proposed an integrated service model in vocational services for people with disabilities in 2003. This was an integrated and seamless vocational service model, specially designed to accommodate the limitations arising from the workers' disabilities, in which they could be provided with work training, develop their social and economic potential, achieve upward mobility in the vocational ladder, and be prepared for potential advancement to open employment. As a result, more than 95% of the service providers (mainly NGOs) opted to change to integrated vocational rehabilitation services centres (IVRSCs), where a one-stop service approach, including sheltered workshop, supported employment, on-the-job training, social enterprise, and other services, was adopted.

iii) The Work Orientation and Placement Scheme

The Work Orientation and Placement Scheme (WOPS) was initiated by the Labour Department on 1 June 2013. Its aim was to offer an incentive to employers, encouraging them to employ people with disabilities. Under this Scheme, employers were granted an allowance for each employee with disabilities they employed for the training/support necessary to facilitate the employee to be retained in the employment. The allowance could be equivalent to the amount of actual salary paid to the employee with disabilities minus $500 per month during the first 2 months of employment, subject to a monthly ceiling of $5,500. After the first 2 months, employers were entitled to an allowance equivalent of two-thirds of the actual monthly salary paid to the employee, subject to a ceiling of $4,000 per month and for a maximum payment period of up to 6 months. Funding was also available to mentors who assisted the employees with disabilities in continuing with the employment after the first 2 months of employment.

iv) Financial Incentive Scheme for Mentors of Employees with Disabilities Receiving Subvented Vocational Rehabilitation Services and the Support Program for Employees with Disabilities

The Social Welfare Department launched the Financial Incentive Scheme for Mentors of Employees with Disabilities in 2013. The Scheme offered cash incentives to mentors of employees with disabilities to facilitate the employees receiving subvented vocational rehabilitation services to adapt smoothly to the new job environment and to enhance their work capability. Mentors rendering assistance for a period of not less than 1 month would receive an incentive payment.

To further facilitate people with disabilities to be retained in open employment, another program, the Support Program for Employees with Disabilities (SPED), began to operate in June 2014. It provided employers of people with disabilities with a one-off subsidy for each such employee to procure assistive rehabilitation devices and/or workplace modifications to facilitate their employment and to enhance their work efficiency. The subsidy was capped at a maximum support level of $20,000 for each employee. Examples include, but are not limited to, accessories or adaptive equipment for computers, optical magnifying devices, hearing and assistive devices, Braille products, and handrails.

v) Statutory Minimum Wage and rights of employees with disabilities

In Hong Kong, the minimum wage issue has been debated for more than a decade. In 2011, the Minimum Wage Ordinance came into force, and statutory minimum wage (SMW) has applied to all employees in Hong Kong since 1 May 2011. Employees with disabilities, like any other employees, are entitled to wages not lower than the SMW rate. Taking account of the possible employment difficulties encountered by some employees with disabilities, a special arrangement termed "productivity assessment" was proposed. Employees with disabilities were entitled to choose to have their productivity assessed to determine whether they should be remunerated at not lower than the SMW rate or at a rate commensurate with their productivity.

According to the Minimum Wage Ordinance, the right to invoke productivity assessment is entirely vested in the employees with disabilities. For employees with disabilities who do not opt to undergo productivity assessment, their employers must pay them at a rate not lower than the SMW rate.

Tax concession and quota systems

A few decades ago, some NGOs and self-help organizations of people with disabilities already urged the Government to introduce a quota system in the labour market and to offer tax concessions to employers employing people with disabilities. However, as early as 1992, the Government had explicitly stated that both proposals were not desirable (Hong Kong Government, 1992). In the recent decade, the Coalition for Securing Job Opportunities and Quota System for People with Disabilities was formed by more than 30 self-help organizations of people with disabilities. This group has repeatedly pressured for such a change, but their efforts have so far been futile.

The Welfare Sector Subvention Reform – change from input control to output control

Last but not least, the Welfare Sector Subvention Reform in the late 1990s, which had caused a drastic change to the welfare sector in Hong Kong, also had a great impact on the disability sector. As early as 1994, the Hong Kong Government started to appoint consultants to review the subvention system with a view to changing from input to output control. Hence, a new monitoring mechanism for enhancing public accountability and cost-effectiveness in welfare service delivery was devised. In 1998, the review that led to extensive discussion and dispute within the sector was concluded, with recommendations for the introduction of the following:

a) A Service Performance Monitoring System (SPMS), which was to be implemented in phases from April 1999;
b) Funding and Service Agreements (FSAs) by October 2000; and
c) 19 Service Quality Standards (SQSs) by 2001/2002 (later trimmed to 16).

The Service Performance Monitoring System (SPMS) was designed to monitor NGOs' services through the establishment of Funding and Service Agreements (FSAs) and Service Quality Standards (SQSs). Each subvented service unit operated by NGOs would have a Funding and Service Agreement with the Social Welfare Department (SWD) defining the social welfare services to be provided and the required performance standards in terms of quality, performance output, and essential service requirements. SQSs defined the level of quality that the service units under the subvented NGOs were expected to attain.

In addition, in 1999, the Government consulted the subvented welfare sector on a proposal to introduce a new funding arrangement in the form of a Lump Sum Grant (LSG), which was officially launched in January 2001. Prior to the inception of the LSG scheme, SWD imposed rigid input controls on NGOs' staffing, salary structures, and individual items of expenditure. Under the LSG funding arrangement, NGOs now had flexibility in deploying their LSG (excluding the provident fund contribution) for staff and other operating expenses within the context of their respective FSAs. They were also encouraged to engage in social enterprises and, in partnership with private businesses, provide paid/free services. Such activities have reduced their reliance on government subvention, and there is more private-sector involvement in the development of social welfare services in Hong Kong.

In fact, apart from the LSG, the SWD also introduced the open tender bidding scheme for new welfare services, such that the private business sector could also bid to deliver social services. As such, the social service sector, which involved only the Government and NGOs as partners in the past, now also extended to the private sector. At present, an emphasis is placed on social entrepreneurship (Lam, 2002) and more business concepts are applied to the social service sector in Hong Kong.

However, with regard to the impact of the LSG scheme, staff unions of the welfare sector were concerned about staff members under the scheme being subject to a lower salary pay scale, compared to their counterparts working in SWD. Such an allegation was supported by the data gathered from a survey conducted by the

Hong Kong Social Workers' General Union (2014). Staff unions also claimed that the tendency of NGOs to employ staff on contract terms could weaken the staff's sense of job security and long-term career planning. Concerns about the high staff wastage and turnover rates in NGOs were also expressed. However, management-wise, contract employment was regarded as a trendy and common human resources practice that could provide greater flexibility to adapt to the uncertain financial condition.

On the question of the impact of the LSG scheme, there are always conflicting views among the senior management and the staff unions. Nonetheless, for the services for people with disabilities, the greatest problem was the negative effects on recruitment and retention of staff in the service team. All along, difficulties in staff recruitment in services for people with disabilities have been well known. With the introduction of the LSG scheme, the situation became worse, particularly for the paramedical staff, since the employment terms in the medical sector were much better than those of the welfare sector. The persistent problem of staff shortages in NGOs serving people with disabilities can be seen in the data collected by a survey conducted by HKCSS (2013), as shown below.

With the implementation of the LSG scheme and SPMS, many positive changes came to the social welfare sector, including the disability sector, particularly flexibility, accountability, and innovation in the use of resources and service delivery. Yet there were certainly adverse effects, especially with regard to the recruitment and ongoing employment of personnel. There has been outcry in the sector demanding change for some time, yet both the Government and the senior management of the sector appear to be satisfied with the present situation. It will take time to see whether, and how, the opposition may gain strength to make a breakthrough.

Table 1 Shortage of staff in 372 service units of 38 agencies for people with disabilities in 2011

Para-medical Staff Category	% of Vacancies (Subvented and Non-subvented Services)	Front-line Staff Category	% of Vacancies (Subvented and Non-subvented Services)
Clinical Psychologist	24.6%	Special Child Care worker	2.2%
Speech Therapist	7.4%	Assistant Social Work Officer	1.9%
Physiotherapist	22.3%	Social Work Assistant	2.4%
Occupational Therapist	11.6%	Welfare Worker	6.8%
Registered Nurse (Psychiatric)	46%	Health Care Worker	4.2%
Registered Nurse (General)	13.1%	Daily Living Care Worker	6.8%
Enrolled Nurse (Psychiatric)	29.9%	Program Assistant	15.5%
Enrolled Nurse (General)	12%	Care Assistant	9.4%

Discussion and conclusion

History is a record of the past and a journey of change. It is the wish of all that such change is for good. For the history of disability, it is only natural that people with disabilities look for positive changes. As revealed in the information of this chapter, it is indisputable that there have been a great many positive changes in the history of disability in Hong Kong. People with disabilities have become more visible, educated, empowered, and independent. Definitely, people with disabilities in Hong Kong live far better lives than was the case in previous decades. Currently, there is less discrimination, and more protection and opportunities to develop physically, socially, and economically. However, do people with disabilities live as equal to people without disabilities? Has the essence of the White paper of 1995 – equal opportunities and full participation of people with disabilities – been realized? The answer is simple and straightforward: certainly *not*!

The mindset of the Government first began to change in 1977, from the non-development of policy to actively formulating policy for people with disabilities. Yet after more than 3 decades, its thinking remains at the "welfare approach" rather than the "right-based approach" as set out in the UNCRPD. The ongoing goal of integration itself, that is, to integrate people with disabilities into the society – in education, social care, employment, and other areas – implies that people with disabilities are *not* included in the mainstream society. They are excluded from the mainstream society.

Adoption of the term "rehabilitation," which is used in all services for people with disabilities, infers that to a certain extent they have to change to adapt to mainstream society. Does such a concept not bear the shadow of an outdated model of disability – that the problem of disability resides in the person himself/herself, but not at all within society? If a society is built for all, if a society takes responsibility for all its citizens, there should be no barriers or handicap. People with disabilities should not need to make extra effort to integrate into society, and there would be no need for any protection policy or anti-discrimination legislation.

Recalling the significant disability-related incidents from the past, it is clear that they have come about as a result of many interconnected factors, locally and internationally, all of which have played an indispensable part in building the present. So far, positive changes have been witnessed, and we believe that with the strengths of the civil society, the spirit of equal opportunities will prevail.

Acknowledgements

The authors would like to thank Ms. Ophelia Chan, the Ex-Assistant Director of Social Welfare Department, for her generous sharing of knowledge about the disability history of Hong Kong.

The authors are also very grateful to Aamir Khan from Toronto, Canada, for his invaluable assistance in editing this chapter.

References

Alliance for Patient's Mutual Help Organization (APMHO). (1996). *Report on Study of Employment of Chronically Ill Patients*. Hong Kong: APMHO.

199

Bach, M. (2007). Changing perspectives on intellectual and developmental disabilities. in I. Brown & M. Percy (Eds.), *A comprehensive guide to intellectual & developmental disabilities* (pp. 35–43). Baltimore: Paul H. Brookes Publishing Co.

Bond, M. (1986). *The Psychology of the Chinese People.* New York: Oxford University Press.

Caritas – Hong Kong. (2010). *Ageing and People with Intellectual Disabilities.* Hong Kong: Caritas.

Castells, M., Goh, L., & Kwok, R. Y. W. (1990). *The Shek Kip Mei Syndrome: Economic Development and Public Housing in Hong Kong and Singapore.* Thousand Oaks, CA: Sage Publications.

Census and Statistics Department. (2008). Special Topics Report No. 48: Persons with disabilities and chronic diseases. Hong Kong: Government Printer.

Census and Statistics Department. (2012). *2011 Population Census, Main Report: Volume I.* Hong Kong: Government Printer.

Census and Statistics Department. (2014). *Hong Kong Statistics.* Hong Kong: Government Printer.

Chan, L. W. C. (1993). Social welfare. in P. K. Choy & L. K. Ho (Eds.), *The Other Hong Kong Report 1993* (pp. 237–263). Hong Kong: The Chinese University Press.

Chan, L. W. C. (1994). Social welfare. in D.H. McMillen & S. W. Man (Eds.), *The Other Hong Kong Report 1994* (pp. 331–349). Hong Kong: The Chinese University Press.

Chesler, M. A. (1991). Mobilizing consumer activism in health care: The role of self-help groups. *Research in Social Movements, Conflicts and Change, 13,* 275–305.

Chow, N. W. S. (1980). *Hong Kong Social Welfare: Policy and Development* [Chinese]. Hong Kong: University of Hong Kong Press.

Community Rehabilitation Network. (1994). Report on the Survey of Employment Situation of People with Kidney Disease [Chinese]. Hong Kong: Author.

Christophos, F., & Renz, P. (1969). A critical examination of special education programs. *Journal of Special Education, 3*(4), 371–380.

Disability Discrimination Ordinance. (1995). *Ordinance No. 86 of 1995.* Hong Kong: Hong Kong Government Printer.

Fan, T. W. (1994). Scraps of history: The asylum day care of the mentally ill in the earlier days of Hong Kong. *Journal of the Hong Kong College of Psychiatrists, 4,* 43–48.

Fang, H. S. Y. (2002). *Rehabilitation: A Life's Work.* Hong Kong: University of Hong Kong Press.

Foo, T. N. (1981). The Mental Health Association of Hong Kong: A brief history. in T. P. Khoo (Ed.), *Aspects of Mental Health Care: Hong Kong 1981* (pp. 85–103). Hong Kong: Mental Health Association of Hong Kong.

Galloway, D. M., & Goodwin, C. (1979). *Educating Slow Learning and Maladjusted Children: Integration or Segregation?* Harlow, United Kingdom: Longman.

Giddens, A. (1986). *Sociology: A Brief but Critical Introduction.* London: Macmillan Education.

Guranlnick, M. J. (1976). The value of integrating handicapped and non-handicapped preschool children. *American Journal of Orthopsychiatry, 46,* 236–245.

Hilliard, L. T. (1960). *Report on the Problem of Mental Deficiency in Hong Kong.* Hong Kong: Government Printer.

Hodge, P. (1981). The politics of welfare. in J. F. Jones (Ed.), *The Common Welfare: Hong Kong's Social Services* (pp. 1–20). Hong Kong: The Chinese University of Hong Kong.

Hong Kong Council of Social Service. (1992). Position paper on Legislative Protection for People with Mental Handicap. Hong Kong: HKCSS.

Hong Kong Council of Social Service. (1993, April). *Welfare Digest.* Hong Kong: HKCSS.

Hong Kong Council of Social Service. (2013, April). Survey on shortage of staff in NGOs. HKCSS *Newsletter.* Hong Kong: HKCSS.

Hong Kong Council of Social Service and the Rehabilitation Development Co-ordinating Committee. (1987). *Survey on Employment Situation of the Disabled.* Hong Kong: Hong Kong Council of Social Services.

Hong Kong Government. (1972). *Mental Health Ordinance.* Hong Kong: Government Printer.

Hong Kong Government. (1974). *Annual Report 1974*. Hong Kong: Government Printer.

Hong Kong Government. (1976). *The Further Development of Rehabilitation Services in Hong Kong*. Hong Kong: Government Printer.

Hong Kong Government. (1977). *White Paper on Integrating the Disabled into the Community: A United Effort*. Hong Kong: Government Printer.

Hong Kong Government. (1986). *Report of the Education Commission No. 2*. Hong Kong: Government Printer.

Hong Kong Government. (1987). *Hong Kong 1987 Review of Rehabilitation Program Plan*. Hong Kong: Government Printer.

Hong Kong Government. (1992). *Equal Opportunities and Full Participation: A Better Tomorrow for All*. Hong Kong: Government Printer.

Hong Kong Government. (1995). White Paper on Rehabilitation – *Equal Opportunities and Full Participation: A Better Tomorrow for All*. Hong Kong: Government Printer.

Hong Kong Government. (2000). *2000 Policy Address, Quality Education, Policy Objective for Education and Manpower Bureau*. Hong Kong: Government Printer.

Hong Kong Government. (2007). *Hong Kong Rehabilitation Program Plan*. Hong Kong: Government Printer.

Hong Kong Government. (2008). *Special Topics Report No.48 – Persons with Disabilities and Chronic Diseases*. Hong Kong: Census and Statistics Department.

Hong Kong Government. (2014). LC Paper No. CB (4) 323/13–1414 (01). *Policy Address Panel on Education, Education Bureau's Policy Initiatives*. Available from http://www.edb.gov.hk/en/about-edb/legco/policy-address/EDB%20Panel%20Paper%20on%20PA%202014(Eng).pdf

Hong Kong Professional Teachers' Union. (2013). LC Paper No. CB (4) 1016/12–13 (01). *Submission on Difficulties Concerning Implementation of Integrated Education to Students with Intellectual Disabilities and Mental Problems*. [Chinese]. Available from http://www.legco.gov.hk/yr12-13/chinese/panels/ed/ed_ie/papers/ed_ic1003cb4-1016-1-c.pdf

Hong Kong Social Workers' General Union. (2014). *Research report on salary and benefits mechanism of NGOs*. [Chinese]. Hong Kong: Research Committee, Hong Kong Social Workers' General Union.

Hong Kong Working Group on Ex-mental Patients with a History of Criminal Violence or Assessed Disposition to Violence. (1983). *Report of the Working Group on Ex-mental Patients with a History of Criminal Violence or Assessed Disposition to Violence*. Hong Kong: The Working Group.

Hughes, R. (1976). *Borrowed place, borrowed time: Hong Kong and its many faces*. London: André Deutsch Limited.

Hui, L. H. M. (2003). Integrated or inclusive education: The future of Hong Kong education - The way ahead. in S.W. Wu & S. P. Lee (Eds.), *Educational development and curriculum reform: The scope and experience of two coasts and four areas* [Chinese] (pp. 255–270). Hong Kong: International Association of Children's Education in Hong Kong and Macau.

Information Services Department. (2013). *Hong Kong: The facts - special education*. Hong Kong: Government Printer.

Information Services Department. (2014). *Hong Kong: The Facts - education*. Hong Kong: Government Printer.

Jones, C. (1990). *Promoting Prosperity: The Hong Kong Way of Social Policy*. Hong Kong: The Chinese University of Hong Kong Press.

Kuhn, T. S. (1962). *The structure of scientific revolutions*. Chicago: Chicago University Press.

Lam, C. (2002). *Invigorating social welfare through the entrepreneurial spirit*. Paper presented in Conference on Building New Capacity for Social Entrepreneurship in Hong Kong, Hong Kong, May 16, 2002.

Lam, C., Tsang, H., Chan, F., & Corrigan, P. (2006). Chinese and American perspectives on stigma. *Rehabilitation Education, 20*(4), 269–279.

Lee, T. K. (1986). The management of aggressive behaviour in mentally handicapped people. Hong Kong: Hong Kong Polytechnic University.

Leung, C. B. J. (1995). Social welfare. In Y. L. S. Cheung & M. H. S. Sex (Eds.), *The other Hong Kong report 1995* (pp. 361–378). Hong Kong: The Chinese University Press.

Ling, K., Cheung, K. F., & Wong, C. M. (1999). Advocating equal rights and full participation of people with disabilities: The case of the peak galleria of Hong Kong. In HKCSS (Ed.), *Convention and innovation: Community development into the 21st century* (pp. 242–255). Hong Kong: HKCSS.

Liu, S. (1990). The new life and I. In *New Life Psychiatric Rehabilitation Association annual report 1990* (pp. 49–51). Hong Kong: New Life Psychiatric Rehabilitation Association.

Lo, W. H. (1981). Government mental health service. in T. P. Khoo (Ed.), *Aspects of mental health care: Hong Kong 1981* (pp. 48–56). Hong Kong: The Mental Health Association of Hong Kong.

Mak, K. (1994). *Employment for disabled people.* Speech presented in the Governor's Summit Meeting on Employment of Disabled People in Hong Kong, February 2, 1994.

Matthews, G., Ma, E. K., & Lui, T. (2008). *Hong Kong, China: Learning to Belong to a Nation.* London: Routledge.

Miners, N. (1975). *The Government and Politics of Hong Kong.* New York: Oxford University Press.

Mok, B. H., Chau, K., & Fung, H. L. (2002). Prevalence and nature of self-help groups in Hong Kong. in D. Shek (Ed.), *Entering a New Millennium: Advances in Social Welfare in Hong Kong* (pp. 331–327). Hong Kong: The Chinese University of Hong Kong Press.

Mok, M. K. (2001). The effectiveness of self-help groups in a Chinese context. *Social Work with Groups, 24*(2), 69–89.

Ng, N. Y. T. (1984). *The Early Population of Hong Kong: Growth, Distribution and Structural Change.* Department of Geography, Occasional Paper No. 61. Hong Kong: The Chinese University of Hong Kong.

New Life Psychiatric Rehabilitation Association. (1990). *Annual Report 1990.* Hong Kong: New Life Psychiatric Rehabilitation Association.

Oliver, M. (1990). *The Politics of Disablement: A Sociological Approach.* London: Palgrave Macmillan.

Oliver, M. (1992). Changing the social relations of research production? *Disability, Handicap and Society, 7*(2), 101–114.

Patton, M. Q. (1990). *Qualitative Evaluation and Research Methods.* Newbury Park, CA: Sage Publications.

Potts, P. (1982). *Origin.* Milton Keynes, United Kingdom: The Open University Press.

Price, P., & Takamine, Y. (2003). The Asian and Pacific decade of disabled persons 1993–2002: What have we learned? *Asia Pacific Disability Rehabilitation Journal, 14*(2), 115–127.

RACSCE. (1999). Rehabilitation Advisory Committee Sub-committee on Employment, Paper 1/99. Hong Kong: Health and Welfare Bureau.

Rappaport, J. (1993). Narrative stories, personal stories, and identity transformation in the mutual help context. *Journal of Applied Behavioral Science, 29*, 239–256.

Rehabilitation Alliance Hong Kong (RAHK). (1993). *Annual Report 92–93.* Hong Kong: RAHK.

Rehabilitation Alliance Hong Kong (RAHK). (1995). *Annual Report 94–95.* Hong Kong: RAHK.

Rehabilitation Alliance Hong Kong (RAHK). (1997). *Annual Report 96–97.* Hong Kong: RAHK.

Schenk, C. (2008). Economic history of Hong Kong. in R. Whaples (Ed.), *E. H. Net Encyclopedia*, March 16, 2008. Available from http://eh.net/encyclopedia/economic-history-of-hong-kong/

Schopler, J., & Galinsky, M. (1981). When groups go wrong. *Social Work, 26*, 424–429.

Spradley, J. R. (1979). *The Ethnographic Interview.* New York: Holt, Rinehart & Winston.

Tang, Y. J. (1999). *Fojiao Yu Zhongguo Wenhua* [Chinese], Beijing: Zhongjiao Wenhua Chubanshe.

Tong, F. (1997). *Implementation of the Disability Discrimination Ordinance in Hong Kong.* Paper presented at the Seoul International Conference on Disability. 24–29 September, South Korea 1997.

Tung Wah Group of Hospitals. (2010). The need of life and death education for people with intellectual disabilities and ex-mentally ill people. Hong Kong: TWGHs.

UNESCO. (1994). The Salamanca Statement and Framework for Action on Special Education. Salamanca: UNESCO.

Warnock, H. M. (1978). Special education needs – Report of the Committee of Enquiry into the Education of Handicapped Children and Young People. London: HMSO.

Wood, P. (1980). *International Classification of Impairments, Disabilities, and Handicaps: A Manual of Classification Relating to the Consequences of Disease.* Geneva: World Health Organization.

Wong, K. P. D. (1993). *Visceral Disability and Social Security: Policy Consideration and Case Study.* Paper presented in Asian Regional Conference on Social Security, September 14–16, 1993, Hong Kong.

Working Party. (1994a). Report of the Working Party on Mentally Handicapped People Giving Evidence in Court. No. 1. Hong Kong: HKCSS.

Working Party. (1994b). Report of the Working Party on Mentally Handicapped People Giving Evidence in Court, No. 2. Hong Kong: HKCSS.

World Health Organization. (1998). *Towards a Common Language for Functioning and Disablement: IIDH-2.* Geneva: World Health Organization.

Yalom, I. D. (1995). *The Theory and Practice of Group Psychotherapy.* New York: Basic Books.

Yee, A. H. (1989). *A People Misruled: Hong Kong and the Chinese Stepping Stone Syndrome.* Hong Kong: API Press.

Yu, M. W. (1989). *Justice and the Politics of Difference.* Princeton: Princeton University Press.

Yung, K. K. (1977). Special education in Hong Kong: Is history repeating itself? *Hong Kong Special Education Forum, 1*(1), 1–19.

11

HISTORICAL DEVELOPMENT OF DISABILITY SERVICES IN SINGAPORE: ENABLING PERSONS WITH DISABILITIES

Kenneth K. Poon and Meng Ee Wong

A British colony with its modern founding attributed to Sir Stamford Raffles in 1819, Singapore is a young island nation with no more than 5 decades since its independence from Britain in 1963 and from Malaysia in 1965. In this relatively short period, it has made tremendous economic progress. For example, it was ranked in 2012 as a country with among the highest GDP per capita in the world (World Bank, 2014). That same year, Mercer ranked Singapore the top Asian city with the highest quality of living, and it emerged 25th out of the 221 cities in an annual global survey (Lee, 2012). Singapore is the third most densely populated country in the world, with about 4.8 million people living in 700 square kilometres of land. It also has a diverse resident population of about 3.77 million in 2010 (Singapore Department of Statistics, 2011): ethnic Chinese form the majority (74.1%), with ethnic Malays (13.4%) and Indians (9.2%) accounting for a significant proportion of the minority.

There are currently no studies providing an estimate of the prevalence of disabilities in Singapore. However, official statistics (Steering Committee on the Enabling Masterplan 2007–2011 [EM1], 2007) estimated an incidence of 3%. Specifically, about 3.2% of preschoolers receive a diagnosis of developmental disabilities, and 2.5% of school-aged children and adults have a diagnosis of disabilities. How are individuals with disabilities supported? What is life like for persons with disabilities? Tracing this development from the lens of economic development, this chapter will put forward the case that the development in services for persons with a disability has occurred over a few discrete phases, each corresponding to shifting conceptualizations of disability over the decades. In particular, there will be a focus on the tacit assumptions underlying the service provision as well as the tensions and contradictions that exist within.

A brief history of service provision for persons with disabilities in Singapore

Service provision for persons with disabilities has its roots in antebellum Singapore under British rule. Following that, service provision developed in discrete phases corresponding to economic development (Poon, Musti-Rao, & Wettasinghe, 2013).

Antebellum Singapore (1940s and 1950s)

The earliest records show that disability services in Singapore started in the 1940s in post-war colonial Singapore, with organizations providing charitable services for people with physical and sensory with frequently coexisting intellectual disabilities. Homes were established as charities mainly for people with physical disabilities: the Trafalgar Home in 1947 for children with leprosy (Quah, 1993), the Home for Crippled Children in 1949 (Quah, 2004), the Fatimah Home in 1952, and the Singapore Cheshire Home in 1957 (Singapore Cheshire Home, 2014). In contrast, services for children with sensory impairments were established largely for education, such as the education for deaf children by the Red Cross Society, and the Singapore Association for the Blind in 1951 (Quah, 2004; Wong & Chia, 2010). The Singapore Association for the Deaf, the Canossian School for the Hearing Impaired, and the School for the Deaf were established in 1955, 1956, and 1963, respectively (Singapore School for the Deaf, 2007; Singapore Association for the Deaf, 2012; Canossian School, 2017).

This phase of development, focused on service provision for persons with physical or sensory impairments, cannot be understood outside the context of Singapore's social and economic development. These services emerged following the traumatic Japanese invasion and occupation from 1942 to 1945, and Singapore's subsequent return to British rule. This was a period when much of Singapore's infrastructure was destroyed, and there was widespread impoverishment, food shortages, disease, and rampant crime (Turnbull, 2009). Given these dire economic conditions and nature of the social services being developed, it comes as no surprise that the underlying premise guiding these advances was charity. However, there is an emerging sense that children with sensory impairments benefit from education, thus marking the advent of special education in Singapore.

Post-independence Singapore (1960s and 1970s)

Special education services during the formative years of Singapore as a nation proliferated during this period, especially for children with intellectual disabilities. The Singapore Association for Retarded Children (SARC) was established in 1962 (Lim & Nam, 2000). Three schools were established by SARC to serve children with moderate to severe intellectual disabilities between 1965 and 1968 (Movement for the Intellectually Disabled of Singapore, 2010). Children with mild intellectual disabilities were not formally provided for in the education system until 1971, when a subcommittee of SARC established two classes for those with mild intellectual disability. These classes marked the beginnings of the Association for the Educationally Subnormal (AESN) and their school in 1976 (Lim & Nam, 2000). Services for children with profound/multiple disabilities were also established in 1979 with the formation of the Handicapped Children's Playgroup by the Asian Women's Welfare Association (AWWA, 2010), and by the Christian Outreach to the Handicapped (Quah, 2004).

These services emerged during a tumultuous period that spanned Singapore's merger with the Federation of Malaya in 1963, military aggression from Indonesia from 1963 to 1966, riots between ethnic groups in 1964, and Singapore's separation from Malaysia in 1965 (Turnbull, 2009). These events took place in the midst of a nation still reeling from the Japanese Occupation during the Second World War.

Significant during this period is an expansion of special education to support not just those with physical and sensory impairments, but also those with intellectual and multiple disabilities. It was also during this phase of development that the organizations that later became MINDS and APSN came into being. It is also noteworthy that the earliest services for students with special needs in mainstream schools were initiated about this period.

Industrializing Singapore (1980s and 1990s)

Similar to the earlier decades, the 1980s and 1990s were characterized by a further proliferation of special schools. SARC continued to establish new schools, with three new schools established between 1983 and 1995 (Quah, 2004). Also significant was the renaming of SARC to the Movement for the Intellectually Disabled of Singapore (MINDS) in 1985 (Lim & Nam, 2000) and the renaming of AESN to the Association for Persons with Special Needs (APSN) in 2000 (Quah, 2004).

Early intervention in Singapore had its genesis during this period. The Early Intervention Programme for Infants and Children (EIPIC) was pioneered and launched by SARC in 1983 for children under 3 years of age with disabilities (Quah, 2004). The Margaret Drive Special School (MDSS) was established in 1987 and took over the early intervention program from MINDS, developing a programme for children with multiple disabilities (Tham-Toh & Poon, 2012). The first programme for children with autism spectrum disorders (ASD) was launched in 1989 (Tham-Toh & Poon, 2012). MDSS gained autonomy from the Singapore Council of Social Service (SCSS, now termed the National Council of Social Service [NCSS]) and was brought under the umbrella of the newly established Rainbow Centre in 1992 (Quah, 2004). A second school under the Rainbow Centre was established in 1995 (Clarke & Sharpe, 2004). Likewise, the playgroup for children with multiple disabilities run by AWWA was expanded into a special school in 1990 offering programs for students with multiple disabilities, ASD, and early intervention (Quah, 2004).

Services for adults with disabilities were also developed and proliferated during this period. The Goodwill, Rehabilitation, and Occupational Workshop (GROW) was established by the Spastic Children's Association School in 1984 (Cerebral Palsy Alliance Singapore, 2017) to provide sheltered employment and job placement for adults with cerebral palsy. Bizlink was established in 1985 to offer employment programs for people with disabilities (Bizlink, 2014). MINDS also set up three Employment Development Centres (EDC) providing employment opportunities for individuals with intellectual disabilities between 1987 and 1991. APSN established a similar centre for adults with mild intellectual disabilities in 1997 (Quah, 2004). Likewise, Day Activity Centres (later named Training and Development Centres) were established by MINDS in 1991 and 1994 to support individuals with intellectual disabilities who needed daytime assistance in daily living (Quah, 2004).

Mirroring the trend in special schools, support for students with disabilities in mainstream schools continued with the establishment of a centre-based educational psychology service by the Students Care Service in 1983. In addition, AWWA established the TEACH ME program in 1990 (Quah, 2004) to integrate students with physical impairments into the preschools, and also established a mobile therapy team to serve similar children in mainstream schools. The Dyslexia Association of Singapore

(DAS) was also established and started providing services via the Students Care Services Centre in 1991 (DAS, 2013). This program was later expanded to primary schools to help students with dyslexia overcome challenges posed by their learning disabilities (Ministry of Education, 2012).

It is evident that services for individuals with disabilities grew rapidly during this period, with services now spanning from early childhood identification into adulthood. In particular, educational services for persons with disabilities were greatly expanded, particularly within the special schools. Special education was established as a profession during this period, with the Institute of Education (later renamed the National Institute of Education) offering training courses for special education teachers. In addition, educational services were being expanded to include younger children with disabilities as well as children with mild disabilities who were educated within the mainstream primary schools.

This period was, thus, marked by the establishment of special education as a discipline in Singapore. It is likely that the high level of economic growth contributed, in part at least, to this development and to the expansion of more general social services for persons with disabilities. Both women and persons with disabilities were employed to a high degree within Singapore's workforce, and this made employment of persons with disabilities a more prominent issue for policymakers. However, special and mainstream education continued to exist as dual systems (Lim & Nam, 2000; Poon et al., 2013). There was limited mobility across the systems, and the dual-system structure was not conducive to inclusion.

Current service provision to persons with disabilities

The current state of services in the twenty-first century is characterized by a pace of development that far outstrips any period previously reported. Apart from Singapore now enjoying a quality of living that is comparable to the top cities of the world, specific steps have been taken to foster inclusion. Commentators have attributed the current Prime Minister's explicit reference to a vision of Singapore as an inclusive society announced shortly after his inauguration (Prime Minister's Office, 2004) as a starting point, and a number of inclusive-oriented policies unfolded in the ensuing years.

Early intervention

Most young children with disabilities now receive some form of early intervention. This early intervention may take the form of educational or therapy services (Ho, 2007). Centres that run an Early Intervention Programme for Infants and Children, or EIPIC, provide one of the pillars of early intervention for young children with moderate to severe disabilities. The number of such centres for young children with disabilities has rapidly increased to 21 (SG Enable, 2017); 2,600 children served in the various EIPIC programmes in 2015 (Ministry of Social and Family Development, 2016). Parents pay for early intervention services at EIPIC-funded centres but receive a government subsidy along with a sliding scale based on their per capita income. In addition, the *Integrated Childcare Program* (ICCP) was initiated in 2003 with currently 17 ICCPs operated by seven providers (SG Enable, 2011). Unlike EIPIC centres that are funded to provide direct support to young children with mild disabilities, ICCPs are childcare centres that serve children aged 2 to 6 years and receive additional funds to further deploy teachers to provide support to young children with disabilities. Like the EIPIC, parents pay for ICCP services along a sliding scale and receive subsidies. All ICCPs provide inclusive education (usually by teachers trained in early childhood education) for students with disabilities alongside typically developing children aged from 18 months to 7 years (Ho, 2007). The *Development Support Program* (DSP) is a government-funded collaboration between anchor providers of preschool services and the hospitals involved with the Child Development Programme. The DSP is a short-term programme focused on the early detection of, and intervention to, preschool children who are at-risk of, or have, mild developmental needs. Preschools receive the support of an external agency to provide support for young children with mild disabilities (EM2, 2012). Under this initiative, young children with disabilities are supported by learning support educators – preschool teachers who receive further training to support children with disabilities.

Educational support within mainstream schools

The Support for Special Needs Initiative was established in 2005 to support the inclusion of students with disabilities in mainstream schools. This took the form of the introduction of one or more Allied Educator–Learning and Behaviour Support (AED-LBS) programmes in all primary and selected secondary schools (Ministry of Education, 2004, 2010). The AED-LBS is a professional who is trained in supporting the learning and behavioural needs of students with disabilities. This support can take the form of in-class support, pull-out support, or indirect support via collaboration with teachers. Apart from that role, many AED-LBSs take on the role of coordinating the support and transition of students with disabilities. In addition, a tenth of all primary school teachers and a fifth of all secondary school teachers receive more than 100 hours of training to support students with disabilities in mainstream schools (Ministry of Education, 2004, 2007). These teachers trained in special needs (TSNs) take on different roles after their training, with most continuing to serve in their role as teachers of students with disabilities. Some have been entrusted with the responsibility of establishing and maintaining school support structures such as case management teams and special needs committees, or mentoring other teachers and school professionals (Poon et al., 2013). In addition, some secondary schools have been resourced to support students with hearing impairment who communicate via sign language with translators and others to support students with visual impairments (Wong & Chia, 2010). To date, there are 62 (or about one-third of) primary schools that provide School-based Dyslexia Remediation (SDR). SDR is provided to children screened at the end of Primary 2, and includes a parent involvement component (Ministry of Education, 2014a).

More recently, the establishment of a Disability Support Office (DSO) within each tertiary institute of learning (e.g., polytechnics, universities) was announced (Ministry of Education, 2014b). The DSO would provide a one-stop support for students with disabilities, support for staff training, and work with the respective schools or colleges to provide the necessary accommodations for lessons, examinations, and other forms of assessments. Further, they would set up a website to provide information on support for students with disabilities. Moreover, students with sensory or physical impairments will receive financial support to purchase assistive technology devices.

Other students who attend mainstream schools also receive further support in centres providing specialized services to groups of children. For instance, the TEACH ME program continues to support children with physical impairments in mainstream schools with an itinerant therapy team (AWWA, 2010). In addition to the school-based intervention programs, DAS also runs learning centres located within some mainstream schools and within the community to provide specialized interventions for children with dyslexia (DAS, 2009). In addition, therapy services such as physiotherapy, occupational, and speech/language therapy services are delivered via Therapy Hubs, operated by voluntary welfare organizations such as the Society for the Physically Disabled (2011).

Education in special schools

There are currently 20 special schools in Singapore serving approximately 5,400 children (EM2, 2012) with a broad range of needs – mild to severe intellectual disabilities, profound/multiple disabilities, autism spectrum disorder, as well as sensory and/or physical impairments. Special schools are run by voluntary welfare organizations and jointly regulated and funded by the Ministry of Education and NCSS. Apart from purpose-built school buildings, features of special schools include differentiated curriculum, better student–teacher ratios in the form of smaller class sizes, presence of teacher aides in classrooms, and related services provided by trained therapists. Special schools, with the exception of the few supporting children with mild disabilities, do not teach the national curriculum and conduct national examinations. In contrast, a specialized curriculum is adopted for their students' needs. Further, an individualized education plan (IEP) is developed for each student that customizes the supports and services that all students receive. In all cases, there is a strong emphasis on life skills with a focus on literacy and numeracy where appropriate. Due to their focus on specific groups of disability conditions, special schools are differentially resourced with equipment and material that support the specific needs of the students. Some examples include specialized facilities (e.g., hydrotherapy pools), augmentative/alternative communication technology (e.g., picture exchange cards, speech-generating devices), and assistive technology (e.g., wheelchairs, individual schedules, and Braille machines) (Poon et al., 2013). Moreover, to foster an increase in the degree of integration of students in special schools, there is a deliberate effort to co-locate special schools beside or near to mainstream schools to open the possibilities for the sharing of facilities such as school canteens (i.e., physical integration), inclusion during non-academic classes (e.g., music), and more recently, satellite classrooms (Ng, 2010).

Blurring of boundaries

Progress notwithstanding, the education system in Singapore remains very much a dual system (Lim & Nam, 2000; Poon et al., 2013). However, an initiative was announced in 2007 to implement more satellite special education classes within mainstream schools (Ministry of Education, 2007). Within such an initiative, students in special schools accessing the mainstream curriculum are provided with the opportunities to attend classes within mainstream schools. This will be further facilitated by, as mentioned, the co-location of mainstream and special schools to facilitate opportunities for physical and social integration between the students. This co-location also offers other opportunities for exchange, including opportunities for cross-training and secondments/work attachments between teachers from mainstream and special education schools.

From these developments, it appears that the traditional chasm existing between the two systems is showing signs of narrowing. Within the special school system, there seems to be movement towards co-location with mainstream schools and when possible, the adaptation of the mainstream curriculum. Similarly, there is also an increased provision of support for students with mild disabilities in mainstream schools and cross training for teachers to support students with special needs. As a result, traditionally impermeable boundaries between the special and mainstream systems are gradually blurring.

Adult services

When compared to the development of early intervention and special education services, the sector providing services for adults with disabilities is relatively less developed. However, employment and residential options exist for adults up to 55 years of age with disabilities (SG Enable, 2017).

Employment. For adults, *job placement and support* services are provided by voluntary welfare organizations to provide support for adults with disabilities who are able to access open (paid) employment. *Sheltered workshops* provide vocational training to adults with moderate to severe disabilities who are considered to be unable to engage in open employment. Within this environment, people with disabilities have the opportunity to acquire basic vocational skills, such as packaging and assembly and, through contracted work to the sheltered workshop, earn an allowance. However, the majority of individuals working in sheltered workshops earn only up to $100 per month (EM1, 2007). Still, the plan is for persons with disabilities to gain work experience in sheltered workshops and perhaps, as a result, have better prospects for employment within competitive settings. There are currently eight sheltered workshops catering to the needs of adults with ASD, intellectual disabilities, and physical impairments. *Day activity centres* (DACs) provide activities that promote the development of vocational and daily living skills to maximize independence and to provide for a transition to a sheltered workshop. Physiotherapy and occupational therapy are also provided at DACs. In addition, they provide a form of respite for caregivers during working hours. There are currently 19 DACs that provide services to adults with ASD, intellectual disabilities, and physical impairments.

Apart from providing direct services to adults with disabilities, there are initiatives in place to support the employment of such individuals. In addition to the tax incentives provided to employers of persons with disabilities, the Open Door Fund (ODF) was launched to encourage employers to redesign jobs, modify workplaces, and provide paid internships to adults with disabilities. Moreover, the Enabling Employers' Network (EEN) was established to advocate for employment opportunities for persons with disabilities. The EEN seeks to do this by recognizing employers who have provided opportunities and who have made efforts to integrate individuals with disabilities into the workforce. It also seeks to create awareness and acceptance of persons with disabilities in the workforce.

Hostels provide short-term residential-based training in work and life skills so that adults with disabilities are able to live independently in their own homes or in alternative assisted residential options. There are currently three hostels in Singapore catering to those with intellectual and physical disabilities. However, some adults with disabilities require higher levels of support in living. Adult residential homes provide short- or long-term residential care for those who do not have the option of living with family members. Recreational activities, as well as therapy and training, are provided within such settings. There are currently eight such homes in Singapore catering to those with intellectual and physical disabilities. Apart from providing such options, there is currently collaboration with a psychiatric hospital to provide on-site consultation and support to such service providers to equip them to better support the behaviour of adults with disabilities (EM1, 2007).

Compared to early intervention and special education, the adult sector is the most underdeveloped sector providing services for persons with disabilities. As such, parents have expressed high levels of anxiety over the long-term care plans for their adult children with disabilities. They have highlighted, amongst other concerns, the need for residential care settings to be environments that focus upon the quality of life of individuals with disabilities (EM2, 2012). Perhaps one characteristic of care for adults with disabilities in Singapore is the relatively affordable option of a live-in foreign domestic worker. Families of persons with disabilities who employ them for their care also receive some rebates on monthly levies that have to be paid for their employment.

Key characteristics of policy and service provision for disability in Singapore

Unlike many economically developed countries, there is no legislation mandating the provision of services for individuals with disabilities in Singapore. Yet services have nonetheless emerged in an orderly fashion, guided by national plans for persons with disabilities. The following sections discuss characteristics of service provision for children with disabilities in Singapore.

National plans and policy development

As mentioned, the lack of legislation mandating the provision of educational services for children with disabilities has not necessarily led to haphazard service provision. Instead, service coordination at a national level was made possible by the formation of national-level planning committees that make recommendations that guide policy. These recommendations have typically received the endorsement and financial support from successive governments. The most significant three planning committees to date are next described.

The Advisory Council on the Disabled (ADC) was convened in the late 1980s after feedback was elicited from stakeholders to chart policy directions (Advisory Council to the Disabled, 1988). This report, published relatively early in Singapore's economic development, laid the foundations for the current system. The recommendations of the ACD include the development of an assessment and diagnostic service for young children, teacher training in special education, better teacher–student ratios in special schools, increased Ministry of Education funding, Ministry of Education oversight of the operating budget and special education practice, and capital funding for purpose-built special education schools (c.f., Quah, 1990). The recommendations of the ACD were foundational for the sector. The assessment and diagnostic service that followed (see Ho, 2007) led to an increase in the number of young children diagnosed with developmental disabilities which, in turn, fuelled the development of the disability support sector. Likewise, the increased funding for special education and schools, when coupled with the formal training for special education teachers, served to build the sector.

The current period is heralded by a similar initiative termed the Enabling Masterplan for the Disability Sector (EM). Comprising representatives from public and private sectors as well as voluntary welfare organizations, the first EM (EM1) was established to guide the development of policy for people with disabilities in Singapore from 2007 to 2011 (EM1, 2007). The years that followed were marked by an increase in early intervention provision in Singapore. Within the primary and secondary schools, the EM1 called for "a continuum of educational models" (EM1, p. vii). In terms of adult services, the EM1 proposed the establishment of the EEN and highlighted the need for increased residential options. Another significant contribution of the EM was its broader focus of how persons with disabilities were supported. The Centre for Enabling Living (later named SG Enable) was established in 2009 as a first-stop centre that provided information needs and coordinated referrals within the disability sector.

A second EM (EM2) was established to guide service provision from 2012 to 2016 (Steering Committee of the Enabling Masterplan 2012–2017, 2012). EM2 continued the focus on increasing the quality of early intervention. Within special education, the EM2 called for an increased involvement of the Ministry of Education in special education. In addition, the EM2 had a stronger focus on vocational training/ employment, especially an increase in both the capacity of the system to function and the quality of its work. It also proposed that Singapore ratify the United Nations' *Convention of Rights for Persons with Disabilities* (United Nations, 2006), and that children with disabilities who are currently exempted from compulsory education (Ministry of Education, 2014c) be included within Singapore's Compulsory Education Act (2001).

Many helping hands and 3P

A tenet of service provision for persons with disabilities in Singapore is the "many helping hands" approach (c.f., Ho, 2007). This philosophy hinges upon the collaboration of public, private, and people sectors (3P) for the provision of social services. This has resulted in a model of service delivery where services for persons with disabilities are provided by voluntary welfare organizations with some regulation from the government. Parents pay for these services but typically receive some government subsidy along a sliding scale. Within such a model, services are further supported by voluntary welfare organizations' fundraising, as many of these voluntary welfare organizations have charitable status and donors receive a tax incentive for donations.

Future directions

As the preceding discussion indicates, the development of services for disabilities has been led by corresponding gains in economic development. This earlier approach of economic pragmatism is understandable, as Singapore in the earlier decades was unable to afford service provision for those with disabilities. However, in recent years Singapore has been rapidly advancing in its economic progress and now ranks as one of the richest countries in the world. If the earlier rationale was to meet economic needs first, now that Singapore has emerged as one of the world's most prosperous nations the time ahead must surely be expected to focus on further provisions for persons with disabilities. Moreover, Singapore's recent signing of the United Nations' *Convention of Rights for Persons with Disabilities* in 2012 (NCSS, 2014) now introduces the rhetoric of and a commitment to rights into the discourse of service provision for persons with disabilities. Coupled with the political rhetoric of an inclusive society (Prime Minister's Office, 2004), it is possible that the issue of rights and equity may now feature more strongly within social discourse regarding disability. Although the ideals of human rights and of economic pragmatism are not necessarily diametric opposites in the delivery of services to persons with disabilities, balancing these two ideological pillars will not be easy once the notion of rights becomes entrenched in the social milieu. A further outgrowth from this transformation is the greater emphasis of the third *P*, that is, people, or in this case persons with disabilities themselves. Thus far, the committee-led initiatives have been mainly government-directed. There is no reason to dismiss the notion that greater involvement will emerge from the ground to advocate for change. The globalized world we live in exposes us to divergent ideas and possibilities. Greater availability of communication channels, such as social media, serves to consolidate diverse views and air collective voices to introduce change. The tasks that need to be addressed are as follows:

- Conversations need to be fostered about the notion of inclusivity within the context of persons with disabilities, and about how to include their voices within this discussion.
- We need to focus on high levels of quality of life as outcome indicators and balancing that against economic outcomes.
- Given that disability issues are complex and impact the lifespan, the support needed cuts across different disciplines and requires an intergovernmental ministry to monitor and advocate for change. As had been previously proposed in the report of the EM1, we need to revisit the idea of a national disability office to spearhead such coordinated needs.
- At a larger, national platform, we need to begin a dialogue to consider the need for, and relevance of, introducing legislation for disability in Singapore.

References

Asian Women's Welfare Association (AWWA). (2010). Milestones. Retrieved from http://www
.awwa.org.sg/index.php?option=com_content&view=article&id=10&Itemid=41
Bizlink. (2014). Background and history. Retrieved from http://www.bizlink.org.sg/about-us/
background-and-history

Canossian School. (2017). Our journey. Retrieved from http://www.canossian.edu.sg/about-us/journey-2

Cerebral Palsy Alliance Singapore. (2017). About GROW. Retrieved from http://www.cpas.org.sg/our-programmes/pro-grow/about-grow/

Clarke, C., & Sharpe, P. (2004). Early intervention. in L. Lim & M. M. Quah (Eds.), Educating Learners with Diverse Abilities (pp. 63–88). Singapore: McGraw-Hill Education (Asia).

Compulsory Education Act (Chapter 51). (2001). Singapore.

Dyslexia Association of Singapore (DAS). (2017). The history of DAS. Retrieved from https://www.das.org.sg/about-das/history

Dyslexia Association of Singapore. (2017). 1989 to 1994 – the early years. Retrieved from http://www.das.org.sg/about-das/history/1989-to-1994

Ho, L.-Y. (2007). The Child Development Program in Singapore 1988–2007. Annals of the Academy of Medicine, 36, 898–910.

Lee, M. (2012, December 5). S'pore ranks highest in quality of living in Asia. Business Times Singapore, p. 2.

Lim, L., & Nam, S. S., (2000). Special education in Singapore. Journal of Special Education, 34, 104–109.

Ministry of Education. (2004). Enhancing support for children with special needs. Retrieved from http://www.moe.gov.sg/press/2004/pr20040918.htm

Ministry of Education. (2007). Levelling up opportunities: Raising the quality of education for children with special educational needs. Retrieved from https://www.moe.gov.sg/press/2007/pr20070307b_print.htm

Ministry of Education (2012). More Specialised Support for Students with Special Needs. Retrieved from https://www.moe.gov.sg/news/press-releases/more-specialised-support-for-students-with-special-needs

Ministry of Education. (2014a). School-based Dyslexia Remediation Programme (SDR). Retrieved from https://www.schoolbag.sg/story/school-based-dyslexia-remediation-programme-(sdr)

Ministry of Education. (2014b). Enhanced support for students to access opportunities in institutes of higher learning (IHLs). Retrieved from https://www.schoolbag.sg/story/enhanced-support-for-students-to-access-opportunities-in-institutes-of-higher-learning-(ihls)

Ministry of Education. (2014c). Compulsory education. Retrieved from http://www.moe.gov.sg/initiatives/compulsory-education/

Movement for the Intellectually Disabled of Singapore. (2010). Milestones. Retrieved from http://www.minds.org.sg/AboutUs.html

National Council of Social Service (NCSS). (2014). United Nations convention on the rights of persons with disabilities: What does it mean to us? Retrieved from http://www.ncss.org.sg/social_service/uncrpd.asp

Ng, E. H. (2010). Speech by Dr Ng Eng Hen, Minister for Education and Second Minister for Defence, at the official opening of the new Pathlight School site on Tuesday, 27 April 2010 at 10.30am. Retrieved from http://www.nas.gov.sg/archivesonline/data/pdf-doc/20100504001/minister_speech.pdf

Poon, K. K., Musti-Rao, S., & Wettasinghe, C. M. (2013). Special Education in Singapore: History, Trends, and Future Directions. Intervention in School and Clinic, 41(Mar/Apr). Retrieved from http://singteach.nie.edu.sg/issue41-bigidea/

Prime Minister's Office. (2004). Speech by Prime Minister Lee Hsien Loong at the opening of the Spastic Children's Association of Singapore's Cerebral Palsy Centre. Retrieved from http://www.nas.gov.sg/archivesonline/speeches/view-html?filename=2004091801.htm

Quah, M. M. (1990). Special education in Singapore. International Journal of Disability, Development and Education, 37(2), 137–148.

Quah, M. L. (1993). Special education in Singapore. in M. L. Quah, S. Gopinathan, & S. C. Chang (Eds.), A review of practice and research in education for all in Singapore.

Country Report submitted to the Southeast Asian Research, Review and Advisory Group (SEARRAG) (pp. 89–102). Singapore: National Institute of Education.

Quah, M. M. (2004). Special education. in L. Lim & M. M. Quah (Eds.), Educating Learners with Diverse Abilities (pp. 29–61). Singapore: McGraw-Hill Education (Asia).

SG Enable. (2011). ICCP service matrix. Retrieved from https://www.sgenable.sg/uploads/EIPIC%20Service%20Matrix.pdf

SG Enable. (2017). EIPIC service matrix. Retrieved from http://www.sgenable.sg/uploads/EIPIC%20Service%20Matrix.pdf

SG Enable. (2017). Services for adults with disabilities. Retrieved from https://www.sgenable.sg/pages/content.aspx?path=/for-adults/

Singapore Association for the Deaf. (2012). History of SADeaf. Retrieved from http://sadeaf.org.sg/about-us/history/

Singapore Cheshire Home. (2014). Profile of the Singapore Cheshire Home. Retrieved from http://www.cheshirehome.org.sg/aboutsch/profile.shtml

Singapore Department of Statistics. (2011). *Census of population 2010 statistical release: Demographic characteristics, education, language, and religion.* Singapore: Ministry of Trade and Industry.

Singapore School for the Deaf. (2007). About SSD. Retrieved from http://www.ssd.edu.sg/about.html

Steering Committee on the Enabling Masterplan 2007–2011 (EM1). (2007). Report on the Enabling Masterplan 2007–2011. Singapore: Ministry of Social and Family Development.

Steering Committee on the Enabling Masterplan 2012–2016 (EM2). (2012). Enabling Masterplan 2012–2016: Maximising potential, embracing differences. Singapore: Ministry of Community Development, Youth and Sports.

Tan, C. J. (2016). Early intervention services for children with speech delay, autism and at risk of moderate to severe disabilities. Retrieved from https://www.msf.gov.sg/media-room/Pages/Early-intervention-services-for-children-with-speech-delay,-autism-and-at-risk-of-moderate-to-severe-disabilities.aspx

Tham-Toh, J. S. Y., & Poon, K. K. (2012). The development of special education in Singapore. in Tham-Toh, J. S. Y., Lyen, K., Poon, K. K., Lee, E. H., & Pathnapuram, M. (Eds.), Rainbow Dreams: A Holistic Approach to Helping Children with Special Needs (pp. 23–34). Singapore: Armour.

Turnbull, C. M. (2009). A History of Modern Singapore, 1819–2005 (Rev. ed.). Singapore: National University of Singapore Press.

United Nations. (2006). Convention on the rights of persons with disabilities. Geneva, Switzerland: Author.

Wong, M. E., & Chia, N. K. H. (2010). Education of the visually impaired in Singapore: An overview of primary and secondary programs. Journal of Visual Impairment and Blindness, 104, 243–247.

World Bank. (2014). *GDP per capita (current US$). The World Bank.* Retrieved from http://data.worldbank.org/indicator/NY.GDP.PCAP.CD

12

SWEDISH DISABILITY POLICIES:
IDEAS, VALUES AND PRACTICES IN
A HISTORICAL PERSPECTIVE

Rafael Lindqvist

Introduction

Swedish conceptions of disability are formed in the context of a centralist state that imposes universalist principles through legislation. By means of legally defined criteria it gives to disability a consistency that it never had before. As shown by Stone (1984), the disability category became important when the welfare state emerged in the last century as a means for redistribution; it became important in order to decide when citizens were so poorly off because of illness and impairment that some form of public aid was necessary. In the Western welfare states this is manifested in legal entitlements to support in terms of social security, disability benefits and social services. In this chapter Swedish disability policies will be analysed in terms of ideas and values about redistribution. What kind of definitions of disability can be discerned during different time periods? Which were the dominant policy ideals, and how were they legitimized during different time periods? To some extent this chapter also describes social policy interventions relating to the dominating policy ideals. A relatively long historical perspective is used for the purpose of providing a background to important changes during the last 5 or 6 decades. The account will necessarily be selective and sketchy since the field is extensive. The time periods that will be focused on are first, the liberal period in the beginning of the last century. Politics targeting disabled people basically consisted of poor relief, workhouses, i.e., institutions with the purpose of infusing work ethics in the inmates. The second era consists of the decades from the end of World War 2 until the 1970s. It is by some scholars described in terms of a 'golden period' for the Swedish welfare state, when social security, social services and an active labour market policy emerged. Next, some important changes in the welfare system will be dealt with, signifying a development away from the universalist model of the 1960s and '70s to a more selective welfare model that also emphasizes human rights as a key element in welfare.

Liberal social policies – poor relief, institutions and work morality

Care, treatment, and education for disabled people were long performed in a variety of (total) institutions, each of them designed for specific categories of disabled people.

The basis for this expansion was shaped from the early 1900s, but the 1950s can be seen as a high-water mark of this approach. In addition to institutional care, poor relief was a key element in social policies in the beginning of the last century. Poor relief rested with the multitude of small municipalities (than about 2,500) facing the general problem of how to provide for the increasing share of older people, disabled and marginalised people. State interventions were called for and manifested in the introduction of a general public old-age pension system in 1913, and a few years later, a workmen's occupational insurance scheme covering a major share of the working male population. According to the moral values embedded in the liberal policies of that time, poor people should be brought up to become virtuous social citizens (Berge, 1995). The challenge was to change individuals' attitudes and values, not society. In this context it became crucial to distinguish between the 'deserving' poor and the 'undeserving', and the ambition was to create

> a social system that provided support to those in real need in a humane and reasonable way at the same time as such support must be deterring enough so that work always was perceived by the client as a better alternative than public aid. (Sjögren, 1997, p. 86)

Workhouses, poor houses and other institutions that aimed to install work ethics were seen as crucial to educate the poor to become useful citizens. Such institutions housed a mix of people: the poor old people, disabled, drinkers and tramps; they were designed to counteract idleness and begging, and also to counteract unjustified claims to get public aid. Poor relief was despised by 'the ordinary man'. The common trait of the inmates was that they were unable to provide for themselves and/or did not have anyone who could assist them to do so.

The idea of a 'people's home' (*folkhemmet*) articulated by the then Social Democratic party leader, Per Albin Hansson, in a parliamentary speech in 1928, came to be seen as a break with the old poor-relief ideology and its strict needs-test procedures. In his vision a universal welfare policy provided for income protection and basic social services. In addition to the general old age pension established in 1913, a small disability pension was introduced in the 1930s, and disability cash allowances for certain groups were also introduced. However, it was not until after World War 2 that universal income-related social security benefits were established.

As a societal counter-reaction towards the unsatisfying poor relief, a differentiated system of institutional care emerged in the beginning of the 20th century. The state early engaged in education of deaf and blind children, while the long-term sick, mobility impaired and crippled had to rely on private and voluntary initiatives (Grunewald & Olsson, 1997, p. 18). Expressions like 'rescue institutions' (*Räddningsinstitut*) for poor and delinquent youth and correction institutions mirror the underlying motives to rescue marginalised people from moral decay in an era when medical expert knowledge was poorly developed. Care and treatment of the mobility impaired and crippled expanded in the 1920s onwards, based on an optimistic faith in the hitherto successful orthopaedic correction and treatment. Orthopaedics was seen as treatment that could soften the consequences of the epidemics of polio that raged at that time.

Institutional care and treatment were based on a medical model, implying that disability was a consequence of decease and impairment, which in turn required segregated measures and a specialization of support and interventions. The medical perspective also required that institutions were big enough to provide for medical expertise (a chief medical doctor), and patients who could be used for various research projects (Söder, 2003, p. 25). But there also were pedagogical and educational ambitions involved, which meant that the inmates must make efforts to train for an occupation for the purpose of maintaining themselves.

One example that illustrates the importance of total institutions in this era was Vipeholms Hospital, opened in 1935, designed for intellectually disabled with a physical impairment or with 'complicated behavior or asocial symptoms' (Forssman & Olow, 1964, p. 79). At most, it housed 1,000 inmates, and it was at that time the biggest institution for intellectually disabled in Sweden. Another illustration is the fact that around 1900 about 4,000 people were incarcerated in mental asylums. During the following decades these figures were to increase many times over.

The ideology of institutional care and treatment contained a complex pattern of motives: ambitions to support and control the inmates as well as to develop the person's work ability were combined (Qvarsell, 1991). One often-used method was inspection that has long traditions in Sweden (practiced by the church and by medical regional officers). Systematic inspections were conducted in disabled persons' home environment by travelling blind inspectors in the early 1900s. Reports on the living conditions of former inmates and pupils written by these inspectors indicated that the main motive was to assess the need for and provide for the future support needs of former pupils, but also to see to it that the blind and visually impaired people were industrious and conscientious. If this was not the case, a negative report was written (Olsson, 2007). Care and control were intertwined in such inspections. It was important that the blind engaged in normatively acceptable work and occupation; everything that smelled of begging was counteracted by the inspectors. Also mobility-impaired people treated and educated in orthopaedic institutions (*Vanföreanstalter*) must be prepared to be inspected. When they left the institution the inspector usually tried to help them to find gainful employment, and/or to provide them with equipment, work materiel, orthopaedic aids etc. to earn their own living (Holme, 1996).

The integration of disabled people in work life was not a key policy issue until the 1950s. The prevailing view implied that the disabled were bound for specific occupations: tailor, shoemaker, carpenter, brush-maker, basketmaker etc. Workhouse, training institutions and home-work agencies were established in the early 1900s, by the poor relief units in the municipalities and by voluntary organizations to help the long-term sick and disabled to maintain themselves. The aim was also to make the burden easier for the poor relief organization in the municipalities (Hallerby, 1988). Such initiatives paved the way for the introduction of broader labour market policies for disabled persons after World War 2.

The emergence of universal welfare policies and the disabled

The period from the 1950s to the late 1970s is generally thought of as the golden years of the Swedish welfare state (Huber & Stephens, 2001). Drake (1999, pp. 98–105) describes Sweden as the maximum welfare state because it combined general social policy measures with selective support to the most needy. Universal income-related social security was established, as well as ambitious labour market policies and expansion of health care and personal social services in the counties and local municipalities. Such developments were strongly related to the ideological conception of 'the strong society', a concept coined by Tage Erlander, Social Democratic prime minister in the 1950s and 1960s. Social engineering and access to generic benefits and services within the framework of an extensive public sector would take care of citizens' various needs (Erlander, 1962). 'We must try to establish a method dealing with the claimants entire needs. An *action plan* [my emphasis] involving all medical and social elements, must be established', contended the general-director of the National Board of Health and Welfare, Bror Rexed (1969, p. 186).

Economic and job growth in the post–World War 2 decades led to lack of labour power. This meant that the potential labour power of disabled people gained increased interest. In 1946 the concept of normalization was used for the first time in policy context by a government commission, the so-called Commission for People with Partial Work Ability (SOU, 1946: 24; Ericsson, 2002). Its mission was to investigate and propose measures to make better use of the work ability of the partially disabled so that they could get or keep gainful employment.

The concept of normalization contained, in this context, ambitions to increase economic growth and to improve the social and labour market chances for persons with disabilities. However, in practice this meant that selective measures like subsidized employment, sheltered employment and measures for work test and training were considered in order to support disabled people with partial work ability. During the formative years of the active labour market policy, it was estimated that one-third of those registered with the public employment offices looking for work were in some respect disabled (SOU, 1983: 22, p. 164). Policies aiming towards full employment also broadened the base for universal welfare policies implying that the need for needs-tested social assistance and other selective measures decreased.

However, faith in segregating institutions was also considerable as late as in the 1950s. From then and onward, political efforts were directed to modernize and improve the standard of the existing institutions (nursing homes, boarding schools, work training institutions) but also to build new institutions (Söder, 2013, p. 27). One example illustrating how modernization played out in practice, in 1953, was Carlslund nursing home (*Carlslunds vårdhem*) for intellectually disabled people (Socialstyrelsen, 1964). The motive, according to the owner, the Stockholm health county organization, was 'to arrange rational caring facilities, where the relevant clientele, could get adequate care and be looked after, and simultaneously the staff was given the opportunity to work under as satisfying conditions as possible' (citation from Grunevald & Olsson, 1997, p. 96). The nursing home had 522 beds and staff composed of medical doctors, psychologist, physiotherapists, speech therapist and nursing staff. It had laboratory equipment, X-ray and ECG for the purpose of providing 'rational somatic care' (Grunevald & Olsson, 1997, p. 293). Carlslund nursing home was phased out from the mid-1970s; then it accommodated 350 persons with intellectual disabilities living there, and 500 personnel (Grunevald & Olsson, 1997, p. 110). The last institution for the mobility impaired and crippled was closed in the early 1970s, and part of its activities was integrated in somatic hospital care. Likewise, special schools for pupils with mobility impairment were phased out, and these children were educated in the mainstream educational system, albeit many of them in special classes. Institutions and special schools were more and more seen as a last resort; they were too large and they could not provide for adequate treatment and support. Reforming institution-based care and treatment turned out to be difficult and time-consuming, since such institutions reflected deep-rooted cultural values and views on disabled people.

Income maintenance and social security

The orientation of Swedish welfare policies towards universal benefits and services was, for many years, regarded as beneficial for disabled people and other vulnerable groups. Such measures were intended to make disabled people less dependent on poor relief and needs-tested benefits. However, in cases where severely disabled people had needs which could not be met through universal welfare measures or disabled persons were not entitled to income-related schemes (social security programs, labour market policies, generic social services, public health care and rehabilitation), services tended to segregate rather than integrate them into the community. This mirrors the fact that Social Democratic welfare policies from the mid-1940s onwards were mainly oriented towards eradicating poverty for broad groups of wage earners and less directed towards improving the living conditions of people with severe and persistent disabilities. The conscious strategy was to make welfare policies bridge over existing status and class differences by including all social strata in a uniform, income-related social security system. The working class was given entry to the welfare state of the middle class (Esping-Andersen, 1990). But it also created new divisions, for instance between those who were established in the labour market and those who were not. Severely disabled people usually belonged to the latter category. In order to economically support the severely disabled, an expanded disability cash allowance (*handikappersättning*) compensating for extra costs necessary in daily life, and a care allowance (*vårdbidrag*) was introduced in the mid-1970s to economically compensate parents having extra costs for a disabled child. These benefits built on forms of support established in the 1930s.

In light of such divisions, two scholars, Gunnar and Maj-Britt (1970, pp. 298–299), contended in their book, *The Unfinished Welfare Policy* (Den ofärdiga välfärden) that welfare policies so far had not abolished class society. Apart from having supported the poorest, the welfare policies had mainly levelled out differences between individuals and families in the life cycle, but not between social strata and classes. Many disabled people, not being let into the labour market, experienced increased inequality compared to others (Ransemar, 1968, p. 77). During the 1970s increased unemployment because of structural change in the labour market and increased work-speed especially hit disabled and older workers (SOU, 1974: 90). Stricter employment protection laws were introduced, according to the principle 'first in – last out'. Other measures in order to support disabled workers were the introduction of longer notice periods and special employment protection for disabled workers in subsidized employment.

Integration, normalization and the expansion of social services

Concepts of normalisation and integration were launched as key ideas in disability policy (Nirje, 1980). The aim was to bring about an environment for disabled people that offered as normal a life as possible (Mallander, 1995). Disability was increasingly conceived of as a relative phenomenon, i.e., as a relationship between the impaired individual and his/her surroundings (SOU 1964: 43, SOU 1976: 20; Söder, 2013). The Swedish approach to disability policy gradually developed into a relational model approach, or what Pfeiffer (2005, p. 33) has called the 'continuum version'. He contended that 'the fit between the environment and the impairments of people produces the issues confronting persons with disabilities', implying that a lot can be done to improve housing, transportation, employment practices etc. that would increase participation in society for disabled persons. When economic growth was high in the 1960s, this facilitated the expansion of the public sector, including care, treatment and social services. This expansion, which mainly took place in counties and municipalities, has been called 'the silent revolution' (Gustafsson, 1988, p. 58). Ideas of normalization and integration were manifested in terms of (round-the-clock) home help services, supported housing, transport services and economic support to adapt the disabled person's apartment, small group homes, special education or support to participate in mainstream education, technical aid in daily life, etc. All these facilities were organized by the counties or municipalities, but subsidized by the state.

Many of the ideas put forward by Swedish politicians, accepted as guiding ideological principles (however far less implemented in practice), also link to the so-called social model of disability elaborated by UK disability researchers (Oliver, 1990, 1996), because barriers in the institutional and physical environment were emphasized. The idea of mainstreaming, i.e., each societal sector must have responsibility to abolish barriers for disabled people, was strongly supported by Swedish disabled policy activists (Ekensteen, 1968). The crucial problem was that society was not accessible for disabled people. Disability issues thus were politicized since there was a shift in focus: from a caring perspective to a social approach. Within a couple of years the major user-organization, *De handikappades riksförbund, DHR och Handikappföreningarnas centralkommitté*, HCK – had a relational view on disability on their agenda. The latter organization, an umbrella association for a number of different disability organizations wrote in its action program, A Society for All (1972) (*Ett samhälle för alla*), that disability first and foremost must be seen as shortcomings in the environment (Handikappsamverkan, 1972, p. 8).

Critique of the welfare state: The dominance of bureaucracy and expert knowledge

During the years 1970–1985 institutions gradually came to be regarded as a last resort. Important impulses leading to this wave of change came from the critique against expert-dominated care institutions which argued that the professional expertise embodied in such institutions led to spatial as well as social segregation, which stigmatised the disabled inmates (Lindqvist, 2000; Mallander, 1995, pp. 45–67). Such critique, which was first and foremost voiced by the Independent Living-movement (established in Sweden in the 1980s), also drew attention to rigid bureaucratic implementation and the domination of staff interests over service-user interests in generic social services in the community. Critique concerned the fact that benefits and services were not responsive enough to the disabled person's needs, and the fact that the whole welfare landscape of agencies was difficult to oversee (Hugemark, 1998, p. 160).

During the 1980s ideas of normalization and integration were put into effect in the new Swedish Care Act of 1986, which prescribed the closing down of traditional total institutions for people with intellectual disabilities. From then on care services, and support for living in the community, would gradually become the responsibility of the municipalities and not the regional health county organisations. By 1995 almost all former institutions were closed and disabled persons moved to either their own dwellings (adjusted to their needs) or to small group residences. A parallel process took place in the field of psychiatric care. From the 1970s onwards a new emphasis on outpatient services led to the closing down of traditional mental hospitals, beginning in the early 1980s. The social services organisation in the municipalities and the local health care centres were given the responsibility to provide for basic support to the long-term mentally ill now living in the community (Markström, Sandlund, & Lindqvist, 2004).

Changes from the 1990s onwards

In the aftermath of the introduction of the relational model of disability, the political debate has come to involve structural and institutional barriers in society. Concepts like normalization and integration seem to have disappeared from the policy agenda, and new emphasis on concepts like accessibility, full participation in society, self-determination, opportunity to live like others, and choice have occurred. Emphasis on rights and choice has replaced talk about normalization and integration. Such conceptual changes came in as important aspects to form the base upon which the disability policy reform of 1994 was constructed. This reform, and the Psychiatric Care Reform of 1995, signified a further shift from a medical perspective to a social-approach perspective and strengthened the development towards a post-de-institutional era where disabled persons are dispersed in the community (Rosenberg, 2009). The fact that such reforms were launched shows that neither universal welfare policies, nor social assistance based on needs-tests, had succeeded in improving living conditions for disabled people (Lewin, 1998).

The disability reform took shape in the Law Concerning Support and Service for Certain Groups of Disabled People, LSS (SFS, *Svensk författningssamling*, 1993: 387), and the Law Concerning Compensation for Assistance, LASS (SFS, *Svensk författningssamling*, 1993: 289). The group that was eligible for services under this law was disabled people with 'large and persistent difficulties in managing daily life', including three subgroups: (1) persons with intellectual impairments, (2) persons with lasting mental dysfunction after damage to the brain brought about by violence or physical illness, and (3) persons with other physical or mental disabilities that are not clearly linked to normal ageing. Ten different services were stated in the law as being specific social rights (SFS, *Svensk författningssamling*, 1993: 387):

1 personal assistance
2 companion services
3 contact person (support person)
4 relief service in the home
5 short-term minding of schoolchildren over age 12
6 short stay away from home (respite care)
7 group homes for children and adults
8 daily activities

9   counselling
10   other personal support

It rests with the local community to provide for the measures stated in LSS. Since some of these services are frequently contracted out (especially personal assistance and group residences) and the implementation of purchaser-provider models, private providers have come to see this as a lucrative business. Hence, a shift from publicly organized disability services to privately organized or NGO-based services has occurred. The most well-known measure was personal assistance. The disabled person also has the right to decide what kind of help the assistant should give and in what way. The decision about personal assistance must state the number of hours per week, at all hours of the day and night. There is no explicit limitation regarding the number of hours per week, but it is not unique that assistance is provided round-the-clock by several assistants taking over from each other.

With the introduction of the Disability Reform, services to disabled people were divided between two legal frameworks: the Social Services Act, SoL (SFS, *Svensk för-fattningssamling*, 2001: 453), which covers all disabled people (provided that need for services can be demonstrated); and LSS/LASS, which covers the severely disabled. The Social Services Act, SoL, builds on traditions of poverty relief and provides services that are needs-tested, i.e., testing the support needs of the individual. LSS/LASS are civil-rights-influenced. Both programmes target people with severe disabilities, but in practice people with severe intellectual and physical disabilities are more or less automatically categorized as having disability-related needs and therefore entitled to LSS services, while people with mental health problems are referred to needs-tested social assistance because their disability-related needs are considered to fluctuate and vary individually.

According to the The Psychiatric Care Reform, passed in 1995, the local communities were given an expanded mandate to arrange social support, housing and occupational activities for the target group. The idea was that municipalities must develop new comprehensive services for persons with psychiatric disabilities (Markström, Sandlund & Lindqvist 2004). As prescribed in the Social Services Act, in Sweden the local social welfare authority must maintain an awareness of living conditions in the municipality for people with mental health problems. However, up to date the development of recovery-oriented measures in terms of psychiatric rehabilitation and supported employment have been sluggish (Lindqvist, Markström & Rosenberg 2010). Persons with psychiatric disabilities also seem to have a weaker position in the welfare system, because the disability law is more ambitious in its aims: it sets out to provide 'good' living conditions, while social services aim to provide a 'reasonable' level of living.

In 2011 the total number of people receiving one or more of the services according to LSS and provided by the municipalities was 67,400 (Socialstyrelsen, 2015). This is a very small number, given that the population of Sweden at that time was about 9,500 000 people (www.scb.se).

Activation – also for the long-term sick and disabled?

In comparison to expanded rights to social support in daily life, there are no mandated rights to work and occupation. Sweden has to a high extent, compared to other countries, established sheltered employment for disabled people (Migliore, 2010) and subsidized employment. In 2014 almost 77,000 persons with a disability had a subsidized position with a public or private employer (*Arbetsförmedlingen*, 2015, p. 75), and the number of people in sheltered employment in Samhall, a nationwide state-subsidized company with the task to provide meaningful employment for persons with disabilities, was about 19,700 (Samhall, 2015).

As in many other countries, work-related activation policies have developed in Sweden during the last two decades. Activation principles in labour market policy as well as social assistance and sickness insurance today emphasise changes to personal responsibility, the obligation to enter work training programs, reinforced condition-ality, and restricted entitlement to sick cash benefits, disability pensions and more tai-lor-made and individualized services for groups of clients (see Giertz, 2004; Handler, 2004; Hvinden & Johansson, 2007; Lødemel & Trickey, 2001). Activation policies tend to change the balance between citizens' rights and duties codified in individual action plans or activity plans.

Combined with emphasis on activation, restrictions in sickness and disability insur-ance have been introduced. Sickness and disability insurance in Sweden covers all workers (employed and unemployed). The compensation level is about 80% of previ-ous income as long as the annual income does not exceed SEK 536, 600 (in 2017), i.e., 7.5 times the basic amount, (*prisbasbelopp*). After one year on sick cash benefits the compensation level is lowered to 70%. The earlier system, implying that sick cash benefits could be paid out for an unlimited time period, was replaced by a so-called rehabilitation chain (*rehabiliteringskedja*) on 1 July 2008, with precise deadlines for the assessment of the claimant's remaining work ability. The rehabilitation chain was intended to bring about active measures during the sick-list period by explic-itly involving the health care organisation in vocational rehabilitation practices. The maximum benefit period was decided to be 2.5 years. However this time limit was abolished in 2016.

If the person has drawn sick cash benefits for more than half a year, and if s/he is not entitled to a disability pension, the person will be referred to the PEO for partici-pation in a 'work life introductory program'. The idea is that the person will be pro-vided with individually adapted measures to cope with the new situation, to develop work motivation, and to acquire knowledge of different occupations and work tasks. After this period of work life introduction, the person can move on and participate in other labour market measures, or educational programs – or, if that is not a realistic option, apply for further sick cash benefits. During the time period 2010–2014 about 80,000 persons who had exhausted their sick cash benefits took part in such work life introduction programs. A majority of the participants, after having participated in the program, found their way to other labour market programs offered by the PEO. However, many of the participants returned to sickness insurance after some months and received sick cash benefits (Arbetsförmedlingen, 2014). This indicates that acti-vation policies combined with entitlement restrictions and benefit cuts may not sup-port the long-term sick and disabled finding gainful employment.

Welfare, anti-discrimination and human rights

From the 1990s tighter eligibility criteria have been introduced in the social secu-rity system, implying less compensation in case of sickness and early retirement.

In parallel there has been a stronger emphasis on activation and vocational rehabilitation for people on paid sick leave. Also in social services entitlement criteria have become stricter, implying that a greater share of social care tends to rest on relatives and next-of-kin (SOU, 2000: 56, p. 171) The fact that welfare agencies cope with the most needy can be interpreted in terms of a new 'deservingness ethics'. On the other hand, the importance of coping with structural aspects of society to improve living conditions for persons with disability can be traced to the national action plan, From Patient to Citizen (*Från patient till medborgare*), decided by the government in 2000 (1999/2000: 79). There, it is stated that a disability perspective must permeate all societal sectors so that accessibility is increased and discriminating attitudes decrease.

Another important shift in disability policies was the introduction of anti-discrimination laws. Several causal factors were of importance. While welfare policies were good in redistribution of material resources, they did not perform well in creating justice in work life, education and to combat discriminating attitudes. It was not until 1 May 1999 that the Prohibition of Discrimination in Working Life of People with Disability Act (*Lag om förbud mot diskriminering arbetslivet på grund av funktionshinder*) came into force (SFS, *Svensk författningssamling*, 1999: 132). The law draws a distinction between direct and indirect discrimination. The former implies that an employer must not be unfair to a disabled job-seeker or an employee by treating them less advantageously than the employer treats other people. The employer is also obliged to investigate and take measures against harassment, i.e. behaviour in the workplace that violates an employee's integrity where such behaviour has a connection with the employee's disability. The employer may have to pay damages to the employee (or job-seeker) if discrimination or harassment has taken place.

A few years later, a law on equal treatment of students at universities was promulgated, as was a law prohibiting discrimination in a broad range of public services. In 2009 the different anti-discrimination laws were included in one new Discrimination Act (SFS, *Svensk författningssamling*, 2003: 567). The purpose was to make Swedish discrimination legislation more effective and comprehensive. The Disability Ombudsman was replaced by an Equality Ombudsman with an expanded remit. Since 2015 lack of accessibility is included in the anti-discrimination law, with the exception of accessibility to dwellings, private activities and workplaces with fewer than ten employees.

In 2010, commissioned by the government, the Swedish Agency for Disability Policy Coordination (Handisam) in cooperation with the National Collaboration for Improved Mental Health (NSPH) launched an anti-stigma campaign intended to raise awareness, change public attitudes and end the discrimination faced by people with mental health conditions. The campaign, called *(H)järnkoll*, started in 2009 and was intended to run for the next 3 years. It used 200 'attitude ambassadors', i.e. people who have experience of mental health problems and who were key people in educational activities, local mobilisation activities and in providing information for and dialogue with employers and unions.

The development towards more effective civil and social rights was taken a step further when the Swedish government ratified the UN Convention on the Rights of Persons with Disabilities (UN CRPD) and its Optional Protocol on 4 December 2008. The Convention and the Protocol came into effect on 14 January 2009.

Table 12.1 The development of Swedish disability policies – some main traits

	1930s	1960s	1990s onwards
Definition of disability	Individual impairment, medical model	Relational model, interaction between individual and environment	Structural model, lack of accessibility, discrimination, practices, etc.
Policy ideals	Segregation, social control, support and protection	Integration, normalisation, social rights	Full participation in social and work life, living like others, human rights
Base of legitimacy	Paternalism, moral ethics, work enforcement	Central steering, bureaucratization, expert knowledge	Local decision-making, user influence, choice
Interventions	Poor relief institutions (for treatment and training) inspection	Care, services in the community (generic and specialized) Living in the community and	Measures to increase accessibility, combat discriminating attitudes and practices
Social status	Client, inmate, patient	service-user	Citizen and consumer

The convention puts pressure on Swedish policymakers and practitioners to see to it that human rights are effectuated in all the life spheres pointed out in the Convention. Research indicates that, although social rights have been established in a number of life spheres, there is an implementation gap indicating that there is plenty of room to improve human rights for persons with disabilities in such areas as community living, life in institutions, group homes and special schools, support in decision-making and access to justice (FRA, European Union Agency for Fundamental Rights, 2012a,b).

In Table 12.1 some main traits of the historical development are pointed out in terms of key words. It is evident that disability is not a culturally and historically fixed and stable phenomena. Definitions, social political ideologies, and support (and control) measures tend to change from one time to another, as do our attitudes and social status that we ascribe to persons with disabilities.

Conclusions

The Swedish welfare state has, from the 1960s onwards, gone through considerable changes regarding definitions of disability, policy ideals and the way such ideals are legitimized and translated into practices and specific measures and interventions (Lindqvist 2010). The social status ascribed to the disabled person has also changed. In terms of policy, all the major social partners and political parties still subscribe to the idea of universal welfare policies covering practically the whole population. However, some important shifts have occurred towards more privatization of services as a result of the introduction of purchaser-provider models, implying that public bodies purchase services provided by private organizations or NGOs according to contracts negotiated between the parties. Increased focus has also been put on selective services, activation and workfare elements, meaning that the claimant must work or demonstrate his or her work motivation in order to be entitled to a specific benefit or service. However, more civil rights, especially in disability policies, have also been emphasized. While the welfare policies developed in the 1960s were to a large extent characterised by centralised steering and control and by an optimistic faith in social engineering, goal-oriented solutions and detailed regulation, there is now more emphasis on decentralisation to municipalities, and focus on the disabled person as consumer. Accordingly, decision-making and the responsibility for various welfare activities have been transferred from higher to lower levels in the welfare system. Consequently a variety of forms have developed in which welfare services are delivered. The choices made by local agencies have become more important in terms of policy outcomes.

While social rights in sickness insurance, and labour market policy and social assistance, including home help, have been circumscribed, services to people with the most severe impairments have expanded. The Disability Reform of 1994 manifests significant social rights for a group of citizens that has up to this date been marginalised from society. In terms of the social model of disability, the various legal measures can be seen as instruments for overcoming at least some of the barriers imposed on disabled people. On the other hand, it has been demonstrated that new barriers have been raised in other fields in terms of restrictions in social security, social assistance, employment and educational arrangements. This also indicates increased focus on the individual, and on his or her responsibility to become employable, and can be interpreted in terms of 'institutionalized individualism' (Beck & Beck-Gernsheim, 2003), i.e. key institutions in the welfare state target individuals instead of social strata. It would be a mistake to characterize this new form of governance in terms of a reduction of the role of the state, or as a transition from the interventionist state to deregulation. The state has been an active player in making entitlement criteria stricter, linking such criteria to activation.

References

Arbetsförmedlingen. (2014). *Arbetsförmedlingens återrapportering. Tidiga insatser för sjukskrivnas återgång i arbete.* [Public employment services: Report on early interventions for return-to-work. Work life introduction]. Stockholm, Sweden.

Arbetsförmedlingen. (2015). *Arbetsförmedlingens Årsredovisning 2014.* [Public employment services: Annual report 2014]. Stockholm, Sweden.

Beck, U., & Beck-Gernsheim, E. (2003). *Individualization: Institutionalized individualism and its social and political consequences.* London, UK: Sage.

Berge, A. (1995). *Medborgarrätt och egenansvar. De sociala försäkringarna i Sverige.* [Civil rights and personal responsibility]. Lund, Sweden: Arkiv.

Drake, P. (1999). *Understanding Disability Policies.* London, UK: Macmillan.

Ekensteen, V. (1968). *På folkhemmets bakgård. En debattbok om de handikappades situation.* [On the backyard of the "people's home"]. Stockholm, Sweden: Prisma, Verdandi Debatt.

Ericsson, K. (2002). *From Institutional Life to Community Participation: Ideas and realities concerning support to persons with intellectual disability.* Uppsala universitet, Sweden: Acta Universitatis Uppsaliensis.

Erlander, T. (1962). *Valfrihetens samhälle.* [Society of choice]. Stockholm, Sweden: Tiden.

Esping-Andersen, G. (1990). *The Three Worlds of Welfare Capitalism.* Cambridge, UK: Polity Press.

Forssman, H., & Olow, I. (1964). *De psykiskt utvecklingsstörda, deras utbildning och vård.* [Education and social care for persons with intellectual disabilities]. Verdandis skriftserie 16. Stockholm, Sweden: Bonniers.

FRA., European Union Agency for Fundamental Rights. (2012a). *Involuntary Placement and Involuntary Treatment of Persons with Mental Health Problems.* Vienna: Author.

FRA., European Union Agency for Fundamental Rights. (2012b). *Choice and Control: The Right to Independent Living: Experiences of Persons with Intellectual Disabilities and persons with mental health problems in nine EU Member States.* Vienna: Author.

Giertz, A. (2004). *Making the Poor Work: Social assistance and activation programs in Sweden.* Lund, Sweden: Department of Social Work, Lund University.

Grunewald, K., & Olsson, T. (1997). *Utan talan. Historia i bild från omsorgerna om utvecklingsstörda.* [No say. History and photographs of social care for persons with intellectual disabilities]. Stockholm, Sweden: Liber.

Gustafsson, B. (1988). *Den tysta revolutionen: Det lokala välfärdssamhällets framväxt. Exemplet Örebro 1945–1982.* [The silent revolution: The emergence of the local welfare state. The example of Örebro]. Stockholm, Sweden: Gidlunds.

Hallerby, N. (1988). *Samhalls rötter: Från fattigvård till industrikoncern.* [The roots of Samhall: From poor relief to manufactory company]. Tullinge, Sweden: Samhall.

Handikappsamverkan. (1972). Ett samhälle för alla. [A Society for All]. Stockholm: HCK, Handikappförbundens centralkommitté.

Handler, J. F. (2004). *Social Citizenship and Workfare in the United States and Western Europe: The paradox of inclusion.* Cambridge, UK: Cambridge University Press.

Holme, L. (1996). *Konsten att göra barn raka: Ortopedi och vanförevård i Sverige till 1920.* [The art of correcting and preventing deformities in children: Orthopaedics and the care of cripples in Sweden up to 1920]. Stockholm, Sweden: Carlssons.

Huber, E., & Stephens, J. D. (2001). *Development and Crises of the Welfare State: Parties and policies in global markets.* Chicago, IL: University of Chicago Press.

Hugemark, A. (1998). Motstridiga tendenser i handikappomsorgen – professionalism versus personlig assistans. [Conflicting tendencies in disability services – professionalism versus personal assistance]. in Lindqvist, R. (Ed.), *Organisation och välfärdsstat.* [Organization and the welfare state]. Lund, Sweden: Studentlitteratur.

Hvinden, B., & Johansson, H. (Eds.) (2007). *Citizenship in Nordic Welfare States: Dynamics of choice, duties and participation in a changing Europe.* London, UK: Routledge.

Inghe, G., & Maj-Britt. (1970). *Den ofärdiga välfärden.* [The unfinished welfare policy]. Stockholm, Sweden: Tidens förlag, Folksam.

Lewin, B. (1998). *Funktionshinder och medborgarskap.* [Disability and citizenship]. Uppsala, Sweden: Socialmedicinsk tidskrifts skriftserie.

Lindqvist, R. (2000). Swedish disability policy: From universal welfare to civil rights? *European Journal of Social Security, 4,* 399–418.

Lindqvist, R. (2010). *Funktionshindrade i välfärdssamhället.* [Disabled people in the welfare state]. Malmö, Sweden: Gleerups.

Lindqvist, R., Markström, U., & Rosenberg, D. (2010). *Psykiska funktionshinder i samhället.* [Psychiatric disability in the community]. Malmö, Sweden: Gleerups.

Lødemel, I., & Trickey. (2001). *'An Offer You Can't Refuse': Workfare in international perspective.* Bristol, England: Policy Press.

Mallander, O. (1995). Planning for normalization. in A. Khakee, I. Elander, & S. Sunesson. (Eds.), *Remaking the Welfare State: Swedish urban planning and policy-making in the 1990s* (pp. 45–67). Aldershot, UK: Avebury.

228

Markström, U., Sandlund, M., & Lindqvist, R. (2004). Who is responsible for supporting "long-term mentally ill" persons? Reforming mental health practices in Sweden. *Canadian Journal of Community Mental health*, *23*(2), 51–63.

Migliore, A. (2010). Sheltered workshops. In *International Encyclopedia of Rehabilitation*. Buffalo, NY: Center for International Rehabilitation Research Information and Exchange (CIRRIE).

Nirje, B. (1980). The normalization principle. in R. Flynn & K. Nitsch (Eds.), *Normalization, Social Integration and Community Services*. Baltimore, MD: University Park Press.

Oliver, M. (1990). *The Politics of Disablement*. London, UK: Macmillan.

Oliver, M. (1996). *Understanding Disability*. London, UK: Macmillan.

Olsson, C. (2007). Omsorg och kontroll. Diskurs och livsvärld. Synskadades roll i samhället. [Care and control. Discourse and life world. Visually impaired people and society]. in R. Lindqvist & L. Sauer (Eds.), *Funktionshinder, kultur och samhälle*. [Disability, culture and society]. Lund, Sweden: Studentlitteratur.

Pfeiffer, D. (2005). The conceptualization of disability. in G. E. May & M. B. Raske (Eds.), *Ending Disability Discrimination: Strategies for social workers*. Boston, MA: Pearson.

Prop. (1999/2000: 79). *Från patient till medborgare. En nationell handlingsplan för handikappolitiken.* [Government bill: From patient to citizen. A national action plan for disability policy].

Qvarsell, R. (1991). *Vårdens idéhistoria*. [An intellectual history of health care]. Stockholm, Sweden: Carlssons.

Ransemar, E. (1968). Efterskrift. [Postscript]. in V. Ekensteen (Ed.), *På folkhemmets bakgård*. Stockholm, Sweden: Prisma, Verdandi Debatt.

Rexed, B. (1969). Socialpolitiken inför 70-talet. [Social policys on the eve of the 1970s]. in L. Andersson (Ed.), *Idéerna som drivkraft. En vänbok till Tage Erlander*. [Ideas as driving forces. Festschrift to Tage Erlander]. Stockholm, Sweden: Tidens förlag.

Rosenberg, D. (2009). *Psychiatric Disability in the Community: Surveying the social landscape in the post-deinstitutional era*. Umeå, Sweden: Department of Social Work, Umeå University.

Samhall. (2015). Års-och hållbarhetsredovisning. [Annual and sustainability report]. Stockholm: Samhall.

SFS., Svensk författningssamling. (1993: 387). *Lag om stöd och service till vissa funktionshindrade.* [Swedish code of statues: Law on support and services for persons with disabilities].

SFS., Svensk författningssamling. (1993: 389). *Lag om assistansersättning* [Swedish code of statues: Law concerning compensation for assistance].

SFS., Svensk författningssamling. (1999: 132). *Lag om förbud mot diskriminering i arbetslivet på grund av funktionshinder*. [Swedish code of statues: Act on prohibition of discrimination in working life of people with disability].

SFS., Svensk författningssamling. (2003). *Lag om diskriminering*. [Swedish code of statues act on prohibition of discrimination].

Sjögren, M. (1997). *Fattigvård och folkuppfostran. Liberal fattigvårdspolitik 1903–1918*. [Poor relief and people's education. Liberal social policy 1903–1918]. Stockholm, Sweden: Carlssons.

Socialstyrelsen. (1964). Sociala meddelanden. Årg. 1964, Nr 5–6 (Stockholms socialvård II). [National Board of Health and Welfare: Social reports].

Socialstyrelsen. (2015). Personer med funktionsnedsättning – insatser enligt LSS år 2014. [National Board of Health and Welfare: Persons with disabilities – support measures according to LSS in 2014].

SOU. (1946: 24). *Förslag till effektiviserad kurators – och arbetsförmedlingsverksamhet för partiellt arbetsföra m.m.* [Swedish government official report: Proposals for efficient social support and public employment services for persons with partial work capacity].

SOU. (1964: 43). *Social omvårdnad av handikappade.* [Swedish government official report: Social care of disabled people].

SOU. (1974: 90). *Arbete åt alla*. [Swedish government official report: Work for all].

SOU. (1983: 22). *Utbildning för arbetslivet*. [Swedish government official report: Educating for work life].

SOU. (2001: 56). *Funktionshinder och välfärd. Kommittén Välfärdsbokslut*. [Swedish government official report: Disability and welfare].

Söder, M. (2003). Normalisering, handikappolitik och forskning. [Normalization, disability policy and research]. in Nirje, B. The Normalization principle. [Normaliseringsprincipen]. Lund Studentlitteratur.

Stone, D. (1984). *The Disabled State*. Philadelphia, PA: Temple University Press.

13

ONE DIFFERENCE IS ENOUGH: TOWARDS A HISTORY OF DISABILITY IN THE BELGIAN-CONGO, 1908–1960

Pieter Verstraete, Evelyne Verhaegen and Marc Depaepe

In 2010, the Democratic Republic of Congo celebrated the 50th anniversary of its independence, which was celebrated in the Democratic Republic of Congo as well as Belgium. Besides the many official gatherings, celebrations and ceremonial processions, it was also a time when the history of Belgian-Congo (1908–1960) and its aftermath was examined through innumerable books, monographs, journal articles and novels (Van Reybrouck, 2010; De Boe et al., 2010; Verlinden, 2010). Interestingly, the subject of disability, however, was rarely mentioned in these celebratory publications. This is not to suggest that none of the texts referred to the existence of persons with disabilities, but it does appear that the histories of disabled Congolese citizens, like the histories of most people with disabilities across the globe, is quite invisible. Bearing in mind Douglas Baynton's far-reaching statement taken from his influential essay on disability, history and inequality, namely that "disability is everywhere in history, once you begin looking for it, but conspicuously absent in the histories we write," this particular neglect of disability in the historiography of Belgian-Congo seemed to be superficial and misleading (Baynton, 2001). Two examples in particular can sustain this suggestion with regard to the way the subject of disability has been omitted from the history of Belgian-Congo, the first having to do with the very start of the Belgian colony, the second one related to the way its complex and challenging history was made public in 2004 by a group of local activists.

Featuring disability in Belgian colonial history

When exploring the history of Belgian-Congo, one can find evidence where disability has played a crucial role in the colonization of the Congo. For example, when one examines the discourse used by Leopold II, King of Belgium, to legitimize his colonization efforts in Central Africa, one immediately becomes aware of the

This chapter is a revised and abbreviated version of Evelyne Verhaegen's unpublished Masters thesis written at the *Centre for the History of Education* of the KU Leuven under the supervision of Pieter Verstraete and Marc Depaepe: Verhaegen, E. (2012).

importance attributed to disability. Leopold II stated at that time that his actions were necessary and legitimate because Belgian colonization would put an end to the widespread reign of Arabic slavery and the related practices of forced mutilation (Hochschild, 1998). The events that led to the creation of the Belgian-Congo in 1908 are rooted in a much earlier history, beginning in 1875 when Leopold II, who himself succeeded his father Leopold I as King of Belgium in 1865, intensified his efforts to conquer the geographical heart of Africa. Among other things it was the expedition of David Livingstone and Henry Morton Stanley which eventually lead to the recognition of Kongo Free State as the personal possession of Leopold II at the International Conference in Berlin in 1884. Interestingly, while Leopold II used the threat of Arabic slavery and mutilation as a principle for Belgium's involvement in Central Africa, it was not long before Belgian atrocities toward the Congolese people replaced the atrocities of others. Within time, greed for resources such as ivory from elephants and later rubber contributed to incredibly harsh and punitive treatment of the Congolese. Indeed, their lives meant little to Belgian colonists, whose main purpose was to extract as much as possible while at the same time paying the workers as little as they could get away with. By the 1890s and early 20th century, with increased demand for rubber the Belgian Kongo Free State was more or less transformed into one big rubber plantation. As the demand for rubber increased, so too did the concern for profit, and the living and working conditions became harsher and harsher, and in a sense a form of slavery. Supervisors at the plantations made use of dehumanising and painful methods, including the severing of a worker's hand or foot as an example to other workers, thus ensuring that quotas were maintained. It is impossible to trace the exact number of mutilated workmen resulting from Leopold II's harsh economic order in the Kongo Free State but photos of the era, published around 1900, clearly attest to the fact that mutilated Congolese people served as an important tool in the colonization process but would later undermine the legitimacy of King Leopold's activity in the Kongo Free State (Figure 13.1).

The record indicates that thousands of Congolese people were disabled as a result of mutilation and amputation, so disability is very much part of the Belgian-Congo's history. Besides the factual existence of disabled people in the Kongo Free State, in examining the role they played in the discourses surrounding the switch from the Kongo Free State to the Belgian-Congo, one also can find references to a more symbolic and metaphorical existence of disability, namely in the way public opinion in Belgium has dealt with its colonial history after its independence. One of the most tangible examples to be given refers to a group of Belgian activists who disagreed with the overall positive tone by which King Leopold was remembered, and they "reconfigured" the statue. The statue in question is built on the dike of Ostend River and depicts black workers standing in adoration of King Leopold II. In order to highlight the cruel reign of Belgium's former king and to trigger a public discussion regarding Belgium's colonizing history as it was and is remembered, one hand of one of the sculpted black men was sawed off in 2004 (Lippens, 2007) Again disability as a form of punishment was placed central in the discussions related to the history and the commemoration of what happened in the Belgian-Congo. It was these kind of references to the real and metaphorical existence of disabled people in the (commemoration of) Belgian-Congo that triggered the question as to why in the histories devoted to

Figure 13.1 Congolese labourers who failed to meet rubber collection quotas were often punished by having their hands cut off. Image courtesy of the USC Digital Library, International Mission Photography Archive ca. 1860–ca. 1960.

Belgium's colony so little reference was made to disability. In what follows we intend to show for one particular historical subdiscipline, namely the history of education, how and why disability has to be taken into account in order to better understand what happened and why some things did not happen in the educational history of Belgian Congo.

The role of Belgian education in the colonization and the oppression of the Congolese people

The history of education in the Belgian-Congo, especially the rise and development of the Catholic missionary system, has been the subject of several in-depth studies (Briffaerts, 2007, 2011). During the reign of Léopold II, Catholic missionaries were given permission to set up a basic school system with the aim of converting the populace to Christianity and Catholicism. The principle of conversation was linked to the Christian Eurocentric ideology of superiority, wherein the people of Congo were viewed by the Belgian missionaries as the exotic, innocent, child-like savages whose souls had to be saved. As far as European elites were concerned, Europe was the centre of culture, progress and development, and Africa, with its vast resources, was theirs for the taking. Colonization was not only considered right and just, but also it was seen as a humane way of bringing civilization to people who were considered godless and primitive. An important task of the missionaries and other persons active within the educational system in the Belgian-Congo thus was to Christianize and "civilize" the so-called savages and in this way bring them closer to what was considered the superior level of civilization of their European colonizers. Vaughan notes this particular appraisal and devaluation of African life as a result of the distinction between nature and culture. He offers the following example: "the 'wild', whether in the form of the moorland, 'woman', of African wildlife was simultaneously romanticized and feared in European culture" (Vaughan, 1991). The belief in white European superiority was not limited to the Belgians; other Europeans, such as Lord Chesterfield, for example, argued in the 18th century that "African people were the most ignorant and primitive inhabitants of the world. At their best they could be placed a little higher than lions, tigers and leopards" (Exposition ASLK Galery, 1984). Indeed, many European elites believed that the further one was removed from the centre of the world (Europe), the more one would encounter humankind in a less-developed form. Starting in the early 1800s many "anthropological" expeditions departed Europe for various parts of the world with the intention of discovering the origins of humankind by watching and observing how populations considered primitive, especially those living in Australia or Africa, behaved, interacted and communicated with each other. During this age of enlightenment, renaissance and the rise of scientific discovery, observing and studying "the other" had become one of the most important instruments that could be used in order to gain knowledge about "the self", about the development of humankind – in short, about the process of civilization.[1] A notable example of the rise of learned institutions in Europe was the *Société de l'observateur de l'homme*. Besides expeditions, however, this society also became known as one of the most important actors in the education of Victor de l'Aveyron, also known as the Wild Boy. Why, some of the spokespersons of this society asked themselves, send out expeditions to faraway countries while we have within our own world people who meet the criteria to be considered savages. "Can we", they continued, "not just study their development and thus reconstruct man's evolution?" (Gineste, 1991). History reveals that no matter where European colonizers traversed the world, they did so with a sense of superiority over the original peoples from North America to South America, from Asia to Australia, and the people of Africa were treated no differently. Indeed, from the perspective of Belgian missionaries and colonizers, the people of Congo were considered to be not completely human. On the contrary, the main aim of the educational system, which was gradually set up in the Congo, was to civilize those who were considered savage people. As one observer stated in 1902,

> when Europeans spoke about or interacted with black people then they do this in such a way as if these locals were not real human beings, but rather a kind of creatures which belonged more to the animal realm than the realm of human kind. (Quoted in Eynikel, 1983)

It will not come as a surprise that in this particular context of Eurocentric notions of superiority and racism, education was considered one of the main instruments for colonizing, "Catholicizing" and "civilizing" those deemed to be less than human by enforcing values and beliefs that were closer to the European ideal of autonomy, cultural identity, knowledge of the sacraments, local self-governance and productivity.

By the early 20th century, a primary objective of bringing religious canon to Congo was replaced with the objective of civilizing the Congo, which in effect meant moulding the populace into pseudo-Europeans. Belgian officials and landowners needed a population of well-behaving, docile yet physically strong men and women who could help increase the production of rubber and other agricultural products like cacao, palm oil, bananas etc. If at the very beginning of the 20th century the Belgian government strived towards the abolition of child labour in the homeland, a complex educational machinery was established in the colony in order to raise good working and well-behaving labourers. Of course there was some attention paid to the intellectual development of the Congolese child; however, the largest part of the day was dedicated to the instruction of working skills, physical exercise and moral instruction. The primary objective of the Belgian colonial educational system, therefore, should not be considered something aimed at the emancipation of the colonized men, women and children. On the contrary, by focussing on vocational training, religious instruction and moral guidance, the Congolese school contributed substantially to a colonial context where the inhabitants were treated – to use a phrase taken from a Dutch historian of education – so as to keep them child-like (Dasberg, 1975). There were a few exceptions which allowed some of the children and youth to continue with a primary and secondary education that was so-called advanced or *évolué*. Keeping in mind that the primary objectives of education and training were the creation and development of a docile and productive labourer or housewife, the students who composed the *évolués* category, the ones who made the most progress on the ladder of civilization, were not expected to meet the standards of reasoning and behaviour that was typical for European people (Kadima-Tshimanga, 1982; Mianda, 2002).

While the educational historiography has produced a great deal of research regarding the moralizing, colonizing and suppressing nature of the Belgian educational system that was built up between 1908 and 1960, it can be said that 'disability' has played a minor role in this history. In the following pages it will be argued that (1) people with disabilities are found in the Belgian Congo era; (2) there were no special educational initiatives set up for these persons before independence in 1960 and (3) from a European colonizing point of view, all the local inhabitants were considered morally and intellectually disabled.

Sparks of disability in the educational history of Black-Africa

The silence that embraces the history of disability in Africa can be quite disturbing. In the opening section of this chapter it becomes clear that the amputation of hands of plantation workers and their subsequent disability was crucial in the discourses surrounding the foundation of Léopold II's Kongo Free State. In addition to the numerous stories pertaining to disability resulting from amputation, there is historical evidence which reveals that disability was often a stigmatized and devalued human condition. Evidence of the social treatment of disabled people can be found through the investigation of records of priests and nuns who were part of the colonizing and Christianizing process as well as through interviews of individuals who served in the Congo. Following a review of documents archived by one of the major congregations that was active during and prior to the independence of the Belgian Congo, namely the *Zusters van Liefde van Jezus en Maria/ Sisters of Love of Jezus and Maria*, the authors

interviewed three nuns who were active in Belgian-Congo in the 1950s and one peda-
gogue who became dean of the faculty of psychology and educational sciences at the
University of Lovanium in Kinshasa. It was found that interviews were necessary, as
the actual written material of the archives provided no evidence of the existence of
people with disabilities, which is quite interesting considering that disablement is part
of human life in all societies. Evidence from the interviews, however, does explain
some of the reasons underpinning the absence of people with disabilities in the written documentation.[2]

> When a child was born and one saw that it had a particular defect then it
> immediately was murdered. I still remember very well the birth of a deaf and
> dumb child. You immediately recognize this … on the basis of the sound the
> child produces … then there is something wrong. Those kind of children were
> murdered because they could not produce anything for the family, but this
> was not considered a murder like we would do. Very often and due to medical
> faults the child was born with malformations, for example six fingers. In that
> case one would tie one of the fingers … it also happened that a child was kept
> alive but not taken care of. (Conversation with Sister van Quekelberghe)

> No, I do not think I have seen children with a disability … but well, one
> hundred years ago this was not that different in Belgium … In Congo those
> kind of people were hidden, many Congolese believed these children were
> so-called witch children … they did not have any future. (Conversation with
> Sister Haussman)

> I cannot say much about the subject you are researching, in the end I also
> only stayed for a couple of years in Belgian Congo, but most disabled chil-
> dren eventually became street children due to their misery … this resulted
> from the fact that the family feared the abnormal a lot. When something
> abnormal happened, like the birth of a disabled child, this was a very bad
> sign for the Congolese people. The Congolese people actually hid their disa-
> bled offspring … in the sense that one did not talk about them … they were
> not really outcast, but rather … rather hidden due to fear or something as
> shame … and then let to starve … once I myself had a disabled assistant
> with an amputated arm, but at that time this was already very exceptional.
> (Conversation with Knapen)

What becomes clear from these excerpts taken from several interviews is that the
absence of disabled people in community life during the Belgian colonizing period
can be explained on the basis of cultural practices and superstitious beliefs held by the
Congolese themselves. For these interviewees, the practice of infanticide was another
practice which reinforced the belief that Congolese people were not as civilized as
Europeans, as the practice of infanticide of infants born with impairments had more
or less discontinued as a common practice in Europe by the early 20th century. It is
evident that the interviewees saw the care and treatment of children with disabilities
in Europe as being superior to that of the Congolese, and in terms of infanticide this
may have been the case. However, European and Western models of institutional care
which emerged by the mid-19th century were very punitive and reflected social norms

where people with disabilities were considered to be of less value than nondisabled people, and thus they had to be put away and segregated from the population. It is important to note that the observations made by the interviewees may have had some truth, but their comments do not truly reflect the complexities of the relationship between disabled and nondisabled peoples of Africa. Simply put, not all disabled infants were killed or left to die, but from the perspective of those involved in the process of colonizing the Congo, the establishment of programs for Congolese people with disabilities helped to justify the process of colonization as well as helped to legitimize their actions and presence in the colony (Pels, 1997). A somewhat recent example of the justification of "civilizing" the Congo and addressing the situation of people with disabilities can been found in the documentary *Homme comme toi: Les villages Bondekos: Centres pour handicaps Kinshasa* (A man like you: Bondekos Villages, Centres for the handicapped in Kinshasa, 1995) Although this documentary originally appeared in 1995, it still has something to say about the way disabled people figured in the colonial discourse before and after the independence of Congo. *Les Villages Bondeko* (which translates as 'villages of friendship') or the Bondeko villages, were founded after independence. One of the interviewed sisters, Sister Marie-Thérèse Haussman, actually worked for a while as educator in these villages. The opening scene of the movie shows a group of disabled Congolese who reside in the Bondeko villages and who sing a song that depicts the situation of disabled people in former times:

> Really God, you are love
> The God of love, GOD
> God, look at us disabled people
> Yesterday, despised as beggars
> Today we are respected
> Really – really
> Today it is like that
> In former times there were parents who hide away their disabled children
> So it was in the past
> Really – really

The text of this song shows the role of missionaries and nuns in changing the social status of children with disabilities from that of being outcasts to that of being included. It is interesting to note the eminent position of religion and the Christian God in changing this social status. While there is no doubt that the Church played an important role in saving children with disabilities, it appears that these children may play a functionary role for colonial propaganda and legitimacy for their continuous missionary activities (Ceuppens, 2003). Interestingly, the song seems to depict that infanticide, hiding disabled children or treating them as beggars was typical of Congo and possibly other African countries, but these same practices were typical of many countries around the world, including many countries in Europe.

Although missionary accounts suggest that the religious moral approach to providing care to people with disabilities helped to create a more positive social attitude toward disabled Congolese, it is quite evident that there had long been a difference in acceptance which was related to the origins of impairment. The historical reality for sure has to be seen in a different light, and although it is of course impossible to reconstruct the divergent local attitudes towards disabled people – not to mention the epistemological difficulty of applying a Western concept to a bygone period in a completely different culture (Ingstadt and Whyte, 2007) – there are instances from which one can deduce that in the Congo one could encounter blind, deaf or physically impaired people. First, there is the example of rubber plantation workers who had their hands, arms and feet amputated as a form of punishment, which is noted in previous sections of this chapter. Second, there is ample evidence of river blindness, medically known as onchocerciasis, which is caused by a parasitic disease caused by infection from a roundworm and can result in the loss of sight when not properly treated. The relationship between blindness and the filarial worm infection had long existed in the Congo before being medically diagnosed in 1930 by the Belgian ophthalmologist, Jean Hissette. After being informed of the high prevalence of blindness by a priest who lived in a village in the Pania-Mutombo region, Hissette asked the priest to send the blind persons to his house: "One beautiful tropical night," Hissette wrote in an autobiographical text,

> I noticed eight blind people arriving in front of my domicile; each of them was holding onto the end of a stick being guided by another person. In order to get here they had walked over 400 km. During the next five months I examined and tested these blind Babindi people almost every day. (Kluxen, 2011)

The documentation that relates to the discovery of river blindness by Jean Hissette and to the amputations of plantation workers clearly shows that the assumption made by missionaries and nuns, that people with disabilities were outcasts, does not reflect the observations made by the doctor. In brief, ostracizing people with disabilities cannot be accepted as a universal practice throughout the Congo, and there may have been many reasons for the rejection or acceptance of disability, some of which may have been linked to causation. For example, some infants born with disabilities may have been seen as evil spirits, whereas those blinded by onchocerciasis or those who were disabled because of the barbaric practice of amputation may have been viewed as unfortunate innocents by the indigenous Congolese as well as the Europeans. The way these persons were perceived and represented by the colonial powers, however, cannot be disconnected from the reigning attitudes and beliefs held towards the black inhabitants even during the latter colonial period just prior to independence, when rehabilitation programs were being offered to Congolese disabled people. In 1950 Doctor Van der Elst, in an article entitled *La prothèse des amputés du membre inférieur*, reported the following:

> Since a couple of years some Congolese who underwent the amputation of the lower limb are given a prosthesis. Those indigenous people, who were so lucky to receive such a prosthesis, in general were sent back to their homes. I had the opportunity to encounter some of these unfortunate people … We learned by experience that it is necessary to keep those indigenous and prosthetic persons in our centre and thus not to send them back to the bush. In this way we can control their equipment; equipment which they, when abandoned to their own very soon demolish. (Van der Elst, 1950)

In his report Doctor Van der Elst represented the indigenous population as one which simply did not understand the advantages of prosthetic instruments and thus could certainly not be put on par with the European spirit of progress and medical development to use the equipment appropriately. It is this general attitude towards disabled people which time and again can be found in the surviving references to their existence during the Belgian colonial period.[3] The connection between the colonial discourse and the presence of disability in the Belgian-Congo, however, is not limited to the fact that disabled people were represented through the widespread lens of superiority of the white race. Disability served a far more substantial cause and affected a lot more persons than only those who could be said to have this or that physical, visual or auditory impairment. Very soon disability appeared in the discourses, used as an important metaphorical instrument to justify the evolutionary distance between the white colonizer and the black savage. In his 1958 study on the psychology of the African people, for example, Dr. Verhaegen summarized at that time there was still widespread conviction that

> with regard to intelligence and capabilities black people experience a lot of difficulties with abstractive activity of all kind. This is something that is confirmed by all researchers ... Also they miss any elementary geometrical knowledge. From this perspective a lot of adult black people do not reach the level of seven or eight year old European children. (Verhaegen, 1958; See also e.g. Flourens, 1863; Rolin, 1931; Simonin, 1891)

Despite Verhaegen's nuanced interpretation of this observed difference, it can be said to exemplify the image of what one tends to present as "*het achterlijke zwartje*/ the feeble-minded negro", which of course was based on the Eurocentric notions of racist superiority. And connected to these racist ideals was the belief that some form of education and training could help save African people, who were considered lost and primitive souls.

Conclusion: One difference is enough?!

Having reached the end of this exploratory and limited journey into the history of disability in a particular colonial context, namely the Belgian-Congo between 1908 and 1960, a couple of interesting findings can be enumerated. First of all, it seemed that during the official colonization of Congo by the Belgian government, no special educational initiative was founded. Although there undoubtedly also existed people in the Belgian-Congo who had a visual, physical or auditory impairment, reference to rehabilitative initiatives were made only in passing.[4] This absence of special education can be explained in two ways. On the one hand, one could say that for the colonizing powers, the difference between the indigenous Congolese peoples and the Europeans was so huge that there was no need to differentiate any further.[5] Or, and intimately linked to the foregoing in a way, one could say that for the colonizing powers, Congolese people could be considered disabled when looked at from the perspective of the European colonizers and their belief in psychological intelligence testing scales. Secondly – and this is based on the observations of Douglas Baynton, who surmised that disability was an important ingredient in the justification of the colonial activity – Europeans colonists with their racist attitudes believed that Congolese people were primitive, backward savages who, instead of believing in the truth of God, made use of superstitious beliefs, such as the disabled as evil spirits, and who simply could not and would not survive without the blessings of colonial and civilizing education. This dominant representational pattern, however – and this is a third finding – needs to be overcome and replaced by a perspective and historical reconstruction of the particular attitudes of the Congolese people themselves towards individuals who could not see, hear or walk. Going beyond the borders of this missionary bias probably will constitute one of the major challenges for disability historians who are interested in crossing that cultural divide which until now has largely remained unchallenged.

Notes

1   See for more information Gineste, T. (1991). *Victor de l'Aveyron. Dernier enfant sauvage. Premier enfant fou.* Paris: Hachette.
2   Conversation with Sister Walburgis van Quekelberghe and Sister Renildis Van Puyvelde (both members of the Flemish congregation *Zusters Annuntiaten*), 20 October 2011; conversation with Sister Marie-Thérèse Hausman (member of the Flemish congregation *Zusters van de jacht*), 8 February 2012, and conversation with Marie-Thérèse Knapen (professor and dean at the Lovanium University), 17 November 2011.
3   In this context one also should mention that at that time there existed leproseries in the Belgian-Congo. In the way these Congolese lepers were represented in, for example, propaganda documentaries like the one directed by Gérard de Boe in 1928 and entitled *Leprosy*, one can see the personal tragedy model walking over the screen, eventually being replaced by the benefits of the missionary model.
4   One of the few examples of special education which can be retraced in the history of the Belgian-Congo has to do with the education of Congolese pupils who apparently have an auditory impairment. In Gérard de Boe's 1958 documentary *Tokende: Les troubadours du roi Baudoin* one can see some deaf Congolese learning to breath and to speak.
5   This hypothesis is derived from a guest lecture given by Professor Jan Kåre Breivik at the KU Leuven. In this lecture he mentioned the fact that within the Deaf community, one can encounter a tendency to disregard those Deaf people who do not meet widespread criteria (of e.g. economic fitness). One difference, namely the one between the Deaf and the hearing, apparently sufficed.

References

Baynton, D. (2001). Disability and the justification of inequality in American history. In: P.K. Longmore and L. Umansky (Eds.), *New Disability History: American Perspectives* (pp. 33–58). New York, NY: New York University Press.

Briffaerts, J. (2007). *Als Congo op de schoolbanken wil: de onderwijspraktijk in het lager-onderwijs in Belgisch-Congo (1925–1960).* Leuven, Belgium: Acco.

Briffaerts, J. (2011). *When Congo Wants to Go to School. Educational realities in a colonial context. An investigation into educational practices in primary education in the Belgian Congo (1925–1960).* Amsterdam, the Netherlands: Rozenberg.

Ceuppens, B. (2003). *Congo Made in Flanders. Koloniale visies op 'blank' en 'zwart' in Belgisch Congo.* Ghent, Belgium: Academia.

Dasberg, L. (1975). *Grootbrengen door kleinhouden.* Meppel, the Netherlands: Boom.

De Boe, G., Cauvin, A. and Genval, E. (2010). *Belgisch Congo Belge.* Brussel: Cinematek [DVD].

Exposition ASLK Galery (1984). *Oriëntalisten en Afrikanisten in de Belgische kunst: 19e en 20e eeuw.* Brussel, Belgium: Algemene Spaar en lijfrentekas, [Tentoonstelling ASLK Galerij].

Eynikel, H. (1983). *Onze Kongo: Portret van een Koloniale samenleving*. Antwerpen, Belgium: Standaard Uitgeverij.

Flourens, P. (1863). *De la phrénologie des études vraies sur le cerveau*. Paris, France: Garnier.

Gineste, T. (1991). *Victor de l'Aveyron. Dernier enfant sauvage. Premier enfant fou*. Paris, France: Hachette.

Hochschild, A. (1998). *King Leopold's Ghost: A story of greed, terror & heroism in colonial Africa*. Boston, MA: Houghton.

Homme comme toi: Les villages Bondeko: Centres pour Handicapés Kinshasa. (1995). Personal collection of Sister Marie-Thérèse Hausmann, [DVD].

Ingstadt, B. and Whyte, S. (2007). *Disability in Local and Global Worlds*. Berkeley, CA: Berkeley University Press.

Kadima-Tshimanga. (1982). *La société sous le vocabulaire: Blancs, noir et évolués du l'ancien congo belge (1955–1959)*. Mots V (5), 25–49.

Kluxen, G. (2011). *Dr. Jean Hissette's Research Expeditions to Elucidate River Blindness*. Heidelberg, Germany: Kaden.

Lippens, J. (2007). De zaak De Stoete Oostendenaore: Humo-journalist in verdenking gesteld als bendeleider. *Humo*, 3472, 12.

Mianda, G. (2002). Colonialism, education and gender relations in the Belgian Congo: The evolue case. In: S. Geiger, N. Musisi and J. Allman (Eds.). *Woman in African Colonial Histories: An introduction*. Bloomington, IN: Indiana University Press, 144–163.

Pels, P. (1997). The anthropology of colonialism: Culture, history, and the emergence of Western governmentality. *Annual Review of Anthropology*, 26, 163–183.

Rolin, C. (1931). *La psychologie du nègre au Congo-Belge*. Bruxelles, Belgium: la pensée Catholique.

Simonin, H.-A. (1891). De la psychologie du nègre: Conférence faite le 14 avril 1891. Paris, France: A. Davy.

Van der Elst. (1950). La prothèse des amputés du membre inférieur au Congo. *Annales de la Société Belge de Médecine Tropicale*, 30, 615–617.

Van Reybrouck, D. (2010). *Congo een geschiedenis*. Amsterdam, the Netherlands: De Bezige Bij.

Vaughan, M. (1991). *Curing Their Ills: Colonial power and African Illness*. Cambridge, UK: Polity Press.

Verhaegen, E. (2012). *One difference is enough. Een historisch-pedagogisch onderzoek naar de zorg voor Congolezen met een handicap in Belgisch-Congo, 1908–1960*. Niet gepubliceerde Masterproef, Centrum voor Historische Pedagogiek, KU Leuven.

Verhaegen, P. (1958). *De psychologie van de Afrikaanse zwarte*. Antwerpen, Belgium: Standaard Boekhandel.

Verlinden, P. (2010). *Belgisch Kongo: 50 jaar koloniale herinneringen*. Leuven, Belgium: Davidsfonds.

241

PART III

HISTORIES OF EDUCATION AND TRAINING
INTRODUCTION TO PART III: HISTORIES OF EDUCATION AND TRAINING

Nancy E. Hansen

History shows that depending on the culture, trades training and educational programs have been offered to various categories of the disabled populations dating back many generations; however, it is not until the later 18th and early 19th centuries that training programs for various disabled populations becomes integral to charitable, religious and state-sanctioned programs for mental and physical defectives. In the following section we explore examples of these sanctioned programs which emerged during the late 1700s and lasted well into the 20th century, particularly in the form of institutionally based programs where different disabled populations were sent to live and to be trained.

The section begins with a very insightful chapter by Martin Atherton, who, through interview processes that require the assistance of sign language interpreters, raises interesting questions about ethical standards of research when it comes to gaining information about the lived experience of Deaf persons. Ever since the 1960s, the groundbreaking work of William Stokoe and others' research concerning sign language has been slowly increasing. However, with regard for any aspect of research conducted via sign language, especially with regard to ethics and acceptable methodology, it remains very much a novelty, and guidelines are lacking. Atherton's chapter, "From their own hands: Practical and ethical issues in signed 'oral' testimony", continues this journey with an investigation of the practical considerations encountered when collecting data amongst sign language users. The chapter, while considering ethics issues, proposes a justification for considering signed testimony as an alternative form of oral history by explaining the role of sign language within the Deaf community on both national and international levels. Research amongst sign language users, whilst growing in scope, is considered largely by Ethics Committees, and so the practical aspects often raise questions that are outside the experience of those tasked with passing judgement.

Myrle Hill and Nancy Hansen's "Exposure and recovery: Tracing disability history in the midst of cultural absence" explores the nature of archival evidence relating to the experiences of the men and women who were employed in the *blind workshops*

243

in late 19th- and early 20th-century Belfast, Northern Ireland. Although Workshops more generally played an important role in the early labour union movement, this early experience of disability remains largely unknown. For, like most of the history of disabled and poor people or those otherwise perceived as vulnerable in this period, surviving records are mainly concerned with validating the work of paternalistic benevolence undertaken by members of voluntary societies. However, closer analysis of the available materials and discourse relating to blind workers carried out by Hill and Hansen challenges the construction of passive, grateful beneficiaries of philanthropy, to reveal the more complex social, economic and cultural history of a neglected sector of society.

The Hill and Hansen chapter is followed by Heather McFarlane's examination of blind people's asylums and missions that existed in Edinburgh and Glasgow, Scotland, between the late 1700s and the early 1900s. McFarlane's chapter examines the institutional ideology which focused on economic independence, good citizenship and utilitarianism as core principles of education and training. Moreover, through this chapter, "Out of sight, out of mind: Edinburgh and Glasgow blind asylums and missions (1792–1900)", McFarlane draws attention to the differences in approaches to educating and training blind men, boys, girls and women. Whereas blind men and boys were educated and trained to work at various trades and/or to become street venders and were expected to move out of the asylums and to become employed beyond the asylum workshops, blind girls and women were not offered the same expectations to become self-sufficient. Indeed, many asylum and mission administrators felt the blind girls and women needed to be cared for, and, as McFarlane suggests, they needed to be protected from the vagaries of a harsh and violent society. Briefly stated, McFarlane charts this gendering of asylum and mission activity, using a range of primary historical sources from the blind asylums and missions in Scotland's two major cities and shows the reader that the provision of trades training and education was influenced by a number of societal factors, including concerns for productive citizenship as well as societal dependency and cultural notions of the "dependent woman".

"The history of access to education for visually impaired people in Great Britain" by Archie Roy and Gisela Dimigen investigates the history of access to special school/college and mainstream education for blind people from the mid 17th century to the late 20th century. The scope of the research focuses on Great Britain and includes lifelong learning from primary schools through to college and university education. Attention is given to the religious and cultural influences of Christianity and philanthropy; these factors are considered from the 1780s until 1900. Attention is also given to the effects of key pieces of British legislation, reform and to the segregation-integration education conflict which lasted throughout the 20th century. The chapter also focuses on visually impaired students in post-16 education and tracks the educational and career progress of all known blind university graduates in Great Britain from 1656 to 1934. The authors complete the chapter with a discussion of the rapid further development and widening of college and university access and the funding and support mechanisms which have facilitated this.

Martin Earl's "Australian histories of intellectual disabilities" traces the history of care provision for people with intellectual disabilities from colonization to the present day. As many students of history know, European colonization of Australia begins in 1788 with the establishment of Australia as a British penal colony. Earl's chapter notes that by the early 19th century, institutions in the form of insane asylums were established in Australia as a means of containing and caring for Australia's "mental defectives and insane" population. Earl traces the establishment of these institutions, and he notes the influence of the British methods of care and treatment wherein medical staff, superintendents and other professions oversaw the development and growth of institutional facilities across Australia. Although the chapter provides an overview of the care and treatment of people with intellectual impairments, it is nonetheless quite comprehensive in that it traces the history from the growth of segregated institutions to the rise of eugenics practices through to the shift in practices that focus on deinstitutionalization and community inclusion.

Wickman's "Between vision and practice – history of special education in Sweden" describes the establishment and development of special education within the Swedish school system from 1842 onwards. The author discusses the views about children with disabilities and their educational needs and how both the societal stereotypes about children with disabilities changed over time and so too did the Swedish education programs for this population. Wickman's chapter pays particular attention to changes in national education policies from the mid 19th century to the contemporary national policies and the current approaches regarding the education of children with disabilities in the Swedish school context.

Participation and quality of life call for living in less restrictive contexts and experiencing the various contexts of what is considered to be a *normal* life, and Sgaramella et al., in their chapter "The Italian path to school and social inclusion: Problems, strengths and perspectives", examine these constructs (participation and quality of life) which call for inclusion. These elements require a guarantee of the right to be included, which involves definitively extinguishing the risk of segregation. In Italy, achieving these goals has involved navigating a difficult and steep slope. Although inclusion is guaranteed at a legal and legislative level, there are still "pockets" of institutionalization that exist to this day. The authors explore the historical context of this discussion, summarizing the contributions of the "pioneers" who have facilitated the first "public" experiences of education for persons with disabilities in Italy at the end of the 19th century. They then analyse the process of change within the *culture of disability*, arriving to some of the current challenges and issues facing in Italy in terms of maintaining high levels of inclusion for people with disabilities.

14

FROM THEIR OWN HANDS: COLLECTING ORAL TESTIMONY IN SIGNING COMMUNITIES

Martin Atherton

Introduction

For almost 20 years, I have been researching Britain's Deaf community, with a significant proportion of that work involving collecting what might be considered as 'oral history' or 'oral testimony'. In doing so, I have faced a number of practical and ethical issues that make aspects of this approach significantly different from similar speech-based data collection exercises. The very concept of gathering "oral histories" from Deaf people gives rise to some interesting issues, most notably of which is the reference of signed language as 'oral: Can testimony provided in sign language – 'signed' testimony – be considered 'oral' testimony, as it is clearly not a 'verbally' spoken language and therefore cannot be 'oral'? However, sign language is the only practical alternative to spoken language for a significant proportion of the Deaf population in any country. Recent data from the UK government suggests as many as 180,000 Britons use British Sign Language (BSL) as their first or preferred language (Department of Health, 2011). For many of these people, spoken language is not a viable communication option, and so signed testimony acts in precisely the same way as oral testimony for those who speak. The argument put forward here is that much of what is considered as oral testimony is not available in any other form, as it is not been written down or recorded elsewhere. This is certainly true of the Deaf community, as there is no written form of any sign language, other than extremely complex and specialist linguistic notation systems that have been devised for research and analysis purposes (Hopkins, 2008). Therefore I contend that the concept of oral testimony and oral history is not confined simply to spoken language, but can be equally applied to signed communication. Signed testimony may not come from Deaf people's voices, but they speak with their hands instead and so what is signed is just as valid as the more traditional interpretation of oral testimony.

Having made an argument (a plea?) for the acceptance of signed testimony, this chapter will first argue that such research at least mirrors many of the factors posed by ethnography, and that many of the practical and ethical issues discussed later are directly linked to an understanding of the world and the way it works that is deeply influenced by deafness. Central to this is a conceptualisation of deafness as 'otherness' that is felt by both Deaf and hearing communities but which results in diametrically opposite perceptions of the consequences of deafness. The chapter will then outline some of the practical considerations I have had to address when collecting data amongst sign language users, before moving on to consider what ethical issues can arise and how I have sought to address these.

Sign language users as an ethnographic minority

It has already been argued that research conducted through the medium of sign language and amongst research subjects who are sign language users themselves is essentially the collection of oral testimony. Di Leonardo (1987) argued that oral history collection represented an 'ethnographic encounter', replicating many of the issues raised by ethnographic research. These include:

- Gaining access to the research group and finding suitable gatekeepers
- Ensuring effective communication between researchers and contributors
- Engendering mutual trust and respect between researchers and interviewees
- Ensuring informed consent can be and is given by contributors and protecting the right of interviewees to edit and amend their contributions
- Balancing external perspectives with those of contributors
- Considering the presentation and representation of the evidence gathered to accurately reflect the views and opinions that arise from this testimony
- Providing access for contributors to results and outputs of the research (Hammersley and Atkinson, 2007)

All these elements present particular challenges to those conducting "oral historical" research through sign language and addressing these issues is a core requirement when investigating the Deaf community. As with so many issues, perception and definition are important factors in determining whether sign language users form an ethnographic group, as has been proposed by various theorists, including Lane (2005), Eckert (2010) and Lane et al. (2010). One of these factors is an understanding of how deafness, and sign language use in particular, can give rise to a very different view of the world. Key amongst these is the perception of many deaf sign language users that they constitute a social, cultural and linguistic minority (Corker, 1998; Ladd, 2003). Rather than viewing their deafness as the loss of a sense, many Deaf people use sign language as opening up a world of shared values, norms, history, experiences and culture. This view contradicts the socially held and medically derived definition of deafness as a disability that restricts its so-called sufferers and for which a variety of 'cures' have been devised, from 18th-century ear trumpets to modern-day cochlear implants and gene therapy.

Whether Deaf sign language users can and should be viewed as an ethnographic group is also dependent on how 'ethnography' is defined. Fetterman (2010) describes ethnography as the art and science used to describe a group or culture, so this certainly applies. Boyle (1994) claims ethnography is always informed by a concept of culture, which aligns closely with how the Deaf community (both nationally and globally) regard themselves. Lambert et al. (2011: 21) list a number of characteristics of ethnography, several of which have cultural significance for studies involving sign language users. These include the following:

- A reliance on collecting data in the natural environment: the natural environment of sign language users is one in which sign language is the primary form of communication.
- Ethnography does not rely totally on what people say, but sees, visualises and creates a picture through first-hand experience: this is the very essence of communication via sign language, which does not rely on verbal or aural descriptions but instead offers a visual representation of how deaf people view the world and those around them.
- Ethnography is about immediate social and cultural contexts and broader socio-economic and political contexts: communication through sign language has to be conducted 'face to face' and so has immediacy. This form of communication also creates its own social and cultural contexts, which must be recognised and respected if meaningful and contextually appropriate communication is to take place. Elements of communication such as turn-taking and eye-gaze have particular cultural significance in sign language and are much more important to an effective exchange of information and ideas than in spoken languages. Sign language use is in itself often an overt political act for many Deaf people, who regard its use as a treasured aspect of their culture rather than as a limited response to disability.
- An intimate relationship is vital between researcher and researched: even after the development of technologies such as webcams, MSN and Skype, which now allow sign language users to enjoy live conversations over long distances, the visual nature of the language still requires face to face communication and produces a sense of intimacy between those involved.

Whilst these are not the only characteristics of ethnographic research outlined by Lambert et al. (2011), these factors have particular resonance when researching Deaf communities and via their preferred communication medium. Without an appreciation of the cultural aspects of sign language use in Deaf communal life, no research into this group can be wholly successful (if at all). Therefore any research involving data collection via sign language must take into account ethnographic methodologies and so must by extension constitute a form of ethnography. This involves understanding and responding to cultural sensitivities and considerations, which in turn give rise to a range of practical and ethical considerations.

Practical issues

Except in circumstances wherein an individual is both blind and Deaf sign languages are used as a visual/gestural mode of communication, which have their own syntax/grammar, and this often differs greatly from the dominant language and culture in which Deaf people find themselves living. For example, in BSL, the simple question, 'What is your name?' is represented by the following signs: 'Name you what?'. However, there is more to sign language that just the syntax of signs, as meaning is also affected by the use of non-manual features (NMF), facial expression and multi-channel signs. In very simple terms, NMF might be considered to be similar to body language amongst speech users but this aspect of sign language is much more important to meaning and understanding than that. In sign language, a question form is denoted by raised eyebrows; in the question above, these might be thought of as a direct replacement for the question mark (Sutton-Spence and Woll, 1999).

Another important use of NMF is to indicate negative statements, for example through a shake of the head. I was Principal Researcher for the Deaf United project UK, which investigated the social history of Deaf football (soccer) players (Atherton, Russell and Turner, 2000). As part of the data collection I conducted interviews in sign language and transcribed the videotaped data into written English. On one occasion, I transcribed what I thought was 'I like to sit in that part of the ground' but this statement did not seem to fit with subsequent information. When I reviewed the tape some time later to try and rectify this anomaly, I noticed a very slight shake of the head that I had not seen previously. It was only then that it became apparent that I had completely misinterpreted what had been told to me; that slight shake of the head changed the meaning to 'I do *not* like to sit in that part of the ground'. A very minor error on my part could have resulted in a very major misrepresentation of data if this had occurred in a different context. Interestingly (and partly in my own defence), as part of the review process I had conferred with two colleagues who are BSL users, and neither had noticed the gesture that so completely altered the meaning of the statement. However, both colleagues stated that if the conversation had been live rather than recorded, then they would have picked up on the anomaly and asked for clarification.

Even when such omissions and errors are avoided, there is still a lack of direct transliteration between BSL and English, as interpreting takes place between modalities as well as languages. BSL is not merely English expressed on the hands but rather presents information in a very visual and graphic mode that often cannot be directly represented in words. To illustrate this point, here is an example taken from the 'Deaf United' project. This excerpt first gives a simple direct transliteration from sign into English and then my interpretation of this data into a more coherent form of English.

Transcript 1: transliteration from sign language

Interviewer:	School Deaf football there?
Respondent:	Football school football yes — lunch break after football — three half after football — match half four home — football every — football
Interviewer:	School team league have?
Respondent:	No, friendly — only friendly — one, two — league nothing school
Interviewer:	Glasgow then — match other Deaf club — Cup, friendly — hearing league include?
Respondent:	League hearing yes
Interviewer:	Other Deaf club — league self?
Respondent:	When finish me — one nine eight nine — set up one nine nine zero Deaf league — break again three, four years finish

Transcript 2: interpretation of the meaning into grammatically correct English

Interviewer:	Was there football at your school for the Deaf?
Respondent:	Yes, we had football at school. We played at lunchtime, and after school finished at 3.30 until 4.30, then we went home. There was football every day.
Interviewer:	Did the school play in a league?
Respondent:	No, just one or two friendlies. We didn't play in a league.
Interviewer:	At that time, Glasgow was playing matches against other Deaf clubs, in the Cup and as friendlies ... were they also playing in a hearing league?
Respondent:	Yes, we played in a hearing league.
Interviewer:	Did the Deaf clubs have a league of their own?
Respondent:	I finished in 1989, and a league was set up in 1990, but it broke up after three or four years.

(Atherton, Russell and Turner, 2000: 116–7)

This second version not only considers the signs used but also factors such as multichannel signs, which have no direct meaning in spoken language but are hugely influential in giving meaning in signed interactions. Other considerations included facial expression and the use of signing space (perhaps best understood as how 'big' someone signs). Someone signing in a large signing space might be considered to be 'shouting' in certain circumstances, or passing on information in an emotional manner in others, with the differences clear only when the context is known. Presenting such subtleties of language is often successfully achieved only by the most gifted sign language interpreters, and even then it cannot always be accurately portrayed in written modes.

Another important factor is the large-scale failure of Deaf education internationally to provide sign language users with adequate fluency in the local majority language. Even in the 21st century, a primary focus of Deaf education is often not to educate but to produce Deaf children who can speak as clearly as possible and who can use lip reading with some degree of certainty (Ladd 2003). The reality is that for many Deaf people, such approaches fail abysmally, with the result that the majority language of their own country is effectively a foreign language for sign language users. This gives rise to numerous consequences for those conducting research with this group of people, which closely reflect several of the considerations outlined earlier for those undertaking ethnographic research.

Communication

Establishing effective methods of communication between the researcher and the interviewees is vital to all investigations of this type, no matter what languages are involved.

When one of those languages is sign language, a plethora of factors arise that might mirror those faced by other ethnographers but which also present particular challenges. The ability of the researcher to communicate directly and effectively in sign language can be a key factor in the success or failure of a project. Jennifer Harris (1995) recounts the difficulties she faced as a novice entering the field of sign language–mediated research. Harris acknowledges that at the time her signing skills were limited and she was not able to communicate fully with her interviewees, but she made the effort to adapt to the cultural demands placed upon her to use the first language of her respondents. Unfortunately for Harris, some people took this as an opportunity to make a political point about the general lack of sign language skills amongst the hearing majority. Although at first happy to modify their language so as to be understood by Harris, several respondents then increased their level of signing, once Harris' own shortcomings became apparent, through constant requests for repetition and clarification. In effect, they made themselves unintelligible to anyone without high levels of signing fluency, with potentially damaging consequences for the success of her work. Fortunately these were mitigated by the majority of her interviewees adopting a more sympathetic and helpful attitude to her communication abilities.

The most obvious response to such situations is to employ the services of a sign language interpreter, but this poses severe financial and logistical burdens on research budgets. In the UK, there are less than 700 qualified British Sign Language/English interpreters available, which has two immediate consequences. Both the demand for their services and the fees charged by interpreters are high, which place restrictions on researchers taking this option to ensuring effective communication. Interpreters usually have to be booked weeks, if not months, in advance, and so juggling such bookings with the availability of interviewees can be a nightmare, if not utterly impossible. There is no guarantee that interpreters will be available in more out-of-the-way places, or be willing to travel (incurring extra research costs in the process), especially if interviews are taking place at evenings or weekends. Other factors include the following:

- The working patterns of sign language interpreters, who cannot work for lengthy periods without a break. This brings other factors into consideration, with the interviewing process being lengthened or even disrupted by the need to stop at regular intervals. The alternative is for interpreters to share the workload, known as co-working, but this just increases the logistical and financial problems exponentially.
- The gender imbalance of the sign language interpreting profession, especially in the UK. The vast majority of interpreters are female (personal and anecdotal evidence suggests in excess of 80%), which can pose difficulties for research into personal and sensitive issues, especially amongst male respondents.
- An associated issue related to personal or sensitive data collection amongst sign language users is that the comparatively small pool of interpreters available locally, coupled with the number of sign language users in an area, means that both parties tend to know or to be known to each other. Despite the Code of Practice all interpreters are bound by and the requirement for confidentiality this places upon them, many potential interviewees may be dissuaded from sharing such

information in front of someone they know and with whom they will probably have to work again in the future (Harrington and Turner, 2001).

Fortunately I can sign sufficiently well so as to not need interpreters present, and I have benefitted from misconceptions about my hearing status on more than one occasion. On several occasions, interviewees presumed I was Deaf simply because I was signing to them, only to realise later that I am hearing. In every instance, the tone of the interview became warmer and more productive after they learnt I was not Deaf after all, but could still communicate clearly and effectively. This is not meant as a criticism of Harris or the invaluable work of sign language interpreters, but it does serve to illustrate some of the barriers that can be unwittingly constructed whilst trying to address these same issues.

Transcription of data

An issue of major logistical and ethical importance is the transcription of data from sign language into written language. The factors involved in this transcription process need careful consideration and forward planning on the part of researchers if the challenges posed by this aspect of sign language based data collection is to be successful.

The first factor to consider is the length of time transcription from sign language takes. I have always undertaken my own transcription, which has the added advantage that I conducted the interviews and so know the context of the questions and answers being transcribed. In my experience, straightforward transcription of a one to one interview involves about one hour of work for every five minutes of signed data. This is partly due to the need to check and double check for factors such as negators and question forms, as illustrated earlier, but also to ensure the context of responses is fully understood. This process can be complicated by respondents using unfamiliar regional signs (these are similar to accents or dialect in spoken languages) which can cause both confusion and delays. Whilst British Sign Language is largely standardised, in the same way that there is a common form of English, there are numerous variations in signs from different parts of the UK or depending on which Deaf school the respondent attended (Sutton-Spence and Woll, 1999). In addition, the same handshape can represent different meanings in different contexts; for example, the handshape for 'plane' can also represent 'telephone', 'milk', 'wine', 'cow' or even 'devil', depending on how the sign is used and in what context. When transcribing, these signs have first to be recognised and then accurately translated in the correct contextual meaning. When interviews involve multiple contributors (such as a discussion group) the time scale increases exponentially, as individual elements of the conversation need to be transcribed and then woven into a collective narrative. One such interview I conducted with four contributors produced around 65 minutes of data but took me 4.5 days to transcribe – a rate of around two minutes per hour.

The obvious answer might be to employ the services of a sign language interpreter, notwithstanding the difficulties and costs highlighted earlier. Interpreting from sign language into English is usually a verbal process and someone would still need to audio-type the interpretation, which is another highly specialised – and expensive – task. However, even highly skilled interpreters can struggle with unfamiliar signs and contexts, especially when there is no opportunity to check with the contributor. I was once transcribing an interview I had conducted and which had presented no communication problems at the time. However, when viewing the tape later, I came across a sign I did not recognise and I could not work out the meaning from the content and context of the conversation. I sought advice from two colleagues, both of whom were Deaf and native BSL users. Between us, we still could not work out the meaning, and other colleagues gradually became involved. Eventually, six people were sat around the video-screen – four Deaf colleagues, an experienced sign language interpreter and myself. The tape was constantly played and rewound, each time going further backwards and forwards in the conversation to try and contextualise the meaning of the sign. After 20 minutes, the conundrum was solved; the sign was 'afternoon' and had no significance in terms of the information that was being offered by the interviewee. However, this could be determined only by going through the laborious process of identifying the sign and its meaning, and this example illustrates the ethical requirement on the researcher to ensure that the views of the contributor were accurately reported and represented. This might seem straightforward enough in theory, but in this instance it took the combined efforts and time of six people, which raises questions about the practical and logistical resources needed to ensure ethical working practices.

Presentation of research findings

One often overlooked aspect of research conducted via sign language is how the outcomes of the research are to be presented. There is an expectation placed on researchers to make the results of their work widely available, and this usually takes written and oral forms, such as conference papers, books and chapters and even television and radio programmes. However, none of these formats are necessarily appropriate to members of a community for whom the spoken word is largely inaccessible and written language is effectively a foreign language. The obvious answer is to present the findings in a visual format that uses sign language as its medium of communication, but this in turn raises both ethical and practical challenges.

Who presents the findings is an important consideration for sign language–based research. It is important that the presenter is highly fluent in sign language in order to ensure accuracy of presentation but also as a mark of respect to the community under investigation. The most appropriate solution is to use a Deaf person who is a native sign language user and preferably well known in the Deaf community to lend credibility to the project. During the final year of my undergraduate studies, I produced a video history of the local Deaf school (Atherton and Hodson, 1997). From the start, it was important to me that the end results were presented in sign language by a member of the Deaf community. Through existing links with the local Deaf club, I was able to find someone who would be the onscreen 'face' of the project. Len acted as my gatekeeper to a number of former pupils, school records and other important materials, which, as Clark (2011) points out, is a vital aspect of this type of data collection. I devised a script based on my research and Len acted as both presenter and interviewer, with the film being recorded on videotape in British Sign Language. The project was highly successful from my point of view, not least because the end product was accessible to the community whose history was being recorded. The biggest problem at the time was making the film accessible to a non-signing audience, which I achieved with the help of fellow students who provided voiced translations that were dubbed onto the tape. In many ways, producing signed outputs in a visual format which are then supplemented with a spoken commentary offers a more viable alternative to trying to make written outputs accessible to a signing audience.

Ethical issues

Further ethical considerations involve amending existing practices, whilst others require researchers to take greater responsibility for their actions and the possible consequences. A basic precept of all research involving human subjects is that ethical approval should be granted by an appropriate authority. In my own experience, this creates significant moral problems when those authorities have no experience of research conducted in sign language. In such instances, I have had to act as my own expert witness and try to foresee what ethical issues might arise, in order to both identify these for the appropriate Ethics Committee and to put forward what I hope are viable and responsible solutions.

Virtually all institutions and authorities require a written consent form to be signed by contributors, which outlines, amongst other details, their willingness to take part in data collection and their rights to edit and amend the information they provide. Once again the issue of written language competency has to be considered and dealt with sensitively. The process I have used in all my research, following approval by Ethics Committees, has been to send a copy of the consent form to contributors in advance. They do not sign this until I have explained the content of the consent form to contributors at the start of the interview process and they have indicated their understanding and willingness to take part. As all my interviews are filmed, this process forms part of the interview. The letter is shown to the camera so that the content can be compared with my signed explanation, before the contributor then signs the letter within view of the camera. To date, no-one has ever objected to this process and no ethical concerns have been raised, but in case of any dispute, a clear record is available for scrutiny. Without this process, I do not feel I can be confident that contributors have been fully informed before giving their consent.

As an extension of this process, I always offer contributors the opportunity to edit and amend my transcription of the interview before I start to use the data. In order to address the second-language issue, I offer copies of the written transcript and the interview film. This provides contributors with the chance to correct any factual errors in the transcript and to make clarifications. Of all the interviews I have conducted, only one contributor has asked for a written transcript, but all have requested a copy of the film. Viewed in the most positive light, it might be claimed that the contributors are demonstrating trust in the researcher by waiving their right to edit the transcript, and this is the perspective I have to work from. However, one consequence of this is that the pressure on the researcher to ensure the accuracy of testimony presented in the findings is significantly increased. In effect, the researcher is putting words into the mouths of people who may not have the skills, abilities or opportunity to know they are being misrepresented. This issue can be further complicated when additional communication barriers exist, as happened when I was involved in the Minimal Language Skills project. In this project, I was part of a team seeking to identify and address communication issues involving Deaf people with mental health conditions which further restricted their communication abilities (Atherton et al. 2002). In this instance there was a very clear process for gaining consent, which was delegated to care providers. Even so, it was imperative to ensure we acted in an ethically and morally defensible manner, as not only consent but the opportunities to edit and amend were also in the hands of others rather than the contributors. From my own point of view, the need to tread extra carefully serves as a motivating factor rather than an additional concern, as I believe this underlying responsibility of all researchers is emphasised by the particular circumstances of sign language–based data collection. All researchers should seek to work in an ethically sound manner, but it does no-one any harm to be regularly reminded of this requirement and to reflect on their practice.

Conclusion

During the last 20 years, I have come to realise that conducting research amongst sign language users presents a particular set of challenges that are not faced by those investigating other groups. At the heart of this difference is the communication barrier that acts as a catalyst for many of the practical and ethical considerations that arise. Some of these mirror ethnographic research, such as the greater responsibility for researchers to act in the best interests of contributors. These problems are not insurmountable, but a degree of innovation is sometimes needed, from both the researchers and those who oversee them. The establishment of trust should also not be seen as solely a matter for researcher and researched; those in authority have to place some degree of trust in the knowledge and experience of the researchers as well.

The need to ensure contributors are active participants in all aspects of data collection might require only minor changes to the data collection process, but suitable planning and funding to ensure effective communication between participants is of paramount importance. Ensuring full access to the presentation of findings and outcomes is less easy to resolve without acknowledgement of the particular communication options open to Deaf people. Even with adequate funding, there are still a number of issues that might mitigate against research results being available to all. However, there are an increasing number of examples of how this can be achieved, and the work of uncovering a largely neglected field of historical research will continue. The challenge for the hearing majority is to ensure that this largely misunderstood and misrepresented community of sign language users are provided with the opportunity to express their own views and perspectives. To research the Deaf community at any level, whether local, national or international, without at least trying to make that research available to those being investigated, is not only unethical but also deeply disrespectful. There are a number of practical issues that still remain but none of these are insurmountable with the right attitude.

References

Atherton, M. and Hodson, L. (1997). The Royal Cross Remembered: Memories of the Royal Cross School for the Deaf, Preston. Privately produced and distributed videotape.

Atherton, M., Gregg, A., Harrington, F., Laugesen, C., Quinn, G., Traynor, N. and Turner, G.H. (2002). *Addressing Communication Disadvantage: Deaf People with Minimal Language Skills.* Preston, Lancashire, UK: University of Central Lancashire.

Atherton, M., Russell, D., and Turner, G.H. (2000). *Deaf United*. Coleford, Gloucestershire, UK: Douglas McLean.

Boyle, J. S. (1994). Styles of ethnography. in J. M. Morse (Ed.), *Critical Issues in Qualitative Research Methods* (pp. 159–185). London, UK: Sage Publications.

Clark, T. (2011). Gaining and maintaining access: exploring the mechanisms that support and challenge the relationship between gatekeepers and researchers. *Qualitative Social Work* 10(4), 485–502.

Corker, M. (1998). *Deaf and Disabled or Deafness Disabled?* Buckingham, London, UK: Open University Press.

Department of Health. (2011). GP Survey 2011. Retrieved from http://www.gp-patient.co.uk/info/.

Di Leonardo, M. (1987). Oral testimony as ethnographic encounter. *Oral History Review* 50, 1–20.

Eckert, R. C. (2010). Toward a theory of Deaf ethnos: Deafnicity ≈ D/Deaf. *Journal of Deaf Studies and Deaf Education* 15(4), 317–333.

Fetterman, D. M. (2010). *Ethnography Step by Step*. London, UK: Sage Publications.

Hammersley, M. and Atkinson, P. (2007). *Ethnography: Principles in practice*. London, UK: Routledge.

Harrington, F. and Turner, G.H. (2001). *Interpreting Interpreting*. Coleford, Gloucestershire, UK: Douglas McLean.

Harris, J. (1995). Boiled eggs and baked beans: a personal account of a hearing researcher's journey through Deaf culture. *Disability and Society* 10(1), 295–308.

Hopkins, J. (2008). Choosing how to write sign language: a sociolinguistic perspective. *International Journal of the Sociology of Language* 192, 75–90.

Ladd, P. (2003). *Understanding Deaf Culture: In Search of Deafhood*. London, UK: Multicultural Matters.

Lambert, V., Glacken, M. and McCarron, M. (2011). Employing an ethnographic approach: key characteristics. *Nurse Researcher* 19(1), 17–24.

Lane, H. (2005). Ethnicity, ethics, and the Deaf-world. *Journal of Deaf Studies and Deaf Education* 10(3), 291–310.

Lane, H., Pillard, R.C. and Hedberg, U. (2010). *People of the Eye: Deaf Ethnicity and Ancestry*. Oxford, UK: Oxford University Press.

Sutton-Spence, R. L. and Woll, B. (1999). *The Linguistics of BSL: An Introduction*. Cambridge, UK: Cambridge University Press.

15

THE HISTORY OF ACCESS TO EDUCATION OF PEOPLE WITH VISUAL IMPAIRMENTS IN GREAT BRITAIN FROM 1656 TO 1999

Archie W.N. Roy and Gisela Dimigen

The history of education of visually impaired people in eighteenth- and nineteenth-century Great Britain has often been considered briefly, perhaps in a cursory resume of Pritchard's (1963) account which stops at 1960, along with a remark or two about later legislation. There are, in fact, relatively few histories at all, and they tend to follow Pritchard's cumulative approach. In his history *Education and the Handicapped*, chapters are organised to lead from early "experiment" to "growth" to "consolidation" and imply ordered progression through time and approval of the then current developments in voluntary and statutory provision, largely to do with special schools. The result is an extremely thorough history of educational provision for the visually impaired which is non-critical in a conceptual or philosophical sense. He is pleased to note that early labels such as "defective" have been replaced by labels such as "sub-normal", the underlying assumption being one of progress. An elaborate and professional system for supporting the visually impaired had thankfully been created. We should add, however, on the positive side, that Pritchard clearly was concerned about recognition of need and provision for visually impaired children. A more recent approach to the subject, contained in the highly influential Warnock Report, which led to Britain's Education Act 1981, was more critical, but its historical content drew greatly from Pritchard's narrative while the *approach* to history contained within it is another example of Pritchard's cumulative one.

Such texts can be the product of subtle implicit bias. Pritchard's and the Warnock Report's accounts may be biased, for instance, towards professionals in voluntary and statutory organisations working together to make educational provision better for disabled children who required educational supports and services. This, in other words, is what progress is and is a perspective drawn from the historical record and the writers' own professional interests. A second source of bias, however, is the patchy historical record itself. If there is no documentary record of some points of view, these positions are hidden from history. It is only relatively recently, for instance, that self-advocacy groups such as the Forums on Disability in Scotland have organised socially and politically to represent and empower specific perspectives.

The history of education of visually impaired people can also be viewed frequently out of its social historical context. This is hardly surprising, given that histories are written usually by special educationalists rather than historians, the former selecting or filtering their facts through their motivating concern: the merits or demerits of special disability-specific schools or the necessity and value of integration. More recently, special educationalists and their conference debates have tended to view simultaneously the benefits of both systems, and hopefully we are relatively free of either concern exclusively, given that we have been aware of the recent effectiveness of some special provision (Dimigen et al., 1993) but have both worked mainly to support visually impaired students in mainstream colleges and universities. However, a useful starting point historically may be not in concern but in the defining characteristics of the society which promoted and experimented with both of them.

Influences of Christianity and philanthropy 1791–1900

From the 1780s until the early 1900s, British society was deeply influenced by Christian philanthropy rooted in traditional Christian teachings of the Roman Catholic Church and the Church of England, as well as the teachings of a rising evangelical movement. Indeed, charitable relief tied to religious affiliation was quite common, and some reports show a vast range of moral and philanthropic deeds, not as a means of salvation of the giver, but because they might lead to others' salvation. In many ways, the concept of religious charitable relief was tied to self-improvement, wherein the receiver of relief was expected to become a productive citizen. An example of this connection between religious philanthropy and self-improvement is evidenced in the opening in 1791 of the Liverpool School for the "Indigent Blind" by the cleric Henry Dannett, wherein the principles of self-discipline, self-reliance and the work ethic were often based on religious conviction. School-based activities and school rules themselves were structured around the twin priorities of religious adherence and economic activity. Day students in music, weaving and basketmaking at the Liverpool School, adults as well as children, were required to produce evidence of regular church attendance to the school superintendent (Pritchard, 1963).

By 1869, more secular models of charitable relief began to emerge throughout Great Britain. Larger urban philanthropic societies united to form Charity Organisation Societies (COS). While one of the primary purposes of philanthropy or charity was to extend kindness to less fortunate citizens, another function of the COS was to develop a scientific basis to charitable relief wherein statistics on individuals, their families and neighbourhood could be gathered. Within time it became routine for charity aid workers to visit homes to carry out detailed assessments of the family's situation, and the gathering of data kept people in need from going from one charitable relief organisation to another as files were kept on individuals. While it can be argued that the charitable relief offered through the COS could be a form of social control of the poorer urban classes, the argument is also made that many reforms in the area of public health and public education came as a result of the actions of COS workers. The period between 1868 and 1983 witnessed the development of various educational reforms, including the 1893 Elementary Education Blind and Deaf Children Act requiring compulsory education for all blind children aged 5 to 16 years.

The nineteenth century witnessed the growth and development of a large number of schools for blind and visually impaired youth, and some schools came into existence to meet the needs of a specific religious constituency. For example, the first Catholic school for the blind opened in Liverpool in 1841 and some institutions offered a higher level of education such as the Worcester College for the Higher Education of the Blind, which opened in 1866, and the Royal Normal College (RNC), which opened in 1872, both of which exist today in different form, renamed and on new sites. There is little evidence of conflict with pioneers such as Barnhill. In fact there is considerable common ground: Barnhill's (1875) report contains letters of support and agreement from the heads of both Worcester College and RNC. Both of these schools departed radically from the fairly typical special school asylum and workshop which focused on trades training. Worcester College pioneered special provision to prepare visually impaired students for university and the professions and was opened by two clergymen who thought there should be a "College where the blind children of opulent parents might obtain an education suitable to their station in life", (Bell, 1966, pp 16). Fortunately, in due course, students from less opulent backgrounds were encouraged to attend along with some sighted students who were readers for their visually impaired peers. This model of education functioned on a quid pro quo basis wherein the sighted students of lesser economic means paid a lower tuition and were able to gain a high-level public school education as reimbursement for being readers and assistants for the blinded students. Curriculum emphasised classics, divinity, English literature, maths and music.

When the RNC school opened in 1872, only two blind students were enrolled, but by 1892 the number of blind students had grown to 160. From the descriptions of the school made by Archdeacon Farrar (1892) in the Alumni Association magazine of the Perkins Institution for the Blind in Boston, Massachusetts, it appears that the facility was quite lavish for the era. He details the extensive gardens with terraces and flights of steps, sets of swings, a lake, rowing boats, trees and adjoining fields. Students even learned the position of turns in the walks and flights of steps by gentle risings in the asphalt pavement. The result of this, according to Farrar, was that "boys and girls and youths and maidens are enjoying it, walking, running, driving tricycles ... and moving about in every direction with the utmost independence" (pp 373). He was also very pleased to note the garden parties, that students gathered around a Christmas tree donated annually by the Archbishop of Canterbury, and the "non-sectarian religious teaching", the children attending different churches and chapels (Figure 15.1).

The end of the Victorian era was a time of substantial social, economic, cultural and political change resulting in less religious influence over British society in general, and the provision of charitable assistance, specifically non-conformist influence, was also in decline in Parliament by 1906 – culturally, Puritan self-denial was gradually supplanted by the desire for self-development through reason, science and qualifications. Specific factors such as the influence of Liberalism, with its tendency towards increasing government responsibility for welfare provision, also caused a decline in the power and sphere of influence of religious-based philanthropic organisations. This is not to suggest that charitable organisations fell out of favour with the populace, as this was not the case, and in fact charities continued to affect and sometimes dictate government legislation, particularly in the field of education.

Figure 15.1 RNC: Driving tricycles in the grounds. (Lithograph from Archdeacon Farrar's account, 1892. Courtesy of RNIB Research Library, London.)

Legislation, reform and the segregation-integration dilemma 1901–1994

Throughout the nineteenth and early twentieth centuries there were many debates in Great Britain regarding the pros and cons of segregated and integrated schools for blind and visually impaired children and youth. In Scotland, for example, Rev. Alexander Barnhill, superintendent of the Glasgow Mission for the Blind, advocated full integration of visually impaired students in classes for sighted students, with parents providing additional home instruction and schools providing aids for the blind students:

> In learning geography, the blind child will acquire much in going over the lessons at home, and in the exercises in the class with the sighted scholars; but it is of importance that he should have the assistance of raised globes or maps to give him a distinct conception of the position, magnitude, and form of the different places, as well as their distance from each other. (Barnhill, 1875, pp 37–38).

Barnhill reported on the social, educational and emotional benefits of integration for visually impaired children and backed this up with successful case histories and testimonies from various Scottish teachers, some of whom had initially been "doubters" of his approach. In Scotland, Barnhill's work had long-term effects and integration expanded in scope, and by 1905, visually impaired students in Aberdeen were being taught alongside sighted students by mainstream teachers with support from specialist peripatetic staff. During the interwar years, continued efforts were made for greater integration of blind students into regular school systems throughout Scotland, the idea being that a special school was desirable only if nothing better existed. This educational philosophy tended to reflect parallel American thinking at the time (Cole, 1989).

Interestingly, while Scottish educators advocated for greater integration, there appears to be less enthusiasm for integration in Wales and England, where there tended to be greater support for segregated special schools for blind children. The 1921 Education Act, for example, required blind children to be registered and be provided for in special schools. Furthermore, the building programme for segregated special schools gained pace, with the number of schools for the blind increasing from 58 in 1919 to 77 in 1929; however, by 1939 the number of schools had decreased to 7. It is interesting to note that there was an attempt during this time to develop schools which reflected the broader elements of British society, wherein some schools for blind students were based on a private boarding school model. The interwar years also saw the opening in 1921 by the National Institute for the Blind (NIB) of a grammar school, Chorleywood, for female "academically able" visually impaired students, as an extension of the English boarding school system, with special provision for visually impaired girls (Figures 15.2 and 15.3). Although unique in some respects, Chorleywood fitted in with government thinking of the time, wherein the prevailing attitude was that blind and visually impaired students should be segregated regardless of their academic ability. Throughout Great Britain the provision of educational instruction for partially sighted students was more mixed. From 1900 to 1918, the educational needs of partially sighted students began to receive attention, and in some schools, "specialized segregated" classes, were established. Besides the segregated classes, partially sighted students attended regular classes whenever they were judged able to cope alongside their sighted peers. Evidence also suggests that partially sighted students were often enrolled in schools for the blind (NIB, 1936), but it appears that the majority of students diagnosed as being partially sighted received their education through the regular school system either in some form of integrated class or in the more common "special education class".

Figure 15.2 Chorleywood Grammar School, science: weighing without sight, 1943. (Courtesy of RNIB Research Library, London.)

Figure 15.3 Chorleywood Grammar School, knitting for the troops, World War II, 1943. (Courtesy of RNIB Research Library, London.)

It is important to note that there was a particular ideology underpinning the segregated classes for partially sighted students, and it was rooted in a theory of "sight saving": between 1908 and 1954, "sight-saving" classes were a popular option for partially sighted students. The medically inspired and anti-integration rationale for this model of education was based on the belief that partially sighted children should be removed from mainstream classes in order to preserve their existing sight, as it was argued that integration would cause them to overuse their sight to the point of damaging or losing it. Sight-saving classes, beginning in Camberwell, London, in 1908, became particularly popular, and by the early 1930s there were 37 such classes provided by 22 local education authorities (LEAs) across Britain. The influence of early twentieth-century ophthalmology is evidenced in the establishment of the sight-saving classes, wherein the students had restricted periods for reading and writing and very limited involvement in games and physical education (Fothergill, 1980). Eventually, sight-saving teaching practices were challenged, and by the mid 1950s ophthalmological opinion had reversed and now favoured maximum use of residual sight.

By the early 1960s, more and more LEAs were integrating partially sighted student and blind students into mainstream classes, and within a 10-year period a number of segregated schools had closed. St Vincent's School for the Blind in Liverpool, for example, began a project in 1962 to integrate some of its students in neighbouring mainstream schools, with Braille educational materials being produced by local prison units. Some schools for blind children, such as the school department within Royal Normal College, closed in 1972. And throughout the 1970s and 1980s, most government reports recommended the closure of segregated schools for blind children and youth. The Warnock Committee's report of 1978 was a major document containing the recommendations of an enquiry into the education of "handicapped children and young people" and was followed in turn by the 1981 Education Act, passed by Margaret Thatcher's government. The Act adopted much of the Warnock Committee's philosophy about children's special educational needs and advocated integration for all children but included certain provisos which in practice continued to limit development. The position was, in fact, not dissimilar to earlier pronouncements by the Scottish Education Department in 1966 that special schools should be a "last resort" alternative, considered when the "sound principle" of integration did not apply in a particular case (Figure 15.4).

The reports and resulting legislation changed provision for visually impaired students substantially. In 1972, only 2 of 39 special schools in England and Wales educated both blind and partially sighted students, and the Report argued that both groups should be educated together, reversing earlier thinking. This would make viable more local schools nearer students' home areas and make placements easier for partially sighted students with little or unpredictable residual vision. The Report did serve to indicate a change but only over the medium term; by 1984, it was clear that the two groups were coming together (Moody, 1987). The Report also commented favourably on an integration project in Sheffield where a number of special school students were chosen to attend a local mainstream school and were given backup from two specialist teachers providing Braille teaching materials and offering support to them and their mainstream staff. The success of the project, measured in terms of students' free mixing with sighted peers and enhancement of a range of skills, was noted by the Vernon Committee along with apparent American and Scandinavian successes with integration to the extent that it advised a limited shift in Britain towards integrated provision.

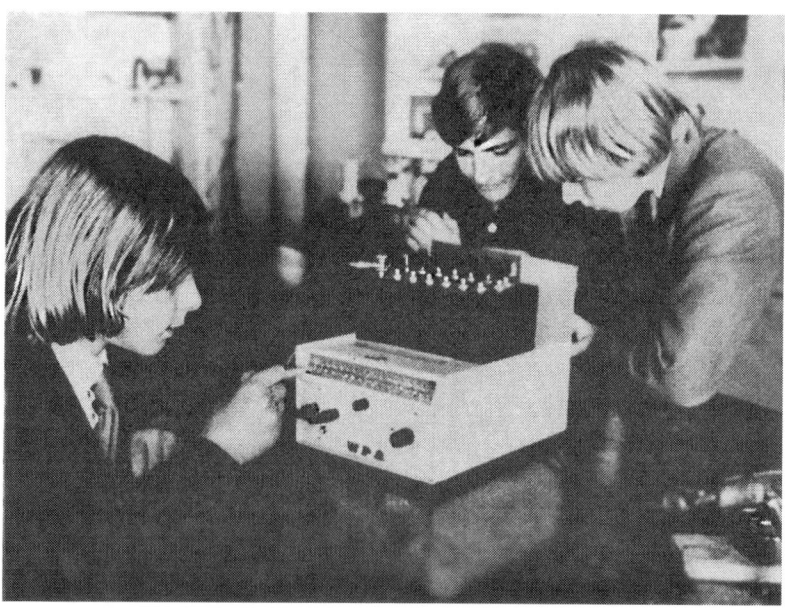

Figure 15.4 Science class, RNIB Worcester College, 1981. (Courtesy of RNIB Research Library, London.)

Yet the push given to integration by the 1981 Act often still failed to materialise on implementation within LEAs. On the one hand, English and Welsh LEAs were given a legal *duty* to provide mainstream education for all children, so long as this concurred with parental wishes and involved efficient resourcing: only children with very severe (often multiple) disabilities would require special schooling. However, many parents used the legislation to ensure placements for their children in special schools despite the LEAs' preferences. Neither did the government provide additional funds to help LEAs implement the new procedures. Moreover, it was and is extremely difficult to integrate children beyond the point at which schools can cope, and LEAs were further hampered by the difficulty of altering the system, ensuring, for instance, that mainstream teaching staff were trained to understand the needs of visually impaired students. Finally, as on many other occasions, Scottish legislators did not concur with English ones, and decided not to place a legal *duty* on Scottish LEAs to integrate special educational needs students. This, they felt, was in complete agreement with the Warnock Report's philosophy: special schools should remain an important option within the range of provision, and a visually impaired child attending a special school for visually impaired students need not mean segregation. Nevertheless, integration gained ground post-Warnock and a support system of peripatetic specialist teachers expanded to cater for the increase in mainstream visually impaired student numbers.

Not all were in agreement with Britain's educational reforms for blind students. Gisela Dimigen et al. (1993), for instance, noted that special schools seemed to equip students well for post-school transition to employment or post-secondary education in the sense that they encouraged optimistic attitudes in school leavers. Similarly, examination results of visually impaired students in various special schools throughout the 1980s indicated that many special schools allowed good curriculum access and enabled students to achieve a high level of academic success. Indeed, knowledge of this often compelled parents of visually impaired children to choose the special school option (Cole, 1989). This and the fact that special schools could work successfully with vocational credentialing bodies such as the Scottish Vocational Education Council conflicts with claims by some that special schools denied children success within the British national curriculum. However, despite this critique, history shows that the integrated education approach became the standard method by providing educational supports and services to blind and partially sighted students throughout Britain.

Visually impaired students in post-16 education

It should be noted that different models of education were offered to some blind and visually impaired students dating back to the seventeenth century. A National Institute for the Blind (1935) survey of literature showed that a small number of blind students attended universities such as Oxford as early as 1656. The NIB study found that between 1656 and 1883 26 blind students graduated from Oxford, and of these 14 went on to pursue "holy orders". The same NIB survey noted the substantial increase of blind graduates after the widespread acceptance in special schools of Braille (see Table 15.1) and the creation of a tradition in which significant numbers of Worcester College school graduates made the transition to Oxford University from 1884 to 1934. Booth (1940) indicated that a dozen blind students could be attending Oxford at any one time, scattered across various colleges. The survey results also

Table 15.1 Estimated total numbers of blind university graduates 1656–1934

Pre-Braille Group 1656–1883		Braille Group 1884–1934			
Career After Graduating	Student Numbers	School	Student Numbers	University	Student Numbers
Holy Orders	14	45 Worcester College	84	Oxford	77
School Teachers	0	17			
Solicitors	1	12 Royal Normal College	20	Durham	19
University Lecturers	1	11			
Musicians	3	8 Royal Blind School, Edinburgh	8	Cambridge	16
Serving Articles (Law) and Barristers	0	8			
Private Teaching	1	4 Schools for the Sighted	6	Edinburgh	10
Social Workers	1	2			
Masseurs	0	2 Chorleywood College	5	London	7
No Information	5	12			
Known to have died at college or shortly after graduating	0	8			
Others	0	16 Others	22	Others	16
TOTAL	26		145		

showed continuity with the pre-Braille era in the careers chosen by university graduates (still largely holy orders, teaching, lecturing and music) and in the above-average performance at university of many in this group. Some examples from the records include seventeenth-century Oxford graduates John Troughton and Richard Lucas, who became distinguished clerics: a Puritan preacher and Prebendary of Westminster Abbey, respectively. While Troughton was able to earn praise from his most critical theological opponent as "a good school divine and metaphysician", Lucas wrote prolifically and was praised by John Wesley. In 1724, a third, John Stanley, became organist at All Hallows, Bread Street, London, at the age of 11, graduated in 1729 as a Bachelor of Music and later was Master of the King's Musick.

Considering the fact that these students attended university during a pre-Braille era, when formal educational supports would not have been provided and during a time wherein people with disabilities were most often kept out of the mainstream, we can assume that this group may have consisted of highly motivated individuals who undoubtedly came from the families of British elites who could afford to pay for educational supports and services that may have been required.

A later study by the Royal National Institute for the Blind survey of 1143 full-time students by Butler (1986) covering the period 1969–1985 shows major shifts in the educational attainment of blind and partially sighted students. Interestingly, the study also shows a shift in the terminology when referring to blind and partially sighted students wherein the term "visual handicap" is applied. Some view the term "visual handicap" as a negative reference but during the period in question the term "handicap" was often used as a broad descriptive reference point such as "the person with a visual handicap", or "person with a mobility handicap" (person using a wheelchair, or person with a hearing handicap in reference to Deaf and hard-of-hearing persons). But in many ways the term "with a handicap" was part of the shifting vernacular of "person-first" wording – such as person with a visual handicap. The person-first language stems from North America and the terminology was meant to reinforce the principle that impairment was only one of many characteristics of the individual. In Britain terms such as "a person with a visual handicap" were used as a broad descriptive term, while "blind" and "partially sighted" were specific categories that were used to describe individuals in terms of the degree of visual loss. Moreover these terms were divided into sub-categories for Butler's study, i.e. no useful sight (39 percent of students surveyed), studying mainly by non-sighted methods (27 percent) and studying mainly by sighted methods but also with visual and non-visual aids (34 percent). During the 1960s, '70s and '80s large numbers of blind and partially sighted students attended and graduated from schools throughout Britain, including Worcester, Chorleywood, Royal National College for the Blind, Exhall Grange and Royal Blind School in Edinburgh. Butler's 1986 study found that there was a dramatic shift in selected careers of the blind and partially sighted students who had graduated. Whereas earlier documentation showed a number of blind and partially sighted students studying in the fields of music and theology, by the 1970s many blind and partially sighted students were studying in the fields of social work, social sciences, law, modern languages, arts, computer studies, maths, science, religious studies and music and upon graduation many were finding employment in these fields of work. No graduates surveyed opted for a religious vocation.

These surveys can give the impression that precise and comprehensive historical figures for visually impaired student numbers are easy to come by. This is not the case, given that organisations such as RNIB have never exercised a monopoly in provision in this area. It would be possible to examine numbers of requests for financial and other assistance from students accepted by the relevant RNIB Education Assistance committees, and it is possible that these numbers would reflect the rise in numbers generally; it is likely that numbers would always tend to indicate the majority of cases of visually impaired students studying over a period of time. From the records of an RNIB Education Assistance Sub-Committee, numbers of students in the late 1940s and early 1950s probably stood at less than 30 per year, most students coming from the special schools listed in Table 15.1. This annual figure for students in higher education (mainly universities) known to RNIB rose to 90 in 1970 and 296 by 1983 (Butler, 1986), with a further 160 studying mainstream open learning courses with the Open University (OU). By 1995, the figure stood at 1792 (Richardson and Roy, 2002). This included students in mainstream further and higher education on part-time and full-time courses but excluded students in special colleges.

There is no knowing the precise relationship between the various causal factors and the increase in visually impaired student numbers in the latter half of the last century: legislation, post-16 advisory support, technology and changes in philosophy and practical awareness have all influenced growth. Certainly, specific legislation has had an effect, though as McGinty and Fish (1992) note, the 1981 Act implementing the Warnock Committee's recommendations omitted completely the area of further and higher education. In fact, much of the legislation already mentioned did not refer to post-school provision at all, and it has only been in recent years that requirements have been recognised and clarified in law.

The effect of legislation

By the late 1980s postsecondary education became more available to students with disabilities throughout Britain but that does not necessarily mean that significant reforms were instituted. The 1988 Education Reform Act, for example, was the first such legislation to involve students with special educational needs in the context of post-16 education. The Education Reform Act required colleges to develop long-term strategic plans wherein they had to institute 3-year development strategies for meeting the needs of *all* students and therefore, to include within the plans a strategy for meeting the needs of students with disabilities. Colleges were also required to clarify cross-college performance indicators to be used in monitoring and evaluating the quality of college provision, for *all* students. However, the wording of the Act did not actually guarantee the provision of supports and services to meet the educational needs of students with disabilities, merely that LEAs would "have regard" about the needs of students with disabilities. In fact, the initial draft of the Education Reform Bill, resulting in the Act, did not even mention visually impaired students or other students with disabilities; these categories were later introduced as a result of lobbying activities of charitable organisations in Great Britain.

Provision of educational supports for visually impaired students in post-16 education also improved through changes in the regulations governing student awards as contained in the Further and Higher Education Acts of 1992. From 1978, students with disabilities were able to claim limited additional funding from their LEA through the Disabled Students Allowance (DSA). This funding was provided in addition to payment of fees and maintenance costs in many cases so that some of the educational expense of disability could be offset but was insufficient for many students' needs, particularly in relation to interpreter costs for deaf students and technology costs for visually impaired students (Patton, 1990). Fortunately, alterations were made to the 1990 Education Mandatory Awards Regulations and from that point, DSA rose to a level which met the personal assistance and technology costs of most students with disabilities studying full-time in higher education. To some extent, these changes were brought about by the detail of information on student need elicited by RNIB and others working with individual students and their various LEA officers. Change was also brought about by effective communication with the Civil Service and lobbying.

One of the most interesting collaborative efforts in lobbying was made as John Major's Conservative government pushed through legislation for the Further and

Higher Education 1992 Acts for Scotland, England and Wales to enact them before the May 1992 general election. In response to this legislation disability organisations combined together to lobby government officials to ensure that legislation creating entirely new funding bodies for British further and higher education would enshrine best practice for meeting the needs of students with disabilities. As a result, the Major government was hit by a well-orchestrated disability campaign, wherein the rights and needs of students with disabilities became the most significant focus for debate during the proceedings and the government was forced to concede a number of issues. Although gains were made, the disability lobby would consider the result of its efforts as one of only partial success. Visually impaired students, for example, who were studying part-time often because of the practical limitations imposed by their condition and other disabilities such as diabetes gained little from the Act. More generally, areas such as adequate college provision for visually impaired students depended entirely on how this was perceived and interpreted by the institution's authorities. Although some institutions would avail themselves of staff development and resourcing opportunities to develop adequate support systems, others remained at a level which did not offer the proper supports for blind and visually impaired students (Dryden, 1993, 1994).

The effects of philosophical change and models of disability during the 1990s

By the mid 1990s disabled people in Britain, including blind and partially sighted individuals, were becoming increasingly more political, and a major paradigm shift away from a medical model of disability toward a social model of disability began to emerge. This shift had a positive influence over blind and partially sighted university students. As a result of this paradigm shift, people with disabilities across Britain, including blind and partially sighted university students, began to challenge long-standing beliefs which viewed disablement in terms of personal loss and failure to a social oppression model of disability (Oliver, 1990) wherein the problems of disabled people were framed in terms of social, political, economic, cultural and historical barriers. As a result of these shifts in disability identification and increased advocacy by disabled people, barriers to accessing the post-school institutions began to be removed.

Todd (1992) provides a historical account of the conceptual change. The medical model applied purely medical logic to label and group individuals according to limitation and handicap, emphasising "defect" and the disability of the individual. Negative rather than positive emphasis was the more likely result. Such a logic clashed with the situational and relative philosophy of special needs education prevalent since Warnock, in which a continuum of ability was emphasised for all students. That is, "a student who has little or no vision … is a whole human being with many intellectual, social, and psychological characteristics. Classification according to one or a few characteristics is minimally useful in planning a total educational programme" (Stainback and Stainback in Todd, 1992, pp 17–18).

While the educational implications of visual impairment should be weighed carefully, visual loss became one of many factors. By the early 1990s, the social model was being accepted by such organisations as the Royal National Institute for the Blind, and to reduce attitudinal and environmental barriers to education for visually impaired students and the academic staff, training programs offered by the RNIB emphasized principles of the social model. The RNIB training programme, for example, challenged the personal attitudes of educators towards visually impaired students and encouraged them to learn and apply good practice in making learning materials and the physical environment accessible to students with visual impairments.

Given the interpretative function of the social interactional or social barriers model, its actual aim was to reduce the significance of disability by influencing the range of causal factors internal and external to the individual concerned. It is also worth noting that this shift of emphasis and the resulting decline in the medical model has been evident in Britain only over approximately the last 30 years, and it is too early to consign to history attitudes dominated by the medical model. But it is apparent that the current impact of the newer approach will include a rise in visually impaired student numbers along with considerable improvement in the quality of post-16 integrated provision.

Yet, given that this philosophical shift is comparatively recent, it cannot account in the main for increased numbers of visually impaired students attending post-secondary institutions throughout the 1970s and 1980s. When the Warnock Report was published, it revealed a general lack of opportunity for school leavers with disabilities beyond the special colleges. Most local further education colleges were not providing integrated places for them. This began to change as the Report's philosophy of integration became influential. Various pioneering projects set out to develop college provision until a "philosophy of inclusiveness" became widely articulated and applied through bodies such as the Further Education Unit (McGinty and Fish, 1993). When the Education Reform Act 1998 was implemented, colleges were required to include their strategies for meeting the learning needs of students with disabilities in their long-term development plans.

It is also true that although they were still under-represented in the post-16 education population, visually impaired students benefited from the adoption of equal opportunities policies. By the mid-1990s, more and more colleges and universities across Britain included an equal opportunities statements within their official policies and procedures. Although colleges and universities varied widely in the extent to which they promoted explicit policies which actually reflected implicit ones, the new autonomy provided by the Further and Higher Education Acts 1992 made them the responsible party for the ethics they adopted.

Conclusion

Over the last two centuries, access to education for visually impaired people improved as a result of direct legislation, the values expounded by Christianity (including the work ethic) and the secularised morality of equity and equal opportunity. Visually impaired people have in the end been included across the widest curriculum range. Nevertheless, if society creates disability, as the social models suggest, this present society's belief in market forces and competition also creates a vulnerability in groups who must strive harder to succeed. Often it is only the wording of legislation which protects these groups from marginalisation and clarifies their rights. The interpretation of legislation is also crucial. Although it should aim to achieve the greatest measure of equity, it should not foster any dependence, demeaning those it attempts to assist. Passive dependence, of course, has rarely been encouraged anyway; replacing dependence on the state by economic self-sufficiency was always a factor in nineteenth-century charity, while more recent legislation for post-16 provision was motivated by a belief in self-sufficiency and economic considerations, especially the desire to reduce the unemployment level.

Rather than engendering passivity, the historical changes in educational provision have, in fact, required an ever-greater striving by visually impaired children and students, ever-greater motivation and application, as the opportunity for success in education has grown. Much of this is extremely positive. Yet while the barriers to education may be falling, the legislation which caused them to fall has usually been fairly reactive, half-hearted, reluctant and patchy. Greater numbers of visually impaired students are now in education than ever before, and it is encouraging that fewer drop out than average when comparisons are drawn with the sighted student population. But can they now succeed as they should, when Great Britain continues to lack a coherent policy in government for people with disabilities which fully covers education, employment and training? Visually impaired students still face considerable barriers, and it is evident that the disability lobby and charities have a major part to play to facilitate their progress in the years ahead. When we look back at historical change, we note that charities have often carried the greatest responsibility, had the greatest vision and involved themselves in much of the most innovative work in this field. We are optimistic that their future efforts will continue to encourage barriers to fall.

References

Barnhill, Alexander. (1875) *A New Era in the Education of Blind Children*. Glasgow, UK: Charles Glass.

Bell, Donald. (1966) (Ed.) *An Experiment in Education: The History of Worcester College for the Blind. 1866–1966*. London, UK: Hutchinson.

Booth, H. (1940) Blind university graduates: A comment on the facts. *The New Beacon*. 24, 113–116.

Butler, Michael. (1986) *Visually Handicapped Students: A Survey 1969–1985*. London, UK: RNIB.

Cole, Ted. (1989) *Apart or A Part? Integration and the Growth of British Special Education*. Milton Keynes, UK: Open University Press.

Dimigen, Gisela, Scott, Fiona, Thackeray, F., Pimm, Mark and Roy, Archie W.N. (1993) Career expectations of British visually impaired students of school-leaving age. *Journal of Visual Impairment and Blindness*. 87(6). 209–210.

Dryden, Gordon. (1993) Letter to the Further Education Funding Council on FEFC consultation circular 93/32 recurrent funding methodology. *Unpublished letter*.

Dryden, Gordon. (1994) Implications of the 1992 Further and Higher Education Act. In David T. Etheridge and Heather L. Mason (Eds.) *The Visually Impaired: Curricular Access and Entitlement in Further Education*. London, UK: David Fulton.

Farrar, F.W. (1892) The Education of the Blind. *The Mentor*. 2(10), 373–386.

Fothergill, Sister Kathleen. (1980) The education of the partially sighted. In D.J. Harvey (Ed.) *Children Who are Partially Sighted*. Birmingham, UK: AEWVH.

McGinty, Jean and Fish, John. (1992) *Learning Support for Young People in Transition*. Buckingham, UK: Open University Press.

McGinty, Jean and Fish, John. (1993) *Further Education in the Market Place: Equity, Opportunity and Individual Learning*. London, UK: Routledge.

Moody, Terry. (1987) Inertia, resistance and change: educational policy for pupils with visual disabilities. In Tony Booth and Will Swann (Eds.) *Including Pupils with Disabilities.* Milton Keynes, UK: Open University Press.

NIB. (1935) *Blind University Graduates.* London, UK: NIB.

NIB. (1936) *The Education of the Blind – A Survey.* London, UK: Edward Arnold.

Oliver, M. (1990) *The Politics of Disablement.* London, UK: MacMillan Press.

Patton, Brian. (1990) A survey of the disabled students' allowance. *Educare.* 36. 3–7.

Pritchard, D.G. (1963) *Education and the Handicapped 1760–1960.* London, UK: Routledge and Kegan Paul.

Richardson, John T.E. and Roy, Archie W.N. (2002) The representation and attainment of students with a visual impairment in higher education. *The British Journal of Visual Impairment.* 20(1), January. 37–48.

Todd, Neil. (1992) *The Integration of Visually Impaired Students in Further Education.* Loughborough University of Technology: unpublished doctoral thesis.

16

OUT OF SIGHT, OUT OF MIND: BLIND ASYLUMS AND MISSIONS IN SCOTLAND

Hazel McFarlane

Introduction

The asylums

Local philanthropists established the Edinburgh and Glasgow Blind Asylums in 1793 and 1827 respectively. The directors, drawn from the medical profession, business and church communities, genuinely desired to have what they considered to be a positive influence on the lives and circumstances of blind people.

> The aim we have in view is to rescue the blind from hopeless despondency and render them useful members of society. (GBAAR 1883:5)

These sentiments indicate a commitment to assisting blind people to acquire education and skills to facilitate their participation in mainstream society. The Edinburgh and Glasgow Blind Asylums admitted mainly young people, who generally had been blind from a young age. Entrance criteria favoured those who could be taught a trade and be employed within the asylum workshops; they did not admit individuals who would possibly become a burden upon the institution (Royal Commission on The Blind 1886(c):44). The asylums proactively created the impression that they accommodated the needs of the majority of blind people in the cities' populations, but, because they admitted only those who could be absorbed as employees into the workshops, they effectively served to assist only a minority of the blind population (Ritchie 1930). Moreover, it would appear that the directors' intentions to make blind people useful members of society were very much gender-orientated. These institutions were opened with the intention of offering blind males, first and foremost, opportunities to access general education, industrial training and employment within the asylum workshops. The asylums met the requirements of mainly blind males, mirroring the cultural expectations of that time, when men were assumed to have responsibilities as providers for their families. These blind males were enabled to fulfil their expected social roles and served a purpose to society, manufacturing the various goods produced in the asylum workshop, but the directorial intentions for females appear to have been very different. Prior to the 1820 opening of the female asylum in Edinburgh,

273

the directors were particularly concerned with the guidance and development of the moral deportment of their female charges. It seems that the directors perceived blind women to be physically and morally vulnerable, and in need of guidance and care. Many of the women initially admitted were assumed to originate from the poorest classes, although they were considered to be among the most respectable characters who were very poor (EBAMB 1805–1825:208). It is apparent that the directors regarded blind females as helpless, and that this misguided perception undoubtedly influenced their adoption of a guardianship role in the women's lives.

Contained spaces

The Edinburgh Asylum for the Relief of the Indigent and Industrious Blind, opened in 1793, was initially located in Waterloo Place in the centre of the city. The requirement for larger workshop premises prompted a move to Nicholson Street on the south side of the city. While located in the south side, a female asylum was opened in 1820, situated in the same street as the male asylum. Further expansion in workshop premises and female accommodation involved the erection of new buildings at Craigmillar Park on the periphery of the city: 'This which is a new building, is just outside the town, in a very healthy and beautiful situation' (Armitage 1878:6). Situated just beyond the city boundary, only a few large dwelling houses were present in the vicinity of the asylum in 1876 (Edinburgh 1877, 1881). House-building proliferated, and by 1893 the area had established itself as an affluent neighbourhood, and large detached and semi-detached dwelling houses had encroached on the fields that bounded the asylum grounds (Edinburgh 1893). The Glasgow Blind Asylum, established in 1827 and based in the former fever hospital, was located to the north of the city, occupying a semi-rural location bounded on the north and east by fields and west and east by newly built large residential dwellings (Maps 1828, 1831, 1832). In the mid 1800s the Asylum moved to a purpose-built site in Castle Street, and the new location positioned the asylum in front of Glasgow Royal Infirmary (Map 1860). The asylum was surrounded by a substantial, 9-feet-high, perimeter wall. A statue of Christ opening the eyes of the blind stood symbolically at the Castle Street entrance. By 1896 the asylum had become completely encompassed by residential developments, and these were large dwellings as opposed to tenements, which would suggest that the asylum was now sited in an increasingly prosperous residential area of Glasgow (Map 1896).

Peripheral locations contributed to the spatial segregation of blind people. Even when residential developments encroached on the asylum boundary, perimeter walls, austere, imposing entrances and long tree-lined avenues leading to the main asylum buildings all acted as physical boundaries between segregated and mainstream spaces. These physical boundaries distanced supposedly 'defective others' away from mainstream normality. These physical features contributed to the mystification of both the activities within such spaces and those who inhabited them.

The blind asylums distributed advertising literature to raise awareness of their charitable work, as well as detailing the items for sale produced by the inmates, such as mattresses, baskets, brushes, knitted shawls, stockings and baby clothes. Annual reports frequently carried adverts for these items, with the text always constructing the institutions positively as philanthropic providers and inmates negatively as passive recipients. This exploitation of inmates as a means of increasing legacies and donations was particularly pronounced during times of financial hardship. A trade depression in the late 1840s was identified as the cause of a decline in sales, donations and legacies, and in order to redress this situation the institutions promoted the need for their continuation:

> The many pressing applications for admission to the institution, from all parts of Scotland and elsewhere, at once show the great helplessness of the blind. The reputation of the asylum for meeting their wants, and the usefulness of the institution in enabling them to raise themselves above entire dependence upon others. (EBAAR 1850:3)

Edinburgh Asylum also projected the fate of inmates had they *not* been admitted into the institution:

> Houselessness, uninstructed, blind – helped through this dreary world, as it were, from hour to hour, groping for aid amid the constant embarrassment of their forlorn condition. (EBAAR 1852:4)

Similarly, Glasgow Asylum forcefully conveyed the institution's supposed role in alleviating the perceived burden that blind people placed on society:

> The Asylum is the only institution in Glasgow or the West of Scotland where a blind person can learn to do something for his or her support, and without which many blind persons would now be wandering about begging or be dependent on their friends, or have to enter the poorhouse. (GBAAR1883:8)

A trade depression in 1886 again dramatically reduced legacies and donations to the institutions and once again placed them in a tenuous financial position. These severe financial circumstances were reflected in an aggressive approach to raising public support and funds for the continuation of the institutions. The asylums clearly indicated their supposed role in society and the manner in which the general public were expected to assist them in undertaking their role:

> To maintain such an institution necessarily involves a considerable outlay, which can only be provided by subscriptions, donations, bequests and purchases of articles manufactured by the blind. (GBAAR 1887: Front Cover)

During financially hard times the institutions kept only profitable lines in production and resorted to using poorer-quality raw materials. Inmates were portrayed as incapable of working efficiently and as such their wages required augmentation:

> It must be remembered that the work of the blind can never be entirely remunerative. There will always be a certain income required from the public to keep the asylum in efficient state. Considerable expense must be incurred in the industrial training of the blind. (GBAAR 1884:9)

Inmates were portrayed as an inefficient, unprofitable workforce who would have little influence on the prosperity of the institutions. The notion, perpetuated by the institutions, that blind individuals worked slower than sighted people meant that blind people were generally considered unsuitable for employment outside the asylum workshops. Consequently, their association with the asylum tended to span their entire working life.

Institutional literature represented inmates as a human group deserving of sympathy and charitable support, while the general public were regarded and positioned as the main means of providing that charitable support. Thus, the general public were believed to have the capacity to influence the prosperity of the institutions and to alter the life circumstances of blind people, rather than this possibility being in the remit of blind people themselves:

> The desire to help the blind was natural in every well-disposed person. The sad loss under which they laboured in the deprivation of sight, and the cheerfulness with which they bore it, commanded the interest and sympathy of those more highly favoured. (GBAAR 1888:8)

The asylums, perhaps unintentionally, created a fearful image of blindness, describing blindness in some annual reports as 'one of the severest of human afflictions' (EBAAR 1857:4). Such descriptions were clearly used to stimulate generous donations, and the language used, combined with the spatial segregation of blind people, created societal fear of blindness and blind people. Therefore blindness was something to be avoided, and giving to charity enabled sighted individuals to distance themselves financially and physically from 'the blind'. Where gender was acknowledged, men were portrayed as competent, undertaking masculine tasks despite being blind. Women, however, were not accredited with adult status, and were instead portrayed as dependent, incapable, recipients who needed the institution to protect them.

> To allow a female in the helpless state of a blind woman to go by herself unprotected through the crowded streets on a Sunday was inexpedient and attended with risk to the pupil herself. (EBAMB 1825–1835:152)

The asylums thus substantially contributed to the social construction of blind women as helpless and vulnerable individuals, women for whom everyday spaces were positioned as dangerous places.

The notion that blind females needed to be taken care of was reflected in statements from annual reports that reinforced the women's supposed unsuitability for work, inferring an incapacity to support themselves within or outwith the institution. Directors promoted their magnanimity towards the women:

> The female asylum in a pecuniary sense, may be considered almost entirely unproductive, the expenses incurred for board, clothing of its inmates, absorbing a large proportion of the subscriptions to the institution. The directors have much satisfaction in believing that this great outlay is compensated by the comfort and happiness experienced by their interesting

charge, through the mental training and sound religious instruction they receive under the superintendence of their respected Matron, Miss Bathgate. (EBAAR 1856: initial page unnumbered)

In general inmates' privacy or feelings were accorded little if any recognition by directors, and in many respects the inmates, especially females, were a commodity perhaps unintentionally exploited (Finkler 2003). For example, in an attempt to increase legacies and donations, members of the public were invited to tour the asylum on a daily basis. Females housed in the asylum in receipt of benevolence effectively became the property of the benefactors – the public. Giving to charity seemingly bought individuals the right to view, inspect and observe inmates at close quarters. For daily tours, no space was out of bounds. Visitors toured the workshops to watch inmates working, as well as the large dormitories where the women slept two to a bed. Female inmates were constantly on display, encouraged and expected to perform for visitors. As objects of public property, any aspect of the females' lives could be scrutinised or questioned by visitors and directors. As recipients of charity, the women were expected to be passive, diligent, obedient and most importantly, grateful.

The directors welcomed expressions of gratitude, and inmates were often invited into directors' meetings to thank them personally, or letters from inmates were read aloud. Despite the restrictive regimes, female inmates did express their gratitude to both the directors and the public. A letter submitted to the directors' meeting of November 1824 read:

The girls of the female blind asylum beg leave at this time humbly to thank the gentlemen of the management, the kind and indulgent public, and master Johnston in particular, for the many favours that are daily conferred on us: and it shall be our earnest prayer and constant endeavour to merit a continuation of the inestimable blessings both temporal and spiritual, which we have received since we entered the asylum. (EBAMB 1805–1825:326)

Containment, morality and purification

The containment of inmates varied considerably depending upon the inmate's gender and the financial position of the institution. Prior to 1820 Edinburgh Blind Asylum admitted only males. The directors considered it highly improper to have males and females living in the same house. Funding constraints and a resultant lack of accommodation prohibited the admission of females for a further 23 years. Boys and unmarried men were boarded within the asylum, and later in a boarding house purchased specifically for the purpose. This arrangement was abandoned in 1830. From this point onwards, boys were lodged with respectable married couples, unmarried men resided in lodgings selected by directors, and married men returned to their families each evening. Therefore, males participated in a segregated working environment during the day, after which they had opportunities, albeit limited, to participate in the everyday life of their local communities.

Women were accepted as home workers onto the roll of the Edinburgh Blind Asylum from 1796 onwards. Women were provided with materials and visited regularly by the overseer to monitor progress and productivity. At this early stage, differential directorial influence over females' lives became apparent. Where women's living conditions were considered to be very poor, the directors of the asylum applied to the parish workhouse on their behalf. If women were accepted, but refused to enter the workhouse, they were denied the benefits of outworking for the Blind Asylum (EBAMB 1805–1825:17). By the early nineteenth century, directors resolved to establish a female asylum. In their deliberations regarding the location, they acknowledged 'the importance of females placed under their care in a more reputable situation and where their whole moral deportment would be under one superintendence' (EBAMB 1805–1825:217). It would seem that the directors did, in fact, assume responsibility for the moral correction and guidance of their female charges. The female asylum opened in 1820, and females admitted into the asylum resided within the walls of the institution. It was not until the middle of the nineteenth century that a few women were boarded out in lodgings selected by the directors. Even so, the majority of female inmates remained resident within the institution.

The directors' perceptions of the women as childlike had spatial consequences, chiefly manifested in the large dormitories with no physical divisions as privacy was not considered a requirement for inmates, especially when housed in single sex accommodation. Directors discussed the possibility of dividing the space with partitions, but took the decision not to do so (GBAMB 1880–1884). It was assumed that blindness, or at best partial sight, negated the need for physical divisions to create private space. For example, toilet facilities in the female dormitory were not equipped with doors until 1881 (GBAMB 1880–1884:58).

Moreover, newspaper descriptions of the female inmates at the time centred on their appearance, suggesting recognition of them as females. As with their sighted counterparts, their appearance indicated their moral stature; a dirty, untidy appearance was thought to signify immorality, while cleanliness and neatness equated with good moral standards (Barret-Ducrocq 1992). However, the description of their conduct also implies an infantile perception of these women:

> In appearance they are clean, tidy and intelligent – in disposition apparently contented and cheerful: they appear less talkative than the males, the silence that reigns in the house being very noteable in a household of women. The fact that they almost never quarrel among themselves is perhaps equally so (*Scotsman* article 1864:71).

In general, children rather than adults would be expected to quarrel amongst themselves. The article also described the men working competently with complex and potentially dangerous pieces of machinery. Female inmates were depicted quite differently, referred to as girls working quietly and passing the time singing; such portrayals distanced the inmates from sighted women.

The majority of asylum inmates originated from poor families. Poor conditions and poverty were routinely associated by the Victorians with dirt, disease and also immorality. Directors therefore assumed that the majority of inmates originated from 'families where good example was not known' (EBAAR 1853:4). Inmates were occasionally admitted into the asylum on a conditional basis, especially when they were considered to come from an immoral background, and inmates were often forced to sever all ties or to limit contact with their relatives. For instance, Eliza Lyell was admitted into the asylum on the condition that she visited her family only with the Matron's permission (RBASEMB 1872–1883:20).

Although the directors perceived female inmates to generally be of good character, by virtue of their social class they were still assumed to have immoral and delinquent habits that had to be corrected through a purifying process of strict adherence to religious regimes. The directors professed their responsibilities towards both the moral and physical deportment of the inmates. 'With so great a responsibility [to] the moral, as well as the physical culture of so many of these almost helpless fellow creatures' (EBAAR 1855: unnumbered), worship, religious instruction, reading and recital of the bible were fundamental elements of daily life in the asylum. The reformatory effects of the religious doctrine were considered to have paramount importance, especially in relation to female inmates. Christianity and expressions of Christian beliefs indicated the taming of a savage, animal-like group, and cleansing females of their immoral, depraved, dirty origins was crucial in the purification process. The female inmates were to be rendered as women of moral stature, living a celibate, moral life and, as such, could more readily gain social acceptability as deserving objects of charity.

Attendance at family worship twice per day, in addition to religious instruction and Sunday worship at the local church, was compulsory for all inmates. Male and female outworkers could choose which church they wished to attend, with their attendance monitored by directors. If monitoring revealed repeated absence, dismissal from the asylum ensued. The directors were convinced of the reformatory effects of religious doctrine:

> The benefits of religious and secular education are afforded to those who might otherwise have remained in mental as well as visual darkness. (EBAAR 1857:4)

Female resident inmates were held to a far higher moral code than were their outworking counterparts. Regulations dictated the church they were to attend, where they were to sit within the church, namely the seats provided for the blind, and the manner in which they should spend Sunday:

> No one living in the house being left to wander about but all to attend the parish church with the mistress and to remain afterwards at home, neither admitting visitors or paying visits. (EBAMB 1825–1835:271)

A few women residents made requests to attend a church of their choice. While the directors anxiously denied any desire to control the conscience or religious creed of the female inmates (EBAMB 1825–1835:272), they exerted their power directly in outright refusals to permit females to attend another church:

> The directors do not want females wandering from church to church and perhaps about the streets or fields. Wandering on the Lord's day without God or good once influencing their mind. (EBAMB 1825–1835:273)

The women's safety and religious ordinance may well have been causes for directorial concern. However, it is highly likely that the directors did not want inmates to be 'aimlessly wandering' in public space, because women whose presence in the street could not be explained by an obvious task, shopping or some other necessary activity, were considered unnatural and their out-of-placeness perceived to signify doubtful morality (Barret-Ducrocq 1992). Also, images of vulnerability and helplessness had been constructed around the female inmates, women for whom public space was regarded as a thoroughly risk-laden place to be. Blind women independently navigating their way through public space would certainly have challenged this social perception of them. The directors' influence hence appears to have limited women's opportunities to participate independently in mainstream society, perhaps as a means of maintaining the created social images of both the incapable female inmates and the supposed necessity of the asylums.

Controlled and surveyed spaces

Strict regimes, rules and regulations formed the framework by which the Blind Asylums operated. The rules and regulations were initially devised to facilitate the efficient running of the institutions. However, as directorships changed over time, so too did the ethos underpinning both their involvement and attitudes towards the inmates. Regulations were introduced which acted to restrict and to control the choices and activities of all inmates to varying extents: for example, swearing, drinking alcohol, impertinent language, idleness and smoking were not tolerated within the asylum. Rules and regulations were frequently read out to inmates, particularly when they had been contravened. The threat of dismissal was unremitting and presence in the asylum was always conditional, dependent on adherence to the rules and diligence in the workshops. Since expulsion from the institution would almost certainly lead to destitution or entry into the workhouse, these actions perpetuated a climate of fear and conformity.

One of the objects of the asylum was to 'educate the young, and to instruct the adult to earn his bread by his own industry' (Alston 1846:37). It was assumed that blind men would have families dependent upon them for support, whereas blind women were not expected to have such responsibilities, but rather to be themselves dependent upon their friends and relatives for support. A gender bias hence existed in the facilities provided within the asylum, mirroring assumed responsibilities and dominant social roles. Expansion of male workshops enabled the enrolment of an increased number of males, and the Edinburgh Asylum Annual Report of 1865 notes 106 men and boys in the male asylum, and 28 females in the female asylum (EBAAR 1865:iv). Males outnumbered females at least three to one. Age limits on admission differed, with 40 years as a maximum age limit for men, compared to 30 years for females (EBAMB 1805–1825). Provision for female inmates was limited to one workroom and two dormitories, accommodating a maximum of 29 women (*Scotsman* 1864:72). The imbalance in provision was somewhat redressed in 1876 when the asylum moved to new buildings in Craigmillar Park, which allowed accommodation for upwards of 100 females (RBASAR 1874).

The directors exerted their influence over all inmates by devising and implementing mechanisms for monitoring conduct and behaviour within and, more significantly, outwith the institutions. All inmates had to seek the permission of the workshop manager prior to taking leave for example, prior to taking a day off work. A regulation was implemented that obligated the inmates to disclose why they wanted time off and where they were going. All outworkers' lodgings were selected and approved by the directors, and a regulation imposed a curfew on the activities of inmates lodged outwith the asylum:

> It is enjoined that the blind shall never be from their homes after nine o'clock at night, unless they can give a satisfactory excuse and if the least appearance of drunkenness is discovered at any time it will be visited by the most severe reprehension of the directors and by dismissal upon repetition. (EBAMB 1825–1835:338)

Outwith the institution female outworkers' activities and conduct were monitored more closely than males. For example, prior to the opening of the female asylum, a few outworkers sang in a choir along with male outworkers, but the directors exerted their influence over the women's activities by instructing the minister that the women were no longer to participate (EBAMB 1805–1825:208). Male outworkers' behaviour was probably observed with a degree of leniency, so that when male inmates McDermid and Watson were found guilty of staying out late with suspicious company, both were admonished for their behaviour but neither was expelled (EAMB1825–1835:292). In November 1827, Paul Ramsay was disciplined for being seen intoxicated, but he was allowed to stay in the asylum on the condition that this would not occur again (EBAMB 1825–1835:80). The directors took this opportunity to remind inmates of 'their determination to punish in the most exemplary manner every delinquency that may arise' (EBAMB 1825–1835:81).

For women, though, the consequences of digressing from the moral limits imposed upon them as females were enforced to a far greater degree. The minutes of a directors' meeting held on the 21 January 1834 record the dismissal of Margaret Bogle, an outworker of the Glasgow Blind Asylum. She was dismissed for misconduct that took place outwith the asylum. The minutes do not detail the nature of the misconduct, but the stance and resolve adopted by the directors following this incident implies that the misconduct took place in Bogle's lodgings. Revealingly, they stated that

> as much care as possible should be taken to find lodgings for blind females working but not boarded or lodged in the asylum. Where they would not only have the benefit of moral example, but observation taken of their conduct and for this purpose authorise the treasurer to allow out of their funds a small gratuity not to exceed £5, to a proper person for finding out such lodgings and taking superintendence and observation of their conduct. (GBAMB 1825–1845:175)

It hence became common practice to pay sighted observers to monitor the conduct of female outworkers and to report any indiscretions to the directors. The likely hidden motive of surveillance measures may have been to prevent women indulging in supposedly immoral behaviour.

The conduct, activities and choices of females resident in the asylum were restricted and controlled by oppressive regimes that punctuated their daily lives. Woken at 7.00 a.m., allowed a limited amount of time to wash, dress, eat breakfast and attend worship before commencing work for the day, the women's working day was then regimented by an inflexible timetable dictating breaks and meal-times. The inmates were supervised constantly, and they had restricted opportunities to exercise choice, while options were usually set within narrow parameters. For example, women could choose from limited options the way in which they wished to pass the time during the evening in the asylum house: either to return to work, read an embossed Braille book, play the piano or engage in conversation with other inmates. Bedtime at 9.00 p.m. ended their day. The daily routine, coupled with surveillance, enabled directors disproportionately to exert their influence and control over female inmates, in particular those accommodated within the asylum.

Female residents were rarely permitted to leave the asylum house unaccompanied. During the week, women were permitted to leave the asylum for 1 hour per day, usually accompanied by a sighted guide. A few of the women considered capable of negotiating the outside environment safely were allowed to take exercise in an area of land adjoining the asylum, which had been purchased specially for that purpose. Some independent freedom was allowed for a few women, then, but this was highly circumscribed:

> At four o'clock the inmates are then taken out for a walk, under the charge of a servant generally straight south to Newington, or round the Meadows. A few who have the inclination and the cash, are able to take care of themselves on the streets, are permitted to indulge in 'shopping'. But all return to tea at five. (*Scotsman* 1864:72)

Ritchie described a group of inmates of a blind institution negotiating public space in his book *Concerning the Blind*:

> the inmates of an institution were taken out like a party of rock climbers, united by a rope. Much more recently in vogue was the 'crocodile', wherein each youngster laid his hand on the shoulder of the one in front. (Ritchie 1930:32)

Female inmates being guided in such a way in public space reinforced an evolving stereotype of blind women as dependent, helpless and different, but this learned helplessness was precisely *not* an option for female outworkers, who had to negotiate their way to and from the asylum on a daily basis.

Directors frequently exerted their powerful influence over female residents by refusing petitions from women wishing to move out of the asylum house. In April 1834, eight females of the Edinburgh Asylum petitioned a representative of the board of directors regarding lodging out of the asylum house (EBAMB 1825–1835:303). Their request was refused. Directors interpreted such requests as insubordination by an unappreciative individual or group. In order to repress such ingratitude, petitions to leave the house were refused and regulation of food was introduced. The gradual erosion of personal autonomy and the necessary support of the directors to leave the house made it extremely difficult for women to change their circumstances.

Women within gender, sexual and eugenic limits

Socially dominant sexual stereotypes influenced female occupations, education, earnings and living arrangements within the asylums. Therefore, on a practical level, in relation to roles and occupations, *females were regarded as women.* Many prevailing social attitudes towards women were mirrored in the asylum. Women pursued socially acceptable, suitably feminine occupations such as plain sewing, knitting, dressmaking, shirt making and fancy needlework. Over and above their work in the asylum workroom, females were also expected to help as much as possible with cleaning and other domestic tasks in the house. Within the asylum workshops, men had the opportunity to earn from 9 to 11 shillings per week (Alston 1846:37), but the comparative insignificance attributed to female earnings within the asylum is evident in the lack of clear indications of the pecuniary reward for work undertaken by the women. Alston simply recorded that 'many of these young women are receiving regular wages from the institution' (Alston 1846:41). Armitage, meanwhile, recorded that women in the asylum were paid far less for their work than men (Armitage 1878:9), presumably making attainment of financial independence and a self-supporting lifestyle virtually impossible. Regulations governing funds established to pay allowances to families of inmates in the event of their death, or to provide sick pay when inmates were unable to work, were based on the premise (as mentioned) that only men would have family responsibilities. In Edinburgh Asylum only men contributed to the fund, whereas in Glasgow both men and women participated, women contributing three pence and men 6 pence per week. When unable to work due to ill health, men then received 6 shillings per week and women received three shillings and six pence per week (Alston 1846:40).

Sex-differentiated education within the asylum also reflected the dominant social culture, where a sound elementary education was considered inappropriate for females. In keeping with this ethos, girls were instructed in various branches of female industry, in principles of religious instruction and in elements of general knowledge, whereas boys received religious instruction and elementary education as well as being taught trades that suited their capabilities and inclination. Annual reports recorded inmates' educational and industrial activities. The activities of males were separated out into those of men and boys, no such distinction between adult and juvenile was made for women they were simply recorded as 'females' or 'girls'. Women in the asylums continued to be called 'girls' even when older, thus positioning them as potential subjects of schooling.

Female inmates were infantilised by the asylum directors, often being referred to as 'girls' in annual reports, advertising literature and newspaper articles. Crucially for this thesis, these inmates were treated as childlike individuals, asexual and sexually immature. Consequently, they were denied recognition as women, and were deprived of the social trappings of womanhood: sexual maturity, sexual activity and the reproductive roles of childbearing and mothering. One aspect of this was ensuring that women and men in the asylums, or when outworking, were not allowed to mix in a manner that might carry any kind of sexual charge, such that gender segregation was indeed also very much a *sexual* segregation. Unsurprisingly, a host of problematic assumptions crowded into the imposition of this strict gendered and *de*sexed geography of asylum life.

Stringently imposed and monitored measures to ensure gender segregation were implemented in both the Glasgow and Edinburgh Blind Asylums. Prior to opening, the directors of the Glasgow institution took the decision to implement a rigid separation of the sexes:

> No intercourse shall be permitted between the male and female branches of the Asylum, nor shall the boys and girls enter the building appropriated to each other's use except when they are attending family worship or religious instruction. (GBAMB 1825–1845:57)

Sexual separation was imposed in various ways, but most obviously in the social segregation, close supervision and monitoring of women resident in the asylum. Resident inmates rarely had time to themselves, or in fact, any time where their behaviour was not being observed. This level of surveillance severely limited their opportunities to express any resistance to the rules and regulations. Separate workrooms indicated a deliberate measure to segregate inmates along gender lines:

> Their apartments are separate from those of the males and no intercourse whatever is permitted. (Alston 1846:41)

Men were engaged in mattress-making, sack-making, brush-making and rope-making (Alston 1846:37, *Scotsman* 1864:67), while women sewed mattress covers (Armitage 1878:6, *Scotsman* 1864:67). The compatibility of these activities does not indicate a necessity for the tasks to take place in separate environments. In addition, men and women worked different hours, with men starting earlier and finishing later (Alston 1846:49). Women who boarded outwith the asylum were obliged to have dinner with resident inmates each evening, rather than carrying on working (Alston 1846:41). Furthermore, one of the Edinburgh Asylum regulations specifically forbade male and female inmates from communicating in any way within and outwith the institution:

> It is hereby most strictly enjoined that the men and boys shall on no account whatever hold any communication whatever with those in the female department of the institution, either on the respective premises or elsewhere. (EBAMB 1825–1835:339)

Men and boys were hence strictly prohibited from communicating with the females, but there is no such documented rule preventing women communicating with men. This omission is revealing of the directors' attitudes towards the sexuality of the inmates, in that men were perceived as sexual beings while the women, however, were not. These measures contributed to spatial separation of men and women at times of the day when they could possibly meet, develop friendships or even form relationships, times when men, with supposedly limited control of their sexuality, might take advantage of vulnerable females.

As a means of preventing the women inmates from engaging in any immoral behaviour, sighted observers monitored the women in both public and private space:

> It has been found advantageous to have an elderly woman, who has sight to take charge and work along with them [female inmates]. (Alston 1846:41)

The Royal Commission on the Blind suggested that

> the supervision of the blind at night should be obtained by a sighted officer sleeping in a cubicle in the same room, or in one with a window looking directly into the dormitory. We attach great importance to this. (Royal Commission on the Blind 1886(a):xliii)

Daily worship in the morning and evenings were the only times when men and women were permitted to share the same space. Even so, women sat in a separate area of the chapel and a sighted elderly woman observed the females' conduct and behaviour throughout the sermon. The sighted observer's principal role was to ensure that women did not engage in any form of communication with the male inmates. The superintendent of the male asylum also observed the men's behaviour throughout family worship.

The various measures to ensure gender and hence sexual segregation suggests that, despite infantilising the women, the directors did acknowledge the potential for sexual activity between inmates – primarily between men and women, since at this point in time the likelihood of same-sex relationships, certainly between women, was simply not recognised as a possibility by asylum directors. Lesbian sexual relations had not been discovered, identified or named.

Separation of the sexes within the asylums was probably influenced by the attitudes and moral stances of those involved in blind welfare. Notable in this respect was Dr T.R. Armitage, founder of the British and Foreign Blind Association, later known as the Royal National Institute for the Blind (Ritchie 1930). He was a prominent figure of the time who disseminated his views on wide-ranging social and moral issues in relation to blind people as a means of, in his estimation, producing healthy public opinion through sound views and correct information. In a paper, "On the Means Employed for Ameliorating the Condition of the Blind of Great Britain and Ireland", presented to the Paris Congress in 1878, he indicated staunch support for morally informed sex segregation within institutions for the blind. Dr Armitage, himself a blind person, acquired a visual impairment later in life, and may have taken a moral stance that did not necessarily impact upon his own lifestyle. In relation to arrangements for achieving sexual separation within institutions for the blind, he stated that

> In one or two blind schools, the arrangements are so bad that inter-marriage among the old pupils is of frequent occurrence. (Armitage 1878:13)

He made reference to a workshop in London where blind men and women worked side by side, and as a result some formed relationships and married. In the few institutions where men and women worked alongside each other, vigilant supervision was implemented and widely supported by those involved in blind welfare (Wagg 1932). It would appear the key function of sex separation, surveillance and imposition of an oppressive influence over blind women's lives was primarily to prevent them forming relationships, engaging in sexual activity and procreating.

The 19th rule, as it became known and implemented within the Edinburgh Asylum, required all inmates to seek the permission of the directors prior to entering into marriage:

> It is expected that when any of the blind think of entering the married state they will intimate their intention to the directors who will be always ready to give their best advice relative the formation of suitable connections. Although the directors do not claim to themselves any power to prevent marriages yet it is to be held imperative that they are to be consulted. (EBAMB 1825–1835:338)

Directors were of the opinion that marriages entered into without due consideration could cause great misery. They rendered the 19th rule imperative, an action they believed to be important for the 'good of the charity and comfort, respectability and happiness of the members' (EBAMB 1825–1835:223). However, such an action undoubtedly placed the directors in a position of power where they could approve or disapprove of the blind person's intended spouse. Even when inmates lived and worked a considerable distance from the asylum, the directors continued to exert their influence over the inmates' lives. It would seem that the directors genuinely thought that their intervention would avoid blind people making a decision that they would later regret. The elevated status of the 19th rule from observed regulation to imperative rule implies that the directors may have indeed questioned the abilities of inmates to make considered and reasoned decisions.

One of the earliest records of an inmate seeking permission to marry is recorded in the Edinburgh Asylum minute of a directors' meeting held on 5 July 1796. Denis McQueen had been sent as an outworker of the asylum to David Dale's cotton mills in Lanark. Denis's written request sought permission to marry a local Lanark woman, and was accompanied by a letter from a Mr Lamb of Lanark vouching for the woman's good character. The directors resolved that they would give their permission if the woman's character withstood the closest scrutiny. The secretary ascertained the woman's age, current earnings, potential earnings and ability to assist Denis. Only when the directors had satisfied themselves that the woman was of good character, could earn her own bread and assist Denis, did they finally give their approval (EBAMB 1792–1805:110). A thorough investigation of archive documents revealed no documented instances of female inmates requesting permission to marry. The absence of female appeals for permission to enter into marriage may well indicate the restrictive effects of surveillance on the women's lives and social activities. The absence of documented instances of men requesting permission to marry female inmates similarly points towards the limiting influence of surveillance.

Later in the century, the emergence of a particular social discourse in relation to blind people marrying undoubtedly influenced the attitudes of asylum managers and others involved in the welfare of blind people. Although blind people marrying was not encouraged, it would seem that blind men marrying sighted women was more palatable to those involved in blind welfare, as it was assumed that sighted women, if necessary, could 'look after' their blind husbands. Also sighted wives of blind men were considered less likely to produce blind children. Whereas blind-blind intermarriages were presumed to be productive of blind children, Dr Armitage, mentioned earlier, was forthright in his views of blind intermarriage, stating to the Paris Congress in 1878 that

> Of all social questions connected with the blind, there is none perhaps on which those who have studied the subject practically are more unanimous than the evils of intermarriage. (Armitage 1878:13)

The Royal Commission on The Blind supported this way of thinking, and their report suggested that

> The intermarriage of the blind should be strongly discouraged. (Royal Commission on the Blind 1886(a):xliii)

Directorial stance and morally informed working practices within the asylums were undoubtedly influenced by such external discourses, this being obvious in the opinion offered to the Royal Commission on The Blind by Mr William Martin, Manager of the Edinburgh Asylum. He believed that "[i]ntermarriage of the blind ought to be prohibited by the State" (Royal Commission on the Blind 1886(b):502).

It almost goes without saying that negative attitudes towards intermarriage of blind people, as held by those in a position of power within the institutions under study here, undoubtedly limited inmates' opportunities to marry.

Dr Armitage was of the opinion that 'intermarriages were followed by the usual bad consequences' (Armitage 1878:13). He did not elaborate on what such consequences might be, but Martin, in his evidence to the Royal Commission, offered his opinion on the consequences of intermarriage:

> I have never seen anything but either blind children or dirt and filth result from the intermarriage of the blind. (Royal Commission on the Blind 1886(b):502)

Institutionalisation of blind women and proactive influences on public opinion colluded to engender widespread moral hostility towards the possibilities of blind people establishing relationships, marrying and bearing children, possibly children with inheritable blindness. It would appear that the moral issue of sexual separation was unquestionably charged with eugenic undertones, and the further notion that blind women's bodies rather than men's were more likely to transmit heritable blindness was illustrated by additional evidence presented to the Royal Commission by Martin:

[Sir Lyon Playfair]	Was there any hereditary blindness in the family of either the man or the woman in the case to which you have just referred?
Answer:	There was hereditary blindness in the case of the female.
[Dr Tindal Robertson]	In the case of the man, was his blindness accidental, or had he been blind from birth?
Answer:	He lost his eyesight gradually when young. He had a brother whose eyesight gave way also when he was young.
[Dr T R Armitage]	Could you state what was the nature of the hereditary taint in the case of the woman?
Answer:	There is a difference of opinion in this case, it is a very peculiar and interesting one. (Royal Commission on the Blind 1886(b):503)

It would appear that the manager of the Blind Asylum associated the female's body with hereditary blindness, indeed perhaps as the source, rather than questioning the male's genetic inheritance. The notion of women's bodies as carriers or sources of inheritable blindness without doubt contributed to a hostile moral climate towards blind women indulging in sexual activity and childbearing. The fear of blind women procreating not only justified precautionary methods of sexual separation, it legitimated their spatial segregation from mainstream society.

Resistance

Resignation and a proper spirit of gratitude for benefits received were the moral postures most highly in favour with the management. (Ritchie 1930:33)

The asylum directors welcomed expressions of gratitude from the inmates. Female resident inmates were expected to be particularly grateful for what they received from the institution: a home, employment, earnings, clothes and food. However, for these benefits women were expected to comply with restrictive rules and regimes.

The directors interpreted acts of resistance to the asylum regime as insubordination, inevitably provoking a hostile or disciplinary response from them. Directors conditioned and convinced inmates that adherence to the rules and obedience was in their best interests. When the directors felt that order within the institution or their authority were being challenged by inmates, they took swift and decisive action to quell such confrontations. Action taken by the directors was dependent upon their interpretation of the gravity of the situation in line with the social moral code of the time. Asylum directors did not want their institution to be associated with immoral, depraved or delinquent behaviour, given the possible ramifications for both themselves (as supposed moral guardians) and levels of donations on which the asylums depended. Directors and the institution as a whole thus had to be distanced immediately from inmates who had transgressed moral boundaries. Instant dismissal facilitated distancing from such supposedly immoral behaviour, and acted as a warning to other inmates contemplating disobedience of the rules.

The age of inmates on admission had a significant influence on whether they expressed resistance to the rules and regimes of 'the house'. In general, the younger inmates were on admission, the less likely they were to test or to contravene the rules. Those who chose to defy the rules expressed resistance in various ways. Some refused to conform with daily regimes, such as attendance at religious ordinance and instruction. Women who absented themselves from religious worship were thought to be exhibiting signs of serious mental instability. When Isabella Gray, an inmate of the Edinburgh Asylum, refused to attend daily worship, the directors considered her to be 'mentally deranged'. They professed her presence in the asylum to be 'extremely injurious to the welfare of the inmates', and she was dismissed for insubordination of the house rules (EBAMB 1825–1835:173). It is reasonable to assume that Gray desired to exercise choice in relation to religious persuasion and attendance at worship, but that the wilfulness displayed in wishing to display such choice – something departing from the infantilised state in which the women inmates were supposed to reside – was perceived by the directors as a threat to order and morality within the institution. The directors hence discredited her actions as those of a deranged and dangerous individual.

A hostile moral background within and outwith the asylums did not encourage marriage between blind people. Prior to entering into marriage, as indicated, all inmates had to seek the permission of the directors, but inmates very occasionally defied this regulation by entering into marriage *without* the directors' consent. Records of the Edinburgh Asylum document the case of John Strachan and Jean Miller, inmates who had contracted their marriage without consulting the directors (EBAMB 1825–1835:104). Following the discovery of this marriage contract, the directors delivered a stern address to the inmates warning of the consequences of such actions:

> That is of those under their protection [who] engage in so serious a contract without advising their best friends [the Directors] – such may expect immediate dismissal. (EBAMB 1825–1835:104)

The justification for the imperative nature of this rule was attributed to the welfare of the inmates, and yet the moral enmity towards blind people marrying was more likely a pertinent factor. The 19th rule placed male inmates in a 'no win' situation, since in the process of seeking permission to marry they had to disclose the identity of their intended. If she was an inmate, they effectively admitted to breaching the rules by forming a relationship, punishable by dismissal. Similarly, not seeking permission, marrying and maintaining a relationship in secret, also risked dismissal. Considered in these terms, it is probable that the 19th rule deterred individuals from entering into marriage. Resistance to this rule nonetheless affirms that a few inmates were indeed capable of making their own decisions, and were prepared to face the consequences.

With no easy access to contraception or abortion (Barret-Ducrocq 1992), the exist-ence of forbidden relationships tended to be discovered when women became preg-nant. Such a discovery was usually followed by an immediate demand by the directors for the name of the father, particularly where the involvement of a male inmate was suspected. An inmate of the Edinburgh Asylum, Agnes Miller, was found to be preg-nant to Thomas Manderson, also an inmate, and both were immediately dismissed. Following their subsequent marriage, Manderson requested to be readmitted into the asylum workshops, and he was allowed to return (EBAMB 1835–1849:370), presum-ably because he had done the honourable thing by marrying Miller (Barret-Ducrocq 1992) and thereby rendering her pregnancy respectable. Later in the century, the directors' response to behaviour that they considered immoral had not changed, as was evidenced when an inmate, Susan White, requested time off because she was in a 'delicate state of health'. The institution physician confirmed her pregnancy. She was instantly dismissed, with the directors ordering her name to be immediately removed from the roll and her family and friends to be informed of her pregnancy (RBASEMB 1872–1883:35). The directors' reactions indicated a revulsion at the manifest fact that, in a biological sense, the women were quite capable of adult sexual activity. Moreover, the implication is undoubtedly that their real sexuality was indeed being denied, repressed by the institutional regime.

Female inmates of Glasgow Asylum also faced dismissal when found to be preg-nant. Christina Mypen and James McLatchie, both inmates of the Glasgow Asylum, were dismissed when Christina was found to be pregnant. Directors were disgusted when McLatchie 'admitted intimacy with the girl, with the knowledge of the girl's parents' (GBAMB 1880–1884:28). Such immoral behaviour reflected negatively upon the institution and its directors, so it was thought, and the institutions were perceived to have failed their moral duty to both inmates and society. It would seem that directors interpreted their moral duty to society as one of keeping blind peo-ple's behaviour within morally acceptable boundaries, although this duty did not then extend to the welfare of those who broke the rules. Individuals, especially preg-nant blind women, dismissed from the asylum for immoral behaviour possibly faced being shunned by their family and friends, or unavoidable entry into the poorhouse.

An institutionalised life for life

Although the main object of the asylums was to render blind people, predominately men, self-supporting, very few inmates left the asylum to enter into mainstream employment or self-employment. The majority of male inmates tended to be associ-ated with the institution for the duration of their working lives. The Edinburgh Blind Asylum Annual Report of 1852 noted of the inmates that 'many of [them] have been there from an early age and have grown grey in the institution' (EBAAR 1852:4). The institutions' founders did not intend to establish a long-term home for blind people. However, the creation of stereotypes and subsequent construction of blind men and women as helpless, passive dependants in need of special facilities, coupled to the simultaneous portrayal of the asylums as the most appropriate places of expert knowl-edge to deal with such a group, all meant that the systematic and long-term segrega-tion of blind people became socially acceptable.

Turner and Harris's 1884 *Guide to Institutions and Charities for the Blind in the United Kingdom* contained survey responses from both the Glasgow and Edinburgh Blind Asylums regarding age of admission and potential length of time inmates might typically remain in the institution. Glasgow Asylum indicated an admission age of 8–14 years and that individuals could remain until their education and apprenticeship were complete, an average of 7 years (Turner and Harris 1884:23). Edinburgh Asylum indicated 5 years and upwards as age of admission and that individuals could remain for life (Turner and Harris 1884:21).

Domineering controls and repressive regimes undoubtedly contributed to the length of time females remained resident in the asylum house. For some women their association with the asylum spanned almost their entire lifetime. Margaret Baxter, from Cupar Angus, was admitted into the Edinburgh Blind Asylum in March 1822, aged 15 years. Prior to admission she had been employed as a spinner. She remained in the asylum for 72 years, until her death on 21 December 1894, aged 87 years (EBA Admissions Register 1793–1938: unnumbered, Register of Deaths 1894). Elizabeth Baird from Innerwick was admitted into the Edinburgh Blind Asylum in November 1832, at the age of 13 years. Prior to admission she had been employed as a servant. She died in the asylum 73 years later on 31 January 1905 (EBA Admissions Register 1793–1938: unnumbered, Register of Deaths 1905). Women's long-term association with an institution was not unique to the Edinburgh institution. Glasgow Blind Asylum 1896 Annual Report records the death of Ann Taylor, who had been admitted into the asylum in July 1831, at the age of 9 years old. She became a knitting instructor, and 'passed more than 64 years of her life in the asylum' (GBAAR 1896:10).

Although men may have remained associated with the asylum for a considerable proportion of their working lives, they did have the opportunity to return to their families, to live outwith the asylum, to take control of their own lives and even to participate to a limited extent in their local communities. Women, as resident inmates, however, had extremely restricted freedoms and little opportunity to engage with mainstream society.

The missions

Since the asylums catered for only a minority of the blind population, even with outworkers in their workshops, Missions to the Out-door Blind were established initially in Edinburgh in 1857, followed by Glasgow in 1859. The Edinburgh Society for Promoting Reading Amongst the Blind and the Glasgow Mission to the Out-door Blind shared similar objectives:

> To seek out the blind, visit them in their homes, conduct meetings among them where convenient, teach them to read with the finger the embossed system of reading, supply them, free of charge, with books from the society's library, and in every way possible seek their spiritual and temporal good. (ESAR 1893:2)

The missions employed missionary teachers and volunteer lady visitors to undertake the duties of seeking out and teaching blind individuals to read embossed books.

As well as visiting blind people in their homes, the missionaries also visited blind people in hospitals, infirmaries and poorhouses.

The Edinburgh and Glasgow Missions encompassed an extensive geographical area. The Edinburgh Missionaries worked within six counties: Edinburgh, Haddington, Peebles, Selkirk, Roxburgh and Berwick. Glasgow missionaries worked in the counties of Glasgow, Lanarkshire, Renfrewshire and Ayrshire. The missionary teachers of both societies went to great lengths to seek out blind people, note their circumstances, develop a register and keep statistical records of the diverse blind population. By 1882 ten Missions had been established, covering the whole of Scotland, and these efforts formed the basis of a voluntary movement of welfare on behalf of blind people. Within 10 years of their establishment, the Edinburgh and Glasgow Missions took the decision to offer assistance only to blind people who were unemployed and those not associated with the Blind Asylums. By 1881, 2,747 blind people were on the rolls of the missions throughout Scotland (Auchincloss Arrol 1886:6). The missions claimed to be doing 'All in their powers to help this helpless class' (GMAR 1884(a):9).

The work of the missions was underpinned by a pervasive religious ethos, unsurprisingly given their very name, and they aimed to seek blind peoples' 'spiritual and temporal good' (ESAR 1893:2). Although their priority was to teach blind people to read, a close second was to save their souls, 'bringing them from darkness into the light' (ESAR 1889:2). Blindness, class and morality were closely connected. Individuals from the poorest classes were often considered to have brought illness or blindness upon themselves through immoral conduct, and women's immorality was particularly linked with loss of sight. In some instances blindness was directly attributed to women's inappropriate conduct.

Journal extracts disseminated in annual reports fuelled this ideology, placing emphasis on the ways in which wayward, wanton women had been reformed following the loss of their sight. Two cases illustrate this belief held by the missionaries and internalised by some blind women. The case of a 28-year-old woman, noted in the 20th Annual Report of the Edinburgh Society, indicates the stance supported by the missions:

> This young woman was trained in a Sabbath School by a kind Christian lady. She left her home when she was a young girl but wandered far away from the paths of virtue and continued year by year to do so; but the Lord arrested her in her downward course by taking away her eyesight. (ESAR 1879:3)

The case of Margaret Wallace, noted in the 1878 annual report, suggests the internalisation of this ideology. The 27-year-old had lost her sight 18 months prior to the report, and had been taught to read by the missionary. She confessed to him:

> I have lived a careless life, and believe God in his love has stopped me in my downward course, by taking from me my eyesight, and through your visits and instruction, I have been taught the way to be saved, and through grace I have taken Jesus as my saviour. (ESAR 1878:3)

The implication was that blindness acted as a warning or punishment from God for living a morally careless life. Furthermore, blindness could seemingly be avoided by living a moral, Christian life.

The missions exploited any opportunity to illustrate the reformatory effects of Christianity on blind people, and a conviction that blind peoples' lives and very character could be reformed by a belief in God was evident in all aspects of the missions' work:

> The eyes of the blind have been opened, and those who were once in darkness are now light in the Lord. (ESAR 1891: initial page unnumbered)

Therefore the rejection of a dark immoral lifestyle and the embracing of a Christian ethos could propel blind people onto a superior spiritual plain. Although they could no longer physically see, they could see spiritually. The reformatory effects of religious instruction subtly hinted at physical transformation: that for those who believed in God and lived a moral life, miracles could happen. In short, those who read their bible each day, prayed and led a Christian lifestyle, might at some point have their eyesight restored. The importance of individuals reading their bible daily is shown in one of the few journal extracts regarding a blind woman with childcare responsibilities. The missionary does not focus on her physical responsibilities, but rather on her spiritual ones:

> R's case is very interesting. She is the Mother of a number of children, and although she has the work of the house to attend to she finds time to read her portion of the word of the Lord. (ESAR 1877:8)

Dissemination of extracts from letters evidenced both blind peoples' gratitude to the society for teaching them to read embossed print and in turn to find salvation, simultaneously publicising the reformatory effects of religious instruction on blind people. Hence one woman was presented as

> Manifesting a cheerful Christian spirit and filled with gratitude for what the mission, and especially the Ladies Auxiliary had done for her. (LAGMAR 1888:5)

A relief fund enabled missionaries to provide limited financial support to unemployed blind people in times of extreme hardship. However, increasing demands made upon this fund for financial assistance influenced their supportive role. The missions undertook to assist blind people capable of working to return to some form of employment. The majority of blind people resident in Glasgow in 1881 were not in employment or in a position of independence:

Blind people in the poorhouse	83
Receiving parochial relief	229
Employed	294
Non productive	899

(*Auchincloss Arrol 1886*:13)

Returning to work and realising the potential of financial self-sufficiency were considered to be of paramount importance for men. The loss of a breadwinner's income was portrayed in the missions' annual reports as a catastrophic turn of events:

> homes once bright and happy, suddenly plunged into deepest poverty and distress, by the terrible calamity overtaking the father or breadwinner. (GMAR 1884(b):2)

Men were generally perceived to fulfil the role of breadwinner, with a family dependent upon them. The loss or deterioration of eyesight did not relieve men of this role. For women with acquired visual impairments, though, it was assumed that they would have an extended family, friends or husband upon whom they could rely for financial support. On this basis, men and women were assisted into very different forms of employment. Men were more likely to have served apprenticeships. Where possible, they were helped to return into their trade on a self-employed basis. Men were generally assisted to set up as tea, firewood, drapery and coal sellers (GMAR 1885:14). The Edinburgh missionary, Mr Brown, reported in 1894 that

> I had the privilege of giving a handbag and a quantity of tea to one of our blind men who has a wife and family dependent upon him, and thus set him agoing as an itinerant tea seller. (ESAR 1894:5)

Furthermore, such employments meant that blind men remained visible in the streets, participated in their communities and provided a service to others. As such, they gained something approaching an equitable status with others eking out a living selling in the streets. The aim of the mission's support was to enable such men to become financially self-supporting, and so, in general, blind men thereby remained active in mainstream society. Blind women's dependence upon their families and friends was socially acceptable, conversely, and they were rarely expected or assisted to become physically or financially independent. Scottish-wide statistics gathered in 1881 illustrate the emphasis placed upon blind men returning to employment. These estimated that 467 blind men were unoccupied and unproductive, whereas 1,172 blind women over the age of 20 years were unoccupied and unproductive (Auchincloss Arrol 1886:6). The minority of blind women who were employed tended to be engaged in industrial and domestic occupations.

The Glasgow Mission to the Out-door Blind established a Ladies Auxiliary Committee in 1865, with the purpose of assisting unoccupied blind women. Their objectives were to teach blind girls and women to knit, to supply them with the necessary materials and to assist in the disposal of the finished articles. Members of the Ladies Auxiliary offered knitting classes to blind women. They resolved to brighten the lives of blind women who attended the classes 'by reading to them and providing them with little treats to relieve their gloom' (Dunbar 1989:55). This aim implies an assumption that blind women lived a miserable existence, brightened only by the knitting classes and cakes provided by the Ladies Auxiliary. Blind women, it would seem, were objects of pity and sympathy, women who lived their lives in a darkened gloom who could not possibly be happy. The description of a new recruit to the knitting class exposed some of these attitudes:

> She is really very dull in spirits having now to face the stern reality of dark-
> ness all through her future in this life, and beginning to experience some of
> the hardships and disadvantages which surround the path of those in such
> circumstances. (LAGMAR 1882:16)

The majority of women mentioned in the mission's annual reports were portrayed as passive recipients and dependants, living with their mothers, relatives or friends:

> BG is about 19 years of age, who has been for years a great sufferer and never
> will be able to work for herself. She can knit a little and takes great pleasure
> in reading. (ESAR 1877:8)

Income generated from knitting and sewing work was meagre, and the main pur-pose of such 'diversional' work was to keep women occupied. Even where the quality of work was so poor that items produced were not saleable, the mission continued to provide materials to those individuals. Regardless of previous work-ing experience, these women were presented with knitting and sewing as the main means to earn a living. One woman mentioned in the Glasgow Ladies Auxiliary Annual Report had successfully managed her own business prior to losing her sight. Nonetheless, she was still provided with knitting and sewing as a means of earning money (LAGMAR 1880:6). Although the nature of this woman's business was not documented, it was noted that she managed the enterprise with 'energy and ability' (LAGMAR 1880:6). It would appear that her capabilities as a business-woman were taken to be annulled by her loss of sight, and her acquired visual impairment was clearly accompanied by a change in the social perception of this woman.

On the rare occasions where women were assisted to attain an independent life-style, their lives were still very much confined to their homes, with little indication of women participating in mainstream society. One journal entry tells the story of a young woman who lived with an aunt. They lived in extreme poverty, and the only prospect for the blind woman was the poorhouse. However, after being taught to read and supplied with knitting, her circumstances significantly altered:

> She has now a neat, clean comfortable house of her own: and being fully
> occupied with her housework, her knitting and her book, is quite contented
> and happy. (LAGMAR 1888:5)

Blind women were not supported or encouraged to become street traders, and instead all were offered work to be done in the home. At the time respectable and moral women's work was strongly associated with the confines of the home, while women's presence in the street was considered unnatural, except where they were involved in tasks such as shopping or running errands (Barret-Ducrocq 1992). Therefore, sup-plying working-class blind women with work to be undertaken in the home removed them from the streets and may have enhanced their moral stature. Since blind women were generally considered to be delicate and vulnerable, home working was perhaps a means of protecting them. Annual reports of the Outdoor Missions evidence the isolation and loneliness experienced by the women, many of who did not venture outside the familiar environment of their home, as illustrated in a missionary's journal extract for 27 May 1875:

> On reaching Ms L I found her much cast down and on hearing my voice she brightened up and exclaimed 'o Mr M is that you? Thank God I am not forgotten yet'. Were it not for my visits, this woman would not have a single friend to take any special interest in her. (LAGMAR 1876:28)

Conclusion

The Blind Asylums established themselves as centres of expertise and knowledge in relation to the training, education and management of blind people. They proactively created the impression that they met the requirements of the majority of blind people in the Glasgow and Edinburgh populations, even if in practice they did not. Numerically, the Outdoor Missions probably worked with more blind people. The working practices of the asylums and missions seem to have been influenced by prevailing cultural stereotypes of female morality and respectability. Consequently, through religious instruction, the aim was to reform working-class blind women's assumed immorality to mirror the moral stature accredited to the asylum or mission with which they were associated. The connections and cross-codings between the women and the 'space' of both the asylum and the mission were hence multiple and enduring, having significant implications for both the women themselves and the perceptions of a wider (sighted) mainstream society.

Similarly, within the asylums the imposition of oppressive regimes, rules and regulations, ones manipulating institutional spaces to impose sexual separation, surveillance and monitoring of women's behaviour and conduct, were probably motivated by a desire on the part of directors to protect the respectable reputation of the institution rather than with genuine concerns for inmate welfare. This being said, we must beware of assuming that no directors held genuine feelings of wishing to improve the lot of inmates, but, even so, such feelings could not but have been framed by dominant discourses about disability, femininity and the 'right' ordering of social and sexual relations. As a result, the oppressive regimes, rules and regulations denied female inmates opportunities to sexual expression, childbearing and mothering. Likewise, changing notions of respectability saw the retreat of respectable women from the streets, and this undoubtedly influenced the imposition of institutional regulations that severely limited blind women's participation in mainstream spaces. The localised, but concentrated, spatial segregation of women resident in asylums, along with the limited presence of respectable women on the streets, combined to deter and virtually to eradicate the participation of blind women in mainstream society. With time, the erosion of blind women's presence in spaces of everyday life rendered them invisible to the majority sighted population. This pervasive invisibility became second nature, to the point where society no longer questioned their absence.

References

Edinburgh Asylum for the Relief of the Indigent Industrious Blind, Minute Books
1792–1805
1805–1825
1825–1835
1835–1849.
Royal Blind Asylum and School, Edinburgh, Minute Book 1872–1883.

Edinburgh Asylum for the Relief of Indigent Industrious Blind, Admissions Register Book.
1793–1938 (including submitted Application Forms 1900–1903).

Edinburgh Asylum for the Relief of the Indigent and Industrious Blind, Annual Reports
1850, for author.
1852, William Burness, Edinburgh.
1853, William Burness, Edinburgh.
1855, William Burness, Edinburgh.
1856, William Burness, Edinburgh.
1857, Mould & Tod, Edinburgh.
1865, William Burness, Edinburgh.
1874 (Royal Blind Asylum and School, Edinburgh), William Burness, Edinburgh.

Edinburgh Society For Promoting Reading Amongst The Blind At Their Own Homes By Moon's System, Annual Reports
18th 1877, for author.
19th 1878, for author.
20th 1879, for author.
30th 1889, for author.
32nd 1891, for author.
34th 1893, for author.
35th 1894, for author.

Glasgow Asylum for the Blind, Minute Books
1825–1845.
1880–1884.

Glasgow Asylum for the Blind, Annual Reports
56th 1883, WG Blackie & Co, Glasgow.
57th 1884, for author.
60th 1887, for author.
61st 1888, for author.
69th 1896, for author.

Mission to the Out-door Blind for Glasgow and the West of Scotland, Annual Reports
24th 1884 (a), John J Rae, Glasgow.
24th 1884 (b), To the Sabbath School Children of Glasgow and the West of Scotland, Glasgow, for author.
25th 1885, John J Rae, Glasgow.

Ladies Auxiliary to the Mission to the Out-door Blind of Glasgow and the West of Scotland, Annual Reports
11th 1876, Charles Glass & Co, Glasgow.
15th 1880, John J Rae, Glasgow.
17th 1882, John J Rae, Glasgow.
23rd 1888, James C Erskine, Glasgow.
Maps relating to the Edinburgh and Glasgow Asylums and Missions
1877 Edinburgh and its Environs, sheet 48/49.
1881 Edinburgh and its Environs, Cannongate, sheet 36.
1893 Edinburgh and its Environs, Mayfield sheet 111.12 23.
1828 Early Glasgow Maps number 52.
1831 Parishes within the Royal Borough of Glasgow, number 59.
1832 Early Glasgow Maps number 60.

1860 Ordinance Survey Map; Barony, Springburn, City, Gorbals, Govan, Calton.

1896 2nd Edition Ordinance Survey Map County of the City of Glasgow.

Death certificates relating to the Edinburgh materials

Register of Deaths, Registers House, Edinburgh

Margaret Baxter, 21 December 1894.

Elizabeth Baird, 31 January 1905.

Also, 1ˢᵗ 1888 Annual Report of The Edinburgh Charities Registration Union, for author.

Alston, J. (1846) *Statement of the Education, Employment and Internal Arrangements Adopted at the Asylum for the Blind Glasgow, with a Short Account of its Founder, and General Observations Applicable to Similar Institutions*, The Asylum, Glasgow.

Armitage T.R. (Ed) (1878) *The Condition of the Blind Of Great Britain and Ireland and Other Papers Presented to the Paris Congress of 1878*, Gilbert and Rivington Printers, London (including papers 'On means employed for ameliorating the condition of the blind of Great Britain and Ireland' and 'Education of the blind in ordinary schools').

Auchincloss Arrol, W. (1886) *A Few Statistics in Connection with the Blind in Scotland*, Royal Commission on the Blind, Committee Paper, Edinburgh.

Barret-Ducrocq, F. (1992) *Love in the Time of Victoria: Sexuality and Desire Among Working-Class Men and Women in Nineteenth-Century London*, Penguin, London, translated by John Howe, originally *L'amour sous Victoria* 1989, Plon, Paris.

Dunbar, H. (1989) *History of The Society for The Blind in Glasgow and the West of Scotland 1859–1989*, Heatherbank Press, Glasgow.

Finkler, L. (2003) Personal communication between Hazel McFarlane and Lilith Finkler, Dalhousie University, Nova Scotia, Canada, 17 December, 2003.

Ritchie, J. M. (1930) *Concerning The Blind: Being a Historical Sketch of Organised Effort on Behalf of the Blind of Great Britain, and Some Thoughts Concerning the Mental Life of a Person Born Blind*, Oliver and Boyd, Edinburgh.

Royal Commission on the Blind, the Deaf and the Dumb (1886) *The Report of The Royal Commission on the Blind, the Deaf and Dumb* (esp. 'The blind'; miscellaneous suggestions, Vol.1, p xliii; Report of visits to Glasgow Asylum for the Blind and Glasgow School Board, Vol.2: Appendix, pp. 48–50; Minutes of evidence presented by Mr W.C. Lester, Secretary, Indigent Blind Visiting Society, Vol.3, p.118; Minutes of evidence presented by Mr William Martin, Manager, Royal Blind Asylum, Edinburgh, Vol. 3, pp. 502–503).

Scotsman Newspaper (1864) 'Edinburgh Asylum', 28th September, in Charitable Institutions in Edinburgh, a collection of Scotsman newspaper articles, located in 'The Edinburgh Room', Central Library, Edinburgh.

Turner, M. and Harris W. (1884) *A Guide to Institutions and Charities for the Blind in the United Kingdom to Which is Added Information Relating to the Blind as to their Manufactures, Books, Types, Education, Appliances, Statistical Figures & c*, Simpkin, Marshall and Co, London.

Wagg J.H. (1932) *A Chronological Survey of the Work for The Blind (with an Appendix on the Prevention of Blindness, and a Bibliography) From the Earliest Records up to the Year 1930*, for the National Institute for the Blind, Great Portland Street, London, Sir Isaac Pitman and Sons Ltd, London.

17

TRACING DISABILITY HISTORY IN THE MIDST OF CULTURAL ABSENCE: AN INVESTIGATION INTO THE BELFAST ASSOCIATION FOR THE EMPLOYMENT OF THE INDUSTRIOUS BLIND

Myrtle Hill and Nancy Hansen

Introduction

Tracing the history of people with disabilities is a project fraught with difficulty. This is especially true if we wish to move beyond the collection of quantitative data or analysis of medicalised discourse. Although there are one billion disabled people worldwide (WHO, 2011), studies of their historical, social and cultural experiences are limited – only more recently coming to the fore through the creative work of disabled people themselves – and even then too frequently omitted from or marginalized within the mainstream cultural agenda. It is our contention that this cultural invisibility must be challenged by a more imaginative and thorough investigation and utilization of archives and artifacts. In addition to bringing to light a wealth of individual and collective experiences, a more probing and sensitive approach to historical materials would both deepen our appreciation of the ways in which the past has helped to shape present attitudes to disability and, perhaps more importantly, increase our understanding of the richness, vibrancy, and texture of life within the disability community past and present.

This chapter aims to make a contribution to that investigation. It focuses on the north of Ireland, where 20 per cent of the population is identified as having some form of disability, which is the highest reported rate of disability in Britain. We will begin with some discussion of the issues surrounding disability history – or the lack of it – in Ireland, before turning to specific examples of Irish history. At this point we note that despite the plethora of books, articles, reports and stories about Ireland – its people, culture and history – there is little material about Ireland's disabled population. By providing this brief history of blind and visually impaired persons, the chapter will add to the limited texts pertaining to disability history.

Like most forms of knowledge, history has been subject to critical scrutiny in recent decades, postmodernism in particular promoting epistemological and contextual interrogation of traditional sources, narratives and methodologies

(Jordanova, 2000, 91; Shapiro 8). While debates continue to both clarify and problematise theoretical positions, there is general agreement that "the writing of history is not an innocent or transparent affair" (Bannerji, 1998, 15). Shaped by outside forces, its inclusions, exclusions, assumptions and interpretations produce partial, often competing versions of the truth, with narratives most usually representing the values and experiences of those in power (French, 2006). This seems particularly true of disability history, which, if it exists at all, is colonized, hidden and most often written from the perspectives of 'professionals' and policy-makers and the non-disabled (French, 2006). However, as most disability activists acknowledge, this omission has serious consequences for those with disabilities in the twenty-first century, with an exploration of the origins of barriers to inclusion critical to our understanding of contemporary social, and indeed governmental, attitudes toward disability (Barnes, 1997). Moreover, as several decades of women's history has taught us, the experiences of even those remote from the exercise of power can be brought to light if we approach the documentary evidence with a critical eye, a degree of sensitivity, a readiness to read between the lines and a close familiarity with the context in which experiences were played out.

Assessing the archives: the workshops for the blind

Our preliminary research on this project, which involved an interrogation of the archives of the Public Records Office Northern Ireland (PRONI) and several phil-anthropic institutions, focused on the experience of the adult men and women who were employed in the Workshops for the Blind in late nineteenth- and early twentieth-century Belfast. Although workshops more generally played an important role in the early labour union movement, this early experience of disability remains largely unknown; we discovered, however, that their records rewarded careful scru-tiny (PRONI, d/3563). In many ways the founding of the Belfast Association for the Employment of the Industrious Blind followed a pattern familiar to the period and the location. Originating with the charitable impulse of a minister's daughter, Mary Hobson, it owed the first 40 years of its development almost entirely to the philanthropic endeavors of a group of prosperous and prominent citizens. Previous research has highlighted the significance of Belfast's middle-class elite – revealing it as a strong and vibrant local subculture which operated through tightly knit net-works centred on family and church, for whom Christian philanthropy was a moral duty, and one which was disproportionately significant in terms of its social influence (McClelland, 2000; Hill, 2007). Although women were not invited onto the governing body of this association, their background work, here as elsewhere, was critical – par-ticularly in terms of fund-raising, where the Ladies Committee engaged in the time-consuming tasks of organizing collections, putting on events and generally ensuring that the public at large were frequently and effectively reminded of their financial obligations to 'those less fortunate'. Mary Hobson in particular was not only instru-mental in creating the organization and heading up the fund-raising campaign, but as Ladies Secretary was a key driving force during the important first two decades of this work (she died in 1891). A formidable character, her frequent interventions were effective in securing contracts and in purchasing and designing impressive new shop premises – against the wishes of the management committee – whose members she overruled on many occasions, in disagreements about personnel appointments or on disciplinary matters: a fine example of yet another strong-willed woman whose role has been overlooked in mainstream historical analysis (Jordan, 1993 97–8, 130–33).

Most commentators on the voluntary organizations of the period agree that, while individuals were motivated by a range of factors, that of religion was particularly strong, and this is clearly reflected in the records of this association. A colonialist missionary zeal was evident in most of their proceedings and in their protective, controlling approach to blind workers. While the practical goal of the organizers was to provide blind individuals with the means of employment (and thus clear the streets of blind beggars and the workhouse of blind inmates) (Jordan, 1993), this was understood in the context of preserving them from 'sin and crime, and to lead them in the paths of virtue and religion' (PRONI, D/3564/AK/1, Annual Report, 1871). Thus the Ladies Committee read extracts from the scriptures to the workers, and established a library where 'improving' lectures and bible classes provided a 'worthy' alternative to the attractions of the local public house. Parallels with missionary interactions with indigenous peoples are again evident in the Association's stereotypical and generalized views of blind people, whom they perceived as passive and dependent. This infantilisation was clearly articulated during the opening speeches, when Reverend Hannay asserted that "unless someone puts them [the blind] in the way of exercising [their remaining] faculties they must remain dormant and useless" (PRONI, D/3564/AK/1, Annual Report, 1871). Lacking individual agency, it was asserted that, left to their own devices, "the blind got drunk and created considerable trouble in the town" (ibid.). On the other hand, they would supposedly respond positively to charitable intervention: "if the blind get any sort of fair play they are of a naturally happy disposition" (ibid.). These assumptions were based on the concept that such charitable interventions represented "a self-imposed moral obligation towards the weaker members of society felt by the more sensitive members of the privileged classes" (Rose, 1970, 126).

On its opening in 1871 the Belfast workshop could accommodate 20 to 30 blind men and women, training them in the making of baskets, mats and mattresses, which were then sold to the general public. By the turn of the century the workers numbered 120; by 1920 the greatly expanded premises held 146 blind men and women. It is perhaps not surprising that the workshops not only met but exceeded their capacity; for example, the 1871 census indicated that there were almost 6,500 blind persons in Ireland, with approximately 1600 in the province of Ulster (Census of Ireland for the year, 1871). Apart from the workhouse and a few asylums in the larger cities, there was little provision of any kind for blind persons throughout the island. And although it has long been claimed that a majority of the Irish blind were situated in workhouses, in fact only 14% of blind persons in Ireland as a whole were workhouse residents, and only 6% of blind in Ulster. Ulster at this time was of course the only part of Ireland where significant opportunities insofar as industry existed, with Belfast itself described as 'a mature and expanding industrial city' (Lynch, 1998), so it is important to keep geographical specificity in mind – generalizations can be misleading. The north of Ireland offered more opportunities for a greater range of employment than elsewhere on the island, and the workshop concept was more viable there. In this pre–social welfare state era, these workshops appeared to present a manageable solution: keeping blind off the streets, specifically keeping them from begging; as much as possible keeping them out of the workhouse (where they represented a drain on the public purse) and providing the 'worthy' poor with the means of earning a living.

Despite the moral underpinning, the workshops' historical evidence suggests that there were clear benefits for the blind employees, as the workshops provided blind men and women with a degree of safety and security, offered them education, training and a market for the goods they produced. Significantly too, the stated intention of the management was to pay blind workers at the same rate as their sighted contemporaries. But, while this ambition, together with the frequently asserted claim that the association was to run as a commercially viable business, is particularly important in that it recognized blind individuals as legitimate employees, it would prove impossible to achieve (Scott, 1967). Recurring personnel problems and operational difficulties reflected the tensions inherent in combining skilful and efficient business management practices with the values of religious benevolence embraced by its founders. It was a major principle, for example, that no worker was dismissed because of a decline in orders (Centenary Publication, 1971, 7). Thus a living wage was achieved only by way of continuous supplements and bonuses. As the author of its centenary publication noted, 'bridging the gap between what the blind could actually produce and the wages necessary to maintain them in decent independence and of meeting the ordinary expenses of the Association' was 'an annual running sore', with losses recorded virtually every year of its operation (1971, 11–12). In many ways, therefore, the workshops operated as a form of social welfare service rather than a business, with winter fuel allowances, Christmas gifts and bonuses, day trips and paid holidays being offered to the blind employees.

Through its constitution and rules, the association attempted to impose standards of behaviour which reflected the charitable and religious values of its founders and indeed contemporary understandings of physical and sensory disability. These are most clearly exemplified in the insistence on compliance with religious observance and in rule 12, which prohibited marriage between blind workers (PRONI, D/3563/BA/3. Manager's Report, 2 Nov. 1898). This latter attempt at social control reflected the eugenic misconception that such a union would produce further generations of blind people. However, and in contrast to both contemporary beliefs and historical representations, the records indicate that the workers themselves were not passive, grateful beneficiaries of charity, but were well prepared to assert their rights and to challenge and resist some of the more traditional aspects of 'benevolence'. For example, even in the opening year of its operations, Catholic workers actively challenged the right of the management to insist on their acquiescence in religious observances – considering such practice 'a grievance' and 'contrary to the laws' of their church (PRONI, D/3563/DB/1, ms. Correspondence, 13 May 1874). This is perhaps particularly significant in a city characterised by religious division and in which Protestantism was dominant. Similarly, there were numerous examples of workers defying the marriage ban. One of the most difficult cases was that of John O'Neill, a Catholic who, in 1886, declared his intention of marrying a 16-year-old Protestant co-worker, thus simultaneously breaking several rules – around age, religion and marriage between blind employees (Jordan, n.d., 1993). Although dismissed by management, after which he went ahead with the marriage, O'Neill refused to go quietly and, following a campaign of protest, he was in fact readmitted (PRONI, D/3653/AA/3, Minute Book, July 1888). Indeed, the willingness of management to compromise – even on their most deeply held principles – reflects a dynamic between patrons and beneficiaries which was highly unusual in charitable institutions, and again points to the ambiguous nature of the workshop situation.

There was, of course, a gendered perspective to the discourse and gendered perceptions determining the treatment and experience of the blind workers. Men outnumbered women by a ratio of two to one and, in keeping with broader practice, men and women were trained in different occupations – the men in basket-, brush- or mat-making, the women knitting or sewing sacks – and, of course, there was a significant difference in rates of pay. A survey of the manuscript correspondence indicates that it was almost always men who engaged in negotiation with the management and the committee, though one Margaret Campsie did complain about the inadequacy of her coal allowance (PRONI, D/3563/DB/1, ms, correspondence; D/3563/BC/4, 15 December 1876, Sub-committee report). Sally French's research suggests that blind women were generally 'perceived to be physically and morally vulnerable, in need of [particular] guidance and care' (French, 2006), and there is no doubt that the association was much more inclined to take up the role of guardian when dealing with females. Thus young women were frequently sent to Homes of Rest, and in 1906 13 'adoptions' were arranged for blind girls, through branches of the Girls Friendly Society. Adopters arranged holidays or outings for their nominated blind adoptee, often sending them treats such as flowers, eggs, butter and cash for special occasions (PRONI/D/3563/AK/1, Annual Report, 1906). Women appear to have been generally acquiescent in this culture of dependency, though there were a couple of exceptions – Margaret Campsie, already mentioned, was dismissed following an accusation of 'gross misconduct' with a male worker, and though she was eventually readmitted following a noisy campaign of protest, it took almost a year, compared to the 2-week-dismissal of the male worker involved. Cassie Marshall provides an example of entrepreneurship – claiming illness as an excuse for her absence from the workshop, she was in fact earning additional cash by giving private piano lessons (PRONI, D/3563/BA/4, 6 January 1909, Manager's Report). These examples from internal reports again suggest that the reality of experience did not always conform to the public image and that the blind community could be as diverse, and indeed as difficult, as any other cohort in society.

That male blind workers regarded themselves first and foremost as paid employees is clearly evidenced in the association's correspondence. Apart from their assertion of personal rights, noted above, they regularly lobbied the committee on matters pertaining to working conditions and to request pay rises (PRONI, D/3563/DB/1, ms. Correspondence, undated letters). This degree of activism, again highly unusual amongst those with disabilities in this period, was both explained by, and evidenced in, trade union membership. The League for the Blind, founded in 1899, had branches in Dublin, Cork and Belfast, as well as throughout Britain, and was primarily concerned to improve the working conditions and salaries of employees of the blind workshops. They were particularly anxious to reject the stigma of charity which surrounded such organizations, arguing that the state should provide all facilities for those disabled by blindness. Although the Belfast records of the league await further investigation, evidence from other sources points to the significance of this organization in furthering the rights of its members. Following the First World War, and a well-publicized radical campaign, the League secured the implementation of the Blind

Persons Act, which led to increased state intervention in workshops and considerable improvements in the welfare of the blind (O'Caithain, 2006).

Thus, while further research is required, what is already clear from these records is that the Belfast Association for the Employment of the Industrious Blind and its workers were not simply binary opposites of powerful patrons and helpless 'beneficiaries' of colonizer and the colonized. This cohort of blind workers, like any other section of society, was made up of a diverse number of individuals – whose experiences differed according to personality, gender and a range of other factors. Similarly, recognizing the need to compromise, this particular voluntary organization was able to work through and around contested spaces of tension to the mutual benefit of themselves and their employees. Sensitive reading reveals the ability to create places of equality and control for blind workers in the midst of contested space, and thus a far more complex and indeed interesting reality emerges than that generally attributed to institutional philanthropy.

The limited degree of academic attention which such materials have received and the virtual exclusion of their analysis from mainstream history could perhaps be interpreted as a literal manifestation of social distancing – a reflection of the perception of social discomfort prompted by a 'difficult' subject area. The narrowness of this intellectual engagement inevitably diminishes the prospect of a broader dissemination and popularisation of more complex understandings of disability past and present. Museums, on the other hand, as major, public depositories of our history and culture, and in contrast to the usual dusty archives scrutinised by professional historians, are accessible in most senses of the word. Presenting us with visual images of the richness and diversity of past experiences, their social significance should not be underestimated. Moreover, in recent years museums have moved away from being areas of observation and display to becoming sites of education, dialogue, interaction and transformation. Increasingly too, representations of marginalized groups are being incorporated into the more developed context of the social, cultural and historical narratives with which they are concerned. Simultaneously, representations of disability which seek to challenge reductive stereotypes have taken innovative and diverse forms. Nonetheless, a recent publication claims that

> while the burgeoning field of disability studies includes investigations of representational practices within film, television, journalism, literature and charity advertising, the museum – as both a site of exclusion and a site for the staging of interventions intended to elicit support for disability rights – has been largely overlooked. (Sandall, Dodd and Garland-Thomson, 2010)

This volume in itself points to the increasing recognition of the need to include disability-related narratives in the growing body of literature on museum studies and, given their potential to challenge and change public perceptions, it is perhaps not surprising that disability scholars and activists are now seeking evidence of their cultural history in such forums.

Cultural reclamation: Disability in the museums

The cultural representation of visible disability in the public arena is, however, perceived to hold particular challenges for practitioners undertaking the task of developing progressive interpretive approaches to subjects that conventionally evoke sentimentality, horror or pity. Rosemary Garland-Thomson, for example, discusses how the presence of disability is often perceived to be disruptive to the natural social order; arguing that the power of the normative gaze and the strength of normative standards forces those individuals labelled as different to blend into the background, present but socially invisible (Garland-Thomson, 2010). A growing number of examples, however, demonstrate how disability activists and scholars, utilizing a critical disability, can move against powerful silencing cultural norms to reshape and reposition the lens of social examination to arrive at a better understanding of impairment and disability. Thus, at Ryerson University in Toronto, Canada in October 2007, a group comprising Disability Studies students, faculty, alumni and community activists put together a 'compelling' exhibition illustrating the hidden history of disabled people's experiences, later shown in the Royal Ontario Museum in Toronto. In the same year the University of Leicester, working with nine museums and art galleries from England and Scotland, initiated a project whereby

> For the first time, objects and pictures connected with the lives of disabled people [were] shown to the public in a project designed to challenge stereotypes and the ways in which visitors think about issues connected with disability. www .le.ac.uk/ebulletin-archive/ebulletin/news/press-releases/2000-2009/2007/10/ nparticle.2007-10-09.html retrieved January 22, 2016.

The Greater Manchester Coalition of Disabled People is currently working on plans for a national archive of material generated by the Disabled People's Movement in Britain (http://gmcdp.com/our-history, retrieved January 22, 2016).

As these examples suggest, the shift from reductive stereotypes to more complex and nuanced portrayals of disability requires an inclusive and imaginative approach which will, it is hoped, be taken up by other public bodies. At the time of writing, however, such representations remain relatively rare and in some places are conspicuously absent. It was against this background that, as part of an ongoing research project, the authors considered the state of the representation of disability culture in Northern Ireland.

Northern Ireland has a significantly high rate of disability; at around one-fifth of the population, it is the highest in the United Kingdom. Moreover, as a region just emerging from a prolonged period of violent civil conflict, physical disablement is just one of the legacies which the new political regime must consider in the often contested discourse of the current 'peace process'. The prevalence of religious and political sectarianism, which may have declined but has not disappeared in the post-conflict era, is just one of the reasons for the lack of a distinctive or robust disability movement in Northern Ireland during recent decades. Contemporaneously, provision for disability rights forms part of the equality agenda contained within the 1998 Belfast Agreement, often regarded as both 'unique and world leading' (Donaghy, 2004, McLaughlin, 2003). Section 75 of that Agreement places a statutory requirement on public authorities to carry out their duties with *due regard* to the need to promote equality across nine grounds, including that of Disability.[1] The process of mainstreaming equality has its critics, however: Eithne McLaughlin points out that 'an excessive focus on process rather than outcome has helped to undermine the political credibility of mainstreaming as an equality practice' (2003: 720). Similarly, a review of the duty revealed a number of operational problems (McLaughlin and Faris, 2004) and in most activist circles an air of cynicism prevails. Probably the most visible sign of change in relation to disability has been round the issue of access: ramps, lifts and 'wheelchair-friendly' toilets are the usual response to such legislation. While such interventions are both necessary and welcome, they reflect a focus on equality of opportunity, rather than a broader-based human rights agenda (Hill et al., 2006).

Since, as we have argued, museums have an important role to play in both reflecting and promoting a cultural diversity which is inclusive of impairment and disability, and are thus pertinent in discussions of a more meaningful equality, we focused our attention on the two major cultural fora of the wider Belfast area: the Ulster Folk & Transport Museum and the newly refurbished Ulster Museum in Belfast, which has just won a £100,000 Arts Fund Prize for its 'cultural rejuvenation'. The acclaim which the museum's reopening received is well deserved; in terms of its architecture, design, its interactive facilities and its collection of 9,000 years of cultural history. But while this magnificent building is said to be 'rooted in the community', the experiences of disabled people do not appear to have been included in that community. Discussions with museum staff on the issue have to date elicited no response apart from references to physical access to the built environment.

Whereas some museums have included portrayals of disablement in their consideration of the legacy of armed conflict, the Ulster Museum contains no reference to the estimated 100,000 local people injured during the 40 years of the 'Troubles'. Indeed it is interesting to note that the Minister for Culture in this province, preoccupied with the issue of identity, recently slated the museum for its lack of or minimalist representation of the Orange Order, the Ulster Scots and the Creationist perspective – a somewhat narrow view of identity reflecting local popular political priorities. But while the loss of opportunity reflected in this example is disappointing, the preoccupations of the past are inevitably resistant to challenge, and as the process of peace-building continues to gather momentum, there is much potential for a more inclusive future.

Conclusion

Museums can be powerful sites of social change. They can play an important role in shifting and changing the dominant social narrative for many marginalized social groups in addition to disabled people. Methodologies tested in this project not only set out to change public attitudes, they are also a form of capacity building and strengthening of the organizations of civil society themselves and of people in the minority social group concerned. While this project is specific to disability, the general methods and lessons learned will be applicable to other social statuses and minority groups. In practicing selective social erasure, we must ask ourselves who really benefits. Certainly, absences in spaces and places of culture have not helped disabled people. If progress is to be made we must come to grips with the messy leaky richness of disability history and recognize and embrace our natural place within and along the historical continuum.

Note

1 Religious belief, political opinion, racial group, age, marital status, sexual orientation

References

Bannerji, Himani. Politics and the writing of history. In Ruth Roach Pierson and Nupur Chaudhuri (eds.), *Nation, Empire, Glory: Historicizing Gender and Race.* Bloomington, IN: Indiana University Press, 1998. 287–301.

Barnes, Colin. A legacy of oppression: A history of disability in Western Europe. In Len Barton and Mike Oliver (eds.), *Disability Studies: Past Present and Future.* Leeds: Disability Studies Press. 1997. 3–24.

The Belfast Association for the Employment of the Industrious Blind. *Centenary of the Workshops for the Blind 1871–1971.* Published by the Workshops for the Blind, Belfast. 1971.

Donaghy, Tahnya. Mainstreaming: Northern Ireland's participative-democratic approach. *Policy and Politics.* Vol. 32. 49–62. 2004.

French, Sally (ed.). *An Oral History of the Education of Visually Impaired People: Telling Stories for Inclusive Futures.* Lewiston, Queenstown, Lampeter: The Edwin Mellen Press. 2006.

Garland-Thomson, Rosemarie. 'Picturing People with Disabilities, Classical portraiture as reconstructive narrative', in Richard Sandell, Jocelyn Dodd and Rosemarie Garland-Thomson, *Representing Disability: Activism and Agency in the Museum,* Routledge, London and New York, 2010

Hill, Myrtle. Gender, culture and 'the spiritual Empire': The Irish protestant female missionary experience. *Women's History Review.* Vol. 16, no. 2. 185–208. April 2007.

Hill, Myrtle, Fran Porter, Caroline McAuley and Eithne McLaughlin. *Eighty Years of Talking about Equality in Northern Ireland,* Queens University Belfast. Working Paper No 5. January 2006.

Jordan, Alison. *Who Cared? Charity in Victorian and Edwardian Belfast.* Belfast: Queen's University of Belfast, Institute of Irish Studies. 1993.

Ludmilla Jordanova, *History in Practice,* Arnold Publishing; London/Oxford University Press, New York 2000

Lynch, John. *A Tale of Three Cities: Comparative Studies in Working Class Life.* London: Macmillan. 1998.

McClelland, Gillian. Evangelical Philanthropy and Social Control or Emancipatory Feminism? *A Case Study of Fisherwick Presbyterian Working Women's Association, 1870–1918.* Unpublished PhD thesis, Queens University Belfast. 2000.

McLaughlin, Eithne. Equality and equity policy. In Mary Hawesworth and Maurice Kogan (eds.), *Encyclopedia of Government and Politics* (2nd Edition). London: Routledge. 2003.

McLaughlin, Eithne and Neil Farris. *Section 75 Review: The Section 75 Equality Duty – An Operational Review.,* Volume 2, Northern Ireland Office, 2004

O'Caithain, Mairti. Blind, but not to the hard facts of life: The blind workers' struggle in Derry, 1928–1940. *Radical History Review.* Winter 2006 vol. 26. No. 4:9–21

Public Records Office of Northern Ireland, The Records of the Belfast Association for the Employment of the Industrious Blind. Ref. D/3653

Rose, June. *Changing Focus: The Development of Blind Welfare in Britain.* London, Hutchinson, 1970.

Sandell, Richard, Jocelyn Dodd, and Rosemarie Garland-Thomson. *Representing Disability: Activism and Agency in the Museum.* New York, NY. Routledge. 2010.

Scott, Robert A. The factory as a social service organization: Goal displacement in workshops for the blind. *Social Problem.* Vol. 15, no. 2. 160–175. 1967.

Shapiro, Ann-Louise. 'Introduction: History and Feminist Theory, or Talking Back to the Beadle' *History and Theory,* Vol. 31, No. 4, Beiheft 31: History and Feminist Theory (Dec., 1992), pp. 1–14.

World Health Organization (2011) World report on disability. who.int/disabilities/world_report/2011/en/ retrieved, January 21, 2016.

18

AUSTRALIAN HISTORIES OF INTELLECTUAL DISABILITIES[1]

Dave Earl

Until recently, Australian historians have relegated people with disabilities, and especially people with intellectual disabilities, to the margins of their study. Over the past decade, however, a number of historians, drawing on principles from the new disability history, have begun to pay closer attention to people previously marginalised in our work. In this chapter, I briefly survey new developments in Australian histories of intellectual disabilities, and present an overview of the major historical shifts regarding these categories in Australia.

Classifications of disability, like other social and cultural categories, are fluid and historically contingent, and subject to change, resistance, and contestation over time (Kudlick, 2003, pp. 764–765; Snyder & Mitchell, 2006, pp. 6–7; Tremain, 2005, pp. 9–11). As categories of disability are reimagined, and new cultural, medical, and scientific understandings are attached to them, their constituents change, and it is possible for different people and types of individuals to move within and through them. "People with intellectual disabilities"[2] is the term currently used in Australia to describe a diverse group of individuals with a range of cognitive impairments, genetic disorders, and various social disabilities, who test markedly below average on standardised tests of intelligence or behavioural development (see Cocks, 1998, p. 39ff). The amorphous nature of intellectual disabilities has led them to being especially liable to being historically reconstituted; there is certainly no reason to assume that people included in current classificatory schedules neatly align with older categories and understandings (see: Brockley, 2001, p. 3; Snyder & Mitchell, 2006, p. 19; Trent (Jr.), 1995, p. 5). We must be wary, as Stainton and McDonagh (2001) remind us, to avoid "trans-historical assumptions about what constitutes … [intellectual] disability. We can study a particular construct in a particular time and context, but once we move away from that frame the concept will begin to destabilize" (2001, p. xi). When constructing survey histories such as presented in this chapter, it is necessary to acknowledge both shifts in the definitions of the disabilities we study, as well as the broader social, medical, and cultural changes which shape them.

In Australia, temporal shifts are further complicated by the frequent employment, at any given time, of a variety of differing labels and classifications by the bewildering array of government bodies, voluntary organisations, and private individuals that have involved themselves with intellectual disabilities. Historically, health and educational services have been a state-based responsibility, and governments in each state have frequently proscribed differing and sometimes contradictory terms to describe the populations we would now call intellectually disabled. One observer summed up the situation in 1965: "a sub-normal child in Queensland is the same as a retarded child in Tasmania, a mentally retarded in Victoria and a slow-learner in Western Australia" (A New Home for the Handicapped in N.S.W.,1965, p. 19).

Most of the older terms Australians employed to describe intellectual disabilities now have pejorative connotations, despite having frequently been introduced with the explicit purpose of supplanting words already seen as offensive (see: Greenspan, 1999, pp. 6–7; Ryan & Thomas, 1980, p. 11). While the shifting language is partially symptomatic of the euphemism treadmill (where older terms are replaced in order to reduce social stigmas attached to them), it also reflects shifting classificatory boundaries and new social and scientific understandings of these classifications. For both these reasons, historians of intellectual disabilities in Australia choose to use terms current at the time we are investigating, even though they may seem outmoded and offensive to contemporary readers. I endorse that approach, and for the purposes of this chapter, consider "people with intellectual disabilities" to be anyone who may have been included in a range of older categories.

Recent historiographical developments

For many years Australian historians disregarded intellectual disabilities as having historical interest. People classified as intellectually disabled occasionally emerged in histories of education, welfare, childhood, and psychiatry, but they were almost invariably dismissed as "chronic incurables" or "problem children," "sufferers" of an unchanging, organic, and unproblematic disorder. In 1996, a landmark collection of essays transformed the field by adopting a social approach to disability history, mapping the construction of intellectual disabilities in the state of Western Australia (Cocks, Fox, Brogan, & Lee, 1996). Subsequently, a growing number of scholars, including Ellmoos (2010), Gothard (2011), Manning (2008), Monk (2010), and Williams (1996, 2000, 2003), have expanded our knowledge of this neglected field, charting the shifting cultural meanings of intellectual disabilities, and examining the changing life outcomes of people considered to be affected by them. Simultaneously, a range of historians examining eugenics, notably Anderson (2005), Garton (2000), Jones (1999, 2009), and Rodwell (1998, 2000), have engaged in incredibly fruitful work revealing the nexus of social concerns which led to the creation of mental deficiency as a new (and ever widening) social category in the early twentieth century. Historians of eugenics have also begun unpacking the complex set of circumstances which led to eugenics' eventual abandonment in the post-war period.

For the most part, Australian historians of intellectual disability have focused upon government agencies, and the power to change discourses of disability has almost exclusively been granted to the professionals who worked within and alongside state services. These studies have somewhat paradoxically revealed that Australia governments have only ever provided adequate services for a small fraction of individuals who might be categorised as intellectually disabled. As was the case overseas, "community care initiatives … [were] the most common historical response to those with … [intellectual] disabilities" (Digby, 1996, p. 15). Recently historians, including Fox (2003a), Coleborne (2010), and myself (2009, 2011) have taken steps to correct this historical oversight, shifting focus away from government services, and towards the families, carers, and non-government and philanthropic groups which have frequently been the primary providers of assistance to people identified as intellectually disabled. In the remainder of this chapter, I draw upon these historians' work to provide a chronology of the major shifts in scientific and popular understandings of intellectual disabilities, and the significant changes in our provision of services for people with intellectual disabilities in Australia.

Colonial period

European occupation of Australia began in 1788 with the establishment of a British penal colony in Sydney. Like settler-colonial centres elsewhere, the city rapidly developed a suite of benevolent homes, orphanages, and other institutional apparatuses to accommodate, and discipline, problematic or otherwise difficult citizens. Administratively, the Governor's Commission provided for direct supervision of all "ideots, lunaticks, and their estates" by the Crown. Research undertaken by Earnshaw (1995) suggests that initial efforts were to employ "ideot" convicts as gainfully as possible, part of a broader policy to engage sick, amputee, and other impaired convicts in productive labour (p. 28ff). By 1811, a disused government barn in Sydney's west had been set aside as a "lunatick asylum" housing around thirty inmates believed too impaired to work, or too unstable to be left at large (Earnshaw, 1995, p. 30).

Over the following decades, as settlement expanded across the continent, asylum provision grew. The New Norfolk Asylum in the colony of Van Diemen's Land (later known as Tasmania) opened in 1827, and housed a heterogeneous assortment of invalids, maniacs, and aments (Fox, 2008, p. 131). By the 1860s, dedicated mental institutions had been established in the colonies of South Australia, Queensland, and Western Australia (Kirkby, 1999, p. 194), and the more populous colonies of Victoria and New South Wales had extended institutional provision to regional centres such as Bendigo and Ballarat (Coleborne, 2010, p. 24ff). A series of *Dangerous Lunatics Acts* provided for the certification of lunatics by medical administrators, allowing individuals identified by two physicians as imbecile or insane to be compulsorily detained (Coleborne, 1995, pp. 88–89).

In practice, it seems that many "idiots" made a living undertaking simple rural and industrial work if male, or domestic service if female. Many idiots probably remained with their families, away from the eyes of authority, and, hence, the documentary record. References to fools occasionally emerge in newspaper reports and other correspondence, described in a rather matter-of-fact and unproblematic manner. Asylum admission papers from the colonial period suggest that certification under the *Acts* usually occurred as a last resort for families facing financial or other pressures, or when previously independent idiots came to the attention of magistrates through petty crimes or other disturbances (Coleborne, 2010, p. 55ff; Fox, 2003b, p. 150; Megahey, 1996, p. 32ff).

During the latter decades of the nineteenth century, a new generation of medically trained and professionalised lunacy administrators emerged in the Colonies. Concerned less with custodialism, and more with the "correct" classification, scientific treatment, and cure of lunacy, the new superintendents, supported by philanthropists, saw the establishment of Australia's first dedicated idiot asylums. New South Wales'

"Newcastle Asylum for Idiots &c." opened in 1877, Victoria's "Kew Idiot Asylum" opened in 1897, and Adelaide's "Minda Home for Weak-Minded Children" opened in 1898. Looking to precedents in Britain (notably the famous Earlswood Asylum in Surrey), these places sought, with a spirit of optimism, to train idiot children in simple manual work, enabling them to contribute to their upkeep, and, ideally, return to the community (F. N. Manning, October 1878, p. 294). Minda was especially successful in galvanising public sympathy, holding frequent fundraisers, fêtes, and appeals to support its activities.

Eugenics

In 1901, the seven colonies joined to form the Commonwealth of Australia, with the federal government assuming control of customs, immigration, and defence, and the colonies (henceforth known as states) remaining residual control of areas such as health, education, and policing. As a state responsibility, lunacy provision evolved independently in each state, though, as previously, there was considerable cross-fertilisation of ideas, policy, and staff between the states, as well as from Britain, and, increasingly, North America.

By the first decades of the twentieth century, the optimism exhibited by late-nine-teenth-century lunacy administrators was being challenged. Politicians, professionals, and philanthropists considered the newly federated nation the world's social laboratory, and a growing number of these influential figures became attracted to eugenic ideas. Medical practitioners, particularly, began regarding the feeble-minded as a threat to Australia's "racial type," and the root cause of crime, vice, and delinquency. Eugenicists generally argued that, while not necessarily being inherent criminals, the weak intellects and poor self-control of feeble-minded people "naturally" led them to drift into criminality when left to their own devices. They therefore needed to be sheltered from the dangers of roaming freely through the community. Their eugenic threat was seen as particularly grave in a newly formed nation:

> In a young, partially developed country like Australia the need for a virile stock to propagate the generations to come is particularly urgent for economic as well as social reasons; and unless steps are taken to ensure the perpetuation of a healthy and normal population before it is too late, we will be inviting an inevitable shipwreck as a people. (Royal Commissioners, 1923, p. xliv)

Throughout the 1910s and '20s, a clique of professional men and women urged governments to introduce eugenically inspired legislation, which usually entailed the compulsory, permanent segregation of mental deficients. Their efforts met with mixed success: although the sections of the press were generally sympathetic, many politicians baulked at the financial implications of the programmes eugenicists proposed.

Eugenic debates tended to be driven by younger, American-trained social workers and psychologists, such as Lorna Hodgkinson, a Harvard-trained psychologist who was employed by the New South Wales Education and Child Welfare Departments in the mid-1920s (Turtle, 1993), and Ethel Stoneman, who studied in America before being appointed as Western Australia's first State Psychologist in 1926 (Gaynor & Fox, 1993). Their positions were given weight by more established commentators, notably Richard Berry, Professor of Anatomy at the University of Melbourne, who initiated a series of nationwide lecture tours publicly promoting the eugenic threat of feeble-mindedness (Jones, 1999, pp. 325–326); and Sir Charles Mackellar, prominent Chair of NSW's State Children Relief Board (later the Child Welfare Department) who, although at first a strident advocate of "nurture" versus "nature," turned cynical in his retirement and published a widely circulated tirade which outlined the dire menace mentally deficient people posed to the young nation (Garton, 1986).

As in much of the modernising world, the firebrand issue of the 1910s, '20s, and '30s was compulsory sterilisation. Australians alternatively looked to the United States and Britain for guidance, with a mix of hesitance, fascination, and disdain. Paul Popenoe's *Sterilisation for Human Betterment* (1930), which outlined California's "successful" sterilisation of just over 6,000 defectives, was popular amongst Australia's more radical eugenicists, and a well-thumbed copy circulated the Commonwealth Parliamentary Library. Nonetheless, many politicians remained wary of accepting that sterilisation was an appropriate solution to the feeble-minded "problem." Some argued that surgical intervention would always be legally questionable; others were concerned that the public would never support such radical measures (Garton, 2000, pp. 13–14; Wyndham, 1996, pp. 318–320). While sterilisation bills were introduced in several Australian states, none were passed. In practice, however, it appears that some women were sterilised at either the urgings of institutional superintendents, or at the request of their parents or carers. Regulations passed in Victoria in 1933, for instance, suggestively "empowered the director [of Mental Hygiene] to consent to any surgical operation or other treatment by any member of the medical staff of a hospital" (Mental Hygiene. New Names Approved. Sterilisation Discussed, 1933, p. 13). More research needs to be undertaken in this area.

Eugenicists and their allies broadly expanded the scope of mental deficiency. Whereas earlier generations of administrators had been satisfied providing for problematic idiots whose families were willing (or compelled) to relinquish them, Hodgkinson, Berry, and their contemporaries focused their efforts towards "hidden" deficients: those who frequently appeared normal to laypeople, and had escaped the eyes of authority. In their logic, it was these hard-to-identify, seemingly unproblematic individuals that posed the greatest threat to the state. The Victorian Mental Defectives Colony Association explained the problem in the 1920s:

> The greatest menace to a proper understanding of mental deficiency is the preconceived notion that the condition is synonymous with idiocy or imbecility, that is, with human beings who are so distorted mentally that it shows, and is obvious, in the outward physical signs. These are the 'Crazy Janes' or 'Silly boys' of the streets and are the least of our troubles. (PROV, VPRS 892 102/1196)

That proponents had to repeatedly emphasise that the mentally defective group expanded beyond the obvious fools suggests how little popular currency their position held. Popular scepticism remained, especially amongst Catholics and liberals. "Let us beware," a typical sceptic wrote in Western Australia, "that in our enthusiasm for legislating for mental deficients, … we do not set up an itch for finding mental deficiency where it does not exist" (Murdoch, 1930, p. 4).

Institutional decline

While eugenic debates continued to occupy specialists, most Australian states developed a bipartite system of care whereby "ineducable" idiots and imbeciles remained the responsibility of lunacy (and later mental hygiene and mental health) departments, and backward and feeble-minded children fell under the jurisdiction of educational departments. Beginning with Victoria in 1913, most states established limited networks of special schools and "opportunity classes" to cater for children identified by counsellors and schoolteachers as problematic. By the middle of the century, these special classes were populated by a motley collection of "mental defectives of any degree down to idiocy, … the crippled, the cerebral palsied, the deaf, the partially sighted and the rest, as well … the more normal child" (Hall, 1956, p. 41). Invariably, waiting lists for these special classes were long, and the usual outcome for a child identified as "special" was simply exclusion from government schooling (Earl, 2011, p. 89ff).

State and philanthropic mental hospitals remained the only formal provision for adult mental defectives until the 1960s and beyond. Through the first half of the century, and into the second, the number of government beds continued to grow; as the quantity of beds increased, the quality of services declined. Asylums had always been underfunded, but by the 1940s a decade of depression followed by war had led to overcrowding and understaffing in almost every institution in Australia. The funnelling of resources into curative psychiatric facilities had left the chronic wards and idiot asylums in a deplorable condition (Garton, 2009, pp. 40–41). A series of scandals in the late 1940s publicly exposed the appalling conditions inside mental hospitals, and when the Commonwealth government commissioned a national enquiry into psychiatric care in 1955, scathing observations were made of mental deficiency wards (Garton, 1987, p. 344). As in previous decades, it appears that many families were reluctant to relinquish family members to government care; with chronic overcrowding and a desperate shortage of beds, even those who wished to do so were finding it increasingly difficult. Examining Victorian provision for mental defectives in 1950, one witness complained that "even if the present institutional accommodation was increased sixfold it could not deal adequately with the number of cases urgently requiring help" (Kennedy, 1950, p. 4).

The parent movement

Beginning in the late 1940s, groups of parents unwilling or unable to institutionalise their children began organising across Australia. Forming associations such as the Slow Learning Children's Group (Western Australia), the Sub Normal Children's Welfare Association (Queensland and New South Wales), and the Helping Hand League for the Mentally Retarded (Victoria), these parent groups launched widespread and highly visible publicity campaigns, calling attention to their children's plight and arguing for a "new deal"" for the mentally retarded. In 1952 most of the parent groups loosely federated under an umbrella organisation known as the Australian

Council for Mentally Retarded Children (ACMRC), with the aim of presenting a "united front" to governments and the public (van Pelt, 1968, p. 5).

Although each parent group had its own particular aims and philosophies, most sought to establish their own, privately run special schools, occupation centres, sheltered workshops, and residential institutions, in the hope of supplementing overcrowded government facilities. Their initiatives were to be financed by private donations raised through fundraising activities such as fêtes, door-knocking, badge draws, and lotteries. By the end of the 1950s, the parent organisations had opened several hundred day centres, and established over a dozen small residential units to permanently accommodate their children. Equally importantly, the groups' fundraisers and appeals had made significant inroads towards dispelling older, eugenic stigmas attached to mental deficiency. Particularly prevalent in their publicity material was the concept that mentally retarded people were like "children who never grew up," an idea which had enjoyed a resurgence in America after the 1950 publication of Pearl S. Buck's *The Child Who Never Grew* (Trent (Jr.), 1995, p. 330ff). Within a handful of years, the mentally retarded had shifted from being an object of public disdain to one of widespread sympathy. One parent explained the change in a 1956 newsletter: "not so long ago, the mentally handicapped children amongst us were looked upon almost as though they were a race apart … that day is gone" (Anonymous, 1956, p. 25).

The parents' cause was bolstered by an ever-increasing number of professionals who allied themselves with the voluntary groups. Prominent educationalists, psychologists, social workers and administrators, notably Eric Cunningham Dax, Fred Schonell, Beatrice Silk, Marie Neale and Bill Piddington, all encouraged the establishment of parent groups, or became involved with them at an early stage. These professionals were particularly influential in encouraging governments to provide partial funding for the associations' activities (Earl, 2011, p. 96). "The movement has been exciting," reported Dax, head of the Victorian Mental Hygiene Authority, it "has caught the public imagination; has stimulated the efforts of many; has resulted in a new deal for the children; relief for their parents, and education for the populace" (January 1963, p. 146).

In conjunction with the parent organisations, this new breed of administrators imported radical treatment philosophies from abroad, particularly from Scandinavia and the Netherlands. Typifying the new regimes was Dax's *Community Programme for the Mentally Retarded* (1961), which, in the late 1950s and early 1960s, replaced large hospital wards with smaller, hostel-like accommodation, and engaged inmates in seemingly productive forms of occupation therapy and work relief. Despite (or perhaps because of) these new approaches, the number of mentally retarded people accommodated in state mental hospitals continued to grow, both in actual numbers, and as a proportion of total inmates.

Normalisation

While the parent groups precipitated a widespread expansion in services for the mentally retarded, their overwhelming belief that their offspring were like eternal children eventually brought them into conflict with professionals and advocates who had begun to preach a new mantra of "normalisation" from the late 1960s. In 1968, it came as a shock and surprise to many members of the groups when visiting international disability advocates Rosemary and Gunnar Dybwad warned of "the continuing danger of benevolent segregation," pointedly noting that "there are those who feel that … the mentally retarded individual should enjoy protection from the pressures of everyday life in the community." "With all due respect," they wrote in a report to the ACMRC, "the question might be raised whether this type of arrangement is not providing more definitely for the security of the parent rather than for the needs of the child" (Dybwad & Dybwad, 1969, p. 270).

The 1970s saw increasing divisions between government agencies, families, and other groups providing services for mentally retarded Australians. As Gothard (2011, p. 152) has argued, a second wave of parent groups emerged throughout this period, tended to focus on specific disorders, such as Prader-Willi Syndrome, or Down's Syndrome. Parents sought disorder-specific facilities, and were more assertive in their demands for government support, rather than earlier self-help. Other groups, such as the Autistic Children's Association of New South Wales, took advantage of new scientific and psychological understandings, and successfully campaigned to have their children, previously thought to be mentally retarded, excised from the category altogether (Bowen, 1975, p. 8). Cocks (1998, pp. 23–25) has observed that many parent organisations, which seemed progressive in previous decades, resisted calls for the closure of "terminal" sheltered workshops, "farm colonies," and other older residential facilities. Although the language of normalisation became increasingly prevalent late in the decade, in practice, most of the older, strikingly segregated forms of custodial care continued.

Deinstitutionalisation

Mentally retarded people also missed out on many of the rights campaigns won by the physically disabled during the 1970s. Although the concept of self-advocacy gradually emerged in Australia during the decade, its adoption was slow. While deinstitutionalisation of psychiatric patients, easily managed with psychopharmaceutical medication, was well underway by the 1980s, most of the large institutions for mentally retarded people – including Minda, Kew, and Newcastle – remained open and overcrowded. Landmark enquiries in Victoria (Victorian Committee on Mental Retardation, 1977) and New South Wales (NSW Department of Health, 1983), eventually set formal programmes of deinstitutionalisation in place, but their implementation was often piecemeal: constrained by cost and bureaucratic hurdles.

Perhaps surprisingly, the families of many institutionalised people were strident opponents of deinstitutionalisation programmes. Fox (2003a) has noted that much of this opposition hinged around the idea of community. Parents of inmates at Kew Cottages, for instance, drew on familiar discourses when they campaigned to prevent the closure of the institution in the mid-1990s, arguing that the "Cottages community" offered "a safe and social environment for residents who are essentially very vulnerable people" (cited in Fox, 2003a, p. 49). Other parents embraced the deinstitutionalisation process, arguing that the "it's for his own good" attitude had to end. "Intellectually handicapped people will often be 'protected' from developing any independence," wrote one father in 1983, "if all your decisions are made for you, then you will never learn to push your point of view." "If we are genuinely interested in the welfare of intellectually disabled people," he suggested, "then the time has come for us to re-examine our assumptions, attitudes and practices" (Barson, December 1983, pp. 37–39).

Post-deinstitutionalisation

From the 1980s onwards, most large institutions were gradually replaced with hostel- or group home–style supported accommodation dispersed throughout suburban Australia. Simultaneously, the provision of community care was largely outsourced to non-governmental, non-profit organisations, many of them conglomerates formed from the remnants of earlier parent groups and other philanthropic organisations. In conjunction with this shift in service provision, a market model and a new language of consumerism was adopted by government agencies and professionals. People with intellectual disabilities, and their families, were reimagined as "clients" who exercised "rights" as buyers and consumers of a customer service (Newell, 1996, pp. 429–431). While most people with intellectual disabilities now located within the community, critics have noted that they are still seldom part of the community, and their personal relationships are generally restricted to professional carers, family members, and other people with disabilities. Disturbingly, the "job" of institutionalising individuals with "challenging" or "antisocial" tendencies has frequently shifted from mental health authorities to judicial and penal ones (Gardner & Glanville, 2005, p. 226). While deinstitutionalisation has been successful for some individuals, the larger project of social and community improvement has remained largely unfulfilled.

Chronic underfunding of services has continued. As institutions have been closed, the financing and expansion of community care facilities has seldom kept pace. The net result has been a continuing burden upon many families with intellectually disabled members, particularly those with high care needs or challenging behaviour. Some parents, often those with several disabled children, or elderly parents who feel they can no longer care for an adult child, one again feel abandoned by the state (Victorian Equal Opportunity & Human Rights Commission, 2012, p. 33ff). This issue has gained political traction, and in recent state and federal elections groups such as the "Carers Alliance" have emerged, campaigning, in part, for the reopening of residential institutions, and opposing "trendy academics" and "know-it-alls" who peddle the "myth" of community care. Some look back nostalgically to a mythological, utopian institutional past where government hospitals provided benevolent care for all (Smith, 2011).

Conclusion

The history of intellectual disabilities in Australia shares many characteristics with similar histories from abroad, particularly from the United States, United Kingdom, and the British settler-colonies of Canada and New Zealand. This is a partial reflection of scientific and cultural transmissions from Europe and North America, and of a continuing exchange of ideas between Australia and the wider world. The superintendent of a newly founded Western Australian institution summarised this transnational mindset when he planned his institute in 1929: "we shall combine what is best in the old world and pick the worth-while ideas from America, mix them, and adapt to our own conditions and circumstances" (McMahon, 1929, p. 13). Yet, these common histories – of government neglect and underfunding punctuated by brief periods of enlightenment; of shifting classificatory boundaries; and of continuing community care from families, laypeople, and voluntary and philanthropic organisations – are also a product of nations and communities undergoing contemporaneous social and cultural changes: from a pre-industrial to an industrial society, to a post-industrial consumer society. These broader social shifts have fed into and transformed our understandings of intellectual disabilities: what they are, what they mean to society, and which individuals should be labelled as possessing them.

Notes

1 Research for this chapter was partially funded by an Australian Pioneers' Club Travel Bursary, and a National Library of Australia Summer Scholarship.
2 This term in largely synonymous with the British "developmental disabilities," and DSM IV's "mental retardation."

References

Anderson, W. (2005). *The Cultivation of Whiteness: Science, Health and Racial Destiny in Australia* (New ed.). Carlton, Victoria: Melbourne University Press.

Anonymous. (July, 1956). Untitled Message, *Welfare News*, p. 25.

Barson, R. (December, 1983). It's for his own good. *Welfare News*, 1(6), 37–39.

Bowen, J. (September 22, 1975). Two extraordinary men speak out: For the future of the autistic child: Dr Andrew Vern-Barnett, working while the world talked, *Australian Women's Weekly*, p. 8.

Brockley, J. A. (2001). Rearing the child that never grew: Parents, professionals and children with intellectual disabilities, 1910–1965. PhD Thesis, Rutgers University, New Brunswick.

Cocks, E. (1998). *An Introduction to Intellectual Disability in Australia* (3rd ed.). Fyshwick: Australian Institute on Intellectual Disability.

Cocks, E., Fox, C., Brogan, M., & Lee, M. (Eds.). (1996). *Under Blue Skies: The Social Construction of Intellectual Disability in Western Australia.* Perth: Centre for Disability Research and Development, Faculty of Health and Human Sciences, Edith Cowan University.

Coleborne, C. (1995). Legislating lunacy and the female lunatic body in nineteenth-century Victoria. in D. Kirkby (Ed.), *Sex, Power and Justice: Historical Perspectives of Law in Australia* (pp. 86–98). Melbourne: Oxford University Press.

Coleborne, C. (2010). *Madness in the Family: Insanity and Institutions in the Australasian Colonial World, 1860–1914.* London: Palgrave Macmillan.

Dax, E. C. (1961). *Asylum to Community: The Development of the Mental Hygiene Service.* Melbourne: F. W. Cheshire.

Dax, E. C. (January, 1963). Guest editorial: Australia and its retarded children. *Australian Children Limited*, vol. 4, 146–147.

Digby, A. (1996). Contexts and perspectives. in D. Wright & A. Digby (Eds.), *From Idiocy to Mental Deficiency: Historical Perspectives on People with Learning Disabilities* (pp. 1–21). London: Routledge.

Dybwad, G., & Dybwad, R. (November, 1969). A report to the Australian Council For Mentally Retarded on a consultation visit during July and August 1968. *Australian Children Limited*, 264–276.

Earl, D. (2009). Help for children and their families: Presenting 'subnormal' and 'spastic' children to the public in 1950s New South Wales. *AntiTHESIS*, 19, 148–161.

Earl, D. (2011). 'A group of parents came together': Parent advocacy groups for children with intellectual disabilities in post–world war II Australia. *Health & History*, 13(2), 84–103.

Earnshaw, B. (June, 1995). The lame, the blind, the mad, the malingerers: Sick and disabled convicts within the colonial community. *Journal of the Royal Australian Historical Society*, 81(1), 25–38.

Ellmoos, L. (2010). *Beneath the Pines: A History of the Stockton Centre*. New South Wales: New South Wales Department of Ageing, Disability and Home Care.

Fox, C. (2003a). Debating deinstitutionalisation: The fire at Kew cottages in 1996 and the idea of community. *Health & History*, 5(2), 37–59.

Fox, C. (2003b). 'Forehead low, Aspect idiotic': Intellectual disability in Victorian asylums, 1870–1887. in C. Coleborne & D. Mackinnon (Eds.), *Madness in Australia: Histories, Heritage and Asylum* (pp. 145–156). St Lucia: University of Queensland Press.

Fox, C. (2008). Exploring 'amentia' in the Tasmanian convict system, 1824–1890. *Tasmanian Historical Studies*, 13, 127–152.

Gardner, J., & Glanville, L. (2005). New forms of institutionalization in the community. in K. Johnson & R. Traustadóttir (Eds.), *Deinstitutionalization and People with Intellectual Disabilities: In and Out of Institutions* (pp. 222–230). Philadelphia, PA: Jessica Kingsley Publishers.

Garton, S. (1986). Sir Charles Mackellar: Psychiatry, eugenics and child welfare in New South Wales. *Historical Studies*, 22, 21–34.

Garton, S. (1987). Changing minds. in A. Curthoys, A. W. Martin & T. Rowse (Eds.), *Australians from 1939* (pp. 343–355).Sydney: Fairfax, Syme and Weldon Associates.

Garton, S. (April 27 and 28, 2000). *Writing Eugenics: A History of Classifying Practices*. Paper presented at the History and Sociology of Eugenics Conference, Customs House, Newcastle, New South Wales, Australia.

Garton, S. (2009). Seeking refuge: Why asylum facilities might still be relevant for mental health care services today. *Health & History*, 11(1), 25–45.

Gaynor, A., & Fox, C. (1993). The birth and death of the clinic: Ethel Stoneman and the state psychology clinic, 1927–1930. *Studies in Western Australian History*, 87–101.

Gothard, J. (2011). *Greater Expectations: Living with Down Syndrome in the 21st Century*. Fremantle: Fremantle Press.

Greenspan, S. (1999). What is meant by mental retardation? *International Journal of Psychiatry*, 11(1), 6–18.

Hall, J. A. (1956). The education of retarded and backward children in Victoria. *Slow Learning Child*, 3(1), 38–45.

Jones, R. (1999). The master potter and the rejected pots: Eugenic legislation in Victoria, 1918–1939. *Australian Historical Studies*, 30(113), 319–342.

Jones, R. (2009). Removing some of the dust from the wheels of civilization: William Ernest Jones and the 1928 Commonwealth Survey of Mental Deficiency. *Australian Historical Studies*, 40(1), 63–78.

Kennedy, A. (1950). Report to the Minister for Health on mental health and mental hygiene services in the State of Victoria. Melbourne, Australia: J.J. Gourley, Government Printer.

Kirkby, K. C. (1999). History of psychiatry in Australia, pre-1960. *History of Psychiatry*, 10(191), 191–204.

Kudlick, C. J. (2003). Disability history: Why we need another 'other'. *American Historical Review*, 108(3), 763–793.

Manning, C. (2008). *Bye-bye Charlie: Stories from the vanishing world of Kew Cottages*. Sydney: University of New South Wales Press.

Manning, F. N. (October, 1878). Statistics of lunacy in New South Wales. *The Australian Medical Journal*, vol. 23, 292–296.

McMahon, R. J. T. (February 16, 1929). Castledare: Our home for sub-normal boys, *The Record*, p. 13.

Megahey, N. (1996). Living in Fremantle Asylum: The colonial experience of disability 1829–1900. in E. Cocks, C. Fox, M. Brogan & M. Lee (Eds.), *Under Blue Skies: The Social Construction of Intellectual Disability in Western Australia* (pp. 13–52). Perth: Centre for Disability Research and Development, Faculty of Health and Human Sciences, Edith Cowan University.

Mental Hygiene. New names approved. Sterilisation discussed. (November 30, 1933). *The Argus*, p. 13.

Monk, L. A. (2010). Exploiting patient labour at Kew Cottages, Australia, 1887–1950. *British Journal of Learning Disabilities*, 38, 86–94.

Murdoch, P. (December 6, 1930). Aren't We All. ...?, *The West Australian*, p. 4.

A New Home for the Handicapped in N.S.W. (April, 1965). *Australian Children Limited*, 200.

Newell, C. (1996). The disability rights movement in Australia: A note from the trenches. *Disability & Society*, 11(3), 429–432.

NSW Department of Health, D. o. P. a. R. (1983). *Inquiry into Health Services for the Psychiatrically Ill and Developmentally Disabled*. Sydney: Haymarket, NSW.

Popenoe, P., & Gosney, E. S. (1930). *Sterilization for Human Betterment*. New York, NY: The Macmillan Company.

PROV [Public Records Office of Victoria], (1906–1929). VPRS 892 Department of Education Special Case Files, 102/1196 *Feebleminded*.

Rodwell, G. (1998). 'If the feeble-minded are to be preserved ...': Special education and eugenics in Tasmania 1900–1930. *Issues in Educational Research*, 8(2), 131–156.

Rodwell, G. (2000). Domestic science, race motherhood and eugenics and Australian state schools, 1900–1960. *History of Education Review*, 29(2), 66–83.

Royal Commissioners. (1923). Report of Royal Commission on lunacy law and administration with notes of evidence and appendices. *Joint Volumes of Papers Presented to the [NSW] Legislative Council and Legislative Assembly*, 1, 651–982.

Ryan, J., & Thomas, F. (1980). *The Politics of Mental Handicap*. Harmondsworth: Penguin.

Smith, A. (May 30, 2011). Report reveals burden on cares to hit crisis point, *Sydney Morning Herald*, p. 5.

Snyder, S. L., & Mitchell, D. T. (2006). *Cultural Locations of Disability*. Chicago, IL: University of Chicago Press.

Stainton, T., & McDonagh, P. (2001). Editorial: Chasing shadows: The historical construction of developmental disability. *Journal on Developmental Disabilities*, 8(2), 9–16.

Tremain, S. (2005). Foucault, governmentality, and critical disability theory. in S. Tremain (Ed.), *Foucault and the Government of Disability* (pp. 1–24). Ann Arbor, MI: The University of Michigan Press.

Trent (Jr.), J. W. (1995). *Inventing the Feeble Mind: A History of Mental Retardation in the United States*. Berkeley, CA: University of California Press.

Turtle, A. M. (1993). The short-lived appointment of the first New South Wales government psychologist, Dr Lorna Hodgkinson. *Australian Historical Studies*, 25(101), 569–588.

van Pelt, J. D. (1968). Parent groups for the mentally retarded in America: A report on the organization and functioning of the National Association for Retarded Children at national, state and local levels. Prepared under a 1967 Rosemary F. Dybwad Grant. Canberra, Australia.

Victorian Committee on Mental Retardation. (1977). *Report to the Premier of Victoria*. Melbourne, Australia: Government Printing Office.

Victorian Equal Opportunity & Human Rights Commission. (2012). *Desperate Measures: The Relinquishment of Children with Disability in State Care in Victoria*. Carlton, Victoria: Victorian Equal Opportunity & Human Rights Commission.

Williams, A. K. (1996). Defining and diagnosing intellectual disability in New South Wales 1898 to 1923. *Journal of Intellectual and Developmental Disability*, 21(4), 253–271.

Williams, A. K. (April 27 and 28, 2000). *'A Terrible and Very Persistent Danger:' Eugenic Responses to the 'Feebleminded' in New South Wales, 1900 to 1930*. Paper presented at the History and Sociology of Eugenics Conference, Customs House, Newcastle, New South Wales, Australia.

Williams, A. K. (2003). Assessing the prevalence and exploring the aetiology of intellectual disability in the early twentieth century: The experience of policy and practice in New South Wales. *Journal of Intellectual and Developmental Disability*, 28(1), 40–50.

Wyndham, D. H. (1996). Striving for National Fitness: Eugenics in Australia, 1910s to 1930s. PhD Thesis, The University of Sydney, Sydney, Australia.

19

HISTORY AND NATIONAL POLICY DOCUMENTS ON SPECIAL EDUCATION IN SWEDEN

Kim Wickman and Margaretha Kristoffersson

Special education in Sweden may be said to have been started in connection with the introduction of general elementary education in 1842 (Hjörne and Säljö, 2008). Up to this year only children in the upper and middle classes could go to school, but when general elementary education was introduced in Sweden, all children were given an opportunity to go to school. This in turn contributed to a discussion about how to relate to pupils who were considered deviant and had difficulties in profiting by the teaching (the Swedish National Agency for Education, 2005; Ahlberg, 2007). In the policy document of education, the Elementary Education Ordinance, there was a mini-course for "the children who did not correspond to the concept of normality implicitly defined by the Elementary Education Ordinance, the children whose parents were worst off financially and children described as maladjusted" (the Swedish National Agency for Education, 2005:18). These children were not given any special support in the teaching, and the measures that were taken were that lower knowledge demands were placed on them than on the other pupils. Blind, deaf and intellectually disabled children were in practice completely outside the school system (Ahlberg, 2007).

Around the turn of the century there was a discussion about the presence of pupils with learning disabilities in elementary education. Pupils with learning disabilities were regarded as a disgrace to education, and many teachers argued that the presence of these pupils made the teaching difficult and that it was trying and hampering for other pupils. There was a dominant conception among teachers who thought that the best course of action for everybody would be to separate the pupils with learning disabilities from the other children (Persson, 2007; Ahlberg, 2007).

The discussions continued in the same vein in the early 20th century and the solution was that pupils in need of support were segregated from the ordinary classes. Special schools were established for children with more severe functional disabilities. At this time the scientific view of human beings was spreading, which contributed to medical and biological diagnoses becoming increasingly common for the purpose of distinguishing those who were not considered normal (the Swedish National Agency for Education, 2005). As a part of this development Binet's intelligence test began to be used in the 1920s in order to establish children's ability, which resulted in so-called special solutions being created for some children, and in the early 1940s special classes were organised for pupils with diagnosed impairments (Ahlberg, 2007).

In an attempt to sort this out, a commission was appointed in 1946 to investigate remedial and special education. The result of the investigation was that in the following year a proposal was presented about establishing a state institute for teachers of intellectually disabled pupils and special classes. Sixteen years later, in 1962, a Government bill was submitted on the issue, in which the Government suggested that a state institute for remedial teacher education be founded in Stockholm (Persson, 2009). The special teacher education comprised two semesters and was targeted at pupils considered to be difficult to bring up and with hampered development (Bladini, 2004). The decision to introduce the remedial teacher education may be said to constitute the origin of special education as a knowledge area of its own in Sweden (Persson, 2009).

In the same year, 1962, that the special teacher education was established, primary and lower secondary education was also introduced in Sweden and thereby "Curriculum for primary and lower secondary education 1962", (Lgr 62). In the curriculum it was clearly stated that the teachers should individualise the teaching according to the pupils' different abilities. In spite of this and by means of generous Government grant decisions, the special education expanded and the number of special classes increased for pupils who for various reasons could not keep the same pace as their classmates. The various different special classes could be remedial class, school readiness class, reading class, observation class, hard-of-hearing class, eyesight class and classes for pupils with Celebral Palsy (the Swedish National Agency for Education, 2005; Persson, 2009; Ahlberg, 2007; Österlind, 1998). Pupils attending ordinary classes could also get special support for short periods at various clinics such as speech clinic and reading clinic. The difficulties were seen from a relatively one-sided perspective, as the individual was considered to be the problem (Österlind, 1998).

Seven years after the introduction of primary and lower secondary education, a new curriculum was launched, "Curriculum for primary and lower secondary education 1969", (Lgr 69), in which the importance of integrating pupils with disabilities was emphasised with focus on the learning environment. The pupils with special needs should as far as possible be given support in order to be able to participate in the regular teaching. So-called coordinated special education was introduced, which implied that the teaching could be designed so that the pupils were given individual teaching or teaching in a small group, in parallel with and coordinated with the ordinary teaching (Vernersson, 2007). In spite of this the special education increased above all in mathematics and Swedish. The introduction of the special classes did not have the expected positive effects. This contributed to a change of the view of pupils in need of special support. The difficulties were no longer considered to be related only to the individual, and the perspective was instead widened to taking into consideration the activities of the entire education system and the social context in which the pupils were included (Ahlberg, 2007).

In the new curriculum that was introduced in 1980, "Curriculum for primary and lower secondary education 1980", (Lgr 80), the focus was directed at decreasing and levelling out the differences between the ordinary teaching and the special education. The most central objective was to counteract pupils encountering obstacles or getting into trouble at school (Persson, 2007). It was thus the mission of schools to see to it that the pupils did not have difficulties in the schoolwork. The teaching was to be adapted to all pupils and schools should strive for integrating pupils in need of support in the ordinary classes, which in turn led to a decrease in the number of special classes in schools (the Swedish National Agency for Education, 2005; Ahlberg, 2007). They claimed that education should be available to everybody regardless of difficulties or disabilities.

This became contradictory, since at the same time worry was spreading among Swedish educational authorities about more pupils failing at school. For this reason the Government appointed in 1982 a working party with the task of investigating the causes of so many pupils leaving lower secondary education with incomplete education. The working party submitted the report "*Utslagningen i grundskolan*" ['Failure in primary and lower secondary education'] (SOU, 1983:63), where they stated a number of factors with a governing impact on the work with special education. The next year the National Agency for Education presented the report "*Elever med svårigheter*" ['Pupils with difficulties'], in which it was concluded that schools had difficulties in coping with pupils' educational failures by means of special education (Persson, 2009).

In order to try to solve these problems, the old remedial teacher education was discontinued in 1989 and a new education started in 1990, special educator education. Originally the special teacher education contained four specialisations: complicated learning situation, deafness and hearing impairment, vision impairment and intellectual disabilities. Unlike the remedial teacher education, which was targeted at pupils in need of special support, the special educator should work with three levels, the individual, group and organisation levels. The special educator also had the task of working with learning, educational development and supervision (Bladini, 2004).

In the 1990s great changes took place in the educational system. Education changed from being the state's responsibility to becoming the municipalities' responsibility. A new curriculum was also issued, "*Läroplan för det obligatoriska skolväsendet, förskoleklassen och fritids-hemmet 1994*" ['the Curriculum for the compulsory school system, the pre-school class and the leisure-time centre'] (Lpo 94). It was the first curriculum that was managed by objectives and results (Persson, 2007). Just as in the previous curriculum, it was emphasised in this one that it was the mission of schools to design the teaching on the basis of all pupils' individuality. The pupils' different preconditions and needs should be taken into consideration. Lpo 94 stressed that schools had a special responsibility for the pupils who for various reasons had difficulties in attaining the objectives. This was the first time that an inclusive perspective was included in the policy documents (Ahlberg, 2007).

The introduction of Lpo 94 took place at the same time as a strong recession in the Swedish economy, which did not affect the number of teaching hours. On the other hand, the special education resource decreased by 30 percent, which in turn contributed to pupils in need of special support not getting the help they were entitled to. This was proved by the fact that the number of reports to the National Agency for Education increased considerably (Persson, 2007).

Because of this, the present special educator programme was introduced in 2001, and in 2008 the now valid special educator programme was reintroduced in order to cope with the insufficient knowledge above all of effective methods for early stimulation of children's learning to read and write, and methods for different forms of support for pupils in need of special support. The idea of this programme is that in a working team there should be a remedial teacher working on the basis of her/his competence and a special educator working in a more overarching manner with investigations, educational development and preventive efforts, e.g. through supervision (Malmgren-Hansen, 2002).

In 2012 both a new Education Act and a new curriculum have come into force. The Education Act makes it clear that inclusion is still advocated, as it says:

> Special support may be given instead of the teaching that the pupil would otherwise have participated in or as a complement to this. The special support must be given in the group of pupils to which the pupil belongs unless something else follows from this act or some other ordinance. (Education Act 2010:800, ch. 3 & 7)

The view of inclusion is strengthened through the curriculum, Lgr 11, describing that everybody who works in the schools' activities must contribute to all pupils experiencing affinity and solidarity. The staff of a school must also actively counteract discrimination and insulting treatment of groups or individuals.

The special educator's professional role

Since 1990, when the new special educator education was introduced, there has been confusion about the tasks of the profession, and in the special education context this is a topic that is constantly being discussed (Malmgren-Hansen, 2002; Backlund, 2007). As early as 1991 Skrtic (1991) discussed and analysed the organisation of the practical construction of special education and emphasised the inconsistent conditions in the special educational activities. Skrtic was supported by Blatini (2004), who argued that the professional area of special education is very unclear. Emanuelsson (2000) also argues that the special educator was in a "market" that was full of conflicts due to irreconcilable wishes and expectations from many different actors both within and outside the field of special education. There are consequently many factors that influence the special educators' professional role, e.g. their own and others' expectations, such as those of teachers, other special educators and school managements, as well as influence from the existing educational policies and different discourses concerning the view of normality and deviance (Lansheim, 2010).

In Sweden since the decentralisation reform of 1994 it is the municipalities that are responsible for making decisions on special education, which has created great variation in how special education is organised (Helldin, 1998; Haug 1998). Yet another explanation of the great variation is, according to Haug (1998), that special education itself has a very unclear definition, which in turn contributes to the lack of guidelines for how it should be organised. Persson (2007) argues that it is the school heads and the special educators in the schools that have the responsibility for organising the work so that it guarantees that all pupils, above all pupils in need of special support, are included in the activities. In this connection Bladini (2004) points out that a functioning management organisation that takes responsibility for the governance of the special educational activities is important for schools to succeed in meeting all pupils' needs. The management should see to it, in an active and conscious way, that the special educators have adequate education and are given reasonable conditions for their work and opportunities to use their communicative and educational knowledge (Bladini, 2004; von Ahlefeld Nisser, 2009).

As regards schools' organisation, international research indicates that it is important for the effects of special education. Schools with successful special education are characterised by an organisation consisting of teamwork, cooperative culture and a shared sense of responsibility by all the staff in the school (McLaughlin, 2002; Schulte, 2002; Grosin, 2003). This is well in accord with Swedish research, where Blossing (2003), among others, also thinks that a cooperative school culture is the most desirable state. The cooperative school culture is characterised by cooperation permeating all work and is maintained through continuous communication among the staff. A school head at a typical school with a cooperative culture stands out as a strong leader and good organiser who is visible and available to the teachers, and an expert in educational issues and well up in research (ibid.). The school culture should be characterised by seeing problem solving as something expected. Traditional school cultures where specialised tasks are supposed to correspond to predetermined solutions experience problems when encountering unexpected circumstances (Ainscow, 1999).

Developing a shared professional language is something that several researchers (Bladini, 2004; Colnerud & Granström, 2002; von Ahlefeld Nisser, 2009) emphasise as important for special educators' profession. What is required is that special educators can make practice out of theory and vice versa. Clarifying points of departure, aims and planned measures will make the activities clearer. To achieve this, a developed professional language is required, a meta-language that is something else than the everyday, concrete language (Bladini, 2004; Colnerud & Granström, 2002; Åman, 2006). By using a professional language the special educators can argue and communicate their message and in that way fulfil the requirements existing in the educational context. According to von Ahlefeld Nisser (2009) it is of paramount importance that the special educators find tools for communicating knowledge so that a development and progression of the field will be possible.

Ahlberg (2001) argues that the three most important parts of the special educational work are the establishment of action programmes, supervision and reflective talks, and school improvement work. Rosenqvist (2007) argues, however, that the professional role is above all a matter of teaching, investigating and developmental. A further designation of the so-called three legs is found in the National Agency for Higher Education's evaluation (Högskoleverket, 2006:10), where the special educator's principal tasks are considered to be advisory, supervisory and developing. Since the special educator is a representative of the special educational expertise, Hjörne (2004) argues that it is of paramount importance constantly to reflect, challenge and critically examine one's own practice through professional talks.

Special educators' educational practice and special educators' view of their professional role in primary and lower secondary education

An empirical investigation from the autumn semester of 2011 comprising qualitative interviews with seven special educators and two school heads in a Swedish municipality shows that the view of the special educator's professional role varies and that there are different designs of the task. None of the special educators state that they have a clear job description. This result finds support in Malmgren-Hansen's (2002) and Backlund's (2007) study, which shows that special educational efforts have always varied and that there are differences in how they are used in different schools.

One of the school heads in the study argues that this is due to what role the special educators take on and what role they are assigned by the school head and colleagues. The school head's views are supported by Emanuelsson (2000) and Lansheim (2010), who think that there are many, e.g. the special educators themselves, the teachers and the school management, who have demands on and expectations of the special educator's professional role. The same school head also points out that it is enormously important that the head of the school makes it clear what is included in a special educator's task, which four of the special educators in the present study also emphasise. This is strengthened by Bladini (2004) and von Ahlefeld Nisser (2009) arguing, in accordance with this study's result, that the school management should actively see to it that the special educators are given opportunities to use their communicative and educational knowledge. This implies that the school management together with the special educator has an important task in the design of the special educator's professional role.

As regards the school culture's importance for the view of the special educator's professional role, a clear indication is that one of the special educators states that there is an open, cooperative climate at the school, which facilitates her work. This is in accord with both international and national research, which indicates that schools with successful special education are characterised by a cooperative school culture (McLaughlin, 2002; Schulte, 2002; Grosin, 2003; Blossing, 2003). It is also shown that schools' culture is to some extent important for the special educator's professional role through the interior governance, e.g. the school's way of regarding pupils in need of special support. This might be one of the reasons why all participants in the study look upon special educators as a mixture between remedial teacher and special educator. A valid question is why it is like this, why this is the case when there are now both a remedial teacher education and a special educator education that are supposed to complement each other (Malmgren-Hansen, 2002; Assarsson, 2009; Olsson & Olsson, 2007; Lansheim, 2010).

One answer to the above question might be that the special educators assume the prototype that Lassbo (2006) calls "The Fortress Builder", which means that the special educator started her/his career by working with counselling in accordance with the education, but this was not positively received and the special educator could just as well work as remedial teacher. The answer to the question might also be, as one of the school heads puts it, that the school heads do not make themselves sufficiently clear about how the special educators' competence should be used. This resembles von Ahlefeld Nisser's (2009) statement about there being recruitment staff without knowledge of the special educator role and who therefore think that it is remedial teachers they are looking for. The answer to the question might also be, as the other school head points out, that the present economic situation does not permit the special educators to work as pure special educators.

According to the current educational system a special educator should work close to the activities, chiefly at the individual level (Chiriac, 2009; Malmgren-Hansen, 2002; Assarsson, 2009; Olsson & Olsson, 2007). All special educators work close to the activities, since in their professional role they often teach pupils in various ways. It also turns out that one of the school heads thinks that this is a part of the special educator's commission. This is entirely in line with what previous researchers have found out. Special educators devote a large part of their working hours to

325

remedial teaching (Malmgren-Hansen, 2002; Lansheim, 2010; von Ahlefeld Nisser, 2009), although this is not explicitly mentioned in the Higher Education Ordinance (Högskoleförordningen, 1993:100). On the other hand, it is described in "*Statens offentliga utredningar*" ['the Swedish Government Official Investigations'] (SOU, 1999:63) that special educators in their overarching responsibility for educational activities can work with targeted efforts, which in our opinion might be interpreted as remedial teaching.

Teaching as a part of the special educational professional role is supported by Rosenqvist (2007), who argues that several researchers think that the special educator's commission implies teaching, investigating and developing. Rosenqvist is not supported by the Agency for Higher Education's evaluation (Högskoleverket, 2006:10), since it emphasises that the special educator's chief tasks are to be advisory, supervisory and development. What is then the reason why so many special educators work with teaching? This is remarkable and has great similarities with the so-called co-education that occurred in the late 1960s, which contributed to the increase in remedial teaching (Vernersson, 2007; Persson, 2007; Ahlberg, 2007), which may be due to the test subjects having a compensatory perspective in several respects. The point of departure in the compensatory perspective is to compensate pupils for their problems (Nilholm, 2003). With this as the starting point, we argue that remedial teaching is natural, i.e. compensating the pupils for their difficulties. Another explanation might be that it is in the special educators' own interest to teach pupils, since several of the special educators state that this is the case in their statements and actions. This theory is supported by Lansheim (2010), who argues that educators' prioritisations and actions are governed by personal values and that the special educational commission is seen as an opportunity to work with something that they themselves are interested in.

In addition to teaching, the result shows that tasks such as surveying, investigating and observing are included in the special educators' professional role. A part of this work is to adapt the learning environment and teaching materials and to remove obstacles. This is in accord with several points in the Higher Education Ordinance (Högskoleförordningen, 1993:100). The Ordinance also mentions supervision, and the result shows that talks of different kinds and supervision are large parts of the special educational professional role. These tasks go hand in hand with previous research, which claims that among other things the work implies conducting continual supervisory talks (von Ahlefeld Nisser, 2009; Malmgren-Hansen, 2002; Lansheim, 2010). Malmgren-Hansen further argues that more than half the special educators in her study devote themselves to establishing, implementing and evaluating action programmes, which is also in accord with the result of this study, in which all special educators see this as a part of their professional role.

The result of the study also shows the same thing as previous research in the respect that the special educator's professional role implies being constantly prepared to be able to "turn out", which is stated by all special educators in this study. This study differs, however, in relation to previous studies as regards the importance of constantly being professional and having the same language. In this study three special educators state that it is enormously important always to be professional, while this is not mentioned in von Ahlefeld Nisser's (2009), Malmgren-Hansen's (2002) and Lansheim's (2010) studies. Several other researchers emphasise, however, the importance of the special educator's profession in which a shared professional language is included (Ainscow, 1999; Bladini, 2004; Colnerud & Granström, 2002; Åman, 2006). Ainscow argues that schools that manage in an effective way to treat all pupils act on research-based knowledge and methods. In view of this it is gratifying that the study shows that four of the special educators state that they base their activities on research in their professional role. It is only the school heads and one of the special educators, however, who state that developing the educational activities is included in special educators' professional role. This may be regarded as noteworthy, since in the Government bill *Hälsa, Lärande och Trygghet* ['Health, Learning and Security'] (Prop. 2000/01:14) it is stressed that the special educator must have an important role in schools' change and development work in order to improve the quality of the learning environments.

It might, however, be possible to interpret this as if all special educators in the study work with school improvement without explicitly expressing it, since they state that they work on all school levels. This is in line with the Higher Education Ordinance's (Högskoleförordningen, 1993:100) statement that the special educator should analyse difficulties at the organisation, group and individual levels. These tasks may be interpreted as a part of the preventive work that is emphasised in the Education Act (2010:800, ch. 3 & 7), where it says that the work with pupils' health must be preventive. In the result one of the special educators says that she agrees with this view, as she wishes that she could do more preventive work. As regards pupils' health the result shows that all special educators are members of the schools' pupils' health teams together with the school nurse, the school head, the welfare officer and the psychologist.

Cultural norms and practices – Physical education and sporting experiences of young women with physical impairments

Is Swedish education inclusive and does it comprise inclusive teaching? Are schools able to handle normal variations of differences among children and young people in the subject of physical education and health? Is there any clear boundary between what are regarded as normal variations and what is perceived and understood as so divergent that there is a need for special measures?

Within a physical education (PE) context, it is evident from research that integration and inclusion of disabled students and special educational needs (SEN) has until recently been more or less a non-issue (Smith & Thomas, 2006; Jerlinder, 2010). Mainly, studies have been based on teachers' perceptions (Fitzgerald, Jobling, & Kirk 2003a, b; Fitzgerald, 2005; Coates & Vickerman, 2010; Vickerman, 2012), with little research on exploring children with SEN's perceptions about their experiences of PE (Smith & Thomas, 2006; Vickerman & Coates, 2009; Jerlinder, 2010; Vickerman, 2012). The few studies that have been conducted with a focus on self-perceived experience (see e.g. Goodwin & Watkinson, 2000; Kristén, Patriksson, & Fridlund, 2002) have shown that disabled children with SEN have positive experiences of PE when they are fully included in lessons and are given the ability to improve their social and physical skills. Despite this knowledge Vickerman, Hayes, and Wetherley (2003), Smith and Thomas (2006), and Vickerman (2012) report that disabled children with SEN tend to take part in a narrow range of PE activities compared to their non-disabled peers.

From a gender perspective, there are numerous studies that have shown that PE disadvantages girls, and even some boys, because of its traditional masculine form (Lundvall & Mackbach, 2003; Carli, 2004; Olofsson, 2005) and that co-education PE classes, which are standard in Sweden, disadvantage girls from influencing the subject and receiving higher grades (O'Sullivan, Bush & Gehring, 2002; Carli, 2004; Quennerstedt, Öhman & Eriksson, 2008; Sandahl, 2005). This problem also includes disabled girls (Wickman, 2008, 2011a) but the area is still relatively unexplored. Consequently, disability and gender seem to be crucial factors for successfully including students in general PE.

The pilot project presented in this section represents ongoing work relating to sport both within and outside the school curriculum. In an attempt to visualize barriers to inclusion and to identify the central themes and issues relatable to children with SEN's experiences of PE, this section sets out to direct attention to young women with physical impairments lives and their experiences of sport.

Physical activity for disabled children with SEN

As has been pointed out previously, physical activity has shown to benefit disabled children with SEN psychologically, socially and physiologically (Kristén et al., 2002; Groff, Lundberg, & Zabriskie, 2009). Therefore, including disabled children with SEN in PE lessons is fundamental to mental and physical development and promotes lifelong physical activity (Coates & Vickerman, 2010; Vickerman, 2012). In contrast to these positive findings reported above, research also shows that when disabled children with SEN are not fully included, they commonly experience PE from a negative point of view. Illustrative examples of exclusion are for instance bullying by peers, restricted access to activities and lack of differentiation from teachers (Goodwin & Watkinson, 2000). Furthermore, children have stated that teachers of PE did not modify their lessons to accommodate their needs, resulting in negative experiences of PE and/or complete exclusion from lessons (Blinde & McCallister, 1998; Goodwin & Watkinson, 2000).

Owing to the fact that there is a close connection in Sweden between organized sport and schools' sport activities and the fact that Swedes devote a large part of their leisure time to participating in various sports at both the competition and the exercise level, there is among many teachers (Larsson, 2009) and students (Engström, 2010) a strong connection to organized sport and its norms and values, which also has an impact on schools' sport activities (Olofsson, 2002, Annerstedt, 2008, Lundvall & Meckbach, 2008). Swedish and international research shows, however, that disabled children and young people are excluded from sport contexts (Vickerman et al., 2003; Wickman, 2011a, b) and that the dropouts are more frequent among disabled children and young people than among non-disabled people of the same age (Trondman, 2005). This implies that disabled children and young people are not offered equal opportunities to develop the "silent knowledge", such as sport skills, manifestations and concepts, which are conveyed within organized sport generally and within individual sports and associations specifically. Such "silent knowledge" is more or less a prerequisite for the individual's communication and interaction with teachers and peers and is relevant to the individual's ability to position herself/himself within a PE context. Sport on equal terms is hence still a goal but not yet a reality in Swedish sport (Wickman, 2011a).

Method and data collection

This pilot study draws on data from semi-structured interviews with five young women with physical impairments. The interviews were conducted in February and March 2012. All participants attending in this study were between 17 and 28 years of age and were all from Swedish middle-class families. The interviews were carried out on the telephone in all cases, except one which was carried out face-to-face. All of the interviewees had extensive experiences of sports on different levels and of physical education and of organized sports in their leisure time. All of the interviewees had varying degrees of impairments. The women were asked to choose where the interview would take place and each woman was interviewed privately for 55–60 minutes. After the interviews were conducted and transcribed, the interviewees had the opportunity to review the transcripts and make corrections or additions. These procedures are accepted among qualitative researchers (Kvale, 1996; Gratton & Jones, 2004). The interview questions were designed to allow the interviewees to talk about issues they felt were important to their own involvement in sport.

In the present pilot study attention is thus directed towards young women with physical impairments and their experiences of sport within and outside school activities. The disadvantage of interviewing young adults about what it is like to be a child in a particular context is, on the one hand, that the child's way of expressing itself and of rendering what happens in real time cannot be captured. On the other hand, the advantage might be that with some distance to previous experiences the narrative can take place without direct influence from the power relationships between the student/child and teacher/adult.

These findings have been organized in the following themes: 1) *Discrimination and exclusion,* 2) *Feelings of self-doubt,* 3) *To be confirmed.*

Direct quotes from interviewees (identified by pseudonyms) are used to illustrate the various themes and concepts from the interviews.

Discrimination and exclusion

As previous research has described many disabled children and young people have experiences of discrimination and exclusion. This is also something that all the *interviewees* have experienced:

> In lower secondary school I was not allowed to take part, or my teacher she told me that I couldn't take part because I sat in a wheelchair and then she would not be able to grade me /.../ I was of course terribly sorry because I felt that I wanted to be with the class and she said that I could have physical education alone with her. I said that it wouldn't develop me... something like that. So we sent a mail to her and my mother called her. I had like two lessons alone with her and I thought it was terribly boring... but then I also said "please can't I be allowed to prove who I am, you don't even know... to 100% who I am, it feels as if you are discriminating against me". Then I was allowed to be with the class and in the end I got a Pass with Distinction. (Vilma, 20)

Sports days are a further example of sports contexts where the interviewees have experienced isolation:

> In lower and upper primary school I was almost always at home on sports days; I thought it was very boring because I wanted of course to be with the others /.../ my friends asked where I was but then I had to say that they hadn't arranged anything for me. But in lower secondary school and high school I took part in the sports days because then I was in a wheelchair class. It was not until then that they [the teachers] organized it and that I felt that I was secure. (Maja, 19)

As the above quotations show a clear norm appears, i.e. that schools' sports activities are adapted to non-disabled students with a sports background. Based on the quotation above, it is more or less up to the students themselves to find solutions to what is regarded as a "problem", namely the students' lack of preconditions for taking part in the ordinary teaching. The above quotations also show the experience of isolation and separation that the students express when they are forced to abstain from fellowship and participation in the relation to their classmates. The support from understanding adults is important in both cases in order for the students to be confirmed and strengthened in their self-esteem. Several of the interviewees also express a feeling of insecurity in connection with the sports lessons, since they seldom know in advance what activity will take place, how the lesson is organized and whether they can participate on the same conditions as their classmates.

Feelings of self-doubt

Maja, who experienced isolation and mobbing during her first 3 years in primary school, chose to change to a class that was especially adapted to students with physical impairments.

> The worry was there, or it had a very negative effect on me. So I became very insecure; even if it had sorted itself out a little, it was still as if I backed out because I was so insecure. But then it was completely different when I began to feel more secure...in the wheelchair class and all that. /.../ My assistant that I had then she always took my side and said "but it will sort itself out, it's OK. I can talk to the teacher." And then I felt secure... in her like. (Maja, 19)

Maja's pedagogical and social participation in the PE lessons improved considerably when changed to a class with other students with motor impairments. In the social context she was successively given an opportunity to strengthen her self-esteem again with support from her personal assistant. Maja's story also shows the importance of adult support for creating security in a learning situation.

Elina's impairment meant that she could move without a wheelchair for short periods. In connection with the PE lessons she chose to take part without a wheelchair, although this resulted in her getting a lot of pain in her body after the lessons:

> I felt it when I was in primary and lower secondary school, because I remember that I sat in a wheelchair a few times. Then it was as if everybody looked strangely

at me, so that's why I stopped doing it. And it has also been like that now in high school in my class; they have looked at me when I've sat in a wheelchair and that, and they've also looked at me when I've stood up and walked. (Elina, 19)

Moa says that all physical activity she took part in during her schooldays was motivated by rehabilitation purpose. Experiencing social fellowship in sports contexts or choosing an activity because it seemed exciting and fun was never an option. Joy and physical activity were incompatible things to her; everything was more or less physiotherapy. She quickly learned to do as the adults in her environment said without questioning or initiating suggestions of her own, which had a negative effect on herself-esteem:

.... and if I fail, I think, "well, okay, just as usual." I don't think it was an isolated occurrence, but I function in a somewhat different way than others. And then one has a little more to work against. So one probably has to think in a somewhat different way. I mean, I won't put the bar too high, because then I'm just nasty to myself. (Moa, 29)

To be confirmed

Being seen and confirmed not only because of one's functional disability is mentioned by several of the interviewees. Vilma and Elina express this in the following way:

Because the worst thing I know is to be given special treatment /.../ I don't want anyone to coddle me or go on like that, but I still want them [the teachers] to show understanding of what a person wants and sit down with the person and go through the syllabus and maybe the sports timetable, if it concerns sport, and be there and encourage the person, even if one is in a class full of walking persons, that they can care about the competence of somebody sitting in a wheelchair /.../ But not to make a lot of demands on the person in the wheelchair, because it's psychologically terribly tough to have to feel all the time that you cannot relax, because they have to think up all sorts of things. (Vilma, 20)

I think it's important that the teacher sees all individuals and understands that they have not all got the same prerequisites. Then they must try to adapt so that everybody can take part. I felt that when I was in the first year at high school, I think it was. Then I had PE with my class and that PE teacher didn't see me; I mean he ignored me and went through his lesson with the class. I remember that they played soccer and I took part... and I sat in a wheelchair and it doesn't work. It's a bit difficult to play soccer if you are sitting in a wheelchair, but the teacher didn't see it. So I suppose it's such occurrences that have irritated me quite a lot. (Elina, 19)

Lisa talks about when she was confirmed in connection with a floorball match and how important this was for her self-esteem:

... one thing that makes me happy even now, it's one of the last floorball matches we took part in, and I was appointed the team's player that day. And

331

that our coach asked 'where the hell have you been all my life". I think that was great. From hardly being noticed on the floor to being appointed the team's player, that's an enormously big step, because I never managed really to score a goal, and things like that. I suppose I was... I tried hard but was still careful. (Lisa, 28)

Conclusion

All the interviewees experienced exposure in relation to school sport and in connection with the lessons. Above all this was about the teacher's lack of ability to adapt the teaching to the student's needs, the student's lack of self-esteem, the feeling of being a nuisance and the insecurity about lessons, since planning in advance and informing the student about the prerequisites were lacking. The interviewees also point out insufficient access to sports aids. It is important to emphasize here that it is not the sports activities in themselves that are experienced as problematic but the circumstances around them.

Some of them experienced the separation from the rest of the student group as very difficult: difficult to be separated for reasons not clearly stated by the teacher. Some interviewees described how they later on in their turn were forced to explain to the other students why they could not participate. The sports days are one example when the students either had to stay at home or to do something completely different from their classmates.

The fact that sport and performance are associated with the non-disabled body contributes to the disabled body often being perceived and understood as if it does not really fit into the sports context. Such normative ideas also influence the acceptance inclination, i.e. who is given access to the sports context. According to the interviewees the teachers had no clear expectations of the student's sports performance. Some of the interviewees seem to have had the most positive experiences of sport outside the school activities.

Several of them also mention advantages of and problems with the assistant's presence. The assistant as a secure present adult – the assistant as an obstacle in the fellowship with the classmates – the assistant as a link between the student and the teacher. It is obvious that the interviewees experience the isolation more tangibly in connection with the subject of PE than in other school subjects. It seems as if the interviewees have rather been in a situation that they have experienced as insulting and discriminating and have very seldom expressed criticism of what they have experienced as wrong. Taken together, the narratives give the impression that the interviewees have had a relatively tough time at school with demands and expectations that they have had difficulty living up to. All the interviewees also state that they were anxious not to worry their parents about their situation in school.

Discussion

In all Nordic countries it has been democratically decided to develop "education for all" (Haug, 1998; Emanuelsson, Persson, & Rosenqvist, 2001; Nilholm, 2003). The basic idea is that all children should have access to educational activities. In the last decade the Swedish state and the civil society have raised increasingly high demands on education to work more actively with *the UN convention on the rights of the child* (the child convention) in order to live up to the political goals and in particular to make visible children with functional impairments (Skolverket, 2007). Such an example is the new Education Act, which among other things strengthens children's legal security. Another example is the strategy for implementing the disability policy in Sweden 2011–2016, the purpose of which is to visualize the concentration of the policy on concrete goals, efforts and results. This implies that all students, regardless of impairment or development levels, are to be offered education in the nearest school together with the other students (SOU, 1974:53). With such an approach, scope is to be given for diversity and variation among the students. The school as an institution is thereby expected via the teachers to adapt the environment, the methods and the pedagogy to all students, rather than that the students should adapt themselves to the school (see also DePauw & Doll-Tepper, 2000; Vickerman, 2012). However, in these new times some critical voices may suggest that such developments have not changed practices in school subjects such as PE, which continue to disadvantage many young people, including disabled girls and boys with SEN (Trondman, 2005; Jerlinder, 2010). The Swedish Schools Inspectorate is a supervisory authority with the task of examining schools and assessing applications for running independent schools. In a recent report (2012:5) the results are presented of a national supervisory quality control with emphasis on school heads and schools' activities for teaching PE in grades 4–6. The report points out the need for teachers of PE to develop more work to translate the curriculum and the syllabus content in teaching. Further, teachers need to be more proactive in preventing and identifying abusive behavior in connection with the PE lessons. Obviously, there is a discrepancy between what the policy documents say the programs should offer and what is actually offered (Sandahl, 2005; Ekberg, 2009; Jerlinder, 2010; Wickman, 2011a).

As observed initially in this chapter, special education is a complex knowledge area containing several different approaches and perspectives. It is thus both a research area and a sphere of activity (Jakobsson & Nilsson, 2011). Traditionally a part of the core of special education has consisted of describing and categorizing different kinds of deviations from what is regarded as normal. The special educational activities are therefore designed differently, depending on the outlook on human beings and knowledge that is prevalent in a society. From an overarching point of view it might be said that special educational issues are about normality and segregation, participation and learning, power and responsibility and consequences of different approaches and perspectives. Thus, in this setting the people, curriculum and organization all have a role to play in embedding and reproducing cultural norms and practices (Kirk & Colquhoun, 1998; Davis & Watson, 2001; Fitzgerald & Kirk, 2009).

There are great shortcomings in the treatment of disabled students with SEN. Meetings between people do not happen unaffected by the prevalent values in society, which is also important for the individual's contacts with sport. It is among other things a matter of how education and the sports movement through rules, categorization, resource allocation, access measures and general values maintain or actively work for a change of the environments and contexts that exclude young disabled people. The treatment is a concern not only for young disabled people, their parents or custodians. It is a democracy issue that concerns everybody. The goal should be to strengthen the individual's self-determination, influence and integrity, and facilitate participation and equality. The treatment of young disabled people in the sports practice includes both parties' expectations of the meeting. They often have different perspectives because their knowledge and experiences differ. The individual, most often a parent or custodian of a disabled girl or boy, bases her/his view on the child's preconditions, while coaches and leaders in organized sport base theirs on the rules, norms, values and conceptions that are prevalent in the given social and cultural context where they are active. These differences in perspectives are of great importance for the quality of the treatment. There must therefore exist a will from both parties to create preconditions jointly for practicing sport without the ultimate responsibility being shifted from schools and the sports movement to the child, its parents or custodians.

There is a risk that activities for young disabled people fall between two stools. It is the adults close to the children that must give them active support and take responsibility for the rights given by the child convention. Thereby it is important for education and the sports movement to think about and make plain to all, teachers, leaders, parents and students how the child perspective should be interpreted and understood in relation to their own activities. What is written in the convention texts and the schools' and sports activities' own policy documents must therefore be concretized so that they have an impact on the sports practice.

References

Ahlberg, A. (2001). *Lärande och delaktighet.* [Learning and participation]. Lund, Sweden: Studentlitteratur.

Ahlberg, A. (2007). Specialpedagogik – ett kunskapsområde i utveckling.[Special Education - an area of knowledge in development]. in Nilholm, C. & Björck-Åkesson, E. (Eds.), *Reflektioner kring specialpedagogik—Sex professorer om forskningsområdet och forskningsfronterna. Vetenskapsrådets rapportserie* 5 (pp. 66–84). Stockholm, Sweden: *Vetenskapsrådets.*

Ainscow, M. (1999). *Understanding the Development of Inclusive Schools.* New York, NY: Routledge Falmer.

Åman, K. (2006). *Ögonblickets pedagogik. Yrkesgrupper i samtal om specialpedagogisk kompetens vid barn- och ungdomshabiliteringen.* [Moment of Pedagogy. Professional Groups in Discussions on Specialist Teacher Training in Child and Youth Habilitation]. Stockholm, Sweden: Stockholms universitet.

Annerstedt, C. (2008).Physical education in Scandinavia with a focus on Sweden: A comparative perspective. *Physical Education and Sport Pedagogy,* 13(4), 303–318.

Assarsson, I. (2009). *Utmaningar i en skola för alla—Några filosofiska trådar.* [Challenges in Education for All—Some Philosophical Topics]. Stockholm, Sweden: Liber.

Backlund, Å. (2007). *Resurser, organisering och praktik.* [Resources, Organization and Practice]. Akademisk avhandling. Stockholm, Sweden: Stockholms universitet. Institutionen för socialt arbete.

Bladini, K. (2004). *Handledning som verktyg och rum för reflektion—En studie av specialpedagogers handledningssamtal.* [Supervision as a Tool and Space for Reflection—A Study of Tutoring Call for Special Educators]. Karlstad, Sweden: Karlstads universitet.

Blinde, E. & McCallister, S.(1998). Listening to the voices of students with physical disabilities. *Journal of Physical Education, Recreation and Dance,* 69(6), 64–68.

Blossing, U. (2003). *Skolförbättring i praktiken.* [School Improvement in Practice]. Lund, Sweden: Studentlitteratur.

Carli, B. (2004). *The making and breaking of a female culture. The history of Swedish physical education 'in a different voice'*. Dissertation. Göteborg, Sweden: Acta Universitatis Gothoburgensis.

Chiriac, E. (2009). *Släpp tankarna loss—Det är nytt, Kvalitetsgranskning av ett reformarbete: ny speciallärarutbildning*. [Let the Thoughts Away – It's New, Quality Review of a Reform: New Special Teacher Training]. Linköping, Sweden: Linköpings universitet, LIU-tryck.

Coates, J. & Vickerman, P. (2010). Empowering children with special educational needs to speak up: Experiences of inclusive physical education. *Disability and Rehabilitation*, 32(18), 1517–1526.

Colnerud, G. & Granström, K. (2002). *Respekt för läraryrket. Om lärares yrkesspråk och yrkesetik.* [Respect for the Teaching Profession. If Teachers' Professional Language and Professional Ethics]. Stockholm, Sweden: HLS Förlag.

Davis, J.M. & Watson, N. (2001) Where are the children's experiences? Analysing social and cultural exclusion in "special" and "mainstream" schools. *Disability and Society*, 16(5), 671–687.

DePauw, K. & Doll-Tepper, G. (2000). Toward progressive inclusion and acceptance. Myth or reality? The inclusion debate and bandwagon discourse. *Adapted Physical Activity Quarterly*, 17, 135–143.

Ekberg, L.-E. (2009). *Mellan fysisk bildning och aktivering—en studie om ämnet idrott och hälsa i skolår 9.* [Between the Physical Formation and Activation - a Study of Physical Education in School Year 9, not available in English]. PhD thesis. Malmö Studies in Educational Science. Malmö, Sweden: Malmö högskola.

Emanuelsson, I. (2000). *Specialpedagogen på marknaden, Att undervisa, År 2000.* [Special Educator in the Market, Teaching in Year 2000] (no. 5, pp. 6–9). Stockholm, Sweden: Liber.

Engström, L.M. (2010). *Smak för motion. Fysisk aktivitet som livsstil och social markör.* [Taste for Exercise. Physical Activity as a Lifestyle and Social Marker, not available in English]. Stockholm, Sweden: Stockholm University.

Fitzgerald, H. & Kirk, D. (2009). Identity work: Young disabled people, family and sport. *Leisure Studies*, 28(4), 469–488.

Goodwin, L. & Watkinson, J. (2000). Inclusive physical education from the perspectives of students with physical disabilities. *Adapted Physical Activity Quarterly*, 17, 144–160.

Gratton, C. & Jones, I. (2004). *Research methods for sport studies*. London, UK: Routledge.

Groff, D., Lundberg, N. & Zabriskie, R. (2009). Influence of adapted sport on quality of life: Perceptions of athletes with cerebral palsy. *Disability and Rehabilitation*, 31(4), 318–326.

Grosin, L. (2003). *Forskning om framgångsrika skolor som grund för skolutveckling*. In Berg, G. & Scherp H.-Å (Eds.), *Skolutvecklingens många ansikten*. [Research on Successful Schools as a Basis for School Improvement]. Stockholm, Sweden: Myndigheten för Skolutveckling.

Haug, P. (1998). *Pedagogiskt dilemma : Specialundervisning*. [Teaching Dilemma: Special Education]. Stockholm, Sweden: Skolverket.

Helldin, R. (1998). *Kommunerna och den specialpedagogiska verksamheten. Nutid och framtid.* [Municipalities and Special Needs Education. Present and Future]. Stockholm, Sweden: HLS Förlag.

Hjörne, E. (2004). *Excluding for Inclusion? Negotiating School Careers and Identities in Pupil Welfare Settings in the Swedish School.* Göteborg Studies in Educational Sciences 213.

Högskoleverket (2006:10) *Utvärdering av specialpedagogprogrammet vid svenska universitet och högskolor.* Rapport 2006: 10R. [Evaluation of Special Education Program at Swedish Universities]. Stockholm, Sweden: Högskoleverket.

Jakobsson, I.-L. & Nilsson, I. (2011). *Specialpedagogik och funktionshinder* [Special Education and Disability, not available in English]. Stockholm, Sweden: Natur och Kultur.

Jerlinder, K. (2010). *Social rättvisa i inkluderande idrottsundervisning för elever med rörelsehinder: en utopi?* [Social Justice in Inclusive Physical Education for Pupils with Physical Disabilities—Reality or Utopia?, not available in English]. PhD thesis. Örebro, Sweden: Örebro universitet.

Kirk, D. & Colquhoun, D. (1998). Health and physical education. *British Journal of Sociology of Education*, 10(4), 417–434.

Kristén, L., Patriksson, G. & Fridlund, B.(2002). Conceptions of children and adolescents with physical disabilities about their participation in a sports programme. *European Physical Education Review*, 8, 139–156.

Kvale, S. (1996). *Interviews. An introduction to qualitative research interviewing*. London, UK: Sage Publications.

Lansheim, B. (2010). *Förståelser av uppdraget specialpedagog. Blivande och nyblivna specialpedagogers yrkeslivsberättelser*. Malmö Studies in Educational Sciences: Licentiate Dissertation Series 2010:14, Malmö högskola. [Understandings of the mission special education. New and expectant special educators career stories]. Malmö: Holmbergs.

Larsson, L. (2009). *Idrott – och helst lite mer idrott. Idrottslärarstudenters möte med utbildningen*. [Sport – and Preferably a Little More Sporting. Sports Teacher Students' Meeting with Education, not available in English]. Dissertation. Studies in Education in Arts och Professions 1, Stockholm, Sweden: Stockholm University.

Lassbo, G. (2006). *It Takes Two to Tango. The professional identity formation processes of Swedish Special Educators in the early 21st century*. Göteborg, Sweden: Göteborg University.

Lundvall, S. & Meckbach, J. (2003). *Ett ämne i rörelse. Gymnastik för kvinnor och män i lärarutbildningen vid Gymnastiska Centralinstitutet/Gymnastik- och idrottshögskolan under åren 1944 till 1992*. [Movement in motion. The subject of gymnastics in the physical education teachertraining programme at the Royal Central Institute of Gymnastics/Stockholm College of Physical Education and Sports during the years 1944 to 1992]. PhD thesis. Stockholm, Sweden: HLS Förlag.

Lundvall, S. & Meckbach, J. (2008), Mind the gap: Physical education and health and the frame factor theory as a tool for analyzing educational settings. *Physical Education & Sport Pedagogy*, 13(4), 345–364.

Malmgren-Hansen, A. (2002). *Specialpedagoger - nybyggare i skolan*.[Special Educators -Settlers in the School]. Stockholm, Sweden: Högskoleförlaget Stockholm.

McLaughlin, M. (2002). Examining special and general education collaborative practices in exemplary schools. *Journal of Educational and Psychological Consultation*, 13, 279–283.

Nilholm, C.(2003). *Perspektiv på specialpedagogik*. [Perspectives on Special Education, not available in English]. Lund, Sweden: Studentlitteratur.

Olofsson, E. (2002). RF och kvinnorna. in Lindroth, J. & Norberg, J. R. (Eds.), *Ett idrottssekel - Riksidrottsförbundet 1903–2000* [The Swedish Sports Confederation and the Women, not available in English] (pp. 379–395). Stockholm, Sweden: Informationsförlaget.

Olofsson, E. (2005). The discursive construction of gender in physical education in Sweden, 1945–2003: Is meeting the learner's needs tantamount to meeting the market's needs? *European Physical Education Review*, 3, 219–238.

Olsson, B.-I. & Olsson, K. (2007). *Att se möjligheter i svårigheter. Barn och ungdomar med koncentrationssvårigheter*. [To See Opportunity in Difficulty. Children and Adolescents with Attention Deficit]. Lund, Sweden: Studentlitteratur.

O'Sullivan, M., Bush, K. & Gehring, M. (2002) Gender equity and physical education: A USA perspective. In Penney, D. (Ed.), *Gender and Physical Education: contemporary issues and future directions*. London, UK: Routledge, 163–189.

Österlind, E. (1998). *Disciplinering via frihet*. [Disciplining Through Freedom]. Uppsala, Sweden: Uppsala universitet.

Persson, B. (2007). Specialpedagogik—Svensk specialpedagogik vid vägskäl eller vägs ände? In Nilholm, C. & Björck-Åkesson, E. (Eds.), *Reflektioner kring specialpedagogik*. [Special Education - Swedish Special Education, at the Crossroads or the End of the Road?]. Stockholm, Sweden: Vetenskapsrådet.

Persson, B. (2009). Finns det en specialpedagogisk agenda? - Om utbildningspolitik och elever i behov av särskilt stöd. *Kritisk utbildningstidskrift.* [Is There a Special Education Agenda? – About Education Policy and Pupils with Special Educational Needs]. 4,11–27.

Quennerstedt, M., Öhman, M. & Eriksson, C. (2008). Physical education in Sweden—A national evaluation, Education-line. Available on the Internet: http://www.leeds.ac.uk/educol/documents/169508.pdf/.

Regeringens proposition 2000/01:14; Healt, Learning and Security. Stockholm, Sweden: Utbildningsdepartementet.

Rosenqvist, J. (2007). Några aktuella specialpedagogiska forskningstrender. in Nilholm, C. & Björck-Åkesson, E. (Eds.), (2007). *Reflektioner kring specialpedagogik—Sex professorer om forskningsområdet och forskningsfronterna. Vetenskapsrådets rapportserie 5* (pp. 36–47). [Some Current Special Education Research Trends].

Sandahl, B. (2005). *Ett ämne för alla? Normer och praktik i grundskolans idrottsundervisning 1962-2002.* [A Subject for All? Norms and Practices in Elementary School and Physical Education from 1962 to 2002, not available in English]. Stockholm, Sweden: Carlssons Bokförlag.

Schulte, A. (2002). Moving from abstract to concrete descriptions of good schools for children with disabilities. *Journal of Educational and Psychological Consultation,* 13, 393–403.

SFS (1993:100) Högskoleförordning [Higher education ordinance]. Available on the Internet: http://www.notisum.se/rnp/sls/lag/19930100.HTM [Retrieved 11.04.04].

SFS. (2010:800). Public Law. Skollagen. Stockholm: Swedish Code of Statutes.

Swedish National Agency for Education. (2005). *Ökat inflytande med individuella utvecklingsplaner.* [Increased influence of individual development, not available in English]. Stockholm, Sweden: Fritzes.

Swedish National Agency for Education. (2007). *Kategorisering av elever med funktionshinder i Skolverkets arbete.* [Categorization of Disabled Students in The Swedish National Agency for Education's Work, not available in English]. Stockholm, Sweden. PM 2007-11–26.

Skrtic, T.M. (1991). *Behind special education.* Denver, CO: Love Publishing Company.

Smith, A. & Thomas, N. (2006). Including pupils with special education needs and disabilities in National Curriculum Physical Education: A brief review. *European Journal of Special Needs Education,* 21(1), 69–83.

SOU. (1974:53). *Skolans arbetsmiljö.* [The Work Environments in School, not available in English]. Stockholm, Sweden: Utbildningsdepartementet [Ministry of education and research].

SOU. (1999:63). *Att lära och leda: En lärarutbildning i samverkan och utveckling: Lärarutbildningskommitténs slutbetänkande.* [Learning and Leading: The Teacher Training in Cooperation and Development: Teacher Training Committee's Final Report, not available in English]. Stockholm, Sweden: Utbildningsdepartementet.

Trondman, M. (2005). *Unga och föreningsidrotten.* [Young People in the Sport Organization, not available in English]. Stockholm, Sweden: Ungdomsstyrelsens skrifter.

Vernersson, I.-L. (2007). *Specialpedagogik i ett inkluderande perspektiv.*[Special Education in an Inclusive Perspective]. Lund, Sweden: Studentlitteratur.

Vickerman, P. (2012). Including children with special educational needs in physical education: Has entitlement and accessibility been realised? *Disability & Society,* 27(2), 249–262

Vickerman, P. & Coates, J. (2009). Trainee and recently qualified physical education teachers perspectives on including children with special educational needs. *Journal of Physical Education and Sport Pedagogy,* 14(2), 137–153.

Vickerman, P., Hayes, S. & Wetherley, A. (2003). Special educational needs and national curriculum physical education. in Hayes, S. & Stidder, G. (Eds.), *Equity in Physical Education* (pp. 47–65). London, UK: Routledge.

von Ahlefeld Nisser, D. (2009). *Vad kommunikation vill säga: En iscensättande studie om specialpedagogers yrkesroll och kunskapande samtal.* [What Communication is: A Staging Study of Special Educators Professional Role and Expertise on Communication]. Akademisk avhandling. Stockholm, Sweden: Stockholms universitet.

Wickman, K. (2011a). *Flickor och pojkar med funktionsnedsättning och deras rättigheter och möjligheter till ett aktivt idrottsliv.* [Disabled Girls and Boys and Their Rights and Opportunities for an Active Sports Life, not available in English]. In Norberg, J. & Pihlblad, J. (Eds.), *För barnets bästa: En antologi om idrott ur ett barnrättsperspektiv.* Stockholm, Sweden: Centrum för idrottsforskning.

Wickman, K. (2011b). The governance of sport, gender and (dis)ability. *International Journal of Sport Policy,* 3(3), 385–399.

20

THE ITALIAN PATH TO SCHOOL AND SOCIAL INCLUSION: PROBLEMS, STRENGTHS AND PERSPECTIVES

Teresa Maria Sgaramella, Laura Nota, Lea Ferrari,
Salvatore Soresi and Aamir Khan

Introduction

In the last few decades, the field of disability studies has adopted a perspective that emphasizes psychological, social, and environmental considerations. This newer way of thinking contrasts with traditional conceptualizations of disability, which focus on characteristics of the human body and on medical intervention. The World Health Organization played an important role in this change with the publication of its *International Classification of Functioning, Disability and Health* (ICF; WHO, 2001). By suggesting a positive approach to disability and emphasizing activities persons with or without *impairments* are able to perform within their environments, levels of effective participation and quality of life for persons with disabilities have improved (Soresi, Nota, & Wehmeyer, 2011).

In our view, participation is one of the most important constructs within the broader term *quality of life*, and there is a significant relationship between the two. Participation refers to the degree of involvement a person has in everyday life situations concerning health, body conditions and functioning, and activities that one is able to perform within specific contextual factors (WHO, 2001). Quality of life is a construct that involves familial and professional relationships, economic well-being, quality of both rehabilitation and living environments, competencies and adaptability, the degree to which the possibility to benefit from education and leisure time activities exists, autonomy, independence and decision-making, and the degrees to which effective participation in social life and control over one's personal life exist (Schalock, Bonham, & Verdugo, 2008; Schalock & Verdugo, 2002).

Participation and quality of life call for living in less restrictive contexts and experiencing the various contexts of what is considered to be a normal life. Both of these constructs (participation and quality of life) call for inclusion. This implies *living with, and acting and making decisions together with others in the community*. These constructs require a guarantee of the right to be included, which involves definitively extinguishing the risk of segregation. This may be achieved by taking necessary steps to ensure that relevant supports are provided to persons with severe disabilities. More specifically, these steps involve providing access to supports that guarantee people with severe disabilities can participate and make decisions in a manner as similar to persons without such disabilities as possible.

In Italy, achieving these goals has involved navigating a difficult and steep slope. Although we can now affirm that inclusion is guaranteed at a legal or legislative level, there are still "pockets" of institutionalization that exist in Italy to this day.

In the first part of our analysis, we will examine the historical context of this discussion. More specifically, we will summarize the contributions of some of the "pioneers" who have facilitated the first "public" experiences of education for persons with disabilities in Italy at the end of the nineteenth century. We will then analyse the process of change within the *culture of disability*, arriving at some of the current challenges and issues we are now facing in Italy in terms of maintaining high levels of inclusion for people with disabilities. Ways in which these problems create difficulties in facilitating further improvements in participation and quality of life as experienced by persons with disabilities will also be discussed (Soresi, 2007).

From the end of the nineteenth to the twentieth century

During the last decades of the nineteenth century, after the Risorgimento concluded and Italy unified as a whole nation, several problems associated with specific areas of societal organization had to be solved. These included slow development of a democratic vision of the state, the first forms of industrialization and a consistent gap between North and South in this development, and finally the rise of farmers and workers revolts.

From a cultural point of view there has historically been a clear paternalistic pattern of progress, which is limited to a generic invitation to fraternity, equality, and understanding of subordinate classes (Guglielmino, 1982). Based on this paradigm, the tendency to consider persons with mental health problems and/or disabilities as people who should be kept isolated due to perceived high levels of needed care has been prevalent. This model historically resulted in real and complete social exclusion. Persons with disabilities were not recognized as possessing their own rights, but as people who should be kept away from the rest of society because they were "un-useful" in terms of education, employment, and family life. Based on this line of thinking, many institutes for the permanent placement of people who were deemed un-useful were established. These places were built in order to house people who were poor, vagrants, criminals, and persons with mental health problems or disabilities. Within these institutions, people were confined and subjected to severe isolation. The same mechanisms that characterized isolation towards people with leprosy – considered as a social scourge, hence individuals affected by it had to be excluded from society – were extended to these newly outcast individuals. People who were housed in this system were relegated to a condition of social exclusion and a strict separation from civil and religious society.

The contributions of Maria Montessori (1870–1952) were a turning point in this historical path. In fact, thanks to the "experimental observations" conducted mainly by Montessori in Italy and, later on, in the rest of Europe and North America, the idea that many of those children (for whom education was considered useless) could learn if properly stimulated began to take shape. Remarkable improvements in the autonomy and skill levels of children receiving this form of intervention were noted, and results began to spread. Montessori was the first in Italy to show that children with severe intellectual impairments could achieve relevant results in reading, writing, and practical skills. This strengthened the idea that the way disability was conceptualized and treated could remarkably alter how it (disability) existed in society as a phenomenon. Montessori's most famous book, *The Method of Scientific Psychology*, was translated into English in the United States in 1912, 3 years after the Italian edition was published. This book received a great deal of international attention. Maria Montessori accepted the central idea of Séguin's proposal, namely that medical diagnosis could and should be overcome and not ignored. Séguin had pointed to education as a method leading to partial or total recovery from the effects and consequences of intellectual impairment. Montessori's view of special education, which was also anchored in paradigms of experimental research, was seen as a form of "social medicine" and was widely used as a reference point for many institutions and experts involved in the treatment of disability.

In 1907, Montessori opened the first *Casa dei bambini* (Children's home), where she applied a new model of nursery school based on an environment in which both furniture and educational tools were child friendly. Activities suggested for children were based on spontaneity and creativity. The teacher's task was to provide help and feedback and to reinforce children without using traditional methods (such as punishment). The goal was to create an environment that fostered intellectual and social development guided by the principles of inclusion.

First half of the twentieth century: The segregation period

In the broader Italian context, the first decades of the twentieth century were characterized by the uneven development of Italy as a nation. The Northern region, in particular, required military and economic investments and the strengthening of communications, which stimulated the idea of Italy as a rising international power. There were, however, frequent cultural tensions as well as economic and political uncertainties. Within this context, Italy, like much of the rest of the world, had no public safeguards for persons with mental health problems or disabilities. People in these circumstances could rely only on some minimal forms of care and assistance provided by various charities and organizations. These social programs were created in several areas of the country, almost exclusively by religious organizations.

Regarding education specifically, officials in several large cities (Rome, Milan, Naples, Genoa, Florence, Venice, and Palermo) began to realize that it was impossible to offer adequate treatment to all children with intellectual disabilities within the existing schools. Adequate treatment in this context referred to education that was in compliance with the suggestions provided by the pioneers of special education (De Sanctis, Monetesano and Bonfigli, and Montessori). As a result, the first special schools for children with intellectual disabilities were opened through municipal initiatives. These were developed as spontaneous, local projects deemed to be in the best interest of the public. Such initiatives were also carried out in areas of cities that were characterized by greater economic means (Soresi, 1981).

After a period of profound separation and social exclusion, institutionalization developed and was considered as the only possible means of giving persons with "special needs" some form of care and assistance. With the rise of fascism in Italy (and other European countries) in the 1920s, the segregation and isolation of persons with disabilities became increasingly apparent. However, at the same time, state-run social programs and the first nonclerical initiatives began to develop with the aim of reducing the supremacy of the church on social service activities. These included services for persons with disabilities.

In the years following World War I, Italy was committed to improving its educational system. As a result, some changes were introduced. These included the provision that compulsory education for children with tuberculosis in special schools would be extended to children with visual or auditory disabilities who did not show other abnormalities or behavioural problems (Royal Decree n.3126, 1923). This led to the *Riforma Gentile* (Royal Decree n.3126, 1923), named after the philosopher Giovanni Gentile. Gentile had been tasked with "drawing" the format of improvement with respect to the education system. He was inspired by neoidealism, a philosophy that was prevalent in Italy at this time. Neoidealism professes that the ultimate end of education is the development of persons and not simply the transmission of knowledge. Gentile provided a new energy to the Italian school system. After this reform, special schools for persons with visual and auditory disabilities were opened.

The year 1928 represented another significant step. Royal Decree 1297 established the formal institution of *Special Classes*. This term refers to classes for children with disabilities that were located inside of schools. Although such classes became frequent in regular schools, there was no real change for children. They remained substantially isolated and segregated from the rest of the school community.

The establishment of special classes within regular schools opened the door to another idea that was even more closely linked to segregation. The idea, borrowed from boarding schools for non-disabled students, brought about the idea that education for children with disabilities could take place within the very institutions where they lived. Thus, schools within isolated institutions became a reality.

The evolving thinking and debates about Italian education in the first half of the twentieth century, then, did not focus on the desirability of greater inclusion, but rather on discussion around how education could be reorganized in more "effective" ways. Unfortunately, such ways were associated with even greater degrees of segregation and isolation, and a new awareness and acceptance of the isolated living conditions of children with disabilities was the result.

Second half of the twentieth century: Disability in Italy after World War II

The end of the World War II resulted in the establishment of the Republic of Italy. In the ensuing years, Italy lived through a dramatically fluctuating economic situation. It was also grappling with the development of the Italian constitution, which stressed equal rights for all citizens and the State's duty to facilitate the full development of citizens without discrimination based on numerous characteristics (e.g., disability). But the fulfilment of constitutional dictates proved to be slow and progressive (Guglielmino, 1982).

The 1950s and 1960s: The separate assistance

With the Italian Constitution of 1946 inequality became outdated. In particular, Article 3 of the Italian Constitution stated that

> All citizens have equal social dignity and are equal before the law, without distinctions based on sex, race, language, religion, political opinions, personal or social condition. It is a duty of the Republic to remove economic and social barriers that limit effective freedom and equality of citizens, prevent the full development of human beings and the effective participation of all workers in the political, economic and social organization of the Country.

Article 3 specified that the State, and consequently the public, are committed to the removal of all inequalities and the guardianship of all persons with psychophysical, sensory, or intellectual impairments.

The Italian Constitution granted several inviolable rights to every child, regardless of living condition. One result of this was that there developed a new social interest towards persons with disabilities and on how the obligations of the Constitution might be addressed. As interest increased, greater attention was paid to impairments and on interventions that might be useful for particular disabling conditions. This focus on intervention and pathology usually involved the testing of new treatments and, at first, these worked in favour of persons with certain disabilities. Because of new medical advances, the life expectancies of people with certain disabilities increased, and persons with disabilities began to receive more attention for medical treatments. However, these interventions tended to favour medical approaches, reinforcing the idea of disability as illness. They also followed a traditional custodial and segregating approach, characterized by various degrees of institutionalization.

During the industrial boom in the 1960s, the socio-medical system developed and implemented during Italy's period of fascism was still active. But these years were also characterized by the development of the first associations of parents of children with disabilities. These included the Italian Association for Assistance to Spastics (*Associazione Italiana Assistenza agli Spastici*, A.I.A.S) in 1953, and the National Association of Families of Persons with Intellectual and/or Relational Disabilities (*Associazione Nazionale Famiglie di Persone con Disabilità Intellettiva e/o Relazionale*, A.N.F.F.A.S.) in 1958. Families gained a more active role in public institutions. These newly created associations began to ask for specialized treatments and rehabilitation for their family members. The disability service system finally acknowledged and responded to the voices and needs of members of these associations. Specialized rehabilitation centres and wards were created. Medical treatments that had been requested were provided, with the main objective of safeguarding and defending persons who were still considered "abnormal" (Pieri, 1991).

Laws formed in this period demonstrated a new attention to children with sensory disabilities for whom specific educational pathways became extended into separate work inclusion programs. In 1952, Law 1463 extended to *all* primary schools mandatory education for children with visual disabilities "eligible for education and in *specific special schools*." Ten years later, in 1962, Law 1859 established that mandatory education for children with visual disabilities would be extended to all intermediate schools.

All of these legislative steps were integral in facilitating an increase in the number of special classes, which increased to 2,247 in the 1963–1964 school year. At that time, though, only 20% of children with disabilities attended school.

The 1970s: The inclusion period

In the middle of the 1960s, there was an increase in acceptance of the Italian Left Party, and a process of social reform began. This reform was important, as it supported the development of an Italian society that was in the process of advanced industrialization. At the same time, Italy began to transform into a society that was predicated on the production and consumption of commodities. With the invention and normalization of products such as televisions and cars, material objects and wealth became highly desired.

These new paradigms could not be translated into reality for all Italian citizens, and this new social context produced protests in 1968. The focus of these protests was a revision of secondary school and university (which were previously viewed as quite sufficient). A second period of protest extended the discussion to the general social and economic assets of the country and how they were managed (Guglielmino, 1982). This movement in 1968 brought about a discussion of both the objectives and the models of "schooling" in Italy.

With respect to education, the Movement for Educational Cooperation (*Movimento di Cooperazione Educativa* or MCE) was created in 1951. This organization unified liberal teachers working in schools of varying orders and levels, from primary to secondary schools, who wanted to reform the educational system. These teachers asked for schools that focused on paying attention to relationships and communication. Development and social inclusion were major factors that this organization also demanded. The teachers who formed the MCE asked for a school where the processes of learning and teaching would be capable of producing a global growth of the student, including affection, cognition, and social skills.

Within this cultural context, a significant role was played by the School of Barbiana. This school was set up by Don Lorenzo Milani during the 1950s in a small village in the mountains near Florence. Don Milani put forward a unique educational proposal for young people living in that community who, for geographical and economic reasons, were disadvantaged when compared to their peers living in the city. He reported the fact that traditional public school, which he defined as "a hospital which takes care of healthy persons and pushes back those who are sick," did not adequately fulfil the educational needs of many children. Don Milani claimed that these schools did not care about helping children in difficulty, but rather valued those who already had a positive familial background. At this new school in Barbiana, Milani implemented school hours that were fixed at unusual times of the day. For example, after work in the fields, children attended school late in the day for 7 days a week. It was an open school, where the teaching program was shared with students. At the same time that Milani's school in Barbiana began operating, a group of healthcare workers began a new movement referred to as "Democratic Psychiatry," guided by Franco Basaglia (1968). Basaglia was dissatisfied with the failure of traditional psychiatric practices, and was successful in gaining public opinion in favour of his new movement to the point that politicians were "forced" to issue the historical Law 118 (March 31, 1971).

This law decreed the end of the psychiatric hospitals (which had to be dismantled) as well as special schools.

A new cultural climate and the efforts of Basaglia led to the creation of Law 118 in 1971. Law 118 defined "protected categories" of citizens and discouraged the development of mental hospitals. Article 28 of Law 118 regularized inclusion for students with disabilities by stating that mandatory education had to take place in regular classes in public schools. This marked the beginning of inclusion of children with disabilities in regular classes. However, children with severe intellectual and physical disabilities whose needs made it very difficult to provide them with meaningful inclusion were still excluded from regular classrooms (Article 28).

At the end of the 1970s, attention shifted towards the inclusion of all children with disabilities in regular classes. There were frequently disputes, which lead to the end of "special schools" and special classes in common schools. It was effectively argued that both were simply social ghettos for people with disabilities. This involvement and resulting change was in keeping with trends in the broader society, where citizens began to participate in a more direct way in terms of public life and began to ask for urgent and effective implementation of the principles stated in the Italian Constitution (Pieri, 1991). Intense discussions developed in favour of persons with disabilities and mental problems based on the principles of equality and international literature (Soresi, 1983). As a result, an increasing attention to inclusion, education, and ultimately a democratic school system open to all people emerged. The diversity of students was to be recognized and accepted within these schools. This change and the commitment from political forces were established in 1977 by Law 517. This law prohibited discrimination towards students with disabilities of any type and severity in attending primary school (Article 2) or intermediate school (Article 7).

Law 517 required the progressive dismantling of special schools and a rapid move towards inclusion. It was finally recognized that teaching and learning should be based on collective responsibility and on educational and didactic planning, which should occur inclusive of certain student's peculiarities. Besides stating principles of participation and collectiveness, Law 517 abolished special classes and established "forms of supports in primary and intermediate schools" (Groppo, 1983; Soresi & Nota, 2001).

While educational efforts and treatments were previously devoted only to students with disabilities who had been defined as "teachable," Law 517 directed society to consider meaningful education for persons with all disabilities as both possible and appropriate. This law forced all schools to provide psycho-educational activities to all persons with disabilities independently, based on their level of severity, and to schedule attendance of regular classes in regular schools if they were of school age. School was finally considered truly open to everyone due to the diversity of the students attending it and because of the role of control and participation parents of children with disabilities were recognized as having.

From the 1980s to the 1990s: The integration period

Law 517/77 required that a support teacher be assigned to a classroom if it included a child with a disability. This support teacher was meant to help facilitate inclusion and to increase educational opportunities for all students. The support teacher was also meant to implement individualized interventions tailored to the needs of each student. In Italy, at the end of the 1970s and at the beginning of the 1980s, the first experiences of school inclusion were realized for students with disabilities. In most cases, these experiences involved an additional teacher (support teacher) in the classroom with the specific aim of helping the main teacher (Sidoli, 2008).

These first experiences of inclusion were frequently characterized by "unruled" conditions (lack of guidelines or regulation). Teachers, including support teachers, did not have specific knowledge with respect to disability and specific issues related to it. As a result, collective planning and support for the whole class was limited. Several difficulties associated with the presence of a support teacher in the class were experienced (Nota & Soresi, 1997; Soresi, 1981, 1983). For example, many children were isolated even though they were included in regular classrooms. This often took the form of the removal of the child with a disability from the class by the support teacher for most of the school day (Nota & Soresi, 1997; Soresi, 1981, 1983). Additionally, since support teachers were not specifically trained, and lacked skills and knowledge related to disability, most activities were left to their experience and goodwill. It is reasonable to assert that students with disabilities were inserted into regular educational classes without adequate supports or instructional knowledge in place (D'Alessio, 2011; Vitello, 1991).

Only during the 1990s did formal courses for support teachers begin to be organized. In the late 1990s, a bachelor's degree, certification as a teacher, and an additional year of study specific to becoming a support teacher became required to work as a support teacher in any classroom, regardless of grade level. The additional year of study for specialized support teachers (*insegnante di sostegno*) is currently based on a set of nationally established training topics. Departments of Educational Sciences in Italian universities have since been charged with the primary responsibility for preparing these specialized teachers.

The 1990s was also the decade of "Europe with no frontiers." The breakdown of communism in central and Eastern Europe precipitated a cohesion of European citizens who showed a growing interest in defending the rights of persons with marked difficulties. With a document produced in Salamanca (Salamanca Statement and Framework for Action on Special Needs Education; UNESCO, 1994), the need to offer a "qualitative high education to all individuals in order to guarantee an effective inclusion" (Evans, 1995) was declared. These documents underline the need to act so that inclusive schools provide a setting that is encouraging to the development of equal opportunities and full participation. These documents emphasize considering not only the perspective of teachers but also those of peers, parents, and volunteers (Soresi & Nota, 2001, 2004).

In agreement with the declarative documents produced in Europe, and with issues raised by Law 517, Law 104 was passed in Italy in 1994. Passage of this law marked a historic change in Italy. Law 104 ruled out discrimination towards persons with disabilities in terms of assistance they may require, social inclusion, and their rights. This law collected and organized all previous rulings on disability and inclusion and organized them in a comprehensive manner, establishing a basis for a more modern and advantageous culture of inclusion. Law 104 extends the rights of persons with disabilities and defines the duties that institutions have toward them. It traces the intervention guidelines for public institutions and private associations, and provides general principles for school and work inclusion as well as parameters for supported employment. Law 104 also emphasizes the removal of barriers in architecture and transports, tax concessions, and the right to vote and to live in a chosen home. Article 2 of the same law underlines "the relevance of prevention (information and education about health; search for and removal from living and work environments all risk factors for genetic malformation and disabling diseases) and of continuing prevention activities which safeguard children from birth."

This significant law (Law 104) was born out of the awareness that the aim of social inclusion is the development of the potential in relationship, communication, learning and social processes (Article 12) for persons with disabilities. The right of students with disabilities to attend all mainstream classes in schools of any order or rank, including university, is also stressed. These rights are affirmed not only with respect to disability but also with respect to other difficulties or any other category of marginalization such as poverty, low sociocultural status of families, lack of parental care, and ethnicity.

In addition to guidelines described in Law 104, a Decree of the President of the Italian Republic (February, 1994) is relevant to this discussion. This decree includes several operational guidelines (known as *"Atto di indirizzo e coordinamento relativo ai compiti delle unità sanitarie locali in materia di alunni portatori di handicap"*) which regulate its application. The decree includes criteria for functional diagnosis of a student with disability (Article 2) and descriptors of a functional diagnosis (Article 3), which, in particular, should take into account learning potential in cognitive, affective and relational dimensions, language, sensory processing, motor and praxis functioning, neuropsychological functioning, and personal and social autonomy. These guidelines outline the development of a document that results in a "Dynamic Functional Profile," which describes the possible level of development a student with a disability is expected to reach in a short (6 months) or long (the next 2 years) period of time.

A year later, in 1995, with Article 13 of the Ministerial Decree number 80, the Individual Educational Plan (*Piano Educativo Individualizzato*) was introduced. This document describes all interventions planned for the student with a disability along a specified period of time and aims to realize the right to education and teaching. Most importantly, this document is expected to be realized and shared by teachers and experts from health and social services. This document must be made in agreement with the family of the child with a disability. Furthermore, this document must also refer to both academic learning and life skills.

At the end of the 1990s, approximately 98% of Italian students with disabilities were attending classes in regular schools as their primary placement. However, even with all the achievements described previously, the problem of allowing children with impairments to "experience" classroom life and to participate in all activities effectively still exists. Most of their activities are, in fact, realized outside of the class, and are constructed around contents and targets that have little to do with school curriculum. In some cases the average percentage of time spent inside the class versus the time out of the regular classroom is unknown (Cottini & Nota, 2007; Giangreco, Doyle, & Suter, 2012).

From school to work inclusion

Work inclusion is considered one of the most objective indexes of an adequate quality of life for adults with disabilities, as well as the effectiveness of habilitation and reha- bilitation efforts (Nota & Soresi, 2004a; Soresi, Nota, & Wehmeyer, 2011; Wehmeyer & Garner, 2003).

It is worth adding that in 1999, in agreement with what was declared in Europe (Article 15 of the European Social Charter, adopted in 1961 and revised in 1996), Law 68/1999 was passed in Italy. This law promoted the inclusion of people with ortho- paedic, psychological, sensory, and intellectual disabilities in the workplace through support services and supported work actions. This inclusion was based on the analysis of work skills of an individual person and of his or her work environment. Work inclu- sion of persons with disabilities and the principle of participation and equal opportu- nities were enhanced as a result.

According to Law 68, 1 out of every 15 employees a company hires must have a dis- ability. Failure to adhere to this regulation results in the company being required to pay a fine. Additionally, government incentives (e.g., tax breaks and salary reimburse- ments) are offered for hiring people with more significant disabilities. Nonetheless, given the absence of systematic economic sanctions, several companies still do not meet law requirements and represent a significant barrier to work inclusion.

We can conclude from this analysis that, although Italy is internationally recog- nized as being one of the first to have subscribed to the inclusion model and to have established a series of norms and laws to support it, there are still many issues to be solved. Several initiatives are needed in order to effectively guarantee real partici- pation in community life for persons with disabilities (Nota & Soresi, 2004b; Nota, Soresi, Ferrari, & Solberg, 2008; Soresi, 2007).

The new century

In the last 20 years the superiority of the inclusion model has certainly been recog- nized in Italy over insertion and institutionalization models. Increasing attention has been paid to the needs and rights of persons with impairments related to their *quality of life, participation, and self-determination* (Nota, Soresi, & Perry, 2006). There is now widespread agreement on the need to personalize interventions, by providing ways for persons with disabilities to make choices from a variety of options that reflect their interests, tastes, and abilities. Services can no longer be satisfied with simply knowing that some interventions have been provided to persons with disabilities. It is now rec- ognized that personalized actions should be carried out, and that their effectiveness in satisfying personal needs and wishes now needs to be "measured."

Besides legal supports, cultural pressure coming from the academic world has certainly contributed to the realization of an inclusion model. There has been an increase in the number of new, specific educational courses offered by several facul- ties for people interested in a career in the study of disability. For example, several years ago at the University of Padova, only a single course on "Psychology of handicap and rehabilitation" existed. The School of Psychology now offers several different courses such as Psychology of Disabilities, Psychology of School and Social Inclusion, Psychology of Career Counselling, and Work Inclusion for Persons with Disabilities,

Models and Programs for Rehabilitation across Lifespan, and so on. Similarly, the number of postgraduate courses has increased. Specialization and Master's level courses, doctoral research grants, and research positions are available for those studying disability and rehabilitation. In terms of other forms of education and training, students can pursue extended professional training. However, this training is not generally provided in Europe (Devecchi, Dettori, Doveston, Sedgwick, & Jament, 2012).

Several national studies and research projects focused on problems associated with disabilities have been conducted. New specialized journals and new book series have been dedicated to rehabilitation and inclusion. This has decreased the gap that has traditionally existed with respect to other countries in terms of disability study and knowledge (Soresi, 2007).

However, it is worth noting that despite the commitment and work of many people, the Italian model has been marked by frequent failure. Inaction and inefficiencies at both the administrative and organizational levels, in addition to problems in everyday practice, have also prevented schools from fully developing a truly effective educational practice for school inclusion (Associazione TreeLLLe, Caritas Italiana & Fondazione Agnelli, 2011; Dettori, 2009; Fondazione Giovanni Agnelli, 2011).

In high school, for instance, inclusion is still limited and is characterized by a rate of inclusion ranging from 0.4 in lyceums to 9.8 % in vocational schools. These data stress the limited presence of persons with disabilities in secondary schools, although this differs widely from school to school (Giangreco, Doyle, & Suter, 2012).

The presence of assistants who provide primarily personal care supports such as feeding, dressing, mobility, and bathroom assistance for students with disabilities may have also contributed to barriers in terms of true inclusion. These supports may result in a series of unintentional negative effects, especially when assistants become too dominant or inappropriately engage in teachers' roles for which they are not qualified. This may result in interference both with teachers and peers, and the imposition of other limitations (Giangreco & Broer, 2007).

It should also be noted that in the first decade of the new century, Italy was experiencing an *influx* of immigration from Eastern Europe, Africa, and Asia. The number of foreign students began to significantly increase in Italian classrooms. This has brought new challenges to Italian schools. In particular, we refer here to the increasing number of students who speak a wide variety of primary languages other than Italian, and some of whom may also have disabilities or other special needs. These changes have contributed to making classrooms more heterogeneous, and it is possible that these new circumstances may facilitate the personalization of teaching, make social exchanges richer, increase openness to difference and, as a consequence, facilitate stronger inclusion of children with disabilities in school classrooms.

Future perspectives

In order to make educational practices sufficiently effective in facilitating school inclusion, it should be clear that "inclusion is not about moving special education into the general education classroom" (Waldron & McLeskey, 2009, p. 39). Creating an inclusion context in school requires sharing an ethos in support of inclusion. Teachers should arrange curriculum and instruction so that they can accommodate a broad range of differences among their students (McLeskey & Waldron, 2007).

The superiority of the inclusion principle should be recognized, but this alone is not enough. School inclusion requires the acceptance of persons with disabilities as a natural part of the school community, as active participants. It also provides the moral purpose for transforming schools in a way that makes student differences ordinary (Dunn, Hanes, Hardie, Leslie & MacDonald, 2008; Waldron & McLeskey, 2009). Several actions have been put forward to help accomplish this. These actions include the following:

> *Strengthening the ability of teachers to personalize interventions.* This should be considered especially when dealing with some of the more static subjects and disciplines, such as mathematics and science. These categories of subjects together with other disciplines are important in order to know and understand the complex reality we live in. Teaching techniques that will improve student motivation, participation, and generalization should be utilized wherever possible (Springer, Pugalee, & Algozzine, 2007).

> *Increase the quality of teaching supplied by intermediate and high schools.* In Italy, teachers of younger students currently have greater access (than teachers of higher grade levels) to training that is specific to teaching students with disabilities. If university-level education and activities have been provided to nursery and primary school teachers working with children with disabilities, the same quality of instruction and training should be provided to teachers of intermediate and high school students. Teachers of all levels must be capable of learning teaching approaches and facilitating the inclusion of students with disabilities. Much more has to be done for intermediate and high school teachers within this context, since education for these teachers has been more limited than that of nursery and primary teachers. This education is often considered as simply an "additional course" they decide to attend in order to have more opportunities to work in schools (Cottini & Nota, 2007; Laporta, Fiorentini, Cambi, Tassinari, & Testi, 2000).

> *Facilitate positive attitudes of teachers towards the futures of persons with disability.* In a study involving public schools that followed a model of inclusion, teachers were asked to describe the future of a hypothetical student with Down syndrome (Nota & Soresi, 2009). The authors observed that only a minority of teachers predicted that a student with Down syndrome would be working in a competitive and inclusive setting, and that he would be able to determine his own future. The teachers paid greater attention to the restrictions that disability can impose and referred frequently to a more traditional conception of disability with focus on limitations and deficits, rather than strengths. This "negative" attitude could be reduced by involving teachers and other professionals in specific in-service training activities useful in increasing their ability to see the potential of individuals with disabilities and to support their development (Carrieri & Sgaramella, 2011; Sgaramella, Carrieri, Meligrana, & Nota, 2009; Soresi, Nota, Ferrari, Sgaramella, & Wehmeyer, 2013).

> *Provide for effective educational and preventive activities that involve the classmates of students with disabilities.* These activities should point to strengthening social skills, problem solving, and cooperation in the class group. This would involve educating all children to know about impairments, disabilities, and other

differences within their classrooms and within their wider communities. This would promote support and cooperative action in terms of advocating for the rights of people with severe disabilities (Nota, Ferrari, & Soresi, 2005).

Increase parental involvement. Educational and social services can no longer consider parents as merely spectators. Instead, Italian society should "stimulate" the ability of parents to support and advocate for inclusion, resulting in benefit to the whole school community. With respect to the parents of children with disabilities, it is crucial to work to try to improve their coping strategies (and those of their children) in terms of dealing with the demands of school. A recent position paper adopted by the Council of the IASSIDD (International Association for the Scientific Study of Intellectual & Developmental Disabilities) on July 9, 2012, (Emerson et al., 2012) supported this premise. If trained, these parents may facilitate an inclusive atmosphere at school and may also support the work of teachers for the entire class group (Ferrari, Pagliai, Benincà, & Concato, 2010; Soresi & Nota, 2001).

1 *Give volunteers a new role.* A reduction of public resources dedicated to facilitating inclusion in Italy has been obvious to even the casual observer. This fact has been reflected by the actual number of support teachers, and by the amount of economic supports provided to persons with disabilities or to their families in order to facilitate participation. As a result, volunteer associations may play an increasingly important role in facilitating actions that promote inclusion in community contexts, based on support and social participation. Volunteers may play new roles (Pancaldi, 2010) and may assume a cultural relevance, promoting information, education, and cultural innovation. Specific training on these topics may enhance the effectiveness of volunteers in helping persons with disabilities achieve inclusion.

Conclusion

The new century seems to be highly characterized by globalization, internationalization, and rapid technological progress. Jobs are now less well defined and predictable, and employment transitions occur more frequently. These factors present more difficult challenges for all people, with and without disabilities (Savickas et al., 2009). Additionally, in Europe and Italy people are living a "global financial crisis" (GFC), with several consequences on work and employment. These include weakened employment protections, reduced benefit entitlements, and reductions in study supports (Heyes, 2011). It is clear that the state is less able or less willing to provide social protection than in the past as a result of this financial crisis. However, potential demands on the state for social support are increasing (Rubery, 2011) and pose considerable challenges to citizens (Bauman, 2006; Sultana, 2011). These challenges are especially relevant to those who are more vulnerable. These more vulnerable groups include persons with disabilities (Soresi, Nota, Ferrari, & Ginevra, 2014; Sgaramella, 2011).

Although this statistic varies by nation, Europe showed an average unemployment rate of 9.74% in 2010 and 2011. This rate was more than double for young workers, migrants, and people with disabilities or mental health problems. Primarily, this was due to the limited access these groups generally have to training and other enabling services (Eurosat, 2012).

We should also consider that Internet technology has significantly modified the way people work. In the last several years, the labour market has systematically begun to become dependent on the Internet, organized around networks, characterized by less rigid hierarchies, built on partnership, and influenced by demographic changes. Within Italian society, which has been defined as a society of knowledge (Castelfranchi, 2007), people need to continuously update their skills throughout their entire lifespans so that they are able to use sophisticated technologies, accept flexibility rather than stability, and maintain requisites to fulfil work expectations and create new opportunities (Savickas et al., 2009). This is true also for persons with disabilities (Ferrari, Sgaramella, & Soresi, 2015).

We believe that in the next several years, we should focus on strengthening the ability of people with disabilities to deal with the complex reality we are facing, encouraging persons with disabilities, their parents, and their teachers to think more about the future and not to concentrate on the past. Barriers and obstacles persons with disabilities encounter every day, or difficulties resulting from their limitations, should not be the main topics of discussion. Specific actions focused on career construction for persons with disabilities should be undertaken. These will provide a link between school and future careers for persons with disabilities.

All of these assertions will assume a particular importance if they are realized in normal and integrated school settings, using teaching techniques that emphasize active participation and give a sense of normalcy to what is proposed in order to increase the feeling of involvement and level of motivation in children and adolescents with disabilities (Soresi, Nota, Ferrari, & Sgaramella, 2013).

Fortunately, some steps toward achieving this goal are under way. As an example, an initiative was undertaken involving the first three authors in Padova, Italy. In order to search for answers in the current hard times, an international research and study group on time perspective, hope, optimism, and resilience has been created. This group, known as the IHRT (International Hope Research Team) involves Italian and international scholars. It has become apparent that it is crucial for professionals in the field of disability and teachers to experience hope, optimism, and positive time perspective as they work with people who have been historically treated quite unjustly. People who can be characterized by higher levels of these positive characteristics also show high levels of professional ability, and exhibit an improved attitude toward inculcating hope and confidence in those who benefit from their work (Nota & Soresi, 2012). We believe that these aspects cannot be "left to chance" and that specific attention should be devoted to them both in terms of research and education.

References

Associazione TreeLLLe, Caritas Italiana & Fondazione Agnelli. (2011). *Gli alunni con disabilità nella scuola italiana. Bilancio e proposte* [Disability students in Italian school: Evaluation and suggestions]. Trento, Italy: Erickson.

Basaglia, F. (1968). *L'istituzione negata* [The denied institution]. Torino, Italy: Einaudi.

Bauman, Z. (2006). *Liquid Times: Living in an Age of Uncertainty*. Cambridge, UK: Polity.

Castelfranchi, C. (2007). Six critical remarks on science and the construction of the knowledge society. *Journal of Science Communication, 6*(4), 1–3.

Carrieri. L., & Sgaramella, T. M. (2011). Predittori cognitivi nello sviluppo professionale del giovane adulto con disabilità. [Cognitive predictors of career development in young adults with disabilities]. In L. Nota & S. Soresi (Eds.), *Nuove sfide per l'orientamento scolastico e professionale* [Challenges for school and work guidance] (pp. 79–98). Firenze, Italy: OS–Giunti.

Cottini, L., & Nota, L. (2007). School inclusion: The Italian model. In J. A. Rondal & A. Rasore-Quartino (Eds.), *Therapies and Rehabilitation in Down Syndrome* (pp. 144–162). Chichester, UK: Wiley.

D'Alessio, S. (2011). *Inclusive Education in Italy: A Critical Analysis of the Policy of Integrazione Scolastica. Rotterdam,* Netherlands: Sense Publishers.

Dettori, F. (2009). La fuga degli insegnanti di sostegno verso il posto comune: Una ricerca sulle storie professionali [The flight of support teachers towards mainstream classes: A study on professional lives]. *L'integrazione scolastica e sociale* [Social and Educational Integration], *8,* 247–258.

Devecchi, C., Dettori, F., Doveston, M., Sedgwick, P., & Jament, J. (2012). Inclusive classrooms in Italy and England: The role of support teachers and teaching assistants. *European Journal of Special Needs Education, 27,* 27–171.

Dunn, P., Hanes, R., Hardie, S., Leslie, D., & MacDonald, J. (2008). Best practices in promoting disability inclusion within Canadian schools of social work. *Disability Studies Quarterly,* vol 28(1). http://dsq-sds.org/article/view/66/66 (2017).

Emerson, E., Barron, D. A., Blacher, J., Brehmer, B., Clinch, S., Davidson, P. W. et al. (2012). *Better Health, Bbetter Lives: Research Priorities.* Copenhagen, Denmark: World Health Organization Regional Office for Europe.

Eurosat. (2012). *Underemployment statistics.* Retrieved from http://epp.eurostat.ec.europa.eu/statistics_explained/index.php/Unemployment_statistics (2017)

Evans, P. (1995). Conclusion and policy implications. In P. Evans (Ed.), *Our Children at Risk* (pp. 137–145). Paris: Center for Educational Research and Innovation, Organization for Economic Co-operation and Development.

Ferrari, L., Pagliai, M., Benincà, A., & Concato, F. (2010, September). *Supporting parents of children with disability with parent training.* Paper presented at the 5th Conference of the European Society on Family Relations, Milan, Italy.

Ferrari, L., Sgaramella, T.M., & Soresi, S. (2015). Bridging disability and work: Contribution and challenges of life design. In L. Nota & J. Rossier (Eds.), *Handbook of Life Design: From Practice to Theory and from Theory to Practice* (pp. 219–232). Gottingen: Hogrefe Publishing.

Fondazione Giovanni Agnelli. (2011). *Rapporto sulla scuola in Italia 2011* [Report on School in Italy in 2011]. Bari, Italy: Edizioni Laterza.

Giangreco, M. F., & Broer, S. M. (2007). School-based screening to determine overreliance on paraprofessionals. *Focus on Autism and Other Developmental Disabilities, 22,* 149–158.

Giangreco, M. F., Doyle, M. B., & Suter, J. C. (2012). Demographic and personnel service delivery data: Implications for including students with disabilities in Italian schools. *Life Span and Disability, 15,* 97–123.

Groppo, M. (1983). Analisi critica dell'integrazione scolastica degli handicappati [A critical analysis of school inclusion]. In L. Silvestrelli (Ed.), *Psicologia ed Handicap* (pp. 70–118). Roma, Italy: Bulzoni Editore.

Guglielmino, S. (1982). *Guida al novecento* [The twentieth century]. Milano, Italy: Principato Editore.

Heyes, J. (2011). Flexicurity, employment protection and the jobs crisis. *Work, Employment & Society, 25*(4), 642–657.

Laporta, R., Fiorentini, C., Cambi, F., Tassinari, G., & Testi, C. (2000). *Aggiornamento e formazione degli insegnanti* [Teachers' training and continuing education]. Firenze, Italy: La Nuova Italia.

McLeskey, J., & Waldron, N. (2007). Making differences ordinary in inclusive classrooms. *Intervention in School and Clinic, 42,* 162–168.

Nota, L., Ferrari, L., & Soresi, S. (2005). Elementary school children's willingness to help and be friends with disabled peers. *International Journal on Disability and Human Development, 4,* 131–137.

Nota, L., & Soresi, S. (1997). *I comportamenti sociali: dall'analisi all'intervento.* Pordenone, Italy: Erip Editrice.

Nota, L., & Soresi, S. (2004a). Vocational guidance for persons with intellectual disability. In J. Rondal, A. Rasore Quartino, & S. Soresi (Eds.), *The Adults with Down Syndrome: A new Challenge for Society* (pp. 251–264). London, UK: Whurr Publishers Limited.

Nota, L., & Soresi, S. (2004b). Social and community inclusion. In J. Rondal, R. Hodapp, S. Soresi, E. Dykens, & L. Nota (Eds.), *Intellectual Disabilities: Genetics, Behavior, and Inclusion* (pp. 157–192). London, UK: Whurr Publishers Limited.

Nota, L., & Soresi, S. (2009). Ideas and thoughts of Italian teachers on the professional future of persons with disability. *Journal of Intellectual Disability Research, 53,* 65–77.

Nota, L., & Soresi, S. (2012, September). *Future time perspective, hope and optimism in Italian career counselors.* Paper presented at the 1st International conference on time perspective. Coimbra, Portugal.

Nota, L., Soresi, S., Ferrari, L., & Solberg, S.V.H. (2008). Career guidance for persons with disabilities. In J. Athanasou & R. Van Esbroeck (Eds.), *International Handbook of Career Guidance* (pp. 405–417). Amsterdam, Netherlands: Kluwer.

Nota, L., Soresi, S., & Perry, J. (2006). Quality of life in adults with an intellectual disability: The evaluation of quality of ife instrument. *Journal of Intellectual Disability Research, 50,* 50–371.

Pancaldi, A. (2010). L'associazionismo nel settore dell'handicap. Storie di "geologia", tra luci e ombre [Associations and handicap: lights and shadows]. In L. Corradi (Ed.), *Movimenti per la salute e associazioni delle persone malate.* Milano, Italy: Franco Angeli.

Pieri, L. (1991). *Breve storia dell'assistenza in Italia dall'unità ad oggi* [Short history of assistance in Italy from unification to today]. Bologna, Italy: Accaparlante e Centro Documentazione Handicap.

Rubery, J. (2011). Reconstruction amid deconstruction: Or why we need more of the social in European social models. *Work, Employment and Society,* 25(4), 658–674.

Savickas, M. L., Nota, L., Rossier, J., Dauwalder, J. P., Duarte, M. E., Guichard, J. et al. (2009). Life designing: A paradigm for career construction in the 21st century. *Journal of Vocational Behaviour, 75,* 239–250.

Schalock, R. L., & Verdugo, M. A. (2002). *Handbook on Quality of Life for Human Service Professionals.* Washington, DC: American Association on Mental Retardation.

Schalock, R. L., Bonham, G. S., & Verdugo. M. A. (2008). The conceptualization and measurement of quality of life: Implications for program planning and evaluation in the field of intellectual disabilities. *Evaluation and Program Planning, 31,* 181–190.

Sgaramella, T. M. (2011, September). *Time perspective and future goals when university students have a disability: Profiles and suggestions for interventions.* Paper presented at the International Conference on Vocational designing and career counseling. Challenges and New Horizons, Padova, Italy.

Sgaramella, T. M., Carrieri, L., Meligrana, L., & Nota, L. (2009). La valutazione delle abilità orientata al lavoro in persone con disabilità cognitiva [The assessment of work oriented abilities in cognitive disability]. *GIPO–Giornale Italiano di Psicologia dell'orientamento* [Italian Journal of Vocational Psychology], *10*(3), 15–23.

Sidoli, R. (2008). *Inclusive Policy in Italy.* Milano, Italy: Catholic University of the Sacred Heart. Retrieved on October 10, 2012, from centridiateneo.unicatt.it/it/cesi_Inclusive_policy_in_Italy_inglese.pdf

Soresi, S. (1981). *Problemi ed esperienze di integrazione scolastica e sociale degli handicappati* [Problems and experiences of school and social inclusion of people with handicaps]. Pordenone, Italia: Erip Editrice.

Soresi, S. (1983). La programmazione dell'integrazione scolastica: Riflessioni a margine di un esperienza [Planning school inclusion: Considerations after an experience]. In S. Soresi (Ed.), *Territorio, comunità educativa, handicappati* [Local areas, educational communities and handicap] (pp.158–178). Pordenone, Italy: Erip Editrice.

Soresi, S., (2007). *Psicologia delle disabilità* [Psychology of disability]. Bologna, Italy: Il Mulino.

Soresi, S., & Nota, L. (2001). *La facilitazione dell'integrazione scolastica* [Facilitating school inclusion]. Pordenone, Italy: Erip Editrice.

Soresi, S., & Nota, L. (2004). School inclusion. In J. Rondal, R. Hodapp, S. Soresi, E. Dykens, & L. Nota (Eds.), *Intellectual Disabilities: Genetics, Behavior, and Inclusion* (pp. 114–156). London, UK: Whurr Publishers Limited.

Soresi, S., Nota, L., Ferrari, L., & Ginevra, M. C. (2014). Parental influences on youths' career construction. In G. Arulmani, A. Bakshi, F. Leong, & T. Watts (Eds.), *Handbook of Career Development: International Perspectives* (pp. 149–172). New York, NY: Springer.

Soresi, S., Nota, L., Ferrari, L., Sgaramella, T. M., & Wehmeyer, M. L. (2013). Career development and career thoughts. *Oxford Handbook of Positive Psychology and Disability* (pp. 239–264). New York, NY: Oxford University Press.

Soresi, S., Nota, L., & Wehmeyer, M. L. (2011). Community involvement in promoting inclusion, participation, and self-determination. *International Journal of Inclusive Education, 15,* 15–28.

Springer, R. M., Pugalee, D., & Algozzine, B. (2007). Improving mathematics skills of high school students. *Clearing House,* 81(1), 37–44.

Sultana, R. G. (2011). Lifelong guidance, citizen rights and the state: Reclaiming the social contract. *British Journal of Guidance & Counselling,* 39(2), 179–186.

UNESCO. (1994). *Salamanca statement and framework for action on special needs education.* Paris, France: UNESCO. Retrieved from http://unesdoc.unesco.org/images/0009/000984/098427eo.pdf (2017)

Vitello, S. (1991). Integration of handicapped students in the United States and Italy: A comparison. *International Journal of Special Education,* 6, 213–222.

Waldron, N., & McLeskey, J. (2009). *Developing schools that are both effective and inclusive.* Proceedings of the International Association of Special Education Conference. Alicante, Spain.

Whemeyer, M., & Garner, N. W. (2003). The impact of personal characteristics of people with intellectual and developmental disability on self-determination and autonomous functioning. *Journal of Applied Research in Intellectual Disabilities,* 16(4), 255–265.

WHO. (2001). *International Classification of Functioning, Disability and Health–ICF.* Geneva, Switzerland: World Health Organization.

21

EDUCATION OF PEOPLE WITH INTELLECTUAL DISABILITIES AND HEARING IMPAIRMENTS IN SPAIN: A HISTORICAL APPROACH

Climent Giné, Carles Llombart, Anna Balcells and Joana Mas

The response of society to disability, from the legal, educational, and care point of view has undergone an enormous transformation throughout history. There have been some common elements to this in various countries that, in general, are based on common beliefs, values, culture, and social and economic conditions. Nevertheless, the specific shapes that these responses have taken within countries have led to some unique aspects, peculiarities that make our broader common perspective richer.

In this chapter, we focus mainly on the education given to people with intellectual disabilities and hearing impairments in Spain. For both groups, we examine the evolution of concepts throughout the centuries leading up to the present (later for people with intellectual disabilities), as well as how those concepts were responded to in real life by society as a whole and by professionals in particular. The idea is to offer neither a simple descriptive account of what has transpired in the education of people with intellectual disabilities and hearing impairments in Spain throughout this time period, nor an erudite exercise on policies, facts, and people. Rather, the real objective of this historical analysis is to contribute to a better understanding of what has occurred in the past and how this has evolved into the current situation, with an emphasis on the resulting opportunities that are opening for people with disabilities today. In carrying out such an analysis, it is also imperative to identify the tensions and threats that seem to fog the horizon. In support of this analysis, we make use of the voices of family members, service providers, professionals, and others.

Education of people with intellectual disability

Little attention was paid to people with intellectual disabilities (ID) in Spain until the 1950s and 1960s, when services tailored for this population began to be developed, in particular in the field of education. Authors (Basil, Bolea, & Soro-Camats, 2003; Giné, 2003) have agreed on the identification of three stages in the evolution of education for people with ID that respond to clearly differentiated conceptual models and, furthermore, that coincide with what occurred in other countries (Scheerenberger, 1984): the welfare model, the medical-rehabilitation model, and the educational model.

The welfare model

In Spain, the welfare model dominated the approach toward people with ID up to the end of the 1940s. During this period, people with disabilities were mostly isolated from society in private homes or housed in large care centres or asylums. The rationale for housing people with disabilities in this way was mainly charitable – it was the best way to care for them – and education was not, in most cases, a priority (Giné, 1990). With regard to people with intellectual disabilities in particular, there were two principal forms of care, partly determined by where people lived and the family's social and economic situation: they could either stay at home, hidden from society; or they could be interned in an institution, which most times was a mental health centre.

A number of voices support this point of view. J. Bofill, former president of a major association of parents of people with ID, explained, "In Spain, before 1950, there was nothing; people didn't even know that there were people with ID, and if they existed they were hidden." Similarly, J. M. Jarque, head of special education in Catalonia, noted, "At that time, there were very few centres ... people with ID were either locked at home or in institutions; lunatic asylums were full." Dr. Júdez, a child neurologist and an eminent figure in the field of care for people with ID, remembered that, when she was at university in the 1950s, she

> went to a friend's to study, and there they heard someone screaming; then her friend said, "You know what happens? My brother is mentally disabled." She then took me to a small room, half dark and without furniture; and I saw a person sitting on a chair.

Dr. T. Vilaltella, a child psychiatrist, stated, "It was not until the 1960s [that] people started to say that subnormal (sic) people should not be at home, should not be hidden" (Giné, 2005, pp. 65–66).

The focus during this period, then, was mainly welfare in character: to protect people with disabilities, and to protect other people from them. People with disabilities were not considered as citizens with rights, but rather as pitiful people. Dr. Meler, professor at the University of Barcelona, remembered, "Society did not pay any attention of them ... or just pitied them" (Giné, 2005, p. 64).

With regard to legislation to support the development of educational systems, Fierro (1984) pointed out that the education of children with ID was first considered in the Primary Education Act (*Ley de Educación Primaria* of 17 July, 1945), but that this was not accompanied by any specific measures for putting it into practice. Prior to this, there were few references to people with ID in legislation. A Decree in 1902 mentioned that people with ID were to be excluded from educational programmes. In 1933, they were to be included in the Vagrancy Act (*Ley de Vagos y Maleantes*), and later in the Dangerousness and Social Rehabilitation Act (*Ley de Peligrosidad y Rehabilitación Social de 6 de agosto de 1970*). It seems clear from this, then, that the lawmakers and public authorities during this time had no concern for the education of children with disabilities, and, for that matter, little concern for the welfare of people with ID at all – they were considered to be a responsibility of their families and best housed in asylums. Consequently, the Administration neither created nor funded any educational services. As J. Bofill, quoted above, noted, "In those years, the Administration ... not a single word!" (García-Dié, 2005, p. 88).

Another factor to be considered was the lack of educational programmes, or even educational emphasis, for people with ID in the centres where they were cared for. Indeed, the professionals who took direct care of them had qualifications in accordance with their roles of invigilation and care particular to psychiatric institutions, and did not have training in teaching or education. This exacerbated the neglect of education in the care centres.

This long stage, dominated by the welfare model, had strong repercussions on the lives of people with ID. It was not difficult to see the negative effects of the many practices that were followed. In particular, there was segregation, social devaluation, and few opportunities for development, and, as a consequence, there was personal deterioration. In turn, such treatment and results strongly conditioned the social "image" others formed of people with disabilities as beings not worthy of education or consideration or any kind beyond basic care.

The medical-rehabilitation model

The medical model dominated the concept of intellectual disability and the approach to providing services to people with ID from the 1950s to the end of the 1970s. The influence of this model was enormous, and is still being felt today. Scientific advances, particularly in the fields of medicine, psychology, and pedagogy – along with the increasing recognition of the abandonment and deterioration of people with ID in large psychiatric institutions and at home – led doctors associated with ID to promote new services with rehabilitation goals, organized around the model with which they were familiar: diagnosis-treatment. Within this model, education was both a complement to therapy and a type of therapy in itself. The needs of people with ID were now seen not from the perspective of "protection" and "pity" but rather as "disease."

Throughout these decades, opportunities for education in Spain were rather scarce – both in quality and quantity – for children with disabilities. In some instances, they were even deplorable. This situation was worsened by the social and economic backwardness of Spain during those years, and by political ostracism by other countries due to the political dictatorship.

The application of the medical model, in clinical practice, began with assessment and culminated in treatment. With regard to assessment, the basis was the use of standardized testing that provided an IQ, but did not usually take into account other developmental aspects nor the context in which individuals were developing. Assessment typically concluded by assigning a diagnostic category (label) according to the deficit revealed by the assessment process. At times, diagnosis was directed toward showing the causes and characteristics of the person's disorder (e.g., Down syndrome), but people with ID were also categorized, as they were in other countries, by their level of severity of ID (typically, borderline, mild, moderate, severe, and profound). The practice of categorizing individuals according to their deficits had two main drawbacks: first, it proscribed the kind of care and rehabilitation that was provided; and, second, the therapy and the relationships within the therapeutic context were polluted with the low expectations that were typical of that category by both professionals and family members.

Another consequence of the medical model was the increase in centre specialization and proliferation of various professionals. Specialization would become a "value" to aim for and was synonymous with quality of response. Indeed, centre specialization for every "pathology" and degree of disability resulted in the consolidation of an important network of schools that operated parallel to mainstream schools. Mrs. E. Garriga, an experienced professional in this field, explained this as follows:

> Specialization has a very important role (in the origin of centres) ... an initial diagnosis practically becomes a final prognosis ... a child with retardation has to go to this centre or, if he is profound, he has to go to this other centre ... and that is final – he'll never get out of there. (Giné, 2005, p. 65)

A characteristic of these decades was the explosion of educational centres – religious or professional institutions – managed by the families themselves due to the lack of initiatives and planning by the Administration. For these centres, there was always a scarcity of resources and a great deal of uncertainty. This is how Mrs. C. Martínez, promoter and director of such a centre that was established in the 1960s, explained it: "I started with a group of children... first 1, then 2, 4, etc. One day, Dr. Folch i Camarasa, renowned psychiatrist, called me and told me I should have them for lunch too ... and that's how I started." Similarly, Mrs. Mariné, who formerly worked in a parents' association, claimed: "At the mainstream school, they didn't want them ... so we started the school in a flat." Finally, Mrs. Obiols, director of a special education centre, said: "They were almost medical institutions ... there was always a doctor in charge. We had children, but it couldn't be called a school exactly" (Giné, 2005, pp. 67, 65, respectively). Thus, these were centres that were defined by two characteristics: the predominance of the medical model (with its therapeutic and rehabilitating goals), and being specialized and segregated in nature.

Nevertheless, these initiatives undoubtedly had a positive impact on the lives of people with intellectual disability. Very slowly, the broader society and the Administration itself would become aware of the existence of the needs of this group of people, and aware that these needs had to be met. The efforts of the many parents and professionals would open the doors to allow for the significant changes of the next period. Two initiatives stand out in this sense. First, the enactment of the General Education Act of 1970 (Ley 14/1970, *General de Educación*) represented a progressive move forward in that it recognised the right of people with disabilities to be attended to in mainstream centres, and even in special education units. As is usually the case, this law was implemented slowly and faced many obstacles that needed to be overcome. Second, an important boost was given to the training of teachers and speech therapists with the aim of improving the quality of teaching that pupils with ID would get at the schools, whether mainstream or special education.

There were many aspects to the medical model and many variables in the family and social context that all influenced the lives of people with intellectual disability in these decades. As is typical when examining a complex situation, we can find both lights and shadows. Overall, though, progress was made during this period. There was a substantive move from ignoring and discriminating against people with intellectual disabilities toward a progressive recognition of their rights and an increasing interest in their welfare.

The educational model

The educational model began to be followed in Spain about the end of the 1970s and the early 1980s. Three initiatives by Parliament and by the Government expressed this conceptual change well, and these led to important transformations in professional practice. We refer to the National Plan of Special Education (Real Patronato, 1979), a policy document of the Spanish Ministry of Education and Science; the *Social Integration of Handicapped People Act* (Ley de Integración Social de los Minusválidos) in 1982; and the regulations published by the educational administration to promote school integration (1985). The adoption of such principles as normalization, school integration, sectorialization of services, and personalized attention implied a change of paradigm in the understanding of people with ID and in the organization of services that appeared in the following years.

All these changes have to be understood within the framework of a deep transformation in attention to people with disability throughout Europe. This transformation is apparent in such things as the policies of normalization in Northern European countries, policies of deinstitutionalization in Italy that represented the end of special education centres (1971), and the Warnock Report (1978), which undoubtedly had a significant influence on policies, professional training, and practices in Spain. Among the many far-reaching and influential questions posed by the Warnock Report, those that particularly stand out are, first, the rejection of categorization of people with ID according to their IQ and, therefore, the rejection of their labels; and second, the adoption of the concept of special educational needs, implying a change of vision from deficit conditions to strengths and from limitations to supports.

The rationale for conceptual changes often came from accepted ideas and principles that had been developed within the field of psychology. For example, the concept of "retardation" and developmental disorders was adopted and adapted from psychology's interactive and ecological approach. Further, the development of a child with "retardation" was said to depend, above all, on the opportunities, experiences, and supports that adults and, in some cases, their peers, offer them in the different life contexts, that is, in the family, the school, and the community.

Testimonies corroborate what has been stated above. M. Trueta, president of the Catalan Down's Syndrome Foundation, explained it this way:

> In 1974, when a doctor from the University of Washington said to me: "Look, this thing you're saying about limits, please don't say it any more, because if you say this, you are just limiting your child." And it's always been a surprise because he has done more than we have ever expected.

Or as E. Llamazares observed, "In 1982, a policy of social integration was started from the Warnock Report and the National Plan for Special Education with the deinstitutionalization of special education centres." (Fontanet & Palau, 2005, pp. 25–26).

It is also important to highlight that these conceptual changes also implied a decisive step towards recognising and acting on rights for people with ID; that is, although the law had addressed the new conceptualization, society in general and organizations in the field of ID in particular now began to put a new approach into practice. As D. Mariné remembered, they started to claim for rights instead of begging for alms: "In

1978–79, we decided that, instead of going out with our collection boxes, we would go out to collect signatures, claiming for rights" (Fontanet & Palau, 2005, p. 26).

All this occurred in a moment when Spanish society was undergoing deep transformations due to the end of the dictatorship and the enactment of the Spanish Constitution (Constitución Española, 1978). The new Constitution represented a circumstance that enabled more advanced trends and ideas to enter the country in all spheres of society: social, cultural, scientific, and others.

Undoubtedly these integration policies, despite their initial limitations and difficulties in implementation, involved a transformation in the very way that people in general society looked at people with ID. This transformation can be seen mainly in three ways:

1 A recognition to the right to education and a quality life;
2 Their public presence; and
3 The role of parents.

From being practically unknown to society in the early 1970s, people with ID to a large degree now had a normalized presence at schools and elsewhere by the late 1980s. They progressively became a part of the neighbourhoods where they lived, and others became aware of them, in the shops, the parks, public transportation, and particularly at school. The image of pity, which did not disappear completely, slowly gave way to the image that they are different people but equally worthy of every respect.

In this process of progressive implementation of the educational model concerning the people with ID, it is essential to recognise the important contribution of the 1992 and 2002 definitions of "mental retardation" (now intellectual and developmental disability) by the American Association on Mental Retardation (AAMR) (since 2006, the American Association on Intellectual and Developmental Disability (AAIDD)). The most recent definition, published in 2010, and the conclusions of the Salamanca Declaration (UNESCO, 1994) also helped open the doors to the transition from "school integration" to "educational inclusion."

Although the most recent Spanish regulations (*Education Act; Ley 2/2006, de Educación*) have opted for the inclusion of people with ID, current reality shows some important shadows. The most important of these are the existence of serious difficulties for inclusion during secondary education; the lack of definition for the role of special education centres in the framework of inclusive schools; updating the training of professionals; the insufficient development of transition into adult life programmes; and particularly the lack of job opportunities in normalized environments, despite the existence of very important initiatives committed to supported work.

The path toward inclusive education has been long, but enormous strides forward have already been taken. There are new and very important challenges to face in order to achieve schools that are respectful of individual differences, and where all students have the opportunity to be admitted, participate, and be academically and personally successful. As J. Font reminded us: "I've always thought that the problem of children with disability is a problem of opportunities; if we don't offer them normalized opportunities, we'll never know what will happen" (Giné, 2005, p. 83).

The gradual construction of deaf people's right to education

"Municipal school for deaf-mutes" of Barcelona

The first Catalan institution for the education of deaf students was established in 1800 in Barcelona, funded by the Barcelona's Town Council. With its 200-year history, the school can be considered representative of how Spanish society has evolved in relation to the education of the deaf during these two centuries. Here, our goal is to present these ways in chronological order to show the various conceptualizations of deaf people that have shaped the curriculum they have been offered. We conclude that the educational curricula offered depended highly on what deaf people were thought to be able to learn and on what their social identity was thought to be. This reflection is an invitation to us today to pledge to continue progressive educational programmes that are based on positive possibilities, as is the case today in socially advanced countries.

Deaf pupils are educable!

Pioneering work in the education of deaf pupils occurred in the 16th century, such as the innovations of Spanish friar Pedro Ponce de León. These and efforts by various others up to the middle of the 17th century were private experiences, featuring individual tutorials, and comprised of a small number of pupils belonging to the higher social classes. It was not until the mid-17th century that the French abbot Charles-Michel de l'Épée founded the first school for deaf pupils in Paris. From that time on, it was not unusual that other schools should open.

In 1799, French presbyter Joan Albert i Martí educated a small group of deaf boys in Barcelona. He carried out this task on his own initiative, with money obtained from public charity. But, after using up all his resources, he went to the Town Council to ask for appropriate premises ("a wide and long room where they can learn to conjugate verbs and put together the parts of a sentence" (Assessoria Tècnica, 1922, p. 236)) in order to continue with his teaching.

The Consistory assigned him a part of the *Saló de Cent*, which is now the most emblematic room in the Town Hall, although at the time it was used only as a storeroom. Joan Albert was in charge of maintenance expenses (blackboards, fungible material, etc.). But before approving the expenses of that "school," Town Council wanted to check that it was actually true that deaf pupils were educable, that they were able to learn things, and that, therefore, money would not be wasted in a utopian project. For this reason, a public examination was called, on 16 February 1800, to clear up any doubts. Many clergymen, members of nobility, and various town councillors attended. Joan Albert carried out the following activity with some of his pupils, which was thus recorded in the minutes of the session:

> Those deaf-mutes that have advanced more, a total of 10, started immediately to explain Catechism and different points of Spanish grammar, everything in writing and distributed on some big cards that everyone could see, with this method: One of the deaf-mutes with a small stick would successively point at the words written on the cards, and for every one of them, the mute that should explain it, with very clear signs that would lead to no confusion, would express their meaning. Once finished this exercise, which everyone did in

turns, they were asked to write the same thing they had already explained, and so they did, by writing it down on their blackboards with elegant letters. (Assessoria Tècnica, 1922, p. 238)

The authorities who were present were astonished to see that it was true that these deaf boys were able to understand and express words and concepts. The minutes clearly show this: "There were tears of tenderness in many among the audience due to the pleasure of seeing those poor boys with education and culture that seemed unattainable for them" (Assessoria Tècnica, 1922, p. 238).

Nevertheless, the aim was not that students would achieve some knowledge that allowed them to understand the world and make it their own. What really concerned that first teacher was that, if the lack of language sentenced these people to an absolute cognitive darkness, they would not have the chance to get to know God or His commandments, and therefore their souls would not go to heaven but would remain in darkness for eternity! But, what tool could make it possible to introduce God's words into their minds? The only imaginable one was language, whether written or spoken, or a sign code. For this reason, that first curriculum, apart from Catechism, also included grammar, though only as the instrument needed for religious education.

An educational model was born, then, which was more like volunteer evangelizing, rather than the expression of a right to education as we understand it today. But Joan Albert went back to France a year later, and the school he initiated was closed until 1806 when another priest – Salvador Vieta – proposed that the Town Council fund the classes again. In this way, the school opened and closed intermittently on the basis of the presence of a teacher, always a clergyman, who was available to volunteer.

These experiences represent an educational model of a redeeming nature, without any direct responsibility on the part of the public institutions. It sprang from a conceptualization of deaf people that defined them as "wretched" and "miserable" people, in a biblical sense, that is, "sufferers of misfortune" and "worthy of mercy" respectively. For example, Dominican friar Manuel Estrada, director of the school when it reopened in 1816, used these adjectives in his opening speech at the beginning of the academic year, and praised the redemption that education could bring to their "unhappy state of stupidity and ignorance" (sic) and that it could free them from "the sentence of vegetating as a beast on earth" (sic).

Following a number of periods of reopening and closing, the last of which was funded by the "Commerce Board of Barcelona" from 1838 to 1840, Barcelona's Town Council finally decided to open the school permanently in 1843. This time it was operated as a municipal public school – Municipal School for Deaf-Mutes – with a teacher and an assistant.

A gradually expanding, but basic level, curriculum

The "Book of registration and classification of Barcelona's School for Deaf-Mutes in Primary Education" provided the register of students and the curriculum of every period. In 1844, the curriculum listed only the following subjects:

- Religion and moral doctrine
- Writing

- Lip reading and dactylology
- Arithmetic
- Study of the state's language (meaning Spanish)

In 1856, the Town Council moved this school for deaf people to the premises of the school for blind people, which had been in operation for some years. Thus, the "Municipal School for Blind and Deaf-Mute People" was created. Although it was one school, it had two separate sections, one for each group of students. This move responded to the philosophy current at the time that all students with "special educational needs" who were considered to be "educable" had to go to the same school. At that time, this included only those students with sensory impairments and not those with mental health or cognitive disabilities, as they were not yet considered to be educable.

Later, curricula were gradually expanded to include new subjects. For example, in 1858, in addition to those subjects mentioned above in 1844, the following subjects were taught:

- Pronunciation
- Mimic (sign) language
- Linear drawing
- Geography
- Useful knowledge (Useful skills or knowledge for daily life)

Sign language, which was referred to at the time as "Mimics," was not actually considered to be a real language. Instead, it was used as a tool, simply to make it easier to transmit content.

Following this expansion of subjects, by 1861 the curriculum, with a training period of 8 years, included all the subjects that hearing students would cover in a mainstream school of Elementary and Higher Primary Education. This did not mean, however, that deaf students were expected to learn the same things as hearing students. They would work on those subjects only in a basic manner, at a level of "General Culture," as they said. In current language, it could be defined as a "curriculum adaptation" of the mainstream curriculum, more or less adapted depending on the abilities of individual students. But the adaptation of that time meant that deaf pupils could not get the Primary Diploma that hearing students received after 8 years of education. Apart from this "*intellectual education*," some types of "*industrial education*" were also offered. These focused on learning a useful trade that would enable them to earn a living at the completion of their studies.

Boys and girls were educated separately, and they were taught some different things. For instance, girls would not learn the decimal system or writing in gothic letters, and those "subjects that might be less applicable or useful for girls were prudently" reduced, and their "industrial education" was basically those "tasks particular to their gender" (Escola de Cecs i de Sords-Muts, 1861, p. 10). Needless to say, this was a reflection of the particular conceptualization of male and female roles that were held by society at that time.

In 1910, two new and interesting things occurred. First, the curriculum included auditory education for the first time and, second, a section for students with cognitive difficulties was created. These moves recognised for this group their right to be educated, as was the case in the more advanced countries in Europe and North America. The school's name was changed and was henceforth named – not politically correct by today's standards – the Municipal School for Blind, Deaf-Mute and Abnormal People.

The 1915 handout for the deaf people's section of the school included the social goals of the school: that students "can be self-sufficient" and taught to "speak and understand spoken language" (Ajuntament de Barcelona, 1915). These specified goals were quite different from the charitable-social motivations of the previous century.

Establishing the "medical model" of education

In 1917, Barcelona's Town Council made the decision to divide that three-purposed school into three separate ones, as they considered that each group of students had unique education needs. The original school then reverted back to its former name, the Municipal School for Deaf-Mutes.

The goal of the school was said to be to "make conscious people that truly deserve the name of citizens." They began to use modern, active teaching methods in place of the simple transmission methods used in earlier years. There was also a fundamental conceptual change inherent in this new school: the deaf pupil was now considered as a "language impaired" person, who needed to "*be rehabilitated to be reintroduced into society*" (Barnils, 1918, p. 7). In support of this, subjects considered as school subjects were taught, but, in addition, a "re-educational" method was adopted, based on "demutization" – systematic phonetic work, articulation of words, auditory education, and so on. Even the director of the school, Pere Barnils, was not a teacher, but a renowned phonetician of that time. In contrast with the teachers who wore habits at the beginning of the 19th century, now the teachers wore white coats – white like that of doctors of that time – in order to stress the scientific-medical character of their educational goals.

This emphasis was accomplished at a cost of sign language. With a teaching method based on articulated words, sign language was given no role at all, and was even contemptuously described as "the show of gestures."

The period from 1918 to 1930 (Pere Barnils' period) was a time of enormous pedagogical innovation and expansion of ideas within this school for the deaf. But this was followed by three decades when there was little progress. With a civil war and a dictatorship regime in Spain in the background, the school was not a priority for the Administration any more, and gradually it lost both its drive and its teachers.

The right to have the primary diploma

In 1970, the Town Council built a new building and provided the school with the best resources available at the time. This new, splendid school was then called Municipal Phono-audiological Centre. The name itself reveals the speech therapeutic orientation that formed the basis of the educational method, as in Pere Barnils' period. But the new young teachers played the major role in achieving a transcendental goal: to go beyond the ceiling of "General Culture" to aim at the curriculum objectives of "General Basic Education." As a consequence, in 1980, the studies given at the school were recognised, and from that point on deaf pupils could get the same Primary diploma as any other hearing pupil studying in a mainstream school. Finally, the deaf child was not a "language impaired" person, but only a pupil.

From special centre to mainstream schools

The recognition of deaf students as full learners, equal to hearing students, raised an important question. If deaf children could study the same as hearing children, why couldn't they do so in the mainstream school? Thus, and following new directives by the Department of Education, Generalitat of Catalonia, a process of externalization began in 1981. This process involved most pupils being schooled in mainstream schools, which is the usual situation at present.

The special centre itself was later transformed into a mainstream school, *Tres Pins*, for the preferential schooling of deaf pupils, and an Educational Resources Centre, where teachers provide speech-therapy support to deaf pupils in mainstream schools. The current model encompasses both the exclusively oral modality, and the "bilingual" one which considers CSL (Catalan sign language) as the language used to learn, along with Catalan and Spanish. The parents or tutors of each pupil choose one or the other modality.

Today nobody is surprised to see deaf people at universities. But this is the result of successive changes in disability as a social construct over time, and the struggles of those in the deaf community and their advocates. This is particularly noteworthy and praiseworthy, because for many centuries they were considered as not educable and suffered from significant restrictions in their rights as citizens.

References

AAIDD. (2010). *Intellectual Disability: Definition, Classification and Systems of Support* (11th ed.). Washington, DC: American Association on Intellectual Disability.

AAMR. (1992). *Mental Retardation: Definition, Classification and Systems of Support* (10th ed.). Washington, DC: American Association on Mental Retardation.

AAMR. (2002). *Mental Retardation: Definition, Classification and Systems of Supports* (9th ed.). Washington, DC: American Association on Mental Retardation.

Ajuntament de Barcelona. (1915). *Escuela Municipal de Ciegos, Sordo-Mudos y Anormales*. Barcelona, Spain.

Assessoria Tècnica de la Comissió de Cultura de l'Ajuntament de Barcelona. (1922). *Les construccions escolars*. Barcelona, Spain: Henrich.

Barnils, P. (1918). *Projecte de l'Escola Municipal de Sords-Muts*. Barcelona, Spain: Inèdit.

Basil, C., Bolea, E., & Soro-Camats, E. (2003). La discapacitat motriu. In C. Giné (Coord.), *Trastorns del desenvolupament i necessitats educatives especials* (pp. 117–127). Barcelona, Spain: EDIUOC.

Constitución Española de 19 de diciembre de. 1978. Constitución Española - BOE.es www.boe.es/legislacion/documentos/ConstitucionCASTELLANO.pdf

Escola de Cecs i de Sords-Muts. (1861). *Reglamento de la Escuela Especial de Ciegos y de Sordo-Mudos establecida en Barcelona á cargo de su Excmo. Ayuntamiento*. Barcelona, Spain: Imprenta de la EECSM.

Escola Municipal de Sords-Muts. (1844 and successive). *Libro de Matrícula y Clasificación*. Barcelona: Imprenta de la EECSM

Fierro, A. (1984). Historia reciente. in R. C. Sheerenberger (Ed.), *Historia del Retraso Mental* (pp. 401–431). San Sebastián, Espana: SIIS.

Fontanet, A., & Palau, R. (2005). El retraso mental: Cambio de Mirada. In C. Giné (Comp.), *Educación y Retraso Mental: Crónica de un proceso* (pp. 15–35). Barcelona, Spain: Edebé.

García-Dié, M. T. (2005). Los padres, promotores de servicios. In C. Giné (Comp.), *Educación y Retraso Mental: Crónica de un proceso* (pp. 85–92). Barcelona, Spain: Edebé.

Giné, C. (1990). La habilitación/rehabilitación basada en la institución escolar. In *Alternativas institucionales en rehabilitación: Documentos y experiencias: Documentos 23/90.* Madrid, Spain: Real Patronato de Educación y Atención a Personas con Minusvalía.

Giné, C. (2003). El retard mental. In C. Giné (Coord.), *Trastorns del desenvolupament i necessitats educatives especials* (pp. 29–47). Barcelona, Spain: EDIUOC.

Giné, C. (2005). Los servicios educativos: De la exclusión a la inclusión. In C. Giné (Comp.), *Educación y retraso mental: Crónica de un proceso* (pp. 61–78). Barcelona, Spain: Edebé.

Ley de vagos y maleantes de 5 de agosto de 1933 (Gaceta de Madrid, Núm. 217).

Ley de 17 de julio de 1945 sobre Educación Primaria (BOE Núm. 199 de 18/07/1945).

Ley 14/1970, de 4 de agosto, General de Educación y Financiación de la Reforma Educativa (BOE Núm. 187 de 06/08/1970).

Ley 16/1970, de 4 de agosto, sobre peligrosidad y rehabilitación social (BOE Núm. 187 de 06/08/1970).

Ley 13/1982, de 7 de abril, de Integración Social de los Minusválidos (BOE Núm. 103 de 30/04/1982).

Ley Orgánica 2/2006, de 3 de mayo, de Educación (BOE Núm. 106 de 4 de mayo de 2006).

Real Patronato de Educación y Atención a Deficientes. (1979). *Plan Nacional de Educación Especial.* Madrid, Spain: Fundación General Mediterránea – SEREM.

Scheerenberger, R. C. (1984). *Historia del retraso mental.* San Sebastián, Espana: SIIS.

UNESCO. (1994). *Declaración de Salamanca y Marco de Acción sobre Necesidades Educativas Especiales.* Geneva, Switzerland: UNESCO.

Warnock, H. M. (1978). *Special Educational Needs. Report of the Committee of Enquiry into the Education of Handicapped Children and Young People.* London, UK: Her Majesty's Stationery Office.

22

THE CASE OF THE "DULL" PUPIL IN THE NORWEGIAN FOLK SCHOOL 1892–1930

Bodil Ravneberg

Some of us might be old enough to remember a group of children who attended our primary schools who were called "dull" pupils. Today, this concept has gone from our vocabulary. However, in the first half of the 20th century, these children received a great deal of attention from teachers, psychiatrists, and psychologists in the Nordic countries.

For 20 years, from 1892 to 1913, the number of dull pupils in the Norwegian capital, Oslo, increased tenfold, from 60 to more than 600 pupils. This was about 2% of the total population of children of compulsory school age in Oslo. The number of dull pupils also increased in the rest of the country[1]. By 1922, ten municipalities had established educational programs for this group of pupils. This indicated a dramatic increase of pupils having "different" behaviour in the Norwegian primary school (also called "folk school") at the beginning of the last century.

Why did the primary schools in the capital of Norway have so many dull children early in the 20th century? What had happened? Did the schools not have dull pupils before the middle of the 19th century? What was special about this period in history regarding these children? My point of departure is that the "problem" with "dull" pupils in the schools was not defined as a social problem until there was a decision taken to do something about it. This might be thought of as a *constructivist approach* in the sense that recognizing and treating dull students was not understood as a social problem until action was taken to be involved with it. A social phenomenon is not necessarily a social problem – until it is understood to be so through experience – as any social phenomenon can be constructed in different ways (Best, 1995).

In this chapter, I wish to argue that the increase in the number of dull pupils did not occur because of any real increase in numbers. Rather, the explanation lies in the fact that a new understanding of the problem with dull pupils developed during this period. For this reason, the chapter deals more with definition processes where certain children came to be seen and defined as a social problem for the folk school, and not so much with the actual discovery of them as "dull" pupils.

The development of the folk (unitary) school

The establishment of the Norwegian folk school system contributes to the explanation of the social construction of the "dull" or the "backward" child. The development of the folk school (or the unitary school) actually presupposed and legitimated a segregation of problem pupils. The Norwegian folk school laws of 1889 represented a major shift from focusing on children's social background to focussing on their *ability* in the classroom, regardless of social background. Initiatives were taken, and by the 1920s, the folk school was consolidated on these values.

The development of the folk school implied stricter entrance requirements for children with special needs (Froestad, 1995, p. 355) and, together with society's growing confidence in experts and professionals, the power of the folk school teachers was strengthened. This opened up the path to specialize in helping dull pupils. The teachers' argument was that these children needed extra help in the classroom. According to jurist Tove Stang Dahl, this was one of the explanations behind the system dividing the children into four new groups. The "normal" children were defined as the genuine pupils of the new folk school, or the new unitary school, in order to make grouping of students more attractive to the middle- and upper-class families (Dahl, 1992). The other three groups of children that were segregated, were the A-group, or the "abnormals," that is, the "blinds," the "deaf" and the "mentally defective"; the B-group, the temporarily "infectious"; and the C-group, the "delinquent" children, who should not enrol in the new folk school because of their own needs and for the smooth operating of the school system. This categorization of children into four groups made the Norwegian folk school narrower than it had previously been, and led to the exclusion of many other groups of children who did not fit into these categories.

The establishment of two special schools in Oslo: Sarsgaten and Ullevålsveien

Beginning in the 1890s, new definitions of deficiency emerged that were connected to an ongoing classification and differentiation debate within the school system. This not only contributed to a new understanding of what was at stake, but also influenced how these questions were to be handled by the folk school. In Oslo, or Kristiania, as the city was called at that time, two special schools were established in order to solve the problem of dull pupils. These two schools were Sarsgaten School in the eastern part of the city, established in 1902, and Ullevålsveien School, established in the western part of the city in 1913. Sarsgaten School was situated in what might be described as a "working class" area of the city, while Ullevålsveien School was situated in an area where more people who were affluent lived. Thus, the children came from different socioeconomic backgrounds, and this was an important aspect in understanding the dull pupil in the school system. Research in the 1920s by doctors working with health promotion illustrated that these social differences between east and west in Oslo mattered. In particular, place of birth (socioeconomic environment) and time spent at school were important factors in the start children had in life (Schiötz, 1927).

The two schools were the result of pressure from teachers, and they were not established with support from the state. In the beginning, the schools were private, with support from the Kristiania municipality. In 1892, Sarsgaten had 10 classes, but by 1921 500 children attended the two special schools in Kristiania, with 40 classes, 30 female teachers, and 10 male teachers (Jacobsen, 1922). By 1920, about 10 municipalities had established some type of program for teaching these children, although these were located only in the larger cities of Norway: Kristiania, Trondheim, Bergen, Kristiansand, and Arendal (Jacobsen, 1922).

The pupils in these schools had originally attended mainstream schools, where they were tested, assigned IQs, and then taken out of the regular schools. Blind and deaf pupils were not included, as these pupils were sent to specialized institutional schools specifically for them. Children with behaviour disorders were also not included, as there also existed special institutions for them.

It was, in fact, not actually clear who these dull children were. Officially, they were called "feeble" and were looked upon as "neither gifted nor talented." They could be hard of hearing, vision impaired, or have speech impediments or other disabilities such as epilepsy, anaemia, spina bifida and so on, that demanded individual treatment (Jacobsen, 1922). In the 1920s, the criteria for being designated a dull pupil became somewhat clearer. Attention was drawn to the pupil's health, intelligence, character, and domestic relations. It was a combination of these differences that determined if the children should be segregated from the normal school and transferred to a special school in Kristiania.

The special schools had two aims: (1) to attend to the needs of the children, and (2) to make society in general satisfied/pleased that the needs of the children were being attended to. An important point was that school segregation presupposed the necessity of medical and psychological interventions, and this acted to legitimize the segregation of the "right" child. Making use of intelligence testing after 1917, the differentiation increased. Statistics showed that it was not the "nasty" or the "mean" child who was assigned to these schools, but rather it was the "weak," the "inactive," or the "restless" child. Many of them came from poor homes. Most of them came from so-called less-adjusted families, although a few came from "well-adjusted families." In fact, the children mainly came from the respectable part of the working class (Det statistiske Centralbyrå, 1926).

The segregation process indicated that the problem was understood in a special way in Oslo. In other cities, special classes were established and integrated within the ordinary schools. In the smaller towns and villages, and in the rural areas, these pupils simply attended regular classes in the schools that were in their communities. The question, therefore, is why special schools for dull pupils were established only in Oslo, and why special classes within the ordinary school system were established in other cities, and not in the countryside. In the following sections, several explanatory factors will be discussed, addressing this big city phenomenon in Oslo.

Changing views of the dull pupil

The new category of pupils in question was a group of children whom Cyril Burt, one of Great Britain's most noted psychologists in the years between the wars, named as the "problem of the borderline child" (Burt, 1935, p. 113). The term "borderline" denoted children who were difficult to diagnose. The dull was a diffuse case, somewhere in between normality and mental deficiency. The problem had to do with the fact that professional groups at the turn of the century – the doctors, the folk school teachers, and the teachers in the schools for mentally defective children – could not agree on whether these children were genuinely normal or whether they were genuinely mentally defective (Nyt Tidsskrift for Abnormvæsenet, 1899, p. 148). The only question they could agree on was that the children were neither genuinely blind nor deaf. Most of the disagreement concerned whether it was possible to separate the dull and the backward children from the mentally defective children, and to retransfer them from the special schools to the regular schools or to other arrangements. The doctors and some of the teachers in the special schools for mentally deficient children argued against the separation of the dulls from this category. The folk school teachers, especially in the capital of Oslo, however, were very much in favour of separating dull children from the mentally deficient children. For several years at the end of the 19th century, a debate occurred about how to name and define the needs of these children and about which living and school placements were the best for them.

This debate took place not only in Norway, but also in the other Scandinavian countries. The teachers within the folk school and the special schools, as well as the doctors working in special schools, disagreed on whether it was a good idea to make a new category of children and name them dull or backward. The teachers and the doctors at the special schools maintained that these children really were mentally deficient and that it was best for them to be sent to the special schools. Their argument was that making new schools for the dulls, as the folk school teachers wanted to do in Oslo at the end of the 19th century, would harm the reputation of the schools for the mentally defective. It would make the dulls an elite group within the mentally defective children, which surely would bring about an undesirable social ranking of the children (Nyt Tidsskrift for Abnormvæsenet, 1899, pp. 73–4).

Who were the dull pupils?

Prior to the first half of the 20th century, it was barely recognized that this category of pupils – the dull – existed, and the doctors and teachers did not look upon mental deficiency as a matter of degree (Burt, 1935, p. 114). Eventually psychologists and psychiatrists realized that the mentally defective actually was the "the tail-end of a more numerous section of the community – the mentally dull" (Burt, 1935, p. 113–114 and 1977, p. 115). From seeing the "mentally dull" as a marginal group within the larger group of people with mental deficiencies, the psychiatrists came to see the mentally dull as a large group that actually outnumbered the mentally defective children. These were children whose progress in the classroom lagged 2 or 3 years behind the progress of their so-called normal peers. In the schools, the teachers and doctors simply called them the dulls and the backwards at the turn of the century. After the Second World War, however, educators changed the term to "slow learners" (Kirk, 1962, p. 85).

These borderline children turned out to be not few in numbers, according to Cyril Burt. He described them as the many marginal cases within the group of mentally defective children, because they, at the turn of the 20th century, caused hesitation among the doctors when they diagnosed and examined the defectives (Burt, 1935, p. 113).

Most of the dull children attended the regular schools in Norway, although some of them attended schools reserved for children who were "mentally deficient." The folk school laws of 1889 had opened up opportunities for the municipalities to establish special arrangements for the dulls. But as long as such arrangements were not compulsory, it was up to the municipalities, based on what they could afford and on their way of understanding the needs of these children, whether or not to make special arrangements.

"Rescuing" children from the special schools for mentally defective

Another issue at stake was that special schools for mentally defective children already were in disgrace among most parents. Sending children to these schools labelled the children as "idiots." The disgrace grew stronger as a result of the growing body of eugenic research that was being carried out in Europe and America, and because of a growing pessimism about the possibility of demonstrating that education of the mentally defective could be successful (Kirkebæk, 1993, p. 23). As a consequence, the doctors took steps to separate the so-called uneducable mentally deficient from those who were considered to be educable, and send the uneducable out of the school system to the social welfare system. This was a step that the teachers within the special schools argued against. They did not cooperate with the doctors in differentiating mentally deficient children in a way that gave them a diagnosis that essentially deemed them to be incapable of receiving benefit from the instruction in the special schools (Nyt tidsskrift for Abnormvæsenet, 1924). The eugenics ideology, widely followed in Europe and North America, did not make the situation better for the parents or the teachers. To a considerable degree, this was the reason why the folk school teachers wanted to define the "borderline" children and rescue them from attending the special schools for the mentally deficient.

Debates among professional groups

In addition to the new arrangements described above that affected how dull children were categorized in the school system, the changing relations among professional groups is also an important aspect of the changing views of the dull child as a social construction (Abbott, 1988). Some of the tasks of the various professional groups involved in the education of dull children overlapped, although each professional group sometimes had its own interests. The psychiatrists were interested in making tests, testing and classifying, and naming and treating the children (Ludvigsen, 1996). The psychologists wanted to use the tests, take care of, differentiate, and treat the children (Hernes, 1996). Some of the teachers who were teaching "normal" pupils wanted to educate the dulls within the ordinary school, while some of the teachers in the special schools for the mentally defective wanted to educate and foster the dulls in the special school reserved for them.

One important outcome of these debates was that a group of folk school teachers in Oslo took charge of the separation of the dull children from the normal and the mentally deficient. One reason for this was that this city had the largest number of pupils, and hence more pupils with special needs than other cities. Another reason was that the working class largely lived in the cities rather than in the countryside, and many of the dull pupils came from the working class[2]. Children from other social classes were also sent to the special schools in Oslo if the psychiatrists advised their families to do so, but these children were fewer in numbers (Statistisk Centralbyrå, 1926).

In Oslo, many female teachers involved themselves in questions on how to teach dull pupils. Most female teachers in the cities came from the middle classes, as compared to the teachers in the countryside (Hagemann, 1992). Some of the teachers' motivation can also be found in the fact that measures to help all dull pupils would also help dull pupils from higher social classes, as most of the children with this class background were sent to one of these schools: the Ullevålsveien School. The argument was that these children would get a better education there than in the regular school or in the school for pupils with mental deficiencies. In addition, many of these children came from, as previously mentioned, the "respectable" parts of the working class, with families that the teachers could identify with themselves.

Modern pedagogical and psychological knowledge

The female teachers in Oslo were very concerned with new pedagogical and psychological ideas coming from Italy, Belgium, Switzerland, England, Germany and France. This becomes evident when studying the activities and interests of the organisation of the female teachers (Norges Lærerinnelag) that was established in 1912. The majority of the female teachers who became members of this organisation came from the cities and, in particular, from Oslo (Hagemann, 1992). This organisation had different interests than its male counterpart organisation, "Norges lærerlag." The female teachers claimed, for instance, that female teachers were better qualified to teach young children than male teachers (Homme, 1993).

Many of the female teachers, especially those who taught the lower grades in Oslo, were also very much inspired by the progressive educational movement called *reform pedagogics*. The reform pedagogic movement (e.g., the pedagogics of Maria Montessori or Ovide Decroly) was optimistic in nature, and believed in the opportunities and the power that education gave children. Important pedagogical principles were independence, self-education, responsibility for the self, self-activity, independent and autonomous learning, and discovery (Myhre, 1991). It was also important to encourage the development of imaginative skills and social learning. The central aim was to aid young people on their way to becoming autonomous human beings, and developing their social skills and common interests as well as their uniqueness. The reform pedagogics was also concerned with the content of the school curriculum – it did not see itself as offering supplementary or alternative content so much as offering a new way of learning traditional content that resulted in additional personal and social skills. In practice, the ideas of reform pedagogy blended into the existing school system and the larger social environment of Norway.

The teachers directed their claims for reform towards the state, the regular school system, and the special school system. The folk school teachers initiated several strategies to further their objectives, as explained below, although these strategies faced barriers from other specialized professional groups that were also interested in the problems with these children, but interested in different ways and for different purposes. These were primarily the psychiatrists and, later, the psychologists (Erichsen, 1996).

The separation of the dulls was a work carried out by the psychiatrists and the folk school teachers working together. This gave the psychiatrists an opportunity to develop new techniques in testing the intelligence of a new type of clientele and to put in place a legitimate sub-speciality within the medical profession. The psychiatrists had, by this time, gained intellectual and advisory jurisdiction over the "mentally dull" children. They were the ones who diagnosed and advised the folk school teachers to separate them from the "normal" pupils. The folk school teachers had, of course, full jurisdiction in teaching the children, but they were in a subordinate position when it came to diagnosing and treating them.

The folk school teachers who engaged in this work developed a somewhat tense relationship towards two other professional groups, psychiatrists and psychologists. The folk school teachers claimed that they could not hand the problem of the dulls over to the other professions as they realized that they, as educators with growing experiences in teaching dull pupils, had the best qualifications to handle the problem and help the children to become independent members of the society. They claimed that the doctors were not able to solve the problem by medical knowledge and techniques alone, as this was an issue of giving the "right" child the "right" education, not only the "right" diagnosis or treatment. They argued that this was a problem related to the school, while the psychologists argued that the solution to the problem was to be found outside the school premises (Hernes, 1996). They also claimed that the ordinary folk school teachers could not deal with the problem as long as they did not have the proper qualifications to do so.

Another strategy for the group of folk school teachers was therefore to become qualified in testing, treating, and teaching the dull children. They did this by establishing educational courses with medical, psychiatric, and psychological knowledge content for the teachers interested in these children.

A big-city phenomenon

As mentioned, Oslo had the largest number of dull pupils in Norway, and most of these attended two special schools located in the western and in the eastern part of the town, respectively. Outside the cities, in the countryside, dull children attended regular classes. Many teachers in the countryside avoided taking up the question of separation of dull pupils, which they claimed was out of respect for the parents and the children. The folk school teachers in Oslo argued that this avoidance was due, rather, to their lack of knowledge about these children.

Thus, the construction of the dull or the backward child was a big-city phenomenon. There were four main reasons for this. First and most obvious, the largest cities had a greater number of children with special needs, and as a result arrangements for their education were established in only the largest cities of Norway. Second, social class division was more visible in the cities. More than half of the dull children had a father classified as a "worker." Children from higher social classes also attended the special schools when a psychiatrist advised their families to do so, but they were fewer in numbers. Third, in defining the needs of the "borderline" children, the folk school teachers in Oslo took the lead. Fourth, gender tensions within the teacher profession itself contributed to this being a city phenomenon. In Oslo, it was to a large extent the female teachers who engaged in this work. Many of the female teachers came from more affluent families in the cities, unlike the teachers from the countryside (Hagemann, 1992). In 1912, the female teachers broke away from the male teacher organisation and established a new organisation only for female teachers to better reflect their interests.

In 1870, the school board in Oslo – or Kristiania, as the city was named at that time—decided to begin teaching "dull" pupils on a probationary basis. There were two arguments for taking up this work. First, there were pedagogical arguments and arguments related to the organization of the school system, namely the development of the unitary school. The view of the school board was that it was possible to educate these children and make them independent and useful members of the society as long as their abilities were not too weak. Second, it was argued that the regular schools had to be relieved of dull pupils who never would benefit from the teaching there, and that these children, according to the existing law, could not demand special arrangements being made especially for them within the folk schools.

Summary

The perspective in this chapter has been a social constructivist one. The point has been to show what mechanisms led to the definition of a new problem pupil at school – "dull" pupils – and why this problem was solved in a special way at this time in history. The main arguments have been that dull pupils became a problem for the school because the teachers wanted to raise the status of the folk school in order to attract children from middle- and upper-class families. Some of the important driving forces behind this were the development of the Norwegian folk school, the changing view of mental deficiency within the special school system, and the changing relations among the occupational groups in the professional field. New therapeutic and pedagogic knowledge, the feminisation of the primary school profession in the larger cities, as well as the society's growing confidence in expert knowledge were also important driving forces in the segregation process.

The female teachers' organization had interests other than those of the male teachers' organization. The female teachers argued that they had better qualifications in teaching small children than did male teachers. They also took a strong interest in the reform pedagogical ideas of the time, and were to a greater degree than the male teacher organisation interested in trying out the new modern pedagogical and psychological ideas in the folk schools.

Jurisdictional disputes among different professions help explain how the view of the dull and the backward child has changed over time, and how the state of being dull has changed to become a "slow learner" and, later, to be "integrated" into the regular school system. Over the decades, teachers gradually began to teach an increasing number of children with a variety of medical diagnoses. This paved the way for the professionalization process of special teachers after the Second World War. It is, however, a dilemma today that diagnosing on medical grounds is so dominant. The dilemma is that such practices are, or can be, a straitjacket for the pupil and the school in the sense that they exclude other ways of defining deficiency and other methods of effective teaching.

Whether the establishment of measures to identify dull pupils in the cities was good or bad for the children is not discussed here, as that is a different question. The point has been to show how the problem with dull pupils was socially constructed, defined as it was as a new social problem for the unitary school, and to explain how this social problem was solved in a particular way at this time in history.

Notes

1 In 1923 there were 613 pupils in "særskolen" in Oslo, whilst there were a number of hard-of-hearing pupils (not deaf) of 2800. In the city of Bergen the numbers were 130 and 1200, Trondheim 31 and 800, Drammen 61 and 400, Arendal 29 and 130 (Statistisk Sentralbyrå 44de bind-1926).

2 Between 1919 and 1923, of a total population of 248 pupils, 156 had a father who was a worker in the cities of Oslo, Bergen, Drammen, Trondheim or Arendal. (Statistiske meddelelser, Det Statistiske Centralbyrå, 44de bind-1926, Oslo).

375

References

Abbott, A. (1988). *The System of Professions. An Essay on the Division of Expert Labour*. Chicago, IL: University of Chicago Press.

Best, J. (1995). Typification and social problems construction. in J. Best (Ed.), *Images of Issues* (pp. 3–15). New York, NY: Aldine de Gruyter.

Burt, C. (1935) and (1977). *The Subnormal Mind*. Oxford: Oxford University Press.

Dahl, T. S. (1992). *Barnevern og samfunnsvern* [Childcare and Protection of Society]. Oslo, Norway: Pax Forlag.

Erichsen, V. (Ed.). (1996). *Profesjonsmakt: På sporet av en norsk helsepolitisk tradisjon* [Professional Power: Tracing a Norwegian Health Political Tradition]. Otta, Norway: Tano Aschehoug.

Froestad, J. (1995). Faglige diskurser, intersektorielle premisstrømmer og variasjoner i offentlig politikk: Døveundervisning og handikapomsorg i Skandinavia på 1800-tallet [Professional discourses, intersectorial premises and variations in public policy: Teaching the Deaf and care for the handicapped in Scandinavia in the 18th century]. Rapport nr. 34. Dr.grads avhandling ved inst. for Adm. Org., Univ. i Bergen.

Hagemann, G. (1992). *Skolefolk: Lærernes historie i Norge* [The History of Teachers in Norway]. Oslo, Norway: Ad notam Gyldendal.

Hernes, S. (1996). Barnevern i 1950-årene: Om psykologiens profesjonalisering [Childcare in the 1950's: About the professionalisation of the psychology]. in V. Erichsen (Ed.), *Profesjonsmakt. På sporet av en norsk helsepolitisk tradisjon* [Professional Power: Tracing a Norwegian Health Political Tradition] (pp. 150–166). Otta, Norway: Tano Aschehoug.

Homme, A. (1993). Vi vil løfte skolen og løfte standen, En studie av feminiserings- og profesjonaliseringsprosessen i læreryrket i Norge, 1890–1912. [We want to raise the school and the profession: A study of feminisation and professionalization processes in the teacher occupation, 1890–1912]. Rapport nr. 21. Hovedfagsoppgave, inst. for Adm. Org, Univ. i Bergen.

Jacobsen, J. (1922). Særskolen, dens maal og midler [The special school, aims and means]. In Jacobsen, J.: *Særtrykk av Skola och Samhalla* [Special Print of School and Society]. Göteborg, Sweden: C. R. Holmquists Boktryckeri.

Kirk, S. A. (1962). *Educating Exceptional Children*. Boston, MA: Houghton Mifflin Company.

Kirkebæk, B. (1993). *Da de åndssvake blev farlige* [When the Mental Deficients Became Dangerous]. Holte, Denmark: Socpol.

Ludvigsen, K. (1996). Barnevern ved århundreskiftet: Om psykiatriens profesjonalisering, [Childcare by the century shift: About the professionalisation of the psychiatry]. in V. Erichsen (Ed.), *Profesjonsmakt: På sporet av en norsk helsepolitisk tradisjon* [Professional Power: Tracing a Norwegian Health Political Tradition] (pp. 130–147). Otta, Norway: Tano Aschehoug.

Myhre, R. (1991). *Grunnlinjer i pedagogikkens historie*. (Main features in the history of pedagogics). Gyldendal Norsk Forlag, Oslo.

Nyt Tidsskrift for Abnormvæsenet omfattende Aandsvage-, Blinde- og Vanføre-sagen i Norden 1899–1943. København/Copenhagen.

Ravneberg, B. (1999). Normalitetsdiskurser og profesjonaliseringsprosesser: En studie av spesialpedagogenes yrkesutvikling 1880–1990. Dr. Gradsavhandling: Rapport nr. 69 (1999), Institutt for administrasjon og organisasjonsvitenskap, Univ. i Bergen. [Discourses of normality and professionalisation processes. A study of the development of the special teacher profession 1880–1990. Doctoral thesis, University of Bergen, Dept. of Administration and Organization Science.]

Schiötz, C. (1927). *Skolealderen. Utviklingsforhold, sygdomslære og hygiene. En utredning for lærere, gymnaster og skolepleiersker*. (School age. Development, nosology and hygiene. A report for teachers, gymnasts and school nurses), J.W. Cappelen, Oslo.

Statistiske meddelelser, Det Statistiske Centralbyrå, 44de bind-1926, Oslo.

PART IV

SPECTACLE, SCIENCE, SERVICES
AND CIVIL RIGHTS

Ivan Brown

In this fourth and final section of the book, we look beyond the development of more general and educational services for people with disabilities and focus on disability as a visible phenomenon over the past 100 years. The central theme of the section is that the way people with disabilities have been seen – and consequently the way they have been treated – by others changed during the latter part of the 20th century to the present day. The six chapters of this section endeavour to depict this transition by presenting how people with disabilities were featured in freak shows, their physical features manipulated through photography, or killed systematically in Nazi Germany forward to a time when supports and services were introduced and then on to an era when national and international civil rights legislation for disabled people emerged as a viable ideology and practical force in societies around the world.

Andrea Zittlau's chapter "The Freak Show Act: Science and spectacle in the nineteenth century" is an excellent place to begin this exploration. Zittlau describes in some detail two key examples of freak shows, the Missing Link and the Aztec Children, that became common features of freak shows that were part of circuses, amusement parks, popular museums, and other public entertainments. She notes that the physical differences of those presented on stage were accompanied by mostly fictitious stories of their origins and histories, and were ostensibly validated by research and science. Although freak shows were carried out as public entertainment, and thus an understanding of them should fully reflect this, the presentation of visible "difference" as a spectacle seems from our current perspective to be not only dehumanizing to those made to act out the shows but also misleading to a gullible public who may have mistaken some of what they saw and heard to be scientific fact rather than mere entertainment.

Martin A. Elks' chapter "Three Illusions in Clinical Photographs of the Feeble-Minded During the Eugenics Era" illustrates a more sinister aspect of presenting physical differences. Although the freak show deliberately promoted enfreakment – the contextualization of physical difference within a fantasy world – it did so with tongue at least partially in cheek and with one eye at least partially winking. Freak show presenters knew they were hoodwinking the public, even if the public may or may not have always caught on to this. On the other hand, Elks' describes how leading scientists of the Eugenics Era actively set out to convince both the scientific community and the general public that there were visible differences among the various "grades" of the feeble-minded. The difficulty with their body of work is that it does not stand up to scrutiny when the categories and descriptions are compared to the visual illustrations presented. Elks provides numerous examples of how scientists of this era tried to manipulate others into their way of thinking by sheer persuasion. Because their descriptions and illustrations were presented as serious science, they were much less likely to be received by the audience as the deliberate fraud that the freak shows were.

The seriousness of false presentation is illustrated by Ivan Brown's chapter entitled "When Is Life Unworthy of Living? Lessons from the systematic killing of children with disabilities in Nazi Germany." In his chapter, Brown argues that the Nazis in Germany built their view that children with disabilities, among others (including about 75,000 people who lived in psychiatric asylums, and about 6 million Jews) were unworthy of living. The program for killing children relied heavily on "scientific" evidence and on the scientific community of professionals to carry it out, although, as Brown argues, there was considerable resistance and non-compliance from families, medical practitioners, and facility operators. The presentation, and ultimately the acceptance, of children with disabilities as "useless eaters" led directly to them being considered to be unworthy of even living.

Taken together, these three chapters illustrate that public presentation, social construction, and ideology can interact in intricate ways, and when they occur in dishonest ways they can lead to horrific and tragic consequences. This is a lesson that is still relevant today, for there are still places in the world where children and adults with disabilities die as a result of similar interactions.

Chapters 25 and 26 illustrate two major ways visible disabilities were treated in the middle decades of the 20th century. The examples are from Canada, but are representative of phenomena present throughout developed countries of the world at the time. Roy Hanes' chapter "The Rise of Services for Crippled Children in Canada: The case example of the Ontario Society for Crippled Children" traces the development of one organization from a local initiative to a large and established structure. More important, Hanes' chapter illustrates how people with disabilities were increasingly viewed as deserving recipients of charity, a view that had been established to lesser degrees many centuries earlier in Europe. Large charitable organizations that provided services to people with disabilities expanded quite dramatically during the 20th century alongside the expansion on government services – each contributing to the rationale for the other.

The chapter that follows by Karen Yoshida and Fady Shanouda, "Breaking of Silence: A culture of silence, polio practices, agency and the self" reminds us that the overall treatment of people with disabilities was not always as charitable as it was made out to be. The authors argue that the experiences of children (and, by extension, others with disabilities) who were "crippled" from polio were mostly silenced during the middle decades of the 20th century, due primarily to a predominant "culture of silence" that prohibited the life experiences of people with disabilities from being validated in open conversation or even known. The charitable aspect of support organizations appears to have been confined, and they may have knowingly or unknowingly exacerbated the culture of silence. The inherent irony of attempting to make visible disabilities invisible through silence may seem self-defeating to us now, but was a powerful force at the time.

The final chapter of this section moves us forward from the dominant tendency to simultaneously segregate and overlook disability within the broader culture toward our current view: that disability is a legitimate and valuable aspect of all cultures and that people with disabilities are valued citizens with full and equal rights and opportunities. Steven E. Brown's chapter "Changing America's Consciousness: A brief history of the Independent Living Civil Rights Movement in the United States" describes for us how this transition took form. Brown notes such a transition involved a major paradigm shift, and that this took several decades to evolve and is still evolving.

The optimism that emerges when the chapters in this section are taken together is that the view of disability by non-disabled people has changed very dramatically over the past 100 years. The current view that people with disabilities have a right to full inclusion and participation in all aspect of societies is one that has taken root. If it has not yet been fully accepted, and certainly not fully implemented, it is a very major step forward from categorizing people with disabilities in questionable ways, using photographs, featuring them in freak shows, and having them killed as unworthy of living.

23

THE FREAK-SHOW ACT: SCIENCE AND SPECTACLE IN THE NINETEENTH CENTURY

Andrea Zittlau

The exhibition of the physical Other – in its broadest sense – has a long tradition. Cave paintings of the Stone Age depict human anomalies and suggest their singular status within society (Garland-Thomson, 1996a, p. 1). Deformity features prominently in several ancient myths, such as in the *Odyssey*, that include Cyclops and giants (see Neumann, 2005, pp. 23–26 for a brief discussion). During the Middle Ages, monsters were imagined to inhabit the outskirts of the world. Maps or treatises testify to that tradition, exhibiting drawings of fantastic bodies (see Daston and Park, 1998, pp. 21–66.). The cabinets of curiosities, popular collecting houses of the Renaissance, entertained Europe's nobility with unusual objects and people (see Arnold, 2006), and during the Enlightenment the tradition of displaying the extraordinary body[1] continued, for example, as part of the growing science of medicine where those bodies became part of anatomical museums (e.g., Zürcher, 2004, pp. 66–82).

But nothing could have predicted the immense success of the display of anomalies of the human body that emerged in the second half of the nineteenth century as the mass entertainment industry.[2] "In a turbulent era of social and material change," as Rosemarie Garland-Thomson wrote, "the spectacle of the extraordinary body stimulated curiosity, ignited speculation, provoked titillation, furnished novelty, filled coffers, confirmed commonality, and certified national identity" (1996a, p. 4). Due to a new understanding of leisure,[3] venues like the dime museum, amusement parks, circuses and vaudeville bloomed – and the so-called *freak show* was at the heart of them all. Although advertised in the shows as human oddities or human curiosities, or described by their specific features, the "freak"[4] and "freak show" quickly became terms used to refer to the shows that staged abnormal bodies within a sensationalist discourse by blurring the boundaries between fact and fiction and by creating characters that violated the rules of civilization. With the help of promotion (published in newspapers, distributed in form of posters, etc.), narratives (published in pamphlets or delivered by a speaker during the show), "expert" lectures, and props, the extraordinary body was contextualized in a fantasy world that was geographically and temporally distant from the audience. This process of fantastic transformation is described as *fantastification* and *enfreakment* (Garland-Thomson, 1996a, p. 10) and was essential to the success of the freak show. Whereas fantastification describes the process of radically othering here, enfreakment refers to the gap thus created between the audience and the performer. Accordingly, extraordinary embodiments induced by congenital or developmental disorders are perceived as cultural (not natural) constructs that have been consistently "stylized, silenced, differentiated and distanced" from the norm by the cultural rituals of ideologically infiltrated (medical, religious, political) representational practices (Kerchy and Zittlau, 2012, p. 1). So the "freaks of nature" become "freaks of culture," since their bodily difference is highlighted and used in cultural rituals to reassure mass identities. This also means that the physical difference as such was not spectacular enough to be staged and stared at.

Perhaps because of their individual talents that were so essential to the freak shows, the performers have been at the centre of popular and academic discussions of this particular form of entertainment. From encyclopaedia-like publications that categorize them by their deformities (Drimmer, 1973; Fiedler, 1981; Scheugl, 1974) to discussions driven by moral concern about their exposed display (e.g., Bogdan, 1990), the performers have been crucial to the understanding of the freak-show phenomenon. Eventually the focus shifted to the broader social issues, particularly in the United States and Victorian Britain, to understand the desire and dynamics of exhibiting the extraordinary bodies for consumer and commercial purposes (Adams, 2001; Garland-Thomson, 2009; Tromp, 2008). In fact, freaks simultaneously performed "gender, race, sexual aberrance, ethnicity, and disability as inextricable yet particular exclusionary systems legitimated by bodily variation" (Garland-Thomson, 1996a, p. 10). But they do not embody the complex fantasies underlying stigmatization; rather, they *enact* them in strictly scripted shows. To be as powerful as the shows were (and to a certain extent still are), the performance has to follow a certain pattern to be able to entertain, educate and reassure middle-class mass identity. Since freak shows not only took place in North America but also toured most European and other developed countries, the acts had to appeal to audiences of various cultural backgrounds but always addressing questions of radical physical and cultural otherness.

The two different acts discussed in this article, the Aztec Children and the Missing Link, both translate (through fantastification and enfreakment) contemporary scientific discoveries to mass audiences. The immense popularity of the two acts as well as their longevity and international circulation and success confirm the promotion of knowledge and ideas on a transnational stage. In both acts performers with microcephaly played a crucial role, and yet their condition was interpreted on stage in entirely different ways.

The freak show is a medium located between Performance Studies and Disability Studies, which, in this particular case, presents disability to audiences as a "scientific" oddity that amalgamates elements of human anatomy with exotic curiosities (highly fictional) from history, geography, anthropology, archaeology, and sociology. The perspective of the freak show is on the performance, rather than on the individuals featured in it. Tapping into the age-old human fascination for human difference, it was presented as stories or shows, in theatrical style, with the displayed people as actors. In doing so, it was neither the person with the disability nor the disability itself that was highlighted, but rather the representation of disability as a remote and awe-inspiring scientific extreme (anatomically, historically, geographically, culturally, etc.) – literally and figuratively "worlds" apart from the experience of the average person in the audience. The real meaning of the freak show, then, is not to better understand disability or the "unfortunate" people with disability, but rather to feed natural human curiosity about difference in the human condition. In doing so, though, disability is understood by the audience as a marvel and ultimately as an "other" condition.

Act 1 – The Aztec Children

The freak show act of the Aztec Children was born in 1849 when a boy and a girl, presented as Maximo and Bartola,[5] appeared on stage in New York City for the first time. "The Two Living Aztec Children" was the headline that never changed throughout their lifetimes, and neither did the essence of their performance. They were "said to be descendants of the sacerdotal caste, now nearly extinct, of the ancient Aztec founders of the ruined temples of Central America and Yucatan" (Barnum, 1860, p. 9). As the almost last of a vanishing people, they were staged as physical evidence that confirmed the widespread notion of the disappearance of the Indigenous population of the Americas – a notion that not only was very present in the Americas themselves but also was a continuous theme on the European continent. The *Vanishing Indian* was made prominent in the public consciousness by the paintings of George Catlin and Karl Bodmer, which received much attention in the United States, Europe, and elsewhere from the 1840s onwards. The Aztecs were claimed to be of special status, mythologized as inhabitants of a golden empire that had perished long ago. They were connected to discovery, not only of people but of unknown lands, to wealth and prestige and to an age in which explorers had been celebrated as heroes because they brought knowledge in the form of people, objects, and stories to European audiences.

In the nineteenth century, the map of the world had been long drawn, but many discoveries were being made – in archaeology, anthropology, biology, medicine, and a set of other sciences that developed at the time. The performance of the Aztec Children built on both a nostalgic longing for discoveries, and relied on the newly developing sciences for their rationales. To prove their Aztec origin, the examination of the bodies of Maximo and Bartola was essential to the performance, during which they were eventually pronounced as "the most extraordinary specimens of the human race ever known" (Barnum, 1860, p. 9). The examination was based on comparative anatomy, a popular method at the time. Since Maximo and Bartola had microcephaly, a neurodevelopmental disorder that often (but not always) produces physical and intellectual disabilities, their heads were of a particular shape characteristic of their condition. This particular shape was often (offensively in the present day) termed as "pinhead" in the freak-show business and was a crucial part of a number of different acts. But the human head was also the focus of a number of sciences, such as phrenology, that were developing at the time, and the obsessive collecting of crania, their measurement, and comparison was crucial to the disciplines of medicine and anthropology (see Morton, 1839).

During the display of Maximo and Bartola, it was stressed that "their form and features [were] unlike any other human being, their heads smaller than an infant's a week old, measuring only thirteen inches in circumference, while that of an ordinary adult measures 22 to 23 inches" (Barnum, 1860, p. 9). Further scientific discourse confirmed them to be "the most wonderful human beings ever brought to the notice of the public" (Barnum, 1860, p. 9), comparing the shape of the heads to drawings of sculptures found during archaeological excavations in Central America, where Maximo and Bartola were said to have been found.

The narrative of their discovery provided a spectacular background to their performance, and it seems that their stage act was solely an illustration of the adventurous story. In a booklet entitled *Memoir of an eventful expedition into central America, resulting in the discovery of the idolatrous city of Iximaya, in an unexplored region; and the possession of two remarkable Aztec children. Maximo (the man) and Bartola (the woman), descendants and specimens of the sacerdotal cast (now nearly extinct), of the ancient Aztec founders of the ruined temples of that country, described by John L. Stephens, Esq., and other travellers* (1850), readers learn about the circumstances of their spectacular discovery in the lost city of Iximaya. As indicated already in the book's title, the mythical city of Iximaya goes back to John Lloyd Stephens' *Incidents of Travel in Central America, Chiapas and Yucatan* (two volumes), which was first published in 1841 and was extremely popular at the time. Stephens was an American writer and explorer with a keen interest in the sciences of anthropology (then in its infancy) and archaeology, particularly concerning Mesoamerica. In his book, he mentioned the existence of "a living city, large and populous, occupied by Indians, precisely in the same state as before the discovery of America" (Stephens, 1841, p. 195). But Stephens and his companions, among them the architect Frederick Catherwood, decided not to climb the sierra, though they had intended to, because the roads were very difficult and it would have added another ten days to their journey just to be able to see the city from the sierra without reaching it.

The *Memoir* about the discovery of Maximo and Bartola makes excessive use of Stephens' work, quoting long passages from his book. For example, they point out that the inhabitants of that mystic city "who speak the Maya language, are aware that a race of white strangers has conquered the whole country around them, and have hence murdered every white man that has since attempted to penetrate their territory" (*Memoir*, 1850, p. 3). This and other statements turn the described expedition by Mr. Huertis of Baltimore, Mr. Hammond from Canada, and the Spaniard Pedro Velasquez (the only survivor and supposed author of the text) into a life-risking mission with a fatal end for several members of their party. The pages detail their difficult paths and complicated but heroic finding of Iximaya, mimicking anthropological and archaeological texts of the time. The Aztec Children appear only briefly, but are crucial to the disastrous end of the narrative, since the expedition feels a responsibility to take them – kidnapping the most sacred element of the city at great risk to themselves. This echoes a number of other stories in which anthropologists nearly sacrificed their lives to "rescue" sacred ritual items, although in fact they were stealing them (see for example Price, 2001, pp. 68–81). As in those narratives, the Aztec Children here are part of a conquest having been "saved" from obscure practises.

The *Memoir* includes Frederick Catherwood's illustrations of the travels of Stephens that depict the particular head shape of the Mayan nobility. These were then compared to the engravings published in 1848 in *Nineveh and Its Remains* by Austen Henry Layard as further proof of the children's noble origin. While in popular culture the over-spectacularized narrative of the discovery of the Aztec children was perceived with scepticism but not thought unlikely, the scientific community invested much time and effort to prove or contradict the findings. But their discussions continuously reassured the possibility of the story narrated in the *Memoir*, since they confirmed the extraordinary status of the Aztec Children, and thus somewhat inadvertently promoted the show: "Both Dr Latham and Professor Owen have critically examined them [Maximo and Bartola]," announced an article entitled "The Aztecs in England" in *Buchanan's Journal of Man* in August 1854, "and both have arrived in the main at similar conclusions." While Professor Owen saw them as "examples of impeded developments in individuals, belonging possibly to a mixed and degraded Indo-Spanish race," Dr Latham fashioned the thought that they had parents of ordinary size, but considered it possible that "other individuals, more or less similar to them, exist in the same region" as a "consequence of the degradation of the race from which they sprung." He is furthermore sure that they are not Aztecs but "descendants of an older race" (p. 240). In Germany, Rudolf Virchow, the renowned pathologist of the time, repeatedly examined Maximo and Bartola and in his discussions concluded that they were microcephalic, but continued to use the narrative of their discovery when talking about their origin (for a discussion see Rothfels, 1996, pp. 158–172).[6]

The freak show allowed the public to seemingly take part in these scientific exchanges, since the discussions were recited during performances often by someone enacting a professor or lecturer. Thus, the show displayed contemporary scientific discourses more than Maximo and Bartola themselves, who were merely seen to be evidence of these discourses. Their part consisted of simply appearing on stage, often dressed in golden robes or other fantastic costumes that used the symbol of the sun to further connect them to the Aztec Empire (as can be seen on a popular carte-de-visite, Rothfels 1996, p. 161). The audience was invited to talk to them or play with them to form their own opinion of their origin.

In their essence, many freak shows remained a riddle to be solved by the spectator, and deception was a well-known part of it. The wife of scientist Richard Owen, for example, reported in her journal to have seen "two most extraordinary dwarf children from Peru [sic], whose minds seem to go no further than those of ordinary children of two or three years old. ... I soon attracted the attention of the boy by drawing objects he was likely to know on a piece of paper. He recognized a duck at once, pointing and nodding his head. A cat was not so familiar. They are very strange beings" (cited in Altick, 1978, pp. 284–5). While her encounter with Maximo and Bartola clearly made an impression on her, she was not interested in who they really were. In contrast to the scientists who measured and examined Maximo and Bartola, the audience interacted with them throughout their lives as children, miniature and cute beings, similar to the performers of tiny people acts such as the "Sicilian Fairy" (who died in the 1820s) or "General Tom Thumb" (performing from the 1840s until his death in 1883).[7] These "midget acts" had been relying on Thomas Langley's English fairy tale "Tom Thumb" of 1621, Jonathan Swift's *Gulliver's Travels* (1724), the fairy tales "Thumbelina" by Hans Christian Andersen (1835) and "Snow White" eventually published by the Grimm Brothers in 1857. In all these stage acts, which in some cases even involved the re-enactment of the fairy tales, the audience was drawn into a fantasy world, a world not dissimilar from the Aztec Children act, and yet the latter played with scientific ideas as opposed to fictitious spheres. Maximo and Bartola never reached the individual doll-like status of a Tom Thumb who, in acting the general or Napoleon, succeeded in escaping claims of inferiority.

As Susan Stewart noticed concerning the miniature, "the child continually enters here as a metaphor" (Stewart, 1993, p. 44). In the case of the Aztec Children, the immature took on further significance, reassuring colonial claims over populations described to be inferior (see also Aguirre, 2004). Savages and primitives were common terms used to describe the ethnic other that was always understood to be mainly a bodily "other." Anthropology treated the subjects of its interests like children who either would eventually learn to assimilate to Western practises or would fail at this difficult task. Although seemingly ethnographic specimens, the Aztec Children were not staged in the fashion of an ethnic show. They did not perform dances, music or quotidian practises foreign to their audiences. Instead, they were singular curiosities, specimens, linked to the animal kingdom often by announcing them not by their names but by their ages, biological sex ("a male and a female"; Barnum 1860, p. 9), and connecting them to their geographical origin.

Maximo and Bartola were not the only Aztecs who were commonly found on the freak show stages. The act was popular, and others, effected likewise by microcephaly, toured the world stages with the same act and similar narratives of discovery (see, for example, Drimmer, 1973, 355f.; Scheugl, 1974, pp. 105–108), although Maximo and Bartola had been the first. Carte-de-visites to be found, for example, in the Felix Adanos collection in Vienna, testify to the popularity of the act and some performers, just like Maximo and Bartola, became celebrities. Among them "Pip and Flip, the Twins from Yucatan," the microcephalic twins Elvira and Jenny Snow from Georgia who gained fame after having appeared in Todd Browning's film *Freaks* (1932). Almost a century after the first staging of the act of the last Aztecs, Elvira and Jenny no longer wore golden costumes, but they were still linked to Yucatan, and thus to the narrative of the discovery of lost worlds.

Besides the geographical and temporal distance created by the original act, the performance itself had, by the 1930s, become a classic. Again, the actors confirmed through their mere presence a narrative that did not lose its fascination, and by continuing to embody this "fascinating" story the Aztec performers in show business could never escape their roles.

The disability of the performers was crucial to the role, and yet the performance never focussed on the disability. Rather, it was merely the subject matter that illustrated, or proved, the scientific findings about civilizations who deliberately deform the heads of their infants to, for example, indicate nobility. The Aztec Children merged ideas of savage anthropology (the last of a vanished race), medicine in its widest sense (pathology, but also comparative anatomy that tried to classify human races by physical measurement and was widely used in physical anthropology), and archaeology (the images of the Mayan ruins and Egyptian hieroglyphs). The scientists were part of the myth; they were as exotic as the "presented specimens" themselves. But, whereas the audiences did not particularly care about the claim for authenticity, since they most likely enjoyed the riddle and the clearly distinguishable performers as the last of the Aztecs during their freak show visits, the scientists worried about fraud and deception (see Virchow (1891) and Owen (Altick, 1978)).

The sheer longevity of the Aztec act testifies to the romantic desire of discovery, the nostalgic idea of the vanished, and the longing for the exotic that was threatened during the nineteenth century, when the scientific approach dominated and was widely accepted. It also testifies to the fact that scientific discourses of anthropology, archaeology, and medicine were popular at the time and continued to be so. Finally, the act illustrates the pathologizing of the body that was crucial in the sciences. The disability of the performers was essential for the role of the Aztecs, but that does not mean that all people with microcephaly toured the world as Aztecs. There were other roles available to them, as the following will illustrate.

Act 2 – The Missing Link

While the Aztec Children relied primarily on the public's interest in archaeology and anthropology, the Missing Link, also called What is It or nondescript,[8] was a particular play that focused on evolutionary themes. Only 3 months after the widely read and discussed publication of Charles Darwin's *The Origin of Species by Means of Natural Selection, or the Preservation of Favoured Races in the Struggle for Life* (1859), Phineas Taylor Barnum,[9] the freak show mastermind, turned the popular man-monkey act into a show he called the *What is It* that relied on knowledge of Darwin's theory. In 1860, he published an edition of the *Memoir* about the Aztec children that also included reference to the Missing Link attraction:

> The What is It? Or, Man or Monkey!, a most singular animal, which, though it has many of the features and characteristics of both, the human and brute, is not, apparently, either, but, in appearance, a mixture of both – the connecting link between humanity and the brute creation. (Cited in Cook, 2005, p. 134)

The performance played on recent scientific discourses and debates that were mirrored in the presentation of the performer, who was presented to the public in the fashion of comparative anatomy. Its foot was said to be "narrow, slim and flat," with "a long heel like that of the native African." "The large toe," the announcement in the *New York Herald* furthermore specified "is more like a man's thumb" (March 19, 1860). The teeth, the arms, and legs were described in similar mode proving to be of unusual proportions (in terms of comparative anatomy). But at the focus of interest and scientific argument was the head, as a lecturer would explain during the show but as it was also included into booklets sold at the event:

> The upper part of the head, and the forehead in particular, instead of being four or five inches broad, as it should be, to resemble a human being, is less than two inches! The head of the What is It is very small. The ears are set back about an inch too far for humanity, and about three-fourths of an inch too high up. They should form a line with the ridge of the nose, to be like that of a human being. As they are now placed, they constitute the perfect head and skull of the Orang Outang, while the lower part of the face is that of the native African. (cited in Cook 2005, pp. 134–135)

The actor on stage was, just like the actors of the Aztec Children, microcephalic, and accordingly had a deformed head. But while the Aztec Children were pronounced to be the most wonderful and extraordinary human beings of ancient and superior status, the nondescript became a case of pathology. In the nineteenth century, scientific practice began to rely heavily on comparison, a quantitative approach that was based on collected data. The definition of physical difference was at the heart of both anthropology and medicine. But while anthropology defined the visual "other" body as different, medicine (and biology) defined anything departing from a statistical standard as pathological, which meant "not normal."[10] In case of the Aztec Children, geography and time were used to distance their bodies, creating a frame of the exceptional. Their humanity was never doubted, although they were presented as specimens in a biological fashion. Speculations concerned only their ethnic origin and also, in scientific circles, their condition. In some of these meta-discussions, they became degraded beings devoid of emotions (see for example Virchow, 1901) because they were further categorized with their disability and classified as intellectually slow. Conclusions drawn reflect the scientific discourses while the public continued to marvel at extraordinary children.[11]

In the case of the nondescript, microcephaly was used to dehumanize the staged character. Speculations did not concern the geographical and temporal origins, but rather the human condition of the actor who was usually said to have been captured by "a party of adventurers who were in search of a gorilla." One explanation, for example, was that

> [w]hile exploring the River Gambia, near the mouth, they fell in with a race of beings never before discovered. ... After considerable exertion the hunters succeeded in capturing three of these oddities ... the present one is the only survivor. (*New York Herald*, March 19, 1860)

As in the case of the Aztec Children, the capture turned out to be a life-threatening mission and, again, the character presented is said to be the very last of his kind.

The deliberate reference to the gorilla is no coincidence, since the nineteenth-century public was familiar with man-monkey performances that made similar claims about missing links but lacked a scientific context in the pre-Darwin era. As early as 1799, Charles Willson Peale presented an orang-utan as "The Wild Man of the Woods" in his museum in Philadelphia. By the 1840s, Barnum had introduced a man-monkey performance in his American Museum. In some of these performances, monkeys had been trained to act like human beings, while in other acts humans played monkeys. These performances reveal the wonder about similarities between the two species, but also recall the stories of feral children and wild men that had been retold for centuries.[12] Instead of comparative anatomy and intensive measurement of the performers, they had often been dressed in fur or had *hypertrichosis*, a condition resulting in the body being covered with hair. Parallels were not only drawn with monkeys, but also with all sorts of animals, resulting in acts like Lionel the Lionman or Jo-Jo the Poodleman. The animals assigned to the people on stage signified hierarchies and assumptions about the animal kingdom: the lion was the king and thus the act received its connotations of nobility; and the monkey was a tricky creature because it could be easily adapted to notions of danger (also evident in stories like Edgar Allan Poe's "The Murder in the Rue Morgue") or act in a harmless and mostly unsuccessful attempt to mimic human civilization.

Among the most tragic freak show celebrities in the monkey role was Julia Pastrana, who toured the American and European stages in the 1850s dancing and singing as the Missing Link or the "most ugly woman on earth." Frederick Drimmer (1973) provided a detailed description of her physical appearance:

> She stood only four and a half feet high. Most of her face, including her forehead, was covered with a shocking growth of shining black hair. Her tinselly

red gown, which left a good part of her arms and bosom bare, revealed large
expanses of hairy skin. [...] Her lip, large and deformed, were surmounted
by a heavy moustache. Her chin was prognathous, giving her an apelike
appearance. (p. 369)

In the public perception, her dancing and singing contrasted her physical appearance (which was successfully stressed by her costumes, as Drimmer also points out),
creating a tension between discourses of (wo)man and animal, of wilderness and
civilization, which was continued after her death in 1860 with the exhibition of her
mummified body.[13]

After the publication of Darwin's book in 1859, the Missing Link moved from the
sphere of curiosity and wonder (in which Pastrana had been exhibited) to the status
of specimen and scientific context. The tensions so popular in the (wo)man monkey
act between brute and human were kept and enacted in, for example, eating habits
(raw meat), walking practices (Barnum's advertisements always depict the actor with
a supporting walking stick), and sound (growling or (un)human laughter). The process of "taming" was staged with a lecturer who explained the progress the Missing
Link had made since its capture.

The audience was not free to interact, as it had been with the Aztec Children.
Handling the Missing Link was a more dangerous interaction with the laws of nature,
as was the idea of evolution, since it fundamentally threatened the Christian world
order. That the performer was in most cases a black man on American stages fuelled
even further controversial discussions, such as human equality and slavery that were
hotly debated as both social and political fodder at the time: Which conclusions could
be drawn from the evidence of the presented body? That there was a species not
human and not animal? What statement was made about African Americans in that
act? (see also Cook, 1996).

But it is not so much about what the act states, but rather about what discourses
it picks up and represents. Scientific conclusions were quickly drawn from Darwin's
book, making assumptions about human races and their relationship to one another,
insisting on the superiority of the Caucasian race. These debates were embodied
in the stage act that ridiculed scientific practices by making them appear absurd.
A growling beast learns to walk and eat in 30 minutes, wears a fur costume, and is
presented in a cage and quickly transforms from animal to human, depending on the
perception of the audience and also on the individual actor.

The actor Harvey Leech was apparently identified by name in 1846 by a member
in the audience in London after only 30 minutes. Leech had legs that were unusually
small compared to the rest of his body, and this qualified him to play several monkey
characters, such as "Jocko, the Brazilian Ape" and "Bibbo, the Patagonian Ape," that
made him famous (Cook, 1996, p. 142); in fact, too famous to act the role any longer.
He was replaced by William Henry Johnson, a microcephalic African American who
acted the role for most of his life and became iconized in the character. Photographs
of him, taken by Matthew Brady, show him holding a walking stick, turning his head
into profile to further stress its shape. On lithographs, in newspapers and programs,
the image was continuously reproduced.

As was the case with the act of the Aztec children, the Missing Link was not short-
lived. William Henry Johnson gained great fame as Zip, a role he enacted until his

death in 1926. While Harvey Leech's fatal embarrassment in London's Egyptian Hall occurred because he had enjoyed fame in a set of different roles, the freak show act demanded its performers to be faithful to singular roles. This way, they became the acts that made fact and fiction undistinguishable and turned the actors not only into extraordinary performers but also into extraordinary beings with a lifelong commitment to the stage.

In principle, the acts outlasted generations of audiences, but it is interesting that crucial details kept changing. The narrative of the discovery of the Aztec Children remained unshattered, but they were married eventually on stage. The Missing Link was not only discovered in Africa near the River Gambia, but also in California, where for the last 10 months it had been living with a tribe of Indians, or later in "the land beyond the moon" (Cook, 2001, p. 133). Late photographs show Zip with a fiddle having transformed the character of the What is It into a clownish persona, a meta-character that relied on the knowledge of the original Missing Link performance to understand its humorous effect. Still dressed in fur in these photographs, the scientific implications in which the act originated remained evident.

Strikingly, the same medical condition created suitable characters for two entirely different acts, supporting the notion of disability as a cultural construct in the figure of the freak. Both characters, the Aztecs and the Missing Link, are supported by the "scientific" evidence of measurement and reveal how the same numbers as outcome of measurements can lead to two entirely different conclusions (a vanished noble race and a brute creation). The *American Phrenological Journal* from September 1, 1855, reported, under the headline "Lunatics," information about an inmate in the Kings County Lunatic Asylum on Long Island near New York City, who resembled the "so-called 'Aztec' children" since the "dimensions of her head in its circumference and the different measurements from ear to ear correspond exactly with those of the elder of the two 'Aztecs'" (p. 66). We learn that the inmate is called "Monkey Mary" by the staff for her "restless vivacity accompanied by a thrusting forward of the head" (p. 66). She is described as cheerful and amazingly strong.

In the description, both characters fuse – the Aztec Children and the Missing Link. The shape of the head, carefully measured and treasured as scientific fundament, is linked to the Aztecs, while her movements and strengths that earn her the name are connected to the monkey performance. But more remarkable is the fact that a report in a scientific journal does not reflect these contradictions. Disability becomes the radical other, defined by measurement as the pathological body, explained by narratives that further radicalize the disabled person. The show acts can be performed only by disabled actors, but beyond the stage every disabled person becomes a potential actor, as Mary in the institution shows.

Conclusion

The freak show was an assembly of displays in which unusual bodies staged popular myths. While ongoing debates about the exploitation of people with disabilities point their finger to the freak shows, most scholars tend to recognize freak shows now as opportunities in which not only bodies but also special talents could be presented. The freak show provided an income for people who may have otherwise disappeared in questionable institutions (such as Mary in the example above). However, the performers were exposed to the stare Garland-Thomson criticises (2009), and only the narrative turned them into respectable human beings or ridiculous, laugh-provoking absurdities.

It is not so much disability that is staged in the freak show, but a theatrical act of scientific findings for which disabled people were thought to be suitable actors, mostly because they enacted scientific narratives that were obsessed with them. This is not to say that the freak is a scientific invention, but rather that it is a character strongly supported by the sciences at the time. And whereas the authenticity of the shows was continuously doubted and discussed by professionals of all relevant disciplines, deception was an accepted part of it for the masses and not the point at all. Instead the freak show was the possibility to view science at its limits and reassure the audience not only of the collective physical identity but also of their intellectual capacity.

Science played a crucial role in those narratives. It provided the scientific rationale for the legitimacy of the act, while at the same time purporting to educate the ignorant by presenting itself in a straightforward way that related to the lives of people in the audience – what we think of today as "pop" science. The freak-show act, as such, translated science to mass audiences. And perhaps it is no coincidence that Stephen Jay Gould, whose books and articles successfully brought science to mass audiences for many years in the late twentieth century, often relied on freak shows as examples to bring his points across.

Acknowledgement

The images of the Aztec Children and Barnum's What is It are in the public domain, and are reproduced here from the Catalogue or Guide Book of Barnum's American Museum, New York: Containing Descriptions and Illustrations of the Various Wonders and Curiosities of the Immense Establishment which have been Collected During the Last Half Century from Every Quarter of the Globe. New York, 186? (AAS). p. 107 (Aztec Children) and 108 (the What is It).

Notes

1 I use Rosemarie Garland-Thomson's term here (1996b) which she coined to describe the physical other not in an anthropological sense but in a medical-cultural context, although the term was commonly used at the time in scientific and popular contexts to describe such bodies.

2 The freak show is roughly set between the 1840s and the 1940s, although similar events before and after testify to a long and persisting tradition.

3 For the changed concept of leisure, see the classic Thorstein Veblen, *The Theory of the Leisure Class*.

4 As Rosemarie Garland-Thomson writes, the term "freak" had not been used for physical abnormality until 1847 (Garland-Thomson, 1996a, p. 4).

5 It was stressed that the names had been given to them after the conversion to Christianity (Velasquez, 1850, p. 5), thus erasing any knowledge of their previous lives from public consciousness.

6 It is also interesting to consider that the staging of freak performers in scientific contexts does not differ significantly from their popular performance. But stripped of all the props, the examination focussed on their physical disability interpreted in the humiliating

discourses of medicine at the time (see Virchow's discussions of Maximo and Bartola 1891 and 1901).

7 The issue of cuteness reappears in case of the Aztec Children, especially concerning Assra, the last of the Aztecs who was presented around 1910 (Scheugl, 1974, p. 105). See also Ngai, Sianne. "The Cuteness of the Avant-Garde" in Critical Inquiry, 31:4 (Summer 2005): pp. 811–47.

8 I use the terms What is It, Missing Link and nondescript synonymous in the following to refer to the same stage act.

9 Phineas Taylor Barnum is probably the most famous showman in the late nineteenth century. His American Museum in New York City and later his circus business included freak-show attractions that he massively advertised. All freak-show celebrities were either first staged in his establishments or were eventually engaged by him.

10 See also Georges Canguilhem's great discussion of *The Normal and the Pathological* (1943).

11 To refresh interest in the act, Maximo and Bartola had been married in 1867 as a stage act and were then presented as husband and wife, although it was argued that a marriage between brother and sister was common in their culture.

12 See for example the case of Marie-Angélique Memmie Le Blanc (Small, 2012), who appeared in 1731 in France and became an attraction.

13 For a gender-specific context and interpretation of the act see Stammberger, 2011.

References

Adams, R. (2001). *Sideshow U.S.A. Freaks and the American Cultural Imagination.* Chicago, IL: University of Chicago Press.

Aguirre, R. (2004). *Informal Empire. Mexico and Central America in Victorian Culture.* Minneapolis, MN: University of Minnesota Press.

Altick, R. D. (1978). The Shows of London. London, UK: Belknap Press.

Arnold, K. (2006). *Cabinets for the Curious: Looking Back at Early English Museums.* Aldershot, UK: Ashgate.

The Aztecs in England. (1853). *Buchanan's Journal of Man,* Vol 4/N VIII August 1854, p. 240. (AAS).

Barnum, P. T. (circa 1860). *Illustrated Catalogue and Guide Book to Barnum's American Museum.* New York, NY: Wynkoop, Hallenbeck & Thomas. Also available at http://www. disabilitymuseum. org/lib/docs/872.htm.

Bogdan, R. (1990). *Freak Show: Presenting Human Oddities for Amusement and Profit.* Chicago, IL: University of Chicago Press.

Canguilhem, G. (1991 [1943]). *The Normal and the Pathological.* New York, NY: Zone Books.

Cook, J. W. (1996). Of men, missing links, and nondescripts. in R. Garland-Thomson (Ed.), *Freakery. Cultural Spectacles of the Extraordinary Body* (pp. 139–157). New York, NY: New York University Press.

Cook, J. W. (2001). The Arts of Deception: Playing with Fraud in the Age of Barnum. Cambridge, MA: Harvard University Press.

Cook, J. (Ed.). (2005). *The Colossal P. T. Barnum Reader. Nothing Else Like It in the Universe.* Urbana and Chicago, IL: University of Illinois Press.

Darwin, C. (1859). *On the Origin of Species by Means of Natural Selection, or the Preservation of Favoured Races in the Struggle for Life.* London, UK: John Murray.

Daston, L., and Park, K. (1998). *Wonders and the Order of Nature 1150–1750.* New York, NY: Zone Books.

Drimmer, F. (1973). *Very Special People.* New York, NY: Amjon Publishers.

Fiedler, L. (1981). *Freaks: Myths and Images of the Secret Self.* New York, NY: Simon and Schuster.

Garland-Thomson, R. (Ed.). (1996a). Introduction: From wonder to error – A genealogy of freak discourse in modernity. In *Freakery: Cultural Spectacles of the Extraordinary Body* (pp. 1–22). New York, NY: New York University Press.

Garland-Thomson, R. (1996b). *Extraordinary Bodies: Figuring Physical Disability in American Culture and Literature.* New York, NY: Columbia University Press.

Garland-Thomson, R. (2009). *Staring: How We Look.* Oxford, UK: Oxford University Press.

Kerchy, A., and Zittlau, A. (Eds.). (2012). *Continental European Freakery and Enfreakment.* Newcastle, UK: Cambridge Scholar Publishing.

Layard, A. H. (1848). *Nineveh and Its Remains.* London, UK: John Murray.

Lunatics. (1855). *American Phrenological Journal.* (AAS). The American Phrenological Journal. A Repository of Science, Literature and General Intelligence. XXII Sept, 1855, p.66.

Morton, S. G. (1839). *Crania Americana; Or a Comparative View of the Skulls of Various Aboriginal Nations of North and South America.* Philadelphia, PA: J. Dobson.

Neumann, J. N. (2005). Der missgebildete Mensch. in M. Hagner (Ed.), *Der falsche Körper: Beiträge zu einer Geschichte der Monstrositäten* (2nd ed., pp. 21–44). Göttingen, Germany: Wallstein.

Ngai, S. (2005). The cuteness of the avant-garde. *Critical Inquiry,* 31(4), 811–847.

Price, S. (2001). Primitive art in civilized places. Chicago, IL: University of Chicago Press.

Rothfels, N. (1996). Aztecs, Aborigines, and Ape-People: Science and freaks in Germany, 1850–1900. in R. Garland-Thomson (Ed.), *Freakery. Cultural Spectacles of the Extraordinary Body* (pp. 158–172). New York, NY: New York University Press.

Scheugl, H. (1974). *Show Freaks & Monsters.* Köln, Germany: Verlag M. DuMont Schauberg.

Small, S. (2012). Frontier girl goes feral in eighteenth century France: The curious case of Marie-Angélique Memmie Le Blanc, the Wild Girl of Champagne. in A. Kerchy and A. Zittlau (Eds.), *Continental European Freakery and Enfreakment* (pp. 74–89). Newcastle, UK: Cambridge Scholar Publishing.

Stammberger, B. (2011). Monster und freaks. Eine Wissensgeschichte außergewöhnlicher Körper im 19. Jahrhundert. Bielefeld: Transcript.

Stephens, J. L. (1969 [1841]). *Incidents of Travel in Central America, Chiapas and Yucatan.* New York, NY: Dover Publications, Inc.

Stewart, S. (1993). *On Longing: Narratives of the Miniature, the Gigantic, the Souvenir, the Collection.* Durham, NC: Duke University Press.

Tromp, M. (Ed.). (2008). *Victorian Freaks: The Social Context of Freakery in Britain.* Columbus, OH: Ohio State University Press.

The What is It. (1860). *New York Herald.* The American Phrenological Journal. A Repository of Science, Literature and General Intelligence. XXII Sept, 1855, p.66. Retrieved from http://www.disabilitymuseum.org/dhm/lib/detail.html?id=2081

Veblen, T. (2009 [1899]). *The Theory of the Leisure Class.* New York, NY: Oxford University Press.

Velasquez of San Salvador, P. (1853). [Illustrated memoir of an eventful expedition into central America, resulting in the discovery of the idolatrous city of Iximaya, in an unexplored region; and the possession of two remarkable Aztec children. Maximo (the man) and Bartolo (the woman), descendants and specimens of the sacerdotal cast (now nearly extinct), of the ancient Aztec founders of the ruined temples of that country, described by John L. Stephens, Esq., and other travellers.] Translated from the Spanish by Pedro Velasquez of San Salvador. 1867. London: R. S. Francis.

Virchow, R. (1891). Die sogenannten Azteken und die Chua. *Verhandlungen der Berliner Gesellschaft für Anthropologie, Ethnologie und Urgeschichte,* 23, 370–377.

Virchow, R. (1901). Die beiden Azteken. *Verhandlungen der Berliner Gesellschaft für Anthropologie, Ethnologie und Urgeschichte,* 33, 348–350.

Zürcher, U. (2004). Monster oder Laune der Natur. *Medizin und die Lehre von den Missbildungen 1780–1914.* Frankfurt am Main: Campus.

24

THREE ILLUSIONS IN CLINICAL PHOTOGRAPHS OF THE FEEBLE-MINDED DURING THE EUGENICS ERA

Martin A. Elks

Much has been written about the early decades of the twentieth century and its dominating eugenics ideology (e.g., Black, 2003; Lombardo, 2011; O'Brien, 2013; Smith & Wehmeyer, 2012). Scholarship has generally relied on written rather than visual sources of data for interpreting this period. Little work has been completed that examines the photographs of the era as primary data, even though we know that journals and textbooks were profusely illustrated. For example, Talbot's text *Degeneracy: Its Causes, Signs and Results*, published in 1901, contained 120 illustrations (many of which were photographs) within its 362 pages. Photographs can provide new avenues of exploration and understanding, and often reveal points of view that are different from the written text (Dowdall & Golden, 1989). Thus, by examining photographs of "the feeble-minded" during the eugenics period, we may be able to increase our understanding of the period in ways that are not available to us through other sources.

Many interesting questions may be asked about these photographs, such as, how are "the feeble-minded" portrayed? What photographic conventions are employed? Were eugenic images obvious and overwhelming in their effects, or subtle and sophisticated?

This chapter addresses some of these questions by documenting the ways in which eugenicists employed photography in their depictions of people labelled the feeble-minded. Specifically, the chapter explores their use of modes of presentation to describe a classification scheme for feeble-mindedness, the mutually amplifying juxtaposition, and other photographic techniques such as printing and grouping.

The eugenics movement

It is hard to downplay the importance and influence of the eugenics era to persons with intellectual disabilities. This period, often referred to as the "indictment" or "genetic alarm" period, was a time when professionals working with people with intellectual disabilities concerned themselves with describing, explaining, and controlling a class of persons thought to be responsible for many of the social problems of the day. For example, inherited feeble-mindedness was widely believed to be the root cause of crime, pauperism, alcoholism, and prostitution. As Goddard remarked, "The feeble-minded person is not desirable, he is a social encumbrance, often a burden to himself. In short it were better both for him and for society had he never been born" (Goddard, 1914a, p. 558).

The goal of the leaders of the time was, therefore, to achieve a final solution to the problem of feeble-mindedness by such means as marriage and immigration laws, segregation, and sterilization of those deemed to be unfit to reproduce. No cost should be spared to this end (Goddard, 1914b), and even euthanasia was suggested as a possible remedy (Elks, 1993a; Hollander, 1989).

Eugenics may be defined as "the science of the improvement of the human race by better breeding" (Davenport, 1911, p. 1). The idea of breeding out problems and breeding in virtues became extremely popular in the final decades of the nineteenth century and the first few decades of the twentieth century. Many famous names were associated with the eugenics movement, such as Leonard Darwin, Winston Churchill, Charles Eliot, Alexander Graham Bell, Sir William Osler, John Maynard Keynes, Samuel Longfellow, Mrs Horace Mann, George Bernard Shaw, H. G. Wells, Margaret Sanger, and others (Cohen, 2016; McLaren, 1990; Popenoe & Johnson, 1918; Saloway, 1990).

By 1914, eugenics was taught at many major American universities, including Harvard, Columbia, Cornel, Brown, Wisconsin, Northwestern, and Clark, among others (Chorover, 1979). Eugenics exhibits could be found at many state fairs, where families would be examined and trophies given to the "fittest" families, and numerous books, journals and associations were devoted to eugenics propaganda or the public dissemination of the movement's ideals and policies. Prominent eugenics associations in the United States included the Eugenics Education Society, the American Breeder's Association, and the Race Betterment Foundation.

Two institutions were responsible for much of the research and popularization of the eugenics message: the Eugenics Record Office, at Cold Spring Harbor, Long Island, New York, for general eugenic research; and the Research Department of the Vineland Training School for Feeble-Minded Boys and Girls at Vineland, New Jersey, for research into intellectual disabilities.

The Research Department at Vineland Training School, created in 1908, had three directors in the period 1906–1931, all of whom were highly regarded in the field of intellectual disabilities during their day – Henry Goddard, S. D. Porteus, and Edgar Doll. It was this research department that was very influential in developing intelligence and other mental tests, and researching the genetic causes of feeble-mindedness (Zenderland, 1998). Goddard's intellectual classification scheme became the standard in the field at its adoption in 1910 by the American Association for the Study of the Feeble-minded, and Goddard's study, "The Kallikak Family," published in 1912, became a classic of both psychology and intellectual disabilities.

The drive to recognize

The nation was aroused. The hunt for the feeble-minded began.
(Davies, 1930, p. 76)

Armed with theories of degeneracy, genetic inheritance, and intellectual disabilities, eugenicists felt compelled to seek out the feeble-minded wherever they might be. This need to recognize the feeble-minded may be seen in Barr and Maloney (1920):

> The information most eagerly sought by those entering upon the work among the feeble-minded is naturally how to easily recognize the various forms of mental defect, in order that they may define, and meet promptly, the special needs of those with whom they are brought in daily contact. (p. vii)

The urge to recognize the feeble-minded dominated the writing and policies of eugenicists. For example, Fernald's (1912) article contains the following statements urging recognition:

> The unrecognized imbecile is a most dangerous element in the community. In a rational policy for controlling feeble-mindedness it is essential that we recognize the condition in childhood. ... The mental defectives in our penal institutions should be recognized and transferred to permanent custody in suitable institutions and farm colonies. ... It is most important that the physician should recognize the so-called "borderline" cases. (pp. 91–97)

Goddard (1915) urged, in relation to the criminal imbecile, that "[u]nless their mental condition is recognized and they are cared for in such a way as to make crime impossible, many of them will repeat the career of Trouson" [a convicted murderer] (p. 81).

Eugenicists had the best of motivations for this drive, thinking that early recognition "might retard the degeneration that ignorance would precipitate, and lead to the seeking of specialized treatment and training in time to secure the best results" (Barr & Maloney, 1920, p. 124).

Clinical photography and eugenics

The use of the camera by eugenicists has received much less attention than their use of mental tests, yet the camera was a technology that played a significant role in the development of the eugenics movement. Both the camera and intelligence tests were used concurrently and to reinforce each other in recognizing feeble-mindedness, often by the same people – Henry Goddard being a notable example.

It was Goddard who, in 1908, brought the Binet intelligence tests to the United States from France and was responsible for developing and revising the tests for use in North America. His fieldworker, Elizabeth Kite, was responsible for translating many of the texts of Binet and Simon into English (Rafter, 1988). In addition, Goddard made extensive use of photographs in two important texts: *The Kallikak Family* (1912), and *Feeble-mindedness: Its Causes and Consequences* (1914a). Martin Barr, another influential professional in the field, also made great use of photographs in his two texts *Mental Defectives* (1904/1913) and *Types of Mental Defectives* (1920.)

Medical and psychiatric illustration has been evident from antiquity, but it was the *camera obscura* (a camera without film) that entered the field in 1733 in which we find the closest forerunner to photography as we know it today (Ollerenshaw, 1961). Even so, it was not until the advent, in 1852, of the work of Hugh Welch Diamond, a psychiatrist, that there was any systematic use of photography in medicine (Gilman, 1976; for a biography, see Tucker, 2004).

The value of photography lay in its ability to "record accurately, rapidly, perhaps cheaply, and repeatedly" (Ollerenshaw, 1961, p. 3). Photography "was held to be the ultimate form of realistic portrayal" and the camera became a "diagnostic tool," providing empirical proof of psychiatric symptomatology and physiognomy (Gilman, 1976, p. 5; Gilman, 1982). Hugh Diamond (1856) wrote:

> [T]he picture speaks for itself with the most marked impression and [arrests] the attention of the thoughtful observer more powerfully than any labored description. … [T]he Photographer secures with unerring accuracy the external phenomena of each passion, as the really certain indication of the internal derangement, and exhibits to the eye the well-known sympathy which exists between the diseased brain and the organs and features of the body. Photography, as is evident from the portraits which illustrate this paper, confirms and extends this [written] description, and that to such a degree as warrants the conclusion that the permanent records thus furnished [by photographs] are at once the most concise and the most comprehensive (pp. 18–21).

This chapter is based on a subset of photographs from a much larger study (Elks, 1993) in which 1,233 photographs depicting people labelled feeble-minded between the years 1900–1930 were analysed using inductive, or grounded theory methods (Bogdan & Biklen, 2011; Corbin & Strauss, 1990; Dowdall & Golden, 1989; Glaser & Strauss, 1967). The vast majority of these photographs in this larger study were found in books and journals of the period, such as *American Breeders Magazine*, *American Journal of Sociology*, *Annals of Eugenics*, *Eugenics*, *Eugenics Review*, *Eugenical News*, *Journal of Heredity*, *Journal of Mental Science*, *Journal of Psycho-Asthenics*, *Mental Hygiene*, and *Proceedings of the Association of Medical Officers at American Institutions for the Idiotic and Feeble-Minded Persons*. In addition, the library and archives of Cold Spring Harbor Laboratory, Long Island, New York; the American Philosophical Library, Philadelphia, Pennsylvania; Vineland Training School, Vineland, New Jersey; and the state Library of New York were also sources of photographs. The period 1900 to 1930 was chosen as best representing the period historians generally recognize as the eugenics era (Haller, 1963; Ludmerer, 1972; Searle, 1976).

Three examples of photographic illusions found in eugenic clinical photography are presented in the following sections.

Caption illusion

Barr (1904/1913) includes a picture of a person with "echolalia" (p. 21). Echolalia is there defined as "a speech affection characterized by a tendency to repeat words or phrases spoken by others" (Barr, 1904/1913, p. 233). Similarly, Barr and Maloney (1920) define echolalia as a "parrot-like repetition of words and sentences which may or may not be fully comprehended by the speaker. Complete echolalia is rarely met with, but partial echolalia, usually well-marked, is not infrequent and is always a concomitant of mental defect" (Barr and Maloney, 1920, p. 157). However, there is no visible photographic feature of echolalia. People do not look "echolalic"; they sound echolalic. The caption in the picture is the only element that leads to an interpretation of echolalia. The belief in the validity of photography in general and this specific photograph lead the viewer to see the caption *in* the photograph (Figure 24.1). The photograph with its caption thus makes something that cannot be seen into something the viewer believes can be seen.

Another example is the illustration in Figure 24.2 of a so-called idiot savant. An idiot savant was defined as a person who was feeble-minded but had unusual skills. For example a person might be incompetent in basic life skills but could accurately add large numerals in their heads. Other savants could tell the day of the week if told a particular date. For example if you told them the date that Abraham Lincoln was killed, they would tell you what day of the week that was.

The photograph's caption forms the viewer's mind into an interpretation of the photograph that would not necessarily be made without the caption. In other words, the same photograph without a caption could be capable of multiple interpretations, including something as simple as "this is a photograph of a well-dressed young man." Thus, a caption uses the authority of the professional and their publisher to influence the viewer to "see" the photograph as illustrating and thereby confirming the content of the caption. A belief in the objectiveness of photography as a mechanical process that captures reality also confirms the scientific basis for this interpretation

ECHOLALIA.

Figure 24.1 Echolalia. (Barr (1904/1913), Plate I, between pages 20 and 21.)

398

Figure 24.2 Case D, Idiot savant. (Barr and Maloney (1920),
Plate XXIII, p. 129.)

by showing that there is a physical basis for this interpretation. Thus, echolalia and idiot savant have a face that can be recognized, and the fear of feeble-mindedness has therefore a basis in observable reality.

When readers see dozens of captioned photographs, they are led to believe, cumulatively, in the validity of eugenic theory and consequently of the validity of the professionals who "discovered" feeble-mindedness and of the social policies these professionals are promoting.

Classification illusion

In the early decades of the twentieth century, professionals working with intellectual disabilities created what they believed to be reliable and complete classifications of feeble-mindedness. There are many reasons why such classification schemes were important to eugenicists. The ability to classify feeble-mindedness would place professionals working with intellectual disabilities on a par with other descriptive scientists such as botanists and geologists. It would also reinforce the need for experts in recognition and classification, since, as Barr and Maloney (1920) pointed out, "A correct classification is of paramount importance in the study of mental defect" (p. 177). This would in turn ensure the future of the intellectual disabilities professional. Classification schemes would also provide experts with an instrument with which to implement the various policies of eugenicists. For example, the need to correctly identify individuals was acknowledged to be very important when a decision to sterilize was being contemplated.

Eugenicists also believed that one could see feeble-mindedness, and hence could photograph it. Photographs were thus used in creating the "visual evidence" for their theoretical classification schemes. One important classification scheme was that of Barr and Maloney (1920), which claimed to discern five major types of mental deficiency (Figure 24.3): idiot, idio-imbecile, imbecile, moral imbecile, and backward or mentally feeble. In addition, each of these major categories could be further divided into four subcategories, yielding a total of 12 classifications and "grades." This classification scheme, first published by Barr (1904/1913), chief physician at Pennsylvania training school for feeble-minded children (now simply referred to as "Elwyn"), was endorsed by physicians and teachers as "the best one as simplifying the tasks of all engaged in the work" (p. vii).

Barr (1904/1913), for example, noted that, "To the student of mental deficiency, the very first requisite is a classification that shall be at once simple and comprehensive, definite and clear" (p. 78). Fernald (1912) added, "The recognized field of mental defect has been gradually extended and widened, and clinical types and degrees of feeble-mindedness are recognized by the alienist which are not yet familiar to the medical profession generally" (p. 97).

It seemed natural to try to illustrate this classification system and thus to understand it more clearly by the use of photography, a popular medium at the time. The "evidence" presented by the photographs was thought to legitimize the classification system, but, since the classification system itself was used as a mode of presentation (different subclasses of the system were presented in different ways), the very mode of presentation that was based on the classification system served to further legitimize the classification system. This was, of course, a deception and, it is argued, a purposeful deception by those with eugenics beliefs.

Barr and Maloney's text, *Types of Mental Defectives* (1920), contains 12 plates of photographs each with up to eight photographs for each of the 12 categories of feeble-mindedness. For example, seven photographs on one page are labelled idiots: profound apathetic (Figure 24.4), and eight photographs are labelled idio-imbecile (e.g., Figure 24.8) and so on. These photographs are important because they reinforce the classification scheme by giving the impression that each type and grade has a characteristic appearance, and that it is possible to learn to recognize and distinguish the different categories and subcategories: "By comparing the picture with the short description of the case accompanying each – including the diagnosis, family history, and notes of mental progress or retrogression – a very fair idea of the type can be gained, and put into practice in daily examination of defective children" (Barr & Maloney, 1920, p. 177).

Thus, "idiots: superficial excitable" supposedly look different from "idiots-superficial apathetic," who look different from "idio-imbeciles," who in turn look different from "middle-grade imbeciles" and so on. Being able to clearly see in photographs the alleged

EDUCATIONAL CLASSIFICATION
OF
MENTAL DEFECTIVES

IDIOT

Asylum Care	Profound	Apathetic — Unimprovable.
		Excitable
	Superficial	Apathetic — Slightly improvable.
		Excitable — Improvable in self-help only.

IDIO-IMBECILE

Improvable in self-help and helpfulness.
Trainable in very limited degree to assist others.

IMBECILE

Long Apprenticeship and Colony Life under Protection

Mentally deficient.
Low-grade—Trainable in industrial and simplest manual occupations.
Middle-grade—Trainable in manual arts and simplest mental acquirements.
High-grade—Trainable in manual and intellectual arts.

MORAL-IMBECILE

Custodial Life and Perpetual Guardianship

Mentally and morally deficient.
Low-grade—Trainable in industrial occupations. Temperament bestial.
Middle-grade—Trainable in industrial and manual occupations. A plotter of mischief.
High-grade—Trainable in manual and intellectual arts: with genius for evil.

BACKWARD or MENTALLY FEEBLE

Trained for a Place in the World.

Mental processes normal, but slow and requiring special training and environment to prevent deterioration. Defect imminent under slightest provocation, such as excitement, overstimulation or illness.

Figure 24.3 Educational classification of mental defectives. (Barr and Maloney (1920), p. 1.)

differences between classifications lends great credibility to any diagnostic schema and hence to its underlying presuppositions about the nature of mental deficiency. Such visual confirmation would also provide an excellent teaching and diagnostic tool.

Thus, if the classification scheme is accurate, one should be able to arrange the photographs side by side – from "profound apathetic idiots" through "high-grade imbeciles" and see, in a progressive fashion, the authors' "ascending scale of mental defect" (Barr & Maloney, 1920, p. 50). However, when one does view the photographs in their progressive order of classification, there appear a number of aspects that greatly diminish the validity of the classification scheme, at least in terms of the photographic evidence.

How, then, do the photographs illustrate the text's classification scheme? For example, what are the visual differences between "idiots: profound apathetic" (Figure 24.4)

Figure 24.4 Idiots: Profound apathetic. (Barr and
Maloney (1920), Plate I, p. 9.)

and "idiots: profound excitable" (Figure 24.5) and how do they illustrate the written
descriptions of the differences?

The text gives the characteristics of idiots in general, and the difference between
these two types of idiots as follows:

> The idiot, commonly dwarfed and under-sized, exhibits those signs of physi-
> cal weakness which at once betray mental degeneration. Mutism or deafness,
> where the cause is proven not local, indicates plainly a cerebral lesion or
> deficiency; so also insensitiveness to touch, inhibition to pain, lack of muscu-
> lar coordination impeding or preventing locomotion, unclean habits, vacant
> expression, and drooling mouth, are all manifest signs of idiocy profound
> or superficial. The profound idiot, apathetic, can give no expression to his
> wants by either speech or motion; he lies simply a breathing mass of helpless-
> ness. The excitable idiot is distinguished from him only by the bleating cry
> and almost constant imperative movements which seem his one gratification
> – the rolling of the head on its axis, the swaying of the body to and fro, and
> the rhythmical movements of fingers before the eyes. Both at any age whatso-
> ever are more helpless that the ordinary normal infant, and have not even an
> intelligent animal existence. (p. 3)

Figure 24.5 Idiots: Profound excitable. (Barr and
Maloney (1920), Plate II, p. 13.)

Of these characteristics, lack of coordination and drooling mouth may be able to
be shown, or at lease implied, in photographs. From the photographs of the apathetic
group (Figure 24.4), we can see several cases of (presumably) poor coordination in the
crossed legs (cases A and F) and curved wrists (cases B and E) of the apathetic group.
The bib (case B) may indicate a drooling mouth, and the diaper (case F) may also imply
severely delayed development. However, the term "lies simply a breathing mass of helplessness" seems to be contradicted by at least two of the cases (E and G) shown standing
up. Similarly, it is difficult to decide which individual has a "vacant expression."

With respect to the profound excitable group (Figure 24.5) the presence of the
attendant's hand around the head, neck, and chin in five of the eight photographs
may indicate attempts to steady the "rolling head on its axis" and the "swaying of the
body" said to be characteristic of this group. Moreover, the seeming resistance shown
in case D to the attendant's hand may be consistent with "excitability" rather than
"apathy." Similarly, cases D and G show more animated facial expression (a grimace
and a smile) than is found in the apathetic group.

Thus, the photographs do seem to illustrate some of the differences between the
two groups described in the text in some cases. From viewing the photographs alone,
however, the clearest examples of the difference between apathetic and excitable profound idiocy appears to be that the apathetic group uses chairs (the case descriptions

Figure 24.6 Idiots: Superficial apathetic. (Barr and
Maloney (1920), Plate III, p. 17.)

accompanying the individual photographs describe those in chairs as paralyzed or
unable to walk), have signs of physical disability (e.g., curved hands and crooked
legs), wearing a bib or diaper, and have a light presence of an attendant's helping
hand (e.g., on the back of the chair), whereas the excitable group are shown all
standing, with heavy presence of helping hands and with more animated expression.
However, it appears that case G of the apathetic type could be better placed in the
excitable category, given her standing position and the heavy presence of the helping
hand. Presumably, however, she is placed in the apathetic category because she is said
to "remain perfectly passive unless roused" (p. 11).

These photographs illustrate the importance of the text and captions in influencing the interpretations of the images. For example, one would not necessarily assume
from the fact that a person is sitting, or even lying down, that she or he couldn't walk.
But when one is informed that he or she is paralyzed, the chair takes on the image of
needed support rather than choice.

With respect to superficial idiots (Figures 24.6 and 24.7), we find the following
descriptions:

With the superficial idiot, whether apathetic or excitable, is found a certain degree of reflex muscular action, but poor coordination. Speech and

Figure 24.7 Idiots: Superficial excitable. (Barr and Maloney
(1920), Plate IV, p. 23.)

locomotion are possible but always imperfect and halting. Mutism is the rule
with apathetics of this type, who, with dribbling saliva will blow bubbles from
their lips and make known their wants by signs and inarticulate cries. The gait
is the uncertain and tottering step of infancy, or, not infrequently, the limbs
are partially or wholly paralyzed and the extremities cold and livid, owing to
poor circulation. The excitable idiot of this class is a very imp of mischief, with
violent temper, willful and irritable under restraint. Restless, always in motion,
curious in the extreme, testing everything with finger and tongue, he will lick
furniture door-knobs etc. and even swallow stones, rags, sticks, and garbage
of every description. His speech is delayed and confined to monosyllables,
short phrases and broken sentences, supplemented by gestures or harsh animal cries. The gait is an unsteady shuffle, with dragging footstep and body
bending forward, especially marked where there is a history of meningitis; or
excessive excitation of temperament is often associated with a peculiar tip-toe
step and automatic movements of head, hands and body. (pp. 3–5)

Here we begin to find the photographs as illustrations of discrete categories less convincing. Photographically, we may see for superficial apathetic idiots (Figure 24.6) an

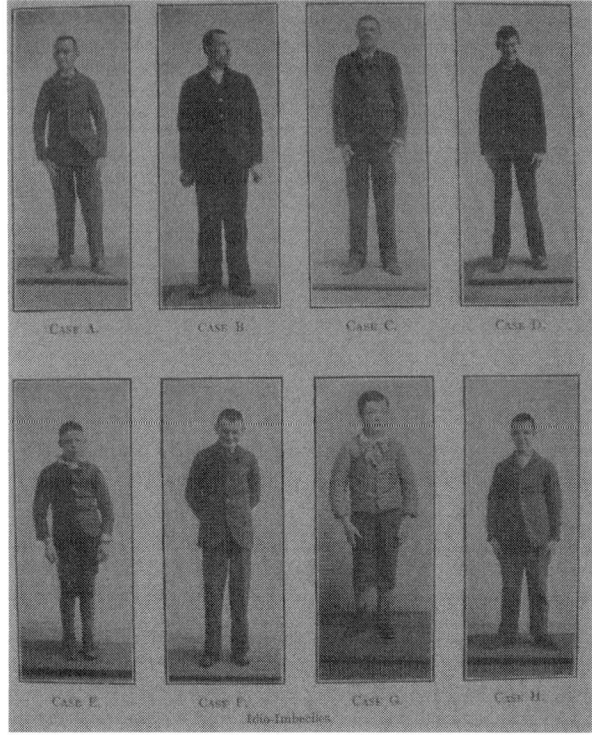

Figure 24.8 Idio-imbeciles. (Barr and Maloney (1920),
Plate V, p. 27.)

uncertain gait (case C) and somewhat awkward stance in general. The downcast faces of cases C, E, and F may also give the impression of apathy. However, two of the males (B & D) seem to fit visually into the profound excitable category, given their stance and the attendant's hands.

How do the photographs show the characteristics of the excitable superficial idiot (Figure 24.7), namely mischief, violent temper, restlessness etc.? Perhaps the crossed arms of case D express some "willfulness" and "irritability," as might the folded arms and turned-away head of case F. Perhaps, also, case B shows a rather mischievous expression. But if "constant motion" is a characteristic of this category, then photographing them standing still seems to be a significant and obvious contradiction. Moreover, cases A, G, and H appear to fit the "superficial apathetic" category as much as the superficial excitable category. In addition, the stronger presence of the helping hand in the superficial excitable, compared to the apathetic category of profound idiocy seen above, does not seem to apply in the case of superficial idiocy where the superficial excitable idiot (Figure 24.7) actually has one less example of an attendant's helping hand than the superficial apathetic group (Figure 24.6). Also, Case E, a "superficial excitable idiot" (Figure 24.7), appears to be very similar to Case F, a "profound excitable idiot" (Figure 24.5).

Perhaps the authors have other information that enables them to place individuals into various categories, but it seems from the photographs that the impression that one can reliably see the features of her/his category is difficult to substantiate.

The ability to discern differences between classifications based on appearance seems to fall apart dramatically with the category of idio-imbecile. The difference between "idiots," "idio-imbeciles," and "imbeciles" (Figures 24.10 through 24.15) is acknowledged by Barr and Maloney (1920) to "merge so imperceptibly that the experienced eye alone can recognize and place him" (p. 4). This statement, however, is contradicted by the inclusion of photographs with their unambiguous captions which imply clear delineations between the various classifications.

The text goes on to describe the characteristics of idio-imbeciles, few of which would be visible in still photographs (such as the idio-imbecile's chatter, and sudden tempers). The basic difference in the photographs of idio-imbeciles and idiots seems to be the relative absence of the attendant's helping hand with idio-imbeciles compared to idiots, and the fact that idio-imbeciles seem to stand more erect and with their hands placed at their sides or clasped in front or behind. In addition, perhaps the women wear more interesting dresses and do not wear aprons.

Case I (Figure 24.9) in interesting. Except for her feet which have their heals together (characteristic of low-grade imbeciles), her posture and head position seem more like case E (Figure 24.6) of the idiot–superficial apathetic class. Thus she is a mixture of both elements – an idio-imbecile.

The text acknowledges that Case P (Figure 24.9) "looked like an idiot" (p. 35) as is evidenced by the helping hand, plain dress, and somewhat awkward stance, but it also noted that "appearances were deceptive as she had quite a little intelligence" (p. 36). But if appearances are deceptive in this instance, why include the photograph?

If relative absence of an attendant's helping hand, posture, and dress distinguish between idiots and idio-imbeciles, what are the distinguishing features between idio-imbeciles and low-grade imbeciles (Figures 24.10 and 24.11)? The only reliable difference between idio-imbecile and low-grade imbecile males appears to be that only low-grade imbeciles stand with their feet together. Perhaps there is some (unstated) neurological reason for this, but such a distinction could hardly be definitive in any case, since three out of the eight low-grade imbeciles stand with their feet apart and are otherwise photographically similar to idio-imbeciles.

For the low-grade imbecile women (Figure 24.11), the four women shown full length have a straight and balanced stance, and perhaps the hands-behind-the-back pose of cases N and P is meant to indicate higher coordination. The presence of the four head-and-shoulder portraits, however, seem to be out of place since they could be included in the middle and high-grade groups. Thus, case O could just as well be placed under middle-grade (Figure 24.13) or high-grade imbeciles (Figure 24.15) as low-grade imbecile. Also, Case I (Figure 24.11), a low-grade imbecile, looks very similar to Case L (Figure 24.9) an idio-imbecile, except Case I has longer hair and is perhaps a little older. Also, Case K (Figure 24.11) a low-grade imbecile looks very similar to Case B (Figure 24.12), a middle-grade imbecile. Thus, for the women at least, the category low-grade imbecile is at least partially created by including the editorial convention of the head-and-shoulder frame (a high-grade convention) which "raises" the image of the page from idio-imbecile to the next level of low-grade imbecile.

Figure 24.9 Idio-imbeciles. (Barr and Maloney (1920),
Plate VI, p. 31.)

Case J (E. G.) and J-1 also seem out of place. They share a common frame, so it is clear they are to be seen as a unit, but how do they represent low-grade imbeciles? Are the photographs of the same person at different ages, or are they two different people but related in some way? The caption indicates they are low-grade imbeciles, and if we consider the accompanying case description as a kind of extended caption, it appears that this is another example of the caption illusion. The text states that J is shown at 15 years of age and that J-1 is her mother. Most members of the family are described as being feeble-minded and living in a 12´ × 20´ cabin with their horse, dog, pig and cow and "in extreme poverty" (Barr & Maloney, 1920, p. 44). E. G. eventually came under the care of Dr. Barr and reached her mental limit "in her 21st year and since then has retrograded until now she does absolutely nothing" (Barr & Maloney, 1920, p. 47). Thus, without the caption and extended caption, the photographs do not seem to display anything other than portraits of two women. With the caption, however, the viewer is primed to see the two women as low-grade imbeciles and members of a notorious family in which feeble-mindedness has been passed on from parent to child.

The presence or absence of the attendant's helping hand seems to be one clear visual demarcation between grades up to and including idio-imbecile being absent in photographs for the remaining higher grades. Thus, the presence of the attendant's hand is a reliable image signifying "lower-grade."

Figure 24.10 Imbeciles: Low-grade. (Barr and Maloney
(1920), Plate VII, p. 39.)

The middle-grade imbecile is "the first to approximate in the slightest degree the normal" (p. 50). It is also the grade at which studio portraits become the majority. However, the first page of photographs devoted to middle-grade imbecility (Figure 24.12) shows an interesting phenomenon – the illusion of the middle-grade. The page comprises two groups of photographs, those showing full-length portraits and those showing three-quarter-length or head-and-shoulder shots. All the full-length photographs could be placed as low-grade imbeciles (Figures 24.10 and 24.11), and the three remaining photographs showing studio portraits and head-and-shoulder shots as high-grade (Figures 24.14 and 24.15) leaving no-one to exemplify the middle-grade. It thus seems possible that the middle-grade page is a visual illusion created by the viewer, who is encouraged to make some sort of visual average or combination between the low-grade (full-length) and the high-grade (studio) images. The presence of the two types of images combine to create an image somewhere between low and high-grade, hence "middle-grade."

Such a notion of averaging out the different influences of a number of separate photographs may not be as implausible as it may sound. The process is reminiscent of the composite photographs Galton produced to illustrate the average physiognomy of groups such as Jew and criminals (Sekula, 1989). This process involved the use of multiple exposures of different individuals onto the one negative to produce an overall, average, or "composite" photograph representative of the entire class.

Figure 24.11 Imbeciles: Low-grade. (Barr and
Maloney (1920), Plate VIII, p. 45.)

Similarly, in Figure 24.13, also of middle-grade imbeciles, all but one of the photographs (cases J and K) could be placed as high-grade imbeciles. Only cases J and K, being full-length (consistent with the low-grade convention) but also shown wearing stylish clothing (high-grade convention) could be classed as middle-grade, having both high- and low-grade imagery. Thus, it would seem that the category "middle-grade imbecile" lacks clear supporting photographic evidence.

The characteristics of the high-grade imbecile (Figures 24.14 and 24.15) include elaborate studio settings (e.g., swings, pedestals), less than full-length framing (three-quarter or head-and-shoulder), a variety of poses (full-frontal being rare), stylish clothing, and the presence of what may be called symbols of civilization or culture (e.g., books, jewellery, military uniforms, and gardens). All of these are editorial in nature, however, and therefore lack the necessary reliability and permanence on which to base a diagnosis of feeble-mindedness. If the feeble-minded people look typical, how do they visually illustrate feeble-mindedness?

The table shows the visually differentiating characteristics between the various categories of feeble-mindedness. Interestingly, photographically the best predictors of idiocy and idio-imbeciles, as distinct from higher grades, are the presence of an attendant's helping hand, women wearing aprons, and males standing with their feet apart,

Figure 24.12 Imbeciles: Middle-grade.
(Barr and Maloney (1920),
Plate IX, p. 51.)

Figure 24.13 Imbeciles: Middle-grade.
(Barr and Maloney (1920),
Plate X, p. 57.)

Figure 24.14 Imbeciles: High-grade. (Barr and Maloney (1920), Plate XI, p. 65.)

Figure 24.15 Imbeciles: High-grade. (Barr and Maloney (192 0), Plate XII, p. 69.)

gaping mouths, and the absence of oval frames, studio settings and accessories. From the table we see that low-grade imbeciles are easy to identify. They are shown full-length in ordinary clothes and standing feet together (males). High-grade imbeciles are also easy to identify (they are shown less than full length, in good clothes, in studio settings.

An interesting use of these conventions may be seen in Case L. Figure 24.15, a before and after illustration of the changes in the level of intelligence achieved by through placement in an institution. The standing photograph is E. S. at age 10; the seated photograph is E. S. at age 25. We are told that E. S. "learned to read, write, and do good housework, and she became a good laundress" (Barr & Maloney, 1920, p. 72). The visual conventions are clearly displayed showing E.S. in the "after" photograph as high-grade (see pose, grooming, jewellery, and half-length) compared to E.S. as low-grade (see the dress, awkward pose, full-length).

Exactly what theory of cognitive functioning could link feeble-mindedness with these photographic conventions is hard to imagine. It seems much more likely that the "ascending scale of mental defect" coincides with the ascending scale of socially valued modes of presentation. The bottom of the scale carries images of abnormality, disability, and dependence (e.g., inability to stand with heals together, poor clothing, and attendant's helping hands), whereas the upper parts of the scale carry images of independence and achievement (studio portraits, stylish clothing, books, and jewellery). There seems to be little reason why studio portraits and good clothes should not be as valid for idiots as for high-grade imbeciles. Moreover, these grades and types are supposed to be real enough to "see," and the camera was believed at the time to provide objective documentation, yet several of the classifications lack visual support, and some photographs even contradict the written text, as when idiots supposedly in constant motion are shown standing still. Of course, one cannot say that these classifications are not justified under other (non-visual) criteria, but the use of photographs to illustrate the categories is highly questionable.

Barr's photography may thus be seen as a style or mode of presentation[1]. Bogdan (1988) defines a mode of presentation as a "standardized set of techniques, strategies, and styles" (p. 104) for depicting particular photographic subjects. Modes of presentation were used to create a certain image, such as that of "freak" in freak-show presentations. A person with a demonstrable physical difference such as extreme height or excessive hair is not a freak until a detailed presentation has been worked up that exaggerates the physical differences by using appropriate clothing, sets, and props, and adding an accompanying historical sketch of the person's birth and early life circumstances. Thus, a "very tall man" only becomes a "Giant" when he is presented in the mode of a Giant (such as with a large hat and arms outstretched). Without these modes of presentation, a "Giant" is merely a "very tall man." In this way freaks were made, not born.

In much the same way, we may see classification of feeble-mindedness as an elaborate presentation of cognitive impairment, using caption and other illusions such as the middle-grade imbecile as well as editorial aspects that have no necessary connection with mental capacity, such as type of clothing, studio setting, and jewellery. For many of these photographs, the conventions were the content. Thus, an alternative way of thinking about feeble-mindedness is not so much as an actual physical entity reflected in a visible difference in appearance (physiognomy) that could be recognized and communicated photographically, but rather as a mode of presentation consisting of various conventions. For example, idiots are people shown with

Table 24.1 Differentiating visual characteristics of photographs in Barr and Maloney (1920)

Idiots	Imbeciles	
	Low-grade	**High-grade**
Helping hand	No helping hand	No helping hand
Gape	Mouth closed	Mouth closed
Full-length	Full-length (sometimes less)	Less than full-length
No studio	Some studio	Mostly studio
Feet apart	Feet together	No feet visible
Less stylish clothes	Less stylish clothes	Stylish clothes
Apron (women)	No aprons	No aprons
No accessories	Some accessories	Symbols of culture

helping hands, poor clothing, and in full length. Morons are people shown in stylish clothing and framed head-and-shoulder. Thus, one could ask, what would happen if idiots were photographed in stylish clothes in a studio setting at three-quarter length or less? Would viewers still see "idiocy"?

In defence of the use of photographs as evidence that subclasses exist, one must also raise the possibility that the photographs themselves may not illustrate the concepts they are supposed to illustrate due to technological limitations. This is acknowledged in the text in some cases. For example, case F (Figure 24.10) has this comment in the case description: the distance between F's eyes is very short; and the head is oxycephalic, although this does not show well in the picture (Barr & Maloney, 1920, p. 42). However, the photograph presumably had enough merit as illustrating something to be included in the text, despite its lack of clarity in certain aspects (Table 24.1).

Scale illusion

The illusion of scale occurs when two opposite images are juxtaposed without an objective neutral image, thereby amplifying the differences between the two images (and what they represent). In this way the viewer has an impression that the differences are larger than they may actually be. This may be called a "mutually amplifying juxtaposition," or the juxtaposition of two opposite extremes. The larger the discrepancy between the two juxtaposed subjects, the greater the illusion, provided there is no neutral image. Juxtaposition with a neutral or "normal" image is simply a comparison, and not an illusion.

For example, the illusion of scale was a particularly popular technique in freak shows (Bogdan, 1988), where a "giant" is juxtaposed to a dwarf, a convention that was actually duplicated in medical textbooks (see Figure 24.16) except that the captions were given a more scientific image via "gigantism" and "dwarfism." The use of the mutually amplifying juxtaposition is to be seen particularly strongly in relation to the depiction of microcephaly. The visibility of the defect and its clear association in the popular mind with intellectual disabilities made it an ideal subject for photographs by eugenicists. It was, in many respects, a paradigm case of feeble-mindedness.

Textbooks on feeble-mindedness typically presented microcephaly juxtaposed with hydrocephaly (see Figure 24.17). This juxtaposition of an abnormally large head with

Figure 24.16 Dwarfism and gigantism.
(Talbot (1901), Frontispiece.)

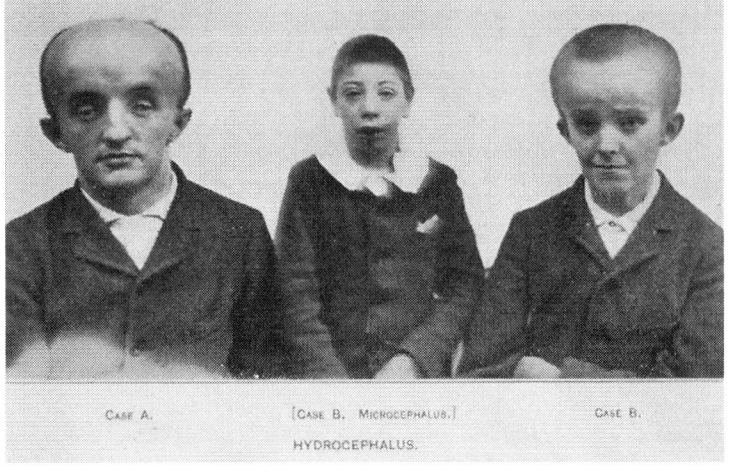

Figure 24.17 Hydrocephalus, (Barr (1904/1913), Plate XLII, p. 237.)

415

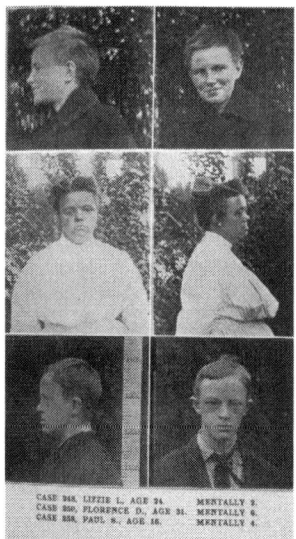

Figure 24.18 Case 248, Case 250,
Case 258. (Goddard
(1914), p. 367.)

an abnormally small head has the effect of exaggerating the two extremes. Thus, an already small head appears even smaller when juxtaposed to a larger-than-normal head, and an already large head becomes even larger when juxtaposed with an (allegedly) abnormally small head. Without an objective standard, any comparison is difficult to adjudicate and hence an illusion, since each extreme renders or amplifies the other. In comparing head sizes, for example, without the use of a ruler one is reacting to the picture which is deceptive because the images are mutually amplifying each others extremes. Thus a small head looks smaller and a large head looks larger. This is an illusion unless there is included a standardized scale. The illusion is also reinforced by the caption, since "micro" means small.

The absence of an objective measure appears to be deliberate since the use of measuring sticks was clearly present on other occasions (see Figure 24.18, Goddard, 1914a)

The mutually amplifying juxtaposition is also evident in iconography of the time. For example, Goddard's (1912) chart of the two lines of descent of the Kallikak family (see Figure 24.19) also represents the juxtaposition of two opposite extremes. The two lines are not just "good" juxtaposed with "bad" but very good and very bad genealogies. Elizabeth Kite, Goddard's fieldworker for the study, described a "veritable gulf" separating the two sides of the family, socially and intellectually (Kite, in Smith, 1985, p. 53). The symbolism of the good (white) and bad (black) lines of descent that have increasing separation between the lines is also mutually amplifying. Even the term "Kallikak" is a mutually amplifying juxtaposition, being a composite from Kalos (good) and Kakos (bad).

The use of the mutually amplifying juxtaposition is not confined to texts on the feeble-minded, but was also employed by eugenicists in other areas. Figure 24.20

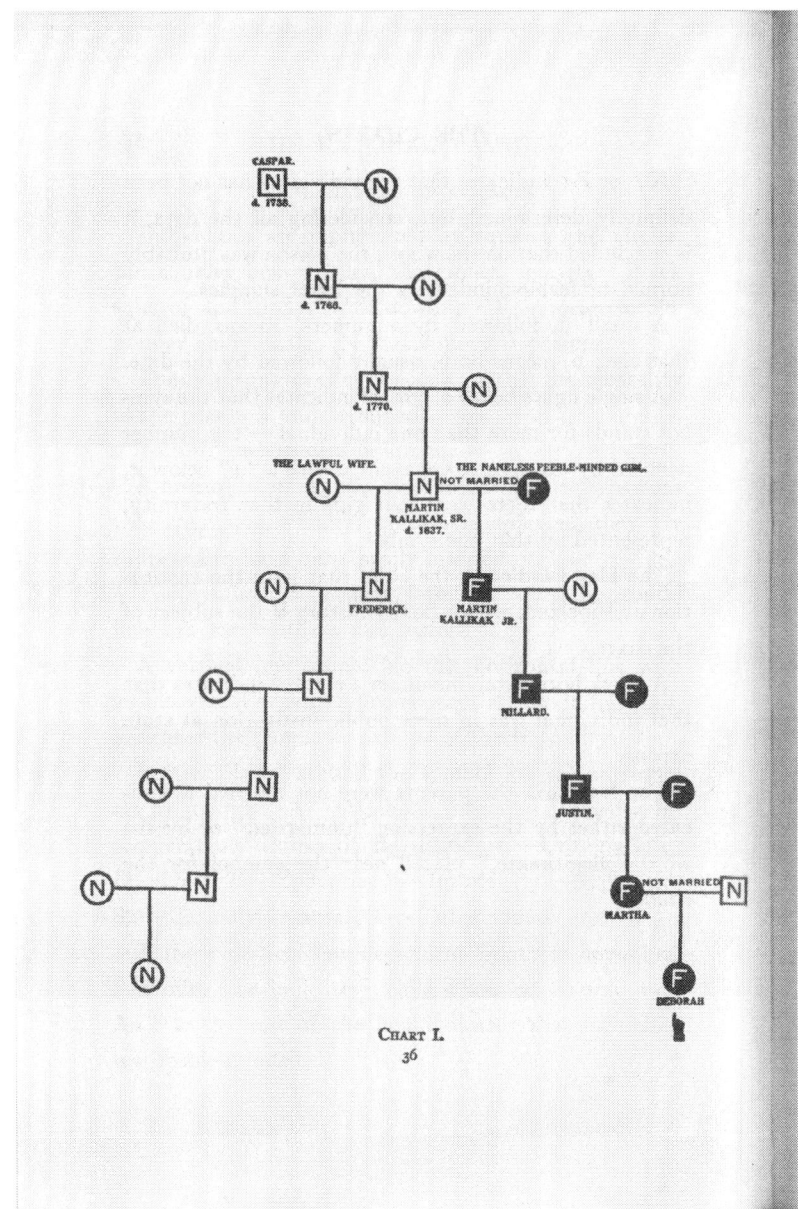

Figure 24.19 Chart I. (Goddard (1912), p. 36.)

(Hague, 1914) presents an extremely blatant example of the mutually amplifying juxtaposition. The two photographs depict evidence of the home of a feeble-minded person contrasted with that of a person of "vigorous mind." The "dirty shack" has the image of a hovel (sloping, wooden building with a porch) except that, in this instance, the shack is actually built into the hillside. The image of slope therefore could not be greater, since this shack slopes all the way to the ground.

The photograph of the white house (taken on a sunny day) represents a great contrast to the dull overcast grey photograph of the feeble-minded person. This house is upright (full of "right" angles) and not sloping at all. There is a garden that is being tended with a watering can and the overall image is one of order (note the even spacing between the people), poise, "upright respectability," and relaxed accomplishment. The image, therefore, seems to reflect an ideal rather than the average.

We do not know whether the white house is large for the time, or of average size. It is, however, a multistorey dwelling with a number of rooms apparently for a number of adults, and is significantly larger when compared to the hovel that seems to comprise little more than a single room. Rafter (1988) remarks that such "imagistic polarities" (p. 75) are also present in the texts of the famous eugenic family studies, such as when descriptions of the good branch employ images of spaciousness and light, but descriptions of the bad branch use images of darkness, enclosure, and descent.

Photography in the service of clinical eugenics

Clinical eugenicists believed that the feeble-minded were a menace and a burden to society. They intended the use of photography as hard, objective, confirmatory evidence that would show not only the existence and appearance of feeble-mindedness but also of its numerous types and grades. Producing a large number of photographs in an apparently logical and orderly sequence gives the strong impression that feeble-mindedness is not only recognizable and understood but that eugenics was based on good science.

Webster's dictionary defines an illusion as a misleading image or a deceptive appearance or impression. Three different kinds of illusions are present in the use of photography by clinical eugenicists, including (1) using a caption to influence the viewer to see a particular image as representing something it would not otherwise represent, (2) grouping photographs (and captions) to create an impression that such groupings represent various classifications of feeble-mindedness, and (3) use of mutually

Figure 24.20 Evidence of a feeble mind, evidence of a vigorous mind. (Hague (1914), located between pages 32 and 33.)

amplifying juxtapositions to visually exaggerate differences that may not appear to be so extreme if not so juxtaposed or if an objective measure were included in the frame.

Caption and classification illusions stem from a mindset that sees taxonomy as an integral component of scientific method. It was important for eugenicists to establish a scientific basis for their views on feeble-mindedness, which was one reason that the rediscovery of Mendel's laws of inheritance in 1900 was so eagerly embraced and exploited. A scientific approach requires detailed definitions and classifications of feeble-mindedness. Clinical photography was intended to establish the objectivity of the classification schemes Barr and others developed. Examination of their photographs, however, reveals that this desire was more wish fulfilment than reality.

The mindset behind the use of the scale illusion is harder to justify. It is true that there was great medical interest in freak-show exhibits showing individuals with microcephaly, referred to as "pinheads," such as Zip and other "Aztec-types" during this period (Bogdan, 1988). The idea that such individuals were biological "throwbacks" could easily be reconciled with eugenics and evolutionary eugenic science. However, the deliberate use of the freak-show convention of the mutually amplifying juxtaposition is not simply deliberately unscientific but also introduces exaggeration and an element of popular entertainment that would have been useful in encouraging the spread of eugenic ideas. They could also be seen as incorporating an element of playfulness and toying with their subjects that does not sit well with an otherwise clinical approach.

These illusions nevertheless severely detract from the persuasiveness of the entire edifice of clinical eugenics. If feeble-mindedness is not so easily recognized and classified as eugenicists believed, then the entire social program of eugenics, such as forced institutionalization, involuntary sterilization, restrictive immigration and marriage laws and positive eugenics such as "fitter family contests" becomes unworkable.

Note

1   Maxwell (2008) recognizes four styles or conventions in eugenic racial photography: anthropometric, prison, social-documentary and publicity.

References

Barr, M., & Maloney, A. B. (1920). *Types of Mental Defectives.* Philadelphia, PA: Blakiston.

Barr, M. W. (1904/1913). *Mental Defectives: Their History, Treatment and Training.* Philadelphia, PA: Blakiston.

Black, E. (2003). *War Against the Weak: Eugenics and America's Campaign to Create a Master Race.* New York, NY: Four Walls Eight Windows.

Bogdan, R. C. (1988). *Freakshow: Presenting Human Oddities for Amusement and Profit.* Chicago, IL: University of Chicago.

Bogdan, R. C., & Biklen, S. (2011). *Qualitative Research for Education: An Introduction to Theory and Methods* (5th Ed.). Upper Saddle River, NJ: Prentice Hall.

Chorover, S. L. (1979). *From Genesis to Genocide: The Meaning of Human Nature and the Power of Behavior Control.* Cambridge, MA: MIT.

Cohen, A. (2016). *Imbeciles: The Supreme Court, American eugenics and the sterilization of Carrie Buck.* New York: Penguin Books.

Corbin, J., & Strauss, A. (1990). Grounded theory research: Procedures, canons and evaluative criteria. *Qualitative Sociology,* 13(1), 3–21.

Davenport, C. B. (1911). *Heredity in Relation to Eugenics.* New York, NY: Henry Holt.

Davies, S. P. (1930). *Social Control of the Mentally Deficient.* New York, NY: Crowell.

Dowdall, G. W., & Golden, J. (1989). Photographs as data: An analysis of images of a mental hospital. *Qualitative Sociology*, 12(2), 183–213.

Elks, M. (1993a). The "lethal chamber": Further evidence for the euthanasia option. *Mental Retardation, 31* (4), 201–207.

Elks, M. (1993b). Visual rhetoric: Photographs of the feeble-minded during the eugenics era. 1900–1930. Ph.D. Dissertation. Ann Arbor, MI: University Microfilms International.

Fernald, W. E. (1912). The burden of feeble-mindedness. *Journal of Psycho-Asthenics*, 17(3), 85–99.

Gilman, S. L. (Ed.). (1976). *The Face of Madness: Hugh Diamond and the Origin of Psychiatric Illustration.* New York, NY: Citadel Press, 19–21.

Gilman, S. L. (1982). *Seeing the Insane.* New York, NY: Wiley.

Glaser, B. G., & Strauss, A. L. (1967). *The Discovery of Grounded Theory.* New York, NY: Aldine.

Goddard, H. H. (1912). *The Kallikak Family: A Study in the Heredity of Feeble-Mindedness.* New York, NY: Macmillan.

Goddard, H. H. (1914a). *Feeblemindedness: Its Causes and Consequences.* New York, NY: Macmillan.

Goddard, H. H. (1914b). *School Training of Defective Children.* New York, NY: World Books.

Goddard, H. H. (1915). *The Criminal Imbecile: An Analysis of Three Remarkable Murder Cases.* New York, NY: Macmillan.

Haller, M. (1963). *Eugenics: Hereditarian Attitudes in American Thought.* New Brunswick, NJ: Rutgers University.

Hague, W. G. (1914). *The Eugenic Marriage: A Personal Guide to the New Sciences of Better Living and Better Babies.* 4 Vols. New York, NY: Review of Reviews.

Hollander, R. (1989). Euthanasia and intellectual disabilities: Suggesting the unthinkable. *Intellectual Disabilities*, 22(2), 55–61.

Kite, E. S. (undated). [Manuscript]. Goddard papers (Box M614, Folder). Akron, Ohio: University of Akron, Bierce Library, Archives of the History of American Psychology, pp. 3–4. In Smith, D. J. (1985). *Minds made feeble: The myth and legacy of the Kallikaks.* Austin, TX: Pro-Ed.

Lombardo, P. A. (Ed.). (2011). *A Century of Eugenics in America: From the Indiana Experiment to the Human Genome Era.* Bloomington, IN: Indiana University Press.

Ludmerer, K. M. (1972). *Genetics and American Society: A Historical Appraisal.* Baltimore, MD: Johns Hopkins University.

Maxwell, A. (2008). *Picture Imperfect: Photography and Eugenics, 1870–1940.* Brighton, UK: Sussex Academic Press

McLaren, A. (1990). *Our Own Master Race: Eugenics in Canada: 1885–1945.* Toronto, Canada: McClelland and Stewart.

O'Brien, G. V. (2013). *Framing the Moron: The Social Construction of Feeble-Mindedness in the American Eugenics Era.* Manchester, UK: Manchester University Press.

Ollerenshaw, R. (1961). Medical illustration in the past. in E. F. Linssen (Ed.), *Medical Photography in Practice: A Symposium* (pp. 1–18). London, UK: Fountain.

Popenoe, P., & Johnson, R. H. (1918). *Applied Eugenics.* New York, NY: Macmillan.

Rafter, N. H. (Ed.). (1988). *White Trash: The Eugenic Family Studies 1877–1919.* Boston, MA: Northeastern University.

Saloway, R. A. (1990). *Demography and Degeneration: Eugenics and the Declining Birthrate in Twentieth-Century Britain.* Chapel Hill, NC: University of North Carolina.

Searle, G. R. (1976). *Eugenics and Politics in Britain 1900–1914.* Leyden, MA: Noordhoff International Publishing.

Sekula, A. (1989). The body and the archive. In Bolton, R. (Ed.). *The contest of meaning: Critical histories of photography, pp. 343–389.* Cambridge, MA: MIT Press.

Smith, J. D., & Wehmeyer, M. L. (2012). *Good Blood Bad Blood: Science, Nature, and the Myth of the Kallikaks.* Washington, DC: American Association on Intellectual and Developmental Disabilities.

Talbot, E. S. (1901). *Degeneracy: Its Causes, Signs, and Results.* London, UK: C. Scribner.

Zenderland, L. (1998). *Measuring Minds: Henry Herbert Goddard and the Origins of American Intelligence Testing.* Cambridge, UK: Cambridge University Press.Author queries

25

WHEN IS LIFE UNWORTHY OF LIVING? LESSONS FROM THE SYSTEMATIC KILLING OF CHILDREN WITH DISABILITIES IN NAZI GERMANY

Ivan Brown[1]

At the time of writing this chapter, the Supreme Court of Canada was considering a case with two central questions: When is life unworthy of living? Who should determine if someone's life is worthy or unworthy of living? In this case, a 60-year-old man had been kept alive by artificial means for 13 months. His physicians assessed that he had no chance of regaining consciousness, described his condition as one of permanent vegetative state, and advocated removing life supports. If he were to be kept alive by artificial means, they believed, he might well survive for a considerable amount of time but without consciousness and at great cost to the healthcare system. Complicating this issue was the fact that his condition had resulted from bacterial meningitis that caused severe brain damage, following surgery for a benign brain tumour in the hospital.

Typically, when such questions arise, those giving consent on behalf of the patient (usually close family members) and physicians discuss the prognosis together and come to an agreement on the best way to proceed. Here, though, family members and physicians did not agree. The physicians did not feel justified in continuing an expensive treatment for which they saw no hope that any improvement would occur. Family members, who understood that their consent is legally required for removal of life support, would not consent to letting the patient die because he was "still alive." The man's physicians and his families had two opposing views on whether his life was worth living.

The decision by the Supreme Court will occur within the legal and cultural context of Canada. There is currently broad acceptance of the need to protect and exercise individual rights and, more specifically related to this case, to sustain life even if serious illness or disability has occurred. Many laws and policies within various social institutions (e.g., health, education, social services) are in place to support such views. In addition, medical advances have made it possible for many people who would have died in earlier times to live with the aid of life supports. Questions have arisen in recent decades about how far such ideology and medical support should be extended (see, for example, Kuhse & Singer, 1985). When should life be saved, and when it is time to let someone die? Moreover, who should decide when is it no longer worthwhile to let someone continue living? The central dilemma is that, although we *can* keep people alive when they otherwise would have died, it does not necessarily follow that we *should* keep them alive in all cases. Cultural customs and mores, social values, personal and spiritual beliefs, perceived and real legal and moral rights, and current technology all factor into the decision, sometimes in complex ways.

The same dilemma has arisen in many societies throughout the world and over the millennia. Often people *could* be kept alive, but it was not always considered that they *should* be kept alive. Children with disabilities are among those who can be identified at many points in history as having been left to die by abandonment or exposure (left alone outside to die from the elements or eaten by wild animals), or as having been deliberated killed – presumably because it had been determined that their lives were not worth living. For example, Western culture contains recorded evidence that the killing of children with disabilities was a common practice in ancient Greek and Roman civilizations (The Society for the Prevention of Infanticide, 1998). This was sometimes supported by the views of leaders (e.g., Aristotle wrote in *Politics*, "[L]et there be a law that no deformed child shall live"), and sometimes by customs and laws (e.g., in Sparta, newborns were examined by a committee of elders to determine if they were worthy of rearing or if they should be exposed because they were not worth bringing up; Baker, 2010). In all cases, such practices were supported by a broadly held ideology that highly valued physical and mental perfection in all its forms, and devalued physical and mental inferiority (Brown & Radford, 2007).

The role of broadly held ideology in determining whose life is worth living and whose life is not worth living can be illustrated in numerous other examples in history. But one of the most poignant examples is the systematic killing of children with disabilities in Nazi Germany during World War II. In this chapter, we explore this example in some detail. Although the facts of this story in and of themselves warrant not only interest, but also horror and alarm, the broader theses explored here are that (1) practices that involve deciding that the lives of people are not worth living cannot take place without both strong ideological acceptance and support from social institutions; and (2) even within this context, other social values or circumstances can be present, curtailing to some degree both the decision and the ensuing action. In the case of Nazi Germany, there was broad acceptance of the Nazi ideology that blended in its own interpretation of *eugenics* (deliberate action to improve the makeup of society), and this ideology had the support of the legal, medical, military, and other systems. These systems were all required for the systematic killing of children to become a reality. Even so, Hitler and his Nazi followers deemed it necessary to carry out their killing program in a great deal of secrecy and under the covers of both medical science and war.

The growth of eugenics in Europe and North America

An ideology of large groups of people or societies is the set of beliefs and values that guides many of their collective goals and determines much of their collective behaviour. In the latter part of the 19th century and the first half of the 20th century, eugenics contributed to the ideology of the times to a very substantial degree in Europe, North America, and countries around the world that were influenced by them (Lombardo, 1996). "Eugenics" literally means "well born" and was coined in 1880 by Sir Frances Galton, a British scientist and a cousin of Charles Darwin.

Galton's idea emerged naturally enough from a few centuries of world exploration and domination of much of the world's lands and oceans by the British, and from the oft-accompanying sense of European racial superiority. Darwin, himself, was a British scientist and world explorer who, in his 1859 book *On the Origin of Species* and other works, promoted the view that animals and plants change over time in accordance with their surroundings, since those more adapted to their environments are likely to survive and those less adapted are likely to perish. Darwin's views of the survival of the fittest and of the evolution of species sparked tremendous controversy, especially when juxtaposed against religious beliefs, but their scientific merit was recognized and soon afterwards the notion of *Social Darwinism* took form.

Social Darwinism was first promoted by the British philosopher Herbert Spencer. Thinking of a society in the same way Darwin thought of a species, Social Darwinism gave rise to the widely accepted notion that race (genetically inherited characteristics), rather than beliefs or learning, primarily determined present and future characteristics and behaviour (Weinstein & Stehr, 1999). Just as physical traits in individual species, such as length of wings or colour of feathers, are determined by genetic inheritance, so too social and societal traits are inherited (Proctor, 1988). And if species change gradually over time by survival of the fittest to adapt better to changing environments, societies do as well. The economic and military domination of European societies over others in the world was seen as clear evidence of a natural survival-of-the-fittest race. Within European countries, the domination of the more socially and financially successful over the less fortunate was considered evidence of natural survival of the fittest classes. Conversely, it was often believed, using resources to support disadvantaged and marginalized members of society undermined such domination and thus interfered with the evolution of natural law.

Eugenics combined these ideas and extended them into a coherent ideology. It held that natural law could be enhanced by deliberate action taken to influence the make-up of society so that it would be improved by having more "well born," and thus it would be more capable of meeting its demands. Galton himself wrote in 1904, "The aim of eugenics is to bring as many influences as can be reasonably employed, to cause the useful classes in the community to contribute *more* than their proportion to the next generation" (par. 5). Thus, in practice, eugenics meant that procreation of those considered desirable was encouraged, while procreation of people who were poor, idiots, insane, underprivileged, or simply undesirable in numerous ways was restricted by measures such as segregated living in institutions and other residences, and through dire warning against the evils of sexual contact by professionals and social leaders of many types (Kanner, 1964; Rotzoll et al., 2006). In a sense, the thinking behind eugenics was not particularly new at all, since people had devised from time immemorial that they could selectively breed animals in such a way as to improve the make-up of their herds, and that they could selectively plant seeds to improve the make-up of their crops' harvests. Eugenics emerged, then, from a background of relevant knowledge and experience, and within a current ideological environment that was sufficiently fertile for it to flourish.

Eugenics had tremendous impact on virtually every aspect of society (Brown & Brown, 2003). For people with disabilities and other social disadvantages, it provided the rationale for building and operating an enormous number of institutions, and it was widely considered that such people "belonged" in an institution (Brown & Radford, 2007; Kanner, 1964). It resulted in millions of unwanted people being encouraged (and at times forced) to move to other, sometimes remote, parts of the world such as North America, Australia, and New Zealand. It strongly influenced numerous laws and the professional ethics of education, medicine, industry and commerce, religion, law, social services, and many others. Today, it is difficult for us to fathom the pervasive influence of eugenics over the thinking and actions of our ancestors in Europe and North America only a hundred years ago.

The setting for eugenics extremism in Nazi Germany

The ideological setting

Eugenics as an ideology was perhaps most strongly perpetuated and practised in Britain and North America, although its influence on other countries, including Germany, was very considerable. At the same time, though, a parallel ideology that emphasized egalitarianism and humanitarianism had earlier emerged and swept France, the United States, and to a lesser extent other countries in Europe. When applied to people with disabilities and social disadvantage, this movement stressed good health, safe housing, and education and training (Buell, Weiss, & Brown, 2011). The result was the building of institutions in the form of safe residences and self-sufficient farms away from the health hazards and physical dangers that plagued city living at the time, and numerous types of schools and training institutions for people with various disabilities and disadvantages (Woodill & Velche, 1995). Medical, educational, and social leaders in France and Germany pioneered this work, which was later expanded considerably, especially in Britain and the United States (Brown, Percy, & Machalek, 2007).

Eugenics and humanitarianism did not always operate separately or in completely opposing ways. Schools and institutions were designed and operated as places of refuge and places of learning, but they were also usually places of segregation where eugenics ideas could be easily implemented. Males and females were typically housed separately and sexual activity among adults was discouraged. Although there was a scientific interest – even excitement – in the possibility of training and rehabilitating people who had formerly been considered untrainable, there was also a strong sense that such people did not belong in the regular schools and did not merit participating in the life of general society. Thus, Germany – much like other European and North American countries – entered the first part of the 20th century with two seemingly incongruous ideologies, although the two ideologies often both influenced the way people's lives were conducted.

Eugenics had always dominated humanitarianism as an ideology, but in Germany following World War I this imbalance increased. Over the 20-year period between the two world wars, a unique brand of eugenics gradually, but very steadily, gained importance in Germany. At first, that brand was not clear. As was the case in the United States and elsewhere, there was a general strong belief in the superiority of the Caucasian race, but the supremacy of the Aryan race and action to ensure the endurance of that supremacy were ideas of only one faction of eugenicists in Germany and these were vigorously debated during the 1920s. Anti-Semitism was a eugenics idea that only gradually took form – although there were long-standing prejudices – with the increasing acceptance and popularity of race science, until it was overtly espoused by the Nazis (Friedlander, 1995).

Regarding disabilities, German eugenics spokespersons were primarily eminent scientists whose views were increasingly hostile to supporting the lives of people with disabilities. In 1920, Karl Binding published his work *Die Freigabe der Vernichtung libensun-werten Lebens*, which is translated in English to mean "authorization for the destruction of life unworthy of life" (Friedlander, 1995, p. 14). Binding argued for the right to an assisted death by those who are terminally ill, and used this argument as a springboard to claim that those whose life was unworthy in other ways might also be assisted in dying. Although those unworthy of life were not precisely defined, Binding unfavourably contrasted the value of vigorous youth dying on the battlefields of World War I with keeping the feeble-minded alive in institutions. He argued that the latter were unworthy of life not only because they suffered without purpose in life, but also because they were an enormous burden on their families and on society (Mostert, 2002).

The following year, the definitive text *Outline of Human Genetics and Racial Hygiene* (Baur, Fischer, & Lenz, 1921) was published in two volumes. This work provided a full scientific rationale for the eugenics idea of racial hygiene, acting as the key reference point for the work by Nazi scientists, lawmakers, and other eugenicists for many years, and helping to inform Hitler's thinking in his 1925 (volume I) and 1926 (volume II) book *Mein Kampf*. Throughout the 1920s, eugenics research centres and university teaching gradually developed throughout Germany until 1933, when such activity proliferated under the new Nazi regime (Berenbaum, 1993).

Only 4 months after Hitler and the Nazis assumed full power in Germany in 1933, a law was enacted that required the sterilization of all people with physical and mental disabilities. Two years later, in 1935, such people and others were prohibited by the Marriage Health Law from getting married and thus creating "unwanted" children. Such eugenics laws emerged parallel to several harsh racial hygiene laws (e.g., the 1935 Reich Citizenship Law and the Law for the Protection of German Blood and German Honour) that primarily targeted Jews, but also Gypsies, Negroes, and other minorities. All had the same overall goal, though: to create a superior and pure Aryan race.

The sterilization and anti-marriage laws against people with disabilities provided a way to identify those who were "suffering" from "hereditary" diseases (including physical disability, mental illness, epilepsy, blindness, deafness, and alcoholism), and a reason to act so they could not procreate and thus perpetuate their "diseases." People could apply themselves for sterilization, although most applications were made by health professionals. Applications were reviewed by a three-man committee of experts whose decisions could not be contested. Thus, once a decision had been made for sterilization, which was the case for about 85%–90% of applicants, the procedure was carried out even against the person's will. Between 1934 and 1937, supported by the ideology and social structures of the time, nearly 200,000 men and women were sterilized, about 52% of whom were "diagnosed as suffering from feeblemindedness" (Friedlander, 1995, p. 28).

The socio-political setting

The harsh financial and social conditions in Germany following World War I contributed strongly to eugenics developing and maturing in an extreme form, and in ways that overlooked much of humanitarianism's set of values. The German military, facing desertion and internal collapse from dwindling resources compared to its opponents, initiated Germany suing for peace in November 1918 at a time when the German military was still fighting on foreign soil and the general population of Germany was not prepared for defeat. Kaiser Wilhelm II abdicated the same month under pressure to improve Germany's chances of being treated more favourably. However, the ensuing Treaty of Versailles, which was signed in June 1919 and set out the conditions that ended the war, imposed harsh economic penalties on Germany and the loss of about 11% of German territory. There was widespread opposition to those who had supported signing the treaty.

The Weimar Republic, Germany's post-war move to democracy, was proclaimed in November 1918, and its constitution was signed in August 1919. The social history of the two decades that followed is complex, and has been fully documented elsewhere (e.g., Burleigh, 2000; Shirer, 1941, 1960). Numerous factors contributed to the fall of the Weimar Republic in 1933, and the rise of the Nazi Party (the *Nationalsozialistische Deutsche Arbeiter Partei*, or National Socialist German Workers' Party, shortened to NSDAP or Nazi), which had been formed in 1920 with Adolph Hitler as its leader. Among the most important of these inter-relating factors are the following:

- The harsh repatriation payments to Britain and France imposed by the *Treaty of Versailles* that Germany could not afford to repay.
- Trade embargos against Germany by Britain, France, and the United States.
- Political turmoil, demonstrations, and sometimes violence in Germany under the Weimar Republic, with multiple parties including extremist parties on both the left and right.
- Enormous inflation during the 1920s and 1930s.
- Moral degeneracy and licence in Germany (especially Berlin) in the 1920s.
- Rampant unemployment in Germany during the 1920s and 1930s.
- The 1929 stock market crash in the United States, and the worldwide economic depression over the next decade.
- The demand, following the 1929 stock market crash, by the United States for Germany to repay its substantial loans.
- The economic collapse of the German government in the early 1930s.
- The election of July 1932 that saw Hilter's Nazi Party win the most votes of any party, with 38% of the total number of votes.
- Hitler being named Weimar Chancellor in January 1933, and the final Weimar Republic vote in March 1933, where the Nazi Party used military force to intimidate other parties but gained only 44% of the votes cast.
- Hitler's open adoption of race hygiene, persistent blaming of the Jews for Germany's economic woes, and accompanying series of highly restrictive and repressive laws.
- The remilitarization of Germany, contrary to the Treaty of Versailles.

Blending of political and scientific ideology

After Hitler and the Nazis assumed complete power in Germany in 1933 and banished all opposition, the political ideology of the Nazis and the scientific ideology of eugenics quickly blended together (Friedlander, 1995). In a country where all social institutions were controlled by the totalitarian Nazi regime, the eugenics notion of improving the human race through genetic means found a way to promote itself easily and quickly. On the other hand, the Nazi notion of developing a superior and pure Aryan race found a scientific basis – and all the power that goes with scientific knowledge – in eugenics and race science (Weinstein & Stehr, 1999). The blossoming of this symbiotic relationship would have dire consequences for many "unworthy" Germans and other Europeans.

The program for killing children with disabilities in Nazi Germany

At the U.S. Military Tribunal after the war, Karl Brandt, Adolf Hilter's personal physician, testified that Hitler had made it clear in 1935 "that once war began he would institute euthanasia" (Friedlander, 1995, p. 39). The war did not begin until the German invasion of Poland in September 1939, but an experiment and organizational efforts prior to that time clearly showed that euthanasia (killing) of children with disabilities was both premeditated and thoroughly planned. These actions also showed that the program was carried out only with the cooperation of both scientists and medical professionals and government officials working together and, for the most part, in secret.

How did the program begin?

In 1938, a family named Knauer had their child admitted to the Leipzig University Children's Clinic, and sent an appeal to Hitler by way of his private chancellery to have the child put to death. The child, whose sex is unknown to this day, was assessed by several physicians whose opinions differed somewhat, but was born with missing arm and leg parts, was probably blind, may have had convulsions, and was diagnosed by some physicians as an idiot (Lewis, 2004). Hitler dispatched his personal physician, Karl Brandt, to assess the child and instructed him to kill the child if his assessment matched the facts set out in the appeal. Brandt's assessment did match, and the child was killed (Friedlander, 1995).

The killing of the Knauer child appears to have been a test case to ascertain the appetite of the medical profession and Hitler's government officials for killing children with disabilities. The action apparently met with little resistance, since shortly afterward a bureaucracy was organized for identifying children with disabilities who were considered to be unworthy of living, inducing them to be admitted to centres where medical staff were willing to kill them, and carrying out the killings (Proctor, 1988).

First, the children had to be identified and "assessed." On August 18, 1939, the ministry in charge of public health circulated its *Requirement to Report Deformed etc. Newborns* with the reporting form attached. In exchange for a small payment, physicians and midwives were required to complete these forms and send them to their local public health offices. These offices then forwarded them to the *Reich Committee for the Scientific Registration of Severe Hereditary Ailments* in Berlin, a fictitious department created to camouflage the real intent of the program. A committee of three medical experts and civil administrators then reviewed the brief information on the forms and, without ever seeing the children, designated the children described briefly on the forms for death, further assessment, or continued living (Aly, 1994).

Next, the children had to be moved to "treatment centres" where further assessment, treatment, and killing could take place. Some already lived in the centres that were eventually established for killing, but most children lived with their families or elsewhere. Families were told that their children should be moved to receive advanced scientific treatment where they might well be cured and, for those who resisted, threats of harm were used to gain consent. Most families did consent, although the true intent of treatment for those designated for killing was usually kept hidden from them. Twenty-two treatment centres throughout Germany were set up during the war, although this took some time because administrators and medical staff willing to kill children – unworthy of life and "useless eaters" in a social order that strove for physical and mental perfection – had to be carefully recruited (Mostert, 2002).

How were the killings carried out?

The first killings took place in October 1939, in keeping with Hitler's plan, just one month after the war began. The last known killing occurred one month after Germany's surrender in the spring of 1945. Between these dates, about 5,200 children with disabilities were killed by various means in Germany (Aly, 1994), and thousands more were probably killed throughout Austria, Poland and other parts of occupied Europe (Burleigh, 1997). One killing method was starvation, where food rations were gradually decreased until the child grew weak and eventually died. The preferred method, though, was overuse of medications that were already used in the centres, such as sedatives, sleeping tablets, and morphine. Medications dissolved in food or drinks, or injections, were administered by medical staff in doses that usually resulted in the child developing, and dying from, another condition such as pneumonia (Friedlander, 1995; Glass, 1997). The children's bodies were then sometimes examined and subjected to various types of medical experimentation. This provided a scientific, and perhaps in a perverse and gruesome way a moral, rationale for the killings – the children's bodies were said to be put to a useful purpose, furthering scientific knowledge and helping advance new treatments (Mostert, 2002).

At first, only infants and young children were included in the killings, but the program quickly expanded. By December 1940, children older than 3 years were being assessed for possible killing, and a year later all children and adolescents with disabilities up to 17 years of age were required to be included in the program (Mostert, 2002).

The high level of secrecy and degree of camouflage that accompanied the killing of children with disabilities strongly support the view that deeming people to be unworthy of living and following through with action requires extraordinary circumstances. Even Hitler, with strong and unopposed military and civil structures putting his ideology into practice, realized that the euthanasia of children with disabilities – and later the killing of about 70,000 adults with disabilities, 6 million Jews, Gypsies, and other minorities in one of the most extensive and horrific planned exterminations of humans in history – could be accomplished only under the umbrella of war, when times are dire and values are fluid. The Reich Committee that ostensibly operated the program for killing children with disabilities was not a government department at all, and its mailing address was only a post office box. Instead, the program's leaders were from other areas of the government. The three-person committee that decided on those who were unworthy of life did not even sign their own names to the documents, preferring instead to use aliases (Friedlander, 1995). Medical professionals who killed children with disabilities and government bureaucrats who administered the program blatantly lied to families about the program's intent, and disguised the causes of the children's deaths (Burleigh, 1994). When all else failed, families were threatened with unspecified "harm" to themselves and their relatives.

How "successful" was the program for killing children with disabilities?

The program for killing children with disabilities served as an example and was repeated in the more extensive killing programs that followed, particularly the killing of adults with disabilities and the much larger number of Jews. The transport of huge numbers of people to concentration camps, and the killing methods of those programs – especially the gas chambers, starvation, and mass shootings – were much more complex and deadly. But the basic elements were the same: give credence to the ideology that genetic inheritance primarily determines present and future characteristics and actions, and thus undesired characteristics and actions can be eradicated only by eradication of the race or group of people that displays them; identify a race or group of people who are unwanted and unworthy to live among a pure Aryan race; develop methods for exterminating them; move them by trickery or by force to the killing centres; and carry out the killings. That Hitler and his close followers chose to begin with the killing of helpless children with disabilities speaks to their mastery of Nazi ideology and eugenics working together and taken to their evil extremes.

Adolf Hitler and his close associates did not have any difficulty determining who was worthy, and who was unworthy, of living. Children with disabilities were among the most unworthy and the least vocal, and thus they were the first to be killed. Hitler was the totalitarian leader of a strong ideology that was quite widely accepted in Germany at the time, and his Reich was in control of all the civil structures in the country. In addition, Hitler's personal popularity with his own German populace between 1938 and 1940 was extremely high (Kershaw, 2008). Traditional values and ways of behaving had been splintered by years of political turmoil and recent military action. The task of killing children with disabilities should have been a relatively easy one in the late 1930s and early 1940s by the Nazis in Germany. Yet, they found it necessary to carry out the program only when national and international attention was highly diverted by the beginning of the war, in a great deal of secrecy from even the German people, and with the help of only a relatively small number of dedicated professionals and bureaucrats.

Why was this? The answer may lie in a further look at the implementation of the program. As mentioned, the 22 known killing centres were set up over time and, although most recruited physicians agreed to take part in the program, some refused to do so and were excused (Friedlander, 1995). A few parents also refused to have their children "treated" even when required, and most did not suspect that the real intent of treatment in many cases was to kill their children. In fact, program officials went to great lengths to cover the truth. Hospitals that admitted children with disabilities conducted their own assessments and diagnoses, sometimes quite thoroughly, and physicians and hospitals did not always report children in all the categories that were demanded by the Reich Committee (Aly, 1994). Of the approximately 100,000 reports that were received, only about one-fifth of these were forwarded by officials to the three-man committee for final review, and of these only a little more than one-quarter (5,200) were approved for killing (Aly, 1994). All this suggests that, although there was certainly a well-planned and sinister program for killing children with disabilities who were considered unworthy of life because of their lack of potential for contributing productively to German society, at the same time the limited "success" of the program suggests that there was also internal resistance and adherence to the scientific merits of rehabilitation among both government and medical officials.

Could such opposing values exist in Nazi Germany alongside the extreme eugenics thrust to deem children with disabilities so unworthy of life that they should be killed? The answer, judging by the limited success of the program, appears to be yes. Although it is little comfort, the plain truth is that a great many more children could have been killed in the program than actually were. The presence of opposing values alongside Nazi ideology appears to have resulted in Hilter – bold leader that he was – being insufficiently bold to ever openly advocate killing German citizens with disabilities, and to take action only when the diversion of war and the secrecy of his own administrators made it safer to do so. It would take the incredibly harsh demands and hardships of World War II that occurred shortly afterward to provide cover for the much more extreme killings that were to follow.

A return to the present

From our present perspective, the killing of children with disabilities in Nazi Germany is an extreme example. Still, it illustrates that, even in these extreme circumstances, making the decision that some people's lives are unworthy of living and acting on that decision are not simple things to do. They require the support of accepted ideology and social structures for legitimacy, and may still meet with considerable resistance. This is understandable, because they involve profound moral and ethical questions.

But as we see from the events that transpired in Nazi Germany, morality (what is considered to be right and wrong) and ethics (what is the best thing to do in a particular situation) can be swayed to a considerable degree by environmental conditions. They can be swayed particularly vigorously if those conditions include war. During wartime, values change (Neitzel & Welzer, 2012). Killing in peacetime is murder, but killing in war is a soldier's job and a military duty. People are put in jail or executed if they kill during times of peace, but soldiers are honoured and receive medals for killing during a war. Hilter appeared to know this well, and chose not to begin killing "unworthy" German citizens and citizens from other countries until the war was under way.

Even in times of peace, though, morality and ethics vary according to whom they are being directed toward. Individuals can usually be killed without reproach if they are seen as enemies of some type. Some countries in the world still execute those who are found guilty of serious crimes by their legal systems because they are seen as enemies of the state and unworthy of citizenship. Almost anywhere in the world, when police shoot and kill a threatening or unwanted criminal, it is typically met with little sympathy and often the action involves little public censure.

People are also killed – or not allowed to continue living – if their lives are not considered worth preserving. All countries have measures, formal or informal, for letting people die when they are born with severe medical conditions or physical disabilities, when they are perceived to be indubitably and unequivocally nearing the end of their lives, or when their lives are so damaged that they are not worth continuing, such as being in a profoundly disabled or vegetative state – whether those measures are moving the person toward death, as is the case with administering substances such as morphine to allow for a peaceful death, or withholding supports that could prolong life, such as feeding tubes and ventilators.

When such measures are used, they reflect views about social and economic worthiness and unworthiness (Mostert, 2002). Nazi ideology stressed racial desirability and physical productivity as the primary criteria for social worth, but current debates about stem cell interventions, organ harvesting, abortion of a foetus with a known abnormality, the cost of innovative therapies, and euthanasia also involve a dialogue about the social worth of those who may live with disabilities, and of those who might lead more socially and economically productive lives if they were to receive intervention.

A large amount of academic literature has explored these phenomena, and reviews for children (e.g., Gillam & Sullivan, 2011), critically ill and disabled adults (e.g., Curtis & Vincent, 2010), and older persons (e.g., Weidemann, 2012) suggest that family members, healthcare professionals, and even legal systems vary quite considerably in their views about making end-of-life decisions and in their desire and ability to do so. Protocols for making such decisions exist in many jurisdictions, although definitive ways to resolve disputes that occur when family members, health professionals, and legal requirements do not coincide are still emerging. The country's legal system is usually considered to have the final word.

In today's world, where ideology and cultural beliefs about life and death can be diverse, and where medical science has developed ways to maintain and prolong life, the delicate distinction between life that is worth living and life that is not worth living may be a more difficult one to make than ever. Differences in opinion exist, and no doubt will continue to exist. When addressing this question, though, it is helpful to understand the roles played by ideology and social structures within current social environments, for both are influential and can turn surprisingly quickly in a horrific direction, as the example of killing children with disabilities in Nazi Germany clearly shows.

Note

1   In numerous places throughout this chapter, I have used terms that were commonly used in the historical era described, but that are no longer used. I recognize that some of these terms are considered derogatory today by disability, mental health, cultural, and other groups. They are used here, though, for the purpose of historical accuracy.

References

Aly, G. (1994). Pure and tainted progress. in G. Aly, P. Chroust, & C. Pross (Eds.), *Cleansing the Fatherland: Nazi Medicine and Facial Hygiene* (pp. 156–237). Baltimore, MD: The Johns Hopkins University Press.

Aristotle. (350 B.C.E.). *Politics.* Book seven, Section XVI., par. 5. Retrieved from http://www.constitution.org/ari/polit_07.htm

Baker, P. S. (2010). *Training Warriors in Ancient Sparta*. Retrieved from http://www.helium. com/items/1896238-training-warriors-in-ancient-sparta

Baur, E., Fischer, E., & Lenz, F. (1921). *The Outline of Human Genetics and Racial Hygiene*. Berlin: Lehmann Publishing.

Berenbaum, M. (1993). *The World Must Know: The History of the Holocaust as Told in the United States Holocaust Memorial Museum*. Boston, MA: Little, Brown and Company.

Brown, I., & Brown, R. I. (2003). *Quality of Life and Disability: An Approach for Community Practitioners*. London, UK: Jessica Kingsley Publishers.

Brown, I., Percy, M., & Machalek, K. (2007). Education for individuals with intellectual and developmental disabilities. in I. Brown & M. Percy (Eds.), *A Comprehensive Guide to Intellectual & Developmental Disabilities* (pp. 489–510). Baltimore, MD: Paul H. Brookes Publishing.

Brown, I., & Radford, J. P. (2007). Historical overview of intellectual and developmental disabilities. in I. Brown & M. Percy (Eds.), *A Comprehensive Guide to Intellectual & Developmental Disabilities* (pp. 17–33). Baltimore, MD: Paul H. Brookes Publishing Company.

Buell, M. K., Weiss, J., & Brown, I. (2011). Lifestyles of adults with developmental disabilities in Ontario. in I. Brown & M. Percy (Eds.), *Developmental Disabilities in Ontario* (3rd ed.) (pp. 831–849). Toronto, ON: Ontario Association on Developmental Disabilities.

Burleigh, M. (1994). *Death and Deliverance*. Cambridge, UK: Cambridge University Press.

Burleigh, M. (1997). *Ethics and Extermination: Reflections on Nazi Genocide*. Cambridge, UK: Cambridge University Press.

Burleigh, M. (2000). *The Third Reich: A New History*. New York, NY: Hill & Wang.

Curtis, J. R., & Vincent, J.-L. (2010). Ethics and end-of-life care for adults in the intensive care unit. *The Lancet, 376*(9749), 1347–1353.

Darwin, C. (1859/2008). *On the Origin of Species*. Oxford, UK: Oxford University Press.

Friedlander, H. (1995). *The Origins of Nazi Genocide: From Euthanasia to the Final Solution*. Chapel Hill, NC: University of North Carolina Press.

Galton, F. (1904). Eugenics: Its definition, scope, and aims. *The American Journal of Sociology, 10*(1), pp. 1–6. Retrieved from http://galton.org/essays/1900–1911/galton-1904-am-journ-soc-eugenics-scope-aims.htm

Glass, J. M. (1997). *"Life Unworthy of Life": Racial Phobia and Mass Murder in Hitler's Germany*. New York, NY: Basic Books.

Gillam, L., & Sullivan, J. (2011). Ethics at the end of life: Who should make decisions about treatment limitations for young children with life-threatening or life-limiting conditions? *Journal of Paediatrics and Child health, 47*, 594–598.

Hitler, A. (1941). *Mein Kampf*. San Francisco, NC: Reynal and Hitchcock. Retrieved from http://archive.org/details/meinkampf035176mbp

Kanner, L. (1964). *A History of the Care and Study of the Mentally Retarded*. Springfield, IL: Charles C. Thomas.

Kershaw, I. (2008). *How Hitler Won Over the German People*. Spiegel Online International. Retrieved from http://www.spiegel.de/international/germany/the-fuehrer-myth-how-hitler-won-over-the-german-people-a-531909.html

Kuhse, H., & Singer, P. (1985). *Should the Baby Live? The Problem of Handicapped Infants*. New York, NY: Oxford University Press.

Lewis, S. E. (2004). *The Holocaust and People with Disabilities*. Chicago, IL: Ivan R. Dee Publisher.

Lombardo, P. A. (2002). Commentary: "The American Breed": Nazi eugenics and the origins of the pioneer fund. Albany Law Review, *65*(3), 743.

Mostert, M. P. (2002). Useless eaters: Disabilities as genocidal marker in Nazi Germany. *Journal of Special Education, 36*, 155–168.

Neitzel, S., & Welzer, H. (2012). *Soldaten: On Fighting, Killing, and Dying: The Secret WWII Transcripts of German POWs* (trans. from German by J. Chase). New York, NY: Knopf.

Proctor, R. (1988). *Racial Hygiene: Medicine Under the Nazis*. Cambridge, MA: Harvard University Press.

Rotzoll, M., Richter, P., Fuchs, P., Hinz-Wessels, A., Topp, S., & Hohehdorf, G. (2006). The first national socialist crime. *International Journal of Mental Health, 35*, 17–29.

Shirer, W. L. (1941). *Berlin Diary: The Journal of a Foreign Correspondent, 1934–1941*. New York, NY: A. A. Knopf.

Shirer, W. L. (1960). *The Rise and Fall of the Third Reich: A History of Nazi Germany.* New York, NY: Simon & Schuster.

The Society for the Prevention of Infanticide. (1998). *A Brief History of Infanticide.* Retrieved from http://infanticide.org/history.htm

Weidemann, E. L. (2012). The ethics of life and death: Advance directives and end-of-life decision making in persons with dementia. *Journal of Forensic Psychology Practice, 12*(1), 81–96.

Weinstein, J., & Stehr, N. (1999). The power of knowledge: Race science, face policy, and the Holocaust. *Social Epistemology, 13*(1), 3–36.

Woodill, G., & Velche, D. (1995). From charity and exclusion to emerging independence: An introduction to the history of disabilities. *Journal on Developmental Disabilities, 4*(1), 1–11.

26

THE GENESIS OF SOCIETIES FOR CRIPPLED CHILDREN IN CANADA AND THEIR AMERICAN ROOTS

Roy Hanes

Introduction

Throughout this chapter the writer uses terms such as 'crippled' and 'defectives'. The use of these terms does not represent the writer's personal convictions, and it is not the writer's intent to offend or discredit persons with disabilities. The chapter addresses the development of charitable services for children with orthopaedic disabilities in Ontario, Canada, during the late 19th and the early 20th centuries, and the terms 'defective' and 'crippled' were applied to these children (Platt, 1898; Thorndike, 1898; Henderson, 1904; Wallace, 1910; Howett,1925). In terms of classification, children with orthopaedic disabilities did not exist during this time, but crippled and defective children did, and in this writer's attempt to be as historically accurate as possible the terminology of the era is used. Moreover, the use of the language and definitions of the era attests to the fluidity and social constructionist nature of the disability category (Scheer and Groce, 1988; Oliver, 1990; Hanes, 1995A; Hansen, 2002, Wendell, 2002; Thomas, 2007).

In recent years there has been a growing debate about the role and purpose of organized charities for persons with disabilities, especially children with disabilities. Throughout the year it seems that the public is constantly bombarded with requests for donations from one charitable organization or another. There are a myriad of activities, including telethons, direct mailing, infomercials, public service announcements, as well as billboard posters and newspaper advertisements, all directed at getting donations, and all contributing to what is often referred to as a Charity Model of Disability (Marks, 1997).

While an increasing number of charitable organizations for persons with disabilities have emerged since the 1960s, some of these charities have been in existence for many generations. One such organization which is grounded in the charity effort for children with disabilities is the Easter Seal Society, and its origins can be found in societies for crippled children which were established in the United States and Canada during the early part of the 20th century.

In this chapter, we examine the rise of the Canadian crippled-child-saving movement commencing in the late 19th century to the origins of the Ontario Society for Crippled Children during the early part of the 20th century. This chapter shows how this organization grew from a small community service project in Elyria, Ohio to an inter-state organization in the US to a province-wide organization in Ontario, Canada which in turn laid the foundation for the establishment of the International Society for Crippled Children. In short, the chapter traces the development of the Ontario Society for Crippled Children: its operational mandate, its ideology, the provision of care and treatment to children with orthopaedic disabilities and its connection to the International Society for Crippled Children and the service club movement.

Cripples: Who were they?[1]

Before undertaking this historical exploration of the development of societies for crippled children in the United States and particularly in Canada, it is important to explore what was meant and implied by the term 'cripple'.

Cripple, suggested Alexander Horowitz, assistant professor of orthopaedic surgery at the Saint Louis University School of Medicine, stemmed from the Anglo-Saxon word 'to creep': 'One who creeps, halts or limps, one who is partially or wholly deprived of the use of one or both limbs, a lame person' (Horowitz, 1923, p. 571). The term 'cripple' represented a broad category and refers to the overall condition of the individual; the term was not used to imply a medical diagnosis nor was it considered to be derogatory. 'From the physician's point of view the diagnosis of cripple, would of course, never be made. The patient would be classified as suffering from Potts' disease (hunchback), clubfoot, infantile paralysis or the like. Yet all these people are cripples' (McMurtrie, 1914, p. 366).

While the term 'cripple' represents a broad category of impairments, there are underlying similarities that are indicative of impairment to the muscular–skeletal system. Horowitz (1923) described the crippled condition 'as that condition used to embrace deformities both congenital and acquired causing malformation to the limb and stature' (Horowitz, 1923, p. 571). Abt (1924) provided a similar definition of the crippled child as 'one who by reasons of congenital or acquired defects of development, disease or trauma is deficient in the use of its body or limbs' (p. 68).

The cripple category was further subdivided to denote the origin of impairment. Jaegar (1914) described three distinct groups of cripples, including 'congenital cripples, cripples from disease and cripples from accident including various amputations' (p. 68). Horowitz (1923) considered congenital cripples to be a prehuman form of life, which had not totally completed its human growth prior to birth. 'A cripple (Congenital cripple) that is, one differing in bodily appearance from the accepted normal, a normal established by us who are the majority', concluded Horowitz, 'is one who at some time in its intrauterine development has met some hindrance which checked further development in all or in part of the organism. It is thus a retrogression from the human to some pre-human type' (1923, p. 571).

Crippled children were also defined according to prognosis. The population of crippled children who exhibited the possibility of improvement was referred to as potential cripples, and those who could not be helped were referred to as actual cripples. (Allison, 1915, p. 69).

Concern for economic independence was an essential component of most cripple definitions. Chapin (1930) provides three categories of cripples, which are based on one's ability to work. The first of Chapin's categories of cripples covered those who were able to be trained and were potentially employable in occupations open to all people regardless of level of physical disability. The second category covered those whose level of impairment prevented them from being employed in the open market but who were able to work in a sheltered environment. The third category covered those who were confined to their homes and for whom there was no potential for employment or training.

Setting the stage: provincial policies of reluctant support and reluctant intervention

Throughout most the 19th century and the early years of the 20th century, the policies of the Province of Ontario that pertained to the care and treatment of persons with disabilities emphasized two themes. First, the province took no direct responsibility for the care and maintenance of any needy persons, including all classes of persons with disabilities. Second, the province supported the development of local institutions as the primary mechanism of relief for the poor and dependent classes. Moreover, the use of institutions as mechanisms to deal with poor, deviant and dependent populations was well established in Ontario prior to Confederation, and the province continued with this practice until the onset of the Depression era. The provincial government's policy was to establish institutional standards and procedures for the provision of care and maintenance, but it was never a provincial government's policy to take responsibility for the direct provision of care and relief for the people residing in the institutions. When the municipal or county authorities were unable to provide the required services, local charitable organizations were expected to fill the gap, not the province, and this was how things remained until the 1930s (Wallace, 1950; Splane, 1965; Pitsula, 1979; Struthers, 1991).

Although it was not until the early years of the 20th century that social reformers and charitable organizations took a direct interest in crippled children, the foundations for this work are rooted in social policies of the 19th century. During the early years of the 19th century the provision of care for crippled children as well as other dependent individuals was considered a family responsibility. When families could not provide for a member (usually an elderly person or a disabled person), these persons were housed in private homes, and funds to cover expenses, such as for food, clothing, shelter and medical care, were provided, most often through municipal taxes and local charities.

By the mid-1800s public support for the provision of care and relief for dependent and defective persons gradually declined, and people of means were less inclined to provide financial support for outdoor relief measures. As a consequence of these changes in public attitude toward dependency, institutional and custodial methods (indoor relief) became the preferred method for providing care and relief. Although custodial institutions were not used in all parts of the province, indoor relief in the form of asylums, alms houses and houses of industry as well as jails came to dominate the provision of care and relief for dependent and defective populations in the larger centres of the province, which were similar to the charitable relief method instituted in the United States (Trattner, 1984) and Great Britain (Guest, 1980) during this era.

These custodial methods dominated care and relief of dependent and defective children until the 1890s, at which time institutional methods were evaluated and

436

revamped as part of the mandate of the Ontario government's Royal Commission on Prisons, Asylums and Public Charities of 1891. (Province of Ontario, 1891) This royal commission led to significant changes in care and relief measures and led to the emergence of the 'child-saving movement' in Ontario. As far as defective children were concerned, the reforms proposed by the Royal Commission on Prisons, Asylums and Public Charities were important in at least two important respects. First, The Royal Commission on Prisons, Asylums and Public Charities proposed that the practice of housing defective and dependent persons in jails as a means of providing care and relief be stopped. Secondly, the royal commission proposed that all classes of dependent, delinquent and defective children had to be cared for in facilities separate from those for adults and as part of these reforms, specialized institutions were constructed to meet the needs of distinct populations. These changes were not only indicative of the social reform in Ontario at the end of the 19th century, but also indicative of similar changes occurring in the United States and Britain at the time. As Leiby (1978) points out, 'men began to distinguish among different kinds of problem people to devise special institutions to deal with them in a more rational and practical way' (p. 47).

These reforms that called for the separation of children from adults in institutions such as asylums and jails had the greatest impact on services for children, as these reforms led to the passing of child welfare legislation (*Act for the Prevention of Cruelty to, and Better Protection of Children*, 1893). In addition, a demand for separate facilities for children also provided the impetus for the establishment of special care facilities for disabled children. An example of such a facility was the Bloorview Home for Incurable Children, which was opened in Toronto in 1896. (Hanes, 1995B) The end of the 19th century witnessed a more reformist approach to dealing with dependent, delinquent and defective classes including dependent and defective classes of children. (Varga,1983; Valverde, 1991). The onset of the child-saving movement laid the foundation for the establishment of charitable associations to provide services for needy children, and these charitable associations later gave impetus to the establishment of charitable organizations such as the Ontario Society for Crippled Children.

Selecting a population: Crippled children versus adults

The child-saving movement (Platt, 1969), with its emphasis on children rather than adults, had a significant spin-off effect on the care and treatment of crippled children, and a population once considered a nuisance came to be viewed redeemable and worth helping. Many medical professionals and social reformers argued that the treatment should be directed at the crippled children rather than the crippled adults. (Abt, 1924, Baker, 1919, Hibbs, 1905, McMurtrie, 1911).

In the late 19th century and early 20th century, as the child-saving movement was gaining support, many professionals actively promoted the idea that the care and treatment should be directed at the crippled children rather than the crippled adults.

Watson (1930) argued that the discovery, treatment and cure of the crippled carried out under a competent voluntary scheme and returning them to the community as sound and promising citizens – "all this appeals not only to common human sentiment, but also impresses that final court of appeal, the hard-headed business man. What does not so much, or in fact hardly at all, appeal to him is the adult cripple, whether the victim of disease or disablement in industry." (p. 34).

Crippled-child-savers, whether they were educators, surgeons or social workers, maintained the similar position – that care and treatment of cripples should be provided for the children and not for adults. Not only was there common concern that services are directed at the children, but there was the unanimous opinion that care and treatment should be directed to making crippled children into economically productive adults. (Bradford, 1898, Buck, 1908) Orthopaedic surgery and follow-up care, with education and trades training, were viewed as the most likely way of averting poverty in the crippled adult. The provision of funds for the care and treatment of crippled children was seen as an investment in the future of both the child and the community (Fish, 1920). Investment in the medical, educational and training needs of crippled children was approached in the same way as a business investment, and the investment in the care and treatment of the crippled child was considered as having long-lasting dividends for both the individual and society.

> The introduction of medical care for crippled children in the early years of the 20th century represented a significant shift in society's expectations of persons with disabilities. It was inevitable that this growing solicitude for the unfortunate, which constitutes one of the richest, if not the richest asset of this democracy, would in time lead to the conservation idea to their treatment and substitute rehabilitation for relief. This conservation idea lends large justification – perhaps its largest justification – in a constructed program for the handicapped. Back of this program are such conservation policies as reducing the human waste pile, helping others to help themselves, the substitution of self help for dependency, the utilization of latent human assets, the practice of real economy in social relief, the removal of social discontent among the less fortunate, the building of a sounder foundation for society, the safeguarding of the future of the nation, and the promotion of individual and collective efficiency of our citizenship. (Prosser, 1927, p. 73).

The interest in providing care and treatment for crippled children emerged in the late 19th century and early 20th century, and the same interest prevailed after World War I, the 1920s, 1930s and 1940s. Crippled children remained the primary focus of orthopaedic programs, despite the fact that tens of thousands of adults had been maimed either through war or through industrial accidents. By the mid-1920s, services and programs established for crippled children had far surpassed any similar programs for crippled adults. This observation was made by Sullivan and Snortum (1926), who concluded that 'distinct services, public and private, have been built up for the crippled child and have reached a far more advanced stage than equivalent work for the adult' (p. 58).

The child-savers' interest in the economic self-sufficiency of the adult raises very important questions about the development of medical specialties, such as orthopaedic surgery, and professional interests in meeting the needs of crippled children. Demands for making crippled children into economically self-sufficient citizens, which were demands made by professionals such as doctors, social workers and educators, were also commonly made by many groups interested in social and moral reform as well as those interested in restructuring organized charitable relief. This change in ideology from seeing cripples as helpless and hopeless dependents to having expectations for their own self-sufficiency, responsibility and productivity represents a significant paradigm shift and a convergence between scientific medicine and scientific charity.

Roots and connections: The Ohio Plan and the
Ontario Society for Crippled Children

The Ontario Society for Crippled Children was established in large part through the influence of other charitable organizations and institutions for crippled children previously established in the United States. In fact, the Ontario Society for Crippled Children has direct links to the Ohio Society for Crippled Children, which was the first organization of its kind to take an active interest in the needs of crippled children in the United States.

The establishment of the Ontario Society for Crippled Children was a step in the direction of achieving the dream of Edgar 'Daddy' Allen, the founder of the Ohio Society for Crippled Children, whose dream was to establish a worldwide affiliation of societies for crippled children across the United States and internationally. (Allen, E. 1924) In many ways the Ontario Society was a clone of the Ohio Society for Crippled Children, and the 'Ohio Plan' became the blueprint for the Ontario Society, mirroring its ideology, daily functioning, relationships with service clubs and association with orthopaedic surgeons. The two societies used the same fund-raising activities, extension programs, surveys, public awareness campaigns and political lobbying techniques.

The Ohio Society for Crippled Children came into existence as a result of the philanthropic work of an Ohio lumber baron, Edgar Allen, whose teenage son died because of injuries sustained in a trolley car accident in the small town of Elyria, Ohio, in May 1907. Homer Allen, along with other passengers, was waiting to disembark when the trolley he was on was struck by another trolley car. 'There were 84 casualties. Edgar Allen's 18 year old son, Homer, and others standing on a crowded rear platform had their feet sheared off at the ankles, and died of want of proper surgical attention' (Palmer, 1946, p. 1). Although the injuries were serious, many of the deaths resulting from this accident could have been prevented. But the town did not have a proper hospital to treat the accident victims. As a result, the citizens of Elyria decided to have a modern hospital built, and Allen became the chairman of the fund-raising activities. (Palmer, 1946)

The hospital was opened on October 30, 1908. It was during Edgar Allen's tenure as the voluntary Director of Finance of the hospital when he became interested in the needs of crippled children. By chance Edgar Allen met a little orphaned boy who was disabled by polio and was a patient at the hospital. Over a course of many months the two became friends, and it was this boy who began referring to Edgar Allen as 'Daddy' and from that time on many people involved in the movement to establish societies for crippled children referred to Edgar Allen as 'Daddy' Allen. (Palmer, 1946)

Thus began Allen's work on behalf of crippled children and it is in Elyria, Ohio where the foundation of societies for crippled children takes root. "A chain of events stemming from a trolley car accident led to what one author referred to as 'the age of the crippled child – the last needy type of person to get the aid of the state'." (Howett, 1926, p. 502)

Allen quickly realized the provision of care and treatment to crippled children would be a long and difficult journey, and Allen approached various community groups and agencies in Elyria, Ohio but he was unable to obtain support for his plans.

After being turned away by the Elyria Chamber of Commerce, the YMCA, various church groups and women's organizations Allen turned to the Elyria Rotary Club. The Rotary Club accepted Allen's request for assistance, as club members considered helping crippled children a legitimate community service and thus began a partnership between crippled children and service clubs which lasts to the present day.

Instead of focusing on the local needs of Elyria, Rotarians from that city decided to direct their community service to all crippled children throughout the state, and to pursue this plan they invited fellow Rotarians across Ohio to attend a meeting in Elyria.

This gathering of Ohio Rotarians took place on April 16, 1919, and as a result of this meeting the crippled-child-saving movement was launched with the creation of the Ohio Society for Crippled Children, with Edgar Allen elected as the first President of the Society. The Ohio Society for Crippled Children was established on April 22, 1919, but the founding date was later changed to May 8, 1919, which was Allen's birthday. (Palmer, 1946)

At the first meeting, the foundation and direction of the work of future crippled children's societies and crippled-child-saving activities began to take shape. At this initial meeting, plans were made to involve all the Rotary clubs across the state; dividing the state into eight districts, with Rotarians from each district forming the board of directors of the society; and establishing extension committees for the advancement of providing services to crippled children across the state. (National Easter Seals of America, 1950). These objectives were reconfirmed and became the foundation of bylaws for the Ohio Society for Crippled Children, passed at the district meeting of the Ohio Rotary Club on January 6, 1920. These bylaws were designed with the following ostensible objectives:

> the establishment of a Central Bureau and organization to initiate, coordinate and direct the securing and compiling of information concerning the care and cure of crippled children. The making of surveys of exact conditions of each county in the state. To assist in solving problems incident to the raising of funds as well as the building, equipping and maintaining of hospitals for the care and cure of crippled children. (National Easter Seals of America, 1950, p. 13)

Although the executive committee of the Ohio Society for Crippled Children, under Allen's direction, planned to establish hospitals in the eight districts of Ohio, this objective was never carried out. Ruth Cummer, the first director of the Ohio Society for Crippled Children, recommended that the society not implement a plan to finance the construction of segregated hospitals across the state. Instead of building new hospitals, Cummer suggested that the society make use of existing facilities in general hospitals or fund orthopaedic clinics within general hospitals. The executive committee of the Ohio Society accepted Cummer's proposals and by the early 1920s, Cummer's recommendation to use existing facilities was accepted. 'It is not our province or intention to build institutions', argued Allen:

> it is our function to see to it that facilities already in existence are used to the benefit of the crippled child; to enlarge upon these facilities state by state where they are needed and everywhere to educate the people to the possibilities that

exist for the crippled child; and lastly after legislation and facilities have been made possible, to see to it that some organization of men and women interested in the crippled child makes the connecting link between the child and the facilities. (Ohio Society For Crippled Children and Adults, 1969, p. 16)

In the final analysis, the Ohio Society for Crippled Children embarked on an extensive program of using existing facilities, and the program became known as the "Ohio Plan".

The Ohio Plan and its adoption by the service clubs

The decentralized plan for providing medical care and treatment as well as follow-up vocational education and training for crippled children, coined the Ohio Plan, became the foundation for most, if not all, subsequent crippled children's societies across the United States and Canada. The Ohio Plan can be described under seven headings:

1 A plan evolves out of 'extension service' as distinguished from institutional service;
2 Lays stress upon dispensary and social service by existing public and private hospitals, schools, convalescent homes and institutions;
3 Fixes necessary costs, when advisable upon the public;
4 Does not include the building of institutions for crippled children until all existing facilities at hand have been given an opportunity to develop adequate capacities and proper standards and until actual facts regarding numbers of existing cases are known and means for operating expenses of proposed institutions are in sight;
5 Includes maintenance costs, physical care and education to the end that the crippled child shall not only be helped physically, but become a self-supporting citizen;
6 Includes legislative authority to increase the extension plan through field service and stimulate cooperation among individuals and agencies dealing with care, cure and education; and
7 Sets up an intelligent constituency for the crippled child in active society, which constantly keeps his needs before interested organizations and the public until such time as his needs are automatically cared for without stimulation from the membership of such a voluntary agency (Ohio Society for Crippled Children and Adults, 1969, p. 16).

Although service club members viewed their service work as charity and they tried to remain as apolitical as possible, Rotarians quickly learned that little could be achieved without advocacy, community support and political activism. Consequently, from the early years forward Rotarians, whether they were at the state, provincial or national levels, maintained an ongoing relationship with politicians, professionals and community leaders:

The Ohio Society and later the National Society, the outgrowth of the Ohio Society, never tried to function without a legislative committee. Chairmen kept day-by-day contacts with legislators and legislation. When new committee chairmen needed to be indoctrinated, when superintendents of city schools or teachers of special classes in smaller classes needed backing or encouragement, when interest lagged in providing funds for care, treatment and education, the Rotarians of the state could be counted on to lift their potent voices. (Ohio Society for Crippled Children and Adults, 1969, p. 16)

This political activity of Rotarians represented a major shift in their approach to community service work, in at least two areas:

1 political lobbying went against Rotary's philosophy of apolitical community service work, and
2 political advocacy indicated long-term commitment, which in itself went against the philosophy of short-term community service.

Getting support from politicians was one thing, but getting support from orthopaedic surgeons was another important matter that had to be seen to. When the Ohio Society for Crippled Children attempted to implement the Ohio Plan, particularly its plan for decentralized service, the society was not initially supported by orthopaedic surgeons. 'Orthopedics at the beginning had expressed fear that interference by laymen would result in careless handling of cases' (Ohio Society for Crippled Children and Adults, 1969, p. 16). Orthopaedic surgeons had to be convinced of the viability of implementing a decentralized system that relied on the use of existing facilities:

> There were many conferences with medical groups, which sufficed to convince the doctors that the society was in earnest and that its plan was practical and should work. That the young movement did succeed in winning the good will and cooperation of orthopedic men was a mark of the soundness of the plan, and of the character of the medical men whose cooperation and influence were so much needed. (National Easter Seal Society, 1950, p. 160)

Within a very short time, orthopaedic surgeons were not only accepting laymen administering programs for crippled children, orthopedic surgeons began endorsing the work of Societies for Crippled Children. Many orthopaedic surgeons became active members on the boards of directors of the societies and many became members of the Rotary Club. To promote the objectives of the Ohio Society for Crippled Children, as well as their own profession and expertise, orthopaedic surgeons gave speeches and held public education forums. "There is no better way" observed Howett, "to bring to the general public the importance of high-grade orthopaedic and medical service. This brings together laymen, social service workers, public health authorities, schoolmen and physicians." (Howett, 1926, p. 502)

Saving crippled children: From local concern to an international movement

When the Ohio Society for Crippled Children was fully operational, Edgar Allen then pursued the establishment of similar societies throughout the United States and around the world and to achieve his objective Allen once again requested help from the Rotary Club.

During the summer of 1921, Allen began to lobby Rotarians at both the national (United States) and international levels for support for the wider application of the Ohio Plan, and while he did not get the full endorsement of his ideals of making crippled-child-saving an international movement, he was nevertheless able to expand his interests beyond Ohio. By 1922, Rotary Clubs in Michigan and New York had established statewide societies for crippled children. With the Ohio Society for Crippled Children, the New York and the Michigan societies united to form the National Society for Crippled Children, and Allen was elected president.

The importance of establishing the National Society for Crippled Children cannot be underestimated, as the establishment of this society represented the first concerted effort to provide care and treatment for crippled children in the United States on an inter-state scale, and the National Society for Crippled Children represented another step toward the founding of an international society for crippled children.

1922 proved to be a watershed year in the history of the crippled-child-saving movement, for it was during this year that societies for crippled children expanded beyond the borders of Ohio to other states, and it was also during this year that the crippled-children's movement took root in Ontario, thus establishing a crippled-child-saving movement on an international level.

The first meeting to establish an international organization was held in Elyria, Ohio, on February 8, 1922:

> On the motion of Hugh E. Van de Walker of Ypsilanti, Michigan, treasurer of the Society, and seconded by Samuel H. Squire, it was voted to change the name from National to International Society for Crippled Children. A committee was appointed to draft a new constitution, and another to prepare an international plan for working out the problem of the care and education of crippled children. (National Easter Seal of America, 1950, p. 35)

Six months later, on November 28, 1922, a meeting was held in Windsor, Ontario between Rotarians from Windsor and other areas of south western Ontario and representatives of the International Society for Crippled Children. As a result of this meeting the Ontario Society for Crippled Children was formed thus making crippled child saving work truly international.

The American Influence over the rise of the Ontario Society for Crippled Children

Within its first two years the Ontario Society for Crippled Children began to incorporate many of the principles of the Ohio Plan, beginning with the division of the province into districts each with a Crippled Children's Committee. Ontario's geographical size of over one million square kilometers proved to be a tremendous challenge, as there were many rural, northern and isolated communities, which made reaching and transporting crippled children to and from hospitals and arranging clinics and follow-up care very difficult. The fact that the Society relied solely on the voluntary services of Rotary clubs also proved to be obstacle to the success of the Society, since the Rotary Club was not established in all areas of the province.

Despite formidable restrictions, the OSCC was very successful at establishing medical care and treatment programs for needy crippled children in most parts of Ontario. By 1925, 'the case load had risen to more than 300 with 200 operations being performed each year... and a supply of 500 appliances was purchased over the first three year period' (Hopper, 1972, p. 3) Within two years of this expansion, the number of crippled children receiving treatment through Society-sponsored programs had tripled, and by 1927 there were 33 Rotary clubs involved in the Society, sponsoring more than 1000 disabled children, with 600 surgeries and 1500 appliances (Hopper, 1972, p. 4).

By 1928, the board of directors realized that the work of the OSCC was more than a voluntary organization could handle. Many of these members advocated for greater provincial government responsibility in the provision of care and treatment for the crippled children of the province:

> It was felt that if there were organizations ready to give time to carry out this work, as it was strictly government work and not to be done except through local organizations of right minded citizens, the least the government could do was to supply the funds. (The Ontario Society for Crippled Children: The First Twenty-Five Years, 1947, p. 3)

The call for greater government involvement was a very important step, for it meant that there was recognition, for the first time, that the provincial government had a responsibility for providing for the needs of crippled children. In the spring of 1928 a group of Rotarians met with Premier Howard Ferguson to discuss the funding of the Society's work, and as a result of this meeting, the premier committed $10,000 to the OSCC. With this funding the Board of Directors established an office in Toronto and hired Reginald Hopper as the executive director of the OSCC (Ontario Society for Crippled Children: First Twenty-Five Years, 1947).

Hopper was the ideal choice. Hopper was a member of the Ottawa Rotary Club and he was an active member of the Crippled Children's Committee for the club. The late 1920s were very important years in the history of the Ontario Society for Crippled Children. The hiring of Hopper meant the Society no longer functioned on a strictly voluntary basis, and funding from the provincial government signalled, for the first time, that the province had some responsibility for the care and treatment of crippled children:

> By the end of 1929 the Society had established a new phase of development, and established a number of principles which were to have an important bearing on future activities. However, these were actually more acknowledgments than any new or radical departures. (Hopper, 1972, p. 7)

With provincial government funding to hire an executive director, the Ontario Society for Crippled Children began to fortify itself in its primary role as a central organizing body with the mandate to represent the various service clubs involved in the Society's work. The executive was given the responsibility of extending services to needy crippled children throughout the province. And as part of this extension of jurisdiction, the Society established the objective of attracting new service clubs to become members. Although various objectives were introduced as new in 1929, they were in fact a reiteration of objectives borrowed from the Ohio Society for Crippled Children and the "Ohio Plan".

Providing care and treatment: The Ohio Plan and the Ontario Society for Crippled Children

As indicated earlier, the Ontario Society for Crippled Children was modelled after the Ohio Society for Crippled Children, and it incorporated many of the principles of the Ohio Plan, including extension of services, local surveys, traveling orthopaedic clinics and follow-up treatment. These activities represented the core of the delivery of services to crippled children in Ontario and were the essence of what was referred to as the Decentralized Plan. Although difficult to determine, it can be speculated that the adaptation of the principles of the Ohio Plan may have prevented the establishment of segregated crippled children hospitals and schools for cripples similar to those that were established in Ontario for blind and Deaf children.

The decentralized plan

The decentralized plan was based on the principle of, when possible, bringing the services to the crippled children instead of bringing the children to the hospital. The decentralized plan relied on the use of the existing services of the large urban hospitals, such as the Ottawa Civic Hospital; the Hamilton General Hospital; the War Memorial Children's Hospital, in London; and the Toronto Hospital for Sick Children. The decentralized plan used traveling orthopaedic clinics for assessing and treating crippled children. At various times during the year, orthopaedic specialists would travel from the large hospitals to work in the smaller towns and villages in the surrounding area. The traveling clinics had two primary purposes:

1 the examination and diagnosis of new 'cases', and
2 the follow-up examination of crippled children who had earlier received treatment.

Through the decentralized plan the province was divided into seven geographical regions, and within each of these districts there was a chair whose role it was to oversee the work of the Society at the district level. Each county in the district had a supervisor whose job was to help organize the orthopaedic clinics and to coordinate all follow-up care and treatment. Although the Society was initially developed as an ad hoc committee in 1922, it soon became a sophisticated organization, with representatives at the local municipal, county, regional and provincial levels. By 1935, the province had been divided into the 'Eastern Ontario District, East Central District, Central District, Hamilton–Niagara District, Western Ontario District and the Northern District' (Ontario Society for Crippled Children 1935, minutes of Sept. 27, 1936). The primary function of the OSCC was to coordinate the provision of care and treatment for all needy crippled children across Ontario, but the actual medical, surgical, convalescent and educational needs of the crippled children were, as much as possible, provided at the local level.

Because of this emphasis on using local resources and local facilities, the provincial government did not develop large facilities specializing in the care and treatment of crippled children. (These facilities – crippled-children treatment centres – did not get established in Ontario until the 1960s and 1970s). Most often care and treatment was provided at the local level, and only when the child's medical needs could not be met locally was the child transferred to Toronto Hospital for Sick Children. Although the decentralized plan relied heavily on the voluntary effort of service club members, the medical and surgical care of crippled children was provided in a very scrupulous manner and included (a) county surveys (to discover crippled children), (b) home visits and assessment, (c) clinic visits, and (d) follow-up treatment.

Local and county surveys

Coordinating and arranging the care and treatment of crippled children followed a specific pattern that varied little over the years and varied minimally from one locale to the next. To begin, a survey of the county and or municipality was conducted by the Crippled Children's Committee of the local service club to discover any crippled children in need of treatment. The survey was exhaustive, and unless the child was hidden away in the home (as was often the case), there was little opportunity for the crippled child to escape the attention of those conducting the survey. The breadth and scope of the county survey is evident from the following account of the activities of the Ontario Society for Crippled Children in 1937:

> the procedure to be employed in conducting such a survey has become sufficiently standardized to be uniformly effective. The cooperation of such individuals throughout the county as may be expected to possess a fairly general acquaintanceship with families and homes of any given area is first of all solicited. This is done by means of a personal survey letter. The letter solicits information with respect to any child under the age of eighteen years of age, who gives evidence of suffering from any form of physical disability which is a physical detriment to the development of that child. The information is treated as confidential and the name of the informant is not divulged. These letters are sent to the following individuals: 1. All teachers of public schools throughout the county. 2. All medical practitioners. 3. All clergymen. 4. All post masters. 5. All county and township clerks. 6. All Public Health, Victorian Order and private nurses. 7. Mayors, Reeves, Deputy Reeves, School Inspectors, Children's Aid Inspectors and school attendance officers. (Prueter, 1937, p. 32)

The survey letter was in fact a report slip, which provided identifying data about the crippled child, and neither the child nor the child's parents were consulted. Once the report slips were returned to the Crippled Children's Committee, the names of the children who were identified through the survey were then passed on to service club members. These members were expected to go to the home of the 'discovered' crippled child to carry out a more detailed investigation of the child and the family (Prueter, 1937, p. 34).

In addition to finding out as much as possible about the child and the family, it was also up to the service club member to persuade the parents to bring the child into the orthopaedic clinic for an assessment. In many cases, the service club members had to do a great deal of convincing, as many parents were sceptical, indeed frightened, about the consequences of surgery:

> During the early years the efforts of the clubs were seriously handicapped by a critical attitude on the part of parents and public generally. Parents hesitated to submit their children for examination, in contemplation of possibly dangerous and unknown surgical treatments. Even in this well enlightened community an attitude of resignation was frequently encountered and a passive acceptance of the decree of fate that a child should be crippled for life, coupled with a conviction that it would be presumption to will it otherwise. The success of major orthopedic operations was unknown. The public was frankly skeptical of the interest that was being taken by comparative strangers in the children of the community. It was not "their own children" that they wished to have "cut up" but the children of other parents who were too poor to provide proper care to the children themselves. The feeling that these children were to be used as subjects for experimentation in surgery was often expressed. (Prueter, 1937, p. 35)

Crippled children were brought into the clinic as long as it was not contrary to the opinion of the family physician. Club members attempted to persuade parents to bring their crippled children into the clinic for treatment and were expected to inform the parents of the benefits of medical intervention, surgery and hospitalization. Service club members were also expected to pay a home visit as a means of assessing the conditions of the home and to include this assessment in their report to the Crippled Children's Committee. And finally, information from the home visit assessment was particularly important when it came time to provide financial assistance to the family (Prueter, 1937, p. 34).

Traveling orthopaedic clinics and follow-up treatment

A third component of the organization of treatment for crippled children (after the survey and the initial home visit) was taking the orthopaedic clinics to the crippled children discovered through the county surveys. These clinics arrived in the county at least once a year, and the hospital authorities were generous enough to provide beds, hospital equipment, X-ray machines, and the services of many nurses in training. Besides hospital staff, several physicians and service club members donated their time to help get the children registered for the clinic and to write up brief intake histories of the patients. Following this intake triage procedure, the children were then examined briefly by the orthopaedic specialists. From descriptions of the clinics (Prueter, 1937), it appears that there was the attempt to make them function with military precision:

> This is accomplished by carefully timing the arrival of the patients and by an efficient system of registration and preliminary examination of each case

447

before it is passed in to be examined by attending specialists. Three stenographers are kept busy during the proceedings, since each of the specialists after careful examination of the child's condition, dictates a complete report of his examination and diagnosis making specific recommendations as required. These reports are then written in triplicate and handed over to the crippled children's committee of the club (Prueter, 1937, p. 35). When all the children had been assessed they were divided into categories, which indicated what type of follow-up treatment would be provided: (a) Cases of major physical disability requiring hospitalization and possible surgical treatment. (b) Cases of minor disability requiring local treatment. (c) Mental cases with specific recommendations if any. (d) Cases already in process of rehabilitation with progress reports on the same. (e) Cases for which nothing can be done. (f) Deferred cases for which immediate treatment is not deemed desirable. (Prueter, 1937, p. 37)

Those new patients who were to receive immediate attention were divided into two groups, those to be treated as inpatients at the hospital, and those to be treated at the clinic. Crippled children who fell into these two categories were then reassigned a service club member, whose responsibility was to arrange follow-up treatment. This began with a visit to the parents and the child. If they agreed to medical and or surgical intervention, then the club member tried to obtain the consent of the family physician. Those needing major surgery which could not be done effectively at the local hospital were most often referred to the Toronto Hospital for Sick Children. Admission to the hospital was arranged by the service club member, and a letter indicating that the hospital expenses of the child would be covered by the service club accompanied the child. The surgeons who operated on the crippled children sponsored by the Ontario Society for Crippled Children did not charge a fee for their work, and the primary expenses having to be covered by the service club were those of the daily maintenance of the child as long as he or she remained at the hospital. Although the fees for hospital care were high, the expense was considered an investment in the child and the child's community:

> If the life of a child, however, can be salvaged for seven hundred dollars and instead of such a child being left to become perpetually dependent, his life can be transformed into one of independent usefulness, there can be no question but that the cost and effort have been a sound investment. (Prueter, 1937, p. 37)

The nursing service

The decentralized plan began to change in 1935. Up until that time, the organizing of clinics, making arrangements for orthopaedic equipment, arranging funding for hospital treatment and orthopaedic appliances, and follow-up visits were made by the local service club members. By the mid-1930s the demands on the Ontario Society for Crippled Children had grown to such an extent that service club members were incapable of seeing to the needs of all the crippled children who had been discovered and referred. It was decided by the Board of Directors of the Ontario Society for Crippled Children to initiate a nursing program to supplement much of the work done by service club members.

In response to this growing demand for service, the Society established a district nursing service as a pilot project in Western Ontario in 1935. After months of meetings, the District Nurses Committee made the following recommendations to the Board of Directors of the Society, in April, 1935:

a) That the work for crippled children will be greatly assisted and improved in any section of Ontario by the establishment of a district nurse centre.

b) The area in which the nurse would work would include from five to ten counties.

c) A centre should only be established in a city where there are good surgeons and good orthopaedic facilities.

d) An experimental centre should be started this year in charge of a nurse who is experienced in public health work, who has a good personality, who knows orthopaedic practice and the possibilities of treatment and who would be competent to supervise all work for crippled children within the district.

e) That such a center be established in the city of London to include the counties of Middlesex and those which touch it.

f) That Miss Greta Ross be employed as the nurse in charge of this district, to commence her work on September 1st, 1935.

g) Minutes of the Quarterly Meeting of the Board of Directors, Sept. 27, 1936

Greta Ross began her work at the Great War Memorial Hospital of London, and her territory included south western counties such as Middlesex, Lambton, Perth, Oxford, Essex, Elgin and Kent. Although Greta Ross was hired by the Society to oversee the provision of care and treatment for crippled children in Western Ontario, her role did not replace that of service club members. On the contrary, Ross maintained a close working relationship with the service club members in the cities, towns and villages in her district and relied on their support in organizing and carrying out the work of the Society in this region of Ontario. The nursing service took the same approach to service as previously established by the service clubs and the Society. Ross initiated local surveys, organized the orthopaedic clinics, arranged for hospital treatment and provided follow-up home visits for crippled children in her district. (Ontario Society for Crippled Children, Minutes of the Quarterly Meeting of the Board of Directors, Sept. 27, 1936).

The satellite program

The development of a nursing service paved the way for the Ontario Society for Crippled Children to continue with the decentralized plan by establishing a 'satellite program' in the mid-1930s. The satellite program was initiated as a pilot project in Western Ontario at the same time that Greta Ross was hired, and the satellite project was affiliated with Dr. George Ramsey, an orthopaedic surgeon at the War Memorial Children's Hospital in London, Ontario. Under the direction of Dr. Ramsey and Greta Ross, the orthopaedic team was expected to travel from the War Memorial Children's Hospital at regular intervals throughout the year to provide clinics. Many of the children may have remained at the clinics for both their examination and treatment, and many of those who went to the War Memorial Children's Hospital attended the clinic as part of their follow-up treatment. If the child was deemed to require hospital treatment, he or she was admitted to the War Memorial Children's Hospital. When the child was ready for discharge, local facilities were used as required, and the local facility in many cases helped to shorten the period of separation for the child and the family (Prueter, 1937, p. 23).

The decentralized plan perpetuated the ideology of service to crippled children of both the provincial government and the Society. A service delivery system incorporating a central facility and local mechanisms of support further entrenched the Society's position that the provision of care and treatment for crippled children was a local responsibility and epitomized the province's long-held position that the local county or municipality had to provide for its own indigent population, including the provision of medical and hospital care.

Although the nursing service played a pivotal role in carrying out the mandate of the district programs, the dominant position of the orthopaedic specialist was not forgotten. In the pre-planning stages of the London project, one of the criteria for selecting a district was the availability of specialists. The nursing committee of the Society proposed that a 'centre should be established only in a city where there are good surgeons and good orthopedic facilities' (Ontario Society for Crippled Children, *Minutes, Meeting of the Board of Directors*, April 25, 1935).

The success of the nursing service and the satellite program in Western Ontario did not go unnoticed, and in 1939 Ross was appointed the supervising nurse of the Society. Because of her expertise, Ross was asked to give up her position in London and relocate to Hamilton, Ontario, to begin organizing another satellite program and nursing service with Dr. James, an orthopaedic specialist from the Hamilton General Hospital. Similar programs were established following World War II, and by the 1960s satellite programs and nursing services were spread all across Ontario. The process of organizing the districts remained the same as for the experiment in London, Ontario, and involved the cooperation of the orthopaedic surgeons, service clubs and local health authorities. The central hospital and satellite clinics remained the core of service delivery until the 1960s, when crippled children's treatment centres were established in each of the districts, crippled children were brought to the centres, and there was less emphasis on the traveling orthopaedic clinics.

Conclusion

The social construction of persons with disabilities, including children with orthopaedic disabilities, varies from one historical epoch to the next, and in many circumstances the social role of persons with orthopaedic disabilities has fluctuated between social acceptance and rejection. Prior to the involvement of medical practitioners in the lives of persons with disabilities, the provision of care for persons with disabilities was considered a social-legal responsibility, and care was either provided by family members or through other avenues closely linked to the provision of care for poor and dependent populations. Since the enactment of English Poor Law in 1601, which codified and established relief for dependent populations, persons with disabilities have gone through four phases in their status from the beginning of the 19th century to the early 20th century: outdoor relief, indoor relief, scientific charity and medical.

This chapter has traced the emergence of methods of care and relief established for dependent and defective persons in Ontario from the late 19th century until the early

20th century. This chapter intended to reveal the process through which the care and treatment of crippled children evolved from a social/legal category to a charitable/medical category. The chapter has shown that Ontario government policies pertaining to the care of dependent and defective persons had a direct influence not only on the founding of the Ontario Society for Crippled Children but also on the mandate of the Society and its delivery of service. The development of Ontario social welfare policies makes apparent that organizations such as the Society suited the provincial government's arm's-length approach to the provision of direct services, yet ensured that the needs of crippled children were apparently met. The Society filled a gap created by provincial government policies, which stipulated that the provincial government had no direct responsibility for the maintenance of dependent and defective populations, regardless of their needs. In many ways charitable organizations such as the Ontario Society for Crippled Children could become an effective tool for promoting the interests of medical professionals as well as middle- and upper-class elites through service club activities, and that the care of crippled children, which might otherwise have been the expression of democratic policies and institutions, could be determined by these private interests.

The founding of the Ontario Society for Crippled Children in November 1922 represents a major transition in the crippled-child-saving movement in Ontario and in Canada. The founding of the Society signified a new beginning in crippled-child-saving work, consolidating the work under the leadership of one organization. The rise of the Society after World War I brought surgeons, nurses and other medical professionals together with service club members and social welfare workers to provide care and treatment for needy crippled children. Despite these developments, the establishment of a partnership between medical professionals, charitable organizations, service club members and social workers did not signify a radical shift in the ideology underpinning concerns about crippled children which existed since the 19th century. There still remained the belief that crippled children were psychologically damaged and had the potential of being a burden to the child's family, the community and the state.

At a first glance, it appeared that societies for crippled children came into existence when they did because of a more enlightened view of all children, which benefited crippled children; a more sympathetic attitude toward persons with disabilities, as a result of the high number of disabled veterans returned home from World War I; some improvements in surgical technique, which could be used to rectify some disabling orthopaedic conditions; and (or) the general acceptance of crippled children as deserving of medical, social and educational benefits. While these factors did play a role in the rise of the Ontario Society for Crippled Children, they do not totally explain its rise to a position of dominance or explain why service club members and medical professionals joined together to provide treatment for crippled children. In fact, the literature suggests that the stigma of disability remained long after World War I, and prejudicial attitudes toward many persons with disabilities continued to persist for many decades. The literature also suggests that improvements in orthopaedic surgical techniques progressed slowly, and the public image of the orthopaedic surgeon as an enlightened helper and skilled technician was much greater than the professions' actual ability to eradicate disabling conditions in crippled children.

Despite the stigma of disability and despite the questionable skills of orthopaedic specialists, there appears to have been a desire to provide care and treatment for crippled children on the part of educators, public officials, service club members, medical professionals and parents. The establishment of specialized programs and services could not have been possible without the cooperation of charitable organizations and orthopaedic specialists. In as much as this focus on crippled children stemmed from a more sympathetic view of the children, the literature pertaining to the care and treatment of crippled children throughout the late 19th century and early 20th century suggests that the focus on crippled children was related to concerns about social dependency and the prevention of pauperism in adulthood. In other words, much of the focus of the work carried out by the Ontario Society for Crippled Children and the surgeons was to make better and more economically productive citizens out of crippled children. It is for these reasons that an examination of the development of provincial policies is relevant to the historical examination of the care and the treatment of crippled children, especially the links, or lack of them, between government policies and charitable organizations.

The rise of the Ontario Society for Crippled Children not only represents a significant development in services for children with orthopaedic disabilities in Ontario, it also represents the development of services on a national and international scale. The Ontario Society for Crippled Children, for example, was the first organization of its kind to be developed outside of the United States, thus providing an international scope to the saving of crippled children. By the late 1920s and early 1930s societies for crippled children were being developed in Britain, across Europe and in Australia. In many ways Edgar 'Daddy' Allen's dream of developing an international child-saving organization (International Association for Crippled Children) began to take shape with a meeting with Rotarians in Windsor, Ontario, in 1922.

On a national level the Ontario Society for Crippled Children was instrumental in establishing societies for crippled children in other provinces as well as a national society for crippled children. By the mid-1920s, provinces such as Quebec had followed Ontario's example, and the Quebec Society for Crippled Children was formed. Beginning in the early 1930s, these two societies had held meetings to lay the groundwork for the establishment of the Canadian Society for Crippled Children, which brought together provincial societies for crippled children as part of a national attempt to bring services to all crippled children in Canada.

Note

1 Some material in the beginning section of the chapter was previously published: Roy Hanes, Ph.D. "Linking Mental Defect to Physical Disability: The Case of Crippled Children in Ontario, 1890-1940." *Journal on Developmental Disability* 4 (1), Nov. 1995.

Bibliography

Abt, HE. (1924). *The Care, Cure and Education of the Crippled Child.* Elyria, OH: International Society for Crippled Children.

Allen, E. (1922). Ohio Plan for care of crippled children. *Nation's Health* 4(2): 114–115

Allen, E. (1924). The International Society for Crippled Children. *Public Health Nurse Journal* 16: 412–413.

Allison, N. (1915). Orthopedic surgery and the cripple. *American Journal for the Care of Cripples* 1 (2) p.69–74.

Baker, S. J. (1919). Reconstruction of the crippled child. *American Journal of Public Health,* 9: 185–192.

Bradford, E. H. (1898). The education of the crippled child, *American Physical Education Review* 3:187–207.

Buck, M. Mc. (1908). Work for the deformed: What is being done to give crippled children a chance to become useful members of society. *The Craftsman,* 121: 193–204.

Chapin, C. (1930). The cripple: A social problem. *Nineteenth Century* 108: 650–656 (1930).

Fish, J. (1920). The institutional care of crippled and deformed children. Proceedings of the National Council on Social Work. p. 224–230.

Guest, D. (1980). The Emergence of Social Security in Canada. Vancouver, BC: The University of British Columbia Press

Hanes, R. (1995A). "Linking Mental Defect to Physical Disability: The Case of Crippled Children in Ontario, 1890–1940. *"Journal on Developmental Disability"* 4 (1) Nov.

Hanes, R. (1995B) The Medicalization of Disability: The rise of the crippled saving movement in Ontario (Canada). McGill University, PhD. Thesis.

Hansen, N. (2002). Passing Through Other people's Spaces: Disabled Women, Geography and Work. Glasgow, Scotland: University of Glasgow, Ph.D. Thesis.

Henderson, C.R. (1904). *An Introduction to the Study of the Dependent, Defective and Delinquent Classes.* London, UK: D.C. Heath.

Hibbs, R.A. (1905). The problem of the chronic cripple. *A Review of Local and General Philanthropy.* Jan. 13 (15) 429–231.

Hopper, R. (1947). *The First Twenty-five Years.* Toronto, Ontario, Canada: Ontario Society for Crippled Children.

Hopper, R. (1975). *Memoirs.* Unpublished paper. Toronto, Ontario, Canada: Files of the Ontario Society for Crippled Children.

Horowitz, A. (1923). The cripple's place in society through the ages. *Nation's Health* 5(8): 565–571.

Howett, H. (1925.) State Programs for Crippled Children. *Proceedings of the National Conference of Social Work, June,* pp. 120–124.

Howett, H. (1926). The care of the crippled child. *Better Health* 7(10): 479, 482, 502.

Irving, A. (1987). *From No Poor Law to the Social Assistance Review: A History of Social Assistance in Ontario, 1791–1987.* A study prepared for the Ontario Social Assistance Review.

Jaegar, C. (1914). Trades training for adult cripples. *American Journal of the Care for Cripples* 1 (2): 67–73.

Leiby, J. (1978). A History of Social Welfare and Social Work in the United States. New York, NY: Columbia University Press.

Marks, D. (1997). Models of disability. *Disability and Rehabilitation.* vol.19, issue 3, p.89–95.

McMurtrie, D. (1911). The need of the care for crippled children. *Western Canada Medical Journal,* 5: 489–492.

McMurtrie, D. (1914). The care of cripples. In C. L. Stedman (Ed.), *The Reference Handbook of the Medical Sciences.* New York, NY: William Wood and Co., pp. 366–367.

National Easter Seals of America (1950). The History of the Easter Seal Society. Chicago, IL: National Easter Seal of America.

Noble, J. (1979). Classifying the poor: Toronto charities 1850–1880. *Studies in Political Economy* 2: 108–128.

Oliver, M. (1990). The Politics of Disablement. London: MacMillan Press.

Ohio Society For Crippled Children and Adults (1969).

Ontario Society for Crippled Children (1935). Minutes, Meeting of the Board of Directors, April 25.

Ontario Society for Crippled Children (1936). Minutes of the Quarterly Meeting of the Board of Directors, Sept. 27.

Province of Ontario (1891). Royal Commission on Prisons, Asylums and Public Charities of 1891.

Province of Ontario (1893). Act for the Prevention of Cruelty to, and Better Protection of Children.

Palmer (1946). Hope + help for the handicapped. *The Rotarian Magazine* (June).

Pitsula (1979). The Relief of Poverty in Toronto, 1880–1930. Ph.D. Thesis, York University.

Platt, A. (1969). The Child Savers/The invention of delinquency. Chicago, IL: University of Chicago Press.

Platt, W.E. (1898). Crippled and Deformed Children. *Proceedings of the 25th National Conference on Charities and Corrections.*

Prueter, H. J. (1937). The Care and Education of Crippled Children in Ontario. Toronto, Ontario, Canada: Ontario Society for Crippled Children.

Prosser, C. (1927). The Rehabilitation of Disabled Persons. *Proceedings of the National Conference of Social Work*, May.

Scheer, J. and N. Groce (1988). Impairment as a Human Constant: Cross-Cultural and Historical perspectives on Variation. *Journal of Social Issues*, Vol. 44., No. 1. pp 23–37.

Splane, R.B. (1965). Social Welfare in Ontario, 1791-1893: A Study of Public Welfare Administration. Toronto, Ontario, Canada: University of Toronto Press.

Struthers, J. (1991). How much is enough? Creating a social minimum in Ontario, 1930–1940. *Canadian Historical Review* 1(72): 39–83.

Sullivan, O. and Snortum, K. (1926). *Disabled People: Their Education and Rehabilitation*. New York, NY: The Century Co.

Thomas, C. (2007). Sociologies of Disabilities and Illness: Contested Ideas in Disability Studies and Medical Sociology. New York: Palgrave MacMillan.

Thorndike, A. (1898). The compensatory education of cripples. *American Physical Education Review* 3: 190–197.

Trattner, W. (1984). From poor law to welfare state: A history of social welfare in America. New York, NY: The Free Press.

Valverde, M. (1991). The age of light, soap and water: Moral reform in English Canada, 1885–1925. Toronto, Ontario, Canada: McClelland and Stewart.

Varga, E. (1983). Institutional Child Care in Nineteenth Century Kingston: A Study of the Orphans' Home, 1857–1900. M.S.W. research paper, Carleton University.

Wallace, C. (1910). Education of the crippled child. *Archives of Pediatrics* 27: 345–352.

Wallace, E. (1950). The Changing Canadian State: A Study of the Changing Conception of the State as Revealed in Canadian Social Legislation, 1867–1948. Ph.D. Thesis, Columbia University.

Watson, F. (1930). *Civilization and the Cripple*. London, England: John Bale and Sons and Danielson, Ltd.

Wendell, S. (2002). "Who is Disabled?" Ch.1 and "The Social Construction of Disability." Ch.2 in *The Rejected Body: Feminist Philosophical Reflections on Disability*. New York: Routledge Publishing.

27

BREAKING THE RULES: SUMMER CAMPING EXPERIENCES AND THE LIVES OF ONTARIO CHILDREN GROWING UP WITH POLIO IN THE 1940S AND 1950S

Karen Yoshida, Susan Ferguson and Fady Shanouda

Introduction

The everyday histories of disabled Canadians remain essentially invisible and unknown in dominant historical narratives of this country (Baynton 2001, 33). The social history of people who lived with polio is no exception (Aitken et al. 2004).[1] One response to the Canadian polio epidemic of 1937 was the development of the Ontario Society for Crippled Children (O.S.C.C.) summer camps for disabled children. Originating in 1937, these camps were conceived as opportunities for disabled children (many with polio) to experience life as a "normal," non-disabled child. The O.S.C.C. philosophy reveals normative ableist notions of disability, most clearly demonstrated in two archival documents from this time – *The History of the Ontario Society for Crippled Children* (1967) and *Summer Camp Objectives* (n.d.). These documents, in particular the *Summer Camp Objectives*, provide fertile ground to analyse the dominant views of disability during this historical time period.

In this paper, we demonstrate how the oral history narratives of our participants who attended these camps and grew up during these times often challenged the dominant negative views of disability reflected within the archival documents. While the veiled and not-so-veiled O.S.C.C. camping objectives presented a dismal picture of disabled children's lives, our participants' narratives often reflected a childhood of participation, mischief and risk-taking. What is clear from the narratives is that participants negotiated taken-for-granted assumptions of disability throughout their everyday lives. This negotiation ranged from acceptance to resistance and open defiance in relation to negative popular conceptions of disability. As our analysis will show, the philosophy of the O.S.C.C. reproduced normative values and subjected disabled children to social practices intended to shape the "development" of "the disabled child." By breaking the rules at camp and in their everyday lives, we argue that many participants negotiated not only their camping experiences but also, more significantly, wider dominant discourses of disability in Canadian society.

This analysis is from a critical disability studies history framework developed for the research project that this chapter is based on. The framework incorporates a disability studies and disability rights perspective. Both disability studies and disability rights focus not on the "disabled" body but on the conditions (social, political, economic, medical and legal circumstances), social practices and specific activities that produce and reproduce "disability." In addition, disability studies and disability rights interrogate what constitutes normalcy in different contexts and challenge and push back against social and legal boundaries and limitations enforced by the construction and naturalization of normative constructs related to disability, gender, sexuality, race, ethnicity, class and citizenship (Meade and Serlin 2006). Our perspective on history is focused on the everyday activities of "ordinary" Canadian people. This focus on everyday lives as history is also central to a feminist oral history approach (Armitage and Gluck 2006).

The framework is also interdisciplinary as we weave key post-modernist concepts (Corker and Shakespeare 2002) compatible with this critical disability studies history approach. In this framework we embrace the following:

1 Non-dualistic and intersectional ways of thinking (e.g. about subjectivities and bodies) that open up space(s) to understand the complexities and subtleties of the lived experience.
2 Historicizing lived experience by situating narratives and meanings within a myriad of historical contexts (i.e. social, cultural, economic and political).
3 Embodying the lived experience within the various spaces of people's daily lives. We conceptualize these spaces not only as physical but also as sociocultural sites that have the potential for multiple presentations of disability (Moss and Dyck 2002).
4 A view of bodies as both discursive and/or material. The meaning of bodies are fluid and contingent on the situation (Bordo 1993; Butler 1999).

In this chapter, we discuss first how the research was conducted using an oral history method and how the analysis was produced. We then provide a historical backdrop in which to describe the development of the five O.S.C.C. camps, the philosophic basis for the camps and the intended goals of the camping program. In our analysis section, we deconstruct the philosophy of the O.S.C.C. and present the overarching themes that we draw from them. Each of the themes illustrates an aspect of the ableist dominant view of disability in relation to understandings of disabled children's lives at that time. In the context of each theme, we also introduce the counter narratives of the participants who attended these camps and their everyday lived experiences.

Methodology

Oral history narratives of individuals living with polio are viewed as the most appropriate and important way to learn about and understand the meaning of polio for Canadians during the time period of 1927–1957 (Hirsch 2004). According to Alessandro Portelli (2006), subjectivity is just as important to history as the "facts." This is because what informants or narrators *believe* is itself a "fact," and people act based on what they believe. This is also what makes oral history different from traditional approaches to history, as we predominantly learn about the meaning of events (daily life, culture etc.) *for people*.[2] Using an oral history methodology in this way has "enabled disabled people to be present socially and politically as vibrant subjects – active and vocal experts on their own lives and collective circumstances" (Church 2008, personal communication).

Our overall methodological orientation is collaborative. This approach is consistent with oral history research approaches and has extended throughout our research from the interviews themselves to our analysis and writing of this chapter. Following this, we believe that the process of creating an oral life history is collaborative and jointly constructed. We realize that these oral life histories of the participants were only a part of their lives, albeit an important one.[3] To better understand this partiality, we historicize these narratives by stating here some of the early issues of our collaborations with participants (Armitage and Gluck 2006).

As researchers, we came to the interview sessions with a detailed set of questions for our participants which emphasized the activism throughout their lives (advocating for oneself, questioning authority, etc.). However we also "followed the lead" of the person with respect to where each individual wanted the interview to go and what he or she wished to focus on – we felt that this was, in itself, a way of making meaning and revealing the social and historical contexts of meaning making with respect to gender, class, race, disability and geography. We learned early that certain words we used as researchers, such as "activism," and words that participants didn't use, such as "disability," created some difficulties for active dialogue, and we took note of these differences and made revisions to questions using words that had meaning for the participants. While each individual's life narrative was unique, at the same time, participants did discuss certain places and experiences that were shared or very similar to one another. One of the most poignant examples, which is the basis of this analysis, was the O.S.C.C. summer camps that a number of our participants attended as children.

To complement the oral narratives we also asked participants if they had personal objects associated with this early time period of polio that were important to them growing up. Material objects have not been part of the oral history tradition in the past because oral history has often focused exclusively on the orality of its approach to capture the histories of non-hegemonic groups of people (Portelli 2006). Jose Sebe Bom Meihy (2003) has called for the radicalization of oral history by incorporating other ways of knowing or learning about the histories of "marginalized" people. In our project, we believe that material culture or the products of a particular culture may provide a complementary way to "get at" histories that have been invisible. Not only did we use material objects as a bridge for remembering during the interviews, but we also believe that these material objects represent a "counter archive" to dominant understandings of what constitutes official archival materials. By bringing participant narratives together with personal material objects, we aim to further disrupt the authority of the official O.S.C.C. historical narrative.[4]

As we mentioned earlier, the O.S.C.C. became a topic of interest to us after several participants told us stories of their experiences at summer camp and, in some instances, shared photos, newsletters and other mementos from their time at camp. Following this, we decided to conduct more in-depth research on the O.S.C.C. to help contextualize what we were learning from participants. After contacting Easter Seals (formerly the O.S.C.C.), we were guided to the Archives of Ontario, where we found O.S.C.C. archival materials from that period – financial documents, correspondence between members, plans for renovations, images of the camps and, most important for our purposes here, the two historical documents on which this analysis is based.

The first document is an unpublished manuscript titled, *The History of the Ontario Society for Crippled Children* (1967). In this document, the origins and development of the O.S.C.C. are highlighted up until the 1960s. The second document is a list of objectives, appropriately titled, *Summer Camp Objectives*. This document is not dated but was attached to a poster/ad for Blue Mountain camp that was dated 1979. While the document itself might have been produced in the 1970s, the ideological under-standing of disability illustrated by the language used in the objectives can be found much earlier, in 1940s and 1950s documents cited within the manuscript. For exam-ple, one of the primary objectives of the summer camps was to encourage children to overcome their disability. It was argued that this could be accomplished by seeing others "equally or more handicapped than himself," which would provide the neces-sary support to overcome the child's own "limitations" (*The Ontario Society for Crippled Children* 1967).[5] The same idea is made reference to in the manuscript when it cites a Blue Mountain Camp report from 1942:

> A new camper coming to Blue Mountain for the first time, looking at a child with a more severe handicap than his own, is stimulated to further efforts and, with the continued encouragement of the staff, frequently accomplishes a great deal. (25)

Furthermore, ideas about the physical limitations of campers are also made refer-ence to in both the manuscript and the objectives throughout the 1950s. Disabled children's lives are characterized as "restricted" and "confining," and even assistive devices are represented as deterrents to participation when children are referred to as "hampered by cumbersome braces, wheelchairs, crutches" (51). Moreover, disa-bled children's bodies, in the manuscript and the objectives alike, are considered fragmented, weak and a hindrance because of their "unruly muscles" (51). Given the continuities across these different O.S.C.C. documents, we estimate that the O.S.C.C. objectives, and their ideological and theoretical understanding of disability, were established circa 1940s and 1950s.

Archival research was also conducted in some of the summer camp regions them-selves. This research was conducted by phone and email with local librarians and archivists. Local documents and information contextualized the camps individually as well as collectively. We also visited the University of Western Ontario in London, Ontario, and the London Central Library, both of which had archival documents about the construction, operation and maintenance of one of the most popular camps, Woodeden.

Our Ontario participants were recruited from a number of sources – polio sup-port groups and individual contacts who knew of a person living with polio. These conversations took place in a location of the participants' choosing (usually in their homes) and we often spoke with the participant on more than one occasion. The ses-sions were tape-recorded, and written notes were also taken. Any one session would last, on average, two to three hours. For this chapter, ten participants (three women and seven men) attended one of the five O.S.C.C. summer camps in Ontario at least once.

To historicize the camping experiences and the lives of our participants, we next present a snapshot of the historical origins of organized camping and those key ideals of the hygiene movement that supported the O.S.C.C. philosophy and, in particular, their rationale for creating and maintaining the summer camps.

Hygiene and Fresh movements: Philosophical foundation of camping movements

The hygiene movement began in the early years of the 20th century. As Heidi Rimke and Alan Hunt (2002) argue, Christian ideologies combined with medicine and science, and "this alliance took the form of the social and moral hygiene movement which played a significant role in the fields of both moral regulation and public hygiene" (61). For our purposes, the fundamental idea of the moral hygiene movement is the conceptualization of individuals' morality and social standing as an essential characteristic to their overall health.

In Canada, the social and moral hygiene movement was exemplified by its presence in the educational health textbooks distributed in schools. Mona Gleason (2006) discusses the incorporation of the hygiene movement in Canadian society. She maintains:

> In keeping with the tenets of Christianity, health lessons conveyed in pre–World War I texts were firmly predicated on notions of Cartesian dualism: the mind and body were distinct and co-existed in a hierarchical, mind over body, relationship. This made possible the recurring reminder in these early textbooks that self-control and an acceptance of one's station in life were signs of good health. (55)

Not only does the Cartesian dualism posit a division between mind and body, but it also participates in wider systems of dichotomous thinking that equate the mind and rationality with action and the body with passivity and emotion – assumptions which are, of course, also highly gendered. The characterization of embodiment in this way is not merely a philosophical matter, however. It also has important social effects in that it both reflects and reproduces dominant power relations (Butler 1999). As Gleason asserts, hygiene ideology employed Cartesian values to articulate a requirement for the acceptance of one's position in the dominant social hierarchy and an understanding that the body could be controlled by the mind. By individuals accepting their position in life – their social standing – and by demonstrating control over the mind and body, they would apparently not burden themselves with striving to achieve a higher social status, since it was assumed 'naturally' impossible to climb social ranks in the early 20th century. By accepting one's social position, the overall health of individuals would be less burdened and thus, they would be less likely to experience ill health.

Within the same textbooks, sickness or disease were attributed to individual actions and behaviour. Individuals with morally ambiguious reputations who had contracted an illness or disease were thought punished and disciplined by God because of their wicked ways. Gleason (2006) argues, "whether through ignorance, wickedness, or willful disobedience, poor health was presented as partly a matter of choice" (56). This emphasis on individual responsibility as denoted by the moral hygiene movement was taken up by the camping movement, such that camp was considered a site where children with "handicaps" could understand their physical and social limitations but also strive to improve themselves. William Schwartz (1960) argues, "organized camping has itself developed into a significant resource for those who regard the circumstances of camp life as providing an *ideal laboratory for observing and changing human behaviour*" (423, emphasis added).

Between the wars, however, a change occurred in the way health and children were viewed. No longer was the individual's moral ambiguity to blame for their illness; rather, conventional medicine became the authority over healthy bodies (Gleason 2006, 62). Still, the hygiene movement did not disappear altogether; it simply shifted within the same sphere of medicine and Christian ideology (Gleason 2006, 62). Therefore, within conventional medicine individuals remained responsible for their health, especially illness. While it may be to a lesser degree contemporarily, conditions, diseases and disabilities are still understood at the level of individual responsibility and attributed to an individual's moral ambiguity and social position within dominant health discourses.

The concept of outdoor camping emerged out of the "descriptive terms of hospital recreations, medical recreations and corrective or adapted physical education" (Gentry 1984, 36). Even though conventional medicine influenced the creation and development of camping experiences, there was still a reliance on the values and practices of the moral hygiene movement and on assumptions regarding the healing qualities of nature. The O.S.C.C. objectives, as we will show, similarly perpetuate the hygienic understanding of illness and disease. However, even more so, it is clearly evident from our participants' recollections and the objectives themselves that camping was established for purposes of healing.

Camping itself was considered an option for many disabled children because of the healing qualities of nature. As we cited above, Schwartz discusses the romanticism of returning to nature to enjoy the healing powers of fresh country air. This became a concern because of the rise of pollution and high population density during the Industrial Revolution. Individuals sought open space and fresh air and therefore the fresh air movement – literally the movement to country spaces for short periods of time – was initiated. As Schwartz (1960) maintains, "the interest in organized camping represented an attempt to remove people, at least briefly, from the unhealthy, crowded conditions of the newly created city slums" (421–22).[6]

Fresh air is still considered an important part of healthcare, especially when combined with the environmental benefits of camping. It is argued that, "play and activity open the way for growth and corrective experience" (Mishna et al. 2002, 155). The benefits of camping besides fresh air include "a return to nature and a respite from city life, increased self-esteem, improved relationships with peers and adults, greater ability to assume responsibility, and improved coordination and physical skills" (Mishna et al. 2002, 156). Fresh air continues to be an important concept when it comes to healing and camping.

Camping movement

Camping has been a recreational activity for centuries. However, organized camping in North America dates back only to the late 19th century (Schwartz 1960, 419). In 1861, Frederick William Gunn, founder of the prep school The Gunnery, organized a camping experience for the students of the school (Schwartz 1960, 419–20). According to Schwartz, this is the first known organized camping experience. Schwartz argues that the camping movement foundation is based on the prevailing notions of the moral hygiene and the fresh air movements. Organized camping differs from other types of camping because emphasis is placed on outdoor skills and activities, while participation in group activities is encouraged and thought to effect personal identity. Schwartz also maintains that organized camping emphasizes improving the quality of the individual, generally accomplished by establishing "specific objectives" (419). Organized camping also stresses the importance of creativity and play and adherence to "an educational-developmental-character building" philosophy (Schwartz 1960, 421).

Social organizations, churches and government agencies began creating organized camps throughout the late 19th and early 20th centuries as they became aware of, and invested in, the opportunity for positive character development through the organized camping experience (Schwartz 1960). Organized camping was also popular amongst individuals interested in the human condition (social workers, psychologists, et al.) because they saw the environment as a new "instrument" and one that could change an individual socially and psychologically (Schwartz 1960). Camp settings provided a controlled environment, far from home. Within this "new" space, relationships between campers had to be fostered quickly, while weaknesses were easily identified and adjusted. However, the summer camp site also provided the opportunity "to get out from under certain home patterns that seem dull, or repressive, or otherwise unsatisfactory" (Schwartz 1960, 422). The organized camping site therefore performed two key roles: first, the camp was a site of conditioning, nurturing and rejuvenation and second, a site of play and fun.

A brief history of the O.S.C.C.

On July 4, 1937, the O.S.C.C. opened its first summer camp: Blue Mountain. Within the next 20 years, the O.S.C.C. would open and successfully operate four more summer camps for physically disabled children. Gordon Leitch, a member of the Rotary Club of Toronto, is attributed with first promoting the idea of providing a summer camping experience for children with physical disabilities (Easter Seals). Leitch had been taking disabled children boating and camping with him for several years before Blue Mountain Camp was open. However, he worried about the safety of the children, especially while loading on and off the docks. He therefore offered to oversee the establishment of a camp which disabled children could visit in the summer. The initial purpose of the camps, as Conn Smyth states, was "to have every crippled child get three weeks at a summer camp" (1933, personal communication). Along with volunteers from clubs like Rotary, Kiwanis, Lions, and other smaller organizations, the O.S.C.C. operated five camps in Ontario: Blue Mountain in Collingwood, Woodeden in London, Merrywood near Perth, Northwood Camp near Kirkland Lake and Lakewood Camp on Lake Erie (History of OSCC, 1967).

Figure 27.1 Postcard of Woodeden Camp by London Camera Club

The locations of the camps were chosen for two reasons. First, traveling was considered impractical for disabled people at that time, and the organization decided to develop multiple campsites in Ontario. The goal of the O.S.C.C. was to provide any disabled child who desired to experience camping with the opportunity to participate. Campsite locations were chosen based on appropriate location (generally near the water) and in areas where interest in the camps was high from parents, children and supportive organizations like the Rotary Club.

The camps were located on large parcels of land and, while each camp had its own particular layout, within each camp the same essential features were present. Cabins were set up so that there were eight children for every two counselors. There was generally a large main building where the children would eat and where large group activities would take place. There were indoor play buildings and a small doctor's office or nurse's station at each camp. Campsites that were not on the water, like Woodeden, had pools constructed so that children could play in the water, and at the same time benefit from the rehabilitative value of swimming. Some of the campsites had tennis courts and accessible jungle gyms. At Merrywood camp, a large swing was built, which several children and a counselor could ride together. Each camp had something different from the others that made it unique to its members. Each camp also had its own crest or symbol.

Early on, parents and children throughout Ontario were made aware of the camps by nurses at local hospitals and by local organizations that were affiliated with the O.S.C.C. or that were knowledgeable about disability issues. As the reputation of the camps grew, open houses were held during the summer months, encouraging children and parents to visit and view the camp experience in progress. Parents who brought their children to camp were not asked to pay the full cost of boarding,

SPECIAL SWING AT MERRYWOOD CAMP

Figure 27.2 Swing at Merrywood Camp

and therefore the O.S.C.C. relied on donations from local organizations, as well as government subsidies. The O.S.C.C. also held large fundraisers throughout the year, raising money in order to operate the camps in the summer.

The camps were open only during the summer, except Woodeden, which was open all year round and operated as a rehabilitation centre and school for individuals living with cerebral palsy. Throughout the summer, rotations between girls and boys, senior and junior, would fill the camps. In its third year, in 1939, Blue Mountain reached full occupancy with 163 children. However, by 1968, 1100 children attended a camp operated by the O.S.C.C. The number of children attending the camps remained steady until the mid 1980s, when several camps were sold due to high maintenance costs and lower attendance levels. As of 2011, two camps remained operational: Merrywood and Woodeden.

Children's health was a major concern at the camps. When Blue Mountain first opened, it was considered a camp as well as a convalescent hospital, and for that reason photographs from that time show many of the camp counselors in the earliest years are wearing nurses uniforms. Also depicted in other photographs are smaller children, upon arrival at the camps being bathed and given medical check-ups. Within each camp there was always medical staff with doctors, several nurses and even a psychologist on site. While it is clear from our participant interviews that the camps were promoted by the O.S.C.C. as a vacation for both parents and children, the camps were also viewed as a chance for children to receive the medical benefits of a natural environment and "fresh country air."

While there was an overarching emphasis on the children's health, a typical day at camp did not focus explicitly on the child's health. Rather, children at the camps participated in many activities, including swimming (in lakes and pools), sit-down boxing, putting on plays and productions, attending local festivals, badminton, tennis, baseball, bowling, croquet, fishing, arts and crafts, singing, reading and playing board games. Moreover, at the end of every camp session, the campers would put together a production of a popular story or play, like *Peter Pan, Oklahoma!* or *Oliver*. These plays would be performed for members of local organizations such as the Rotary Club and Kiwanis. The campers also participated in a closing religious ceremony; however, it is not clear whether the O.S.C.C. is affiliated with any particular religious organization.

Figure 27.3 Children performing a play at Woodeden Camp, July 18, 1955
(University of Western Ontario Archives).

The O.S.C.C. summer camp objectives

Reading the O.S.C.C. texts in critical reflexive engagement with other narratives is an important political and epistemological strategy for disrupting dominant discourses of disability. As Tanya Titchkosky argues, texts such as the O.S.C.C. objectives and mandate are alive, and common-sense understandings of disability have important social consequences that must be interrogated:

> Pity, charity and even simply caring are common practices grounded in taken for granted conceptions of disability. Still, they are practices that are not necessarily self-reflective – they are not forms of analysis, even though these practices are grounded upon all sorts of truth claims. Claiming to know disability, while not experiencing a need to reflect upon the assumptions, organization, and consequences of this knowledge is a common yet potentially oppressive social practice. (Titchkosky 2007, 39–40)

The O.S.C.C. summer camp objectives reveal a great deal about the everyday ideologies and practices surrounding disability, and what it meant to be a child and a person, in 1940s and 1950s Canada. In this section, we present an overview of what the O.S.C.C. summer camp objectives tell us more broadly about understandings of disability at that time as a way of contextualizing the in-depth narrative analysis that follows.

Disability is most immediately present in the O.S.C.C. summer camp objectives as a form of undesirable difference that limits and confines children, their bodies and their participation in everyday social life. Ultimately, these objectives suggest, disability limits children in such a way that their development, growth and potential is diminished – measures of successful personhood that are themselves saturated by the artificial construct of the norm (Davis 1995). Implicit here is the assumption that disabled personhood does not constitute a form of viable life (Butler 2004) unless disability can be overcome. Reflecting a society that was (and remains) deeply invested in normative notions of embodiment, these objectives conflate physical impairment and subjectivity in a very negative way, while concealing the social practices that produce disability as an embodied experience.

This dominant medicalized narrative of disability is accomplished through particular social and discursive practices embedded within the O.S.C.C. objectives and as they are contextualized by the camping experience itself. Perhaps most striking is the rhetoric of competition woven throughout the objectives, which is presented as the key means by which one overcomes disability. Each of the five objectives – Participation, Self-Expression, Independence, Sense of Personal Worth and Socialization – invoke social comparison or competition of some kind to generate the demand for movement beyond the confined and limited disabled self towards an improved and more developed self. In some cases, children were to compete against themselves and their disability, while in other cases, children were to feel motivated by comparing themselves to other disabled children. Regardless of the orientation towards this rhetoric of competition, the emphasis on self-improvement suggests that disability represents a constraint in the child that can (and must) be overcome (although ironically, this is to occur at the same time as the disability must be accepted).

The notion of competing against one's disability treats the disabled body as the body-object and produces a profoundly objectified relationship to one's embodiment. As we suggested earlier in this chapter, Cartesian philosophy and its objectification of the body has lived effects in that it reproduces oppressive social hierarchies (Butler 1999). The discursive production of disabled children's bodies as objects in these summer camp objectives thus participates in the maintenance of social relations and ideologies which characterize disabled people, like other marginalized groups, as other and inferior in relation to a white, male, able-bodied norm (Garland-Thomson 1997).

The rhetoric of competition also invokes the passivity of disabled embodiment and subjectivity by implying that it is only through a hyperactive construct such as competition, within the outdoor camp setting, that the passive disabled child will be capable of action and self-improvement. The headings of the objectives utilize active phrases such as "Participation" and "Independence," suggesting that disabled children can hope to achieve these aims only with the help of able-bodied society and special programming. Not only does this invoke the charity model of disability, but it also renders invisible the agency of disabled children and denies the possibility that disability can be a source of creative capacity or a valued form of social difference (McRuer and Wilkerson 2003; Michalko 2002).

The notion of disability as something that resides in individual bodies and which diminishes the function, value and subjectivity of those bodies in relation to an able-bodied norm is the dominant, taken-for-granted understanding of disability in Western society (Longmore 2003; Michalko 2002; Oliver 1996). As disability studies has shown, however, disability is not an individual, medical matter but rather is a social accomplishment produced through interactions with other people, institutions and texts (Titchkosky 2007). Reading these objectives alongside our participant narratives clearly reveals the sociality of disability, both within and beyond the summer camp experience. In the remainder of this chapter, we examine the social production of disability and disabled subjectivity in the everyday life narratives of disabled people themselves, and reveal how dominant ideologies of disability were negotiated and resisted by our participants. In highlighting these negotiations, we show that the objectives, mandate and practices of the O.S.C.C. summer camps were not static discourses that were imposed singularly upon disabled children and their families but, rather, required interactive engagement with people and wider culture to invest them with meaning(s).

While we highlight particular objectives at the beginning of each section, the themes we have identified are actually woven across the different objectives. We begin with an analysis of the notion that disability is represented as a site of physical limitation and deficit. We then consider how the objectives treat isolation as a natural and inevitable outcome of being disabled, thereby stripping isolation of its sociality. We conclude the chapter with a discussion of disabled children's embodied subjectivities.

Disability as limitation / Disability as experience

Participation
Outdoor activities are stressed so that a child may enjoy games popular with his non-handicapped friends at his own pace. Here, rather than competing with other children, he competes against his disability.

Self-expression
Involvement in plays and skits, cabin activities, games and crafts encourage
a child to develop new skills and interests which can be carried on at home
during the confining winter months.
— "Summer Camp Objectives," O.S.C.C. Archival Document

Reading these two objectives carefully, a perception of disabled children is revealed
where disability is understood as limiting. Beginning with the first two objectives,
"Participation" and "Self-Expression," disabled children are considered capable only
of activities conducted indoors. As a result, within the document, the camps are constructed as sites where children should be encouraged to experience "new" activities,
both outside with their non-disabled peers and inside during the winter. The assumption here is that children do not play outside when they are home, do not interact
with non-disabled peers in a playing manner and are inside during the winter as their
disability allows them little physical movement. Disability is clearly established as a
hindrance to so-called normal participation. This is a popular perception of disabled people and more specifically, disabled children. Anne Finger (2006) argues that
representations of disabled people are generally confined. While being interviewed,
Anne was asked about her confined childhood, which she responded to with laughter,
arguing, "I laughed because my childhood was so physically expansive" (67). Finger
(2006) maintains that the media, and we would argue many other forms of representation, depict disabled individuals as "confined, not only inside buildings, but [also]
our bodies themselves contained" (67).

Within the objectives, outdoor activities are highlighted and encouraged and
as a result, a distinction is made between children who play indoors – those "with
disabilities" – and children who play outdoors – those "without disabilities." Thus,
a hierarchy is created between indoor games considered popular amongst disabled
children and outdoor games that non-disabled children play. Outdoor games, which
are encouraged, are associated with non-disabled bodies. Disabled children are motivated to leave the house and participate with their non-disabled peers in games considered superior to games played indoors. Therefore, encouragement focuses on
changing the disabled body to behave like non-disabled bodies. Furthermore, these
assumptions about what counts as participation and what forms of participation are
more valued are highly gendered. The indoor/outdoor binary reinforces the passive/
active binary that suggests that girls and women (and disabled people) are naturally
passive while boys and men (and non-disabled people) are active and action-oriented
in a society that highly values purposeful, rational action. The emphasis on the physi-
cality of the outdoors as the key means of achieving the value of full participation is
thus underwritten by gendered, ableist assumptions as what counts as valuable participation from the outset.

At the same time, it is made clear within the "Participation" objective that disabled children cannot compete at the same level as their non-disabled peers and
should only participate at their "own pace." While it may seem practical that some
children will not be physically capable of competing in the same way as their non-
disabled peers, it is nevertheless paternalistic in its assumption regarding disabled
individuals' physical capacity. In addition, the statement assumes that a disabled
child's only possible friends are non-disabled, and that disabled children do not – or

should not[7] – play together. Therefore, these objectives assume that disabled children do not participate in outdoor games at home, are incapable of competing at the same level as their non-disabled peers and are overall "too disabled" to leave the house during the winter.

Our participants revealed that while there were moments where their impairments prevented them from participating fully according to normative criteria of participation, they actually played both indoor and outdoor games with their peers, both disabled and non-disabled. A counter narrative to the notion of disability as hindrance is present within almost every interview conducted in this research project. Sam, for example, shared his story about a dressing competition, which he won for a Boy Scouts badge. The badge was for the quickest dresser. Sam told us that he could not stand for long periods of time and that he had been dressing himself methodically and systematically for many years. During the competition, he was therefore able to outmanoeuvre non-disabled boys who were haphazardly throwing on all their clothes at once. In this example, disability is constructed as a positive attribute, where Sam competed against his non-disabled peers and won the competition because of his experiences of disability.

Participants also discussed outdoor experiences they had as children, both with non-disabled peers, and in the winter. Sam also told us that he hunted in the winter as a pre-teen:

> Going out in the middle of winter on the farm and that all by myself. Take the two dogs and put a sleigh-toboggan. Load up some food and sandwiches and apples and that; my 22 gun and ammunition and a blanket and head off in the back of the woods all by myself … with my crutches dragging … going hunting.

Sam's narrative demonstrates that disabled children were not all confined to their homes during the winter months. On the contrary, disabled children were capable of activities – even dangerous ones – which their non-disabled peers may also have taken part in. Another participant, Geraldine, told us that she and her non-disabled friend went skating every Sunday for years. She first learned to skate with a red chair on Lake Simcoe and later, she and her friend would make a weekly visit to an ice rink in Orillia. Here, two assumptions found within the objectives are fragmented. This participant reveals that disabled individuals were both active in the winter and had non-disabled peers. In fact, many of our participants did not have disabled friends, a result of often being the only disabled child in their communities. The O.S.C.C. fails to acknowledge the possibility of positive community and friendship with other disabled children.

The wrong kind of independence

Independence
A brief absence from adults upon which the child is accustomed to depend can lead to greater physical independence and aid emotional growth toward maturity. The encouragement and example of other campers can be a powerful motivation for the child to attempt new things for himself.
— "Summer Camp Objectives," O.S.C.C. Archival Document"

This next objective purports the same ideological understanding of disability as a hindrance or limiting. It is different, however, from the two objectives above in that dependence on parents is considered a rationalization that allows disabled individuals a continued excuse for their limited physical ability. Disabled children are viewed, once again, as weak and incapable of experiencing new things, like independence outside the camp without the assistance of able-bodied individuals.

Parents or adults are conceptualized in this statement as weights that literally restrain disabled children from physical independence, and consequently, from maturity. Besides the notion that camp will garner individuals a sense of independence, the statement also problematically assumes that independence equates maturity. Dependence on parents or other adults may be a necessity for disabled children; to argue that such assistance or accommodation is harmful to a child's development is therefore very problematic.

At the same time, the objectives encourage disabled children to improve themselves through comparison to other children equally or more disabled than themselves. However, motivation here develops into pressures and demands on disabled children to act in a normative manner deemed socially appropriate. Overall, the contention of the document is that external motivation, from peers at camp and from society in general, is necessary to appropriately break dependence and immaturity.

Independence, for many of our participants, was not gained during a 3-week stay at one of the summer camps. In fact, most had experienced long periods in hospitals and rehabilitations centres throughout their childhoods, away from parents, siblings and friends, and many had early on gained the independence that the O.S.C.C. incorrectly perceived them to be lacking due to ableist stereotypes. Many of our participants demonstrated great capacity and resourcefulness as children. Lynn recalls babysitting her younger sister:

> I used to babysit my little sister a lot. My mother was … – well my mother was eight months pregnant when I got polio, and I had a year-and-a-half-old sister. And anyway, I used to babysit Laura a lot. I was the older daughter. I looked after her a lot.

At age ten, and having only had polio for a short period of time, Lynn was in charge of her one-and-a-half-year-old sister. While the independence this reveals may well have been invisible and devalued given the naturalization of gendered labour such as caregiving and babysitting, we would argue that this narrative reflects a high degree of competence in an important area of familial responsibility. Lynn's parents were not a hindrance to her independence or her maturity. Rather, Lynn's parents, like many other participants' parents, supported their child's becoming independent.

Another participant, Kathleen, shared a story about her camping experience at Blue Mountain. In this example, independence is obviously present; however, it is the wrong kind of independence from the perspective of the O.S.C.C. objectives:

> … But we wanted to go to the store; two other girls and myself. So we slithered across this field out to the highway so nobody would see us. Now … this girl Jane had one crutch. Of course we couldn't go to the store with a crutch

cause then she might have known that we were from camp. Right? So we had to ditch the crutch in the ditch. [...] Now this other girl, Tracy, had a shrivelled arm. But that was okay, they wouldn't notice that. And then I walked with a limp. So we go into the store. We figure nobody will know we're from camp. Right? So we buy all this crap; it was candy. And we come back. And now we can't find her crutch. So we got to walk up and down the highway to find her crutch because we threw it in the ditch. (laughing) So we got her crutch. We slithered all the way back to camp, and there was the head nurse waiting for us. Nurse Cameron. And she went over every inch of our body with a bar of Sunlight soap that was just wet and rubbed on, because this field was full of poison ivy. (Lynn)

Kathleen told us that following this incident, she was not asked to return to camp. While Kathleen clearly performed independence of a particular variety, it was apparently not the right kind of independence, defined by the O.S.C.C. as physically autonomous, but passive and obedient in every other way. Kathleen's story illustrates the independence and resourcefulness that disabled children possess; in general, the narratives revealed that disabled people participate in an array of physical activities and that dominant conceptions of disability as limiting are overly simplified and inaccurate. The document therefore inappropriately represents the physical abilities of disabled children.

Not always "happy campers": socializing at camp and at home

Socialization

Youngsters sometimes bear the additional burden of isolation because of their handicap. At camp, many lasting friendships originate and a heightened awareness of the needs of others develops. This is noted in those children who start to show a willingness to help those more handicapped than they and assist with cabin duties and other responsibilities within the limits of their ability.

— "Summer Camp Objectives," O.S.C.C. Archival Document"

Thus far, we have discussed how the O.S.C.C. documents represent disability as an inherently limited and constrained form of physical embodiment. This characterization of disability not only shaped the way disabled children were represented and understood in terms of their individual capabilities, however. It also shaped an understanding of the relationship between disabled children and their participation in wider social life. In this section, we will show how the O.S.C.C. summer camps (re)produced an understanding of disability that was grounded in an assumption of the biological materiality of impairment and its totalizing effects upon the embodied subjectivities of disabled children.[8] Our study reveals, however, that this dominant understanding of disability was negotiated with complex, changeable and uneven consequences for our participants, and that their social context, setting and interactions mediated their experiences of disability and disabled subjectivity.

The objectives consistently represent individual children in a way that strips disability, and disabled subjectivity, of its sociality. Indeed, the individualization of disability here creates the appearance of a line demarcating the individual and the social – disabled children, these objectives tell us, inhabit bodies that inherently limit their engagement with daily social life and render them isolated, without recourse. Recall the objective above, for example: "Youngsters sometimes bear the additional burden of isolation because of their handicap." This notion of isolation is also evoked in another objective, which notes that disabled children need to develop "skills and interests which can be carried on at home during the confining winter months."

Ironically, isolation is positioned throughout the objectives as somehow outside the social and residing naturally and inevitably within the disabled child's experience – concealing the fact that isolation is a social phenomenon produced by the organization of communities, institutions and relationships with others. While social isolation is a genuine historical and contemporary reality for many disabled people, it is not a natural outcome of being disabled but is, rather, the consequence of oppressive social structures and ideologies in Western society that privilege normative embodiment, shape the ability to move throughout social space and marginalize disabled embodiments and other forms of social difference.

While the summer camp objectives rest upon the assumption that disabled children lead lonely, isolated lives and need to attend summer camp with other disabled children in order to socialize with others, our participants described social engagement with diverse peer groups comprised of both disabled and non-disabled peers throughout their childhoods, and indeed, throughout their lives. Although not all social experiences were happy ones, and many of our respondents described experiences of exclusion, bullying and stigma, most discussed these negative experiences amidst a backdrop of more diverse and positive social interactions with friends, neighbours and family members. Furthermore, our analysis shows that experiences of bullying and exclusion were located within a wider social context whereby ableist, gendered, classed, racialized and heteronormative ideologies and power relations gave rise to these individualized interactions and experiences. Regardless of the quality of the social interactions, the organization of everyday household and community life constituted the meanings and experiences of living with disability for our participants – despite the suggestion within the O.S.C.C. objectives that physical impairment leads naturally and inevitably to a kind of social impairment for disabled children.

The organization of social networks was a significant factor in our participants' experiences of community and peer interaction. For some people, living in a small Ontario town meant that they experienced strong family and community support that contributed to a sense of well-being and connectedness. Marsha, for example, grew up in Stratford and stated that until she moved to Toronto as a young adult, "no one ever really made an issue about me being any different. I was just one of the gang." She described being an active participant with her peer group whereby accommodations were made "automatically" by other children so that she could play with them:

> I remember in grade school in the nice weather kids would play baseball for gym class. And it was just automatic [that] I would have my turn at bat, and if I hit the ball somebody else ran the bases for me. It just worked.

Many of our participants similarly described creative and inclusive practices of play as children and youth. Recall Geraldine, for example, who learned to skate using a red chair on the frozen lake near her home and whose friend skated alongside her for many winters in a row. Geraldine expressed a strong sense of security and connection to her friend as a result. Others went even further, suggesting that their disability became a resource for fun – when they had wheelchair races down steep hills, for example – and became a source of positive disabled identity when they played with other disabled children.

Not all our participants experienced the apparent practice of inclusion in the same way, however. Kay, for example, felt strongly that "playing baseball by proxy" in a similar manner to that described above was "plain stupid." Significantly, though, playing baseball in this manner was a forced activity during summer camp for Kay – suggesting that it is the context of the activity that shapes its quality and fulfilment rather than its mere status as a form of participation.

For Marsha, and other participants who grew up in small towns, the ability to negotiate inclusion within a variety of social settings, from playing with friends to attending school field trips, was predicated on the proximate social relationships and strong social networks that existed within the small town community and the social resources of their family. Participants who grew up without strong social networks and community connections often described different and more uneven social experiences, however. For Penny, having polio and growing up poor and disabled in Toronto's West End led to several experiences of social stigma that negatively impacted both herself and her family. Penny describes how she was ostracized from playing with other children on the street due to the perception that polio was contagious:

> I played on the next street, Armadale. And when they had the polio epidemic in the thirties, that sure didn't help my popularity cause the mothers would see me on the street, [and] they'd pull their kids in … my friends weren't allowed to play with me because of that …

As Penny pointed out, this was especially upsetting because this occurred 5 years after she had polio.[9] The organization of neighbourhoods and social networks within Toronto at that time seemed to strongly shape Penny's experience of stigma and alienation from her peer group. Urban settings were also associated with poor hygiene and other conditions that facilitated the spread of polio during the epidemics, so a sense of health panic may have been at work during the years after the epidemics themselves (Rogers 1995).

While social interaction is apparently encouraged within the O.S.C.C. objectives and mandate, it is accomplished through an overdetermined individualized framework that rests upon oppressive assumptions about disability and its role within families and communities, assumptions which return disability once again to the space of the individual. The problematic character of these assumptions regarding disabled children's socialization and their experiences of isolation is exemplified by Kay's narrative of her camping experience.

Kay attended Merrywood summer camp for several years during her early adolescence. While she was ultimately to make some lasting friendships at camp, during her first year there, Kay was quite unhappy because she would have preferred to join her family on a summer vacation to visit her grandparents in Saskatchewan. At this time, Kay and her family had just moved back to Canada after living in England for a number of years, and she was very lonely. Whereas in England, Kay went to school and had friends, in Ottawa she lived in a new subdivision outside the city with very few other houses. Compounding matters was the fact that she was not permitted to go to school because she was "too disabled." Against this backdrop of feeling socially disconnected, Kay describes how she came to attend Merrywood summer:

> I remember the Easter Seals nurse came around and told my folks about this camp where they could send me so they could have some parent relief. Which certainly didn't do anything for your self-image, right? So I got sent to camp and the rest of the family went out West to visit my grandparents and relatives, that I hadn't seen in years ... So you see this is part of the reason why camp was not fun. And it was to relieve my parents of me. Of the burden of me.

Being noticeably unhappy at camp proved troublesome, though, and Kay recalls "feeling like a failure as a camper":

> ... I wasn't outgoing. I wasn't happy. And I felt like I was being judged. So then the next year I would go back determined to be what I was supposed to be ... Happy, outgoing ... Everything they wanted campers to be.

Kay embraced the task of being a "happy camper" during her second summer at camp, and recalls making a concerted effort to be cheerful and sociable so that the staff would not wonder about her. In reality, though, Kay recalls that she was "faking it" as part of her determined effort to perform being the kind of sociable, happy camper that she was supposed to be.

Interestingly, it was the exclusion Kay felt as a result of being away from her family that most impacted her sociability. This exclusion was fostered by ableist ideology that regards disabled people as a burden to their families and society, and which was imposed upon Kay and her family when the Easter Seals nurse encouraged her parents to send her to camp. Despite the O.S.C.C. objective which sought to break the isolation of disabled children, going to camp that first summer actually isolated Kay from family life and disallowed the possibility of a sense of strengthened social connection with extended family at a critical time in her life.

As Sara Ahmed (2010) has argued, the demand to be happy is commonly imposed upon marginalized groups and functions as a way to obscure social inequalities. Kay clearly experienced this demand and sought to perform being the "happy camper" as a way to redress her failure to fulfil that demand. However, her self-reflexive engagement with the demand to be happy, revealed through her acknowledgement that she knew she was "faking it," destabilizes both the demand and the apparent accomplishment of the O.S.C.C. objective. In so doing, Kay's narrative brings to the fore the social processes and practices shaping the experience of unhappiness and marginalization in the first place, suggesting that it is towards these social ideological contexts that we must direct our critiques and attention.

Because the notion of isolation in the O.S.C.C. summer camp objectives and mandate is grounded in an understanding of disability as an individual, biological matter, isolation is made to appear as if it is a natural and inevitable outcome of disability, as if isolation experienced by disabled children is by virtue of their impairment alone. Following this, the objectives suggest that disabled children require an external agent – an expert representative of normate society – to socialize them, break their isolation and provide social engagement and support that are allegedly not possible or present within their everyday lives. In positioning itself as an appropriate agent for providing these opportunities for socialization, and the summer camp experience as an essential site of socialization, the O.S.C.C. reveals a deep investment in the notion of disability as a troublesome and tragic form of embodiment that requires saving from itself.

Our participants navigated these notions of disability in a variety of ways, however, making and unmaking the meanings of disability during their summer camp experiences and throughout their lives. While many children made long-lasting friendships at camp that continue to this day, for other children the structure and organization of the social interactions and hierarchies that flowed from them felt like a reiteration of wider social processes of othering. It is to this theme of disabled subjectivity and selfhood that we now turn.

Embodied subjectivities: Beyond binaries of acceptance and resistance

Sense of Personal Worth
Helping a child to accept his handicap is important. Seeing others equally or more handicapped than himself at camp may provide the necessary encouragement and moral support.
— "Summer Camp Objectives," O.S.C.C. Archival Document

In this theme of embodied subjectivities we discussed parts of the O.S.C.C. objectives that relate to notions of selfhood. The previous themes of physical limitation and social participation have demonstrated the contradictory embodiment(s) of the participants. This tension is also evident within the O.S.C.C. objectives related to issues of selfhood, as disabled children needed to view their disability or difference as something to overcome and at the same time, acquiesce to their disability. Besides these negative views of disability, views of heteronormative gender were also evident in camping practices.

Ultimately, this paradox of struggle against disability, while at the same time accepting the limitations associated with it, serves to place the participants in subordinate positions within many circumstances of everyday life. This means at different times accepting normative expectations by pushing oneself to do things despite disability and accepting normative expectations of one's limits by just "trying activities." However, participants also rejected normative views of disability by not accepting limits imposed by others, resisting prescribed and ableist social practices and generally challenging those boundaries imposed on them. In doing so, participants enacted and negotiated multiple subjectivities at the camps. This negotiating was contingent and represented a diversity of action or agency beyond a binary categorization of acceptance or resistance (Mahmood 2001).

To illustrate these tensions we discuss specific social practices of camping life: (1) the spatial arrangements of the camp cabins and the varied responses of participants, (2) how hetero-normative gender subjectivities are (re)produced by camp activities, and (3) the absence of "future" subjectivities of disabled children.

Devaluing/resisting/reclaiming a sense of personal worth

The structural organization of these camps also reproduced a dominant negative discourse of disability. This was reflected in the spatial arrangements of placing campers in cabins based on their physical abilities. Cabin numbers further contributed to this designation. The higher the cabin number, the more abled-bodied the person was in the cabin. This practice was evident in the O.S.C.C. objectives and in a number of the camps, based on our participants' narratives.

A few participants attended the Blue Mountain Camp in Collingwood where this practice took place. One participant, Ann, attended this camp in 1955:

> These are all the counselors, and campers, and … And it depended on your ability what cabin you would be put in. If you weren't very mobile you were in cabins one, two, three, and so on. And then cabin number nine was for kids that were very mobile … And I was in cabin number nine.

These spatial arrangements of the cabins was aligned with early social work research that "adjustment" could be seen as a social process and related to individuals' process of acceptance by and of the group they were in. This thinking of the late 1930s reinforced the O.S.C.C. objective to have a camper "learn to accept his/her handicap which seem to be best done in the company of others with the same abilities" (Newstetter 1938). This practice was supposed to promote a "positive self worth" for the individual; however, it does so at the expense of others as it reinforces the notion of a disability hierarchy – that some were better than others. Kay, who went to Merrywood camp, also described segregated cabins based on ability. Not only did Kay experience the hierarchy among the campers based on ability, though, but she also described feeling the "hierarchy" between the disabled campers and the counselors, who were not much older than she was and who might otherwise have been her peers.

However, some of the participants negotiated their view of self, and often it was not aligned with O.S.C.C. objectives, i.e. not accepting one's disability. For example, while Ann "felt special" being in cabin nine, she also stated that she felt very "able-bodied" at camp. Ann's embodied ableist subjectivity at camp reinforced to her a desire to be "able-bodied" in everyday life. This was particularly evident later in life in her capacity as mother to her children, in which she did everything that other mothers did – volunteered in her children's class at school, attended class trips, etc. – pushing herself to fulfil the gendered role of mother. In this way, she rejected her disabled subjectivity and her polio, effectively silencing her disabled embodiment in her daily life.

Another camper, Nick, attended Lakeview camp in the early 1960s. When I asked him about his camping experience, he discussed his feelings about being around other children with a range of disabilities:

> Everyone had a range of disabilities. I must admit though that I did feel … a little bit ambivalent because in that time period … as I mentioned earlier … I really didn't perceive myself as being disabled … Although intellectually I

knew I was, and intellectually I knew I had to have some assistance in different things. But I didn't see myself ... in that light. And sometimes being with
disabled – other disabled kids who were ... really disabled, it ... it was bothersome to me. I didn't like it.

Nick's statement reflects a great uncertainty on his part. This may be understandable,
given the time period, because, similar to other participants, Nick was the only child
with polio that he was aware of in his community. Thus attending camp and being
around other disabled children was a new experience. Nick's stated ambivalence is
poignant as he acknowledged his need for assistance at times, but at the same time he
admits that he sometimes did not like being around kids who were "really disabled."
Nick occupies a "liminal subjectivity" created by the tension of acknowledging his
personal limitations but rejecting other disabled campers. For Ann and Nick, being
with other disabled children reproduced oppressive and subordinate relations. While
camps brought together children with a range of abilities, for these participants the
disability community was essentially a subordinate one.

Kathleen's response to the structural organization of the segregated cabins on the
surface was more in line with O.S.C.C. objectives; however, it illustrates a person willing to push boundaries in some spaces but acquiesce to conventional expectations at
other times. When asked about how she viewed her polio, she spoke about her camping experiences and specifically referenced the segregation and grading of cabins
and helping others. For Kathleen, it crystallized her understanding of who she was:

I have always felt that I was fortunate enough because I can sit right on the
fence because when I'm dealing with people who are handicapped and it's a
'poor me' situation, then I can get after them for that, because at that point
in time I am a handicapped as well as they are. OR if I'm talking with someone who is quote "normal" and they are complaining and complaining; well
then I can be normal as well and be on their back as well. So I figure I got the
best ... the best of two worlds here.

Kathleen's account illustrates how she saw her subjectivity as both "normal" and
"handicapped." She believed she was fortunate as she held status in both able-bodied
and disabled communities. Her response illustrates not a denial of disability but an
acceptance of competing against the self by telling people not to complain and take
pity on themselves. At the same time, for Kathleen, helping other children in the
other cabins was something she had no trouble doing and demonstrates her comfort
with others:

And so when we were in the highest number we looked after the ones who were
in a lower number cabin. So, you know, you learned a lot about ... about the
kids that were there. And ... well one of the little girls I had ... she did have a
colostomy; she had to wear a bag. And as young and all as we were, I would take
her to the bathhouse, or the shower house, what you want to call it, and during
the day and I would take that bag off her and ... put it in the toilet, and flush
the toilet but hold on to the straps, of course; clean it out, throw it in the bin so

they could sterilize it. And then I'd come back and wash her and put a bag back on her, and we'd go on our merry ways. And it was like that with all of us, like us older ones. Not even necessarily older … I was 12, you know, 12 or under.

For Kathleen, this helping attitude was demonstrated later in life when she babysat children of single moms during the 1960s and 1970s. Single mothers at that time would have been stigmatized, and her helping illustrates a progressive stance. However, she also wanted people to get off of their butts and do something, which is consistent with her views of people not complaining and not taking pity upon themselves.

Gendered subjectivities, social practice and performances within the camps

Camp practices reproduced heteronormative gender subjectivities through various camping activities. Camping activities such as drama productions, physical camping activities and camp songs reproduced traditional binary subjectivities of female/male and handicapped/normal of the 1940–50s. Many participants spoke of their enjoyment of participating in summer camp productions of plays popular at this time. For the women participants, dressing up, wearing make-up and singing on stage were an important part of the camping experience.

Sandra was one young girl living in southern Ontario, close to the Woodeden Camp. Her family knew the family that owned the property before it was sold to the O.S.C.C, so they thought it would be good for her to attend. By "good," her parents thought that the camp would be a social outlet for her, which would also allow her mother to take a break from looking after her care. Sandra did not want to attend the camp, but she did in 1950 at age 12. She was able to go as a senior girl (age 12–14 years) for 3 weeks in the summer. The camp was for girls only. Sandra talked about how the camp was for her:

> I actually loved it! I loved the counselors, the programs were fun and I made friends that I stayed in touch with for many years … We did drama [and] musicals at the camp. That year, we did a Gilbert and Sullivan play and I was a good singer and got one of the lead parts.

However, Sandra was not enthusiastic about all aspects of the camping experience. She mentioned that she was not "artsy and crafty" and did not participate in these activities, common at the girls' camps. Sandra took up some and rejected other gendered practices at the camp.

Another participant, Ann, attended Blue Mountain Camp in Collingwood, Ontario. The first time she attended was in 1955 at the age of 8 years, and then again between 1960 and 1964. Ann describes doing a variety of different activities at camp in which she also embodied a traditional female subjectivity:

> Well I loved doing arts and crafts. And we had swimming and archery … we put on plays. We put on Oklahoma. We put on Oliver. That type of thing. It was a lot of … a lot of fun.

Similar to Sandra, Ann especially enjoyed dressing up in costumes and putting on make-up as actors in these plays. These practices can be seen as preparatory to traditional female subjectivities of wearing feminine attire and the future use of beauty products. Veronica Strong-Boag (1988) discusses how, beginning in the 1920s and 1930s, there was a growing focus on health and beauty products so women could market their "assets" to enhance their marriage prospects and, once married, to maintain their assets.

Traditional masculine subjectivities were reproduced in the camping activities as well, through a range of physical camping activities like canoeing, kayaking and badminton. Sam stressed that they were encouraged to try any activity that they wanted:

> Anything that you really wanted to TRY [his emphasis] and do. Because you were physically limited didn't limit you to trying. And I think the encouragement of it was that as long as you had the gumption to get up and try it, no matter how you … looked, or felt, as long as you wanted to try it they gave you the opportunity to.

While Sam lauded the encouragement of the camping environment for campers to try things, the camping objectives had implicit negative assumptions about activity and disability. There was an implicit assumption that these activities were only offered or tried only within the camping environment and that the children would be limited in their ability to do the activity as it was clearly conceived that the activity should be done in a particular (non-disabled) way. Thus, the emphasis is on the encouragement of "trying" the activity, rather than "doing" the activity and "succeeding" with it. This negative assumption of trying (and not succeeding, by normative standards) is epitomized by Sam's gendered account of sit-down boxing. Sam recalled the enjoyment of sit-down boxing, and at a previous meeting, Sam talked about how much he enjoyed giving someone a "bloody nose" when he boxed. However, he mentions, "Once someone was injured that activity was stopped." This was an activity that was only "tried" once and not offered again during Sam's time at camp. Sam's account also demonstrates Daniel Wilson's (2004) point that young boys and men who contracted polio could construct a form of heteronormal masculinity by "fighting the polio like a man." This sense of masculinity was bolstered by post war and Protestant ideologies that emphasized strength, aggressiveness, toughness, activity, perseverance, and achievement.

Traditional understandings of gender were also reproduced by the camp songs that were sung during the 1940s, 1950s and 1960s. One participant, Ann, showed us her O.S.C.C. Songbook (Ontario Society for Crippled Children n.d.). This appears to be an official O.S.C.C. camp songbook that was used by all five of the camps – Blue Mountain, Lakewood, Merrywood, Northwood and Woodeden – as each camp location had a camp song within this book.

Many of the songs were centred on boy/girl relationships, and there were also a number of Christian religious songs, military war songs, and songs that reflected southern American origin. Traditional heteronormative female subjectivities were prevalent in a number of camp songs, such as "Peggy O'Neil"[10] and "I Want a Girl (Just like the Girl that Married Dear Old Dad."[11] The lyrics in these songs reproduce traditional and idealized female-type desired behaviours. The lyrics of "Peggy O'Neil," for example, emphasized an always smiling and fun-loving girl. She was mischievous, but sweet. This is complemented by the other song, "I Want a Girl" who is like the girl that married the singer's dad. The girl is old-fashioned, faithful, truthful to the core (The Mudcat Café 2011). These camp songs reproduce gendered female behaviours that girls growing up at this time were encouraged to emulate, as they were behaviours that were important to attract a husband (Strong-Boag 1983).

Camp songs also reproduced traditional heteronormal masculine subjectivities. Some of the camp songs were military anthems or hymns such as "Men of Harlech"[12] and the "The Marine Song."[13] Both of these songs were war songs that spoke of fighting and defending their countries (Britain and the United States). For example, the song "March of Men of Harlech" has its origins in Harlech Castle in North Wales. The original Welsh tune, "*Rhyfelgyrch Fwyr Harlech*," is of unknown origin, but it probably dates to either the siege of Harlech, a castle in Britain in which the army held the castle under great odds (Data Wales-Index & Search 2011). The Marine song (really a hymn) became the military anthem of the United States Marine Corps in 1929 (Heritage Press International 2011). The martial tone of these songs and the notion of fighting on, perseverance and never giving up were hallmarks of this genre of songs. These songs reinforced the competitive spirit that permeated the camping environment.

Future narratives

The O.S.C.C. objectives focus on the immediate and present time of the camper. The present time emphasized in the objectives reinforced the view of the camp as a space or respite for children to get away from everyday life. For children with disabilities, the camp was seen as a break from their bleak existence. The O.S.C.C. objective, "Personal Worth" centres on acceptance of one's handicap and thus signifies that one's personal worth is limited. This limited personal worth also implies a limited future, as illustrated by the "absences" within the objectives. Nowhere in any of the objectives is there any mention of the growth potential and actualization of the individuals to adulthood. There are only fleeting references to the "future" for disabled children in the O.S.C.C. objectives, and those references point to only the short-term, and local future (winter months), occurring in particular spaces of home and school. Harriet McBryde Johnson (2006) poignantly talks about her own awareness of her lack of a future through the idea that she was going to die young. She describes viewing a Muscular Dystrophy Association television advertisement, as a 3- or 4-year-old, in which the boy in the ad is active and enjoying himself playing baseball and other games but then dies, as symbolized by the narration, "little Billy's toy soldiers have lost their general." For her, this representation of muscular dystrophy became her knowledge of her "future," and she says that she began to think of herself as a dying child at the age of 5. McBryde Johnson (2006) goes on to live a rich life and not a limited nor short life – she becomes "too late to die young."

Only one participant mentioned participating in camp activities that promoted a sense of future – a theme week on the various Canadian political parties and campers represented a post-secondary school during this week. Nick spoke specifically about how he viewed his last year at summer camp as a transition out of childhood:

> … in one sense it was a closing of childhood – if I can use sort of a … slightly lyrical phrase, because … you know, once I was finished with there – and

maybe it was because of my age and stage maybe it was just went up to grade eight. I'm not sure. But ... but I don't remember either going back in high school, or wanting to go back. It was just kind of ... that was it. Yeah.

The narratives shared by Nick and many other participants indicated that their parents saw a future for them, and that they subsequently imagined a future for themselves. Often this future involved schooling or work. One may suggest that the decision for schooling for young women was seen as necessary, as women participants mentioned that getting married was not assumed for them.

In general, all the participants who attended the O.S.C.C. camps went on to have rich lives – and they continue to do so today. Participants went to school for varying lengths of time, worked outside and inside the home, had relationships and got married, had children (Ann) and engaged in everyday and collective forms of activism (Stephen) that challenged normative assumptions about living with a disability. As mentioned earlier, for example, Kathleen decided while raising her own children (during the late 1950s) that she would babysit children of only young single mothers. Both Sandra and Stephen got involved in a cross-disability activist group in Southern Ontario during the 1970s that was instrumental in developing the structures and organization for supportive housing and accessibility. Nick became a journalist and worked in government. Thus, participants led lives that illustrate personal growth, mutiple achievements, opportunities, and reflections of their own lives with polio.

In these three themes of limitations/experiences, isolation/social participation and embodied subjectivities beyond acceptance/resistance, participants demonstrated how they challenged, rejected, acquiesed to during camp and in their daily lives the dominant negative discourses of disability. Participants lives reflected the complex intersections of polio, gender, and disability for them growing up during this time period. Thus their negotiations were fluid, contingent and multiple. Their negotiations reflected their fluctuating personal, familial and community agency against dominant practices that exist within and beyond the lived spaces of these children's lives.

Conclusion

The O.S.C.C. summer camps represent the epitome of able-bodiedness through their emphasis on independence and outdoor activity. The O.S.C.C. objectives are presented as common-sense values, and the O.S.C.C. is represented as an authority on how to achieve these values. Thus, the O.S.C.C. documents represent the camps as the key site where these values can be achieved. In doing so, it minimizes the support and actions of families and communities to the participants. The camps did bring together children with a range of abilities and some participants spoke about the friendships that began at camp and continued throughout their lives, into the present day. Both Sandra and Kay spoke about important and supportive friendships with others with different disabilities.

In this paper, participants provided accounts of how they "broke the rules" within the camps and in everyday life related to these dominant negative views of disability. In effect, by breaking the rules, these participants transformed the camping site as a site of regulation and control to a site of chosen and expanded opportunities as active agents in their lives

This agency is foretelling. Of the two camps that are still in existence – Woodeden and Merrywood – both operate as recreation camps today. Ironically, Woodeden camp has been a space of active resistance, allowing for the broader disability community in Southern Ontario to meet and organize around the push for Self Directed Attendant Services in Ontario during the late 1980s and 1990s. Kathy Martinez has spoken about how camping experience has fostered friendships and the beginning of building a disabled community for future activism (personal communication).

Our analysis has shown that the O.S.C.C. objectives conceal the complex everyday interactions and practices that constantly make and unmake disability and its relation to wider social life. While these summer camp objectives are drawn from a historical document, these ideologies persist today. For example, the *Toronto Star*, a prominent city newspaper, founded the Toronto Star Fresh Air Fund in 1901 by Joseph Atkinson. Its focus now, as it was in 1901, is to provide children relief from the "harsh realities and responsibilities of life" and to help "the development of a child's emotional, mental and physical well-being" (Toronto Star). We have also found global examples of the same sentiment and focus (Kearns and Collins 2000). Our analysis helps to illustrate the continuities across different representations, sites and time periods of disability such that we might better understand the social and historical contexts shaping the present.

Notes

1 This chapter is based on research in which we investigate the oral histories of disabled Canadians who contracted polio pre 1955. The project team included academic and community disability activists. The overarching purpose of the research project is the investigation of the extent of activism in the lives of this generation of disabled Canadians. This project is important, because Canadian polio epidemic survivors (1920–1955) represent the earliest contingent of independent living pioneers, and their numbers are diminishing with age, we need to uncover their social histories in order to write our Disability Histories, emphasize our cultural roots and to support contemporary campaigns for equality (Longmore and Umanski 2001).

2 One of the main criticisms of oral histories is whether or not the oral source is credible, as often the oral sources may be removed from events and this distance may alter the memory of the event. However, Portelli (2006) suggests quite rightly, that the same criticism can be said about written documents. He argues that the personal involvement of the informant (i.e. oral sources can be questioned directly and often within the oral history tradition) may compensate for the chronological distance issue.

3 This collaborative approach extends to our analytical process. The research analysis team has read the majority of the transcribed interviews independently. We have met as a group to describe each interview – what was the person saying? What were s/he emphasizing that was important to her/him? How were they framing or positioning their lives? We also wrote up analytical "hunches" about what we were starting to see across the different narratives. This descriptive process was important: it provided the foundation for our group meetings in which we developed conceptually distinct but related key themes.

4 Throughout our analysis of the O.S.C.C. documents, we will refer to these archival documents as "text(s)".

5 Further references to this text will appear as page numbers in parentheses.

6 The origins of the fresh air movement are not during the Industrial Revolution. Kaven's (1993) maintains that Thomas Sydenham was the first to consider the healthy properties of fresh air in 1666. He developed the fresh air treatment specifically for individuals coping with tuberculosis. He would advise his patients to go horseback riding in "fresh kindly air" (123). For this reason, the treatment was called the equestrian cure (123). Over the centuries the equestrian cure continued to be an important instrument for healthcare professionals and continues to be an important part of our society's health vernacular – "just grab some fresh air, it'll make you feel better."

7 The objectives suggest that disabled children should only play together to encourage each other to overcome their disability. The argument then follows that if two disabled children play together there might be a dependence upon each other's so-called (in)abilities and they would hold each other back.

8 The biological facticity of the impaired body is the most common orientation towards disability, both historically and in the present, and is shared by both medicine (dominant society) and the social model of disability (Michalko 2002). See Hughes and Paterson (1997) for a critique.

9 The stigma associated with polio also impacted Penny's family some years earlier, when their home above the family tailoring business storefront was quarantined, with negative economic effects for the family.

10 "Peggy O'Neil." 1921.

11 "I Want a Girl (Just like the Girl that Married Dear Old Dad)." 1912.

12 There is no known date for the song "Men of Harlech." It has origins in songs sung in Northern Wales, estimated to have been created in the year 1408.

13 "The Marine Song." 1929.

References

Ahmed, Sara. 2010. *The Promise of Happiness*. Durham, UK: Duke University Press.

Aitken Sally, Helen D'Orazio, and Stewart Valin. 2004. *Walking Finders: The Story of Polio and Those Who Lived with It*. Quebec, Canada: Vehicule Press

Armitage, Susan H. and Sherna B. Gluck. 2006. Reflections on women's oral history: An exchange. In: Robert Perks and Alistair Thomson (Eds.). *The Oral History Reader*. 2nd ed. London, UK: Routledge. 73–82.

Baynton, Douglas C. 2001. Disability and the justification of inequality in American history. In: Paul Longmore and Lauri Umanski (Eds.). *The New Disability History: American Perspectives*. New York, NY: New York University Press. 33–57.

Bordo, Susan. 1993. *Unbearable Weight: Feminism, Western Culture, and the Body*. California, CA: University of California Press.

Butler, Judith. 1999. *Gender Trouble*. New York, NY: Routledge.

Butler, Judith. 2004. *Undoing Gender*. New York, NY: Routledge.

Camp Song Book. n.d. *Ontario Society for Crippled Children*. Toronto, Ontario, Canada.

Corker, Mairian and Thomas Shakespeare. 2002. *Disability and Post Modernity: Embodying Disability Theory*. Continuum International Publishing Group, London

Data Wales-Index & Search. 2011. *Men of Harlech*. http://www.data-wales.co.uk/harlech2.htm (July 28, 2017)

Davis, Lennard. 1995. *Enforcing Normalcy: Disability, Deafness and the Body*. London, UK: Verso Press.

Finger, Anne. 2006. *Elegy for a Disease: A Personal and Cultural History of Polio*. New York, NY: St. Martin's Press.

Garland-Thomson, Rosemarie. 1997. *Extraordinary Bodies: Figuring Physical Disability in American Culture and Literature*. New York, NY: Columbia University Press.

Gentry, Martha E. 1984. Developments in Activity Analysis. *Social Work with Groups* 7,1 (Spring): 35–44.

Gleason, Mona. 2005. From 'disgraceful carelessness' to 'intelligent precaution': Accidents and the public child in English-Canada, 1900–1950. *Journal of Family History* 30, 2. (April): 230–241.

Heritage Press International. 2011. *History of the Marines' Hymn*. http://www.usmcpress.com/heritage/marine_hymn.htm (July 28, 2017)

Hirsch, Karen. 2004. Culture and disability: The role of oral history. In: Robert Perks and Alistair Thomson (Eds.). *The Oral History Reader*. London, UK: Routledge.

History of the Ontario Society of Crippled Children, The. 1967. History of OSCC, Ontario Society for Crippled Children. 1–55. *The Archives of Ontario.*

Hughes, Bill and Kevin Paterson. 1997. The social model of disability and the disappearing body: Towards a sociology of impairment. *Disability & Society*, 12, 3. (July): 325–340.

Kearns, Robin A. and Damian Collins. 2000. New Zealand children's health camps: Therapeutic landscapes meet the contract state. *Social Science and Medicine* 51. 1047–1059.

Longmore, Paul. 2003. *Why I Burned My Book and Other Essays on Disability*. Philadelphia, PA: Temple University Press.

Longmore, Paul and Lauri Umanski. 2001. *The New Disability History: American Perspectives*. New York, NY: New York University Press.

Mahmood, Saba. 2001. Feminist theory, embodiment and the docile agent: Some reflections on the Egyptian Islamic Revival. *Cultural Anthropology* 16, 2. (May): 202–236.

McBryde Johnson, Harriet. 2006. *Too Late to Die Young: Nearly True Stories From a Life*. New York, NY. Henry Holt and Company.

McRuer, Robert and Abby L. Wilkerson. 2003. Desiring disability: Queer theory meets disability studies. *GLQ: A Journal of Lesbian and Gay Studies* 9, 1–2. 1–24.

Meade, Teresa and David Serlin. 2006. Editor's introduction. *Radical History Review* 94. (Winter): 1–8.

Michalko, Rod. 2002. *The Difference That Disability Makes*. Philadelphia, PA: Temple University Press.

Mishna, Faye, Joseph Michalski, and Richard Cummings. 2002. Camps as social work interventions: Returning to our roots. *Social Work with Groups* 24, 3 (November): 153–171.

Moss, Pamela and Isabel Dyck. 2002. *Women, Body, Illness: Space and Identity in the Everyday Lives of Women with Chronic Illness*. New York, NY: Rowman & Littlefield Publishers, Inc.

The Mudcat Café. 2011. I Want a Girl. http://mudcat.org/@displaysong.cfm?SongID=2879 - July 28, 2017.

Newstetter, Wilber Irvin. 1938. *Group Adjustment: A study in Experimental Sociology*. Cleveland, OH: School of Applied Social Sciences, Western Reserve University.

Oliver, Mike. 1996. *Understanding Disability: from Theory to Practice*. New York, NY: St. Martin's Press.

Portelli, Alesssandro. 2006. What makes oral history different. In: Perks, Robert and Thomson, Alistair (Eds.). *The Oral History Reader*. 2nd ed. London, UK: Routledge. 33–42.

Rimke, Heidi and Alan Hunt. 2002. From sinner to degenerates: The medicalization of morality in the 19th century. *History of the Human Sciences*. 15, 1. (January): 59–88.

Rogers, Naomi. 1995. A disease of cleanliness: Polio in New York City, 1900–1990. In David Rosner (Ed.). *Hives of Sickness: Public Health and Epidemics in New York City*. Rutgers University Press, New Jersey. 115–130.

Schwartz, William. 1960/1994. Characteristics of the group experience in residential camping. In: T. Berman-Rossi (Ed.). *Social Work: The Collected Writings of William Schwartz*. Itasca, IL: Peacock Publishers.

Sebe Bom Meihy, Jose. 2003. The radicalization of oral history: *Words & Silences: Journal of The International Oral History Association* 2, 1, (June): 31–41.

Strong-Boag, Veronica. 1988. *The New Day Recalled: Lives of Girls and Women in English Canada.* Copp Clark Pitman, Toronto. 233

Summer Camping Objectives. n.d. Summer Camps in 1976–1977, Ontario Society for Crippled Children. *The Archives of Ontario.*

Titchkosky, Tanya. 2007. *Reading and writing disability differently: The textured life of embodiment.* Toronto, Canada: University of Toronto Press.

Wilson, Daniel. 2004. Fighting polio like a man. In: Bonnie G. Smith and Beth Hutchison (Eds.). *Gendering Disability.* Rutgers University Press, New Jersey. 119–133.

28

CHANGING AMERICA'S CONSCIOUSNESS: A BRIEF HISTORY OF THE INDEPENDENT LIVING CIVIL RIGHTS MOVEMENT IN THE UNITED STATES

Steven E. Brown

An era ends

'I am not a victim of polio'. On Sunday, March 19, 1995, about 1,000 people watched a clip of Ed Roberts, a man significantly physically impaired from the neck down with quadriplegia since a young age by the onset of polio, a person who required the aid of a portable respirator and an 'iron lung' for breathing, inform national talk show host Larry King that he did not consider himself a victim. We travelled to Berkeley, California, from all over the nation to say goodbye to Ed.

Compared to Martin Luther King Jr., Mahatma Gandhi, and Cesar Chavez, for his leadership in the American and later worldwide disability rights movement, Ed broke many barriers during his life, including those at Berkeley University and the California Department of Rehabilitation. At the time of his death, he was President of the World Institute on Disability (WID), a public policy institute located in Oakland, California – the first such organization run by people with disabilities.

At Ed's memorial service, two of the most important people in Ed's life were in attendance: his mother, Zona, and his son, Lee. It is fitting that Ed linked generations, because his accomplishments reflected struggles that preceded his life and continued following his death.

Historical perceptions

Until the publication of this book, no detailed international histories of people with disabilities exists, even though archaeological evidence suggests that disabled persons have been part of the human experience long before the rise of *Homo sapiens* to the present era. Archaeologists repeatedly uncover evidence of individuals with disabilities, recently as far back as 530,000 years ago (Barth, 2009). There is also a long history of attempts to deal with the needs of people with disabilities. One ancient example is Roman law providing assistance to people with disabilities with the expectation those individuals would then become peaceful citizens (Mackelprang & Salsgiver, 1996).

Yet, despite the evidence of people with disabilities existing in the same social groupings with their nondisabled peers for hundreds of thousands of years, there remains limited historical material pertaining to people with disabilities living in the United States. No comprehensive histories yet exist about people with disabilities in the United States, or elsewhere (though, in fall 2012, Nielsen will publish *A Disability History of the United States*). Indeed, even incomplete histories are few. Journalist Joe Shapiro, in *No Pity* (1993), offered a post–Americans with Disabilities Act history of disability rights. Charlton (1998) skilfully weaved American and international disability rights activities into *Nothing About Us Without Us*. Perhaps our best-known historian, Paul Longmore, who passed away in 2010, contributed two books to this legacy: he co-edited *The New Disability History* (Longmore & Umansky, 2001) and published *Why I Burned My Book and Other Essays about Disability* (2003). Interestingly, the compiling of American history of disability experiences is no different than that of most of the world, wherein most developed and developing countries have paid little or no attention to the histories of people with disabilities. The following chapter attempts to address some of the American disability experiences by providing an insight into the rise of the disability rights movement in the United States.

First perception: Paternalism, or attics, closets and almshouses

Colonial America's law and tradition, including those affecting individuals with disabilities, often continued European precedents, particularly from England and the Netherlands, two countries that colonized the eastern portion of what became the United States of America. The social-legal category of disabled persons first became institutionalized in England's Elizabethan Poor Laws (1598–1601). They were, in part, a reaction to England's world dominance and increase in commerce and industry, which contributed to the creation of a group of unemployed and discontented workers. As the country's economic focus changed from agrarian to industrial, entrepreneurs believed each individual harboured personal responsibility for their unemployment, perspectives which were exported to the colonies (Connors, 1985) (Table 28.1).

Individuals considered ill or physically and or mentally impaired who were unable to work were legally defined as being unemployable social dependents (Connors, 1985). This meant families and communities shared voluntary responsibility for ensuring that their relatives and neighbours with disabilities were respected and part of community life. If this did not happen, individuals with disabilities became burdens, an unwanted and often unhappy appendage of a family or community, leading to many nightmarish stories: people locked up all their lives in closets or attics, treated like animals, doing little more than waiting for death (Benavraham, 1985; Lenihan, 1976–1977).

When families were unavailable or unwilling to care for their relatives with disabilities, the community became responsible either by taking disabled people into their homes or supporting them in their own homes. This method of relief was known as outdoor relief, and it remained the dominant form of social support for disabled citizens until the mid nineteenth century, at which time there was less and less community support for needy citizens and this population were viewed as a nuisance population. This shift from social acceptance to social rejection led to the rise of institutions such as workhouses, almshouses and asylums and in contemporary social

Table 28.1: Historical perceptions of people with disabilities in the United States

General Time Frame	First Perception	Second Perception	Third Perception	Fourth Perception	Fifth Perception
Colonial Period	Paternalism, Or, Attics, Closets, and Almshouses				
Early Nineteenth Century		Competition and Deviance, Or, Schools, Prisons, and Asylums			
Early Twentieth Century			Dominance and Fragility, Or, Purity, Reform, and a President in Disguise		
Mid-Twentieth Century				Rehabilitation, and Independence, Or, Movements, Sit-ins and Disability Rights	
Late Twentieth Century					Charity and Celebration, Or Telethons, Paradigm Shifts, and Disability Culture

Source: Brown (1994).

welfare parlance is referred to as 'indoor relief'. These generic institutions which often housed the poor, the derelict, as well as physically disabled and mentally ill individuals and their families provided only a minimum of shelter, clothing and food to those unable to fend for themselves (Trattner, 1998; Lenihan, 1976–1977; Connors, 1985). Interestingly, there appears to be a differentiation in the provision of aid to different populations of disabled persons. For example, aid and support were provided to combat-wounded army veterans as early as 1636 in Plymouth, Massachusetts, and hospitals were later established along America's eastern seaboard for injured seamen (Lenihan, 1976–1977).

The prevalent theme of these early American years was persons with disabilities who could financially care for themselves and could work were expected to do and those who were unable to do so were then expected to seek assistance from their families. When familial aid was not forthcoming, the local authorities provided minimal aid through punitive and institutional living such as the almshouse, the asylum or the workhouse. Remnants of these first categorizations of the deserving poor and the undeserving poor, alongside the mixed perceptions of paternalism and punishment, as well as the societal will, albeit reluctant at times, to provide care of those who cannot care for themselves, remain to this day.

Despite these colonial beliefs about nuisance disabled populations as well as the rise of segregated institutions, evidence does suggest that for the most part, people with disabilities were part of the broader society and in fact were often leaders of their communities. Stephen Hopkins, for example, who signed the Declaration of Independence, declared, 'My hand trembles, but my heart does not', a reference to cerebral palsy (Lenihan, 1976–1977, p. 12) and Gouverneur Morris, often described as the financier of the American Revolution, was an amputee. Although both men were Revolutionaries, neither were social rebels advocating for the rights of people with disabilities, as they did not perceive disability differently than the majority of their American brethren (Lenihan, 1976–1977).

Second perception: Competition and deviance, or, schools, prisons, and asylums

Certain technological and organizational innovations – standardization of parts, development of assembly lines, and mass production – began in the U.S. in the early nineteenth century, with inventors and refiners of products such as the cotton gin and the rifle (Davis, 1990). Standardizing mechanical parts and inaugurating assembly lines worked so well in American factory and industrial settings, many people thought these advances could be transferred to the broader society with equally notable results. Many twenty-first-century institutions have discernible roots in early nineteenth-century social reforms.

Schools, for example, traditionally place people of the same age in the same grade, teach them the same subjects, and give them the same tests. We allow this pattern in the majority of our educational settings despite knowing people of the same age possess different skill levels, aptitudes, and abilities. The nineteenth-century founders of the school system consciously patterned U.S. educational institutions after the newly established factory system. Moreover, the early American prison system became another object of the reformers' vision. Criminals were to be punished, removed from society, placed in isolated institutions, clothed in identical uniforms, expected to conform to the same time rituals, and, with a minimum of variation, required to perform comparable menial tasks. In many ways, the rise of public schools for children and creation of prisons for criminals had as their primary purpose the creation of citizens who could and would adhere to the moral standards created to meet the demands and needs of an industrial capitalist society.

But what about people with disabilities? Like the criminal, people with disabilities were outcasts, and like the youngster, people with disabilities were seen as childlike, those whose minds and bodies could be moulded in such a way as to meet the needs of society. If institutions such as public schools and prisons could be modelled after the factory and were considered to be advantageous for schoolchildren and criminals, logically the same kind of reforms would benefit those with disabilities.

The classic asylum, or state hospital, was constructed as far away from society as possible. Interestingly, schools and prisons were designed to reform and mould citizens, but for disabled individuals placed in institutions such as hospitals and asylums, segregation and isolation seemed to be the dominating principle for existence. The asylum reflected society's belief that disability was a medical problem, an individual defect. Within a short period of time such institutions became medically oriented, caretaking facilities offering little hope that patients or inmates would ever rejoin the social mainstream (Rothman, 1971).

Disability had evolved from a sympathetic characteristic, rendering its victims unable to meet basic needs, to an unacceptable social aberration warranting social isolation. Whether in a psychiatric hospital, convalescent home, sanitarium, or other variation of this theme, individuals with disabilities were isolated, and often forcibly incarcerated, because society believed disability was deviant and hence people with disabilities had to be segregated from society (Bowe, 1978).

Bridging centuries: The Civil War

The national bloodletting unleashed during the American Civil War between 1860 and 1864, despite its widespread nation-building impact, had minimal positive consequences on the day-to-day lives of Americans with disabilities. Two primary effects resulted from the fighting itself. First, it increased the use of anaesthesia, accelerating scientific medical and surgical advances – a common theme of war (Albin, 2000). Second, hundreds of thousands of combatants were severely injured, dramatically increasing the numbers of people with disabilities in America.

For the most part there was greater public empathy for disabled Civil War veterans than there was for others who may have become disabled as a result of a work-related injury, accident or illness, and Americans, in and out of government, recognized a need to assist those injured in battle. Public aid, in the form of family and community support as it existed in colonial America, no longer held much appeal. Asylums did not seem the proper resort for soldiers who had risked their lives for their country. The government did not favour national relief programs, so concerned citizens formed voluntary associations.

The United States Sanitary Commission brought together many of these voluntary groups to offer private and philanthropical assistance to disabled veterans. Their efforts led to the establishment of a National Home for disabled Union veterans in 1866. Lodging and medical care were provided in 11 more homes opened during the next 60 years (Lenihan, 1976–1977).

Veterans' disability issues pertaining to financial supports, services and training assumed utmost importance in many of the political debates of the latter nineteenth century and throughout the twentieth century, especially following World War 1 and World War 2. And, as a result of the services and supports provided to veterans, the wider disabled American public benefitted with greater provision of supports and services through public aid, workers' compensation and private insurance programs.

Third perception: Dominance and fragility, or, purity, reform and a president in disguise

Many late nineteenth-century scholars believed in the omnipotence of the scientific method. New disciplines, like psychology, sociology, and political science advertised themselves as social sciences or scientific disciplines applicable to society (Stallybrass

& White, 1993). Faith in these social sciences, combined with recently ascertained laws of genetics, led to aspirations of creating a civic utopia. For late nineteenth- and early twentieth-century Americans, this meant a white, intellectually rigorous, middle-class society. Interestingly, we find a paradoxical situation when it comes to the place and role of people with disabilities in American society. On the one hand, individuals with disabilities benefitted through many reforms which offered greater opportunities for social care, vocational training and education, and on the other hand, many suffered as a result of this era's social multiple reforms which emphasized sterilization, eugenics and institutional segregation.

An early indication of what became an early twentieth-century nightmare was the transformation of the word 'defective'. Originally an adjective, by the 1880s, defective became a noun. Defectives, like people with disabilities, were considered threats to genteel society (Finger, 1985). The first public policies advocating for eugenics, or genetic engineering, to control defective populations occurred in 1907 in the state of Indiana, where sterilization laws were first enacted to prevent congenital 'mental retardation', and with a short period of time similar legislation followed in other states across America (Lenihan, 1976–1977). Individuals with disabilities untouched by these statutes often encountered others laws equally repellent. Many cities had ordinances which prevented someone who was 'unsightly' from appearing in public (Longmore, 1985; Schweik, 2009).

Although not often acknowledged, Nazi Germany emulated much of the eugenics legislation initiated in the U.S., and as result of German eugenics policies, tens of thousands of 'mental and physical defectives' were put to death. In fact, history notes that it was people with disabilities that was the first large population to be put to death, and the lessons learned in gassing people with disabilities were applied to millions of other 'undesirable individuals' between 1939 and 1945 (Gallagher, 1990).

Other reform crusades affecting the lives of people with disabilities coexisted with the rise of eugenics. Employers, for example, were rarely held responsible for occupational hazards. On-the-job injuries meant unpaid leave or worse. By the early 1900s, many government and business leaders, along with reformers, realized this entailed a social cost and potential social unrest. This led to laws providing a minimal safety net. Worker's compensation, providing payments to workers injured on the job, sometimes called the first modern disability law, began in 1911 (Berkowitz, 1987).

Fear of civic unrest, concern about social impurities from inferior Eastern European immigrants, who spoke different languages, practiced different religions and dressed differently, along with a desire to inculcate fundamental American notions of government and civility, led to mandatory educational attendance (Fredrickson, 1987), which in turn led to development of vocational education, while nineteenth-century discoveries in antibiotics, bacteria, and causes of diseases enabled people with disabling conditions to live longer. Combining medical breakthroughs with vocational education led to 'vocational rehabilitation', the idea that some people with disabilities could and should enter or re-enter the workplace.

After President Woodrow Wilson declared U.S. entry into World War I, additional numbers of veterans with disabilities returned home. During the final year of World War I, Congress passed the Smith-Hughes Law (Vocational Education Act) of 1917, the first of many vocational laws designed, first for combat veterans, which eventually expanded to just about anyone with a disability who wanted to become educated, trained and work (Lenihan, 1976–1977; Walker, 1985; Scotch, 1984; Shapiro, 1993).

Interestingly, disability and quality of life were very much connected to class affiliation, and notable individuals such as President Franklin D. Roosevelt (FDR) lived quite well in an era of widespread stigma of people with disabilities. FDR, President during much of the Depression and World War II, remains the only President elected to the office with a clear and visible disability. Yet he consciously disguised his disability from the American public, and one author has referred to this as 'FDR's splendid deception' (Gallagher, 1985).

A personable and vigorous young man, FDR emulated his cousin, President Theodore Roosevelt, first in joining the Navy, then becoming a politician. FDR's first foray into presidential politics resulted in a loss as the 1920 Democratic vice-presidential candidate. Shortly thereafter, his political future uncertain, he became ill with polio, lost functional use of his legs and required the use of braces, canes and wheelchairs for mobility.

FDR's wealth and contacts enabled him to pursue physical rehabilitation almost anywhere in the world, let alone America, and he went to the spa at Warm Springs, Georgia. While at this facility and later, he donated energy and financial largesse into building a modern rehabilitation facility at the site, and he encouraged other polio survivors to take advantage of the putative healing properties of Warm Springs.

Many historical accounts of FDR's bout with polio treated it as a brief, isolated incident, which probably proved to his political benefit, showing even someone with FDR's breeding and riches could be vulnerable to disease and disability. Following a long period of rehabilitation, FDR re-entered politics and eventually, with the support of his well-known wife, Eleanor, he was elected as governor of the state of New York in 1928, and in 1932 he was elected President of the United States. Gallagher's (1985) groundbreaking study of FDR showed that America of the 1920s to the 1940s had little understanding of causation of disabling diseases such as polio and there was a great deal of stigma attached to disability. Although FDR recovered from the polio virus itself, his disabilities remained, and he went to great lengths to hide the extent of his impairment from the public view.

Though the polio virus was gone and his consequent impairments did not technically make FDR 'sick', that was how he and the American public viewed disability. The word 'invalid' is used to describe someone incapable of caring for themselves. This was the perception of those with disabilities. While illness or sickness is not necessarily a permanent aspect of disability, it is an inherent concept of invalidism. Since no distinction was made between an invalid and a disabled person, a disabled individual was considered sick.

As a person whose polio had caused paralysis and wheelchair use, FDR fit the classic invalid social construct of early twentieth-century America, so when he resumed his political career, first as state governor and later as President of the United States, he required that he never be portrayed in the persona of the 'invalid'. Simply stated, he needed to convince the American public he could fulfil the duties of public office, and to do that required conscious planning, massive assistance, and, from today's vantage, unbelievable media corroboration and collusion.

When FDR appeared in public he did not use his wheelchair. He rose from a seated position with the aid of braces and crutches and staff members, though he was neither stable nor graceful. Once standing, FDR shuffled along with the assistance of a complement of strong men, or he often leaned against a podium or sat behind a table when giving a speech. For all intents and purposes, FDR appeared to be a healthy politician, not a sickly invalid.

The media supported FDR's efforts to hide the extent of his disability. Radio, newspaper and film correspondents simply did not discuss FDR's paralysis. Thirty-five thousand photographs were shot of FDR as President, but only two show him seated in his wheelchair (Hevey, 1992). Even political cartoonists never drew FDR in his wheelchair, but standing, walking – or running, or flying!

This was FDR's 'splendid deception' because it enabled him to rise to the presidency during a time when everyone was convinced no invalid could aspire to that position.

What did FDR's cloaking of his paralysis and wheelchair use mean for people with disabilities? For many people with disabilities FDR was and remains a hero, a person with a disability who achieved the nation's most coveted office and for a time became the most powerful person in the world, and he helped develop a world-renowned rehabilitation hospital at Warm Springs, Georgia. But despite his great political achievements, this massive cover-up not only reflected the societal perception of his time, it also reflected his own perception that disability meant individual and familial shame, illness, weakness and invalidism; the cover-up also contributed to future generations harbouring those same oppressive beliefs.

Fourth perception: Rehabilitation and independence, or, movements, sit-ins and disability rights

Because of the carnage and widespread injuries stemming from World War II, the federally funded Vocational Rehabilitation services amassed larger budgets. Mary Switzer, appointed agency director in 1950, spent two decades expanding its role (Walker, 1985). She persuaded Congress to fund research and development in medicine and rehabilitation engineering, in-service training programs, rehabilitation centres, and sheltered workshops (Scotch, 1984). By the late 1970s, disability researcher Frank Bowe praised rehabilitation as one of the best social investments ever made, citing studies estimating a return of from five to seventy dollars for every tax dollar invested (1978). But rehabilitation programs and services were built upon an individualized medical construct of disability with an emphasis on professional guidance and individual change, but most importantly rehabilitation often missed a key component: people with disabilities guiding their own destinies. It was not until the World War II era that organizations created *by* and for people with disabilities emerge with a focus toward advocacy and greater societal change. Indeed, the period between the early 1940s to the late 1960s shows evidence of the growing desire for people with disabilities being in control of supports and services programs as well as having a greater say in the development of public disability policy. During this time we find the rise of disability advocacy organizations such as the American Federation of the Physically Handicapped founded in 1940 (Berkowitz, 1987) and the Paralyzed Veterans of America (1947). Organizations such as these helped move disability rights in America forward, and over time there was development of committees such as the President's Committee for the Employment of the Handicapped, which was instituted by President Eisenhower in 1954 (Scotch, 1984). By the late 1960s Congress had passed legislation which addressed barrier removal for people with disabilities in America, and an example of this legislation was the Architectural Barriers Access Act of 1968, which became the first major piece of legislation to promote architectural access for people with disabilities (Scotch, 1984; Bowe, 1978).

While incremental reforms dealing with issues of greater access and inclusion began to emerge in post World War II America, the most significant changes appear during the late 1960s and early 1970s with the rise of the Disability Rights Movement, commonly referred to as the Independent Living Movement (ILM). An important leader of the ILM in the United States was Ed Roberts.

Ed Roberts entered the University of California–Berkeley in 1962. Roberts' post-polio impairments included quadriplegia, as he could move only one finger and he required breathing assistance through a portable respirator as well an iron lung. Ed Roberts was to the Disability Rights Movement what Dr. Martin Luther King Jr. was to the Civil Rights Movement. Barrier-breaking action is celebrated by many in the disability community, including California's annual Ed Roberts Day, but few others know of his achievements, despite print and media documentation (Brown, 2003; Shapiro, 1993; Ó hÉochaidh, 2012)

In the 1960s, when Roberts enrolled at UC–Berkeley, he lived in the on-campus hospital, where he received as much personal assistance as he required. The hospital, unlike dormitories, also provided an architecturally accessible room, big enough for his iron lung. From the University's perspective, it enabled them to keep an eye on a potentially vulnerable student.

Within several years about a dozen other students with disabilities joined Ed. They identified themselves as the Rolling Quads. These students soon began advocating for greater control over the day-to-day personal services that they needed, and through their efforts the UC–Berkeley's Physically Disabled Students' Program (PDSP) came into being.

The Rolling Quads moved beyond the university boundaries to tackle the inaccessibility of public places of the city of Berkeley, California. First the group addressed the lack of curb cuts by wielding sledgehammers and pouring tar to make make-shift ramps. They also requested the City Council redress the problem and in 1971, Berkeley approved building of curb cuts in sidewalks, thus becoming one of the first cities in the United States to address inaccessibility. These actions on the part of disabled university students at the University of California–Berkeley may have been considered radical for the time, but they reflected the growing discontent of other people with disabilities across America at the time. As the Rolling Quads increased in number and identified more issues, the city of Berkeley budgeted money for an office to address these problems and barriers. In 1972, the Center for Independent Living (CIL), Berkeley, California, came into existence, partly staffed by the Rolling Quads, who believed political action and change was necessary to attain equal societal access (Brown, 1994, 2003; Shapiro, 1993). The success of CIL and other independent living centres from the early 1970s became nationally known. All over the U.S. people with disabilities sought ways to achieve comparable services. The independent living centre model seemed to be a mechanism to achieve the goals of disabled people: equal social, political, economic, educational, and cultural options. Funding of CIL completed a circle. A number of individuals with disabilities who had been told by members of the helping professions (doctors, nurses, psychologists, social workers, rehabilitation counsellors, among others) they could never work because of their disabilities now became executives of an organization deemed more fit to work with disabled people than the so-called experts.

Other disability activists, in Houston, Ann Arbor, St. Louis, Boston and elsewhere, like the founders of Berkeley CIL, and in concert with empathetic rehabilitation workers and progressive Congressional colleagues, collaborated in the early 1970s to implement a new and broader agenda for Federal vocational rehabilitation services. Aware of the pervasive discrimination against people with disabilities endemic in all of society, advocates worked to make revision of the rehabilitation act legislation a major shift in the early 1970s. This led to the first real fight of the nascent disability rights community in the United States and laid the foundation for the activism, social justice advocacy and civil disobedience that were core elements of the early disability rights movement in the United States.

A first major success in addressing legislative and policy change was a change to the wording of the American Rehabilitation Act. In 43 words, Section 504 of the Rehabilitation Act of 1973 prohibited programs and activities receiving Federal financial assistance from discriminating against qualified disabled people, guaranteeing disabled individuals civil rights for the first time in U.S. history.

The trouble with Section 504 came from a recalcitrance among government agencies to implement the law. The Action League for Physically Handicapped Adults sued the government in 1975 for issuance of 504 regulations. The next year, disability activists from across the United States demonstrated in Washington, D.C. at the U.S. Cabinet Office of Health, Education, and Welfare (HEW) and they threatened to picket the 1976 Republican Convention.

During the 1976 presidential campaign, Philadelphia's Disabled in Action group invited Republicans and Democrats to a press conference. Out of that meeting the recently formed American Coalition of Citizens with Disabilities (ACCD) became the national organizer for Jimmy Carter (Brown, 2000; D. Pfeiffer, personal communication, July 20, 1999), who went on to become President of the United States.

Passage of 504 regulations became a battle cry of disability activists throughout the country, and within 2 days after Carter's inauguration in January 1977, a group of approximately 15 activists went to see HEW Secretary Joseph Califano to advocate for rapid implementation of regulations. The Carter administration received a deadline of April 4, 1977, to issue regulations, or disability advocates would pursue an alternative course. Secretary of Health, Education and Welfare Joseph Califano, fearing that both actual and administrative costs would be more far-reaching than anyone imagined, stalled the implementation of the 504 Regulations (Eunice Fiorito in *We Won't Go Away...* 1981; Scotch, 1984).

Disability advocates scheduled demonstrations in 10 cities across the United States. The most successful action occurred in San Francisco, where more than 150 people took over the federal building and remained for 28 days. Well-known advocates such as Ed Roberts and Judy Heumann added their voices to the protests. Ed Roberts left his new office as Director of the California Department of Rehabilitation to join the protest. Judith Heumann crossed the Bay from the Centre of Independent Living in Berkeley to become one of the leaders of the takeover. Early in the action, Heumann declared, 'we will no longer allow the government to oppress disabled individuals…we will accept no more discussion of segregation' (*We Won't Go Away*…1981).

San Francisco mayor George Moscone ordered law enforcement personnel to leave the protesters alone. The protestors were supported by other civil rights activist groups such as the Black Panthers and the Gray Panthers, who brought in donated food, and they also assisted with the personal care needs of some disabled activists (Shapiro, 1993).

Later, Judith Heumann led a San Francisco delegation to Washington to talk personally with Califano. When he refused to meet with them, and after 25 days of occupation of the HEW building, Califano signed regulations. The siege was the longest takeover of a federal building by any group in American history (Shapiro, 1993).

One year after the demonstrations in San Francisco, another important disability activist group emerged in the United States, and this group, American Disabled for Accessible Public Transit (ADAPT), advocated for accessible public transportation for Americans with disabilities. At the time transportation was an issue of obvious and symbolic importance. In the 1950s, Black Civil Rights activists protested state laws forcing African Americans to sit at the back of buses; disabled people protested because they could not get on the bus. The most noted group, a group of 19 Denver, Colorado, activists, organized American Disabled for Accessible Public Transit in July 1978.

ADAPT chapters and similar organizations soon formed throughout the country. They blocked buses, proclaiming if disabled people could not use the buses then neither could anyone else. Police quickly arrived to arrest the protesters. But it was not such a simple process. First, police often still thought of disabled people as sick and vulnerable and were either cautious about injuring them or careless about not doing so. Second, police vehicles such as vans, like the buses, were inaccessible, so police could not transfer the disabled protesters to jail. Moreover, even if the police found a way to transport the protesters, the jails were often inaccessible, and the protests for accessible public transportation continued across America until cities such as Denver acquiesced and made accessible public transportation a priority.

The same year that ADAPT began, Congress formally recognized the personal and fiscal value of independent living centres by ensuring their funding through the Rehabilitation Act, and the first 10 independent living centres funded through this legislation began receiving financial assistance in 1979 (Dunning et al., 1994; M. Shreve, personal communication, September 9, 1994).

Despite these successes during the 1970s, '80s, and '90s, more than $200 billion of public funding was spent on programs and services that maintained disabled people in dependent care-giving environments such as long-term care facilities and nursing homes, and less than $1 billion supporting people with disabilities to live in their own homes and apartments to enable their participation in mainstream America (Leon, 1992).

Fifth perception: Charity and celebration, or, telethons, paradigm shifts and disability culture

Among the scores of protesters taking over San Francisco's federal building in 1977, Jeff Moyer brought his guitar, becoming known as the demonstration's resident musician.

This role represented a significant change in disabled people's self-image. In a turnabout from the discounting and devaluation inherent in the first three perceptions of this saga, the Disability Rights Movement encouraged a celebration of disability.

The idea of celebrating disability which had historically been viewed from incompetence to deviance to tragedy remained an anathema to a society generally still guided by the concepts of the medical model, which underpinned the popular view of disabled people as 'needy' and has been moulded by various charities through the United States.

Photographer David Hevey, in his 1992 book, *The Creatures Time Forgot*, exposed charities creating what the public perceives as the 'one voice' of people with disabilities. But in reality, disabled people wait at the end of the line of the disability industry's priorities.

Foremost among any charity's goals are survival and ensuring those individuals who contribute to the agency's success feel good about themselves. This can be accomplished by attaining the dual objectives of raising money for the organization and determining how to distribute it to the organization's 'needy' clientele.

One result of this model is that the needs of the charity, or disability industry, surpass all other concerns. A more invidious consequence of the way charities feel good about their selfless contributions to those less fortunate than themselves is to have a perpetual supply of victims.

In the 1990s, the idea of having pride in one's existence as a person with a disability was novel and begged paradigm analysis. The author composed Table 28.2 to explore two paradigms that included aspects of all five perceptions discussed in this chapter.

Legacies

Since 1994, when the first publication of the following chart and the monograph in which it appeared, Disability Culture has advanced so rapidly, a recent Web search (May 13, 2012) for 'disability culture' returned 117,00 hits on Yahoo and 105,000 hits on Google. This is one of the many legacies of the independent living movement. There are many others, including the Disabled Students Services Program at University of California–Berkeley, leading to almost every university and community college including such a service. There are now hundreds of independent living centres in the U.S. and across the world. Ed Roberts, instrumental in the creation of both these entities, became the first individual with significant impairments to go to college and to be Director of a State Department of Rehabilitation, but many more followed.

The pervasiveness of these changes affected multiple constituencies. Grassroots efforts – such as the development of independent living centres; organizations that believed in street protests, especially ADAPT; and groups representing a variety of constituencies, like People First, which focuses on cognitive disabilities – reflect the movement's roots. Academic interest sparked the growth of multidisciplinary Disability Studies programs worldwide.

Like Ed Roberts, many independent living movement leaders who have passed left legacies in deeds and words, to guide those who follow in their wake. In a 1992 WID publication, Ed wrote an incisive description of what independent living continues to signify: 'every one of us (and not just people with disabilities) has the right and the capacity to participate in all of society's activities' (Leon, p. 3).

Table 28.2: The chart: Disability rights/culture/pride paradigm

	Community Assistance/Medical/ Charity Paradigms	Disability Rights/Culture/Pride Paradigm
Definitions of Problems	Physical or mental impairments; lack of socio-economic, political, educational, and cultural skills	Dependence on professionals, family members, and others; hostile attitudes and environments; lack of legal protections or recognition of inherent worth of disabled people
Locus of Problems	In individual (who is broken or sick and needs fixing or curing)	In socio-economic, political, educational, and cultural environments and perceptions
Social Roles	Patients, clients, charity recipients, non-existent	Family and community members, customers, co-workers, advocates, same as anyone else
Solutions to Problems	Professional and volunteer interventions and treatments	Equitable socio-economic, political, educational, and cultural options
Who Controls	Professional and/or volunteer	Individual or group of individual's choice
Desired Outcomes	Maximum self-care; no social misfits	Pride in unique talents and attributes of each individual and positive disability identity

Note: Parts of this chart have been extrapolated from DeJong (1978), (1983); Racino (1992); Shreve (1994).

References

Albin, M. S. (2000). The use of anesthetics during the Civil War, 1861–1865. *Pharmacy in History,* *42*(3 & 4), 99–114.

Barth, A. (2009). Humans took care of the disabled over 500,000 years ago. *Discover Magazine.* Retrieved from http://discovermagazine.com/2010/jan-feb/082

Benavraham, T. (1985). Orthodox handicapable chicken soup. In S. E. Browne, D. Connors, & N. Stern (Eds.), *With the Power of Each Breath* (pp. 327–29). Pittsburgh and San Francisco, CA: Cleis Press.

Berkowitz, E. D. (1987). *Disabled Policy: America's program for the handicapped.* Cambridge, UK: Cambridge University Press.

Bowe, F. (1978). *Handicapping America.* New York, NY: Harper & Row.

Brown, S. E. (1994). *Investigating a Culture of Disability: Final report.* Las Cruces, NM: Institute on Disability Culture.

Brown, S. E. (2000). *Freedom of Movement: Independent living history and philosophy.* Houston, TX: Independent Living Research Utilization.

Brown, S. E. (2003). *Movie Stars and Sensuous Scars: Essays on the journey from disability shame to disability pride.* New York, NY: People with Disabilities Press.

Brown, S. E. (2008). Breaking barriers: The pioneering disability students services program at the University of Illinois, 1948–1960. In E. Tamura (Ed.), *The History of Discrimination in U.S. Education: Marginality, agency, and power* (pp. 165–92). New York, NY: Palgrave Macmillan.

Charlton, J. I. (1998). *Nothing About Us Without Us: Disability oppression and empowerment.* Berkeley, CA: University of. California Press.

Connors, D. (1985). Disability, sexism, and the social order. In S. E. Browne, D. Connors, & N. Stern (Eds.), *With the Power of Each Breath* (pp. 92–107). Pittsburgh and San Francisco, CA: Cleis Press.

Davis, K. C. (1990). *Don't Know Much about History: Everything you need to know about American history but never learned.* New York, NY: Avon.

DeJong, G. (1978). *The Movement for Independent Living: Origins, ideology, and implications for disability research.* Boston, MA: Tufts-New England Medical Center, Medical Rehabilitation Institute.

DeJong, G. (1983). Defining and implementing the independent living concept. In N. Crewe & I. K. Zola (Eds.), *Independent Living for Physically Disabled People.* San Francisco, CA: Jossey-Bass.

Dunning, T., King, K., & Smith, L. (1994). *1994 Disability Media Calendar.* Houston, TX: Independent Living Research Utilization.

Ed Roberts. (1988). *Sixty Minutes* [Video]. Available from World Institute on Disability, www.wid.org

Education Act, Ch, 3 & 7. The development of children and students towards the goals. (2010:800). Retrieved from: https://www.riksdagen.se/sv/dokument-lagar/dokument/svensk-forfattningssamlingskollag-2010800_sfs-2010-800.

Emanuelsson, I., Persson, B., & Rosenqvist, J. (2001). Research in special needs education: A systematic review. Stockholm: Skolverket.

Finger, A. (1985). Claiming all of our bodies: Reproductive rights and disability. In S. E. Browne, D. Connors & N. Stern (Eds.), *With the Power of Each Breath* (pp. 292–307). Pittsburgh & San Francisco, CA: Cleis Press.

Fiorito, E. (1981). *We won't go away...* [Video]. (Available from World Institute on Disability, 510 16th St., Oakland, CA 94612).

Fitzgerald, H., Jobling, A. & Kirk, D. (2003a). 'Valuing the voices of young disabled people: exploring experience of physical education and sport'. *Physical Education & Sport Pedagogy, 8* (2), p. 175–200.

Fitzgerald, H., Jobling, A. & Kirk, D. (2003b) 'Listening to the "voices" of students with severe learning difficulties through a task-based approach to research and learning in physical education'. *Support for Learning, 18* (3), p. 123–129.

Fitzgerald, H. (2005). Still feeling like a spare piece of luggage? Embodied experiences of (dis) ability in physical education and school sport. *Physical Education & Sport Pedagogy, 10*(1), 95–108.

Fredrickson, G. M. (1987). *The Black Image in the White Mind: The debate on Afro-American character and destiny, 1817–1914.* New York, NY: Harper & Row.

Gallagher, H. G. (1985). *FDR's Splendid Deception.* New York, NY: Dodd, Mead.

Gallagher, H. G. (1990). *By Trust Betrayed: Patients, physicians and the license to kill in the Third Reich.* New York, NY: Henry Holt.

Hevey, D. (1992). *The Creatures Time Forgot: Photography and disability imagery.* London, UK: Routledge.

Hjörne, E & Säljö, R. (2008) To place in a school for all. Student Health and Negotiation on Normality in Swedish schools.

Lenihan, J. (Nov-Dec. 1976–Jan. 1977). *Disabled Americans: A history. Performance, XXVII(5-7).* Washington, DC: President's Committee on Employment of the Handicapped.

Leon, J. (Ed.). (1992). *Just like everyone else.* Oakland, CA: World Institute on Disability.

Longmore, P. (1985). The life of Randolph Bourne and the need for a history of disabled people. Review of Bruce Clayton *Forgotten Prophet: The Life of Randolph Bourne,* In *Reviews in American History,* 13, pp. 581–87.

Longmore, P. K. (2003). *Why I Burned My Book and Other Essays on Disability*. Philadelphia, PA: Temple.

Longmore, P. K. & Umansky, L. (Eds.) (2001). *The New Disability History: American perspectives*. New York, NY: New York University.

Mackelprang, R. W. & Salsgiver, R. O. (1996). People with disabilities and social work: Historical and contemporary issues. *Social Work*, 41, 7–14.

Moyer, J. Music from the heart. Retrieved from www.jeffmoyer.com (year missing)

Nielsen, K. E. (2012). *A Disability History of the United States*. Boston, MA: Beacon.

Ó hÉochaidh, R. (Jan. 24, 2012). Community celebrates Ed Roberts Day. UC Berkeley News Center. Retrieved from http://newscenter.berkeley.edu/2012/01/24/ed-roberts-day-2012/

Racino, J. A. (1992). Living in the community: Independence, support, and transition. In F. R. Rusch, L. DeStefano, J. Chadsey-Rusch, L. A. Phelps, & E. Symanski (Eds.), *Transition from School to Adult Life: Models, Linkages, and Policy*. Sycamore, IL: Sycamore.

Rothman, D. J. (1971). *The Discovery of the Asylum: Social order and disorder in the new republic*. Boston, MA: Little, Brown.

Schweik, S. M. (2009). *The Ugly Laws: Disability in public*. New York, NY: New York University.

Scotch, R. K. (1984). *From Good Will to Civil Rights: Transforming federal disability policy*. Philadelphia, PA: Temple.

Shapiro, J. P. (1993). *No Pity: People with disabilities forging a new civil rights movement*. New York, NY: Times Books.

Shreve. M. (1994). *Independent Living and the Rehab Act: Regional training*. Houston, TX: National Council on Independent Living/Independent Living Research Utilization.

SOU (1983:63) Exclusion in elementary school - Analysis of how the rules for customized study programs, exemption from school and special education are applied in practice. Stockholm, Sweden: Ministry of Education.

Stallybrass, P. & White, A. (1993). Bourgeois hysteria and the carnivalesque. In S. During, (Ed.), *The Cultural Studies Reader* (pp. 284–92). London, UK: Routledge.

Trattner, W. (1998). *From Poor Law to Welfare State, 6th edition: A history of social welfare in America*. New York, NY: The Free Press.

Walker, M. L. (1985). *Beyond Bureaucracy: Mary Elizabeth Switzer and rehabilitation*. Lanham, MD: University Press

Wickman, K., 2008. 'I do not compete in disability': how wheelchair racers challenge the discourse of ableism through action and resistance. *European journal for sport and society, 4* (2), 151–167.

CONCLUDING REMARKS

The 28 chapters of this text trace various cultural and societal conceptualizations of disability from the Greek era to the present day, and they draw upon numerous contributions provided by authors from across the globe. The authors note that despite the comprehensiveness of the text, the story – the history of people with disabilities offered in the preceding pages – is only a beginning, and the many stories within it merely scratch the surface of the multitude of issues which still need addressing when it comes to disability history. However, notwithstanding the limitations of addressing disability in a historical context, this text draws attention to the huge gap evident in historical research which seems to minimize or not deal with disabled peoples' histories at all. Similarly, this text adds to the emerging field of disability studies, and it adds to discourses evidenced in critical disability theory by contextualizing disability according to various historical epochs and cultures which in turn reveal a complex relationship between disabled and nondisabled persons. Interestingly, the historical accounts offered in this text not only highlight the complexity of relationships between disabled and nondisabled citizenships no matter the time or place, but also the various chapters suggest that the relationship was more than a person-to-person, or group-to-group, interaction. Indeed, this text suggests that relationships were and remain to this very day a process that was and is shaped by broader religious, cultural, societal, economic and political entities rooted in history.

While the editors of this text are well informed as to the merits of critical disability theory and the contributions made in the field of disability studies, we are also well aware of the oppressive and discriminatory practices that millions of disabled individuals around the world face on a daily basis. Moreover, much of this contemporary oppression and discriminatory practices have deep historical roots that can be traced back decades, even centuries, and this is where our histories of disabilities text displays its worth and validity. It shows that even the enormous contributions made by critical disability theory – which in turn is heavily informed by critical race, feminist and gender theories wherein contemporary social constructs pertaining to the human form and especially disability are debunked – are not enough. Through the examination of disability histories offered in this text, we learn that while concepts of disability vary from one cultural context to the next, we also learn that discrimination, marginalization and oppression of disabled people have deep historical roots which theoretical debates alone cannot and will not address. This text shows that attitudes, stigma and practices are so deeply entrenched in history and societal norms that most people do not recognize their own role in perpetuating oppression through various forms of systemic ableism. It is hoped that the readers will gain a new insight into the histories of disabled people and, just as important, it is hoped that readers will use the lessons learned from the past as a way of reconfiguring the present status of disabled people so that more progressive change can be introduced in such a way as to change the future.

The editors hope that through an examination of history, nondisabled people can and will ally with disabled members of society to not only develop progressive theories for examining and teaching disability theories but to also work together toward greater societal change. The theme then is to use this history text to learn about disability over time and then to use this knowledge as a way and means for action and change. Throughout the text, the reader will note that there are many examples of what are considered today as being regressive measures, such as the development of segregated institutions, misplaced ideologies of training and education based on gender, inappropriate pseudo-sciences such as eugenics as well as other examples which are rooted in oppression and stigma. But the reader will also note the connection between the rise of awareness through the actions of disability civil rights movements, changes in national and international legislation, shifts in service delivery and their connections to history. Progressive change does not happen in a vacuum, and history teaches us that education is organic in the sense that education and the development of knowledge is not only about the learning of theory, it is also about informing people so that they can take action. As important as it is to deconstruct disability concepts through disability studies and critical disability theory, it is just as important that students of disability learn about the importance of developing a three-pronged approach which includes the development of critical disability theory wherein disability history can play a significant role; the development of well-rounded day-to-day services and supports for disabled individuals and their families; and the need for greater local, national and international legislation which addresses disability oppression through broader structural and systemic change and instills the rights of all disabled people. We should all recognize that we are part of history, and we should be aware as to how we will be written about and judged in the future. And when it comes to affecting the history of disabled people, we should ask ourselves if we did a better job than our predecessors.

INDEX

Printed in Great Britain
by Amazon

85599630R00307